THE
GREAT
STAIN

THE GREAT STAIN

WITNESSING AMERICAN SLAVERY

NOEL RAE

THE OVERLOOK PRESS
NEW YORK, NY

This edition first published in hardcover in the United States in 2018 by
The Overlook Press, Peter Mayer Publishers, Inc.
141 Wooster Street
New York, NY 10012
www.overlookpress.com
For bulk and special sales, please contact sales@overlookny.com
or write to us at the above address.

Cataloging-in-Publication Data is available from the Library of Congress

Book design and type formatting by Bernard Schleifer
Manufactured in the United States of America
FIRST EDITION
1 3 5 7 9 10 8 6 4 2
ISBN 978-1-4683-1513-4

CONTENTS

THE
GREAT
STAIN

INTRODUCTION

"WHAT IS A SLAVE?" ASKED WILLIAM WELLS BROWN IN A LECTURE TO THE Female Anti-Slavery Society of Salem, delivered on November 18, 1847. One of the abolitionist movement's most effective black orators, Brown had himself been a slave, and knew what he was talking about. "A slave is one that is in the power of an owner. He is a chattel; he is a thing; he is a piece of property. A master can dispose of him, can dispose of his labor, can dispose of his wife, can dispose of his offspring, can dispose of everything that belongs to the slave, and the slave shall have no right to speak; he shall have nothing to say." And what was a chattel? According to the then-current edition of Webster's dictionary, "Chattels personal are things movable, as animals, furniture." The word chattel is derived from cattle. The word slave derives from *sclavus,* the medieval Latin word for Slav—probably because so many of that nation were enslaved by the Holy Roman Emperor, Otto the Great, in the tenth century.

Long before the term was defined the fact of slavery had existed in almost every part of the world and in almost every period of recorded history, and indeed still exists in some countries today. While always entailing the unlimited power of one person over another, it has varied greatly from place to place and time to time. Until they became part of the United States as a result of the Alaska Purchase, the Tlingit Indians made slaves of their Aleutian or Athabascan neighbors, sometimes setting them free when celebrating a potlatch, and more often sacrificing them to bring good luck when building a new house. In ancient Rome a slave might be a gladiator or private secretary to a statesman, and if freed could become a citizen. In the late fourteenth century the Ottoman Sultan Murad I formed a bodyguard of Christian slaves, recruited mostly from the Balkans and called Janissaries, who were paid for their service and could retire on a pension. In pre-colonial Africa slavery was widespread; some of its victims were put to work in the salt mines and millions were sold to traders for re-sale in the Barbary states or for shipment across the Atlantic; but many others, especially domestic servants, were treated as virtual members of the family.

For most of history nobody saw anything wrong with all this. Until the great revolution in thinking that came with the Enlightenment, slavery was accepted as part of the natural order—man was not born free and had no right to life, liberty and the pursuit of happiness. A person who was enslaved was unlucky, to be sure, but he was not the victim of injustice. When, in 1838, President John Quincy Adams called slavery "a deadly disease . . . the great and foul stain upon the North American Union," he was expressing an opinion that a mere hundred years earlier was held only by a few political philosophers and a handful of eccentric Quakers.

And not only was it generally accepted, but just about everyone who had a chance to benefit joined in: African rulers who waged war on their neighbors for the sole purpose of capturing and selling them (or, more simply, condemned and sold their own people on trumped-up charges); the Duke of York who, along with other seventeenth-century English aristocrats, invested heavily in the newly-formed Royal African Company; the Society for the Propagation of the Gospel in Foreign Parts, which owned a large sugar-cane plantation in Barbados; the Rev. Cotton Mather, Boston's leading clergyman, who gratefully accepted a household slave as a gift from his appreciative congregation; Brown and other American universities which had no qualms about taking endowments funded by slave traders. And then there were those more immediately involved in the business: New England distillers whose rum was an important part of almost every purchase; artisans in Germany and Italy who made the colored beads that were popular trading goods; shops in Liverpool that sold thumbscrews and shackles; Northern bankers who advanced the money to buy slaves, insurers who sold policies on their lives, and brokers who handled the cotton business. Even ordinary people in other parts of the world who wore cotton clothing could be considered complicit.

Harsh though the subject is, slavery in America has long been an interest of mine, partly because it is of such intense human interest, partly because it has given rise to so many gripping stories, and partly because it lies at the root of so much that ails America today. As I long ago found (and as listed in the bibliography), there are already a great many books on the topic—straightforward narrative histories; biographies of abolitionists and of apologists; scholarly books explaining slavery in academic terms; works by cliometricians and economists, full of charts and columns of statistics; specialized books on some particular aspect of the topic; books about politics; and, unavoidably, novels, most notably *Uncle Tom's Cabin* and some of the "anti-Tom" novels written in rebuttal. Nearly all these books are important and helpful for understanding the subject, but only a few conveyed a sense of what slavery was actually like. Most of them were like those military histories that tell the reader all about the strategy of a war but nothing about the actual fighting.

And so it seemed to me that there was a place for a book that filled this gap, that brought the reader face-to-face with the everyday reality of life as experienced by the slaves themselves. The question I ask, and try to answer, is not "What happened, and why?" but "What was it like?" And the way to do this was to accumulate as much eyewitness material as I could find and then arrange it into a coherent narrative that told the whole story from first to last in the words of those who were actually there. My role would be to research, select and provide explanatory and connective bridges. To be sure, there are already a number of other books that use firsthand material to tell of some particular period or topic, but none that covers the complete story from the start of the trans-Atlantic trade in the fifteenth century to slavery's demise with the close of the Civil War and the ratification of the 13th, 14th and 15th Amendments. Listening to the words and voices of those who were actually there is surely the closest we can come to fully understanding their experiences.

Five years of research have gone into compiling the book, much longer than expected due to the abundance of material. First there were the writings of contemporaries who had firsthand knowledge of the business, beginning with the court historian, Gomes de Azurara, who chronicled the first raids carried out by Portuguese on the west coast of Africa in the fifteenth century. After him there was the Venetian Alvise da Cadamosto, who wrote glowingly of the beauties of Africa, and after Cadamosto the buccaneering English, sword in one hand, Bible in the other, who soon came to dominate the trade. It is from such participants as these that we learn firsthand how the slave trade actually worked, how

humans were bartered for brandy and guns and gew-gaws, and how perilous the whole business was to the traders themselves due to fevers, sickness and the constant risk of uprisings, many of them successful. It is
from these sources also that we have the best accounts of the horrible
conditions aboard the slave ships when crossing the Atlantic and the brutal way slaves were sold on arrival. Much of the testimony about slavery
during the colonial period also comes from white people: a Virginia aris-
tocrat who filled his diary with complaints about the ingratitude of his
"servants"; the trial record of The Great Negro Plot of 1741 (whose
alleged aim was to burn New York to the ground); George Washington's
underhand attempts to recover Martha's slave, Oney Judd, who had
escaped to New Hampshire; and, later on, Alexis de Tocqueville's observations on the pernicious effects that slavery had on the character and
well-being of white people.

But of course the most valuable and relevant material came from
the slaves themselves. Because most of them were from parts of Africa
that did not have a written language, and because the owning class,
aware that illiteracy was an effective means of control, made it a crime
to teach a slave to read and write, there is a dearth of such material for
the early parts of the story—of the ten to twelve million enslaved Africans
who were shipped across the Atlantic only a handful have left a written
record. When, as a boy, Frederick Douglass, the abolition movement's
charismatic leader, broke the law and taught himself to read he was con-
scious that doing so was one of his first steps to freedom; and as the nineteenth century progressed there were many others who followed his
example—William Wells Brown, Josiah Henson and Harriet Jacobs
among them. Many others, such as Harriet Tubman and Charles Ball,
told their stories to better-educated sympathizers, who may have added
some literary flourishes but got their stories from the mouths of the ex-
slaves themselves.

Some of the most powerful accounts told of acts of resistance, a topic
that was largely ignored in many of the early histories and in the self-
censoring antebellum southern press—which liked to pretend that such
things did not exist—but was a major theme in the stories told by slaves.
Resistance ran the gamut from infuriating "masters" by slacking off,
malingering and deliberately misunderstanding orders, to running away
to the North or to Canada, and to open acts of defiance, sometimes col-

lective as in the various famous uprisings, and sometimes individual, of which there are many instances in the book. The final chapter deals with the Civil War, and includes both the small part played by a few slaves in the service of the South and the vital part played by free blacks in the armies of the North.

My years of research resulted in several thousand pages of text, now winnowed down to a few hundred. I hope you will find them worth reading. I say this not from author's vanity, because although I am the researcher, compiler, fact-checker, arranger, editor, and provider of a fair amount of explanatory and connective material, I am not the author. That title belongs to those whose first-person accounts form the essence of the book.

Cape Coast Castle, owned by the Royal African Company, and one of the many fortified trading posts established by Europeans along what they called the Gold Coast (now Ghana). The castles were built to dominate the local people, fend off rival traders, and warehouse slaves brought down to the coast from far inland. The two large houses were for the traders and the garrison. For the slaves there was a dungeon large enough to hold over a thousand men and women. When they embarked they left by what was known as the Gate of No Return.

CHAPTER 1

OUT OF AFRICA

BROADLY SPEAKING, AND SETTING ASIDE EGYPT, THERE WERE FOUR DISTINCT branches of slavery and the slave trade in Africa, all of them dating back to well before the start of the Christian Era.

First, there was slavery of the domestic kind, the result of wars, law enforcement or the system of money-lending whereby a member of a family was put up as collateral for a loan and became a slave to the lender if the debt was not repaid. Domestic slavery varied from region to region but was widespread and long-established; by some estimates nearly half the continent's population was held in this kind of bondage. But this was not slavery as practiced in the New World: it was free of color prejudice; those who served as domestics were generally treated as members of the family; those who became soldiers could rise to high rank; the children of concubines were usually free; except for those sent to the salt mines, they were not worked to death; and they could own property, including other slaves. In fact so relaxed was this system—"benign" is the word usually used to describe it—that there are those who say that it does not even deserve to be called slavery.

However, "benign" is not a word that could be applied to the second kind of African slavery, which operated on the continent's east coast, from Somalia down to Mozambique, including the Comoros Islands and Madagascar. This trade was largely in the hands of the Arabs, who set up business in ports such as Mogadishu, Mombasa and Zanzibar, and from there sent raiding parties as far inland as the Congo. For hundreds of years, until brought to an end in the late nineteenth century by the European colonizing powers, which had their own ways of exploiting the natives, a common sight in East Africa was gangs of slaves roped or chained together by the neck and ankle, shuffling along on their way to the coast, guarded by a few well-armed Arabs. These gangs of slaves were known as "coffles", from the Arabic word *qafilah*, meaning caravan or traveling group. Once on the coast they were put on board small ships called dhows and sold in Arabia, Persia, India, and even as far off as China. This was sometimes called the Indian Ocean Trade, and accounted for many millions.

Then there was the sea-going slave trade based in North Africa, whose victims were mostly Europeans. This had a long history, but greatly increased after North Africa was invaded by Arabs in the ninth century and many Berbers and Moors converted to Islam. Like the Christians, Muslims were not supposed to enslave their co-religionists, but everyone else was fair game. From such bases as Algiers, Tunis and Tripoli, these corsairs were so relentless in their raids on the coasts of Spain, southern France and Italy that the inhabitants either abandoned the coastal areas entirely or took to living in fortified hill-towns. Corsairs also ventured up the Volga River and out into the Atlantic as far north as Iceland. Most of their victims were sold in the slave markets in North Africa, Rome or Constantinople. Not until the French invaded Algeria in the nineteenth century were the Barbary corsairs put out of business.

Also based in North Africa was the trans-Saharan trade. This is thought to date as far back as 1000 BC, but did not really take off until the invading Arabs introduced not just an expansionary Islam, but also the dromedary camel. A much-traveled beast, the dromedary had originated in North America, crossed over to Asia on the Bering land bridge, and been domesticated in Arabia in the third millennium BC. It was well-suited to the trade: it could carry heavy loads, it did not sweat and so could go several days without water, it could close its nostrils during sand storms, its dung could be used for fuel, the protein-rich milk of the female could be drunk by humans, and, in emergencies, the animal itself could be killed, cooked and eaten. According to the sixteenth-century Moorish diplomat Leo Africanus, dromedaries were "gentle and domestical beasts," but during the mating season they "will deadly wound such persons as have done them any injury. And whomsoever they lay hold on with their teeth, they lift him up on high and cast him down again, trampling on him with their feet."

On their way south the camels were loaded with such trading goods as expensive cloth, brightly colored glass beads, and, above all, salt, of which there was a dearth throughout the southern parts of west Africa. On arrival at trading towns on or near the Niger River, such as Gao, Timbuktu or Aoudaghast, these goods were exchanged for gold, ivory and slaves. Most of the slaves came from countries to the south, known as the Land of the Blacks, and were acquired in raids or by purchase from local rulers. In addition to all their other miseries, these unfortunates then faced a journey on foot over the stony plateaus of the Sahel and the sands of the Sahara, well over a thousand miles, and ending in a slave market. Slow-going and piecemeal though it was, this trade is estimated to have brought as many as four million slaves to the north.

One of the first to describe the trans-Saharan trade was the Sunni Moroccan, Ibn Battuta (full version: Hajji Abu Abdullah Muhammad Ibn Abdullah Al Lawati Al Tanji Ibn Battuta—"Hajji" meaning that he had made the pilgrimage to Mecca, and "Tanji" that he had been born in Tangiers). A scholar and a jurist, Ibn Battuta was also a great traveler, who ventured as far north as Siberia, as far east as China and as far south as the Niger River. On his final return to Morocco he set down the story of his travels in a book called *A Gift to Those Who Contemplate the Wonders of Cities and the Marvels of Travel*, more generally known as the *Rihla*, or Journey.

Battuta's journey to the south was undertaken at the behest of the Sultan of Morocco ("May God support him!"), and began at the capital city of Fez ("May God protect it!"). From Fez he went to the inland city of Sijilmassa, on one of the principal north-south caravan routes, "and one of the finest cities, where there is an abundance of excellent dates." Here he stayed with a *faqih*, or theologian, "whose brother I had met at Qanjanfu in China. How far apart from one another they are! He treated me with great hospitality. Here I bought camels and fed them for four months and then, at the beginning of God's month of Muharram in the year 753 [February, 1352], I set off with a caravan of merchants whose leader was Abu Muhammad Yandakan al-Masufi, may God have mercy on him!

"After twenty-five days we arrived at Taghaza, a miserable village whose houses and mosque are made of rock salt with camel skins for roofs. It has no trees, and is nothing but sand and a salt mine. No one lives there except the slaves who mine the salt, digging it from the earth where it lies in great slabs, one on top of the other. A camel can carry two of these slabs. This salt can sometimes sell for eight to ten *mithqals* in Iwalatan, and for twenty to thirty, and sometimes even forty *mithqals* in the city of Mali." (A *mithqal* was one-eighth of an ounce of gold.)

After stopping and resting three days at Taghaza the caravans prepared to enter the great desert, "in which there is neither water, bird nor tree; but only sand and hills of sand, which are so blown about by the wind that no vestige of a track remains among them." According to an earlier traveler, Abu Hamid al-Gharnati, another obstacle in crossing the desert was the Wadi al-Sabt, the River of the Sabbath, "which is a river of sand that flows like water. No one may enter it and survive"—except on the Sabbath, when the sand stopped flowing and the river could be safely crossed. "This is what is said," added Abu Hamid al-Gharnati, "but God knows best." He also mentioned the race of "people who have no heads. Their eyes are in the shoulders, and their mouths in their chests. They are harmless, and have no intelligence."

On arrival at Mali, Ibn Battuta went to live in the White Quarter, that part of the town where, when compared with the Negroes, the relatively white Moors and Arabs resided. He was gratified to receive from local notables several "reception gifts, including a cow and a bullock" and from the sultan, Mansa Sulayman, a gift of thirty-three and a third *mithqals* of gold. Soon after, he was present when the sultan sat in council.

"A dais with three steps, called a *banbi*, is set up under a tree; it is richly upholstered in silk and cushions are spread about. Above it there is a dome-shaped canopy of silk surmounted by a golden bird the size of a falcon. The sultan comes out of his palace with a bow in his hand and a quiver of arrows on his back. On his head he wears a *shashiyya* [skull-cap] made of gold and tied with golden straps. His clothes are made of soft red cloth brought from Europe.

"He is preceded by singers carrying gold and silver instruments and followed by three hundred armed slaves. He walks slowly, with great deliberation, occasionally pausing. When he reaches the dais he stands looking at the people and then mounts it slowly, much as a *khatib* [priest] mounts his pulpit. As he sits drums are beaten and trumpets sounded. His deputy and the military commanders are sum-

moned by three slaves. They enter and take their seats; at the same
time two horses are brought in, as well as two goats as protection
against the evil eye.

"The sultan's bodyguard is armed with quivers made of gold
and silver, swords and scabbards also of gold and silver, and clubs
of crystal. Next to him stand four emirs whisking away the flies, their
hands decorated with silver ornaments. The military commanders
and the priests sit according to custom. Then Dugha, the interpreter,
comes in with the sultan's four wives and his slave girls. There are
about four hundred of these, all wearing fine clothes, and on their
heads bands of gold and silver adorned with gold and silver balls.
Dugha then takes his places on a special seat and plays an instrument
made of reed with little gourds underneath, and sings poetry in praise
of the sultan, recalling his campaigns and heroic deeds; the women
and slave girls also play stringed instruments and join in the singing."

On the whole, Ibn Battuta found much to approve in Mali: "the
lack of oppression . . . the security that prevails throughout the country
so that a traveler has nothing to fear . . . their honesty when dealing with
the property of a white man [i.e. an Arab] . . . their assiduity in prayer . . .
their dressing in fine white clothes on Fridays . . . their eagerness to learn
the great Koran and their practice of punishing their children by putting
them in chains if they fail to memorize it." On the other hand he disapproved of the way "their female servants and slave girls appear before
men completely naked." He also didn't like the way people "sprinkled
dust and ashes on their heads as a sign of good manners" and their habit
of "eating carrion, dogs and donkeys."

After spending eight months there, Ibn Battuta left Mali for Timbuktu.
On his way he saw some hippopotami in the Niger River "swimming in
the water, raising their heads and snorting." After traveling "in a small
boat carved out of a single piece of wood" down the Niger, which like
many other travelers of the time he thought was a branch of the Nile, he
eventually reached Timbuktu, still prosperous as a center of trade but,
following an invasion by Moors from the north, no longer the great city
it had once been. He also visited a town he calls Kawkaw, "a great town
on the Niger River, one of the largest, finest and most fertile cities of the
Sudan, where there is much rice, chickens, milk and fish and incompara-

ble cucumbers. Its people use cowrie shells when buying and selling, just like the people of Mali." From there he headed north for Takkada, traveling with a big caravan and passing through "the country of the Bardama, a tribe of Berber nomads. Their women are most beautiful and most pleasing to the eye, being very white and plump. I never saw in any country women as plump as they are."

On reaching Takkada he was invited to stay in the Moroccan quarter. "The people of the town have no occupation other than trade. They travel each year to Egypt and import all kinds of goods, including cloth of a very fine quality. The people are well off and are proud of the number of male and female slaves they have." He also visited the nearby copper mines, which were worked by male and female slaves and whose product was exported to Mali, where it sold for two thirds of its weight in gold. The copper was also sold to "the land of Burnu, which is a distance of forty days from Takkada. The people of Burnu are Muslims. They have a king called Idris, who never appears before the people and addresses them only from behind a curtain. In exchange for the copper the traders receive good-looking slave girls as well young male slaves, and cloth dyed with saffron."

These adventures all came to an end when, while still at Takkada, he received a message "from our Lord, the Commander of the Faithful, the Champion of Religion, the One who Trusts in the Lord of the Worlds, [i.e. the Sultan of Morocco] commanding me to appear before his lofty seat. I obeyed at once, buying two camels for thirty-seven and a half *mithqals* and, since no wheat is to be found between Takkada and Tuwat, provisions for seventy days. I departed from Takkada on Thursday 11 Shaban 754 [September 11, 1353,] in a very large caravan that included about six hundred slave girls."

Those slave girls who accompanied Ibn Battuta on his journey back north, which he made on the back of a camel and they on foot, almost certainly outnumbered the male slaves, for whom there was less demand. So far from having any color prejudice, Europeans of that time greatly appreciated what the Andalusian-Arab geographer, Al-Bakri, described as "good-looking young women with sleek, elegant figures, whose breasts are firm, whose waists are slender, and whose backsides are well-rounded." Another Arab chronicler, Al-Sharishi, wrote that "God has endowed the slave girls of Ghana with laudable characteristics, both physical and moral, more than can be desired. Their bodies are smooth, their black skins are lustrous, their eyes are beautiful, their noses well shaped, their teeth are white, and their smell is fragrant."

And it was not just their good looks. According to Al-Bakri, in the town of Aoudaghast, in Ghana, "where the market is so thronged and the hubbub so loud that you can hardly hear what the person sitting next to you is saying, some of the Negresses are sold for over a hundred gold pieces. This is because of their great skill as cooks. Among the appetizing dishes they know how to prepare are *djouzincat*, a kind of nut cake, *cataif*, which is macaroni and honey, and all kinds of sweetmeats."

To be sure, not all the people of Ghana were so desirable, particularly the Ququ, who, according to Al-Gharnati, "have short necks, flattened noses, and red eyes. Their hair is like peppercorns and their smell is abominable, like that of burnt horn. They shoot arrows poisoned with the blood of yellow snakes; within an hour of being struck with such an arrow a person's flesh begins to fall off his bones. They eat vipers and other kinds of snakes, except the yellow snake, and serpents. Their arrows are short and have points made of tree thorns that are as strong as iron; when shooting they can hit the pupil of an eye. They are the worst kind of Sudanese. The others are useful as slaves and laborers but not the Ququ, who have no good qualities, except in war."

Sixty-two years after Ibn Battuta arrived back in Fez, a Portuguese army captured the Moroccan port of Ceuta, opposite Gibraltar. This victory was part of the campaign that had been going for hundreds of years to drive the Moors out of the Iberian Peninsula, back across the Mediterranean and eventually out of the so-called Holy Places in Palestine. According to *The Chronicle of the Discovery and Conquest of Guinea* by Gomes Eannes de Azurara, Keeper of the Royal Archives at Lisbon and Chief Chronicler, it was while he was in Ceuta that the Portuguese commander, Prince Henry, first heard of the trans-Saharan trade; this is not very likely, but it is certainly true that Henry, who was generally known as Henry the Navigator—*Henrique o Navegador*—was a major promoter of Portuguese exploration along the west coast of Africa.

According to Keeper of the Archives Azurara, Henry had several motives: First was "the noble spirit of this Prince, which was ever urging him to carry out great deeds." Second was the calculation that the trans-Saharan trade could be carried on at much lower cost if the goods were transported by ship rather than on foot—"a trade which would bring us great profit." Third, "the power of the Moors in that part of Africa was thought to be great, and it was natural prudence to know the power of the enemy and the extent of their territory. Fourth, during the one and thirty years he had been fighting the Moors, not a single Christian king had for the love of Our Lord Jesus Christ come to his aid. But perhaps there were Christian princes in those lands who from charity and the love of Christ would join him in the fight against those enemies of the faith."

This was a reference to the enduring legend of the powerful and fabulously rich Christian ruler called Prester, or Presbyter (i.e. priest), John, whose kingdom was first thought to be located in central Asia, then in India, and then in east Africa—where there was in fact the Christian kingdom of Ethiopia. According to a famous travel book of the time, the *Libro del Conoscimiento*, the inhabitants, who were "as black as pitch, burned the sign of the Cross on their foreheads to show that they had been baptized." That was the kind of religious spirit Prince Henry liked to see. According to the *Libro*, Prester John's kingdom could be reached quite easily via the Sinus Aethiopicus, a huge gulf that began in west Africa and stretched almost all the way across the continent. The fact that this gulf was also sometimes spoken of as the Rio del Oro—the River of Gold—made its existence all the more credible.

> "The fifth reason was the salvation of souls, his great desire to bring to Our Lord Jesus Christ all those who would be saved by understanding the mystery of his Incarnation, Death and Passion. No better offering could be made to the Lord than this, for according to God's promise he will be rewarded in heaven a hundred times over for saving so many souls. And I, the Chronicler of this History, have seen so many men and women who came from those parts turned to the Holy Faith that even if the Prince had been a heathen, their prayers on his behalf would have been enough to obtain his salvation."

Prince Henry the Navigator, promoter of Portuguese exploration and raids along the west coast of Africa—an extension, in his view, of the ongoing Crusade against infidels, and a way of saving the souls of pagan Africans by bringing them to a Christian country.

There was also a sixth reason: if Portuguese ships could eventually find their way around the Cape of Good Hope and across the Indian Ocean, they would be able to horn in on the immensely profitable luxury trade that now made its laborious way overland from India and East Asia along the famous Silk Road.

But before any of those good things could happen, someone had to be bold enough to round the dreaded Cabo Bojador, the "bulging cape" on the west coast of Africa, whose Arab name was Abu Khatar, the "father of danger," a place "of widespread and ancient rumors that had been cherished by mariners from Spain from generation to generation." Not since the fifth century BC, when an expedition from Carthage under Hanno had reached the Senegal River, had any vessel been known to venture beyond this point. And for good reason: the sea was dangerously shallow and would sometimes seethe and throw up an alarming mist (it turned out that this was caused by huge shoals of sardines); at other times the magnetic compass needles would spin wildly (this was due to ferrous rocks on the seabed); enormous sand-storms blown from the Sahara desert would blot out the sky. Moreover, according to the "widespread and ancient rumors," beyond Bojador lay the Green Sea of Darkness, its waters thick with scum and teeming with serpents and sea-monsters, its shores inhabited by giants who would wade out into the sea, grab hold of ships and smash them to pieces. It was a region belonging to Satan, and God would punish any Christian who ventured there by turning him black.

"The Prince always received home again with great patience those whom he had sent out as captains of his ships in search of that land," wrote Azurara; "never upbraiding them for their failure, but with gracious countenance listening to their stories, rewarding them as was his wont, and then either sending them back to search again or dispatching other picked men." Among those thus dispatched was a young courtier named Gil Eannes, who in 1433 "followed the course that others had taken; but touched by the self-same terror, he went only as far as the Canary Islands, where he took some captives and returned to the Kingdom." Next year the prince sent him out again, after first reminding him that "You cannot find a peril so great that the hope of reward will not be greater."

And so, in 1434, "despising all danger," Gil Eannes doubled Cape Bojador in a small ship called a barca "and found the lands beyond quite contrary to what he had expected." He went ashore in the ship's boat, but "without finding people or signs of habitation." But feeling that he should bring back "some token of the land, I gathered these herbs which I hereby present to Your Grace. They are what we call Roses of Saint Mary."

For his success in rounding the cape Eannes was rewarded "with honors and possessions" and then promptly sent out yet again in his barca. After going "fifty leagues beyond the Cape they found the land without dwellings, but showing footmarks of men and camels." Other probing voyages followed, always with orders to push on a bit further and, if possible, bring back a native who could be taught Portuguese and would then serve as an interpreter. Then, in 1441, Antam Goncalvez, "a very young man," was sent out with orders to do no more than explore a little further and bring home a cargo of the "skins and oil of sea-wolves." But Goncalvez was ambitious for glory, and after collecting his cargo he addressed his fellow crew members, who numbered twenty-one: "How fair a thing it would be if we, who have come to this land for a cargo of such petty merchandise, were to meet with the good fortune to bring the first captives to our prince." Everyone agreed that this was a good idea "so long as you will introduce no other novelty that might increase the danger."

They landed at night and found a path leading inland, and when they had gone three leagues, "they found the footmarks of forty to fifty men and youths, but these led in the direction from which they were coming." So they decided to turn back in pursuit of their prey, and soon came upon a naked man following a camel, with two assegais—short spears— in his hand. "Our men pursued him, but though he was only one, and saw that they were many, yet he began to defend himself boldly. But when Affonso Goterres wounded him with a javelin he threw down his weapons as if defeated." After capturing the naked man they decided to return to their ship, "and as they were going on their way they saw a black Mooress coming along," so they seized her too.

Soon Antam Goncalvez was joined by Nuno Tristam, "a youthful knight, very valiant and ardent," who came in an armed caravel—a ship much better suited to these waters than Goncalvez's barca, as it could carry a larger cargo and, with its lateen rigging, could sail into the wind. Nuno Tristam's mission was to explore still farther along the coast as well as "to capture some of the people of the country." He had brought along an Arab to serve as interpreter with the locals, "but they were not able to understand him because the language of these people was not Moorish, but Azaneguy [Tuaregs] of Sahara." So instead of negotiating, Goncalvez and Tristam joined forces for a night attack on two nearby encampments. Four men were killed and ten prisoners, including women and boys, were taken back to the ships, among them a chief called Adahu, who was able to converse with the interpreter in Arabic. Next day the interpreter was sent ashore with a message offering to sell the prisoners back to the natives and to discuss other trading matters.

However, two days later, instead of traders, "there came about a hundred and fifty Moors on foot and thirty-five on horses and camels." Not only did they appear "barbarous and bestial," they also tried to lure the Portuguese into an ambush near the shore; but this act of "treachery" was detected before they landed. Returning to their ships, and abandoning the Arab interpreter, they partitioned the captives, and then Antam Goncalves returned to Portugal, while Nuno Tristam explored farther along the coast.

According to Azurara, Prince Henry expressed "pleasure and delight" at the arrival of Goncalves' captives, not because they and the others that would surely follow promised "a sum of riches," but because of "his holy purpose to seek salvation for the lost souls of the heathen, as I have already mentioned in chapter seven." Indeed, it was the captives who were the lucky ones, "for although their bodies were now brought into some subjection, that was a small matter when compared with the true freedom that their souls would now possess for evermore."

Meanwhile, these events attracted the notice of the Vatican, whose support Henry was keen to obtain. At that time canon law allowed the enslavement of captives only if they were taken in a just war, such as a crusade, and only if they were not Christians. But if the current pope, Eugenius IV, could be persuaded to extend the definition of the long-approved crusade against the Moors to include Henry's West African ventures, then they could proceed with a clear conscience and a guarantee of "the salvation of the souls of those who should meet their end in that conquest."

But while willing to extend to the Portuguese raiders the offer of "complete forgiveness of all their sins, of which they shall be truly penitent at heart," Eugenius not only confirmed the ban on enslaving Christians but extended it to those likely to be converted, as he explained in an encyclical known as *Sicut Dudum* (Latin for "Not long ago") issued on January 13, 1435.

> "To our venerable brothers, peace and apostolic benediction, etcetera.
>
> "Not long ago, we learned from our brother Ferdinand, bishop of Rubicon and representative of the faithful who are residents of the Canary Islands . . . the following facts." Among these facts was that "some Christians (we speak of this with sorrow) have approached the said islands by ship, and with armed forces taken captive and even carried off to lands overseas many persons of both sexes. Some of these people were already baptized; others were tricked and deceived

by the promise of Baptism, having been made a promise of safety that was not kept. They have deprived the natives of their property, or turned it to their own use, and have subjected some of the inhabitants of the said islands to perpetual slavery." As a consequence, many other islanders "have abandoned their intention of receiving Baptism, thus offending the majesty of God, putting their souls in danger, and causing no little harm to the Christian religion." Therefore, "with a holy and fatherly concern for the suffering of the inhabitants," it was ordered that everyone concerned should immediately "desist from the aforementioned deeds," and all natives held captive were "to be totally and perpetually free, and to be released."

However, while easy to promulgate, encyclicals were hard to enforce; and anyway, it was not long before *Sicut Dudum* was replaced with other decrees, and the conquest of west Africa declared to qualify as a crusade. And so, when Prince Henry dispatched six armed caravels on yet another raid, he ordered that "banners should be made with the Cross of the Order of Jesus Christ, one to be hoisted on each caravel."

This expedition, commanded by Lancarote da Ilha and Gil Eannes, the first to round Cape Bojador, was a big success. First they landed on an island near the mainland, where they made a dawn assault on a seaside village. "Shouting 'Santiago!' 'San Jorge!' [Saint George, the dragon slayer], and 'Portugal!' they attacked at once, killing and taking all they could. Then might you see mothers forsaking their children, and husbands their wives, each striving to escape as he could. Some were drowned in the water; others thought to escape by hiding under their huts; others stowed their children among the seaweed where our men found them. And at last our Lord God, who giveth a reward for every good deed, willed that for all the labor and expense they had undergone in His service they should that day obtain victory over their enemies, and they took captive of those Moors, what with men, women and children, one hundred and sixty-five, not counting those that perished and were killed. And when the battle was over, all praised God for the great mercy that he had shown them in giving them such a victory."

Soon afterward, on another island, Lancarote and his men came upon "nine natives, male and female, going along with ten or twelves asses laden with turtles." These were easily taken prisoner, "bound tightly and placed in the boats." Another easy capture took place when "our men saw some of the womenfolk walking along the beach to a creek to collect shell-fish. They captured one of them, who seemed to be about thirty years old, along with her son who was about four and a young girl of fourteen, who was well-shaped and nice-looking, for a Guinea. But the strength of the woman was astonishing, for although three men came upon her and seized her she struggled so fiercely that they were not able to get her into the boat. So one of our men, worried about the delay this was causing and fearing that some of the natives might appear on the scene, hit upon the expedient of snatching her son away from her, and carrying him to the boat; and love of her child compelled the mother to follow behind without any pressure from the two men who were bringing her along."

On August 7, 1444, the fleet arrived back at Lagos. "Moved by curiosity, the townspeople hurried down to the beach, where some of them got into boats and rowed out to the ships to welcome their relatives and friends." The officers went ashore to "kiss the hand of the Prince, their Lord, and to give him a short account of their exploits; after which they took their rest, as men who had returned to their fatherland and homes.

"And the next day Lancarote, as commander of the expedition, said to the Prince, 'My Lord, as your Grace is well aware, you are to receive one fifth of these Moors, and of everything else that we have won in those countries where you sent us for the service of God and yourself. But now these Moors, because of the long time we have been at sea, and because of the great sorrow they must feel at finding themselves far from the land of their birth, and being held in captivity, and not knowing what will happen to them; and also because they are not used to life on board a ship—for all these reasons they are in a poor condition, so I suggest that early tomorrow morning they should be landed and taken to the field just outside the city gate, where they will be divided into five parts, according to custom. And if your Grace will attend, you may choose whichever part you prefer.'

"On the next day, very early in the morning because of the great heat, the seamen began to make ready their boats and bring their captives ashore. And these people, placed all together in that field, were a sight to be wondered at; for some among them were quite white and fair, and well-proportioned; others were less white and more like mulattoes; others again were as black as Ethiops.

"But who could be so hard-hearted as not to be filled with pity at the sight of those people? For some kept their heads low, their faces bathed in tears as they looked at each other, while others stood groaning piteously, looking up to heaven and exclaiming loudly, as if asking for help from the Father of Nature; others struck their faces with the palms of their hands, throwing themselves full length upon the ground, and still others made dirge-like lamentations, after the manner of their country. And though we could not understand their words, the sounds they made were full of sadness.

"To add to their suffering the officials responsible for dividing the captives now arrived, and began separating them from each other into five equal parts; and so fathers were separated from sons, husbands from wives, brothers from brothers.

"Completing the partition was very difficult, for as often as sons were placed in one part, seeing their fathers in another, they would rush over to join them; mothers threw themselves on the ground, clasping their children in their arms and ignoring the blows that rained down on them. Moreover, to make matters worse, the field was invaded by crowds of people who had taken the day off from work and had come out from the town, and from the nearby countryside and villages, and were now causing such tumult and confusion as to make the business of handling and dividing the captives even more difficult.

"The Prince was there, mounted on a powerful steed and accompanied by his retinue. He showed little interest in his share of the profits and very soon had given away the forty-six captives that came to him as his fifth. His chief reward and greatest pleasure lay in the thought that so many lost souls would now be brought to salvation.

"Nor was this expectation in vain, for as soon as they had learned our language these people at once became Christians. And I, who composed this work of history, have seen in the town of Lagos boys and girls who were the children and grandchildren of those first captives, born in this country, and now as good and true Christians as if they had descended directly from those who were first baptized."

Furthermore,

"As our people did not find them hardened in the belief of the other Moorish infidels, but came with a good will to the law of Christ, they made no difference between them and their free servants, born in this country. Those who were still young were taught the mechanical arts, and those who were capable of managing property were set free and married to Portuguese women, sharing their property just like other people. Yea, and some widows of good family who had bought some of these female slaves either adopted them or left them part of their estates in their wills, so that later on they made good marriages. Moreover I never once saw any of these slaves put in irons like other captives, and scarcely any who did not turn Christian and was not very well treated.

"And so their lot was quite different from what it had been. Before their capture they had lived in perdition of their souls and of their bodies—of their souls because they were pagans, without the clearness and light of the Holy Faith; and of their bodies because they had lived like beasts, without any of the habits or customs of civilized beings."

Chief Chronicler Azurara concluded his work in 1448, when he estimated that a total of nine hundred and twenty-seven "infidels had been brought from those lands to this, through the virtue and talents of our glorious Prince Henry." He promised that another book "would record the rest of the Prince's deeds, although the events that followed were not accomplished with such toil and bravery as in the past. For after this year the affairs of that region were carried out more by the trading and bargaining of merchants than by bravery and force of arms."

This change of policy was to be expected. In their first raids the Portuguese had enjoyed the advantage of surprise, but this did not last long and, once on the alert, their intended victims put up a fierce resistance. Sometimes this was collective, as when one of Lancarote's raiding parties sent two men to scout ahead, who soon came running back to warn the others, "telling them to run as fast as they could because a powerful force of Moors was headed their way. So they at once made for the boats, while the Moors came after them as fast as they could. And then it pleased our Lord God, who succors all those who go in his service, that the Christians should reach the shore before the Moors could come up with them. But before they could get safely into the boats, the Moors came up and began to attack them, and it was only with great difficulty that they managed to embark. There were about three hundred of these fighting Moors who made it very clear that they meant to defend their land." (By now the Portuguese had ventured "more than 110 leagues beyond Cape Verde," and often used the terms Moors, Guineas and Negroes more or less interchangeably.)

At other times the resistance was individual, as in this incident which took place when, soon after landing, some soldiers commanded by Dinis Diaz came across footprints in the sand. Following these tracks they soon caught sight of some Moors, gave chase and captured nine of them, men and women. While the main party went on, six of the raiders were ordered to bind these prisoners and take them back to the ship, but this turned out to be more difficult than expected. "And since women are usually stubborn, one of the women prisoners refused to walk, throwing herself on the ground and letting herself be dragged along by her hair and legs, having no pity on herself; and because of her over-great stubbornness our men were forced to leave her there on the ground, intending to return for her another day. And while they were arguing about this the other prisoners began to scatter, some running in one direction and others in another direction, so that two of them got away; and though our men tried to catch them they failed to do so, for they were in a spot where there were plenty of places to hide. So in the end they were able to bring only six captives to the place where they had landed, and where they were joined by the rest of their party. Some of them wanted to go back for the Mooress who had been left in bonds, but as it was very late and the sea was dangerous they gave up the attempt and embarked in their boat, which set sail at once. And so the foolishly stubborn Mooress was left behind strongly bound in that place, where she no doubt met with a troublesome death."

Such acts of resistance increased. Soon after the encounter with the Mooress, Dinis Diaz found it impossible even to get on shore, "for though our men tried to land many times, they always encountered such a bold defense that they dared not come to close quarters." Moreover "the people of this land are not so easy to capture as we desire, for the men are very strong, alert and well prepared for combat, and their arrows are poisoned with a very dangerous herb. Therefore it seemed best to us that we ought to turn back, for if we tried to attack these people it would be the cause of our deaths. So they mended their sails and prepared to depart."

The new policy of "trading and bargaining" rather than "bravery and force of arms" was in place by the time a young Venetian named Alvise da Ca' da Mosto, also known as Luigi Cadamosto, entered the service of Prince Henry. This happened in 1454 when Cadamosto, then aged twenty-two, and "having sailed to various parts of our Mediterranean Sea, decided to return to Flanders, where I had been once before, in the hope of profit." While passing the coast of Portugal the Venetian ships were forced by bad weather to stop off at Cape St. Vincent, not far from Sagres, where Prince Henry had his palace. Hearing of them, Henry dispatched Antam Goncalves and some others to invite them ashore, and while doing so Goncalves, who had been the first to bring captives back to Portugal, filled Cadamosto's head with stories of "seas that had never before been sailed and lands of many strange races where marvels abound, and where they had wrought great gain, turning one *soldo* into six or ten. On my asking, I was told that Prince Henry allowed anyone who wanted to go there to do so, under one of two conditions; either the trader would fit out a caravel and load it with merchandise at his own expense, in which case he would on his return pay the prince a quarter of all his profits; or the prince would provide the ship and the trader would provide the cargo, in which case the profits would be divided evenly."

When all this was confirmed by Prince Henry himself, "I made up my mind to go, for I was young, well-fitted to endure all hardships, desirous of seeing things never before seen by anyone of our nation, and also hoped to win honors and profit. I therefore consigned to a relative my share of the cargo going to Flanders and disembarked." A new caravel was fitted out and on March 22, 1455, "furnished with all necessities, we set sail in God's name and with high hopes." Three days later, aided by a north-northeasterly wind, they reached Madeira, six hundred miles away. After a stop-over there, they went on to Cape Blanco, near Arguim, "where begins the sandy country, which desert the Berbers call Sarra [Sahara]. It is a very great desert which takes well-mounted men fifty to sixty days to cross." The people there were "Muhammadans, and very hostile to Christians; they never remain settled in one place but are always wandering over these deserts; these are the men who go down to the Land of the Blacks, and also up to Barbary. They are very numerous and have many camels on which they carry brass and silver and other things from Barbary to Tanbutu [Timbuktu] and to the Land of the Blacks; and from there they bring away gold and pepper. These people are brown-complexioned and wear white cloaks edged with a red stripe. On their heads the men wear turbans in the Moorish style, and are always barefooted. In these sandy districts there are many lions, leopards and ostriches, whose eggs I have often eaten and found good."

On orders from Prince Henry a fortified trading post had been built on the island of Arguim where resident merchants could trade with the Arabs, selling them woolen cloth, cotton, silver, carpets and grain—"for they are always short of food"—and obtaining in return "slaves whom the Arabs bring from the Land of the Blacks, and gold dust. The Arabs also have many Berber horses which they take to the Land of the Blacks, exchanging them with the rulers for slaves. Ten or fifteen slaves are given for one horse, depending on its quality." Cadamosto estimated that every year a thousand slaves were sent from Arguim to Portugal.

From Capo Blanco they sailed nearly four hundred miles to the mouth of the Senegal River "which separates the Black people from the brown Azanaghi. Beyond the river all the men are very black, tall and big, their bodies well-formed, and the whole country green, full of trees and fertile; while on this side the men are brownish, lean, ill-nourished and small in stature, and their country sterile and arid." However, the kingdom of Senegal, which was populated by Jalofs (also known as Wolofs), was quite poor, "having no cities, only villages of straw huts."

"The kingdom is also very small, extending no more than two hundred miles along the coast and about the same inland. The king has no income from taxes but every year the lords who want to win his favor offer him horses, which are highly valued because of their scarcity, food, goats and cows, vegetables, and so on. He also supports himself by raiding his own or the neighboring countries and taking many slaves. These he either employs in cultivating his land or sells to the Azanaghi traders in exchange for horses and other goods. He also sells them to Christians, now that we have begun to engage in this trade.

"The faith of these Blacks is Muhammadanism, but unlike the white Moors they are not very resolute in this faith, especially the common people. The chiefs are Muhammadans because they have Azanaghi or Arab priests around them, who give them some instruction, but since they have had contact with Christians their faith has lessened, for they like our customs and realize that our wealth and skills exceed theirs. The people are talkative, and never at a loss for something to say. Most of them are great liars and cheats, but on the other hand they are charitable and generous, ready to welcome strangers and provide meals and a night's lodging without charge.

"After passing the Senegal River in my caravel I sailed fifty miles to the east along a low flat coast to the country of Budomel. There I anchored my caravel, for I wanted to meet him, some Portuguese having told me that he was a notable and upright ruler who could be trusted and who paid royally for what he bought. Since I had with me some Spanish horses, which were in great demand in the country of the Blacks, as well as some other goods such as woolen cloth and Moorish silk, I decided to try my luck with this lord. Accordingly I cast my anchor at a place on the coast which is a roadstead, and not a port, and sent my Negro interpreter to announce my arrival. On being informed of this the lord mounted his horse and rode down to the sea-shore escorted by fifteen horsemen and a hundred and fifty foot soldiers. He sent a message inviting me ashore and saying that I would be treated with honor and respect, and knowing of his high reputation I complied. He entertained me with a great feast, and then asked me to go inland for some days to his house about two hundred and fifty [actually more like twenty-five] miles from the coast, where he would pay me generously for the goods I had brought, promising me one hundred slaves. So I handed over the horses along with their harnesses and other goods, which together had cost me about three hundred ducats, and agreed to go with him."

On his arrival in the interior Cadamosto was lodged with Budomel's nephew, Bisboror, lord of a village where he stayed a month and "saw much of the manner of life of this land." For example, "the dwelling of the king is never fixed; instead he has a number of villages which support his wives and families. In the village where I stayed there were from forty to fifty grass huts close together in a circle, surrounded by hedges and groves of large trees, leaving only a couple of gaps as entrances. In this village Budomel had nine wives, as well as other wives in other villages. Each wife had five or six young Negro girls to attend her, and it is lawful for the lord to sleep with these attendants as well as with his wives, who do not take offense as it is the custom of the country. These Negroes, both men and women, are extremely lascivious. Having been given to understand that Christians know how to do many things, Budomel kept asking me if by chance I could provide him with the means of satisfying many women, offering me a large reward if I did. The men are also very jealous and allow no one, not even their own sons, to enter the huts where their wives live.

"This Budomel is always accompanied by at least two hundred Negroes, and many others come to see him from various places. He often displays great haughtiness, appearing only for an hour in the morning and for a short time in the evening. When an audience is granted, great ceremony is observed: on entering Budomel's courtyard the suitor, no matter how nobly born, strips himself naked except for a leather girdle, throws himself down on his knees, bows his head to the ground and with both hands scatters sand on his naked shoulders and head. He remains in this posture for a long time and then, without rising but grovelling on his hands and knees, draws nearer. When within two paces he begins to state his business, still scattering sand and keeping his head bowed as a sign of the greatest humility. Meanwhile, the lord scarcely deigns to take notice of him, but continues talking with his attendants. When the suitor has finished, he replies briefly and in an arrogant manner. If God himself were to come to earth I do not think that these people could show Him more honor and reverence than they do to their king. I believe that this is due to the great fear and dread in which they hold him, since for the most trivial misdeed he seizes their wives and children and sells them for slaves."

Thanks to Budomel's friendship, Cadamosto was allowed to attend evening service at the mosque, where they

"prayed in this fashion: standing upright and often looking up, then taking two paces forward and reciting some words in a low voice, and then bowing down several times and kissing the ground. When he had finished, Budomel asked me what I thought of it, and also asked me to recite some of the articles of our faith. In the end I told him that his faith was false, that those who had instructed him in it were ignorant of the truth, and that only our faith was true and holy. At this he laughed, and said that our faith must be good because God had bestowed so many gifts and such knowledge on the Christians; nevertheless it stood to reason that his people were more likely to win salvation, for God was just, and having given Christians so many benefits in this world, and having given the Negroes almost nothing, it followed that in the hereafter He would reward them with paradise."

Cadamosto took note of many other features of Senegalese life—their inability to raise corn, rye or barley, "which they had obtained of us Christians," because of the great heat and long droughts, and their success with crops of millet and beans, especially kidney beans, "the largest and finest in the world, all spotted with different colors, as though painted, and very beautiful to the eye. They are sown in July and harvested in September, during the rainy season. The people are very bad laborers, unwilling to exert themselves to sow more than will barely support them through the year. Few trouble to raise supplies for the market." On the other hand, "The women of this country are very pleasant and light-hearted, always ready to sing and dance, especially the young girls. However, they dance only at night, by the light of the moon."

Having completed his business with Budomel, Cadamosto decided to continue beyond Cape Verde. "For before leaving Portugal I had understood from the Prince that not far beyond this first kingdom of Senega there was another one called Gambra [Gambia], where the Negroes who had been taken to Portugal said there was gold in large amounts, and that any Christian who went there would become rich." Just as he was setting sail, two other caravels appeared, one captained by Antoniotto Usodimare, a Genoese, the other by "certain squires of the Prince." Since their plans were similar to Cadamosto's, they joined forces and "set a course for Cape Verde, always keeping in sight of land." Next day they reached the cape, which "was very handsome and lofty, with two small hills on the point. It runs far out into the sea, and on it there are many grass huts belonging to the Negroes." Beyond Cape Verde the coast was "low and covered with very fine, tall green trees which never shed their leaves. These trees come right down to within a bow-shot of the beach, so that it appears as if they were growing in the sea—a very beautiful sight."

With the wind behind them they continued along the coast, "anchoring each evening in about six fathoms of water, and four or five miles from the shore. At dawn we made sail, always stationing one man aloft and two men in the bows to watch for breakers, which would disclose the presence of shoals.

> "Sailing thus we reached the mouth of a river as large as the River of Senega. We cast anchor and debated whether we should send one of our interpreters ashore, for each ship had brought from Portugal Negro interpreters who had been sold by the rulers of Senega to the first Portuguese to discover the Land of the Blacks. Lots were drawn to decide which one was to go ashore, and it fell to the one belonging to the Genoese [Antoniotto Usodimare]. A boat was made ready and the interpreter was instructed to find out about the country and its ruler, and whether any gold or other valuables were to be obtained there. When he had landed, and the boat had pulled back a short distance, he was suddenly confronted by a great number of Negroes who had seen the ships approaching and had lain hidden with bows and arrows and other weapons. They talked for a short while, and what he said to them we do not know; but they began to strike at him furiously with their short Moorish swords, and quickly put him to death, those in the boat being unable to help him."

Assuming that if this was how they treated one of their own they would be even less friendly to white men, the adventurers hoisted their sails and resumed their journey. When they reached the mouth of the Gambia they sent the smallest of the caravels and a boat of armed men to explore the river.

> "Their instructions were that if the Negroes attacked them they should return at once, without attempting to fight back, because we had come there to trade peacefully and with their consent. So the boats went two miles up the river, taking soundings; but the higher they went, the more it twisted and turned, so they decided to come back.

"And as they were returning three canoes, made from the hollowed-out trunks of large trees, came out from a stream that flows into the great river. When our men saw them they suspected that they were about to be attacked, and although they were numerous enough to have defended themselves, they were under instructions to avoid a quarrel; and having been warned by other Negroes that in Gambra all the bowmen used poisoned arrows, they bent to their oars and returned with all possible speed. But fast though they were, by the time they reached our ships the canoes were close behind them. After getting on board, our men began to make signs to the canoes to draw near. They slowed down, but came no closer. They remained there for a while staring at things neither they nor their fathers had ever seen before, that is ships and white men, but they showed no desire to parley, despite all our attempts to engage them, and went away about their own affairs. And so that day passed without further incident."

Early the next morning the two larger caravels crossed the bar at the mouth of the river and all three ships then sailed upstream "hoping that we might find more civilized people than those in the canoes. The small caravel led the way over the shallows, and we followed one behind the other.

"Having sailed about four miles upstream we suddenly perceived several canoes, which seemed to have appeared from nowhere, coming up behind us as fast as they could. Seeing this, we turned upon them and stood to our stations, although we were poorly armed, and did what we could to protect ourselves from their poisoned arrows. In a short time they reached us. Being in the leading ship I thrust into the middle of the canoes, scattering them apart. There were seventeen of them, all of them quite large. Checking their course and lifting up their paddles, their crews stared at us as if at a marvel. We estimated that they numbered at most about a hundred and fifty men; they were very well-built, exceedingly black and clothed in white cotton shirts. Some of them wore small white caps on their heads, very like the German style, except that on each side they had a white wing and in the middle a feather, perhaps to show that they were fighting men. A Negro stood in the prow of each canoe with a round shield made of leather on his arm. They made no movement towards us, nor we to them. Then they saw the two other ships coming up behind

Raising the sail on an Arab dhow, the ship generally used in the East African slave trade. Though not crammed in below deck as on European ships, the slaves huddled in the prow had a hard time when exposed to the tropical sun and monsoon rain storms.

us, and headed towards them, and on reaching them they at once threw down their paddles and began to shoot their arrows.

"On being attacked our ships at once discharged four bombards [cannon that fired stone balls]. Astonished by the roar, the Negroes threw down their bows and stood in amazement while the shots fell into the river; but after thus gaping for a while, and seeing no more shots coming at them, and hearing no more thunder-claps from the bombards, they took up their bows and renewed their shooting, coming to within a stone's throw of the ships. The sailors then began to fire their cross-bows at them, and one of them hit a Negro in the chest, so that he fell dead in his canoe. His companions pulled out the arrow and examined it closely, astonished at such a weapon; but this did not stop them from shooting vigorously at the ships. Our crews responded no less vigorously, so that in a short time a large number of Negroes were wounded. However, by the Grace of God, not one Christian was hit.

"When they saw how many had been killed and wounded, all the canoes with one accord made for the stern of the small caravel, where a stiff fight followed, for her crew were few and ill-armed. Seeing this I made sail for the small ship and towed her between our two large ships, which continued to discharge our bombards and cross-bows. At this the Negroes drew off. We lashed our three ships together with chains, dropped anchor and then attempted to parley with the Negroes.

"After much gesticulating and shouting by our interpreters one of the canoes returned within bow-shot. We asked them why they had attacked us since we were men of peace and traders, who had established friendly relations with the people of Senega and would now like to be on the same terms with them. Furthermore, we had come from a distant land and brought gifts for their ruler from the king of Portugal, who desired to be on terms of peace and friendship with them.

"They replied that they had had news of our coming, and of our trade with the Negroes of Senega, who must be bad men if they were friendly to us. They were convinced that we Christians ate human flesh and bought Negroes only in order to eat them. Under no circumstances did they wish to be our friends, but would rather kill us all.

"At this moment the wind freshened; and since they were so hostile we decided to sail straight at them and run them down. But before we could reach them they scattered in all directions, heading for the land. And thus ended our encounter with them.

"We then discussed whether we should proceed further up the river, in the hope of finding more friendly people. But our sailors were unwilling to face any more dangers and wanted to return home. With one accord they began to complain, declaring that they would not consent to such a plan, and that what had been done was enough for that voyage. When we saw that they were all of one mind we gave way in order to avoid trouble, for they were pig-headed and obstinate men. And so the following day we left that place, shaping our course for Cape Verde and from there, in God's name, for Spain."

Henry the Navigator died in 1460, but his expansionary policies were continued by other Portuguese rulers, notably King Joao II, "a very Christian prince and lord of great prudence." One of his first acts was to order the building of a fortress-cum-trading post, known as El Mina and located near

Axim—"the place where our men usually trafficked for gold." (These quotations are from the sixteenth-century Portuguese historian, Joao de Barros.) As usual, the king's stated purpose had little to do with making money; rather it was that "the bait offered by worldly goods might lead those people to receive our Faith." Indeed, "the possibility of getting even one soul baptized into the Faith through the fortress outweighed all the inconveniences." Nevertheless, "since the work was to God's praise, He would see to it that his people made a profit." As well as saving souls, other reasons for building the fort were to enforce the trading monopoly recently conferred by various popes, provide safe-keeping for the gold and slaves awaiting shipment, and intimidate the locals.

The fort was largely prefabricated, the building materials—"hewed stone, tiles and wood"—being prepared beforehand in Portugal and then put on board a fleet of twelve ships that also carried "munitions and provisions for six hundred men, of whom one hundred were craftsmen and five hundred were soldiers. Diogo de Azambuja, a man very experienced in the art of war, was Captain-major." They arrived on January 19, 1482, and a message was at once sent to the local ruler, Caramanca (perhaps a corruption of Kwamin Ansa, i.e. King Ansa), asking for a meeting. When Caramanca replied "expressing delight at his coming," Azambuja landed "with all his people, dressed in their best clothes, but with concealed arms in case of need. He then took possession of a big tree on a small hill near the village, a place very suitable for a fortress; on this tree he raised a banner with the king's arms, and at the foot of the hill an altar was set up at which the first mass in those parts of Ethiopia was said. [The term Ethiopia was often used to describe any region south of the Sahara.] This mass was heard by our men with copious tears of devotion and thanks to God for allowing them to praise and glorify Him in the midst of those idolaters."

After mass, Azambuja drew up his men in ranks to await Caramanca, who "arrived seated on a high chair and wearing a jerkin of brocade with a golden collar of precious stones."

"His captains were all dressed in silk, and his men were drawn up in long ranks so as to form a broad avenue, up which Caramanca proceeded with many people in a war-like manner, with a deafening hubbub of kettle-drums, trumpets, bells and other instruments. Most of his people were naked, their skin gleaming with oil, which made them look even blacker; their privy parts were covered with pouches made of monkey skin or woven palm leaves. All of them were armed, some with spears and shields, others with bows and arrows; instead of helmets they wore monkey skins studded with animal teeth. Noblemen were followed by two pages, one carrying a round wooden stool so that they could sit down and rest whenever they wished, and the other a war shield. [In fact, these stools were emblems of chieftainship.] These lords wore rings and golden jewels on their heads and in their beards.

"Their king, Caramanca, came in their midst. His legs and arms were covered with gold bracelets and rings, around his neck he wore a collar from which hung small bells, and gold bars were plaited into his beard. To add to his dignity, he walked very slowly and lightly, never once looking to either side. When he had drawn near, Diogo de Azambuja went forward to meet him. Caramanca took his hand, then let it go and snapped his fingers while saying '*Bere, bere*' which means 'Peace, peace.' This snapping of fingers is a sign among them of the greatest courtesy." The king then stepped aside so that his lords could greet Azambuja, "but the manner in which they snapped their fingers was different: wetting their fingers in their mouths and wiping them on their chests, they cracked them from the little finger to the index finger. This is a custom used only when greeting princes, for they say that fingers can carry poison if not cleaned in this manner."

When these and other courtesies were completed, Azambuja, with the aid of an interpreter, launched into a lengthy speech—part flattering, part cajoling, and part threatening—whose gist was that they wanted to build a fortress in Caramanca's town. This would be greatly to the king's benefit: the fortress would safeguard "the rich merchandise never before seen in that land," and the trade would make him so wealthy and powerful that he would become "lord of his neighbors, for no one would dare challenge him since that building, and the power of the King of Portugal, would be there to defend him."

Although, according to the narrator, Joao de Barros, Caramanca "was a savage, he was also a man of good understanding, and he not only listened carefully to the interpreter but also observed Diogo de Azambuja closely. He and his men were perfectly silent; no one so much as spat." When the speech was over Caramanca remained silent, staring at the ground, and then made his reply: he appreciated the king's concern, which he certainly deserved since he had always treated the Portuguese who came to trade faithfully and honestly; he was impressed by how well dressed his visitors were and pleased that they wanted to establish a residence in his land. But there were problems: someone so important as the Captain, and the gallant officers who accompanied him, "would require that everything should always be on a lavish scale. Such high-spirited noblemen could not be expected to endure the poverty and simplicity of so savage a land as Guinea. This would lead to quarrels and passions." Also, as a general rule, "friends who meet only occasionally remain better friends than if they are neighbors." He therefore hoped that they "would be pleased to depart, and allow things to go on as before."

Azambuja was having none of this. In a reply that was as menacing as it was flowery, he explained that he had no choice but to carry out the orders of a king "whose subjects feared to disobey him more than they feared death itself. In this matter of establishing peace and erecting a fortress he would sooner lose his life than fail. At these words, Caramanca clapped his hands as a sign of agreement, and all the Negroes did the same." No doubt the presence of five hundred Portuguese soldiers, whose weapons were probably not all that well concealed, also helped win the argument.

Over the years to come, many other European countries would build their own fortresses on the Guinea coast, as much because of their mutual rivalries as they were a means of cowing the natives; but none were so famous as El Mina, formally known as Sao Jorge da Mina, with its own Gate of No Return, and its chapel "where God is praised not only by our own men but also by the Ethiopians, who having been baptized are included among the faithful. And in this church a mass is said every day for the soul of the Infante Don Henrique, the author of these discoveries."

Among those visiting El Mina during the next few years, either as one of Azambuja's officers or during a trading voyage to the Guinea coast, and while there no doubt attending the fort's chapel and praying for the soul of Prince Henry the Navigator, was that other dreamer with large ambitions, Christopher Columbus.

On his return from his first voyage to the West Indies, which to the end of his life he persisted in believing were offshore islands belonging to

Christopher Columbus, Discoverer of the New World, and originator of the trans-
Atlantic slave trade—not the one that went from Africa to America, but from west
to east, the cargoes being natives of the West Indies. The trade was not a success, as
most died in transit or soon after arriving in Spain.

Cipango (Japan) and Cathay (China), Columbus wrote his royal patrons,
Ferdinand and Isabella, a glowing description of how, after a voyage of
thirty-three days, he had discovered "a great many islands, inhabited by
numberless people; and of these I have taken possession for their Highnesses by proclamation and by displaying the Royal Standard." While
performing these ceremonies many natives had gathered round, and "as
I saw that they were very friendly to us, and could be more easily converted to our Holy Faith by gentle means rather than by force, I gave
them some red caps, and strings of beads to wear round their necks, and
other trifles. They were delighted with these gifts and became very
friendly, and later they came swimming out to our ships, bringing parrots,
balls of cotton and other things which they traded with us."

Of all the islands that he visited, Columbus was especially pleased
with Hispaniola, where "the trees are as green and lovely as the trees in

Spain in the month of May" and where "the nightingales sing even in November. Its hills and mountains, fine plains and open country, are rich and fertile, suitable for planting and for pasturage. It has splendid seaports, magnificent rivers, abundant spices and vast mines of gold and other metals. The people have no iron or steel, nor any weapons, nor would these be of any use to them, for though they are well-made and robust, they appear to be exceptionally timid. Their only arms are sticks of cane sharpened at one end, and even these they are afraid to use." They were also very generous—"they never refuse anything that is asked for and in return are satisfied with the merest trifle"—and were ripe for conversion, having no religion of their own. And they had the highest opinion of Columbus and his crew, for "they firmly believe that I, with my ships and men, came from heaven." Indeed, as he explored the island, "wherever I went, they would run on ahead, going from house to house and calling out 'Come! Come and see the men from heaven!' Then all the people, men and women, young and old, would gather about us, bringing something to eat and drink, which they offered with wonderful kindness."

These people were Tainos. Other islands were inhabited by Caribs, "a wild and mischievous people," according to Pietro Martire. "There is no man able to behold them but he shall feel his bowels grate with a certain horror." The Caribs often raided the Tainos, seizing young boys and castrating them "to make them fat, as we do cock chickens and young hogs, and eat them when they are well fed." However "they abstain from eating of women, and count it vile. Therefore such young women as they take they keep for increase, as we do hens to lay eggs. The old women, they make them drudges." The Tainos were no match for the Caribs and "confess that ten of the Cannibals are able to overcome a hundred of them."

Concluding his letter, Columbus promised "to send their Highnesses as much gold as they desire," along with spices, cotton, aromatic gum, aloe wood and "as many slaves as they choose to send for, all of them heathens." But then, disappointingly, it turned out that there was little gold or cotton to send, and that the spices were of the wrong kind, and so slaves became the only apparently profitable export. By implication these slaves would be Caribs, but the Tainos were much easier to capture, and soon a shipment of fifteen hundred was on its way. But then came another disappointment: hundreds died on the way over, and those who survived did not last long.

And the Tainos weren't the only inhabitants of the New World who failed to give satisfaction. When Ponce de Leon set out to "govern and conquer" Florida, "the Indians came out and fought valiantly until they defeated him, slaying almost all the men with him. He escaped with only six companions and sailed for the island of Cuba, where all died of the wounds." Not long after, Lucas Vazquez de Ayllon "armed two ships and sent them out among the islands to capture Indians who would be put to work in the gold mines. But because of bad weather they got lost and landed at a place they called Santa Elena [possibly Cape Fear in North Carolina]." Soon after they had landed, "the Indians approached in great fear and amazement to see such strange vessels and men with beards and wearing clothes. Nevertheless they treated each other in a friendly manner and exchanged gifts . . . After this the ships took on supplies of wood and water, and the Spaniards invited their new friends to come on board and take a closer look. Trusting the good faith of men who had treated them so kindly, and wishing to see things so new to them, more than a hundred and thirty went on board. Then, when they were below deck, the Spaniards locked them in, weighed anchor and set sail for Santo Domingo. However, during the voyage one of the ships was lost at sea, and though the other arrived safely it was found that all the Indians had died of sorrow and starvation, for being angry at the way they had been betrayed under the guise of friendship, they had refused to eat anything at all." (This account is by Garcilaso de la Vega.)

So, with little gold to be found and a dearth of slaves suitable for export, the Spanish took to exploiting the land, dividing it up into large holdings known as *repartimientos* and setting up a system of *encomiendas*, whereby in return for "protection" and being taught the Holy Faith, the natives were required to work the land without pay. Since the Tainos were reluctant to adopt this system, they had to be forced into it, usually at the point of a sword. In addition, the Spaniards brought with them smallpox and measles, diseases to which the natives had no immunity.

The result of all this was described by someone who, before his religious conversion and taking holy orders, had himself been one of the conquistadors—Bartolomeo de las Casas, who had arrived in Hispaniola in 1502 and spent several years as a planter and slave-owner. As he became convinced that the treatment of the natives was a great sin, endangering the souls of the Spaniards as well as destroying the lives of the natives, Las Casas began a campaign of denunciation, testifying back in Spain before the Council of the Indies and the monarch himself, and publishing a book, *Brevissima Relacion de la Destruccion de las Indias— A Brief Account of the Devastation of the Indies*. What he wrote came "from my own knowledge, having been an eye-witness to many of the deeds" of his fellow Spaniards, who he described as "ravening wild beasts, wolves, tigers, or lions that had been starved for many days." Greed and ambition were the causes—"the Christians' insatiable desire to acquire as much gold as they can, as fast as they can, and to rise to a status far beyond their merits." Here is some of what he had to say:

"The Island Hispaniola was where the Spaniards first landed, and where they carried out their first ravages against the native people, destroying and devastating as they went, seizing and abusing the women and children, devouring their food, and forcing many to flee to the mountains. The Indians then began to resist, but their weapons were almost useless, and the Christians with their horses and swords and pikes began to carry out massacres and strange cruelties. When they attacked towns they spared neither the children nor the aged, nor pregnant women, nor women in child-bed, not only stabbing them but cutting them to pieces as if they were sheep in a slaughterhouse. They laid bets as to who, with one stroke of the sword, could split a man in two or cut off his head. Other victims were wrapped in straw and then burned alive. Still others had their hands cut off and then tied around their necks and were told to carry this message to those who had fled to the mountains. And because all those who could do so fled to the mountains the Spanish captains pursued them with fierce dogs specially trained to follow and attack the Indians, tearing them to pieces and devouring their flesh.

"And when the wars and killing came to an end, the survivors were distributed among the Christians to be slaves. The pretext for this *repartimiento* was that it would facilitate the instruction of the Indians in the Christian Faith—as if those cruel, greedy and vicious Christians could be caretakers of souls! And indeed all the care they took was to send the men to the mines to dig for gold, which is unbearably hard labor, and the women to the fields to hoe and till the land, which is work suitable only for strong men. Nor did either the men or the women get enough to eat, and so the milk in the breasts of the mothers who were nursing dried up and their infants soon died. And since the men and women were kept apart there could be no marital relations. And the men died in the mines and the women died on the ranches from the same causes, exhaustion and hunger. And thus was depopulated that island, which had once been so densely populated."

Thanks largely to Las Casas' advocacy, a number of reforms known as the New Laws were promulgated in 1542; but, as always, promulgation and enforcement were not the same thing, and the oppression and depopulation went on. So, with the Taino population reduced in Hispaniola alone from perhaps half a million to a few thousand, and the Caribs too fierce and savage to be subdued, who was to dig the gold, plant and harvest the crops, or do the work around the haciendas? Certainly not the conquistadors, who scorned to labor; peasants and farmers from Spain were too few in number and too ambitious to become *encomienderos* themselves; Jews, Muslims, Protestants and other heretics were not allowed. That left only one answer. Among those in favor of importing slaves from Africa was Las Casas himself. Like almost everyone else of that period, he was not opposed to slavery as such, just to what were considered its abuses—for example, enslaving someone in a war that had not officially been declared "just." And in fact it was precisely this requirement that later made him realize what a mistake he had made, for on reading Chief Chronicler Azurara's account of Henry the Navigator and the doings of the Portuguese in Africa, it dawned on him that the wars in which the Africans had been made prisoners were not, in fact, just: apart from some of the Moors taken in the early days, the slaves were not Muslim heretics, and so did not qualify for being enslaved. For his mistake Las Casas "judged himself guilty through ignorance." Many others have also blamed Las Casas, but the suggestion of one man is hardly likely to have given rise to so vast a trade.

And vast it certainly was. Over the centuries, well over ten million Africans were brought to the Americas, the vast majority going to the sugar and coffee plantations in the West Indies and Brazil, and only about four hundred thousand coming to what are now the United States. It was an extremely lucrative business, and the Spanish and Portuguese authorities at first tried to maintain a monopoly; but they lacked the means to enforce it, nor could their slavers meet the ever-increasing demand. Other sea-going nations were not slow to take notice and join in.

The first of these were the English. Led by the buccaneering Sir John Hawkins, they burst in upon the African slave trade in their usual vigorous and self-righteous manner—a drawn sword in one hand, a Bible in the other. An added incentive to their intrusion was the bitter rivalry between Protestant England and Catholic Spain—when translated into English, the *Brevissima Relacion* bore the title *Popery Truly Display'd in its Bloody Colours*.

According to the chronicler Richard Hakluyt, "The first Voyage of the right worshipful and valiant Knight, Sir John Hawkins, made to the West Indies," took place in 1562. After lining up several wealthy investors—Adventurers, as they were then called—he outfitted three ships, set sail, and reached Sierra Leone in October. Here he "got into his possession, partly by the sword, and partly by other means, to the number of three hundred Negroes at the least, besides other merchandise which that country yieldeth. With this prey, he sailed over the ocean sea unto the island of Hispaniola, and arrived first at the port of Isabella; and there he had reasonable utterance of his English commodities, as also of some part of his Negroes; trusting the Spaniards no further than that, by his own strength, he was able still to master them. From the port of Isabella he went to Porte de Plata, where he made like sales; standing always upon his guard." In exchange for his slaves and English goods, Hawkins received "such a quantity of merchandise that he did not only lade his three ships with hides, ginger, sugar and some quantity of pearls; but he freighted also two other hulks with hides and other like commodities. And so, with prosperous success, and much gain to himself and the aforesaid Adventurers, he came home, and arrived in the month of September, 1563." (That harmless-sounding phrase, "and partly by other means," included attacking a Portuguese ship and robbing it of its cargo of slaves.)

The second voyage did not go so well. On arrival at Sierra Leone they were told of a town called Bimba, "where was not only a great store of gold but also there were not above forty men, and a hundred women and children in the town." Hearing this, Hawkins "prepared his men in armour and weapons, together to the number of forty men." But the raid fizzled. "We landing, boat after boat, and divers of our men scattering themselves (contrary to the Captain's will) by one or two in a company, for the hope they had to find gold in their houses, ransacking the same; in the meantime the Negroes came upon them and hurt many, being thus scattered. Being driven down to take their boats, they were followed so hardly by a rout of Negroes that not only some of them, but others standing on the shore not looking for any such matter . . . were suddenly so set upon that some, with great hurt, recovered their boats; othersome, not able to recover the same, took to the water and perished by means of the ooze."

Despite such difficulties they were able to collect a cargo of slaves and set sail for the West Indies. On their way they were becalmed for twenty-eight days, "which put us in great fear that many never thought to have reached the Indies without great death of the Negroes and of themselves. But the Almighty God (who never suffereth His elect to perish!) sent us the 16th of February the ordinary breeze, which is the Northwest wind, which never left us till we came to an island of the cannibals called Dominica." But though Spanish plantation owners were eager to buy slaves, "the Governor of the island would neither come to speak with our Captain, neither yet give him any license to traffic."

Hawkins' response was to use much the same method selling his merchandise as when acquiring it. Thus when told at Rio de la Hacha that "they durst not traffic with us," Hawkins and one hundred men in armor went ashore. There followed a one-sided parley, after which Hawkins' "requests" were granted, "and we made our traffic quietly with them." After other stops to load up with hides, and stopping over in Florida, where they rescued some starving French settlers, and the New-foundland Banks, where "we took a great number of fresh codfish," they "came, the 20th of September [1565] to Padstow in Cornwall, God be thanked! in safety: with the loss of twenty persons in all the voyage; as with great profit to the Venturers of the said voyage, so also to the whole realm, in bringing home both gold, silver, pearls and other jewels in great store. His Name therefore be praised for evermore! Amen."

After one more voyage, Hawkins gave up slaving in favor of other ventures, though he did write a short book, *An Alliance to Raid for Slaves*, in which he advocated joint operations with African rulers. He is also credited with introducing the potato to Europe, and with establishing the Triangular Trade: buying goods in the home country, exchanging them for slaves in Africa, bartering the slaves in the West Indies for gold, sugar, hides, ginger, pearls and other local products, then selling these on his return home, and making a large profit at each corner of the triangle.

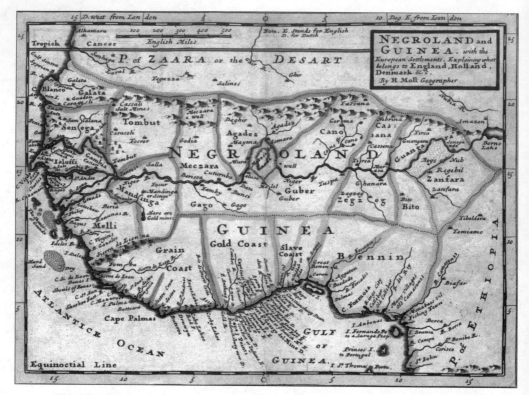

This late eighteenth-century map reflects the way the slave trade worked: capturing slaves and bringing them to the coast was done by Africans, shipping them overseas by Europeans. Hence the precise depiction of the coastline with its forts and trading stations, while much of the interior is either blank or inaccurate—the bottom right-hand corner is marked "P. [part] of Ethiopia," a country on the other side of the continent; and the Niger River, which flows in an arc from west to east, is shown flowing in a fairly straight line from east to west, and reaching the sea in Gambia rather than in Nigeria.

CHAPTER 2

THE TRADE

THE TRANS-ATLANTIC SLAVE TRADE HAD TWO DISTINCT BRANCHES: THERE was the Southern Trade, from the Congo and Angola to South America, primarily Brazil; this was run largely by the Dutch and the Portuguese. And there was the Northern Trade, engaged in by all the sea-going countries of northwest Europe, with Great Britain emerging in the eighteenth century as the leader.

Slaves were needed because the local people could not be coerced into working the gold and silver mines, acting as servants, or raising large crops of tobacco, coffee, rice, cotton and, above all, sugar. The first eastward shipment of sugar from the Spanish West Indies was made in 1515, and the first westward shipment of slaves from Africa in 1518. From its probable origin in the South Pacific, the business of growing and refining cane sugar had spread westward to the Middle East, then to Cyprus, Crete and Sicily, and from there to the islands off the west African coast— Madeira, Cape Verde and the Canaries; and then across the Atlantic. It had a huge and ever-expanding market in Europe, and its two by-products, molasses and rum, also sold well. But raising sugar was labor-intensive, and the work was so exhausting, the conditions so brutal, the birth rate so low and the mortality rate so high, that on average West Indian plantation owners had to replace one tenth of their workers every year. This may have seemed wasteful, but the planters had worked it out and the consensus among them was that it was "cheaper to buy than to breed."

Every European power that took part in the slave trade tried to corner at least part of it but, with the exception of Brazil, monopolies were not a success. Governments were too limited and their agents often too venal for effective enforcement, and buyers disliked them because, as usual, monopolies meant higher prices. One example was the Royal

African Company, set up in 1672 with the backing, among others, of Charles II of England; his brother, the Duke of York; his cousin Prince Rupert; and the political philosopher John Locke, the expert on civil liberty. Their closed market was to be Jamaica, St. Kitts, Antigua, Monserrat, Barbados and Virginia. To supply them, the R.A.C. had a number of fortified trading stations on the West African coast, most notably Cape Coast Castle, also known as Cabo Corso, an elaborate fortress, expensive to garrison and maintain. When the trade went according to plan, ships from the Royal African Company would put into Cape Coast Castle, unload their trading goods, load the slaves that had been collected there and set off across the Atlantic. This way of doing business was known as the "fort trade."

There was also the free enterprise "ship trade," unofficial and often unrecorded, which is one reason why firm numbers are so hard to arrive at. Under this system, ships would moor out at sea, or near the mouth of a river, and send in boats to do business with local rulers or merchants. Sometimes these would have slaves on hand, sometimes they would have to send inland for them, and nearly always a ship would have to make several stops to obtain a full cargo. This way of doing business, flexible and with much lower overheads, soon outstripped the official fort trade—in the ten years from 1698 to 1708, private traders shipped some 75,000 slaves across the Atlantic, and the R.A.C. a mere 18,000 (of whom six thousand went to Virginia, and twenty-two hundred to Maryland). About two thirds of those shipped were men. The peak years of the trade were 1741 to 1810, when some 60,000 were shipped each year.

It was not an easy trade. Just getting from the home port to the African coast was often full of danger, especially during those frequent periods when England and France were at war. For example, this is what happened to Captain Phillips of the *Hannibal*, a ship with thirty-six guns and a crew of 103, which had set sail from London on September 5, 1693, "on a trading voyage to Guinea for elephants' teeth, gold and negro slaves." Two weeks later, while off Tenerife, they saw a ship "standing off to us with all sails set, whereupon we tacked to the north to have time to put our ship in a posture of defense, in case she proved an enemy." By afternoon of the next day, "the ship that stood after us was got within random gun-shot of us, appearing a fine, long, snug frigate; so that now we no longer doubted but she was an enemy." Further proof came when the frigate unfurled the French *fleur de lys*, whereupon "I perceived he was ready to pluck a crow with me. Therefore, after drinking a dram and encouraging all, ordered all my men to their guns, to behave themselves courageously, and expected his broadside, which when within pistol shot he gave us, and his volley of small shot. We returned his civility very heartily with ours; after which he shot ahead of us and brought to, and fell alongside our larboard side and gave us his other broadside, as we did him; then each of us loaded and fired as fast we could, until ten o'clock at night, when his foretop mast came by the board; then he fell astern of us."

The fight was over, but the *Hannibal* "was most miserably shattered and torn in her mast and rigging. We had five men killed outright, and about thirty-two wounded; among the last was my brother, my gunner, carpenter and boatswain; the carpenter had his arm shot off, and three others their legs; five or six of my best men were dreadfully blown up by their carelessness in laying the lighted matches among some cartridges of powder; our harper had his skull fractured by a small shot; the rest are but slight small shot and splinter wounds, and bruises."

Such stories were seized upon by English apologists for the slave trade who claimed that it was vital to the nation's security by training sailors who in time of war could be recruited into the Royal Navy. But in fact, rather than being "a nursery for seamen," the trade was closer to being their graveyard, for the life of sailors on board a slaver was so harsh, and the discipline so savage, that their death rate while at sea was actually higher than that of the slaves—about twenty and thirteen per cent respectively. Only those in desperate straits volunteered; many were shanghaied by "crimps" who got them drunk in the brothels and low taverns that flourished in the home ports. "Every allurement and artifice is held out to entice them into these infamous dens," wrote the English reformer, James Stansfield, himself a former sailor. "Festivity and music lay hold of the deluded senses; prostitution throws in a fascinating spell with too much success, and intoxication generally gives the business its fatal period. . . . I have known many seamen who fancied themselves cunning enough to evade these practices, go with the crimps to some of their houses, boasting that they would cheat the merchant out of a night's merriment, and firmly resolved to oppose every artifice that could be offered, yet have they, in their state of drunkenness, signed articles with the very men whose purposes they were aware of, and have been plunged into a situation of which they had known the horrors."

One account of a seaman's life was written by Silas Told. At the age of eleven Silas had been apprenticed to Timothy Tucker, "commander of the *Royal George*, bound for Guinea and the West Indies." When at home, Captain Tucker "assumed the character and temper of a saint," but at sea he became another person.

"The first demonstration of his notorious conduct was given to the ship's company in the enforcement of a white woman out of her native country, and selling her to a Black Prince of Bonny, on the African coast. The next proof of his villainy was the vile and blasphemous language wherewith he perpetually governed the seamen." Then there was his brutal treatment of the ship's cook. "The poor man had nothing but green wood to make his furnace boil with, on which account it was impossible for him to get the food ready in time: therefore the captain habituated himself to certain practices, such as horse-whipping him, and stabbing a knife into his face, so that the poor man's life was grievously burthensome to him; indeed he oftentimes hinted to us that he would throw himself overboard, but we endeavoured to dissuade him from it; yet one morning, about eight o'clock, poor John Bundy plunged himself into the sea without our knowledge." Only when they "saw a hat swimming astern" did they realize what had happened to him. (As to the white woman who was to be sold to the Black Prince of Bonny, shortly before they arrived she "died in a shocking manner, was sewed up in a hammock, and thrown overboard with a bag of ballast at her feet in order to sink her; but in the course of a week afterwards the corpse of the woman was observed to float upon the waters. I believe God had suffered this uncommon circumstance to happen in order to open the eyes of our wicked captain; but he had no dread or remorse in him.")

Also testifying about the harsh conditions endured by English seamen was John "Amazing Grace" Newton, who before taking up hymn-writing and entering holy orders had himself been a slaver. In his *Thoughts upon the African Slave Trade* Newton wrote of the "inflammatory fever" and harm caused by exposure to those engaged in the "ship trade." "If trade be scarce the ships which arrive in the fair or dry season often remain till the rains return before they can complete their purchase. A proper shelter from the weather in an open boat, when the rain is incessant, night and day, for weeks and months, is impracticable. And during the fair season tornadoes, or violent storms of wind, thunder and heavy rain are very frequent, though they seldom last long. In fact, the boats seldom return without bringing some of the people ill of dangerous fevers or fluxes." There were also the sudden onsets of a wind called the *harmatan* which, according to the Anglo-French trader John Barbot, brought "a sharp piercing cold air, no sun appearing all the while; but the weather was thick, close, cold and raw, which very much affected the eyes, and put many into an anguish temper."

Having reached the African coast, sloops and small boats would be sent up the Senegal and the Gambia Rivers, but here too, wrote Barbot, the going was hard. "Through continual toils and hardships the best part of the sailors sickened and died, whilst others perish'd by the intolerable scorching heat, which threw them into burning fevers; and those who had been proof against that intolerable fatigue were destroyed either by the vile perfidiousness of the native Blacks of the country, or devoured alive by alligators, a sort of crocodiles which swarm in the cross rivers, as well as in the Senega, some of them above ten foot long, lying close among the bull-rushes, or under the water along the banks, and ever ready to seize and prey on man, when opportunity offers."

Along with the crocodiles in the rivers, the whole coast was infested with sharks, "extraordinary ravenous" and "of a vast size, some of them being twenty, and some thirty foot long, very large and thick, their head broad and flat, and the snout sharp-pointed. If a man happens to fall overboard, and these monsters are at hand, they soon make him their prey . . . Its eyes, tho' very small in proportion to the body, and round, look like a bright flaming fire." The mouth was "of prodigious width and bigness, within which are three rows, above and below, of very sharp and strong teeth, which at once cut off a man's arms, leg, head, or any other part of the body. It swims incredibly swift, and great multitudes of them usually follow our slave-ships some hundred leagues at sea, as they sail out from the gulph of Guinea, as if they knew we were to throw some dead corpse overboard almost every day."

Another, much smaller, menace was described by a Dutch trader, David van Nyendael, when writing about the Rio Formosa, in Benin. This was "the innumerable millions of gnats, which the Portuguese call musquitoes," and which "sting so severely that several persons have been so marked with pustules that it was impossible to know them. This torment, which deprives us of our natural rest, heightened by the unwholesomeness of the climate, continually occasions a great mortality amongst our men. This is my second voyage to this river. The first time I was here we lost half our men, and at present the number of dead on board is not less, and the remainder are most of them sick."

Then there was the weather, which in Senegal, wrote John Barbot, "is in the main very unhealthy, especially near the rivers and marshy grounds, and in woody places; but most of all to white men in July, August and September, which is the rainy season." Nor was the rest of the year much better, for "from September to June the heats are almost intolerable, and produce many fatal distempers in the Europeans who reside here on the account of trade."

Many of the Europeans who garrisoned the forts or worked in the "factories," as the trading posts were called, were generally what Barbot described as "necessitous persons, who cannot live at home," and operated "without regard to the principles of Christianity." They looked "poor and thin," their countenances "shriveled and dismal. They are generally men of no education or principles, void of foresight, careless, prodigal, addicted to strong liquors, as palm wine, brandy and punch, which they will drink to excess." Also, "some, and perhaps no small number, are over-fond of the black women, whose natural hot and lewd tempers soon wastes their bodies, and consumes that little substance they have." As a result "they fall into several distempers, daily exposing their lives to danger, very many being carried off through these excesses, in a very deplorable condition, by fevers, fluxes, colicks, consumption, asthmas, small-pox, coughs, and sometimes worms and dropsies." According to ship's surgeon Alexander Falconbridge, at the Bight of Benin, "the bodies of the sailors who die there are buried on a sandy point, called Bonny Point, which lies about a quarter of a mile from the town. It is covered at high water; and as the bodies are buried but a small depth below the surface of the sand, the stench arising from them is sometimes very noxious."

Derived from the Arabic word qafila, *coffles were used by traders to secure slaves while traveling from the interior to the coast. As well as being chained or yoked neck to neck, adults, especially males, often had their hands bound; many also had to carry loads on their heads. Those unable to keep up were put to death.*

In addition to this loss of life, there was "the dreadful effects of this trade upon the minds of those who are engaged in it," wrote John Newton. "In general I know of no method of getting money, not even that of robbing for it upon the highway, which has so direct a tendency to efface the moral sense, to rob the heart of every gentle and humane disposition, and to harden it, like steel, against all impressions of sensibility." Another "dreadful effect" was racial prejudice. Unlike the aristocratic Portuguese adventurers, who waged war on Africans but did not despise them, the middle- and lower-class north Europeans were soon complaining about the innate vices of the people they were busy enslaving. According to John Barbot, the Yarays were "perfidious" and "expert at stealing"; the Senegalese were "lazy to excess . . . knavish, revengeful, impudent, liars, impertinent, gluttonous, extravagant"; the natives of Guinea were "the greatest and most cunning thieves that can be imagined"; the Camina women "made no scruple to prostitute themselves to the Europeans for a very slender profit." The Dutchman, Willem Bosman, writing of the Gold Coast, declared that "the Negroes are all, without exception crafty, villainous and fraudulent . . . These degenerate vices are accompanied with their sisters, sloth and idleness, to which they are so prone that nothing but the utmost necessity can force them to labour."

But what did the Africans themselves have to say about their own country and people? Having no written language, very few were able to record their opinions and experiences, but an outstanding exception was the eighteenth-century Ibo, sometimes called Gustavus Vassa but more generally known as Olaudah Equiano. After a lifetime of many adventures, some of which will appear later, Equiano settled down in England where, in 1789, he wrote the story of his life, which had begun in the rich and powerful kingdom of Benin.

> "This kingdom is divided into many provinces or districts, in one of the most remote and fertile of which I was born, in the year 1745, situated in a charming fruitful vale, named Essaka. The distance of this province from the capital of Benin and the sea coast must be very considerable, for I had never heard of white men or Europeans, nor of the sea; and our subjection to the king of Benin was little more than nominal.
>
> "Our manner of living is entirely plain; for as yet the natives are unacquainted with those refinements in cookery which debauch the taste; bullocks, goats, and poultry supply the greatest part of their food. These constitute likewise the principal wealth of the country, and the chief articles of its commerce. The flesh is usually stewed in a pan; to make it savory we sometimes use pepper, and other spices, and we have salt made of wood ashes. Our vegetables are mostly plantains, eadas, yams, beans, and Indian corn. The head of the family usually eats alone; his wives and slaves have also their separate tables. Before we taste food we always wash our hands; indeed, our cleanliness on all occasions is extreme, but on this it is an indispensable ceremony. After washing, libation is made by pouring out a small portion of the drink on the floor, and tossing a small quantity of the food in a certain place, for the spirits of departed relations, which the natives suppose to preside over their conduct and guard them from evil.

"They are totally unacquainted with strong or spirituous liquors; and their principal beverage is palm wine. This is got from a tree of that name, by tapping it at the top and fastening a large gourd to it; and sometimes one tree will yield three or four gallons in a night. When just drawn it is of a most delicious sweetness; but in a few days it acquires a tartish and more spirituous flavor, though I never saw anyone intoxicated by it. The same tree also produces nuts and oil. Our principal luxury is in perfumes: one sort of these is an odoriferous wood of delicious fragrance, the other a kind of earth, a small portion of which thrown into the fire diffuses a most powerful odor. We beat this wood into powder, and mix it with palm oil, with which both men and women perfume themselves.

"In our buildings we study convenience rather than ornament. Each master of a family has a large square piece of ground, surrounded with a moat or fence, or enclosed with a wall made of red earth tempered, which, when dry, is as hard as brick. Within this, are his houses to accommodate his family and slaves, which, if numerous, frequently present the appearance of a village. In the middle, stands the principal building, appropriated to the sole use of the master and consisting of two apartments; in one of which he sits in the day with his family, the other is left apart for the reception of his friends. He has besides these a distinct apartment in which he sleeps, together with his male children. On each side are the apartments of his wives, who have also their separate day and night houses. The habitations of the slaves and their families are distributed throughout the rest of the enclosure. These houses never exceed one story in height; they are always built of wood, or stakes driven into the ground, crossed with wattles, and neatly plastered within and without. The roof is thatched with reeds. Our day houses are left open at the sides; but those in which we sleep are always covered, and plastered in the inside with a composition mixed with cow-dung, to keep off the different insects which annoy us during the night.

"As we live in a country where nature is prodigal of her favors, our wants are few and easily supplied. Of course, we have few manufactures. They consist for the most part of calicoes, earthenware, ornaments, and instruments of war and husbandry . . . We have also markets, at which I have been frequently with my mother. These are sometimes visited by stout mahogany-colored men from the south-west of us: we call them Oye Eboe, which term signifies red men living at a distance. They generally bring us fire-arms, gun-powder, hats, beads, and dried fish. The last we esteemed a great rarity, as our waters were only brooks and springs. These articles they barter with us for odoriferous woods and earth, and our salt of wood ashes. They always carry slaves through our land; but the strictest account is exacted of their manner of procuring them before they are suffered to pass. Sometimes, indeed, we sold slaves to them, but they were only prisoners of war, or such among us as had been convicted of kidnapping, or adultery, and some other crimes which we esteemed heinous. This practice of kidnapping induces me to think that, notwithstanding all our strictness, their principal business among us was to trepan our people. I remember too, they carried great sacks along with them, which not long after I had an opportunity of fatally seeing applied to that infamous purpose.

"Our tillage is exercised in a large plain or common, some hour's walk from our dwellings, and all the neighbors resort thither in a body. They use no beasts of husbandry; and their only instruments are hoes, axes, shovels, and beaks, or pointed iron, to dig with. Sometimes we are visited by locusts, which come in large clouds, so as to darken the air and destroy our harvest. This, however, happens rarely, but when it does, a famine is produced by it. I remember an instance or two wherein this happened. This common is often the theatre of war; and therefore when our people go out to till their land, they not only go in a body, but generally take their arms with them for fear of a surprise; and when they apprehend an invasion, they guard the avenues to their dwellings by driving sticks into the ground, which are so sharp at one end as to pierce the foot, and are generally dipt in poison. From what I can recollect of these battles, they appear to have been irruptions of one little state or district on the other, to obtain prisoners or booty. Perhaps they were incited to this by those traders who brought the European goods I mentioned amongst us. Such a mode of obtaining slaves in Africa is common; and I believe more are procured this way, and by kidnapping, than any other.

"We have fire-arms, bows and arrows, broad two-edged swords and javelins; we have shields also which cover a man from head to foot. All are taught the use of these weapons; even our women are warriors, and march boldly out to fight along with the men. Our whole district is a kind of militia: on a certain signal given, such as the firing of a gun at night, they all rise in arms and rush upon their enemy . . . When our people march to the field a red flag or banner is borne before them.

"I was once a witness to a battle in our common. We had been all at work in it one day as usual, when our people were suddenly attacked. I climbed a tree at some distance, from which I beheld the fight. There were many women as well as men on both sides; among others my mother was there, and armed with a broad sword. After fighting for a considerable time with great fury, and many had been killed, our people obtained the victory, and took their enemy's Chief a prisoner. He was carried off in great triumph, and, though he offered a large ransom for his life, he was put to death. A virgin of note among our enemies had been slain in the battle, and her arm was exposed in our market-place, where our trophies were always exhibited. The spoils were divided according to the merit of the warriors. Those prisoners which were not sold or redeemed, we kept as slaves; but how different was their condition from that of the slaves in the West Indies! With us, they do no more work than other members of the community, even their master; their food, clothing, and lodging were nearly the same as theirs (except that they were not permitted to eat with those who were free-born); and there was scarce any other difference between them, than a superior degree of importance which the head of a family possesses in our state, and that authority which, as such, he exercises over every part of his household. Some of these slaves even have slaves under them as their own property, and for their own use.

"As to religion, the natives believe that there is one Creator of all things, and that he lives in the sun, and is girted round with a belt; that he may never eat or drink, but, according to some, he smokes a pipe, which is our own favorite luxury. They believe he governs events, especially our deaths or captivity; but, as for the doctrine of eternity, I do not remember to have ever heard of it; some, however, believe in the transmigration of souls in a certain degree. Those spirits which were not transmigrated, such as their dear friends or relations, they believe always attend them, and guard them from the bad spirits or their foes. For this reason they always, before eating, as I have observed, put some small portion of the meat, and pour some of their drink, on the ground for them; and they often make oblations of the blood of beasts or fowls at their graves.

"We practised circumcision like the Jews, and made offerings and feasts on that occasion, in the same manner as they did. Like them also, our children were named from some event, some circumstance, or fancied foreboding, at the time of their birth. I was named Olaudah, which in our language signifies vicissitude, or fortunate; also, one favored, and having a loud voice and well spoken.

"My father, besides many slaves, had a numerous family, of which seven lived to grow up, including myself and sister, who was the only daughter. As I was the youngest of the sons, I became, of course, the greatest favorite with my mother, and was always with her; and she used to take particular pains to form my mind. I was trained up from my earliest years in the art of war: my daily exercise was shooting and throwing javelins, and my mother adorned me with emblems, after the manner of our greatest warriors. In this way I grew up till I had turned the age of eleven, when an end was put to my happiness."

More of Equiano's story will appear later. In the meantime, here is another positive report on another part of Africa, this one by Francis Moore, who worked for the Royal African Company, first as a "writer," i.e. clerk, then as a factor, or agent. He arrived at the mouth of the Gambia River in November, 1730.

"As we sailed up that river near the shore, the country appeared very beautiful, being for the most part woody; and between the woods were pleasant green rice grounds, which after the rice is cut are stocked with cattle. On the 11th we landed at James's Island, which is situated in the middle of the river, that is here at least seven miles broad. This island lies about ten leagues from the river's mouth, and is about three quarters of a mile in circumference. Upon it is a square stone fort, regularly built, with four bastions, and upon each are seven guns well mounted.

"There are many different kingdoms on the banks of the Gambia, inhabited by several races of people. The most numerous are called Mundingoes, as is likewise the country they inhabit; these are generally of a black colour, and well set. On the north side of the River Gambia, and from thence inland, are a people called Jollioffs, whose country extends to the River Senegal. These people are much blacker and handsomer than the Mundingoes.

"In every kingdom and country on each side of the river are people of a tawney colour, called Pholeys, who resemble the Arabs, whose language most of them speak, for it is taught in the schools; and the Koran, which is also their law, is in that language . . . They live in hordes or clans, build towns, and are not subject to any of the kings of the country, though they live in their territories; for if they are used ill in one nation they break up their towns and move to another. They have chiefs of their own, who rule with such moderation that every act of the government seems rather an act of the people than of one man. This form of government is easily administered because the people are of a good and quiet disposition, and so well instructed in what is just and right that a man who does ill is the abomination of all.

"The behaviour of the natives to strangers is really not so disagreeable as people are apt to imagine; for when I went through any of their towns they almost all came to shake hands with me, except some of the women, who having never before seen a white man, ran away from me as fast as they could, and would not by any means be persuaded to come near me. Some of the men invited me to their houses, and brought their wives and daughters to see me; who then sat down by me and always found something to wonder at and admire, as my boots, spurs, clothes or wig.

"Some of the Mundingoes have many slaves in their houses, and in these they pride themselves. They live so well and easily that it is sometimes difficult to know the slaves from the masters and mistresses; they being frequently better clothed, especially the females, who have sometimes coral, amber and silver about their wrists, to the value of twenty or thirty pounds sterling. In almost every town they have a kind of drum of a very large size, called a *tangtong*, which they only beat at the approach of an enemy, or

on some very extraordinary occasion, to call the inhabitants of the
neighbouring towns to their assistance; and this in the night-time
may be heard six or seven miles."

Two years after he arrived, Moore went on an excursion upriver.

"We left Joar, and proceeded in a sloop up the Gambia. The next
day we arrived at Yanimarew, which is the pleasantest port on the
whole river, the country being delightfully shaded with palm and palmetto trees. The company here have a small house, with a black factor, to purchase corn for the use of the fort.

   "On my arrival at Nackway the natives welcomed me with the
music of the *balafeu* which, at about one hundred yards distance,
sounds something like a small organ. It is composed of about twenty
pipes of very hard wood finely polished, which diminish by little and
little, both in length and breadth, and are tied together by thongs of
very fine leather. These thongs are twisted about small round wands,
put between the pipes to keep them at a distance; and underneath
the pipes are fastened twelve to fourteen calabashes of different sizes.
This instrument they play upon with two sticks, covered with a thin
skin taken from the trunk of the palmetto tree, or with fine leather,
to make the sound less harsh. Both men and women dance to this
music, which they much admire, and are highly delighted to have a
white man dance with them.

   "On the 20th of November, in the evening, was a total eclipse
of the moon; and the Mundingoes told me the darkness was occasioned by a cat's putting her paw between the moon and the earth.
The Mahometans in this country were singing and dancing the whole
time, because they expect their prophet to come in an eclipse."

The Anglo-French trader John Barbot was also impressed by the
beauty of the country. Here he is on his return from a visit upriver to a
local ruler to trade for ivory and rice:

"It was just after sunset when I parted from king Barsaw, when I
paid him the first visit at his village, and a most sweet lovely evening
in the month of December. We ran down the river, carried only by

the tide, very slowly, between the banks which are magnificently adorned and shaded with evergreen trees of many different sorts and forms, most of which stretch their boughs far out over the river, in the figure of an amphitheater. This, with the profound silence on the water, and the various notes of a multitude of many sorts of birds lodged in the woods, with the shrieking and chattering of a vast number of monkeys and apes skipping and jumping from bough to bough over our heads; and the sweet gentle noise of the Blacks paddling the several canoes which accompanied us, made our journey very delightful and charming."

Another place widely praised was Whydah, also known as Fida, a small but thickly settled kingdom between Popo and Ardra on the eastern part of the Guinea coast. According to William Smith, a ship's officer, "All who have ever been here allow this to be one of the most delightful countries in the world." Its inhabitants were "the most gentleman-like Negroes in Guinea, abounding with good manners and ceremony to each other. The inferior pay the utmost deference and respect to the superior, as do wives to their husbands, and children to their parents. All here are naturally industrious, and find constant employment, the men in agriculture and the women in spinning and weaving cotton, of which they make clothes."

The main drawback to Whydah was that "this of all other places in Guinea is most difficult to land at." Because the water was exceptionally shallow for a long way out, "the sea breaks and rolls at such a vast distance from the shore that no European boat can come within two hundred yards of it, but must come to anchor a good way off and wait for a canoe to come and carry the passengers or goods ashore." This was accomplished "without any other damage than a little washing. I was amaz'd when we came among the breakers, (which to me seem'd large enough to founder our ship) to see with what wondrous dexterity [the boatmen] carried us through them, and ran their canoe on the top of those rolling waves a good way upon the shore. Which done, they all leap'd out, and dragg'd the canoe up the beach several yards, from the power of the next returning wave."

This was the procedure followed by Captain Phillips of the *Hannibal* who, following the fight with the French ship off Tenerife, arrived at

Whydah on the morning of May 21, 1694, dropping anchor "in eight fathom water, about two miles off shore."

"May the 21st. This morning I went ashore at Whydah, accompanied by my doctor and purser, Mr. Clay, the present captain of the *East-India Merchant*, his doctor and purser, and about a dozen of our seamen for our guard, armed, in order here to reside till we could purchase 1300 negro slaves, which was the number we both wanted, to complete 700 for the *Hannibal* and 600 for the *East-India Merchant*, according to our agreement in our charter-parties with the Royal African Company; in procuring which quantity of slaves we spent about nine weeks, during which time what observations my indisposition, with convulsions in my head, etc, would permit me to make on this country, its trade, manners, etc, are as follows:

"Whydah, or Quedaw, lies in the latitude of 6 degrees 10 inches north latitude, being the pleasantest country I have seen in Guinea, consisting of champaigns [open countryside] and small ascending hills, beautified with always green shady groves of lime, wild orange and other trees, and irrigated with divers broad fresh rivers, which yield plenty of good fish. Towards the sea-shore it is very marshy, and has divers large swamps. Our factory [trading station] lies about three miles from the sea-side, where we were carried in hammocks, which the factor, Mr. Joseph Peirson, sent to attend our landing, with several armed blacks that belonged to him for our guard; we were soon trussed in a bag, tossed upon Negroes' heads, and conveyed to our factory; and this way of traveling being rarely used anywhere except in Africa I think it may not be amiss to give some description of it.

"The hammock is a large cloth made of cotton generally, but the factors have them very fine of silk or broad-cloth. It's about nine foot long and six or seven broad, slung at both ends with several small cords or ribbons, which draw up the ends of the hammocks like a purse; at the end of which is a noose fitted to slip over the ends of a pole, about nine foot long, which cloth or hammock the traveler gets into, and either lies along or sits, as he is disposed; then he is mounted on the heads of two Negroes, which have small rolls of linen betwixt the ends of the pole and their heads, and away they will walk and run as fast as most horses can trot, cheerfully singing in parts to each other till they are quite tired when, upon notice given, they are relieved by two fresh, and they in course by two more, there always being six Negroes to attend the hammock, which are styled hammock-men . . . This country admits of no other kind of traveling for Europeans, by reason of the extraordinary and violent heat of the sun, in which an Englishman can scarcely walk half a mile without fainting; but the hammock traveling relieves us much, for as we sit or lie in that there is a thin cloth thrown over the pole which keeps the sun's heat off, and lying down hollow on each side of the hammock, with the motion of the Negroes, attracts a fine cooling air. I have often taken pleasant naps in them traveling."

Their trading station, known as a "factory", was located a short way inland, "near the marshes, which renders it a very unhealthy place to live in, the white men the African Company send there seldom returning to tell their tale. It is compassed round with a mud wall, about six foot high, and on the south side is the gate; within is a large yard, a mud thatched house, where the factor lives with the white men; also a store house, a trunk [holding pen] for slaves, and a place where they bury their dead white men called, very improperly, the hog-yard; there is also a good forge and some other small houses. The factory is about 200 yards in circumference and a most wretched place to live in by reason of the swamps adjacent, whence proceed noisome stinks, and vast swarms of little flies called mosquitoes, which are so intolerably troublesome that if one does not take opium, laudanum or some other soporific it is impossible to get any sleep in the night." Phillips also complained of the heat—the air "appearing as intensely hot to an European as if he sucked in the heat at the mouth of an oven"—and the heavy rains that were "more like fountains than drops, and as hot as if warmed over a fire."

Soon a message came from the king summoning them to his presence, so Phillips and his officers got into their hammocks and set off, taking an armed guard of twelve men with them.

"From the factory to the king's town is about four miles, through very pleasant fields full of India and Guinea corn, potatoes, yams, in great plenty, of which they have two harvests yearly. On the road to the king's town are several little villages, or parcels of houses, which

the Negroes call *crooms,* and have each of them a captain, few of
the houses being above five yards high, having no light but at the
door, except the chief houses, which may have a hole bored through
the walls; they are much like our sheep-houses in Wales, having for
most part but one room, where they eat and sleep together, the gen-
erality on the bare ground; the cappashiers [leading men] may have
a mat spread under them, and a stone or hard bundle for a pillow.

"When we came to the palace (which was the meanest I ever
saw, being low mud walls, the roof thatched, the floor the bare
ground, with some pools of water and dirt in it) we were met at the
entrance by several cappashiers with the usual ceremony of clapping
their hands and taking and shaking us by ours, with great demonstration of affection. When we entered the palace yard they all fell
on their knees near the door of the room where the king was, clapping their hands, knocking the ground with their foreheads and kissing it, which they repeated three times, being their usual ceremony
when they approached his majesty, we standing and observing till
they had done; then rising, they led us to the room where the king
was, which we found covered with his nobility on their knees, and
those that introduced us fell on theirs, and crawled to their several
stations, and so they continued all the time we were with the king
then, and all other times when we saw him.

"When we entered the king peeped upon us from behind a curtain, and beckoned us to him; whereupon we approached close to
his throne, which was of clay, raised about two foot from the ground,
and about six foot square, surrounded with old dirty curtains, always
drawn betwixt him and his cappashiers, whom he will not allow the
sight of his handsome phiz. He had two or three little black children
with him and was smoking tobacco in a long wooden pipe, the bole
of which, I dare say, would hold an ounce, and rested upon his
throne, with a bottle of brandy and a little dirty silver cup by his side.
His head was tied about with a roll of coarse calico, and he had a
loose gown of red damask to cover him.

"We saluted him with our hats and he took us by the hands,
snapped our fingers and told us we were very welcome, that he was
glad to see us, that he longed for it, and that he loved Englishmen
dearly, that we were his brothers and that he would do us all the good

offices that he could; we returned him thanks by his interpreter and assured him how great affection our masters, the Royal African Company of England, bore to him for his civility and fair and just dealing with their captains; and that notwithstanding there were many other places [with] more plenty of Negro slaves that begged their custom, they had rejected all the advantageous offers made them out of their good will to him, and therefore had sent us to trade with him . . .

"He answered that the African Company was a very good brave man, that he loved him, that we should be fairly dealt with and not imposed upon. He desired us to sit down upon a bench close by him, which we did; then he drank to us his brother the king of England's health, the African Company's, our welcome etc. in brandy and pitto, which is a pleasant liquor made of Indian corn soaked in water, some so strong that it will keep three months, and two quarts will fuddle a man; it drinks much like new ale. We had not stayed long before there came a repast on a little square table, with an old sheet for cloth, old battered pewter plates and spoons, with a large pewter basin of the same hue with his majesty's complexion, filled with stewed fowls and broth, and a wooden bowl of boiled potatoes to serve instead of bread; we had no napkins, knives nor forks laid us, nor do they ever use any, but always tear their meat; and indeed we had no occasion for any, for our fowls were boiled to such mash that they would not bear carving. We had no great stomach to our dainties; however, in complaisance to his majesty we supped two or three spoonfuls of the broth, which was very well relished with malagetta and red pepper; we often drank to the king out of a cup made of a cocoa-nut shell, which was all the plate I saw he had, except a little silver dram cup. He would bow to us, kiss his hand, and burst out often in loud screaming laughter. When we had signified to his majesty that we had satisfied our stomachs with his dainties, he gave some of the fowls out of the broth, with his own hands, to the little children that were with him, and the rest among his nobles, who scrambled for it on their bellies like so many dogs, making spoons of their hands, which they would dip into the broth and then licked them."

The next day the traders returned "with samples of our goods, and made our agreement about the prices, though not without much difficulty; he and his cappashiers exacted very high. Next day we paid our customs to the king and cappashiers, as will appear hereafter; then the bell was ordered to go about to give notice to all people to bring their slaves to the trunk to sell us. This bell is a hollow piece of iron in shape of a sugar loaf, the cavity of which would contain about 50 pounds of cowries. This a man carried about and beat with a stick, which made a small dead sound."

Cowries, also known as boogies, were "little Indian shells, called in England 'Blackamoors' Teeth,' bought at one shilling and sold here at two shillings and six pence per pound." The reason they were so cheap to buy was that these small polished shells could be scooped up in large quantities from the beaches of the Maldive Islands by passing English ships. They had long been accepted as currency through much of West Africa, where they were often also used for jewelry. The *Hannibal* also carried many other goods for trade: iron bars, brass basins, pewter jugs, knives, "coral, large, smooth and of a deep red," broad-cloth, chintz, Indian calicoes, bangles and bracelets, and, above all, muskets, bullets, gunpowder, and brandy—for which cheap West Indian rum or English gin would later be substituted. "With the above goods a ship cannot want slaves here, and may purchase them for about three pounds fifteen shillings a head.

"We were every morning, during our stay here, invited to breakfast with the king, where we always found the same dish of stewed fowls and potatoes; he also would send us a hog, goat, sheep or pot of pitto every day for our table, and we usually returned his civility with three or four bottles of brandy, which was his *summum bonum*. We had our cook ashore and ate as well as we could, provisions being plenty and cheap; but we soon lost our stomachs by sickness, most of my men having fevers, and myself such convulsions and aches in my head that I could barely stand or go to the trunk without assistance, and there often fainted with the horrid stink of the Negroes, it being an old house where all the slaves are kept together, and evacuate nature where they lie, so that no jakes [latrines] can stink worse; there being forced to sit three or four hours a day quite ruined my health, but there was no help."

In the meantime Phillips and Captain Clay of the *East India Merchant* had agreed to avoid any "disagreement in our trade." Rather than bid against each other, "as often happens when there are here more ships than one, and the commanders can't set their horses together," they took turns going to the trunk to buy slaves. Even so, they found it hard to drive a bargain.

"When we were at the trunk, the king's slaves, if he had any, were the first offered to sale, which the cappashiers would be very urgent with us to buy, and would in a manner force us to ere they would show us any other, saying they were the *Rey's Cosa* [king's property] and we must not refuse them; though, as I observed, they were generally the worst slaves in the trunk, and we paid more for them than any others, which we could not remedy, it being one of his majesty's prerogatives. Then the cappashiers each brought out his slaves according to his degree and quality, the greatest first &c. and our surgeon examined them well in all kinds to see that they were sound of wind and limb, making them jump, stretch out their arms swiftly, looking into their mouths to judge of their age; for the cappashiers are so cunning that they shave them all close before we see them, so that let them be never so old we can see no grey hairs in their heads or beards; and then having liquored them well and sleek with palm oil it is no easy matter to know an old one from a middle-aged one, but by the teeth's decay; but our greatest care of all is to buy none that are poxed, lest they should infect the rest aboard; for though we separate the men and women aboard by partitions and bulkheads, to prevent quarrels and wranglings among them, yet do what we can they will come together, and that distemper which they call the yaws is very common here, and discovers itself by almost the same symptoms as *Lues Venerea*, or clap, does with us; therefore our surgeon is forced to examine the privities of both men and women with the nicest scrutiny, which is a great slavery, but what can't be omitted.

"When we had selected from the rest such as we liked, we agreed in what goods to pay for them, the prices being already stated before the king, how much of each sort of merchandise we were to give for a man, woman, and child, which gave us much ease and saved abundance of disputes and wranglings, and gave the owner a note signifying our agreement of the sorts of goods, upon delivery of which the next day he received them; then we marked the slaves we had bought in the breast or shoulder with a hot iron, having the letter of the ship's name on it, the place being before anointed with a little palm oil, which caused but little pain, the mark being usually well in four or five days, appearing very plain and white after.

"When we had purchased to the number of 50 or 60 we would send them aboard, there being a cappashier intitled the captain of the slaves whose care it was to secure them to the water-side and see them all off; and if in carrying to the marine any were lost he was bound to make them good to us, the captain of the trunk being obliged to do the like, if any ran away while under his care, for after we buy them we give him charge of them till the captain of the slaves comes to carry them away. These are two officers appointed by the king for this purpose, to each of which every ship pays the value of a slave in what goods they like best for their trouble when they have done trading; and indeed they discharged their duty to us very faithfully, we not having lost one slave through their neglect in 1300 we bought here.

"There is likewise a captain of the sand who is appointed to take care of the merchandise we have come ashore to trade with, that the Negroes do not plunder them, we being often forced to leave goods a whole night on the sea shore for want of porters to bring them up; but notwithstanding his care and authority we often came by the loss, and could have no redress.

"When our slaves were come to the seaside our canoes were ready to carry them off to the longboat, if the sea permitted, and she conveyed them aboard ship, where the men were all put in irons, two and two shackled together, to prevent their mutiny or swimming ashore. The Negroes are so willful and so loth to leave their own country that they have often leaped out of the canoes, boat and ship, into the sea, and kept under water until they were drowned, to avoid being taken up and saved by our boats, which pursued them; they having a more dreadful apprehension of Barbados than we can have of hell, though in reality they live much better there than in their own country; but home is home &c. We have likewise seen divers of them eaten by the sharks, of which a prodigious number kept about the ships in this place, and I have been told will follow her hence to Barbados for the dead Negroes that are thrown overboard in the passage.

"We had about twelve Negroes did willfully drown themselves, and others starved themselves to death; for 'tis their belief that when they die they return home to their own country and friends again. I have been informed that some commanders have cut off the legs or arms of the most willful to terrify the rest, for they believe if they lose a member they cannot return home again. I was advised by some of my officers to do the same, but I could not be persuaded to entertain the least thought of it, much less to put in practice such barbarity and cruelty to poor creatures who, excepting their want of Christianity and true religion (their misfortune more than fault) are as much the works of God's hands, and no doubt as dear to him as ourselves; nor can I imagine why they should be despised for their colour, being what they cannot help, and the effect of the climate it has pleased God to appoint them."

Francis Moore, the "writer" for the Royal African Company stationed on the Gambia River, had a much harder time than Captain Phillips when doing business. His job was to trade for "gold, slaves, elephants' teeth and bees-wax." The problem was not the quality of the goods themselves, for "the gold is finer than sterling." The ivory was also of good quality, and the supply of slaves abundant—in some years amounting to two thousand, "most of whom they say are prisoners of war and bought of the different princes by whom they are taken. The way of bringing them is by tying them by the neck with leather thongs, at about a yard distance from each other, thirty or forty in a string, having generally a bundle of corn or an elephant' tooth upon each of their heads."

Unlike most slave traders, Moore was troubled in his conscience. "Besides the slaves brought down by the negro merchants, there are many bought along the river who are either taken in war like the former, or condemned for crimes, or stolen by the people; but the Company's servants never buy any which they suspect to be of the last sort till they have sent for the *alcalde* [local ruler] and consulted with him. Since this slave trade has been used, all punishments are changed into slavery; and the natives reaping advantage from such condemnations, they strain hard for crimes in order to obtain the benefit of selling the criminal; hence not only murder, adultery, and theft are here punished by selling the male-factor, but every trifling crime is also punished in the same manner. Thus at Cantore a man seeing a tyger eating a deer, which he himself had killed and hung up near his house, fired at the tyger but unhappily shot a man; when the king had not only the cruelty to condemn him for this accident, but had the injustice and inhumanity to order also his mother, his three brothers and his three sisters, to be sold. They were brought down to me at Yamyamacunda, when it made my heart ache to see them; but on my refusing to make this cruel purchase, they were sent farther down the river and sold to some separate trader at Joar, and the vile avaricious king had the benefit of the goods for which they were sold."

Another villain was the king of Barsally, who, whenever he "wants goods or brandy, sends to the governor of James's Fort to desire him to send a sloop there with a proper cargo; which is readily complied with. Meanwhile the king goes and ransacks some of his enemies' towns, and seizing the innocent people sells them to the factors in the sloop for such commodities as he wants, as brandy, rum, guns, gunpowder, ball, pistols and cutlasses for his attendants and soldiers, with coral and silver for his wives and concubines. But in case he is not at war with any neighbouring king, then he falls upon one of his own towns, which are very numerous, and uses them in the same manner, selling those for slaves whom he is bound by every obligation to protect.

"Soon after my arrival at Joar, the king of Barsally came thither, attended by three of his brothers, above one hundred horsemen and as many foot; and though he had a house of his own in the town he insisted on lying out at the factory. Mr. Roberts, Mr. Harrison, who were factors, and I, were all the English there. The king immediately took possession of Mr. Robert's bed; and then having drank brandy until he was drunk, ordered Mr. Roberts to be held while he himself took out of his pocket the keys of the storehouse, into which he and several of his people went, and took what they pleased. He searched chiefly for brandy, of which there happened to be but one anchor [a cask holding ten gallons]; he took that, and having drank till he was dead drunk, was put to bed. This anchor lasted him three days, and it was no sooner empty than he went all over the house to look for more.

"This king, as well as his attendants, are of the Mahometan religion, notwithstanding their being such drunkards; and this monster, when he is sober, even prays. His people, as well as himself, always wear white clothes and white caps; and as they are exceeding black this dress makes them look exceeding well. This tyrant is tall, and so passionate that when any of his men affront him, he makes no scruple of shooting them; and sometimes when he goes aboard a company's sloop at Cohone, where he usually resides, he inhumanly shows his dexterity by shooting at the canoes that pass by, frequently killing one or two men a day."

For thirty years following Captain Phillips' visit, Whydah continued to prosper as a market-place for slaves brought down to the coast from the interior. "This trade," wrote John Barbot, "was so very considerable that it is computed, while it was in a flourishing state, there were above twenty thousand Negroes yearly exported from thence, by the English, French, Dutch and Portuguese." But this came to an end in 1727 when Whydah was attacked and devastated by the Dahomeys, a powerful inland kingdom.

William Snelgrave, an English slaver, who arrived soon after the war, gave three reasons for the defeat. First, prosperity had made the people of Whydah "so proud, effeminate and luxurious" that they had lost their fighting spirit. Second, their present king was "indolent and lascivious, having in his court several thousands of women, by whom he was served in all capacities," and "being thus softened by his pleasures he grew entirely negligent of his affairs." And third, when the "politic and courageous" king of Dahomey, "a far inland prince, who for some years past had rendered himself famous by many victories gained over his neighbours," sent a message to the king of Whydah "requesting to have an open traffic to the sea side, and offering to pay him his usual customs on Negroes exported," his request was snubbed, an insult that the king of Dahomey "resolved to resent when opportunity offered."

This opportunity came when yet another local ruler, the king of neighboring Ardra, "much injured his own brother." This brother then turned to the king of Dahomey for help in avenging his injury. Hearing of this, the king of Ardra sent a message to the king of Whydah proposing an alliance, but this was refused. "So, being obliged to encounter alone the king of Dahomey, he"—the king of Ardra—"met him with all the forces he could raise," but "was totally defeated, and himself taken prisoner. Soon after which he was beheaded in his conqueror's presence according to the barbarous custom of these black princes."

After this the king of Dahomey had no trouble in taking on and defeating the "proud, effeminate" Whydahs and their "indolent and lascivious" king. He had also been "so politic as to send to the Europeans then residing at Whydaw to assure them, if they stood neuter, and were not found in arms, they should receive no damage in their persons or goods in case he proved the conqueror; and that he would ease their trade and remove divers impositions laid on it by the king of Whydaw."

On his arrival at Whydah, Snelgrave heard from the merchants at the English factory "a full account of the great calamity fallen on the country. It was a lamentable story to hear, and a dismal sight to see, the desolation of so fine a country, lately exceeding populous, now destroyed in such a manner by fire and sword. The carnage of the inhabitants was, above all, a most moving spectacle, the fields being strewed with their bones. Moreover the concern for the interest of my voyage affected me not a little. But knowing it highly necessary to keep up my spirits in so hot a country, I resolved (humbly relying on Providence) not to be wanting in my endeavours for the interest I had under my care; and I met with far greater success than any way I could have reasonably expected, considering the melancholy prospect I had then of affairs."

This is how, with the help of Providence, Snelgrave achieved his commercial success: after sailing a few miles along the coast to a town in neighboring Ardra called Jaqueen, he was sought out by an English-speaking messenger from the king of Dahomey who invited him to the king's camp, about forty miles inland. When Snelgrave hesitated, the messenger added "that if I did not go it would highly offend the king; that he feared I should not be permitted to trade, besides other bad consequences might follow." So Snelgrave decided to go. A Dutch captain offered to go with him, "likewise the lord of Jaqueen offered to send his brother to pay his duty with great presents to the king." Three days later they set off, accompanied by one hundred black servants. The white men and the lord of Jaqueen's brother were carried in hammocks, "the usual way of traveling in this country for gentlemen either white or black."

The all-powerful king of Dahomey holds court. At his feet a supplicant grovels on the ground and pours earth over his head as a sign of abasement. To his left are seated some white men wearing three-cornered hats, undoubtedly slave traders. Behind him are members of his all-female bodyguard, known as the Ahosi ("king's wives"). Women also formed one of Dahomey's élite regiments.

"The country as we travelled along appeared beautiful and pleasant, and the roads good; but desolated by the war, for we saw the remains of abundance of towns and villages with a great quantity of the late inhabitants' bones strewed about the fields." The next day, as they neared the camp, they stopped to change into their best clothes. Then the king, "to do us the more honour, sent the principal person of his court (whom the Negroes distinguished to us by the title of Great Captain) to receive us, which he did in a very extraordinary manner; for he came in the midst of five hundred soldiers who had fire-arms, drawn swords, shields and banners in their hands, using so many odd and ridiculous ceremonies (as they appeared to us) that at first we could not judge whether they meant us well or ill; for the Great Captain, with some of his officers, approached us with their swords drawn, flourishing them over our heads, then pointing them to our breasts, and skipping and jumping about us like so many monkeys, showing as many tricks and postures as that animal generally does. At last, after some time spent in this manner, the great man settled into a sedate temper; then he gave us his hand, welcoming us in the king's name and drank to us in palm wine, which is a juice drawn from the palm-tree, which is very common in that country. We returned the compliment, drinking the king's heath both in wine and beer we had brought with us; and all ceremonies being ended, he desired us to go with him towards the camp; and accordingly we proceeded, the soldiers guarding us, and the musical instruments making a dismal noise."

Most of those in the camp had come from far inland and had never seen a white man before, and "such numbers of people flocked about us that if the officers had not ordered the soldiers to keep the multitude off we should have been in danger of being smothered." They were then shown into a thatched house and "the great man took his leave of us, but left a guard to prevent any of the people from disturbing us, and he went to the king to give his majesty an account of our arrival." They lunched on "cold ham and fowls which we had brought with us," but were plagued with "such an infinite number of flies that though we had several servants with flappers to keep them off our victuals, yet it was hardly possible to put a bit of meat into our mouths without some of those vermin with it. These flies, it seems, were bred by a great number of dead men's heads, which were piled on stages, not far from our tent, though we did not know so much at the time." (Their interpreter later informed them that "they were the heads of four thousand of the Whydahs, who had been sacrificed by the Dahomeys to their god about three weeks before, as an acknowledgment of the great conquest they had obtained.")

"Next morning, at nine o'clock, an officer came from the king to acquaint us we should have an audience forthwith. Accordingly we prepared ourselves, and then going to the king's gate were soon after introduced into his presence. His majesty was in a large court palisadoed round, sitting (contrary to the custom of the country) on a fine gilt chair, which he had taken from the king of Whydah. There were held over his head, by women, three large umbrellas to shade him from the sun; and four other women stood behind the chair of state, with fusils [guns] on their shoulders. I observed the women were finely dressed from the middle downward (the custom of the country being not to cover the body upward, of either sex); moreover they had on their arms many large manelloes, or rings of gold, of great value; and round their necks and in their hair abundance of their country's jewels, which are a sort of beads of divers colours, brought from a far inland country where they are dug out of the earth, and in the same esteem with the Negroes as diamonds amongst the Europeans.

"The king had a gown on flowered with gold, which reached as low as his ankles; an European embroidered hat on his head; with sandals on his feet. We being brought within ten yards of the chair of state were desired to stand still. The king then ordered the linguist to bid us welcome, on which we paid his majesty the respect of our hats, bowing our heads at the same time very low, as the interpreter directed us. Then I ordered the linguist to acquaint the king 'that on his majesty's sending to desire me to come to his camp I forthwith resolved on the journey, that I might have the pleasure of seeing so great and good a king, as I heard he was; relying entirely on the promises his messenger had made me in his majesty's name.' The king seemed well pleased with what I said and assured us of his protection and kind usage. Then chairs being brought we were desired to sit down, and the king drank our healths; and then liquor being brought us by his order, we drank his majesty's. After this the interpreter told us 'it was his majesty's desire we should stay some time with him, to see the method of paying the soldiers for captives taken in war, and the heads of the slain.'

"It so happened that in the evening of the day we came into the camp there were brought above eighteen hundred captives from a country called Tuffoe, at the distance of six days' journey. The occasion of warring on them the linguist thus related: 'That at the time his king was wholly employed in contriving the destruction of the Whydahs, these people had presumed to attack five hundred of his soldiers, sent by his majesty as a guard to twelve of his wives, who were going with a large quantity of goods and fine things, carried by slaves, to the country of Dahomey. The guard being routed and the women slain, the Tuffoes possessed themselves of the goods; for which outrage, as soon as the conquest of the Whydahs was completed, the king sent part of his army against them, to revenge him for their villainy; in which they had all desirable success.' It was necessary to mention this affair for the better understanding of what follows, it being so very remarkable.

"The king at the time we were present ordered the captive Tuffoes to be brought into the court; which being accordingly done, he chose himself a great number out of them to be sacrificed to his fetish, or guardian angel; the others being kept for slaves for his own use, or to be sold to the Europeans. There were proper officers who received the captives from the soldiers' hands, and paid them the value of twenty shillings sterling for every man, in cowries (which is a shell brought from the East Indies and carried in large quantities to Whydah by the Europeans, being the current money of all the neighbouring countries far and near), and ten shillings for a woman, boy, or girl. There were likewise brought by the soldiers some thousands of dead people's heads into the court; every soldier, as he had success, bringing in his hand one, two, three or more heads hanging on a string; and as the proper officers received them they paid the soldiers five shillings for each head. Then several people carried them away in order to be thrown on a great heap of other heads that lay near the camp, the linguist telling us that his majesty designs to build a monument with them and the heads of other enemies formerly conquered and killed."

According to Snelgrave, though he never actually witnessed such an event, the decapitated bodies were then eaten as "holy food"—as the interpreter put it, "the head of the victim was for the king; the blood for the fetish, or god; and the body for the common people." In addition to its religious importance, this practice seems to have been an effective military tactic, for "discoursing afterwards with some of the people of Ardra and Whydah, who had escaped the conqueror's sword, and telling them what a reproach and disgrace it was to the latter nation to quit their country to the Dahomeys in so cowardly a manner as they had done; they answered it was not possible to resist such cannibals, the very report of which had extremely intimidated their whole nation . . .The thoughts of being eaten by their own species were far more terrible to them than the apprehensions of being killed.'"

As a trader, Snelgrave deplored such waste, observing to an officer in the Dahomey army "that I wondered they should sacrifice so many people of whom they might otherwise make good advantage by selling them." To this the officer replied that "it had ever been the custom of their nation, after any conquest, to offer to their god a certain number of captives, which were always chosen out from among the prisoners by the king himself; for they firmly believed, should this be omitted, no more successes would attend them."

Not long afterward Snelgrave had another audience with the king, who this time "was sitting cross-legged on a carpet of silk spread on the ground." Through the interpreter the king asked "'What I had to desire of him?' To which I answered, 'That as my business was to trade, so I relied on his majesty's goodness to give me a quick dispatch, and fill my ship with Negroes; by which means I should return into my own country in a short time, where I should make it known how great and powerful a king I had seen.' To this the king replied by the linguist 'That my desire should be fulfilled, but the first business to be settled was his customs.'"

Most slaves were branded at least twice: first when bought in Africa, with a mark such as DY, for Duke of York, patron of the Royal African Company, and again when re-sold on arrival. Brands for identification were made on the shoulder or chest, brands for punishment on the hands or face.

After negotiating a favorable customs rate (half that formerly charged by the king of Whydah), Snelgrave and his companions were given leave to return to the coast, which they did as soon as they could—"our hammock-men had no need of being pressed to make haste and travel fast, for the impression made on their minds by the sacrificing the poor people of Tuffoe still so much affected them that they ran full speed with us, even beyond their strength; so that by five o'clock in the evening they brought us into Jaqueen Town, where the people received us with much joy, having been under great apprehensions for our safety.

"The next day, being the 15th of April, 1727, I paid the King of Dahomey's officers the custom agreed on; and in two days after a great many slaves came to town, being sent by his majesty for me to choose such as I liked of them." It took a while to complete his business—"the porters refused to bring my goods from the sea-side except I would pay them double the price I did at my first coming." Also, "I was taken ill of a fever; my surgeon, a very eminent man for trade as well as his profession, died in a few days after my being taken ill; and the rainy season coming on, my white people both on board and on shore grew sickly." No less provokingly, the captain of another ship decided not to come to Jaqueen but to trade instead at war-ravaged Whydah, "where he had great success; for that people being in a starving condition, and obliged to sell their servants and children for money and goods to buy food from their neighbours of Popoe, his ship was soon filled with Negroes, and he had the good fortune to sail from the coast three days before me." But at length his cargo was complete and "I got on board to my great satisfaction, having through the goodness of Providence completed my affairs much beyond my expectation. The first of July, 1727, we sailed from the road of Jaqueen, having on board 600 Negroes. I had a tedious passage to the West-Indies of seventeen weeks . . . but at length we arrived at Antigua, where the cargo of Negroes (who had stood very well) came to a good market; and having lain there for a cargo of sugars, we sailed from thence at the latter end of February, and got safe into the river of Thames the 25th of April, 1728, having been sixteen months on this remarkable voyage."

Later in his memoirs Snelgrave acknowledged that "several objections have often been raised against the lawfulness of this trade" and that "to traffick in human creatures may, at first sight, appear barbarous, inhuman and unnatural." But closer inspection would put matters in their true light:

"First, it is evident that abundance of captives in war would be in-humanly destroyed was there not an opportunity of disposing of them to the Europeans. So that at least many lives are saved, and great numbers of useful persons kept in being.

"Secondly, when they are carried to the plantations, they gen-erally live much better there than they ever did in their own country; for as the planters pay a great price for them, 'tis their interest to take care of them.

"Thirdly, by this means the English plantations have been so much improved that 'tis almost incredible what great advantages have accrued to the nation thereby; especially to the Sugar Islands, which lying in a climate near as hot as the coast of Guinea, the Negroes are fitter to cultivate the lands there than white people.

"Then as to the criminals among the Negroes, they are by this means effectually transported, never to return again; a benefit we very much want here"—that is, in England, which in fact would soon start shipping its criminals to Georgia.

"In a word, from this trade proceed benefits far outweighing all, either real or imagined, mischiefs and inconveniences. And let the worst that can be said of it, it will be found, like all other earthly advantages, tempered with a mixture of good and evil."

One of the very few Africans ever to return home, Job ben Solomon owed his good fortune to the chance discovery, while in Maryland, that he was "no common slave" but "the high priest of Bonda in the country of Foota." With the help of English philanthropists he was bought and freed, and while on a stop-over in London was taken up by high society. When writing up his story he appears to have had a good deal of help from his English friends, which may explain the many compliments to his aristocratic patrons and the Royal African Company. This portrait appeared as the book's frontispiece.

CHAPTER 3

PERSONAL STORIES

Of the millions who were taken captive and sent across the ocean, only a handful ever had a chance to tell their story; and often their story is the only thing we know about them—not even their names have survived.

One of these was the anonymous friend of Charles Ball, who before escaping to freedom spent many years on a cotton plantation in South Carolina. Although by then the slave trade had become illegal, several of his companions had been smuggled in from Africa. Some of these were Muslims, including a man "who prayed five times every day, always turning his face to the east when in the performance of his devotion." Ball befriended the newcomer, who told him the story of his life, and many years later, after his escape, Ball included the story in his book, *Fifty Years in Chains*. Perhaps to protect his friend from reprisals, his name was never mentioned. The book was not actually written by Ball, but dictated to Isaac Fisher, a Pennsylvania lawyer and abolitionist, who insisted that "all the facts which relate personally to the fugitive were received from his own lips." With Fisher's help, Ball jumped straight into the story.

"This man told me he formerly lived on the confines of a country which had no trees nor grass upon it; and that in some places no water was to be found for several days' journey; that this barren country was, nevertheless, inhabited by a race of men who had many camels and goats, and some horses. They had no settled place of residence, but moved from one part of the country to another in quest of places where green herbage was to be found—their chief food being the milk of their camels and goats; but that they also ate the flesh of these animals, sometimes. The hair of these people was not short and woolly, like that of the Negroes, nor were they were of a shining black. They were continually at war with some of the neigh-boring people, and very often with his own countrymen. He was himself once taken prisoner by them, when a lad, in a great battle fought between them and his own people, in which his party were defeated. The victors kept him in their possession more than two years, compelling him to attend to their camels and goats."

However, though a prisoner he was not a slave, since his captors "professed the same religion that he did, and it was forbidden by its pre-cepts for one man to sell another into slavery, who held the same faith with himself." After a while he became "so familiar with their customs and manner of life that they seemed almost to regard me as one of their own nation." When they camped one of his jobs was to tie together the camels' fore-feet, so that they could graze, but not go far.

"When I had been a captive with them fully two years, we came one evening and encamped at a little well." The water was "very sweet and good," but "there was no herbage hereabout, except a few stunted and thorny bushes; and on wandering abroad in quest of something to eat, one of the best and fleetest camels entangled the rope which bound its fore-feet amongst these bushes, and broke it. I found part of the rope fast to a bush in the morning; but the camel was at a great distance from us, towards the setting sun.

"The chief of our party ordered me to mount another camel and go with a long rope in pursuit of the stray; and told me that they should travel towards the south that day and encamp at a place where there was much grass. I went in pursuit of the lost camel, but when I came near him he took off at a great trot." This went on all day until "a while before sundown I approached a small grove of tall, straight trees, which are greatly valued in Africa, and which bear large quan-tities of nuts of a very good quality. Under and about these trees was a small tract of ground, covered with long green grass; and here my stray camel stopped.

"When I came up to the trees I dismounted from the camel I rode, and tying its feet together with a short rope, preserved my long one for the purpose of taking the runaway. I gathered as many nuts as I could eat, and after satisfying my hunger, lay down to sleep."

Then, "fearful that some wild beast might fall in with me," he got up and climbed one of the trees. The moon was full and the night clear. Then, "when I had been in the tree about an hour I heard, at a great distance, a loud sullen noise, between a growl and a roar, which I knew to proceed from a lion . . . I was greatly terrified by this circumstance; not for my own safety, for I knew that no beast of prey could reach me in the tree, but I feared that my camels might be devoured, and I be left to perish in the desert. Keeping my eye steadily directed towards the point from which the sound had proceeded, it was not long before I saw some object, moving over the naked plain.

"It was a monstrous lion, of the black-maned species. It was now within one hundred paces of me, and the poor camels raised their heads as high as they could towards me, and crouched close to the trunk of the tree, apparently so stupefied by fear as to be incapable of attempting to fly. The lion approached with a kind of circular motion; and at length dropping on his belly, glided along the ground until within about ten yards of the tree, when uttering a terrific roar, which shook the stillness of the night for many a league around, he sprang upon and seized the unbound camel by the neck.

"The animal, after striving in vain to shake off his assailant, rushed out upon the open plain, carrying on his back the lion, which I could perceive had already fastened upon the throat of his victim, which did not go more than a stone's cast from the trees before he fell, and after a short struggle ceased to move his limbs. The lion held the poor beast by the throat for some time after he was dead, and until, I suppose, the blood had ceased to flow from his veins. Then, quitting the neck, he turned to the side of the slain, and tearing a hole into the cavity of the body, extracted the intestines, and devoured the liver and heart, before he began to gorge himself with the flesh.

"The moon was now high in the heavens, and shone with such exceeding brilliancy that I could see distinctly for many miles round me." But to his great alarm, there was no sign of the other camel, which had apparently broken the cord tying its fore-feet and fled, "leaving me alone and without any means of escaping from the desert.

"I slept none this night—but from my couch in the boughs watched the motions of the lion which, after swallowing at least one third of the camel, stretched himself at full length on his belly, about twenty paces from it, and laying his head between his fore-feet, prepared to guard his spoil against all the intruders of the night. In this position he remained until the sun was up in the morning, when, rising and stretching himself, he walked slowly towards the grove, passed under me, went to the other side of the trees and entered some very tall herbage, where I heard him lap water." After slaking his thirst, the lion came to the tree, "rubbed himself against the trunk . . . and then lying down on his side in the shade, appeared to fall into a deep sleep. Great as was my anxiety to leave my present lodgings, I dared not attempt to pass the sentinel that kept guard at the root of the tree, even though he slept at his post; for whenever I made the least rustling in the branches I perceived that he moved his ears and opened his eyes, but closed the latter again when the noise ceased. The lion lay all day under the tree, only removing so as to place himself in the shade in the afternoon." Even when night came, the lion stayed nearby and "I remained in the tree, burning with thirst, until the moon was elevated high in the heavens, when the silence was interrupted by the roaring of a lion"—*another* lion—"at a great distance, which was again repeated after a short interval. At the end of half an hour I again heard the same lion, apparently not far off. Casting my eye in the direction of the sound I saw the beast advancing rapidly . . . coming to partake of the dead camel, whose flesh or blood he had doubtlessly smelled . . . I knew the nature of the lion too well to suppose that the stranger was going to get his supper free of cost; and before he had reached the carcass, my jailer quitted his post and set off to defend his acquisition of the last night.

"The newcomer arrived first, and fell upon the dead camel with the fury of a hungry lion—as he was; but he had scarcely swallowed a second morsel when the rightful owner, uttering a roar yet more dreadful than any that had preceded it, leapt upon the intruder and brought him to the ground. For a moment I heard nothing but the gnashing of teeth, the clashing of talons and the sounds caused by the lacerations of the flesh and hides of the combatants." The battle lasted more than an hour; but in the end the black-maned lion lost and walked off, while the stranger "returned to the remnant of the camel and lay down panting beside it. After he had taken time to breathe, he recommenced his attack and consumed far the larger part of the carcass. Having eaten to fullness, he took up the bones and remaining flesh of the camel and set off across the desert.

"Parched as my throat was, but afraid to descend from my place of safety, I remained on the tree until the light of the next morning, when I examined carefully around to see that there was no beast of prey lurking around the place where I knew the water to be. Perceiving no danger, I descended before the sun was up, and going to the water knelt down and drank as long and as much as I thought I could with safety.

"I walked out upon the desert and prayed to be delivered from the perils that environed me. At the distance of two or three miles I now observed a small sand hill, rising to the height of eight or ten feet." Climbing to the top of this hill he saw a "hollow place on the side opposite to that by which I had ascended; and on coming to this spot, beheld my camel crouched down close to the ground, with his neck extended at full length. My joy was unbounded—I leaped with delight, and was wild for some minutes with a delirium of gladness. I hastened to loose his feet from the cords with which I had bound them, mounted upon his back, and was quickly at the watering place. I filled my two water skins with water, and gathering as many nuts as my sacks would contain, caused my camel to take a full draught, and fill his stomach with grass, and then directed my course to the south, with a quick pace.

"I pursued my route without anything worthy of relating happening to me until the eighth day, when I discovered trees and all the appearance of a woody country before me. Soon after entering the forest I came to a small stream of water. Descending this stream a few miles, I found some people who were cutting grass for the purpose of making mats to sleep on. These people spoke my own language. They took me and my camel to their village and treated me very kindly, promising me that after I had recovered from my fatigue they would go with me to my friends.

"My protectors were at war with a nation whose religion was different from ours; and about a month after I came to the village we were alarmed one morning, just at break of day, by the horrible uproar caused by mingled shouts of men and blows given with heavy sticks upon large wooden drums. The village was surrounded by enemies who attacked us with clubs, long wooden spears, and bows and arrows. After fighting for more than an hour, those who were not fortunate enough to run away were made prisoners. It was not the object of our enemies to kill; they wished to take us alive and sell us as slaves. I was knocked down by a heavy blow of a club, and when I recovered from the stupor that followed I found myself tied fast with the long rope that I had brought from the desert, and with which I had formerly led the camels of my masters.

"We were immediately led away from the village through the forest, and were compelled to travel all day as fast as we could walk. We had nothing to eat on this journey but a small quantity of grain, taken with ourselves. This grain we were compelled to carry on our backs and roast by the fires which we kindled at nights to frighten away the wild beasts. We traveled three weeks in the woods—sometimes without any path at all; and arrived one day at a large river, with a rapid current. Here we were forced to help our conquerors to roll a great number of dead trees into the water, from a vast pile that had been thrown together by high floods.

"These trees being dry and light floated high out of the water; and when several of them were fastened together with the tough branches of young trees, formed a raft upon which we all placed ourselves and descended the river for three days, when we came in sight of what appeared to me the most wonderful object in the world: this was a large ship at anchor in the river. When our raft came near the ship, the white people—for such they were on board—assisted to take us on deck, and the logs were suffered to float down the river.

"I had never seen white people before, and they appeared to me the ugliest creatures in the world. The persons who brought us down the river received payment for us of the people in the ship in various articles, of which I remember that a keg of liquor and some yards of blue and red cotton cloth were the principal. At the time we came into this ship she was full of black people, who were all confined in a dark and low place, in irons. The women were in irons as well as the men.

"About twenty persons were seized in our village at the time I was; and among these were three children so young that they were not able to walk or to eat any hard substance. The mothers of these children had brought them all the way with them, and had them in their arms when we were taken on board this ship. When they put us in irons, to be sent to our place of confinement in the ship, the men who fastened the irons on these mothers took the children out of their hands and threw them over the side of the ship into the water. When this was done, two of the women leaped overboard after the children—the third was already confined by a chain to another woman and could not get into the water, but in struggling to disengage herself she broke her arm and died a few days after of a fever. One of the two women who were in the river was carried down by the weight of her irons before she could be rescued; but the other was taken up by some men in a boat, and brought on board. This woman threw herself overboard one night when we were at sea.

"The weather was very hot whilst we lay in the river and many of us died every day; but the number brought on board greatly exceeded those who died, and at the end of two weeks the place in which we were confined was so full that no one could lie down, and we were obliged to sit all the time, for the room was not high enough for us to stand. When our prison would hold no more the ship sailed down the river, and on the night of the second day after she sailed I heard the roaring of the ocean as it dashed against her sides."

The story ends as abruptly as it began: "More than one third of us died on the passage; and when we arrived at Charleston I was not able to stand. It was more than a week after I left the ship before I could straighten my limbs. I was bought by a trader with several others, brought up the country, and sold to our present master. I have been here five years."

Another African Muslim came to a happier end. This was the upper-class Job ben Solomon, whose brief biography was published in England early in the eighteenth century. The book's full title told the reader what to expect: *Some Memoirs of the Life of Job, the Son of Solomon, the High Priest of Boonda in Africa; Who was a slave about two years in Maryland; and afterwards being brought to England was set free, and sent to his native land in the year 1734. By Thomas Bluett, Gentleman, who was intimately acquainted with him in America and came over to England with him. London. MDCCXXXIV. Price, one shilling.*

"Job's name in his own country is Hyuba, Boon Salumena, Boon Hibrahema, i.e. Job, the Son of Solomon, the Son of Abraham. The surname of his family is Jallo. Job, who is now about 31 or 32 years of age was born at a town called Boonda, in the county of Galumbo in the kingdom of Futa in Africa, which lies on both sides the River Senegal, and on the south side reaches as far as the River Gambia.

"About fifty years ago Hibrahim, the grandfather of Job, founded the town of Boonda, in the reign of Bubaker, then king of Futa, and was by his permission sole Lord Proprietor and Governor, and at the same time High Priest, or Alpha; so that he had a power to make what laws and regulations he thought proper for the increase and good government of his new city. Among other institutions one was that no person who flies thither for protection shall be made a slave. This privilege is in force there to this day, and is extended to all in general that can read and know God, as they express it; and it has contributed much to the peopling of this place, which is now very large and flourishing.

"Some time after the settlement of this town Hibrahim died; and as the priesthood is hereditary there Salumen, his son, the father of Job, became High Priest. About the same time Bubaker, the king, dying, his brother Gelazi, who was next heir, succeeded him. Gelazi had a son named Sambo, whom he put under the care of Salumen, Job's father, to learn the Koran and the Arabic language. Job was at this time also companion to Sambo, and studied along with him. Sambo, upon the death of Gelazi, was made king of Futa and reigns there at present.

"When Job was fifteen years old he assisted his father as Emaum, or sub-priest. About this age he married the daughter of the Alpha of Tombut, who was then only eleven years old. By her he had a son (when she was thirteen years old) called Abdolah; and after that two more sons, called Hibrahim and Sambo. About two years before his captivity he married a second wife, daughter of the Alpha of Tomga, by whom he had a daughter named Fatima, after the daughter of the Prophet Mahommed. Both these wives, with their children, were alive when he came from home.

"In February, 1730, Job's father, hearing of an English ship at Gambia River, sent him with two servants to attend him to sell Negroes and to buy paper and some other necessaries; but desired him not to venture over the river because the country of the Mandingoes, who are enemies to the people of Futa, lies on the other side. Job not agreeing with Captain Pike (who commanded the ship lying then at Gambia,) sent back the two servants to acquaint his father with it, and to let him know that he intended to go farther. Accordingly, having agreed with another man, named Loumein Ybai, who understood the Mandingo language, to go with him as his interpreter, he crossed the River Gambia and disposed of his Negroes for some cows.

"As he was returning home he stopped for some refreshment at the house of an old acquaintance, and the weather being very hot he hung up his arms in the house while he refreshed himself. Those arms were very valuable, consisting of a gold-hilted sword, a gold knife, which they wear by their side, and a rich quiver of arrows, which King Sambo had made him a present of. It happened that a company of the Mandingoes, who live upon plunder, passing by at that time, and observing him unarmed, rushed in to the number of seven or eight at once, at a back door, and pinioned Job before he could get to his arms, together with his servant, who is a slave in Maryland still. They then shaved their heads and beards, which Job and his man resented as the highest indignity, though the Mandingoes meant no more by it than to make them appear like slaves taken in war.

"On the 27th of February, 1730, they carried them to Captain Pike at Gambia, who purchased them; and on the first of March they were put on board. Soon after Job found means to acquaint Captain Pike that he was the same person that came to trade with him a few days before, and after what manner he had been taken. Upon this Captain Pike gave him leave to redeem himself and his man; and Job sent to an acquaintance of his father's near Gambia, who promised to send to Job's father to inform him of what had happened, that he might take some course to set him at liberty. But it being a fortnight's journey between that friend's house and his father's, and the ship sailing in about a week after, Job was brought with the rest of the slaves

to Annapolis in Maryland, and delivered to Mr. Vachell Denton, factor to Mr. Hunt. Job heard since by vessels that came from Gambia
that his father sent down several slaves a little after Captain Pike
sailed in order to procure his redemption; and that Sambo, king of
Futa, had made war upon the Mandingoes and cut off great numbers
of them upon account of the injury they had done his schoolfellow.

"Mr. Vachell Denton sold Job to one Mr. Tolsey, in Kent Island
in Maryland, who put him to work in making tobacco; but he was
soon convinced that Job had never been used to such labour. He
every day showed more and more uneasiness under this exercise, and
at last grew sick, being no way able to bear it; so that his master was
obliged to find easier work for him, and therefore put him to tend
the cattle. Job would often leave the cattle and withdraw into the
woods to pray; but a white boy frequently watched him and whilst
he was at his devotion would mock him, and throw dirt in his face.
This very much disturbed Job and added to his other misfortunes;
all which were increased by his ignorance of the English language,
which prevented his complaining or telling his case to any person
about him. Grown in some measure desperate by reason of his present hardships, he resolved to travel at a venture, thinking he might
possibly be taken up by some master who would use him better, or
otherwise meet with some lucky accident to divert or abate his grief."

And a lucky accident was exactly what he did meet with. Arrested
for traveling without a pass, he was held prisoner in a tavern in the
county of Kent on Delaware Bay, the tavern-keeper being also the local
jailer. The county court was then in session and among those attending
was Mr. Bluett, the narrator of Job's story, who along with some other
gentlemen went to have a look at the prisoner. "He was brought into the
tavern to us, but could not speak one word of English. Upon our talking
and making signs to him he wrote a line or two before us and when he
read it pronounced the words *Allah* and *Mahommed*, by which, and his
refusing a glass of wine we offered him, we perceived he was a Mahometan;
but could not imagine of what country he was, or how he got thither, for by
his affable carriage and the easy composure of his countenance we could
perceive he was no common slave. An old Negro man, who lived in that
neighbourhood and could speak the Jalloff language, which Job also under-

stood, went to him and conversed with him. By this the Negro's keeper was informed to whom Job belonged, and what was the cause of his leaving his master. The keeper thereupon wrote to his master, who soon after fetched him home, and was much kinder to him than before, allowing him a place to pray in."

Several other letters were also written, one of them by Job "in Arabick to his father, acquainting him with his misfortunes, hoping he might yet find means to redeem him." This letter was given to Mr. Vachell Denton to forward to the Royal African Company in London and there be given to Captain Pike to deliver when next in Africa. But the letter arrived just after Captain Pike had sailed, so it was passed on to General Oglethorpe, founder of Georgia and a director of the R.A.C. After sending it to a scholar at Oxford for translation, Oglethorpe wrote to Denton asking him to buy Job from his present master. Denton had no trouble doing so, "his master being very willing to part with him, as finding him no ways fit for his business."

Accompanied by Mr. Bluett, Job arrived in London, in April, 1733. By now he had learned to speak English quite fluently and was taken up by fashionable society. To ensure his freedom and cover his expenses, a subscription was got up, with contributions amounting to fifty-nine pounds, six shillings and eleven pence halfpenny. "Job's mind being now perfectly easy, and being himself more known, he went cheerfully among his friends to several places, both in town and country. One day, being at Sir Hans Sloane's, he expressed his great desire to see the Royal Family. Sir Hans promised to get him introduced," and soon afterward Job, "clothed in a rich silk dress, made up after his own country fashion," was "introduced to their Majesties and the rest of the Royal Family. Her Majesty was pleased to present him with a rich gold watch, and the same day he had the honour to dine with his Grace the Duke of Montague and some others of the nobility, who were pleased to make him a handsome present after dinner."

The duke, who was interested in scientific agriculture, also took Job to his place in the country and showed him "the tools that are necessary for tilling the ground, both in gardens and fields, and made his servants show him how to use them"; and on Job's departure he presented him with a large chest full of such instruments to take back to Africa. Finally, "at about the latter end of July last, he embarked on board one of the Africa Company's ships, bound for Gambia, where we hope he is safely

arrived, to the great joy of his friends, and the honour of the English nation." Furthermore, added Bluett, "considering the singular obligations
he is under to the English" there was good reason to hope that he "would
upon all occasions use his best endeavours to promote the English trade
before any other."

Job arrived from London at James's Fort on the Gambia River, on
August 8, 1734, where one of the first people he met was Francis Moore,
the writer for the Royal African Company, who had by now been promoted to the rank of factor, or chief agent. Moore was about to go upriver, so Job went with him. "We arrived at the creek of Damasensa; and
having some old acquaintances at the town of that name, Job and I went
in the yawl. In the way going up a narrow place for about half a mile,
we saw several monkeys of a beautiful blue and red, which the natives
told me never set their feet on the ground, but live entirely among the
trees, leaping from one to another, at such great distances as would appear improbable to any but an eyewitness.

"In the evening, as my friend Job and I were sitting under a great
tree at Damasensa, there came six or seven of the very people who,
three years before, had robbed and made a slave of him, at about
thirty miles distant from that place. Job, though naturally possessed
of a very even temper, could not contain himself on seeing them. He
was filled with rage and indignation, and was for attacking them
with his broadsword and pistols, which he always took care to have
about him. I had much ado to dissuade him from rushing upon them;
but at length representing the ill consequences that would infallibly
attend so rash an action, and the impossibility that either of us should
escape alive, I made him lay aside the attempt, and persuading him
to sit down, and pretending not to know them, to ask them questions
about himself; which he accordingly did; and they told him the truth.
At last he enquired how the king their master did? They replied that
he was dead; and by further inquiry we found that amongst the
goods for which he sold Job to Captain Pike there was a pistol, which
the king used commonly to wear slung by a string about his neck;
and as they never carry arms without their being loaded, the pistol
one day accidentally went off, and the ball lodging in his throat, he
presently died. Job was so transported at the close of this story that

he immediately fell on his knees and returned thanks to Mahomet for making him die by the very goods for which he sold him into slavery. Then returning to me, he cried, 'You see now, Mr. Moore, that God Almighty was displeased at this man's making me a slave, and therefore made him die by the very pistol for which he sold me. Yet I ought to forgive him, because had I not been sold I should neither have known anything of the English tongue, nor have had any of the fine, useful, and valuable things which I have brought with me; nor have known that there is such a place in the world as England; nor such noble, good and generous people as Queen Caroline, Prince William, the Duke of Montague, the Earl of Pembroke, Mr. Holden, Mr. Oglethorpe and the Royal African Company."

Another relatively fortunate slave was Louis Asa-Asa, who when still a boy had been taken prisoner, brought down to the coast and put on board a French ship bound for the West Indies. His luck changed when, as it started on its way across the Atlantic, the ship was driven by a storm on to the coast of Cornwall, where he and four other youths were rescued twice—once from the waves, and then, thanks to a writ of *habeas corpus* brought by George Stephen of the Anti-Slavery Society, from the ship's captain. A prosperous London family then took Louis in and made him a member of their household staff. While there he was interviewed by George Stephen, who wrote up his story, keeping the somewhat artless style in which Louis told it, and published it under the title *The Narrative of Louis Asa-Asa, A Captured African.*

"My father's name was Clashoquin; mine is Asa-Asa. We lived in a country called Bycla, near Egie, a large town. I had five brothers and sisters. We all lived together with my father and mother; he kept a horse and was respectable, but not one of the great men. My uncle was one of the great men of Egie: he could make men come and work for him; his name was Otou. He had a great deal of land and cattle. My father sometimes worked on his own land and used to make charcoal. I was too little to work; my eldest brother used to work on the land, and we were all very happy.

"A great many people who we called Adinyes set fire to Egie in the morning before daybreak; there were some thousands of them. They killed a great many and burnt all their houses. They stayed two days and then carried away all the people whom they did not kill.

"They came again every now and then for a month, as long as they could find people to carry away. They used to tie them by the feet, except when they were taking them off, and then they let them loose; but if they offered to run away they would shoot them. I lost a great many friends and relatives, at Egie; about a dozen. They sold all they carried away, to be slaves. They were sold for cloth or gunpowder, sometimes for salt or guns; sometimes they got four or five guns for a man . . . The Adinyes burnt a great many places besides Egie. They burnt all the country wherever they found villages; they used to shoot men, women and children if they ran away.

"They came to us about eleven o'clock one day, and directly they came they set our house on fire. All of us had run away. We kept together and went into the woods and stopped there two days. The Adinyes then went away and we returned home and found everything burnt. We tried to build a little shed, and were beginning to get comfortable again. We found several of our neighbours lying about wounded; they had been shot. I saw the bodies of four or five little children whom they had killed with blows on the head. They had carried away their fathers and mothers, but the children were too small for slaves so they killed them. They had killed several others, but these were all that I saw. I saw them lying in the street like dead dogs.

"In about a week after we got back, the Adinyes returned and burnt all the sheds and houses they had left standing. We all ran away again; we went into the woods as we had done before. They followed us the next day. We went farther into the woods and stayed there about four days and nights; we were half starved; we only got a few potatoes. My uncle Otou was with us. At the end of this time the Adinyes found us. We ran away. They called my uncle to go to them, but he refused and they shot him immediately; they killed him. The rest of us ran on and they did not get at us till the next day. I ran up into a tree; they followed me and brought me down. They tied my feet. I do not know if they found my father and mother, and brothers and sisters; they had run faster than me and were half a mile farther when I got up into the tree. I have never seen them since.

"They carried away about twenty besides me. They carried us to the sea. They did not beat us; they only killed one man, who was very ill and too weak to carry his load. They made all of us carry chickens and meat for our food, but this poor man could not carry his load and they ran him through the body with a sword. He was a neighbour of ours. When we got to the sea they sold all of us, but not to the same person. I was sold six times over, sometimes for money, sometimes for cloth, and sometimes for a gun . . . In about six months we got to a ship, in which we first saw white people; they were French. They bought us. We found here a great many other slaves; there were about eighty, including women and children. The Frenchmen sent away all but five of us into another very large ship. We five stayed on board till we got to England, which was about five or six months."

Of the five enslaved youths who were shipwrecked on the English coast, two died of measles while in London and two were sent to Sierra Leone. When offered the chance of going back to Africa, Louis is reported to have replied, "Me no father, no mother now; me stay with you." And, concluded the Anti-Slavery Society's account, "here he has ever since remained, conducting himself in a way to gain the good will and respect of all who know him. He is remarkably intelligent, understands our language perfectly, and can read and write well...On one occasion in particular, he was heard saying to himself in the kitchen, while sitting by the fire apparently in deep thought, 'Me think—me think—' A fellow-servant inquired what he meant; and he added, 'Me think what a good thing I came to England! Here I know what God is, and read my Bible; in my country they have no God, no Bible.'" On another occasion he said, "'I should very much like to see my friends again, but I do not now wish to go back to them; for if I go back to my own country, I might be taken as a slave again. I would rather stay here, where I am free.'"

The story of an unfortunate young woman called Nealee is told by Mungo Park, a young Scottish physician who had volunteered to lead a small expedition to discover the source of the Niger River, an exploration financed by *The Association for Promoting the Discovery of the Inland Part of the Continent of Africa*. (Mungo, though a fairly common name among slaves in America, was common also in Scotland in honor of St. Mungo, the patron saint of Glasgow.) After arriving on the Gambia River, Park prepared himself by getting used to the climate, a process known as "seasoning," and learning the language of the Mandingoes. He then set off with a few native companions into the interior. After more than a year's hard travel, during which he barely survived several close brushes with death (from starvation, fever, drowning, the beasts of the forest and hostile Moors), he found himself several hundred miles from the coast, at a place called Kamalia. Here he met Karfa Taura, a Bushreen (Negro Muslim) slave trader, who was preparing to set off for Gambia with a coffle of slaves as soon as he had completed his purchases and the rainy season had come to an end. Impressed by Park's ability to read (from a copy of the The Book of Common Prayer that had somehow found its way to this remote village), Karfa Taura invited him to join his expedition, and Park—so yellowed by malaria and so blackened by the sun that he had difficulty passing as a white man—was happy to accept the offer. "Thus was I delivered by the friendly care of this benevolent Negro from a situation truly deplorable. Distress and famine pressed hard upon me; I had before me the gloomy wilds of Jallonkadoo, where the traveller sees no habitation for five successive days . . . I had almost marked out that place where I was doomed, I thought, to perish, when this friendly Negro stretched out his hospitable hand for my relief." Park continues:

> "On the 24th of January [1796], Karfa returned to Kamalia with a number of people, and thirteen prime slaves he had purchased. He likewise brought with him a young girl whom he had married at Kancaba, as his fourth wife, and had given her parents three prime slaves for her. She was kindly received at the door of the *baloon* [guest house] by Karfa's other wives, who conducted their new acquaintance and co-partner into one of the best huts, which they had caused to be swept and white-washed on purpose to receive her.
>
> "My clothes were by this time become so very ragged that I was almost ashamed to appear out of doors; but Karfa, on the day after his arrival, generously presented me with such a garment and trousers as are commonly worn in this country. The slaves which Karfa had

A young Scottish physician, Mungo Park was dispatched in 1795 to discover the source of the River Niger and Timbuktu, the "lost city of gold." Although he found neither, his widely-read book, Travels in the Interior Districts of Africa, *with its vivid accounts of the slave trade, did much to help British abolitionists bring the trade to an end.*

brought with him were all of them prisoners of war. Eleven of them confessed to me that they had been slaves from their infancy; but the other two refused to give any account of their former condition. They were all very inquisitive; but they viewed me at first with looks of horror, and repeatedly asked if my countrymen were cannibals. They were very desirous to know what became of the slaves after they had crossed the salt water. I told them that they were employed in cultivating the land; but they would not believe me, and one of them, putting his hand upon the ground, said with great simplicity, 'Have you really got such ground as this, to set your feet upon?'

"A deeply rooted idea, that the whites purchase Negroes for the purpose of devouring them, or of selling them to others that they may be devoured hereafter, naturally makes the slaves contemplate a journey towards the Coast with great terror; insomuch that the Slatees [black slave traders] are forced to keep them constantly in irons, and watch them very closely, to prevent their escape. They are commonly secured by putting the right leg of one, and the left of another, into the same pair of fetters. By supporting the fetters with a string, they can walk, though very slowly. Every four slaves are likewise fastened together by the necks, with a strong rope of twisted thongs; and in the night an additional pair of fetters is put on their hands, and sometimes a light iron chain passed round their necks.

"Such of them as evince marks of discontent are secured in a different manner. A thick billet of wood is cut about three feet long, and a smooth notch being made upon one side of it, the ankle of the slave is bolted to the smooth part by means of a strong iron staple, one prong of which passes on each side of the ankle. All these fetters and bolts are made from native iron; in the present case they were put on by the blacksmith as soon as the slaves arrived from Kancaba, and were not taken off until the morning on which the coffle departed for Gambia.

"In other respects, the treatment of the slaves during their stay at Kamalia was far from being harsh or cruel. They were led out in their fetters every morning to the shade of the tamarind tree, where they were encouraged to play at games of hazard and sing diverting songs to keep up their spirits; for though some of them sustained the hardships of their situation with amazing fortitude, the greater part were very much dejected, and would sit all day in a sort of sullen melancholy, with their eyes fixed upon the ground. In the evening their irons were examined, and their hand fetters put on; after which they were conducted into two large huts, where they were guarded during the night by Karfa's domestic slaves. But notwithstanding all this, about a week after their arrival, one of the slaves had the address to procure a small knife with which he opened the rings of his fetters, cut the rope, and made his escape. More of them would probably have got off, had they assisted each other; but the slave no sooner found himself at liberty, than he refused to stop and assist in breaking the chain which was fastened round the necks of his companions."

Their departure was delayed for several reasons, including the observation of Ramadan. "When the fast month was almost at an end, the Bushreens assembled to watch for the appearance of the new moon; but the evening being rather cloudy they were for some time disappointed, and a number of them had gone home, when on a sudden this delightful object showed her sharp horns from behind a cloud, and was welcomed with the clapping of hands, beating of drums, firing muskets, and other marks of rejoicing. As this moon is reckoned extremely lucky, Karfa gave orders that all the people belonging to the coffle should immediately pack up their dry provisions and hold themselves in readiness.

"April 19th. The long wished-for day of our departure was at length arrived, and the Slatees, having taken the irons from their slaves, assembled with them at the door of Karfa's house, where the bundles were all tied up and everyone had his load assigned him. The coffle consisted of of twenty-seven slaves for sale, the property of Karfa and four other Slatees; but we were afterwards joined by five at Maraboo, and three at Bala; making in all thirty-five slaves. The free men were fourteen in number, but most of them had one or two wives, and some domestic slaves; and the schoolmaster [a friend of Karfa], who was now upon his return for Woradoo, the place of his nativity, took with him eight of his scholars; so that the number of free people and domestic slaves amounted to thirty-eight, and the whole amount of the coffle was seventy-three. Among the free men were six Jillikeas (singing men), whose musical talents were frequently exerted either to divert our fatigue, or obtain us a welcome from strangers.

"When we departed from Kamalia, we were followed for about half a mile by most of the inhabitants of the town, some of them crying, and others shaking hands with their relations who were now about to leave them; and when we had gained a piece of rising ground from which we had a view of Kamalia, all the people belonging to the coffle were ordered to sit down in one place, with their faces towards the west, and the townspeople were desired to sit down in another place, with their faces towards Kamalia. In this situation, the schoolmaster, with two of the principal Slatees, having taken their places between the two parties, pronounced a long and solemn prayer; after which they walked three times round the coffle, making an impression on the ground with the ends of their spears, and muttering something by way of charm. When this ceremony was ended, all the people belonging to the coffle sprang up, and without taking a formal farewell of their friends, set forwards.

"As many of the slaves had remained for years in irons, the sudden exertion of walking quick, with heavy loads upon their heads, occasioned spasmodic contractions of their legs; and we had not proceeded above a mile before it was found necessary to take two of them from the rope and allow them to walk more slowly until we reached Maraboo, a walled village, where some people were waiting to join the coffle. Here we stopped about two hours, to allow the strangers time to pack up their provisions, and then continued our route to Bala, which town we reached about four in the afternoon. The inhabitants of Bala, at this season of the year, subsist chiefly on fish, which they take in great plenty from the streams in the neighbourhood. We remained here until the afternoon of the next day, the 20th, when we proceeded to Worumbang, the frontier village of Manding towards Jallonkadoo.

On the 21st, "about sunset we came in sight of Kinytakooro, a considerable town, nearly square, situated in the middle of a large and well-cultivated plain. Before we entered the town we halted until the people who had fallen behind came up. During this day's travel, two slaves, a woman and girl belonging to a Slatee of Bala, were so much fatigued that they could not keep up with the coffle; they were severely whipped, and dragged along until about three o'clock in the afternoon, when they were both affected with vomiting, by which it was discovered that they had eaten clay. This practice is by no means uncommon amongst the Negroes; but whether it arises from a vitiated appetite, or from a settled intention to destroy themselves, I cannot affirm. They were permitted to lie down in the woods, and three people remained with them until they had rested themselves; but they did not arrive at the town until past midnight; and were then so much exhausted that the Slatee gave up all thoughts of taking them across the woods in their present condition, and determined to return with them to Bala, and wait for another opportunity.

"As this was the first town beyond the limits of Manding, greater etiquette than usual was observed. Every person was ordered to keep in his proper station, and we marched towards the town in a sort of procession, nearly as follows: In front, five or six singing men, all of them belonging to the coffle; these were followed by the other free people; then came the slaves fastened in the usual way by a rope round their necks, four of them to a rope, and a man with a spear be-

tween each four; after them came the domestic slaves, and in the rear
the women of free condition, wives of the Slatees, &c. In this manner
we proceeded until we came within a hundred yards of the gate, when
the singing men began a loud song, well calculated to flatter the vanity
of the inhabitants, by extolling their known hospitality to strangers,
and their particular friendship for the Mandingoes. When we entered
the town we proceeded to the *bentang* [town platform] where the people gathered round us to hear our *dentegi* (history). This was related
publicly by two of the singing men. They enumerated every little circumstance which had happened to the coffle, beginning with the
events of the present day, and relating everything, in a backward series, until they reached Kamalia. When this history was ended, the
master of the town gave them a small present; and all the people of
the coffle, both free and enslaved, were invited by some person or
other and accommodated with lodging and provisions for the night.

"At daybreak the next day we departed from this village and
entered the Jallonka Wilderness. We passed, in the course of the
morning, the ruins of two small towns, which had lately been burnt
by the Foulahs. The fire must have been very intense; for I observed
the walls of many of the huts were slightly vitrified, and appeared at
a distance as if covered with a red varnish. About ten o'clock we
came to the river Wonda, which is somewhat larger than the river
Kokoro; but the stream was at this time rather muddy, which Karfa
assured me was caused by amazing shoals of fish. They were indeed
seen in all directions, and in such abundance that I fancied the water
itself tasted and smelt fishy. As soon as we had crossed the river,
Karfa gave orders that all the people in the coffle should in future
keep close together, and travel in their proper station. The guides and
young men were accordingly placed in the van, the women and slaves
in the centre, and the free men in the rear. In this order, we travelled
with uncommon expedition through a woody but beautiful country,
interspersed with a pleasing variety of hill and dale, and abounding
with partridges, guinea-fowls, and deer, until sunset.

"April 24th. Before daybreak the Bushreens said their morning
prayers, and most of the free people drank a little *moening* (a sort of
gruel), part of which was likewise given to such of the slaves as appeared least able to sustain the fatigues of the day. One of Karfa's fe-

male slaves was very sulky, and when some gruel was offered to her, she refused to drink it. As soon as day dawned we set out, and travelled the whole morning over a wild and rocky country, by which my feet were much bruised; and I was sadly apprehensive that I should not be able to keep up with the coffle during the day; but I was in a great measure relieved from this anxiety when I observed that others were more exhausted than myself. In particular, the woman slave who had refused victuals in the morning now began to lag behind, and complain dreadfully of pains in her legs. Her load was taken from her and given to another slave, and she was ordered to keep in the front of the coffle.

"About eleven o'clock, as we were resting by a small rivulet, some of the people discovered a hive of bees in a hollow tree, and they were proceeding to obtain the honey when the largest swarm I ever beheld flew out, and attacking the people of the coffle, made us fly in all directions. I took the alarm first, and I believe was the only person who escaped with impunity. When our enemies thought fit to desist from pursuing us, and every person was employed in picking out the stings he had received, it was discovered that the poor woman above-mentioned, whose name was Nealee, was not come up; and as many of the slaves in their retreat had left their bundles behind them, it became necessary for some persons to return, and bring them. In order to do this with safety, fire was set to the grass a considerable way to the eastward of the hive, and the wind driving the fire furiously along, the party pushed through the smoke and recovered the bundles. They likewise brought with them poor Nealee, whom they found lying by the rivulet. She was very much exhausted, and had crept to the stream in hopes to defend herself from the bees by throwing water over her body; but this proved ineffectual, for she was stung in the most dreadful manner.

"When the Slatees had picked out the stings as far as they could, she was washed with water, and then rubbed with bruised leaves; but the wretched woman obstinately refused to proceed any farther, declaring that she would rather die than walk another step. As entreaties and threats were used in vain, the whip was at length applied; and after bearing patiently a few strokes, she started up and walked with tolerable expedition for four or five hours longer, when she made an attempt to run away from the coffle, but was so very weak that she fell down in the grass. Though she was unable to rise, the whip was a second time applied, but without effect; upon which Karfa desired two of the Slatees to place her upon the ass which carried our dry provisions; but she could not sit erect, and the ass being very refractory, it was found impossible to carry her forward in that manner. The Slatees, however, were unwilling to abandon her, the day's journey being nearly ended. They therefore made a sort of litter of bamboo canes, upon which she was placed, and tied on it with slips of bark. This litter was carried upon the heads of two slaves, one walking before the other, and they were followed by two others, who relieved them occasionally. In this manner the woman was carried forward until it was dark, when we reached a stream of water at the foot of a high hill called Gankaran-Kooro; and here we stopped for the night, and set about preparing our supper. As we had only eaten one handful of meal since the preceding night, and travelled all day in a hot sun, many of the slaves, who had loads upon their heads, were very much fatigued; and some of them snapped their fingers, which among the Negroes is a sure sign of desperation. The Slatees immediately put them all in irons; and such of them as had evinced signs of great despondency were kept apart from the rest and had their hands tied. In the morning they were found greatly recovered.

"April 25th. At daybreak poor Nealee was awakened; but her limbs were now become so stiff and painful that she could neither walk nor stand. She was therefore lifted, like a corpse, upon the back of the ass, and the Slatees endeavoured to secure her in that situation by fastening her hands together under the ass's neck, and her feet under the belly, with long slips of bark; but the ass was so very unruly that no sort of treatment could induce him to proceed with his load; and as Nealee made no exertion to prevent herself from falling, she was quickly thrown off, and had one of her legs much bruised. Every attempt to carry her forward being thus found ineffectual, the general cry of the coffle was 'Kang-tegi! Kang-tegi!' ('Cut her throat! Cut her throat!') an operation I did not wish to see performed, and therefore marched onwards with the foremost of the coffle. I had not walked above a mile when one of Karfa's domestic slaves came up to me, with poor Nealee's garment upon the end of his bow, and exclaimed 'Nealee affeeleeta' ('Nealee is lost.') I asked him whether the

Slatees had given him the garment as a reward for cutting her throat. He replied that Karfa and the schoolmaster would not consent to that measure, but had left her on the road; where undoubtedly she soon perished, and was probably devoured by wild beasts.

"The sad fate of this wretched woman, notwithstanding the outcry before-mentioned, made a strong impression on the minds of the whole coffle, and the schoolmaster fasted the whole of the ensuing day, in consequence of it. We proceeded in deep silence, and soon afterward crossed the river Furkoomah . . . About noon we saw a large herd of elephants, but they suffered us to pass unmolested."

When he was eleven, Olaudah Equiano, who earlier described the pleasant and peaceful life of the Ibos of Benin, was suddenly captured and enslaved. This is how it happened:

"One day, when all our people were gone out to their work as usual, and only I and my sister were left to mind the house, two men and a woman got over our walls, and in a moment seized us both; and without giving us time to cry out, or to make any resistance, they stopped our mouths and ran off with us into the nearest wood. Here they tied our hands, and continued to carry us as far as they could till night came on, when we reached a small house, where the robbers halted for refreshment and spent the night. We were then unbound, but were unable to take any food; and being quite overpowered with fatigue and grief, our only relief was some sleep, which allayed our misfortune for a short time.

"The next morning we left the house and continued travelling all the day. For a long time we had kept the woods, but at last we came into a road which I believed I knew. I had now some hopes of being delivered; for we had advanced but a little way before I discovered some people at a distance, on which I began to cry out for their assistance; but my cries had no other effect than to make them tie me faster and stop my mouth; they then put me into a large sack. They also stopped my sister's mouth and tied her hands; and in this manner we proceeded till we were out of sight of these people. The

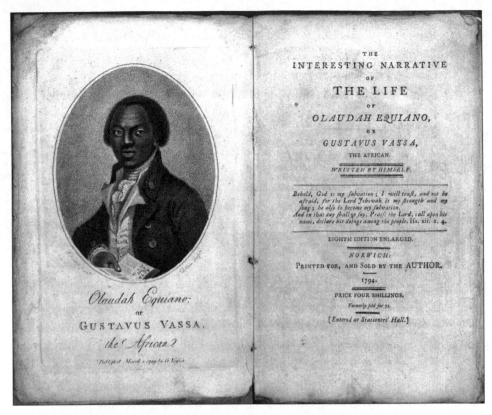

Known for most of his life as Gustavus Vassa, the name foisted on him by one of his owners, Olaudah Equiano reclaimed his rightful name when publishing his "interesting narrative" in England in 1789. The book sold well, for his story was full of adventures, and had a happy ending—married and the father of two daughters, an active abolitionist, and living comfortably in Cambridge, England.

next day—"one of greater sorrow than I had yet experienced"—he and his sister were separated. During the following months he was sold several times over, once as an apprentice to a goldsmith, who re-sold him when he tried to run away, and another time to a wealthy widow who thought he would make a good companion for her son of about the same age. "The language of these people resembled ours so nearly that we understood each other perfectly," and "their treatment of me made me forget that I was a slave." But just as "I began to think that I was to be adopted into this family," the widow, without warning or explanation, got rid of him and "I was awakened out of my reveries to fresh sorrow, and hurried away."

Soon he came to a country where the language was different and the people "ate without washing their hands. They cooked their provisions also in iron pots, and had European cutlasses and crossbows, which were unknown to us; and fought with their fists among themselves. The women were not so modest as ours, for they ate, drank and slept with their men. But, above all, I was amazed to see no sacrifices or offerings among them. In some of those places the people ornamented themselves with scars, and likewise filed their teeth very sharp. They sometimes wanted to ornament me in the same manner, but I would not suffer them; hoping that I might sometime be among a people who did not thus disfigure themselves."

But such hopes of a return were not to be; instead, he was put into a canoe and taken on a long journey down an unnamed river, through a fertile countryside with large crops of vegetables and tobacco, and where cotton grew wild. Finally, they reached the river's mouth. "The first object that saluted my eyes when I arrived on the coast was the sea, and a slave ship, which was then riding at anchor and waiting for its cargo." He was taken on board where he "was immediately handled and tossed up to see if I was sound, by some of the crew; and I was now persuaded that I had got into a world of bad spirits, and that they were going to kill me. Their complexions too, differing so much from ours, their long hair, the language they spoke, which was very different from any I had ever heard, united to confirm me in this belief . . . When I looked round the ship too, and saw a large furnace or copper boiling, and a multitude of black people of every description chained together, every one of their countenances expressing dejection and sorrow, I no longer doubted of my fate; and, quite overpowered with horror and anguish, I fell motionless on the deck, and fainted.

"When I recovered a little I found some black people about me, who I believed were some of those who brought me on board and had been receiving their pay; they talked to me in order to cheer me, but all in vain. I asked them if we were not to be eaten by those white men with horrible looks, red faces and long hair. They told me I was not, and one of the crew brought me a small portion of spirituous liquor in a wine glass; but being afraid of him I would not take it out of his hand. One of the blacks therefore took it from him and gave it to me, and I took a little down my palate, which, instead of reviving me, as they thought it would, threw me into the greatest consternation at the strange feeling it produced, having never tasted any such liquor before. Soon after this the blacks who brought me on board went off and left me abandoned to despair.

"I was not long suffered to indulge my grief. I was soon put down under the decks, and there I received such a salutation in my nostrils as I had never experienced in my life; so that, with the loathsomeness of the stench, and with my crying together, I became so sick and low that I was not able to eat, nor had I the least desire to taste anything. I now wished for the last friend, death, to relieve me; but soon, to my grief, two of the white men offered me eatables; and on my refusing to eat one of them held me fast by the hands and laid me across, I think, the windlass, and tied my feet, while the other flogged me severely. I had never experienced anything of this kind before, and although, not being used to the water, I naturally feared that element the first time I saw it, yet nevertheless, could I have got over the nettings, I would have jumped over the side, but I could not; and besides, the crew used to watch us very closely, who were not chained down to the decks, lest we should leap into the water. I have seen some of these poor African prisoners most severely cut for attempting to do so, and hourly whipped for not eating. This indeed was often the case with myself.

"In a little time after, amongst the poor chained men, I found some of my own nation, which in a small degree gave ease to my mind. I inquired of these what was to be done with us. They gave me to understand we were to be carried to these white people's country to work for them. I was then a little revived, and thought if it were no worse than working my situation was not so desperate. But still I feared I should be put to death, the white people looked and acted, as I thought, in so savage a manner; for I had never seen among any people such instances of brutal cruelty; and this is not only shown towards us blacks but also to some of the whites themselves. One white man in particular I saw, when we were permitted to be on deck, flogged so unmercifully with a large rope near the foremast that he died in consequence of it; and they tossed him over the side as they would have done a brute. This made me fear these people even more; and I expected nothing less than to be treated in the same manner.

"At last, when the ship in which we were had got in all her cargo, they made ready with many fearful noises, and we were all put under deck so that we could not see how they managed the vessel. But this disappointment was the least of my grief. The stench of the hold while we were on the coast was so intolerably loathsome that it was dangerous to remain there for any time, and some of us had been permitted to stay on the deck for the fresh air; but now that the whole ship's cargo were confined together, it became absolutely pestilential. The closeness of the place and the heat of the climate, added to the number in the ship being so crowded that each had scarcely room to turn himself, almost suffocated us. This produced copious perspiration so that the air soon became unfit for respiration, from a variety of loathsome smells, and brought on a sickness among the slaves of which many died, thus falling victims to the improvident avarice, as I may call it, of their purchasers. This deplorable situation was again aggravated by the galling of the chains, now become insupportable; and the filth of the necessary tubs, into which the children often fell and were almost suffocated. The shrieks of the women and the groans of the dying rendered it a scene of horror almost inconceivable. Happily, perhaps, for myself, I was soon reduced so low here that it was thought necessary to keep me almost continually on deck; and from my extreme youth, I was not put in fetters.

"One day, when we had a smooth sea and moderate wind, two of my wearied countrymen, who were chained together, (I was near them at the time,) preferring death to such a life of misery, somehow made through the nettings and jumped into the sea. Immediately, another quite dejected fellow, who on account of his illness was suffered to be out of irons also followed their example; and I believe many more would very soon have done the same if they had not been prevented by the ship's crew, who were instantly alarmed. Those of us who were the most active were in a moment put down under the deck, and there was such a noise and confusion amongst the people of the ship as I never heard before, to stop her and get the boat out to go after the slaves. However, two of the wretches were drowned; but they got the other, and afterward flogged him unmercifully for thus attempting to prefer death to slavery."

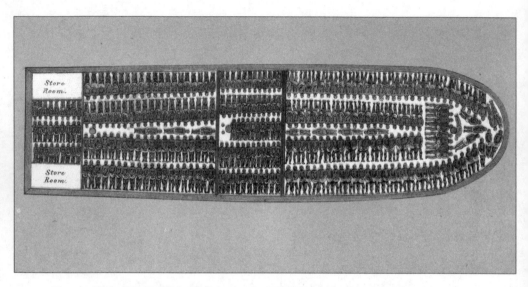

First published by English abolitionists in 1788, this picture of the slave ship Brookes *soon became iconic. An accompanying text explained that by allowing a space of six feet by one foot four inches for a man, and a little less for a woman, the ship could hold 454 slaves; however, on earlier voyages the* Brookes *had carried over six hundred. Slave ships were easy to recognize at sea by the netting draped over the sides to prevent suicides, by their overpowering stench, and by the sharks that followed, waiting to devour the dead bodies thrown overboard almost every day.*

Store
Room.

Store
Room.

CHAPTER 4

THE MIDDLE PASSAGE

WE RETURN NOW TO CAPTAIN PHILLIPS OF THE *HANNIBAL* WHO EARLIER described how he had fought the French and successfully traded for slaves with the king of Whydah. "Having bought my complement of 700 slaves, viz. 480 men and 220 women, and finished all my business at Whydah, I took my leave of the old king and his cappashiers and parted with many affectionate expressions on both sides." After a few formalities, "I set sail the 27th of July [1694] in the morning, accompanied by the *East-India Merchant*, who had bought 650 slaves, for the island of St. Thomas [Sao Thomé], with the wind at the west-south-west."

Before continuing his log, Phillips described how he handled his cargo: "When our slaves are aboard we shackle the men two and two while we lie in port and in sight of their own country, for 'tis then they attempt to make their escape, and mutiny; to prevent which we always keep sentinels upon the hatch-ways, and have a chest of small arms ready loaden and primed constantly lying at hand upon the quarter-deck, together with some granada shells; and two of our quarter-deck guns pointing on the deck thence, and two more out of the steerage, the door of which is always kept shut and well barred. They are fed twice a day, at 10 in the morning and 4 in the evening, which is the time they are aptest to mutiny, being all upon deck; therefore all that time what of our men are not employed in distributing their victuals to them and settling them, stand to their arms; and some with lighted matches at the great guns that yaun upon them, loaden with partridge [small shot] till they have done and gone down to their kennels between decks.

"Their chief diet is called *dabbadabb*, being Indian corn ground as small as oatmeal in iron mills which we carry for that purpose; and after mixed with water and boiled well in a large copper furnace till 'tis as thick as a pudding; about a peckful of which in vessels called crews is allowed to ten men, with a little salt, malagetta and palm oil to relish. They are divided into messes of ten each for the easier and better order in serving them. Three days a week they have horse-beans boiled for their dinner and supper, great quantities of which the African Company do send aboard us for that purpose; these beans the Negroes extremely love and desire, beating their breasts eating them and crying *Pram! Pram!* which is *Very good!* They are indeed the best diet for them, having a binding quality and consequently good to prevent the flux [dysentery], which is the inveterate distemper that most affects them and ruins our voyages by their mortality. The men are all fed upon the main deck and forecastle, that we may have them all under command of our guns from the quarter-deck, in case of any disturbance; the women eat upon the quarter-deck with us, and the boys and girls upon the poop. After they are once divided into messes and appointed their places, they will readily run there in good order of themselves.

"When they have eaten their victuals clean up, (which we force them to for to thrive better,) they are ordered down between decks and everyone as he passes has a pint of water to drink after his meat, which is served them by the cooper out of a large tub, filled beforehand ready for them. When they have occasion to ease nature they are permitted by the sentinels to come up and go to conveniencies which are provided for that purpose on each side the ship, each of which will contain a dozen of them at once, and have broad ladders to ascend them with the greater ease.

"When we come to sea we let them all out of irons, they never attempting then to rebel, considering that should they kill or master us they could not tell how to manage the ship, or must trust us, who would carry them where we pleased. Therefore the only danger is while we are in sight of their own country, which they are loth to part with; but once out of sight, out of mind. I never heard that they mutinied in any ships of consequence that had a good number of men and the least care; but in small tools [ships] where they had but few men, and those negligent or drunk, then they surprised and butchered them, cut the cables and let the vessel drive ashore, and everyone shift

For slavers, the most dangerous time was while still on the coast; hence the shackles and handcuffs as the slaves came on board. Children were often allowed to run free, and women were generally unshackled since they were thought to be more docile, which was not always the case.

for himself. However, we have some 30 or 40 Gold Coast Negroes, which we buy and are procured us there by our factors to make guardians and overseers of the Whydah Negroes, and sleep among them to keep them from quarreling, and in order as well to give us notice, if they can discover any caballing or plotting among them, which trust they will discharge with great diligence. They also take care to make the Negroes scrape the decks where they lodge every morning very clean to eschew any distempers that may engender from filth and nastiness. When we constitute a guardian we give him a cat of nine tails as a badge of his office, which he is not a little proud of and will exercise with great authority. We often at sea in the evenings would let the slaves come up into the sun to air themselves, and make them jump and dance for an hour or two to our bag-pipes, harp and fiddle, by which exercise to preserve them in health."

Resuming his log, Phillips wrote:

"Monday the 6th [of August]. This morning we crossed the line, being by our observations in 10 minutes south latitude; at which time our Negroes being all upon deck at their dinners, a young tiger I had aboard, which was given to me by Mr. Ronan at Cape Corce castle, and which I kept in a wooden cage upon the quarter deck, broke out of it, seized upon a Negro woman's leg, and in instant, before any of us could come to her rescue, tore the calf quite off, which as soon as one of our quarter-masters perceived, he ran to him, and giving him a little blow with the flat of a cutlass, the tiger couched down like a spaniel dog and the man took him up in his arms, dragged him along, and without any resistance or harm pent him up in his coop again.

"'Twas strange to me to observe this ravenous wild creature, that he would be as familiar with our white men as a spaniel, letting them play with him, stroak him, take him by the tongue or paw, and would wantonly lick their hands, pat them with his foot like a cat, without offering the least injury; but when he saw a black, tho' at a distance, he would grow raving mad, bounce and leap in his cage as if he would break it to pieces, and his eyes would look like perfect fire, so that I was forced to get a larger and stronger coop made for him; and always hang an old sail before it to blind him while the slaves were at victuals, else there was no appeasing of him.

"We spent in our passage from St. Thomas to Barbadoes two months eleven days, from the 25th of August to the 4th of November following, in which time there happened such sickness and mortality among my poor men and Negroes that of the first we buried 14 and of the last 320, which was a great detriment to our voyage, the Royal African Company losing ten pounds by every slave that died, and the owners of the ship ten pounds ten shillings, being the freight agreed on to be paid them by the charter party for every Negro delivered alive ashore to the African Company's agents at Barbadoes; whereby the loss in all amounted to near 6560 pounds sterling. The distemper which my men as well as the blacks mostly died of was the white flux, which was so violent and inveterate that no medicine would in the least check it; so that when any of our men were seized with it we esteemed him a dead man, as he generally proved. I cannot imagine what should cause it in them so suddenly, they being free from it till about a week after we left the island of St. Thomas. And next to the malignity of the climate I can attribute it to nothing else but the unpurged black sugar and raw unwholesome rum they bought there, of which they drank in punch to great excess, and which it was not in my power to hinder, having chastised several of them and flung overboard what rum and sugar I could find; and was forced to clap one Lord, our trumpeter, in irons for his being the promoter of their unseasonable carousing bouts, and going in one of his drunken fits with his knife to kill the boatswain in his bed, and committing other enormities." Small-pox also "went through the ship, yet we lost not a dozen by it . . . But what the small-pox spared, the flux swept off."

As he contemplated his losses, Phillips was overcome with sorrow and pity, not for the dead sailors and slaves, but for himself. "After all our pains and care to give them their messes in due order and season, keeping their lodgings as clean and sweet as possible, and enduring so much misery and stench so long among a parcel of creatures nastier than swine; and after all our expectations, to be defeated by their mortality. No gold-finders can endure so much noisome slavery as they do who carry Negroes; for those have some respite and satisfaction, but we endure twice the misery, and yet by their mortality our voyages are ruined, and we pine and fret ourselves to death, to think that we should undergo so much misery, and take so much pains to so little purpose." The net result: "I delivered alive at Barbadoes to the company's factor 372, which being sold came out at about nineteen pounds per head one with another." The return voyage, loaded with sugar, cotton and ginger, was uneventful except for the misfortune that "befell one of my cabin boys, who playing with the tiger in his cage, with his hand, a long time without any offence; at length he scratched his hand against the point of a nail, so that it bled a little. As soon as the tiger saw the blood, he seized upon his hand and in an instant tore it to pieces, almost as far as the wrist ere we could disengage him, the ends of the nerves and torn sinews hanging about like strings, most dismal to behold."

Although it does not of course excuse the hardships inflicted on slaves, crossing the Atlantic in the age of sail was also a grim business for poor whites. Here, briefly, is the story of Philip Drake, a destitute orphan brought up in a workhouse in the English Midlands. When he was twelve, the board of overseers—"three stout, red-faced men in powdered wigs who sat at a green-covered table with snuff-boxes before them"— decided to rid the parish of the expense of maintaining him; and since he was known to have an uncle in America, they booked him passage on the cheapest ship available, fitted him out with a set of cheap new clothes, and gave him one shilling for expenses, along with a letter addressed to "Maurice Halter, Boston, United States." Soon after, with all his possessions tied up in an old handkerchief, "with some forty other English paupers from various parishes, I found myself dumped among four hundred Irish emigrants in the steerage of the ship *Polly* of Waterford." This was in 1802.

> "She was 202 tons burden and carried 450-odd steerage passengers. They were so thick between decks that the air became putrid and whenever her sick squads were ordered up the gangways, one or more was sure to gasp and die with the first gulp of pure air. The steerage became pestilential before our voyage was half made, for the emigrants' beds were never cleaned, and whole families literally wallowed in poisonous filth. The bodies of men and women, and their tattered garments, were crusted and impregnated with the most offensive matter. Typhus fever and dysentery soon broke out, and then mortality raged fearfully . . . I can remember one day in particular, when I had clambered to the deck and crept out to a coil of chain near the capstan. Thirty corpses were hauled up during the morning and cast overboard, to feed a school of hungry sharks that constantly followed the vessel. Most of the bodies were women, with long hair tangled in their filthy garments. No sooner did one of them strike the water than two or three sharks snapped at it, till the ship's track was marked with blood. It was a sight that no after horror ever effaced from my mind." When, after seventy-seven days at sea, the ship reached Cape Ann, "we had 186 left out of 450 odd passengers."

In 1789, after hearing a great deal of evidence, a committee of England's Privy Council concluded that, on average, four and a half per cent of

"View of chained African slaves in cargo hold of slave ship, measuring three feet and three inches high." 19th century woodcut. Schomburg Center for Research in Black Culture, Photographs and Prints Division, The New York Public Library, Digital Collections.

slaves died while being held in factories and forts before sailing; twelve and a half per cent died during the crossing; and thirty-three per cent died during their first year in the colonies, a period known as "seasoning." No estimates were made of the numbers killed in the raids and wars that provided so many of the captives, or of those who died during the long trek from the interior to the coast. In their campaign to end the slave trade, English abolitionists focused on the twelve and half per cent who died during the crossing. Among those testifying on their behalf was Alexander Falconbridge, a ship's doctor:

"It frequently happens that the Negroes, on being purchased by the Europeans, become raving mad; and many of them die in that state, particularly the women. While I was one day ashore at Bonny I saw a middle-aged, stout woman, who had been brought down from a fair the preceding day, chained to the post of a black trader's door, in a state of furious insanity. On board a ship in Bonny River I saw a young negro woman chained to the deck, who had lost her senses soon after she was purchased and taken on board. In a former voyage, on board a ship to which I belonged, we were obliged to confine a female negro of about twenty-three years of age, on her becoming a lunatic. She was afterwards sold during one of her lucid intervals.

"The men Negroes, on being brought aboard the ship, are immediately fastened together, two and two, by hand-cuffs on their wrists, and by irons riveted on their legs. They are then sent down between the decks and placed in an apartment partitioned off for that purpose. The women are likewise placed in a separate apartment between decks, but without being ironed. And an adjoining room, on the same deck, is besides appointed for the boys. Thus are they all placed in different apartments.

"But at the same time they are frequently stowed so close as to admit of no other posture than lying on their sides. Neither will the height between decks, unless directly under the grating, permit them the indulgence of an erect posture, especially where there are platforms, which is generally the case. These platforms are a kind of shelf, about eight or nine feet in breadth, extending from the side of the ship towards the centre. They are placed nearly midways between the decks, at the distance of two or three feet from each deck. Upon these the Negroes are stowed in the same manner as they are on the deck underneath.

"In each of the apartments are placed three or four large buckets, of a conical form, being near two feet in diameter at the bottom and only one foot at the top, and in depth about twenty-eight inches; to which, when necessary, the Negroes have recourse. It often happens that those who are placed at a distance from the buckets, in endeavouring to get to them, tumble over their companions in consequence of their being shackled. These accidents, although unavoidable, are productive of continual quarrels in which some of them are always bruised. In this distressed situation, unable to proceed, and prevented from getting to the tubs, they desist from the attempt and, as the necessities of nature are not to be repelled, ease themselves as they lie. This becomes a fresh source of broils and disturbances, and tends to render the condition of the poor captive wretches still more uncomfortable. The nuisance arising from these circumstances is not infrequently increased by the tubs being much too small for the purpose intended, and their being usually emptied but once every day.

"About eight o'clock in the morning the Negroes are generally brought up on deck. Their irons being examined, a long chain, which is locked to a ring-bolt fixed in the deck, is run through the rings of the shackles of the men, and then locked to another ring-bolt, fixed also in the deck. By this means fifty or sixty, and sometimes more, are fastened to one chain in order to prevent them from rising or endeavouring to escape. If the weather proves favourable they are permitted to remain in that situation till four or five in the afternoon, when they are disengaged from the chain and sent down.

"Their food is served up to them in tubs, about the size of a small water bucket. They are placed round these tubs in companies of ten to each tub, out of which they feed themselves with wooden spoons. These they soon lose, and when they are not allowed others they feed themselves with their hands. In favourable weather they are fed upon deck, but in bad weather their food is given them below. Numberless quarrels take place among them during their meals; more especially when they are put upon short allowance, which frequently happens if the passage from the coast of Guinea to the West India islands proves of unusual length. In that case the weak are obliged to be content with a very scanty portion. Their allowance of water is about half a pint each at every meal.

"Upon the Negroes refusing to take sustenance I have seen coals of fire, glowing hot, put on a shovel and placed so near their lips as to scorch and burn them. And this has been accompanied with threats of forcing them to swallow the coals if they any longer

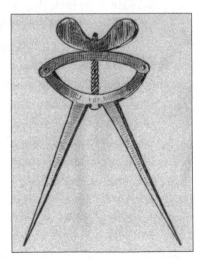

A medical instrument for prying open the mouths of patients with lockjaw, the speculum oris was also used to force-feed slaves who tried to starve themselves to death. To operate, the two points were closed to form a spike which was then forced between the slave's teeth, then the screw was turned by the butterfly nut, the jaws were forced open, and liquid food poured down the throat.

persisted in refusing to eat. These means have generally had the desired effect.

"Exercise being deemed necessary for the preservation of their health they are sometimes obliged to dance when the weather will permit their coming on deck. If they go about it reluctantly, or do not move with agility, they are flogged, a person standing by them all the time with a cat-o'-nine-tails in his hand for that purpose. Their musick upon these occasions consists of a drum, sometimes with only one head; and when that is worn out they do not scruple to make use of the bottom of one of the tubs before described. The poor wretches are frequently compelled to sing also; but when they do, their songs are generally, as may naturally be expected, melancholy lamentations of their exile from their native country.

"The women are furnished with beads for the purpose of affording them some diversion. But this end is generally defeated by the squabbles which are occasioned in consequence of their stealing them from each other. On board some ships the common sailors are allowed to have intercourse with such of the black women whose consent they can procure. The officers are permitted to indulge their passions among them at pleasure, and sometimes are guilty of such brutal excesses as disgrace human nature.

"The hardships and inconveniences suffered by the Negroes during the passage are scarcely to be enumerated or conceived. They are far more violently affected by the sea-sickness than the Europeans; it frequently terminates in death, especially among the women. But the exclusion of the fresh air is among the most intolerable. For the purpose of admitting this needful refreshment, most of the ships in the slave-trade are provided between decks with five or six air-ports on each side of the ship, of about six inches in length and four in breadth; in addition to which some few ships, but not one in twenty, have what they denominate wind-sails. But whenever the sea is rough and the rains heavy it becomes necessary to shut these and every other conveyance by which the air is admitted. The fresh air being thus excluded, the Negroes' rooms very soon grow intolerably hot. The confined air, rendered noxious by the effluvia exhaled from their bodies, and by being repeatedly breathed, soon produces fevers and fluxes, which generally carries off great numbers of them.

"During the voyages I made I was frequently a witness to the fatal effects of this exclusion of the fresh air. I will give one instance, as it serves to convey some idea, though a very faint one, of the sufferings of those unhappy beings whom we wantonly drag from their native country and doom to perpetual labour and captivity. Some wet and blowing weather having occasioned the port-holes to be shut and the grating to be covered, fluxes and fevers among the Negroes ensued. While they were in this situation, my profession requiring it, I frequently went down among them, till at length their apartments became so extremely hot as to be only sufferable for a very short time. But the excessive heat was not the only thing that rendered their situation intolerable. The deck, that is, the floor of their rooms, was so covered with the blood and mucus which had proceeded from them in consequence of the flux that it resembled a slaughter-house. It is not in the power of the human imagination to picture to itself a situation more dreadful or disgusting. Numbers of the slaves having fainted, they were carried up on deck, where several of them died, and the rest were, with great difficulty, restored. It had nearly proved fatal to me also. The climate was too warm to admit the wearing of any clothing but a shirt, and that I had pulled off before I went down; notwithstanding which, by only continuing among them for about a quarter of an hour, I was so overcome with the heat, stench, and foul air, that I had nearly fainted; and it was not without assistance that I could get upon deck.

"The place allotted for the sick Negroes is under the half-deck, where they lie on the bare planks. By this means those who are emaciated frequently have their skin, and even their flesh, entirely rubbed off by the motion of the ship from the prominent parts of the shoulders, elbows and hips, so as to render the bones in those parts quite bare. The excruciating pain which the poor sufferers feel from being obliged to continue in such a dreadful situation, frequently for several weeks, in case they happen to live so long, is not to be conceived or described. Few indeed are ever able to withstand the fatal effects of it.

"The surgeon, upon going between decks in the morning to examine the situation of the slaves, frequently finds several dead; and among the men sometimes a dead and living negro fastened by their irons together. When this is the case they are brought up on the deck and being laid on the grating the living negro is disengaged and the dead one thrown overboard.

"One morning, upon examining the place allotted for the sick Negroes, I perceived that one of them, who was so emaciated as scarcely to be able to walk, was missing, and was convinced that he must have gone overboard in the night, probably to put a more expeditious period to his sufferings. And, to conclude on this subject, I could not help being sensibly affected, on a former voyage, at observing with what apparent eagerness a black woman seized some dirt from off an African yam, and put it into her mouth, seeming to rejoice at the opportunity of possessing some of her native earth."

Slave uprisings—or, as the traders preferred to call them, mutinies—occurred on about one in ten of the ships, mostly while they were still on the African coast. They were of course expected, and precautions were taken: when on deck the slaves were usually chained; the hilts of the swords and cutlasses carried by the sailors were tied to their wrists by lanyards so that they could not be snatched away; and an eight-foot wooden wall called a *barricado* was built across the rear part of the deck, with only one small door so that it could not be rushed. If the slaves rebelled, the crew would retreat behind this wall, fire at them through loopholes, and work the guns that were mounted on the upper deck and were loaded with small shot. Captain Snelgrave, who had earlier described his visit to the victorious king of Dahomey, considered himself something of an expert on the subject of uprisings:

"I have been several voyages when there has been no attempt made by our negroes to mutiny; which, I believe, was owing chiefly to their being kindly used, and to my officers' care in keeping good watch. But sometimes we meet with stout stubborn people amongst them who are never to be made easy; and these are generally some of the Cormantines, a nation of the Gold Coast. I went in the year 1721, in the *Henry* of London, a voyage to that part of the Coast and bought a good many of these people. We were obliged to secure them very well in irons and watch them narrowly; yet they nevertheless mutinied, though they had little prospect of succeeding. I lay at that time at a place called Mumfort, on the Gold Coast, having near five hundred Negroes on board, three hundred of which were men. Our ship's company consisted of fifty white people, all in health. And I had very good officers, so that I was very easy in all respects.

"This mutiny began at midnight, the moon then shining very bright, in this manner: two men that stood sentry at the fore hatchway, where the men slaves came up to go to the house of office [latrines], permitted four to go to that place; but neglected to lay the gratings again, as they should have done. Whereupon four more Negroes came on deck who had got their irons off, and the four in the house of office having done the same, all eight fell on the two sentries, who immediately called out for help. The Negroes endeavoured to get their cutlasses from them, but the lineyards (that is the lines by which the handles of the cutlasses were fastened to the men's wrists) were so twisted in the scuffle that they could not get them off before we came to their assistance. The Negroes perceiving several white men coming towards them, with arms in their hands, quitted the sentries and jumped over the ship's side into the sea.

"I being by this time come forward on the deck, my first care was to secure the gratings, to prevent any more Negroes from coming up; and then I ordered my people to get into the boat and save those that had jumped over-board, which they luckily did; for they found them all clinging to the cables the ship was moored by.

"After we had secured these people I called the linguists [interpreters] and ordered them to bid the men-Negroes between decks be quiet (for there was a great noise amongst them.) On their being silent I asked, 'What had induced them to mutiny?' They answered, 'I was a great rogue to buy them, in order to carry them away from their own country; and that they were resolved to regain their liberty if possible.' I replied, 'That they had forfeited their freedom before I bought them, either by crimes or being taken in war, according to the custom of their country; and they being now my property I was resolved to let them feel my resentment if they abused my kindness;' asking at the same time, 'Whether they had been ill used by the white men, or had wanted for anything the ship afforded?' To this they replied, 'They had nothing to complain of.' Then I observed to them, 'That if they should gain their point and escape to the shore it would be no advantage to them, because their countrymen would catch them and sell them to other ships.' This served my purpose, and they seemed to be convinced of their fault, begging 'I would forgive them, and promising for the future to be obedient, and never mutiny again, if I would not punish them this time.' This I readily granted, and so they went to sleep. When daylight came we called the men-Negroes up on deck and examining their irons, found them all secure. So this affair happily ended, which I was very glad of; for these people are the stoutest and most sensible Negroes on the Coast."

Soon afterward the *Henry* left Mumfort and arrived at Annamaboe, a fort on the Gold Coast, where they met up with another ship, the *Elizabeth*, whose captain and chief mate having died was now commanded by the second mate. Since both ships belonged to the same owner, Snelgrave outranked the other officer and used his authority to oblige him to transfer the slaves he had already acquired to the *Henry*. Snelgrave would then transfer the remainder of his trading goods to the *Elizabeth*, and, his cargo complete, be free to cross the Atlantic. Unsurprisingly, the crew of the *Elizabeth* objected strongly, but Snelgrave overruled them. "But that very night, which was near a month after the mutiny on board of us at Mumfort, the moon shining now very bright as it did then, we heard, about ten a-clock, two or three muskets fired on board the *Elizabeth*. Upon that I ordered all our boats to be manned, and having secured everything in our ship to prevent our slaves from mutinying, I went myself in our pinnace (the other boats following me) on board the *Elizabeth*. In our way we saw two Negroes swimming from her, but before we could reach them with our boats, some sharks rose from the bottom and tore them to pieces.

"We came presently along the side of the ship where we found two men-Negroes holding by a rope, with their heads just above water; they were afraid, it seems, to swim from the ship's side, having seen their companions devoured just before by the sharks. These two slaves we took into our boat, and then went into the ship, where we found the Negroes very quiet, and all under deck." These slaves had all been bought earlier, "did not understand a word of the Gold Coast language, and so had not been in the plot," which was the work of a few recently acquired Cormantines. Snelgrave also found the crew cowering behind the barricade on the quarter-deck, where "they all stood with arms in their hands," and, in the forepart of the ship, "the cooper lying on his back, quite dead, his skull having been cleft asunder with a hatchet that lay by him." One of the two Negroes found clinging to the ship's rope—both of them Cormantines—accused the other, who "readily confessed." Hearing this, "the white men wanted to have cut him to pieces; but I prevented it, and carried him to my own ship."

Next morning he invited the commanders of the eight other slave ships then lying at Annamaboe to join him on board the *Henry*, "and I having acquainted them with the whole matter, and they also having heard the Negro's confession, 'That he had killed the white man,' they unanimously advised me to put him to death, arguing, 'That blood required blood by all laws both divine and human; especially as there was in this case the clearest proof, namely, the murderer's confession. Moreover this would in all probability prevent future mischiefs, for by publicly executing this person at the ship's fore-yardarm, the Negroes on board their ships would see it, and as they were very much disposed to mutiny, it might prevent them from attempting it.' These reasons, with my being in the same circumstances, made me comply.

"Accordingly we acquainted the negro that he was to die in an hour's time for murdering the white man. He answered, 'He must confess it was a rash action in him to kill him; but he desired me to consider that if I put him to death, I should lose all the money I had paid for him.' To this I bid the interpreter reply, 'That though I knew it was customary in his country to commute for murder by a sum of money, yet it was not so with us; and he should find that I had no regard for my profit in this respect; for as soon as an hour-glass, just then turned, was run out, he should be put to death.' At which I observed he showed no concern.

"Hereupon the other commanders went on board their respective ships in order to have all their Negroes upon deck at the time of the execution, and to inform them of the occasion of it. The hourglass being run out, the murderer was carried on the ship's forecastle, where he had a rope fastened under his arms in order to be hoisted up to the fore-yardarm, to be shot to death. This some of his countrymen observing, they told him (as the linguist informed me afterwards), 'That they would not have him be frightened, for it was plain I did not design to put him to death, otherwise the rope would have been put about his neck, to hang him.' For it seems they had no thought of his being shot, judging he was only to be hoisted up to the yardarm, in order to scare him. But they immediately saw the contrary, for as soon as he was hoisted up, ten white men who were placed behind the *barricado* on the quarter-deck fired their muskets, and instantly killed him. This struck a sudden damp on our negromen, who thought that on account of my profit I would not have executed him.

"The body being cut down upon the deck, the head was cut off and thrown overboard. This last part was done to let our Negroes see that all who offended thus should be served in the same manner. For many of the blacks believe that if they are put to death and not dismembered they shall return again to their own country, after they are thrown overboard.

"When the execution was over I ordered the linguist to acquaint the men-Negroes, 'That now they might judge, no one that killed a white man should be spared.' And I thought proper now to acquaint them once for all, 'That if they attempted to mutiny again, I should be obliged to punish the ringleaders with death, in order to prevent further mischief.' Upon this they all promised to be obedient, and I assured them they should be kindly used if they kept their promise; which they faithfully did. For we sailed two days after from Annamaboe for Jamaica; and though they were on board near four months, from our going off the coast till they were sold at that island, they never gave us the least reasons to be jealous of them; which doubtless was owing to the execution of the white man's murderer."

Captain Snelgrave also told the story of Captain Messervy, of the *Ferres Galley*, of London, "who, by his overcare, and too great kindness to the Negroes on board his ship, was destroyed by them." Snelgrave had "met this gentleman at Annamaboe on the coast of Guinea in January, 1722. At his coming on board my ship he informed me of his good fortune, in that he had purchased near three hundred Negroes in a few days

The captain's nightmare—an uprising on board ship. These were expected, and most ships were provided with a stout wooden barrier, called a barricado (visible just to the right of the rigging on the rear mast), which kept the insurgents at bay while the crew fired on them.

at a place called Cetre-Crue on the windward part of the coast of Guinea."

Messervy's good fortune was due to his having arrived at Cetre-Crue just as a war between the people of the coast and the people inland came to an end with the triumph of the coasters, and he thus "had the opportunity of purchasing a great many of the captives at an easy rate." For their part, the conquerors were glad to sell as otherwise "they would have been obliged to have killed most of the men-captives for their own security." Since this was Messervy's first voyage to Guinea, Snelgrave "took the liberty to observe to him, 'That as he had on board so many Negroes of one town and language, it required the utmost care and management to keep them from mutinying.'" Messervy thanked him for this advice, and invited Snelgrave to visit his ship the next day.

"I went accordingly aboard his ship about three o'clock in the afternoon. About four o'clock the Negroes went to supper, and Captain Messervy desired me to excuse him for a quarter of an hour whilst he went forward to see the men-Negroes served with victuals. I observed from the quarter-deck that he himself put pepper and palm oil amongst the rice they were going to eat. When he came back to me I could not forbear observing to him, 'How imprudent it was in him to do so; for though it was proper for a commander sometimes to go forward and observe how things were managed, yet he ought to take a proper time, and have a good many of his white people in arms when he went; or else their having him so much in their power might encourage the slaves to mutiny. For he might depend upon it, they always aim at the chief person in the ship, whom they soon distinguish by the respect shown him by the rest of the people.

"He thanked me for this advice but did not seem to relish it, saying, 'He thought the old proverb good, that The master's eye makes the horse fat.' We then fell into other discourse, and among other things he told me, 'He designed to go away in a few days.' Accordingly he sailed three days after for Jamaica. Some months after I went for that place where, at my arrival, I found his ship, and had the following melancholy account of his death, which happened about ten days after he left the coast of Guinea, in this manner: Being on the forecastle of the ship, amongst the men-Negroes when they were eating their victuals, they laid hold on him and beat out his brains with the little tubs out of which they eat their boiled rice. This mutiny having been plotted amongst all the grown Negroes on board, they ran to the forepart of the ship in a body and endeavoured to force the *barricado* on the quarter-deck, not regarding the muskets or half-pikes that were presented to their breasts by the white men through the loopholes. So that at last the chief mate was obliged to order one of the quarter-deck guns laden with partridge shot [small bullets] to be fired amongst them; which occasioned a terrible destruction, for there were near eighty Negroes killed and drowned, many jumping overboard when the gun was fired.

"This indeed put an end to the mutiny, but most of the slaves that remained alive grew so sullen that several of them were starved to death, obstinately refusing to take any sustenance. And after the ship was arrived at Jamaica they attempted twice to mutiny before the sale of them began. This, with their former misbehaviour, coming to be publicly known, none of the planters cared to buy them, though offered at a low price. So that this proved a very unsuccessful voyage, for the ship was detained many months at Jamaica on that account, and at last was lost there in a hurricane."

By no means all insurrections ended in failure. *The Gentleman's Magazine* of February, 1753, had this story:

"By Captain Wright of the *Endeavour*, from the coast of Guinea, we had the following account of the loss of the *Marlborough*, Captain Codd, of Bristol, by an insurrection of the Negroes the beginning of October last. Capt. Codd, having indulged 28 Gold Coast Negroes with their liberty on deck to assist in navigating the ship, they behaved for some time in a very tractable, civil manner. But on the third day after he sailed from the bar of Bonny, while most of the crew were below cleaning the rooms, and none but the captain and two white men, armed with cutlasses, left above to take care of the ship, all of a sudden the Negroes on deck snatched the arms from them, wounded the captain, and forced him up the fore-shrouds, where they shot him dead. The rest of the Negroes securing the quarter deck and small arms, became soon masters of the ship, and spent the rest of the day in most cruelly butchering the crew (who were in number 35), except the boatswain and the cabin-boy, whom they saved to conduct the ship back again; which they did after 8 days, and came to an anchor within the bar of Bonny. About the same time, the *Hawk*, Captain Jones, of Bristol, arrived at that place, and hearing of the affair, bore down on her with an intent to re-take her; but the Negroes were so expert at the great guns and small-arms that they soon repelled him. After putting the Bight Negroes ashore that chose it, in number 270, the remainder, consisting of 150, weighed anchor, set their sails and stood out to sea with intent, as it is supposed, to go to their own country, tho' the undertaking was extremely hazardous, as they had no one to navigate the ship, the boatswain having jumped overboard the night before they sailed, and got to the *Hawk*."

No doubt the story of this escape lived on for many years in the memories of the people of Guinea—and was forgotten as soon as possible by the white traders. And there were plenty of other stories for them to forget, such as these that appeared in a Charleston newspaper in July, 1759: "The ship *Polly*, Capt. Hamilton, and the ship *Mercury*, Capt. Ingledieu, both of Bristol, were lately lost on the coast of Africa. Capt. Hamilton was destined for this port with a cargo of slaves. A sloop commanded by a brother of the above Capt. Ingledieu, slaving up the River Gambia, was attacked by a number of the natives about the 27th of February last, and made a good defense; but the captain, finding himself desperately wounded, rather than fall into the hands of such merciless wretches, when about 80 Negroes had boarded his vessel, discharged his pistol into his magazine and blew her up; himself and every soul on board perished." And in the same issue: "The snow [a two-masted ship] *Perfect*, Capt. William Potter, of Liverpool, bound for this port, is also cut off by the Negroes in the River Gambia and every man on board murdered, and the vessel lost."

The *Rhode Island News Letter* carried this story, written by George Scott, master of the sloop *Little George*, which left the coast of Guinea on June 1, 1730, "having on board ninety-six slaves, thirty-five of which were men. On the 6th of said month, at half an hour past four of the clock in the morning, being about 100 leagues from land, the men slaves got off their irons, and making their way thro' the bulkhead of the deck, killed the watch, consisting of John Harris, doctor, Jonathan Ebens, cooper, and Thomas Ham, sailor; who were, 'tis thought, all asleep. I being then in my cabin and hearing a noise upon deck (they throwing the watch overboard) took my pistol directly and fired up the scuttle which was abaft, which made all the slaves that were loose run forwards, except one or two men, who seemed to laugh at the cowardice of the rest, and defiance of us, being but four men and a boy."

The mutineers then closed the cover of the scuttle, or hatch, confining Scott and his companions below, where they had little food but plenty of weapons and gunpowder. After "consulting together" they "filled two round bottles with powder, putting fuses to them, in order to send them among the slaves, with a design at the same time to issue out upon them, and either suppress them or lose our lives." But before they could do that, one of the bottles accidentally exploded, igniting a keg of gunpowder and causing a second explosion which "rais'd up the deck, blew open the cabin doors and windows, discharged all our fire arms but one, destroyed our clothes and burnt the man that had the bottle in his hand in a most miserable manner, and myself with the rest very much hurt thereby."

Their next move was to send up the cabin-boy "in order (if possible) to bring them to terms, but they slighted our message." The mutineers then got hold of a swivel gun, but couldn't get it to fire down the scuttle because of the wet weather, while the crew kept them at bay by firing up at them with muskets. Next the mutineers "took pieces of boards and laid them over the scuttle," then "laid the tarpawlin with a great weight upon them to prevent our coming up." This stand-off went on for nine days while the ship drifted back toward the coast, "in which time the boy, being forced by hunger, run up among the slaves, who immediately put him in irons.

"Finding ourselves grow very weak thro' these hardships and for want of sustenance, we thought it proper before our strength was quite spent to take some desperate course." This was to "bore some holes thro' the vessel's bottom, which being approved of, was directly done, and let in about three feet of water. I then called the slaves and told them I would drown them all, which frightened them exceedingly. They then sent the boy to the cabin door to tell us that they had but just made the land, and that when they got a little nearer the shore they would take the boat and leave with the young slaves. I told them if they would do that I would not sink her. They stood in for the land about twelve a clock at night, struck upon the bar of the Sierra Leone River, and were in great danger of being lost. The vessel being strong beat over the bar, and they run ashore about three leagues up the river, on the north side, being then high water."

As the *Little George* came to rest, well-armed locals waded out from the shore and would "have fain tried to overcome us, but were per-suaded from it by the slaves on board, who told them we would shoot them if they appeared in our sight. They persuaded the grown slaves to go ashore, and drove the young ones overboard and then followed them, making the vessel shake at their departure. Our boy assuring us the slaves had all left the vessel, we immediately went up with our arms and saw the slaves just ashore. As we hoisted out our boat the natives mustered very thick on the shore and fired at us divers times. We made what haste we could to the other side of the river, where we rowed down about two leagues, and found a sloop riding in Frenchman's Bay belonging to *Monserrat*, James Collingwood commander, where we refreshed ourselves, being all of us in a weak and miserable condition, having had nothing to subsist upon during the nine days we were under this affliction but raw rice."

Then there is this story told by Captain Hugh Crow, an Englishman, which took place at Bonny, on the African coast:

"Among twelve or fourteen sail of vessels that lay in the river was the ship *Bolton* of Liverpool. She had on board about a hundred and twenty negroes, and these men not being properly guarded contrived to free themselves in the night from their irons and, rising upon the officers and crew, they took possession of the ship. Unfortunately, the trade powder, [i.e. gunpowder] in quantity about two hundred barrels, was stowed in the fore peak, and to this the insurgents, in their rage for mischief, soon found access. At daylight, by which time the circumstance became known, the several masters of the vessels in the river held a meeting to determine how the ship and cargo might be redeemed. The result was that I and some others were appointed to go on board the *Bolton*, and endeavour, if possible, to save the blacks from that destruction to which, in their ignorance, they were so fearfully exposed.

"They consisted chiefly of Quaws, a most desperate race of men. Before we got on board they had brought up many barrels of the gunpowder, which they had started and spread all loose between decks. It would have been madness for any of us to go below amongst them, for a single spark thrown by one of them amongst the powder would have involved us in instant destruction. We prevailed upon a few Eboes to leave the vessel, and these, with all the women, were taken aboard some of the other ships. The Quaws were deaf to all our entreaties and warnings—until evening, when a number of them also gave themselves up. The ringleaders, however, to the number of about a dozen, obstinately remained among the loose powder.

"In this situation they remained until the afternoon of the next day, when we observed the ship to be on fire, and as she was the headmost vessel in the river we manned all our boats in order, if possible, to tow her off, lest she might fall amongst us. We had been but a few minutes in the boats when, with all the unfortunate creatures on board of her, she blew up with a tremendous explosion. I was in our boat with eight or nine of my best men—and only about a hundred yards from her when the catastrophe occurred; and such was the violence of the shock that the poor fellows fell down in the bottom of the boat. The smoke, the pieces of the wreck, the clothes and other articles of trade that flew about in every direction presented a truly awful scene. Several of the latter fell into our boat, and many articles were afterwards found blown as far as Bonny.

"After this misfortune it became necessary to be more watchful of the blacks, and particularly of the Quaws"—who were probably the same people as the viper-eating Ghanaian Ququs, described earlier by Al-Gharnati as having "short necks, flattened noses, and red eyes. Their hair is like peppercorns and their smell is abominable, like that of burnt horn."

In spite of all these hazards and disasters, the trade flourished and soon had well-established procedures for every phase, including the sale of their cargoes. Alexander Falconbridge describes how this was carried out in the West Indies:

"Sometimes the mode of disposal is that of selling them by what is termed a scramble; and a day is soon fixed for that purpose. But previous thereto the sick, or refuse, slaves, of which there are frequently many, are usually conveyed on shore and sold at a tavern by *vendue*, or public auction. These, in general, are purchased by the Jews and surgeons, but chiefly the former, upon speculation, at so low a price as five or six dollars a head. I was informed by a mulatto woman that she purchased a sick slave at Grenada upon speculation for the small sum of one dollar, as the poor wretch was apparently dying of the flux. It seldom happens that any who are carried ashore in the emaciated state to which they are generally reduced by that disorder long survive the landing. I once saw sixteen conveyed on shore and sold in the foregoing manner, the whole of whom died before I left the island, which was within a short time after. Sometimes the captains march their slaves through the town at which they intend to dispose of them, and then place them in rows where they are examined and purchased."

As to selling by scramble, "Being some years ago at one of the islands in the West Indies, I was witness to a sale by scramble whereby about two hundred and fifty Negroes were sold. Upon this occasion all the Negroes scrambled for bear an equal price, which is agreed upon between the captains and the purchasers before the sale begins.

"On a day appointed, the Negroes were landed and placed together in a large yard belonging to the merchants to whom the ship was consigned. As soon as the hour agreed on arrived, the doors of the yard were suddenly thrown open and in rushed a considerable number of purchasers with all the ferocity of brutes. Some instantly seized such of the Negroes as they could conveniently lay hold of with their hands; others, being prepared with several handkerchiefs tied together, encircled with these as many as they were able; while others, by means of a rope, effected the same purpose. It is scarcely possible to describe the confusion of which this mode of selling is productive. It likewise causes much animosity among the purchasers who, not unfrequently upon these occasions, fall out and quarrel with each other. The poor astonished Negroes were so much terrified by these proceedings that several of them, through fear, climbed over the walls of the courtyard and ran wild about the town; but were soon hunted down and retaken.

"On board a ship lying at Port Maria, in Jamaica, I saw another scramble in which, as usual, the poor Negroes were greatly terrified. The women in particular clang to each other in agonies scarcely to be conceived, shrieking through excess of terror at the savage manner in which their brutal purchasers rushed upon and seized them. Though humanity, one should imagine, would dictate the captains to apprize the poor Negroes of the mode by which they were to be sold, and by that means to guard them in some degree against the surprise and terror which must attend it, I never knew that any notice of the scramble was given to them.

"Various are the deceptions made use of in the disposal of the sick slaves, and many of these such as must excite in every humane mind the liveliest sensations of horror. I have been well informed that a Liverpool captain boasted of his having cheated some Jews by the following stratagem: a lot of slaves afflicted with the flux being about to be landed for sale, he directed the surgeon to stop the anus of each of them with oakum. Thus prepared, they were landed and taken to the accustomed place of sale where, being unable to stand but for a very short time, they are usually permitted to sit. The Jews, when they examine them, oblige them to stand up in order to see if there be any discharge; and when they do not see this appearance they consider it as a symptom of recovery. In the present instance, such an appearance being prevented, the bargain was struck, and they were accordingly sold. But it was not long before a discovery ensued. The excruciating pain, which the prevention of a discharge of such an acrimonious nature occasioned, not being to be borne by the poor wretches, the temporary obstruction was removed and the deluded purchasers were speedily convinced of the imposition."

Because he was so young, Olaudah Equiano had been allowed to remain unfettered and on the deck for most of the crossing, and arrived in the West Indies in fairly good health.

"At last we came in sight of the island of Barbadoes, at which the whites on board gave a great shout, and made many signs of joy to us. We did not know what to think of this, but as the vessel drew nearer we plainly saw the harbour, and other ships of different kinds and sizes; and we soon anchored amongst them off Bridge Town. Many merchants and planters now came on board, though it was in the evening. They put us in several parcels and examined us attentively. They also made us jump, and pointed to the land, signifying we were to go there." Once again it was rumored that they were to be sold to cannibals, so "the white people got some old slaves from the land to pacify us. They told us we were not to be eaten, but to work, and were soon to go on land, where we should see many of our country people. This report eased us much."

Soon after they had landed a scramble was held, much as Falcon-bridge had described: "On a signal given, such as the beat of a drum, the buyers rush at once into the yard where the slaves are confined, and make choice of that parcel they like best. The noise and clamour with which this is attended, and the eagerness visible in the countenances of the buy-ers, serve not a little to increase the apprehensions of the terrified Africans . . . In this manner, without scruple, are relations and friends separated, most of them never to see each other again." Because he was small for his age, which was still only eleven, Equiano would have been of little use on a sugar plantation and so was one of the few slaves that remained unsold. But all his fellow countrymen were taken away, and "the women, too, who used to wash and take care of me, were all gone different ways, and I never saw one of them afterwards.

"I stayed in this island for a few days—I believe it could not be above a fortnight, when I and some few more slaves, who from very much fretting were not saleable among the rest, were shipped off in a sloop for North America. On the passage we were better treated than when coming from Africa, and we had plenty of rice and fat pork. We landed up a river a good way from the sea, about Virginia county, where we saw few of our native Africans, and not one soul who could talk to me. I was a few weeks weeding grass and gather-ing stones in a plantation; and at last all my companions were dis-tributed different ways, and only myself was left. I was now exceedingly miserable, and thought myself worse off than any of the rest of my companions; for they could talk to each other, but I had no person to speak to that I could understand.

"While I was in this plantation the gentleman to whom I sup-pose the estate belonged being unwell, I was one day sent for to his dwelling-house to fan him. When I came into the room where he was, I was very much affrighted at some things I saw, and the more so as I had seen a black woman slave as I came through the house, who was cooking the dinner, and the poor creature was cruelly loaded with various kinds of iron machines; she had one particularly on her head which locked her mouth so fast that she could scarcely speak, and could not eat or drink. I was much astonished and shocked at this contrivance, which I afterwards learned was called the iron muzzle.

"Soon after I had a fan put into my hand, to fan the gentleman while he slept; and so I did indeed, with great fear. While he was fast asleep I indulged a great deal in looking about the room, which to me appeared very fine and curious. The first object that engaged my attention was a watch, which hung on the chimney, and was going. I was quite surprised at the noise it made, and was afraid it would tell the gentleman anything I might do amiss; and when I immediately after observed a picture hanging in the room which appeared constantly to look at me, I was still more affrighted, having never seen such things as these before. At one time I thought it was something relative to magic, and not seeing it move I thought it might be some way the whites had to keep their great men when they died, and offer them libations, as we used to do to our friendly spirits. In this state of anxiety I remained till my master awoke, when I was dismissed out of the room, to my no small satisfaction and relief."

And then, all of a sudden, his luck turned. "I had been some time in this miserable, forlorn and much dejected state, without anyone to talk to, which made my life a burden, when the kind and unknown hand of the Creator, who in every deed leads the blind in a way they know not, now began to appear to my comfort; for one day the captain of a merchant ship called the *Industrious Bee* came on some business to my master's house. This gentleman, whose name was Michael Henry Pascal, was a lieutenant in the Royal Navy but now commanded this trading ship, which was somewhere in the confines of the county many miles off. While he was at my master's house it happened that he saw me, and liked me so well that he made a purchase of me." Lieut. Pascal paid between £30 and £40 for Equiano, intending him as a present for friends in England, and then sent him on ahead to the *Industrious Bee*. "When I arrived I was carried on board a fine large ship, loaded with tobacco &c. and just ready to sail for England. I now thought my condition much mended, having sails to lie on and plenty of good victuals to eat, and everybody on board used me very kindly, quite contrary to what I had seen of any white people before; I therefore began to think that they were not all of the same disposition. A few days after I was on board we sailed for England. I was still at a loss to conjecture my destiny. By this time however I could smatter a little imperfect English, and I wanted to know as well as I could where we were going. Some of the people of the ship used to tell me they were going to carry me back to my own country, and this made me very happy. I was quite rejoiced at the idea of going back; and thought if I should get home what wonders I should have to tell. But I was reserved for another fate, and was soon undeceived when we came within sight of the English coast."

By then he had undergone a standard procedure of the slave system: his name was changed at the whim of his owner. At his birth he had been given the name Olaudah; on the ship that brought him from Barbados he was called Michael and on the Virginia plantation Jacob; and now Lieut. Pascal decided that he should be re-named Gustavus Vassa. "And when I refused to answer to my new name, which at first I did, it gained me many a cuff; so at length I submitted." Like Caesar and Pompey, names of famous Romans commonly given to slaves, Gustavus Vassa was a mock-heroic put-down, that being the name of the warrior king who had founded the Swedish royal family.

A varied and often exciting life awaited him. He served in the Royal Navy as a member of a gun crew during a battle against the French, and on another ship that explored the Arctic. He became a trader in the West Indies, where he saved enough to buy his freedom, and was active in the campaign to end the slave trade, joining with the English abolitionist Granville Sharp in making notorious the case of the *Zong*, whose captain had ordered his crew to throw one hundred and twenty-two sickly slaves overboard. (As the captain explained, "if the slaves died a natural death, it would be the loss of the owners of the ship; but if they were thrown alive into the sea, it would be the loss of the underwriters.") He worked hard to help found Sierra Leone as a colony for poor blacks living in England, and after his conversion to Christianity hoped to return to Africa as a missionary; but the Bishop of London, who was in charge of overseas missions, had "some scruples" about giving his approval, and so he remained in England, where he ended his days happily married to an Englishwoman, the father of two daughters, and the author of an autobiography that sold well and bore the title *The Interesting Narrative of the Life of Olaudah Equiano, or Gustavus Vassa, the African, Writen by Himself.*

Equiano's story was of course exceptional. A far more typical account of arriving in America was this story that appeared in the *Charleston Courier* on April 21, 1807: "A jury of inquest was held on Sunday afternoon on the body of an African negro woman found floating near the market dock—it appeared to the jurors, from its having on the usual dress of a blue flannel frock, to have belonged to one of the slave ships in the harbour, and thrown into the river to save the expense of burial; a custom too prevalent in this port with the officers of slave ships, and in itself shocking to humanity. The jury brought in a verdict that she came to her death by the visitation of God."

The "Ethiopian Poetess" and probably the best-known African-American of the eighteenth century, Phillis Wheatley was about eight years old when she was put up for sale on a Boston dock. Ten years later, thanks to her obvious talent, and to the enlightened Wheatley family who owned her, she was immersed in the classics, and before long produced a volume titled Poems on Various Subjects, Religious and Moral. Since many Bostonians refused to believe that a black woman could have written such a book, she was examined by a committee that included the governor and John Hancock, who then signed a statement—included in the preface to her book—that she was indeed its author.

THE COLONIES

NEW ENGLAND

FOR VARIOUS REASONS—THE ABUNDANCE OF WORKING-CLASS IMMIGRANTS from England, a rural economy of small farms and an urban economy of small businesses—slavery never really caught on in New England, other than as a source of domestic servants. And because slavery did not exist in the Mother Country, the early settlers had to make up their own rules as they went along, often basing them on the teachings of the Bible.

Just how out of step New England was with the rest of the world in the matter of slavery was made clear in 1645, when a ship called the *Rainbow* arrived in Boston from the West Indies, having on board some Negroes—variously called "Negeres, negars, neager, or Mores"—who, the captain admitted, had been "fraudulently and injuriously taken and brought from Ginny." The General Court took cognizance of the matter, "conceiving themselves bound by the first opportunity to bear witness against the heinous and crying sin of man-stealing . . . justly abhorred of all good and just men," and ordered "that the Negro interpreter, with others unlawfully taken, be, by the first opportunity, (at the charge of the country for the present), sent to his native country of Ginny, and a letter with him of the indignation of the Court."

And not only did the people of Massachusetts condemn man-stealing as a sin, they failed to realize that in the New World slavery was to be reserved exclusively for people of color. Thus, from the court calendar: "December 1638. William Androws, having made assault upon his master, Henry Coggan, and not only so, but did conspire against the peace of this whole commonwealth, was censured to be severely whipped, and delivered up a slave to whom the Court shall appoint." And in 1639:

"John Kempe, for filthy, unclean attempts with 3 young girls, was censured to be whipped both here, at Roxbury, and at Salem, very severely, and was committed for a slave to Lieut. Davenport." In another deviation from what was to be standard practice, this slavery was temporary rather than for life.

However, when it came to Indians, Massachusetts was more up to date. The Body of Liberties, drawn up in 1641, stated that "There shall never be any bond slaverie, villinage or captivitie amongst us, unles it be lawful captives taken in just warres." Since in the eyes of the colonists all wars against the Indians were just wars, this cleared the way for the deportation of Pequots and other prisoners to the West Indies, where they were either sold or exchanged for Negro slaves. Later, this practice was extended to Indian criminals taken in peacetime. Thus "an Indian called Hoken, that hath been a notorious thief," and was also "insolent in his carriage [conduct]" and "lyeth shirking and lurking about, whereby many persons are greatly in fear and danger of him" was ordered "to be apprehended and sold or sent to the Barbadoes, for to satisfy his debts and to free the Colony from so ill a member."

As New England prospered, qualms about enslaving non-Indians abated. Her ships took part in the African slave trade, and in supplying the West Indian plantations with food and lumber; refining the sugar and molasses they brought back was also an important business. With prosperity there also came a growing demand for domestic help, far more important then than now, what with a list of chores that included having to cook everything from scratch, scrub and sand the floors, boil the laundry, split cords of firewood, lug heavy wooden buckets of water from the well, empty the toilets, shovel the snow, mend and darn clothes, and be at all times at the beck and call of the master or mistress. Small wonder that a good servant was hard to find, and harder to keep; but if the servant were a slave, then he or she *had* to stay. Many of those bought for domestic service were children—easier to train, cheaper to buy, and immediately employable. Prompted by fears of miscegenation, there was some opposition to these imports, and in 1705 Massachusetts passed an act "for the Better Preventing of a Spurious and Mixt Issue," which imposed a duty of £4 on imported slaves. Nevertheless, the imports went on, resulting in these stories:

Mr. Maverick's Negro Woman.

In 1639, the English traveler John Josselyn, who was staying with Mr. Maverick on Noddle's Island (now part of Boston), made this entry in his journal: "The second of October, about nine of the clock in the morning, Mr. Maverick's Negro woman came to my chamber window, and in her own country language and tune sang very loud and shrill. Going out to her, she used a great deal of respect toward me, and willingly would have expressed her grief in English; but I apprehended it by her countenance and deportment, whereupon I repaired to my host, to learn of him the cause, and resolved to entreat him on her behalf, for that I understood before that she had been a queen in her own country, and observed a very humble and dutiful garb [manner] used toward her by another Negro, who was her maid." It was then explained to Josselyn that "Mr. Maverick was desirous to have a breed of Negroes, and therefore, seeing she would not yield by persuasions to company with a Negro young man he had in his house, he [Mr. Maverick] commanded him [the young man] will'd she nill'd she [willy nilly] to go to bed to her; which was no sooner done but she kicked him out again. This she took in high disdain beyond her slavery, and this was the cause of her grief." (The story ends here. Josselyn's next adventure was to go for a walk in the woods where he found "a fruit as I thought like a pine apple," which, on his picking it up, turned out to be a hornets' nest.)

Onesimus.

Like other Puritans, the Rev. Cotton Mather, for many years Boston's leading clergyman, tried to base his life on the teachings of the Bible. One of his ways of doing so was to utter what he called "ejaculatory prayers." Thus "upon the sight of a tall man," his prayer was "Lord, give that man high attainments in Christianity." If he saw a Negro it would be, "Lord, wash that poor soul white in the blood of thy Son."

In December, 1706, Mather wrote in his diary, "This day a surprising thing befell me. Some gentlemen of our Church, understanding that I wanted a good servant at the expense of between forty and fifty pounds, purchased for me a very likely slave; a young man who is a Negro of a promising aspect and temper, and this day they presented him unto me. It seems to be a mighty smile of Heaven upon my family; and it arrives at an observable time unto me. I put upon him the name of Onesimus; and I resolved with the help of the Lord, that I would use the best endeavours to make him a servant of Christ."

Onesimus no doubt already had a name of his own, but whatever it might have been the Rev. Mather would have felt that his choice was an improvement, for the original Onesimus was the subject of one of St. Paul's Epistles in the New Testament. He had run away from his master, Philemon, and joined Paul, then at Ephesus. Paul converted him and then sent him back with a letter asking Philemon to pardon him for running away and receive him back kindly—"not as a servant, but above a servant, as a beloved brother." Over the years this story was to be endlessly quoted by pro-slavery clergymen who claimed that since the Apostle sent Onesimus back to his owner, and did not ask Philemon to free him, therefore he, St. Paul—and by extension all the other founding Christians— did not disapprove of slavery.

For the next ten years Mather mentions his Onesimus only occasionally. In a letter to the Royal Society in London about preventing smallpox, he mentions that "my Negro-man Onesimus, who is a pretty intelligent fellow," had been inoculated in his native Africa, a common practice there but not in Europe. But in the meantime there had been problems, Mather noting in his diary that he had had to keep "a strict eye" on his servant, "especially with regard unto his company." There had also been "some actions of a thievish aspect." Nevertheless, Mather persevered in his attempts to make Onesimus "a Servant of Christ," teaching him the catechism, and how to read and write. But all to no avail, and after ten years together Mather wrote in his diary, "my servant Onesimus proves wicked and grows useless, froward [disobedient] and immorigerous [rude and rebellious]." A separation was negotiated, with Onesimus obtaining his freedom but having to contribute toward the purchase of Obadiah, another slave; also, he still had to perform certain chores such as shoveling snow, fetching water and cutting firewood. And he had to pay back the £5 he had stolen.

Tituba.

Long before his unfortunate experience with Onesimus, the Rev. Cotton Mather had played a major part in promoting the Salem Witch Trials of 1692. The trouble in Salem had begun when, in the words of the skeptical Robert Calef, author of *More Wonders of the Invisible World*, "divers young persons," including nine year old Betty, daughter of the minister, the Rev. Samuel Parris, and her cousin, Abigail Williams, "began to act after a strange and unusual manner, viz. as by getting into holes, and creeping under chairs and stools, and to use sundry odd postures and antick gestures, uttering foolish, ridiculous speeches, which neither they themselves nor any others could make sense of. The physicians that were called could assign no reason for this; but it seems one of them, having recourse to the old shift, told them he was afraid they were bewitched." In response, "Mr. Parris invited several neighbouring ministers to join with him in keeping a solemn day of prayer at his own house."

"A few days before this solemn day of prayer, Mr. Parris's Indian man and woman made a cake of rye meal, with the children's water, and baked it in the ashes and, as is said, gave it to the dog; this was done as a means to discover witchcraft; soon after which those ill-affected or afflicted persons named several that they said they saw, when in their fits, afflicting them. The first complained of was the said Indian woman, Tituba," a slave and maid-of-all-work that the Parris family had brought with them on their return from a sojourn in Barbados.

It then emerged that some time earlier, hoping to foretell the future, Tituba and the two girls had dropped the white of an egg into a glass of water, to see what shape it took. Alarmingly, the shape was that of a coffin, seeming to foretell a death. It was also established that when the cake made of rye meal mixed with the girls' urine, and known as a "witchcake," was fed to the Parris dog, in the hope that the dog would reveal who was tormenting the children, the dog refused to eat it. When he heard about the witchcake, the Rev. Mr. Parris punished Tituba with a beating, apparently not for the first time. Soon after, several other girls were afflicted—"bitten and pinched by invisible agents; their arms, necks, and backs turned this way and that way, and returned back gain."

The question facing the authorities was not whether witchcraft really existed—almost everybody knew that it did—but why it had broken out at this particular time and place. This was where the Rev. Cotton Mather came in. "The New-Englanders," he wrote in *The Wonders of the Invisible World*, "are a people of God, settled in those which were once the Devil's territories; and it may easily be supposed that the Devil was exceedingly disturbed when he perceived such a people here." To assist him in re-establishing his dominion over the American colonies, the Devil "has decoy'd a fearful knot of proud, froward, ignorant, envious and malicious creatures to list themselves in his horrid service, by entering their names in a book." After meeting in "hellish randezvouses," these witches "associated themselves to do no less a thing than to destroy the Kingdom of our Lord Jesus Christ in these parts of the world; and in order thereunto, first they each of them have their spectres, or devils," who "seize poor people about the country with various and bloudy torments." The object of such persecution was to get the victims "to sign the Devil's laws in a Spectral Book laid before them." Once they had signed "they have immediately been released from all their miseries."

When the court convened on March 1, 1692, Tituba was the first to be examined. Almost the first question put to her—"Why do you hurt these poor Children?"—set the tone for the rest of the proceedings: it was not an inquiry into whether she had done anything wrong, but why. To deny the accusation, which she at first did—"I no hurt them at all"— only made matters worse, for the judges construed denial as defiance. So Tituba, who had spent most of her life as a slave, first in Barbados and then in Salem, and along the way had surely learned how to placate her masters by telling them what they wanted to hear, when asked "Why have you done it?" replied "I can't tell when the Devil works." That was better, and soon she was explaining that "the Devil came to me and bid me serve him," and naming others who also served him. Told to describe the devil, she replied that "sometimes it is like a hog, and sometimes it is like a great black dog." "What did it say to you?" "The black dog said, Serve me. But I said, I am afraid. He said if I did not he would do worse to me." Later the dog turned into a man who "had a yellow bird that kept with him." She had also seen "two rats, a red rat and a black rat," and they too had told her to serve them.

Tituba also described how she and other witches had traveled to their meetings—"we ride upon sticks and are there presently." She told of seeing "a thing with a head like a woman, with two legs and wings," and another "thing all over hairy, all the face hairy, and a long nose," that "goeth upright and is about two or three foot high." Also "a tall man with white hair" and wearing black clothes "tell me he god, and I must believe him and serve him six years and he would give me many fine things." This man had a book and ordered her to "write and set my name to it." "Did you write?" "Yes, once I made my mark in the book, and made it with red blood."

Following her testimony the jurors resolved "That Tittapa an Indian woman servant to Mr. Samuel Parris of Salem Village . . . Wickedly & felloniously A Covenant with the Devill did make & Signed the Devills Booke with a marke like A: C by which Wicked Covenanting with the Devill she the said Tittapa is become A detestable Witch."

More than a hundred others were charged with witchcraft. Nineteen were hanged; one man, who had defied the court by refusing to confess, was pressed to death by being pinioned to the ground and then having heavy stones laid on his chest; several others died in prison. Tituba herself spent over a year there, and according to Calef "lay there till sold for her fees [the cost of being kept in prison, payable even if all charges were dropped]. The account she since gives of it is that her master did beat her, to make her confess and accuse (such as he called) her sister-witches; and that whatsoever she said by way of confessing, or accusing others, was the effect of such usage."

In the aftermath of the Salem trials there was an attempt to put the blame on Tituba and depict her as some kind of African voodoo witch; but though she may have been partly Negro, she was mostly Arawak, probably born in Guyana before moving to Barbados. As to voodoo, baking a witchcake of rye and urine, and trying to foretell the future by dropping the white of an egg into a glass of water, were traditional English folkloric practices that the colonists had brought over with them.

Samuel Sewall.

Tituba was not the only one to recant. Samuel Sewall, who had been one of the judges passing sentences of death, later came to realize that he had made a terrible mistake and—virtually unique in the history of the judiciary—acknowledged it publicly, once a year standing up in church while the minister read out his confession, taking upon himself "the shame and the blame."

A few years later, in 1700, Sewall was once again troubled in his conscience, this time by the "numerousness of slaves at this day in the province, and the uneasiness of them under their slavery." The result was a short pamphlet, *The Selling of Joseph* (the son of Jacob, who had been sold into Egyptian slavery by his brothers). Sewall based his main argument on the Scriptures: "Originally and naturally, there is no such thing as slavery. Joseph was rightfully no more a slave to his brethren than they were to him; and they had no more authority to sell him than to slay him. . . . God hath said, He that stealeth a man and selleth him, or if he be found in his hand, he shall surely be put to death. (Exodus. 21. 16)."

There were also practical considerations: "All things considered, it would conduce more to the welfare of the province to have white servants for a term of years than to have slaves for life. Few can endure to hear of a Negro's being made free, and indeed they can seldom use their freedom well; yet their continual aspiring after their forbidden liberty renders them unwilling servants. And there is such a disparity in their conditions, colour and hair, that they can never embody with us, and grow up into orderly families, to the peopling of the land; but still remain in our body politic as a kind of extravasat [alien] blood."

Finally: "Our blessed Saviour has altered the measures of the ancient love-song, and set it to a most excellent new tune, which all ought to be ambitious of learning. (Matt. 5.43. John 13.34.) ['A new commandment I give unto you, That ye love one another.'] These Ethiopians, as black as they are, seeing they are the sons and daughters of the first Adam, the brethren and sisters of the last Adam [Christ], and the offspring of God, they ought to be treated with a respect agreeable."

As he ruefully noted in his diary, Sewall's tract was greeted with "frowns and hard words." Soon a counter-blast appeared, *The Negro*

Chief Justice of the Massachusetts Supreme Court, Samuel Sewall was one of the judges at the Salem Witch Trials of 1692, a role he came to regret. Eight years later he produced a pamphlet, The Selling of Joseph, *which criticized slavery on biblical grounds; it was soon rebutted by the Rev. Cotton Mather, Boston's leading clergyman and an unrepentant supporter of the Salem Trials.*

Christianized, by the Rev. Cotton Mather, who in no way regretted his part in the Salem witch trials. Like Sewall, Mather also quoted the commandment to love thy neighbor, agreed that "thy Negro is thy neighbour," but rather than concluding that he should be treated with respect, saw it as an obligation to convert him—"Canst thou love thy Negro and be willing to see him lie under the rage of sin, and the wrath of God? Canst thou love him and yet refuse to do anything that his miserable soul may be rescued from eternal miseries?"

As usual with the Puritans, good deeds would have their rewards here on earth, as well as in heaven. "The pious masters that have instituted their servants in Christian piety will even in this life have sensible recompense . . . Your servants will be the better servants for being made Christian." They would become "exceeding faithful in their business, and afraid of speaking or doing anything that may justly displease you."

But from the owners' point of view there was this risk: "If the Negroes are Christianized they will be baptized; and their baptism will presently entitle them to their freedom; so our money is thrown away." Not so, said Mather. "What law is it that sets the baptized slave at liberty? Not the law of Christianity; that allows slavery . . . Will the canon law do it? No . . . Will the civil law do it? No. Tell, if you can, any part of Christendom wherein slaves are not frequently to be met withal." In sum: "The baptized then are not thereby entitled unto their liberty." (This view was later endorsed by the Bishop of London, who in 1727 addressed a public letter to *The Masters and Mistresses of Families in the English Plantations Abroad*: "Christianity, and the embracing of the Gospel, does not make the least Alteration in Civil Property, or in any of the Duties which belong to Civil Relations; but in all these Respects it continues Persons just in the same State as it found them. The Freedom which Christianity gives is a Freedom from the Bondage of Sin and Satan, and from the Dominion of Men's Lusts and Passions and inordinate Desires; but as to their outward Condition, whatever that was before, whether bond or free, their being baptiz'd and becoming Christians makes no Manner of Change in it.")

Phillis Wheatley.

Known in her time as the "Ethiopian poetess," Phillis had been enslaved in Africa when aged about seven, and shipped directly to Boston where, dressed only "in a quantity of dirty carpet," she was fortunate enough to be bought on arrival by a kindly and prosperous family called Wheatley. "I was a poor little outcast and a stranger when she [Mrs. Wheatley] took me in," wrote Phillis in 1774, when she was not yet twenty, "not only into her house, but I presently became a sharer in her most tender affections. I was treated by her more like her child than her servant; no opportunity was left unimproved in giving me the best advice; but in terms how tender! how engaging! This I hope ever to keep in remembrance." Phillis was very pious, and at the age of sixteen was admitted a member of the Old South Church, although, like all other slaves, she had to sit up in the gallery. She was also very bright, studied the Bible, Latin and Greek, and then began writing poetry. Though praised by many, her works were skillful rather than inspired. Her most famous was titled *On Being Brought from Africa* to *America*, and echoed the argument, often used by slave-traders, that to bring Africans to this country was to do them a great favor, since only here could they be exposed to the Word of God and given the chance to become Christians. (The poem begins: "'Twas Mercy brought me from my Pagan land/ Taught my benighted Soul to understand/ That there's a God, that there's a Saviour too . . ." and concludes : "Remember, Christians, Negroes black as Cain/ May be refined and join the angelic Strain.")

Another poem, an ode on the death of the renowned evangelist George Whitfield, whom she had once heard preach to a vast crowd on Boston Common, was forwarded to the Countess of Huntingdon, the "patriarchess of the Methodists." As a consequence, when the Wheatleys, thinking that a sea voyage would be good for her fragile health, sent Phillis to England, she was invited to meet that august personage, who also helped to get her poems published. As a phenomenon—a black bluestocking— she was taken up by London society, was presented with a copy of *Paradise Lost* by the Lord Mayor, and was escorted by the abolitionist Granville Sharp to see the lions in the menagerie at the Tower of London. There were even plans for her to be presented to the king and queen, but then came news came that Mrs. Wheatley was sick, so Phillis hurried back to Boston. Meanwhile, although her volume of poems got only condescending reviews in England ("of no astonishing powers of genius," said one), Boston booksellers loyally ordered three hundred copies, a huge number for that time. But then came the Tea Party, followed by the Coercive Acts which closed the port, and all imports, including *Poems on Various Subjects, Religious and Moral* had to be sent back.

But that did not deter her from writing. Soon after taking command of the American army outside Boston in the fall of 1775, George Washington received an ode whose opening lines ran: "Celestial choir! Enthron'd in realms of light,/ Columbia's scenes of glorious toils I write./ While freedom's cause her anxious breast alarms,/ She flashes dreadful in refulgent arms . . ." The general, or more probably one of his staff officers, sent a courteous note thanking the author for "the elegant lines," complimenting her on "her great poetical talents," extending the invitation that "if you should ever come to Cambridge, or near Head Quarters, I shall be happy to see a person so favoured by the Muses," and signing himself "with great respect, Your obedient humble servant." Such a meeting seems never to have taken place, though if it had, what on earth would the literal-minded, fox-hunting, slave-owning Father of his Country have found to say to the Ethiopian poetess?

After that it was all downhill. The Wheatleys died and she became free, but the loss was greater than the gain. She married a grocer called John Peters, a handsome ne'er-do-well who later went bankrupt. Unlike Phillis, who "knew her place," and when dining with white people insisted on eating at a side table, Peters had ideas "above his station" (he "wore a wig, carried a cane, and quite acted out the gentleman"). No one wanted to publish her more recent poems. Two of her three children died early and she ended her days as a housemaid scrubbing the floors in a cheap boarding house. When she died, at the age of thirty-one, her third child was so sickly that it survived her by only a few hours. "It is painful to dwell upon the closing scene," wrote the editor of a later edition of her works. "In a filthy apartment, in an obscure part of the metropolis, lay the dying mother and the wasting child. The woman who had stood honored and respected in the presence of the wise and the good, who had graced the ancient halls of Old England, and rolled about in the splendid equipages of the proud nobles of Britain, was now numbering the last hours of life in a state of most abject misery, surrounded by the emblems of squalid poverty."

NEW YORK

Fifty years after the Salem Witch Trials, New York put on its own show trial, bigger and more elaborate, though still on a very small stage, the city then containing only some twelve thousand inhabitants, of whom nearly a quarter were slaves. The official report of the trial bore the title *A Journal of the Proceedings in the Detection of the Conspiracy Formed by some White People, in Conjunction with Negro and other Slaves, for Burning the City of New York in America, and Murdering the Inhabitants.* This was later, and significantly, modified to *The Great Negro Plot.* The author was Daniel Horsmanden, who played a major role in stage-managing the events that followed the supposed conspiracy, he being a judge on the province's supreme court while also holding the post of city recorder. His motives in going to so much "drudgery" in writing up his lengthy account were, first, to refute those "wanton, wrong-headed persons amongst us, who took the liberty to arraign the justice of the proceedings," some even going so far as to declare "that there was no plot at all!" And second, to warn "every one that has Negroes to keep a very watchful eye over them, and not to indulge them with too great liberties," but rather to "keep themselves upon a strict guard against these enemies of their own household."

The opening scene took place on the night of Saturday, February 28, 1741, when "a robbery was committed at the house of Mr. Robert Hogg, in the city of New-York, merchant, from whence were taken divers pieces of linen and other goods, and several silver coins, chiefly Spanish, and medals, and wrought silver, etc. to the value in the whole of sixty pounds and upwards." Among those planning the robbery was "one Wilson, a lad of about seventeen or eighteen, belonging to the *Flamborough*, man of war, on this station," who often came to Mr. Hogg's house to visit friends who lodged there. "Wilson, it seems, had a more familiar acquaintance with some Negroes of very suspicious character, particularly Caesar, belonging to John Vaarck, baker; Prince, to Mr. John Auboyneau, merchant; and Cuffee, to Adolph Philipse, Esq." These three "catched at the proposal" to rob the store "and the scheme was communicated by them to John Hughson, who kept a public house by the North [Hudson] River, in this city, a place where numbers of Negroes used to resort, and be entertained privately (in defiance of the laws) at all hours . . . Thither they used to bring such goods as they stole from their masters or others, and Hughson, his wife and family"—who were white—"received them." Later on, a grand jury was to bring in a complaint about "the mean alehouses and tippling houses within this city, who make it a practice (and a most wicked and pernicious one it is,) of entertaining Negroes and the scum and dregs of white people in conjunction; who to support such expense are tempted and abetted to pilfer and steal, that they may debauch each other upon the plunder and spoils of their masters and neighbours."

"At Hughson's lodged one Margaret Sorubiero, alias Salingburgh, alias Kerry, commonly called Peggy, or the Newfoundland Irish Beauty, a young woman about one or two and twenty; she pretended to be married, but no husband appeared; she was a person of infamous character, a notorious prostitute, and also of the worst sort, a prostitute to Negroes. She was here lodged and supported by Caesar, before mentioned, and took share (in common with Hughson's family) of the spoils and plunder, the effects of Caesar's thefts, which he brought to Hughson's;

and she may be supposed to have been in most of their wicked secrets
. . . With this Peggy, as she will be hereafter commonly called, Caesar
used frequently to sleep at Hughson's with the knowledge and permission of the family; and Caesar bargained with and paid Hughson for
her board. She came there to lodge a second time in the fall, not long
before Christmas, 1740, big with child by Caesar, as was supposed,
and was brought to bed there not many days before the robbery at
Hogg's, of a baby largely partaking of the black complexion."

Soon after the robbery there was an outbreak of suspicious fires,
starting on Wednesday, March 18, at the governor's house, which formed
part of Fort George; the house and fort, like most of the city's buildings
were of wood. "Upon the chapel bell's ringing, great numbers of people,
gentlemen and others, came to the assistance of the lieutenant-governor
and his family. Most of the household goods, etc. were removed out and
saved, and the fire engines were in a little time brought thither; but the
wind blowing a violent gale at S.E., soon as the fire appeared in different
places of the roof, it was judged impossible to save the house and
chapel." Moreover, "an alarm being given that there was gunpowder in
the fort" many left the scene. It was suspected that this alarm "was given
by some of the conspirators themselves, with artful design to intimidate
the people and frighten them from giving further assistance."

"Wednesday, April 1. A fire broke out at the storehouse of Mr. Van
Zant, towards the east end of the town. It was an old wooden building, stored with deal boards, and hay at one end of it; the fire was
said to be occasioned by a man's smoking a pipe there, which set fire
to the hay; but it is said the fire was first discovered in the N.E. side
of the roof, before it had taken the hay." Neighbors rallied around
and "threw buckets of water with such extraordinary activity it
stopped the progress of the fire."

Three days later fire was discovered in the kitchen of a house nearby.
It was soon put out, but "upon examination it was found that the fire had
been put between a straw and another bed laid together, whereon a Negro
slept." Next day "a discovery was made in the morning early that some
coals had been put under a haystack standing near the coach-house and

stables of Joseph Murray, Esq. in the Broadway and near some dwelling-houses, which had it taken fire would have been in great danger; but the coals went out of themselves." However, "there were coals and ashes traced along from the fence to a neighbouring house next adjoining the stables, which caused a suspicion of the Negro that lived there."

Next Sunday, "as three Negroes were walking up the Broadway towards the English church, about service time, Mrs. Earle, looking out of her window, overheard one of them saying to his companions, with a vapouring [bragging] sort of an air, 'Fire, Fire, Scorch, Scorch, A LITTLE, damn it, BY-AND-BY,' and threw up his hands and laughed; the woman conceived great jealousy at these words, and thought it very odd behaviour." Mrs. Earle shared her suspicions with her neighbor, Mrs. George, who told her local alderman, "who informed the rest of the justices thereof at their meeting the next day."

The fires continued. "Monday, April 6. About ten o'clock in the morning there was an alarm of a fire at the house of Serjeant Burns, opposite Fort Garden. This, it was said, was only a chimney; which, upon inquiry, the man declared had been swept the Friday before; but from the great smother in the house, there were grounds to suspect a villainous design in it." Then another fire broke out in another house, but "being timely discovered," was soon put out. However, "upon view, it was plain that the fire must have been purposely laid." But "who did it was a question remained to be determined. But there was a cry among the people, *The Spanish Negroes! The Spanish Negroes! Take up the Spanish Negroes!*" These were sailors who had been taken captive in the war then going on against Spain (The War of Jenkins' Ear), brought to New York, and despite their claims that they had been free men in their own country were condemned by the Admiralty court to be sold as slaves. Some of them then "began to grumble at their hard usage of being sold as slaves." That afternoon fire broke out at Col. Philipse's storehouse, "a small streak of fire running up the shingles, like wildfire, from near the bottom to the top of the roof, on the side directly against the wind as it then blew." It was soon brought under control, but then there was yet another cry of fire, and "a man who had been on the top of the house assisting in extinguishing the fire saw a Negro leap out at the end window of one of them, from thence making over several garden fences in great haste, which occasioned him to cry out *A Negro! A Negro!* The Negro made very good speed home to his master's. He was generally known," and the cry changed yet again, this time to "*Cuff Philipse! Cuff Philipse!* The people ran to Mr. Philipse's house in quest of him; he was got in at the back door and being found was dragged out of the house and carried to jail, borne upon the people's shoulders. He was a fellow of general ill character." Several other Negroes "who were met in the streets after the alarm of their rising, were hurried away to jail."

In the meantime, John Hughson and his wife, Sarah, and Peggy, the "Newfoundland Irish Beauty," were committed to jail, "being charged as accessories to divers felonies and misdemeanours," including receiving stolen goods; and on May 8, Mr. Vaarck's Caesar [Peggy's lover] and Mr. Auboyneau's Prince were tried for the robbery at Mr. Hogg's. They pleaded not guilty, but were easily convicted, the judge telling them that being "wicked fellows, hardened sinners, and ripe as well as ready for the most enormous and daring enterprizes," they were also undoubtedly involved in the plot "to burn this city and to destroy its inhabitants." He urged them to confess all they knew about the plot; if they did not, then "be assured God Almighty will punish you for it." When passing sentence, the judge told them that they were "to be taken hence to the place from whence you came, and from thence to the place of execution, and there you, and each of you, are to be hanged by the neck until you be dead. And I pray the Lord to have mercy on your souls." The judge also ordered that after the execution "the body of Caesar be hung in chains." The sentence was carried out two days later. "They died very stubbornly, without confessing anything about the conspiracy."

Next up for trial were Philipse's Cuffee and Roosevelt's Quack, both charged with arson, Cuffee, for setting fire to his owner's storehouse, and Quack for setting fire to Fort George. Cuffee claimed an alibi: "he had been sawing wood that afternoon with a white boy," which the white boy confirmed. Some neighbors also declared that they had seen him well away from the scene of the fire when the bell rang, "but an old man who had known Cuffee for several years deposed that he had seen him at the storehouse, and that he stood next him. There seemed to be some objection against the man's evidence; it was thought he might be mistaken, being very near sighted." However, the old man was able to distinguish colors, so his evidence was accepted, and Cuffee was held for trial.

Further damaging evidence came from Mary Burton, an illiterate sixteen-year-old orphan recently arrived from England and now working for the Hughsons as an indentured servant—a form of temporary slavery to pay the costs of her passage to America. At first she refused to testify, but "after the lieutenant governor's proclamation was read to her, promising indemnity and the reward of one hundred pounds to any person, confederate or not, who should make discovery" of the conspiracy, "she considered the better of it." Through all the trials that followed her testimony was crucial.

Among the statements made by Mary Burton were: "'That Caesar, Prince, and Mr. Philipse's Negro man (Cuffee) used to meet frequently at her master's [Hughson's] house, and that she had heard them talk frequently of burning the fort; and that they would go down to the Fly [the east end of the city] and burn the whole town; and that her master and mistress said they would aid and assist them as much as they could . . . That when all this was done, Caesar should be governor, and Hughson, her master, should be king . . . That Cuffee used to say that a great many people had too much, and others too little . . . That when they set fire to the town, they would do it in the night, and as the white people came to extinguish it, they would kill and destroy them . . . That Hughson and her mistress used to threaten that if she, the deponent, ever made mention of the goods stolen from Mr. Hogg they would poison her; and the Negroes swore if ever she published or discovered the design of burning the town, they would burn her.'"

"The evidence of a conspiracy, not only to burn the city but also destroy and murder the people, was most astonishing to the grand jury," wrote Horsmanden. "And that any white people should become so abandoned as to confederate with slaves in such an execrable and detestable purpose, could not but be very amazing to every one that heard it. This was a scheme of such villainy" there had to be "a conspiracy of deeper design and more dangerous contrivance than the slaves themselves were capable of." (Throughout his record of the trials, Horsmanden kept harping on this idea that the slaves were mentally incapable of planning a major conspiracy. This was not to excuse them, but it did help to explain things.)

On May 29, Quack and Cuffee were brought to trial, Quack for "wickedly, voluntarily, feloniously and maliciously conspiring, combining and confederating with Cuffee and with divers other Negroes to kill and murder the inhabitants of this city; and also for setting on fire, burning and consuming the house of our sovereign lord the king"; and Cuffee "for wickedly, etc. conspiring, etc. with Quack and divers other Negroes to kill and murder the inhabitants of this city; and also for setting on fire and burning an out-house belonging to Frederick Philipse, Esq." Both men pleaded not guilty. Neither of them, nor indeed any of the other accused, had a lawyer.

After outlining his case, the Attorney General summoned Mary Burton, who repeated the hearsay evidence she had given earlier.

Other witnesses against Cuffee included Sarah Higgins, who said "that on Sunday, the day before Col. Philipse's store house was set on fire, she saw four Negroes lurking about the garden behind that storehouse" and that one of them was Cuffee. Isaac Gardner said that at the fire at the fort he "observed Cuffee when the flames of the house blazed very high, he huzza'd, danced, whistled and sung, and that the witness said to him, 'You black dog, is this a time for you to dance and make game upon such a sad accident?' And he only laughed . . ."

As to Quack, his master, Mr. Roosevelt, the butcher, declared "that Quack was employed most part that morning the fort was fired, from the time they got up, in cutting away the ice out of the yard; that he was hardly ever out of their sight all that morning." But, as usual, evidence given by an owner on behalf of his slave was discounted, since it was supposed that his motive was to protect his property rather than tell the truth.

Addressing the jury of twelve white men, a prosecutor named Smith then summed up for the prosecution: "No scheme more monstrous could have been invented" than "this most horrid conspiracy" whereby "the white men should be all killed, and the women become the prey to the rapacious lust of these villains!"

One aspect of the prisoners' conduct was especially heinous: "Gentlemen, the monstrous ingratitude of this black tribe is what exceedingly aggravates their guilt. Their slavery among us is generally softened with great indulgence; they live without care, and are commonly better fed and clothed, and put to less labour, than the poor of most Christian countries. They are indeed slaves, but under the protection of the law; none can hurt them with impunity. They are really more happy in this place than in the midst of the continual plunder, cruelty and rapine of their native countries; but notwithstanding all the kindness and tenderness with which they have been treated amongst us, yet this is the second attempt of the same kind that this brutish and bloody species of mankind have made within one age." (A reference to the plot of 1712, described later.)

"Then the jury were charged, and a constable was sworn to attend them as usual; and they withdrew; and being soon returned found the prisoners guilty." After which one of the judges passed sentence, but not until he too had expressed amazement at the ingratitude and folly that prompted them to take part in "so vile, so wicked, so monstrous, so execrable and hellish a scheme, as to murder and destroy your own masters and benefactors." He also urged them to reveal everything they knew about the conspiracy, as only by doing so could they obtain "mercy at the hands of God, before whose judgment seat ye are so soon to appear." He then passed sentence: "That you and each of you be carried from hence to the place from whence you came, and from thence to the place of execution, where you and each of you shall be chained to a stake, and burnt to death; and the Lord have mercy upon your poor, wretched souls." This sentence was carried out the next day in front of a large and hostile crowd, "their resentment being raised to the utmost pitch against them, and no wonder."

After that, the focus was on Hughson, "the contriver and chief schemist of the conspiracy." He, his wife, his daughter Sarah, and Margaret Kerry, alias Peggy, alias the Newfoundland Irish Beauty were "indicted for conspiring, confederating and combining with divers Negroes and others to burn the city of New York, and also to kill and destroy the inhabitants thereof." Though never apparently much more than a petty crook who dealt in stolen goods and ran a low-life tavern where he drank too much and talked too wildly, at his trial John Hughson was presented as the master-mind behind "all this mystery of iniquity."

Particular importance was given to the evidence of Mary Burton, the Hughsons' servant, despite the fact that she evidently bore a grudge and stood to benefit from the lieutenant governor's reward of £100 and freedom from her indentured servitude. Clearly aware of what was expected of her, Mary often mentioned the interracial fraternizing—"there were many Negroes frequently at Hughson's at nights, ever since she came to the house, eating and drinking; that she has seen twenty or thirty at a time there, but most of a Sunday . . . that Hughson, his wife and daughter, and Peggy, used at such meetings to be amongst the Negroes; and that they talked of burning the town and killing the people."

Another witness, who lived next door, also complained of the way Hughson had kept "a very disorderly house, and sold liquor to, and entertained Negroes there; he had often seen many of them there at a time, at nights as well as in the day time. Once in particular he remembers, in the evening, he saw a great many of them in the room dancing to a fiddle, and Hughson's wife and daughter along with them."

Mr. Comfort's slave, Jack, also testified that one Sunday afternoon he had met a friend, Ben, also a slave, who said " 'Brother, go to Hughson's. All our company is come down.' He went with Ben thither, and went round the house and went in at the back door; when he came there they all sat round the table, and had a goose, a quarter of mutton, a fowl, and two loaves of bread. Hughson took a flask of rum out of a case and set it on the table, and two bowls of punch were made. Two or three tables were put together to make it long. Hughson's daughter brought in the victuals, and just as he came in Sarah brought the cloth and laid it. Peggy came downstairs and sat down by Hughson's wife at the table, and ate with them; when they were eating they began all to talk about setting the houses on fire . . ."

Fueled no doubt by the bowls of punch, a lot of wild talk followed—"when the whole city was on fire they were all to meet together and destroy the people as fast as they came out; they were to have penknives to cut their throats." Hughson said that "he would go before and be their king," and then "they all swore; some said d—n, some said by G-d, and other oaths; a Spanish Negro swore by thunder; Hughson swore by G-d, if they would be true to him he would take this country."

Whether all this heated talk, acquisition of penknives to cut throats and downing of bowls of punch really amounted to a conspiracy was doubted by many at the time, and many more since, but not by Horsmanden, the other judges or the jury. Hughson, his wife, his daughter Sarah, and Peggy were all sentenced to be hanged, Hughson's body then to hang in chains, as a warning to others and as a mark of contempt. Sarah later confessed, and for thus implicitly confirming the rightness of the verdict, was pardoned. The other three "protested their innocence to the last." A total of eighteen Negroes were hanged, thirteen were burned at the stake, and seventy were transported out of the colony to "the dominion of some foreign prince or state," rather than to any of the English colonies in the West Indies—a nicety which just went to show "how tender we have been of their peace and security, by using all the precaution in our power that none of our rogues should be imposed on them."

In fairness to Horsmanden and his judicial colleagues it should be mentioned that some thirty years earlier there had been another Negro conspiracy, one whose reality no one could doubt. According to the governor's official report, it began at midnight on April 6, 1712, when about two dozen Negro slaves, "some provided with fire-arms, some with swords and others with knives and hatchets" met in an orchard in the middle of the town. "One Coffee, a Negro slave to one Vantilburgh, set fire to an outhouse of his master's, and then repairing to the place where the rest were, they all sallied out together with their arms and marched to the fire. By this time the noise of the fire spreading through the town, the people began to flock to it. Upon the approach of several, the slaves fired and killed them. The noise of the guns gave the alarm, and some escaping their shot soon published the cause of the fire, which was the reason that not above nine Christians were killed, and about five or six wounded." On hearing the news, the governor "ordered a detachment from the fort under a proper officer to march against them, but the slaves made their retreat into the woods, by favour of the night. Having ordered sentries the next day in the most proper places on the island to prevent their escape, I caused the day following the militia of this town and of the county of west Chester to drive the island, and by this means and strict searches of the town, we found all that had put the design into execution. Six of these having first laid violent hands upon themselves, the rest were forthwith brought to trial before the justices of this place, who are authorized by Act of Assembly to hold a court in such cases. In that court were twenty-seven condemned, whereof twenty-one were executed, one being a woman with child her execution by that means suspended. Some were burnt, others were hanged, one broke on the wheel, and one hung alive in chains in the town, so that there has been the most exemplary punishment inflicted that could be possibly thought of."

PENNSYLVANIA

FOR SALE: "A likely negro Wench about fifteen Years old, has had the Smallpox, been in the Country above a Year and talks English. Enquire of the Printer hereof." Also "A likely negro Girl, about 14 Years of Age, bred in the Country but fit for either Town or Country Business. Enquire of the Printer hereof."

"Hereof" was the *Pennsylvania Gazette*, and the Printer thereof was Benjamin Franklin, who had taken over the paper in 1732, at the age of twenty-six. Along with advertisements for likely Negro wenches, he also ran notices for runaways, white as well as black, the former being indentured servants unwilling to serve out their time—rather like Franklin himself, who had been bound as an apprentice when he skipped out of Boston nine years earlier.

Another advertisement was for "a very likely Negro Woman" who "can wash and iron very well, cook victuals, sew, spin on the linen wheel, milk cows, and do all sorts of House-work well. She has a Boy of about Two Years old, which is to go with her." Also for sale was "another very likely Boy, aged about Six Years, who is the Son of the above-said Woman. He will be sold with his Mother, or by himself, as the Buyer pleases." Since he was free to decline printing the advertisement, Franklin presumably saw nothing wrong with selling away from his mother a boy of six. Not long after, writing in favor of a plan to raise a militia, he urged that it would be a defense not only against the French and Indians, but also against "the wanton and unbridled rage, rapine and lust of Negroes."

But, just as he was to evolve from a fervent supporter of the British Empire to a no less fervent supporter of American Independence, so Franklin was to discard his early prejudices and end his days as President of Pennsylvania's *Society for Promoting the Abolition of Slavery*. Here are some of the steps on his road from acceptance to rejection:

Ever the pragmatist, he began by questioning the economic justification. "'Tis an ill-grounded opinion that by the labour of slaves America may possibly vie in cheapness of manufactures with Britain," he wrote in 1755 in *Observations Concerning the Increase of Mankind*. "The labour of slaves can never be so cheap here as the labour of working men is in Britain. Anyone may compute it. Interest of money is in the colonies from six to ten per cent. Slaves, one with another, cost £30 per head. Reckon then the interest of the first purchase of a slave, the insurance or risque on his life, his cloathing and diet, expenses in his sickness and loss of time, loss by his neglect of business (neglect is natural to the man who is not to be benefited by his own care or diligence), expense of a driver to keep him at work, and his pilfering from time to time, almost every slave being by nature a thief, and compare the whole amount with the wages of a manufacturer of iron or wool in England, you will see that labour is much cheaper there than it can ever be by Negroes here." (Twenty years later, in *The Wealth of Nations*, Adam Smith would make the same point: "The experience of all ages and nations, I believe, demonstrates that the work done by slaves, though it appears to cost only their maintenance, is in the end the dearest of any. A person who can acquire no property can have no other interest but to eat as much and to labour as little as possible.") Another Observation held that slaves "pejorate [degrade] the families that use them; the white children become proud, disgusted with labour, and being educated in idleness, are rendered unfit to get a living."

In 1757 Franklin went to London as agent for the Pennsylvania assembly in its dispute with the rich and selfish Penn family, who refused to pay any taxes on their vast landholdings. He left behind his homely wife, Deborah, to manage his affairs, but took with him his son, William, and two slaves as domestic servants, King and Peter. Before leaving, Franklin drew up manumission papers for both in case he died while abroad, but it was not long before King, who had "often been in mischief," manumitted himself by running away. Franklin did not try to reclaim him, but later reported to Deborah that King had fallen on his feet. He was now living in the country, "where he had been taken in the service of a lady that was very fond of the merit of making him a Christian, and contributing to his education and improvement." The lady "sent him to school, has him taught to read and write, to play the violin and the French horn, with some other accomplishments more useful in a servant." That is the last we hear of King. As to Peter, he "behaves as well as I can expect. We rub on pretty comfortably."

While in London Franklin was asked by the Rev. John Waring, secretary of the philanthropy known as *The Associates of Dr. Bray*, to help establish a school in Philadelphia to educate and Christianize black children. Franklin exerted himself, and the school opened a year later with thirty pupils. On his return to Philadelphia, he paid it a visit and wrote to the Rev. Waring that, "I was on the whole much pleased; and from what I then saw, have conceived a higher opinion of the natural capacities of the black race than I had ever before entertained. Their apprehension seems as quick, their memory as strong, and their docility in every respect equal to that of white children." Soon after, in a revised edition of *Observations*, the statement about "almost every slave being by nature a thief," became "almost every slave being from the nature of slavery a thief."

Then came some backsliding. In 1770, back in London, Franklin wrote *A Conversation Between an Englishman, a Scotchman and an American on the Subject of Slavery*, in response to the English abolitionist, Granville Sharp, who had recently criticized Americans for owning slaves. In the *Conversation*, Franklin has the American agree with some of Sharp's strictures, but others were "too severe." Many regions had few or no slaves and "in truth, there is not, take North-America through, one family in a hundred that has a slave in it. Many thousands there abhor the slave trade as much as Mr. Sharp." It was unfair to blame the whole country. For example, "if one man in a hundred in England were dishonest, would it be right from thence to characterize the nation, and say the English are rogues and thieves? But farther, of those who do keep slaves, all are not tyrants and oppressors. Many treat their slaves with great humanity, and provide full as well for them in sickness as in health." Also, "Remember, sir, that she [England] began the slave trade," and ever since had been forcing slaves on unwilling colonials. "Several laws heretofore made in our colonies to discourage the importation of slaves by laying a heavy duty, payable by the importer, have been disapproved and repealed by your government here, as being prejudicial, forsooth, to the interests of the Africa Company."

In fact, the Portuguese, not the English, began the Atlantic slave trade; few traders can force customers to buy goods they do not want; in Philadelphia about one household in twelve, not one in a hundred, had a domestic slave; the proposed duty was not so much to discourage the importation of slaves as to keep up the price of those raised at home. But worse was to come, for when the Englishman complains of "the severe laws you have made," the American replies that the severity of laws must be in proportion to the "wickedness of the people to be governed. Perhaps you may imagine the Negroes to be a mild-tempered, tractable kind of people. Some of them indeed are so. But the majority are of a plotting disposition, dark and sullen, malicious, revengeful and cruel in the highest degree."

But the aberration was temporary, and two years later Franklin was writing to the *London Chronicle* decrying "the constant butchery of the human species by this pestilent, detestable traffic in the bodies and souls of men." Then, while in Paris to enlist French support for the American cause, he circulated *A Thought Concerning the Sugar Islands* in which he wrote that "when he considered the wars made in Africa for prisoners to raise sugar in America, the numbers slain in those wars, the numbers that, being crowded in ships, perish in the transportation, and the numbers that die under the severities of slavery, he could scarce look on a morsel of sugar without conceiving it spotted with human blood."

In November, 1789, soon after his final return to Philadelphia, he published an *Address to the Public*, in which he argued that "slavery is such an atrocious debasement of human nature," that mere abolition would not be enough; positive, remedial action would also be needed. "To instruct, to advise, to qualify those who have been restored to freedom, for the exercise and enjoyment of civil liberty; to promote in them habits of industry; to furnish them with employments suited to their age, sex, talents, and other circumstances; and to procure their children an education calculated for their future situation in life: these are the great outline of the annexed plan . . ." As might be expected of him, the plan was quite specific, with an emphasis on education and job training. Still energetic at the age of eighty-four, Franklin would surely have pushed the scheme ahead, but he had only a few months to live.

Another Pennsylvanian abolitionist was also called Benjamin, but in every other way different from the worldly and successful Franklin. This was Benjamin Lay, a hunchback not much more than four feet tall, with a pigeon-chest and long beard that as he aged became snow-white. Born in England in 1682, he had spent some time in Barbados, which was

Barely four feet tall, hunchbacked, and with arms longer than his spindly legs, Benjamin Lay (1682-1759) was a forceful polemicist in his campaign against fellow Quakers who owned slaves, a campaign he eventually won. Benjamin Franklin was a great admirer, and kept a portrait of Lay in his living room.

clearly the wrong place for him, and eventually settled in the country near Philadelphia. There he and his wife, who was about the same height, lived a life of extreme simplicity: their dwelling was sometimes described as a cottage and sometimes as a cave; their diet was entirely vegetarian; Lay wove his own cloth and made his own clothes, but because indigo was the product of slave labor, he refused to dye them, leaving them a distinctive pale yellow; he once nearly killed himself by trying to follow the example of Jesus and fasting for forty days and forty nights.

Lay was a Quaker, but at the time of his arrival this sect, while well-established, had not yet officially declared against slavery. This led to a number of run-ins, as when he flouted the Society's rule that nothing was to be published without being approved by the Overseers of the Press. Although he described himself as a man of "very mean capacity and little learning," Lay nevertheless wrote a book, *All Slave-Keepers that Keep the Innocent in Bondage, Apostates*. It was printed by Benjamin Franklin, who though a friend and admirer—he kept a portrait of Lay in his living room—was careful not to put his name on the book as the printer thereof. Franklin also did some editing to tidy up Lay's ranting, but clearly not enough. "For custom in sin hides, covers, as it were takes away the guilt of sin," ran a typical passage. "Long custom, the conveniency of slaves working for us, waiting and tending continually on us, besides the washing, cleaning, scouring, cooking very nicely, fine and curious, sewing, knitting, darning, almost ever at hand and command; and in other places milking, churning, cheese-making, and all the drudgery in dairy and kitchen, within doors and without. And the proud, dainty, lazy daughters sit with their hands before 'em, like some of the worst sort of gentlewomen, and if they want a trifle, rather than rise from their seats, call the poor slave from her drudgery to come and wait upon them. These things have been the utter ruin of more than a few, and yet encouraged by their own parents, for whom my spirit is grieved, and some of which were and are preachers in great repute, as well as others."

As for slaves, "were they at liberty, as we are; had the same education, learning, conversation, books, sweet communion in our religious assemblies, they would exceed many of their tyrant masters in piety, virtue and godliness." But instead of being allowed to live virtuous lives, they had to "plow, sow, thresh, winnow, split rails, cut wood, clear land, make ditches and fences, fodder cattle, run and fetch up the horses, or fine curious pacing mares, for young Madam and Sir to ride about on, impudently and proudly gossiping from house to house, stuffing their lazy ungodly bellies . . ."

Lay also favored direct action. Several times he was forcibly ejected from Quaker meetings for disruptive conduct; when that happened, rather than depart, he would lie on the ground just outside the doorway until the meeting was over, so that those leaving had to step over his body. After his wife died, he demonstrated his disapproval of drinking tea, in itself a luxury and usually taken with slave-made sugar, by standing in the market-place of the local town with a chest containing his late wife's china which he then smashed to pieces with a hammer.

Lay's most famous direct action took place at a meeting of the Society of Friends, held at Burlington in New Jersey. "Having previously prepared a sufficient quantity of the juice of pokeberry [a bright-red, strong-smelling, poisonous berry that leaves a permanent stain] to fill a bladder, he contrived to conceal it within the cover of a large folio volume, the leaves of which were removed. He then put on a military coat, and belted a small sword by his side; over the whole of this dress he threw his great-coat, which was made in the most ample manner, and secured it upon himself with a single button. Thus equipped, he entered the Meeting House"—where swords and military coats were taboo, but large volumes, presumably Bibles, were welcome—"and placed himself in a conspicuous position, from which he addressed the audience in substance as follows:

> "'Oh all you Negro masters who are contentedly holding your fellow creatures in a state of slavery during life, well knowing the cruel sufferings these innocent captives undergo in their state of bondage . . . and especially you who profess to do unto all men as you would they should do unto you, and yet, in direct opposition to any principle of reason, humanity and religion, you are forcibly retaining your fellow men, from one generation to another, in a state of unconditional servitude; you might as well throw off the plain coat, as I do'—here he loosed the button, and the great-coat falling behind him, his warlike appearance was exhibited to his astonished audience, and proceeded—'It would be as justifiable in the sight of the Almighty, who beholds and respects all nations and colours of men with an equal regard, if you should thrust a sword through their hearts, as I do through this book.' He then drew his sword and pierced the bladder, sprinkling its contents over those who sat near him."

As a result of—or perhaps in spite of—these tactics, in 1759 the Quakers came "to the determination to disown such of their members as could not be persuaded to desist from the practice of holding slaves, or were concerned in the importation of slaves." Lay, aged 82, was on his death-bed when the news was brought to him. "The venerable and constant friend and advocate of that oppressed race of men attentively listened to this heart-cheering intelligence, and after a few moments' reflection on what he had heard, he rose from his chair, and in an attitude of devotional reverence, poured forth this pious ejaculation: 'Thanksgiving and praise be rendered unto the Lord God!' After a short pause, he added, 'I can now die in peace.'"

Another Pennsylvania reformer was Anthony Benezet. Like Benjamin Lay, he dressed poorly, but "though mean in his personal appearance, such was the courtesy of his manners, and so evident the purity of his intentions, that he had ready access to people of all descriptions, and obtained the respect of the few whom he failed to influence." After dabbling in business, Benezet became a schoolteacher at the Friends' English School in Philadelphia. Soon he added night classes for slaves, declaring, "The notion, entertained by some, that the blacks are inferior in their capacities, is a vulgar prejudice, founded on the pride or ignorance of their lordly masters." Later he set up the first public school for girls, and then, in 1770, the Negro School at Philadelphia. When he found that he couldn't manage both schools, he left the first, and higher salaried, position. "Better is honest poverty than all the riches bought by the tears, and sweat, and blood of our fellow-creatures," he wrote.

Benezet wrote several anti-slavery works: *A Short Account of the Slave Trade*, then *A Caution and Warning to Great Britain and her Colonies*, followed soon after by an expanded version of *A Short Account*, which was widely distributed in England, where, in the opinion of the abolitionist Thomas Clarkson, it "became instrumental beyond any other work ever before published in disseminating a proper knowledge and detestation of this trade." Slavery, said Benezet, was "an evil of so deep a dye, and attended with such dreadful consequences that no well-disposed person (anxious for the welfare of himself, his country or posterity,) who knows the tyranny, oppression and cruelty with which this iniquitous trade is carried on, can be a silent and innocent spectator."

After citing a number of horror stories, he set out to refute "the common arguments alleged in defense of the trade." First, "That the slaves sold to the Europeans are captives taken in war, who would be destroyed by their conquerors if not thus purchased." This "is without foundation. For altho' there were doubtless wars amongst the Negroes before the Europeans began to trade with them, yet certain it is that since that time those calamities have prodigiously increased, which is principally owing to the solicitations of the white people, who have instigated the poor Africans by every method, even the most iniquitous and cruel, to procure slaves to load their Vessels." Moreover "Government was instituted for the good of mankind; kings, princes, governors, are not proprietors of those who are subject to their authority; they have not a right to make them miserable. On the contrary, their authority is vested in them that they may, by the just exercise of it, promote the happiness of their people. Of course they have not a right to dispose of their liberty and to sell them for slaves."

Another "common argument" was "that the Negroes are generally a stupid, savage people, whose situation in their own country is necessitous and unhappy, which has induced many to believe that the bringing them from their native land is rather a kindness than an injury." But in fact, "The African blacks are as properly and truly men as the European whites; they are both of the same species, and are originally descended from the same parents; they have the same rational powers as we have; they are free moral agents, as we are, and many of them have as good natural genius, as good and brave a spirit as any of those to whom they are made slaves. To trade in blacks, then, is to trade in men. He that made us, made them, and all of the same clay. We are all the workmanship of His hands . . . For one man therefore to assault another, and by mere force to make a captive of him, not for any crime that he has been guilty of, but to make a penny of him, considering him as part of his possessions or goods with which he can do what he pleases, is robbing of God, which is sacrilege."

This brought him to one of his main objectives: to warn his fellow-citizens of what would happen on Judgment Day. "Think of a future reckoning. Consider how you shall come off in the great and awful Day of Account. You now heap up riches, and live in pleasure. But oh! What will you do in the end thereof? And that is not far off. What if death should seize upon you, and hurry you out of this world under all that load of blood-guiltiness that now lies upon your souls? The Gospel expressly declares that thieves and murderers shall not inherit the Kingdom of God. Consider that at the same time, and by the same means you now treasure up worldly riches, you are treasuring up to yourselves wrath against the Day of Wrath, and vengeance that shall come upon the workers of iniquity, unless prevented by a timely repentance. And what greater

iniquity, what crime that is more heinous, that carries in it more complicated guilt, can you name than that in the habitual deliberate practice of
which you now live? Good God! How can you pray for mercy to Him
that made you, or hope for any favour from Him that formed you, while
you go on thus grossly and openly to dishonour him in debasing and destroying the noblest workmanship of his hands, in this lower world? He
is the Father of Men; and do you think he will not resent such treatment
of his offspring whom he hath so loved as to give his only begotten Son,
that whosoever believeth in him might not perish, but have everlasting
life? This love of God to man, revealed in the Gospel, is a great aggravation of your guilt; for if God so loved us, we ought also to love one another." And so: "God grant that you may be made sensible of your guilt,
and repent in time."

VIRGINIA

Thanks to Captain John Smith, savior of the Jamestown colony, and
other chroniclers, we know quite a lot about the early English settlers in
Virginia; but we know very little about the first Africans. "About the last
of August came in a Dutch man-of-war that sold us twenty Negars,"
wrote John Rolfe (Pocahontas' husband) to Sir Edwyn Sandys in London
in 1619. That's all, nothing about where they came from, or whether
they were bought as slaves or as indentured servants. This was an important distinction, for although both classes were treated much the
same—that is, quite badly—slaves served for life, but indentured servants
only for a fixed period, usually between four to seven years. In return for
their service they received free passage across the Atlantic, board and
lodging, and when their time was up some new clothes, and perhaps also
some land. After that they were free. During the colonial period, about
half of all white newcomers came as indentured servants or as redemp-
tioners—immigrants who paid for their passage by agreeing to be sold
into temporary servitude on arrival.

Servants also differed from slaves in that they entered these indenture contracts more or less voluntarily, and if cheated or maltreated could
appeal to a court for redress. This is what happened to an English serving
girl called Charity Dallen, whose case was heard in Lower Norfolk
County in July, 1649: "The deposition of Joseph Mulders, aged 23 or

thereabouts, sworn and examined sayeth: That Deborah Fernehaugh, the Mistress of this deponent, did beat her maid servant in the quartering house before the dresser more liken a dog than a Christian, and that at a certain time I felt her head, which was beaten as soft as a sponge in one place, and that as there she was a-weeding she complained and said her back bone as she thought was broken with beating, and that I did see the maid's arm naked which was full of black and blue bruises and pinches, and her neck likewise; and very often afterwards the said maid would have shown me how she had been beaten, but I refused to have seen it, saying it concerns me not, I will do my work and if my Mistress abuse you, you may complain." This she did, and Mulders' evidence being confirmed by other witnesses, the court ordered that the said "Charity Dallen shall no longer remain in the house or service of her said mistress." With very few exceptions, no such rescue was ever afforded a slave.

For a while Virginians tried importing "Indians of the Carib Islands," probably Arawaks, the same nation that had produced Tituba, the star witness for the Salem Witch Trials. The experiment was not a success, a court declaring that "the said Indians have run away and hid themselves in the woods, attempting to go to the Indians of this country, as some of them have revealed and confessed. And for that they have stolen away divers goods, and attempted to kill some of our people, and for that especially they may hereafter be a means to overthrow the whole colony, have adjudged them to be presently taken and hanged till they be dead."

During the seventeenth century the number of Negro slaves in Virginia was small—some three to five hundred in 1650, and about 6000 in 1700. Probably most came from the West Indies, rather than direct from Africa. There were also a number of free blacks, some of them landowners. One of them appears in this deposition made by Edwin Connaway, clerk of the Northampton court, in 1645: "That being at the house of Capt. Taylor, about the tenth day of July" he "did see Capt. Taylor and Anthony the Negro going into the corn field; and when they returned from the said corn field, the said Negro told this deponent, saying, 'Now Mr. Taylor and I have divided our corn, and I am very glad of it now I know mine own. He finds fault with me that I do not work, but now I know mine own ground I will work when I please and play when I please.' And the said Capt. Taylor asked the said Negro, saying, 'Are you content with what you have?' And the Negro answered, saying,

'I am very well content with what I have,' or words to that effect."

Ten years later Anthony the Negro was the subject of another deposition, this one concerning the indenture of John Casor, also a Negro,
"who demanded his freedom of his master Anthony Johnson; and further
said that Johnson had kept him his servant seven years longer than he
ought." Johnson denied that Casor was indentured, and claimed him as
a slave; but when several other witnesses said they had seen the indenture
"Johnson was in fear," and "his wife and his two sons persuaded the said
Anthony Johnson to set the said John Casor free."

As the number of slaves increased, the Virginia General Assembly kept
pace with laws that reduced the rights of free blacks and turned slaves
into chattels, with no rights at all:

> 1662. "Whereas some doubts have arisen whether children got by any
> Englishman upon a Negro woman should be slave or Free, Be it therefore
> enacted and declared by this present Grand Assembly, that all children
> born in this country shall be held bond or free only according to the con-
> dition of the mother." (This was a major departure from English law, where
> a person's status was derived from the father.)

> 1667. "Whereas some doubts have arisen whether children that are slaves
> by birth, and by the charity and piety of their owners are made partakers
> of the blessed sacrament of baptism, should by virtue of their baptism be
> made free, It is enacted and declared . . . that the conferring of baptism
> doth not alter the condition of the person as to his bondage or freedom."

> 1669. "Be it enacted . . . if any slave resist his master, and by the extremity
> of the correction should chance to die, that his death shall not be accounted
> Felony."

> 1680. "Whereas the frequent meeting of considerable numbers of Negro
> slaves under pretense of feasts and burials is judged of dangerous conse-
> quence; for prevention whereof for the future, Be it enacted . . . that from
> and after the publication of this law, it shall not be lawful for any Negro

or other slave to carry or arm himself with any club, staff, gun, sword or any other weapon of defense or offense, nor to go or depart from his master's ground without a certificate from his master, mistress or overseer." Also "if any Negro or other slave shall presume to lift up his hand in opposition against any Christian, shall for every such offense, upon due proof thereof by the oath of the party before a magistrate, have and receive thirty lashes on his bare back, well laid on." Also "if any Negro or other slave shall absent himself from his master's service and lie hid and lurking in obscure places, committing injuries to the inhabitants, and shall resist any person or persons that shall by any lawful authority be employed to apprehend and take the said Negro, that then in case of such resistance it shall be lawful for such person or persons to kill the said Negro or slave so lying out and resisting."

1691. "For prevention of that abominable mixture and spurious issue which hereafter may increase in this dominion, as well by Negroes, Mulattoes and Indians intermarrying with English or other white women, as by their unlawful accompanying with one another, Be it enacted . . . that for the time to come whatsoever English or other white man or woman being free shall intermarry with a Negro, Mulatto or Indian man or woman, bond or free, shall within three months after such marriage be banished and removed from this dominion for ever." Also "if any English woman being free shall have a bastard child by any Negro or Mulatto, she pay the sum of fifteen pounds sterling"—a huge sum in those days—"within one month after such bastard child shall be born to the church wardens of the parish where she shall be delivered of such child, and in default of such payment she shall be taken into the possession of the said church wardens and disposed of [i.e. sold] for five years." After this "the bastard child" would be "bound out as a servant by the said Church until he or she shall attain the age of thirty years." Also "forasmuch as great inconveniences may happen to this country by the setting of Negroes and Mulattoes free, by their either entertaining Negro slaves from their master's service, or receiving stolen goods, or being grown old bringing a charge upon the country; for prevention thereof Be it enacted . . . that no Negro or Mulatto be after the end of this present session of assembly set free by any person or persons whatsoever, unless such person or persons, their heirs, executors or administrators pay for the transportation of such Negro or Negroes out of the country within six months."

1723. "When any Negro or mulatto shall be found upon due proof . . . to have given false testimony, every such offender shall, without further trial, have his ears successively nailed to the pillory for the space of an hour, and then cut off, and moreover receive thirty-nine lashes on his bare back."

Some of the laws may have been prompted by recent incidents. For example, the one against the "abominable mixture" between the races followed a trial in the Lower Norfolk County court where it was established that "Mary Williamson hath committed the filthy sin of fornication with William, a Negro belonging to William Basnett, squire." For this offense Mary was fined five hundred pounds of tobacco "for the use of Linhaven Parish." As for William, who as well as committing the above outrage, "hath very arrogantly behaved himself in Linhaven Church in the face of the congregation," the sheriff was to take him "into his custody and give him thirty lashes on his bare back."

In 1730, the governor estimated Virginia's population to be 114,000, of whom 30,000 were blacks—a dangerous ratio in the opinion of many. Writing to a friend in England, the aristocratic William Byrd worried about the "many bad consequences of multiplying these Ethiopians amongst us. They blow up the pride, and ruin the industry of our white people, who seeing a rank of poor creatures below them, detest work for fear it should make them look like slaves . . . Another unhappy effect of many Negroes is the necessity of being severe. Numbers make them insolent, and then foul means must do what fair will not. We have, however, nothing like the inhumanity that is practiced in the islands [West Indies] and God forbid we ever should. But these base tempers require to be ridden with a taut rein, or they will be apt to throw their rider . . . And in case there should arise a man of desperate courage" to act as a leader, there might well be an insurrection that would "tinge our rivers, as wide as they are, with blood."

As it happened, there were no uprisings in colonial Virginia, but this did not mean that the slaves were reconciled to their lot. Rather than take up arms, they resorted to passive resistance. This took many forms: doing as little work as possible, as slowly as possible, and then doing it badly; breaking tools; driving cattle into bogs and swamps where they drowned and wagons into ruts that would break their wheels; getting drunk; pilfering; malingering and running away; feigning stupidity, and pretending not to understand orders, no matter how clearly given. "Nothing can be conceived more inert than a slave," wrote William Strickland, an English visitor. "His unwilling labor is discovered in every step he takes; he moves not if he can avoid it; if the eyes of the overseer be off him, he sleeps; the ox and the horse, driven by the slave, appear to sleep also; all is listless inactivity; all motion is evidently compulsory."

Passive resistance also offered the reward of infuriating masters, as in the case of Colonel Landon Carter of Sabine Hall, owner of more than 500 slaves and 50,000 acres in various plantations. With no sense of irony, Landon Carter was a leader in the opposition to what he called the "tyrannic despotism" of George III. Like that misguided monarch, he was convinced that he was a benevolent and wise patriarch—"always generous and kind to those under me"—whose good deeds were all too often repaid with ingratitude. Here is his diary for just one month:

March 9, 1770. "The cattle that have died this year are 8 in Lawson's penn, 5 in Dolmon's, and 2 steers killed in the same place by Mr. Manuel and the Boy Kit. They were ordered to drive them to the Fork to be raised where they had plenty of food, and they drove them through the same marsh in the corn field where each mired and died. When people can do this notwithstanding they have a plain level road, to be sure correction can never be called severity. ("The Fork" was another of Carter's plantations. "Correction" was a common term for punishment, usually a whipping. His calling Manuel and other slaves "Mr" is an example of his heavy sarcasm.)

March 14. "One of my draught oxen, well fed this whole winter with corn, pea vines, rye straw and wheat straw, the night before last broke his neck, entirely by Manuel's carelessness. He fed the creature and then turned him out of the cow yard, and I suppose going naturally in search of grass it stepped into the ditch or gully and so broke his neck. This is the third draught steer put to a violent death by that cursed villain.

March 15. "Mr. Tony shall as certainly receive ample correction for his behaviour to me as that he and I live. The day before yesterday he began to pale [fence] in the garden and only fitted the rails to seven posts. When he began to put them up I was riding out and ordered him to leave the gateway into the garden as wide as the two piers next the gate on each side. Nay, I measured the ground off to him and showed him where the two concluding posts were to stand, and . . . asked him if he understood me. He said he did and would do it so. I had been 2 hours out and when I came home nothing was done and he was gone about another job. I asked him why he served me so. He told me because it would not answer his design. The villain had so constantly interrupted my orders that I had given him about every job this year that I struck him upon the shoulders with my stick"—which being old and brittle "shivered all to pieces; and this morning, for that stroke, which did not raise the least swelling nor prevent the idle dog from putting up the posts as I directed . . . I say this morning he has laid himself up with a pain in that shoulder and will not even come out . . . I might as well give up every Negro if I submit to this impudence.

March 16. "I do believe my old carpenters intend to be my greatest rascals. Guy does not go about any job, be it ever so trifling, that he does not make three weeks or a month of it at least. The silling of my mudhouse, a job of not more than 3 days, he has already been above a fortnight about, and this morning when my people went to help to put the sills in, though he said he was ready for them, he [still] had the rotten sills to cut out; and because I told him he should certainly be called to account for it, as I came back truly he was gone, and nobody knew where, and had been gone for some time, but not about my house. Mr. Tony, another rascal, pretends he is full of pain, though he looks much better than any Negro I have.

March 17. "Tony came abroad [out of his cabin] and was well entertained for his impudence. Perhaps now he may think of working a little. Guy actually ran away. Outlawries are sent out against him for tomorrow's publication. One [lamb] died last night through Johnny's carelessness. He wants his correction.

March 22. "Guy came home yesterday and had his correction for runaway in sight of the people. The two Sarahs came up yesterday pretending to be violent ill with pains in their sides. They look very well, had no fever, and I ordered them down to their work upon pain of a whipping. They went, worked very well with no grunting about pain, but one of them, to wit Manuel's Sarah, taking advantage of Lawson's [the overseer] ride to the Fork, swore she would not work any longer and run away and is still out. There is a curiosity in this creature. She worked none last year, pretending to be with child, and this she was full eleven months before she was brought to bed. She has now the same pretense and thinks to pursue the same course, but as I have full warning of her deceit, if I live, I will break her of that trick.

Tuesday, March 27. "Ball [an overseer] yesterday found some shelled corn as well as eared corn in Manuel's quarter with one of my bags. Thus has that rascal made good my suspicion either of not giving all the corn he was allowed to the oxen he drove . . . or else has robbed me of corn as he brought from Mangorike. I have contrived that he shall not fail of a good whipping.

March 28. "Tony began yesterday to nail my pales up.

March 30. "I think my man Tony is determined to struggle whether he shall not do as he pleases." The problem this time was that the ground where the fence was to be built was uneven. Carter told Tony to level the ground, and then rode out; when he returned he found that nothing had been done, so he gave Tony "one small rap" on his shoulder, whereupon Tony "pretended he could not drive a nail, his arm was so sore. I made Nassau"—another slave—"strip his clothes off and examined the whole arm. Not the least swelling upon it . . . He said the stroke was in his bone, which made all his body ache. At last, looking full upon him, I discovered the Gentleman completely drunk. This I have suspected a great while. I then locked him up for Monday morning' chastisement."

And so it continued.

June, 1770: "Kindness to a Negro by way of reward for having done well is the surest way to spoil him." **May, 1772:** "Every day I discover the sordidness of a slave." **June, 1773:** "I find it almost impossible to make a Negro do his work well." **July, 1774:** "Nothing so certain as spoiling your slaves by allowing them but little to do; so sure are they from thence to learn to do nothing at all." **August, 1778:** "Indeed, slaves are devils, and to make them otherwise than slaves will be to set devils free."

Running away was common, though frequently ending in recapture:

Virginia Gazette, **April, 1766.** Run away from the subscriber in Hanover about the middle of December last, a likely Negro man named Damon, about 5 feet 9 or 10 inches, has a scar on his forehead and cheek, is a brisk, lively fellow, speaks good English, was born in the West Indies, beats the drum tolerably well, which he is very fond of, and loves liquor; had on when he went away Negro cotton clothes, and an old hat bound round with linen. Whoever takes up the said Negro and contrives him to me, shall have 3 pounds reward.   —SARAH GIST

Virginia Gazette, **March, 1767.** Run away about the 15th of December last, a small yellow Negro wench named Hannah, about 35 years of age; had on when she went away a green plains petticoat, and sundry other clothes, but what sort I do not know, as she stole many from the other Negroes. She has remarkably long hair, or wool, is much scarified under the throat from one ear to the other, and has many scars on her back, occasioned by whipping. She pretends much to the religion the Negroes of late have practised, and may probably endeavour to pass for a free woman, as I understand she intended when she went away, by the Negroes in the neighbourhood. She is supposed to have made for Carolina. Whoever takes up the said slave, and secures her so that I get her again, shall be rewarded according to their trouble.
—STEPHEN DENCE

Virginia Gazette, **April, 1767.** Run away from the subscriber in Norfolk, about the 20th of October last, two young Negro fellows, viz. Will, about 5 feet 8 inches high, middling black, well made, is an outlandish fellow [i.e. born in Africa], and when he is surprised the whites of his eyes turn red; I bought him of Mr. Moss, about 8 miles below York, and imagine he is gone that way, or somewhere between York and Williamsburg. Peter, about 5 feet 9 inches high, a very black slim fellow, has a wife at Little Town, and a father at Mr. Philip Burt's quarter, near the half-way house between Williamsburg and York. He formerly belonged to Parson Fontaine, and I bought him of Doctor James Carter. They are both outlawed; and ten pounds a piece offered to any person that will kill the said Negroes and bring me their heads, or thirty shillings for each if brought home alive.   —JOHN BROWN

Virginia Gazette, **September, 1769.** Run away from the subscriber in Albermarle, a Mulatto slave called Sandy, about 35 years of age, his stature is rather low, inclining to corpulence, and his complexion light; he is a shoemaker by trade, in which he uses his left hand principally, can do coarse carpenters work, and is something of a horse jockey; he is greatly addicted to drink, and when drunk is insolent and disorderly; in his conversation he swears much, and in his behavior is artful and knavish. He took with him a white horse, much scarred with traces, of which it is expected he will endeavour to dispose; he also carried his shoemakers tools, and will probably endeavour to get employment that way.   —THOMAS JEFFERSON

Runaways who formed maroon communities in places like the Great Dismal Swamp, or headed west, were another worry for white colonists. In his 1729 report home Lt. Gov. William Gooch wrote that "a number of Negroes, about fifteen, belonging to a new plantation on the head of James River formed a design to withdraw from their master and to fix themselves in the fastnesses of the neighbouring mountains. They had found means to get into their possession some arms & ammunition, and they took along with them some provisions, their cloaths, bedding and working tools; but the gentleman to whom they belonged with a party of men made such diligent pursuit after them that he soon found them out in their new settlement, a very obscure place among the mountains, where they had already begun to clear the ground, and obliged them, after exchanging a shot or two by which one of the slaves was wounded, to surrender and return back, and so prevented for this time a design which might have proved as dangerous to this country as is that of the Negroes in the mountains of Jamaica to the inhabitants of that island. Tho' this attempt has happily been defeated, it ought nevertheless to awaken us into some effectual measures for preventing the like hereafter, it being certain that a very small number of Negroes once settled in those parts would very soon be encreas'd by the accession of other runaways."

SOUTH CAROLINA

As worrying to the authorities as the maroon communities was the problem of fugitives heading south to Florida, at that time a Spanish colony. Reporting back to London in October, 1739, General Oglethorpe, the military commander of South Carolina and Georgia's first governor, explained the situation:

"Sometime since there was a proclamation published at Augustine in which the King of Spain promised protection and freedom to all Negro slaves that would resort thither." At this time there were still no slaves in Georgia, but there were plenty in South Carolina, some of whom got word of this offer and escaped to St. Augustine, either by working their way through the back country, or by stealing a boat and sailing there. "They were demanded by General Oglethorpe who sent Lieutenant Demere to Augustine, and the governor assured him of his sincere friendship, but at the same time showed his orders from the Court of Spain, by which he was to receive all runaway Negroes. Of this other Negroes having notice . . . some of whom belonged to Captain Macpherson, ran away with his horses, wounded his son and killed another man. These marched for Georgia and were pursued, but . . . reached Augustine, one only being killed and another wounded by the Indians in their flight. They were received there with great honours, one of them had a commission given to him, and a coat faced with velvet."

This happened at a time when the long-standing hostility between the Bourbon Alliance (France and Spain) against England was about to result in the War of Jenkins' Ear, and it was supposed by the English that the Spanish promise of freedom was a stratagem to undermine South Carolina. Proof of this came when examining the causes of the Stono Rebellion of 1739. According to an official report:

> "On the 9th day of September last, being Sunday, which is the day the planters allow them to work for themselves, some Angola Negroes assembled, to the number of twenty; and one who was called Jemmy was their captain. They surprised a warehouse belonging to Mr. Hutchenson at a place called Stonehow; they there killed Mr. Robert Bathurst and Mr. Gibbs, plundered the house and took a pretty many small arms and powder, which were there for sale. Next they plundered and burnt Mr. Godfrey's house, and killed him, his daughter and son. They then turned back and marched southward along Pons Pons, which is the road through Georgia to Augustine. They passed Mr. Wallace's tavern towards daybreak, and said they would not hurt him, for he was a good man and kind to his slaves, but they broke open and plundered Mr. Lemy's house, and killed him, his wife and child. They marched on towards Mr. Rose's resolving to kill him; but he was saved by a Negro, who having hid him went out and pacified the others. Several Negroes joined them, they calling out 'Liberty!', marched on with colours displayed, and two drums beating, pursuing all the white people they met with, and killing man, woman and child when they could come up to them. Colonel Bull, Lieutenant Governor of South Carolina, who was then riding along the road, discovered them, was pursued and with much difficulty escaped & raised the country. They burnt Colonel Hext's house and killed his overseer and his Wife. They then burnt Mr. Sprye's house, then Mr. Sacheverell's, and then Mr. Nash's house, all lying upon the Pons Pons Road, and killed all the white people they found in them. Mr. Bullock got off, but they burnt his house.
>
> "By this time many of them were drunk with the rum they had taken in the houses. They increased every minute by new Negroes coming to them, so that they were above sixty, some say a hundred, on which they halted in a field, and set to dancing, singing and beat-

ing drums, to draw more Negroes to them, thinking they were now victorious over the whole province, having marched ten miles & burnt all before them without opposition; but the militia being raised, the planters with great briskness pursued them, and when they came up, dismounting, charged them on foot. The Negroes were soon routed, though they behaved boldly, several being killed on the spot. Many ran back to their plantations thinking they had not been missed, but they were there taken and shot. Such as were taken in the field also were, after being examined, shot on the spot. And this is to be said to the honour of the Carolina planters, that notwithstanding the provocation they had received from so many murders, they did not torture one Negro, but only put them to an easy death. All that proved to be forced and were not concerned in the murders and burnings were pardoned. And this sudden courage in the field, and the humanity afterwards, hath had so good an effect that there hath been no farther attempt, and the very spirit of revolt seems over." Another report mentioned that "fifty of these villains attempted to go home but were taken by the planters who cut off their heads and set them up every mile post."

Stono was the largest slave insurrection in the English colonies, but it was not the only one. There had been revolts in South Carolina in 1711 and 1714. In 1720 occurred "a very wicked and barbarous plot of the Negroes rising with a design to destroy all the white people in the country and then to take the town [Charleston]," but, through "God's will," the plot "was discovered, and many of them taken prisoners and some burnt, some hang'd and some banish'd." Some of the plotters "thought to get to Augustine," and fourteen got as far as Savannah before being caught and executed. Ten years later, the *Boston Weekly News-Letter* published a letter from Charleston describing "a bloody tragedy which was to have been executed here last Saturday night by the Negroes, who had conspired to rise and destroy us, and had almost bro't it to pass: but it pleased God to appear for us, and confound their councils. For some of them propos'd that the Negroes of every plantation should destroy their own masters; but others were for rising in a body, and giving the blow at once on surprise; and thus they differ'd. They soon made a great body at the back of the town, and had a great dance, and expected the country

Negroes to come & join them; and had not an overruling Providence dis-covered their intrigues, we had been all in blood . . ." That same year, 1730, another conspiracy was uncovered in Charleston whose alleged purpose was to massacre all the whites, except the young women.

There were also alarming stories in the Charleston newspapers, such as this from 1729: "We have an account from Guinea by way of Antigua that the Clare galley, Capt. Murrell, having compleated her number of Negroes, had taken her departure from the coast of Guinea for South Carolina; but was not got ten leagues on her way before the Negroes rose, and making themselves masters of the gunpowder and fire-arms, the captain and the ship's crew took to their long boat and got ashore near Cape Coast Castle. The Negroes ran the ship on shore within a few leagues of the said castle, and made their escape." Three years later, "Captain John Major, in a schooner from New Hampshire, was treach-erously murdered, and his vessel and cargo seized by Negroes." Later that same year, "the slaves on board a Guinea-man belonging to Bristol, rose and destroyed the whole crew, cutting off the captain's head, legs and arms."

Most whites agreed about the causes of insurrections: slaves dangerously outnumbered them by well over two to one; more than half of all slaves had been imported from Africa, and these were more likely to rebel than those born in the colony. Also, about three quarters of them came from Angola and the Congo and shared a common background, which made it easier for them to act in concert. Whites could also agree that they had been too good-natured and easy-going, and had not done enough to re-cruit the assistance of the Chickasaw, Catawbaw, Creek and other Indian tribes by offering them "suitable reward to pursue and if possible to bring back the deserters."

Another, much less discussed, cause of the uprisings was the way the slaves were treated. One of the few to bear witness to this was the Anglican missionary, Dr. Francis Le Jau, who had been sent out from England by the recently-founded Society for the Propagation of the Gospel. In his reports back home, Le Jau, though cautious and conser-vative, was often unable to restrain his indignation at what he saw, but could not prevent. "I must inform you of a most cruel contrivance a man has invented to punish small faults in his slaves," he wrote. "He puts them in a coffin where they are crushed almost to death, and he keeps them in that hellish machine for 24 hours, commonly with their feet chained out and a lid pressing upon their stomach." On another occasion he wrote of the "unjust, profane and inhumane practices which I thought it was my duty to declare against. A poor slave-woman was barbarously burnt alive near my door without any positive proof of the crime she was accused of, which was the burning of her master's house, and protested her innocence even to myself to the last. Many masters can't be persuaded that Negroes and Indians are otherwise than beasts." Le Jau also complained of a law "in relation to runaway Negroes" whereby "such a Negro must be mutilated by amputation of testicles if it be a man, and of ears if a woman. I have openly declared against such punishment grounded upon the Law of God, which sets a slave at liberty if he should lose an eye or a tooth when he is corrected. *Exodus, 21.*" (Verses 26 and 27: "And if a man strike the eye of his servant, or the eye of his maid, that it perish; he shall let him go free for his eye's sake. And if he smite out his manservant's tooth, or his maidservant's tooth; he shall let him go free for his tooth's sake.")

Le Jau was not the only white witness to the brutality of slave owners. In his *Journal*, Charles Wesley, one of the founders of Methodism, wrote that "Colonel Lynch cut off the legs of a poor Negro, and he kills several of them every year by his barbarities. Mr. Hill, a dancing-master in Charleston, whipped a female slave so long that she fell down at his feet, in appearance dead; but when, with the help of a physician, she was so far recovered as to show signs of life, he repeated the whipping with equal rigour, and concluded the punishment by dropping scalding wax upon her flesh. Her only crime was over-filling a tea-cup." And Olaudah Equiano, who since his sudden purchase by the captain of the *Industrious Bee* had spent much of his life at sea, described how in 1764 the ship on which he served as supercargo arrived in Georgia, where, "one Sunday night, as I was with some Negroes in their master's yard, in the town of Savannah, it happened that their master, one Dr. Perkins, who was a very severe and cruel man, came in drunk; and not liking to see any strange Negroes in his yard, he and a ruffian of a white man he had in his service beset me in an instant . . . they beat and mangled me in a shameful manner, leaving me near dead. I lost so much blood from the wounds I received that I lay quite motionless, and was so benumbed that I could not feel anything for many hours. Early in the morning they took me away to the jail" where, fortunately, he was found by his ship's captain, who had been searching for him. "He soon got me out of jail to his lodgings, and immediately sent for the best doctors in the place, who at first declared it as their opinion that I could not recover. My captain on this went to all the lawyers in the town for their advice, but they told him they could do nothing for me as I was a Negro."

Before Stono, South Carolina already had some pretty severe laws for "the better ordering and governing Negroes and other slaves," and for preventing the "disorders, rapines and inhumanity to which they are naturally prone and inclined." After Stono, it seemed clear that these laws had not gone far enough, and so the Assembly debated and passed an act "for the better keeping slaves in due order and subjection." Among the more than fifty other clauses: if any slave was caught off a plantation without a ticket of leave and refused to "undergo the examination of any white person, it shall be lawful for any such white person to pursue, apprehend, and moderately correct such slave; and if any such slave shall assault and strike such white person, such slave may be lawfully killed." Also any slave who shall "endeavour to delude or entice any slave to run away and leave this Province, every such slave and slaves, and his and their accomplices, aiders and abettors shall, upon conviction as aforesaid, suffer death." Also "if any slave, free Negro, mulatto, Indian or mustizo [part white, part Indian] shall willfully and maliciously burn or destroy any sack of rice, corn or other grain," or "any tar kiln, barrels of pitch, tar, turpentine, or rosin," or "shall feloniously steal, take or carry away any slave, being the property of another," then all such persons "shall suffer death as a felon." Also "for that as it is absolutely necessary to the safety of this Province that all due care be taken to restrain the wanderings and meetings of Negroes and other slaves at all times, and more especially on Saturday nights, Sundays, and other holidays, and their using and . . . keeping of drums, horns or other loud instruments, which may call together or give sign or notice to one another of their wicked designs and purposes," then "whatsoever master, owner or overseer" who permitted such activities "shall forfeit ten pounds, current money." Also "whereas many of the slaves in this Province wear clothes much above the condition of slaves, for the procuring whereof they use sinister and evil methods," they were henceforth to wear only "Negro duffels, kerseys," and other cheap clothing; and any constable who found a slave wearing "any sort of garment or apparel whatsoever finer than or of greater value than Negro cloths, duffels, coarse kerseys" and so on, "could seize and take away the same to his own use, benefit and behoof."

There was more: "To the end that owners of slaves may not be tempted to conceal the crimes of their slaves to the prejudice of the public," any slave condemned to death would be appraised before execution "at any sum not exceeding two hundred pounds," the money to be paid to the owner by the public treasurer. "And whereas several owners of slaves have permitted them to keep canoes, and to breed and raise horses, neat cattle and hogs, and to traffic and barter in several parts of this Province . . . by which means they have not only an opportunity of receiving and concealing stolen goods, but to plot and confederate together, and form conspiracies dangerous to the peace and safety of the whole Province . . ." all such activities were banned and all such property confiscated. And "whereas the having of slaves taught to write, or suffering them to be employed in writing, may be attended with great inconveniences," any person "who shall hereafter teach, or cause any slave or slaves to be taught to write . . . shall for every such offence forfeit the sum of one hundred pounds current money." Next to last: "And whereas many disobedient and evil-minded Negroes and other slaves, being the property of his Majesty's subjects of this Province, have lately deserted the service of their owners, and have fled to St. Augustine and other places in Florida in hopes of being there received and protected; and whereas many other slaves have attempted to follow the same evil and pernicious example," therefore any white person or Indian "who shall, on the south side of the Savannah River, take and secure, and shall from thence bring to the work-house in Charlestown any Negroes or other slaves," would be rewarded according to the following scale: "For each grown man slave brought alive, the sum of fifty pounds; for every grown woman or boy slave above the age of twelve years brought alive, the sum of twenty pounds; for every Negro child under the age of twelve years, brought alive, the sum of five pounds; for every scalp of a grown Negro slave, with the two ears, twenty pounds."

Perhaps as a sop to their consciences, and also to ensure approval from the London government, which reviewed all colonial laws, legislators added some clauses that would appear to benefit their slaves. Thus any owner who made a slave work on a Sunday could be fined ten pounds, which sounds benevolent except for the loophole: "works of absolute necessity and the necessary occasions of the family only excepted." Also, "if any Negro or other slave who shall be employed in the lawful business or service of his master . . . shall be beaten, bruised, maimed or disabled by any person not having sufficient cause or lawful authority for so doing," then the offender would be fined forty shillings; however, this money would go not to the slave who had been unlawfully beaten and bruised but "to the use of the [white] poor of that parish in which such offense shall be committed." Also, if any owner "shall deny, neglect or refuse to allow such slave or slaves under his or her charge sufficient clothing, covering or food, it shall and may be lawful for any person or persons"—i.e. white person or persons—"on behalf of such slave or slaves to make complaint to the next neighboring justice" who could then order relief for such slave or slaves. Also, if any owner or overseer "shall work or put to labor any such slave or slaves more than fifteen hours in four and twenty hours, from the 25th day of March to the 25th day of September, or more than fourteen hours in four and twenty hours from the 25th day of September to the 25th day of March, every such person shall forfeit a sum not exceeding twenty pounds."

Most notable among these apparent reforms was Clause XXXVII:

"And whereas cruelty is not only highly unbecoming those who profess themselves Christians, but is odious in the eyes of all men who have any sense of virtue or humanity; therefore to restrain and prevent barbarity being exercised towards slaves, Be it enacted by the authority aforesaid, That . . . if any person shall, on a sudden heat or passion, or by undue correction, kill his own slave, or the slave of another person, he shall forfeit the sum of three hundred and fifty pounds, current money. And in case any person or persons shall, willfully cut out the tongue, put out the eye, castrate, or cruelly scald, burn or deprive any slave of any limb or member, or shall inflict any other cruel punishment, other than by whipping or beating . . . every such person shall, for every such offense, forfeit the sum of one hundred pounds, current money."

South Carolinians were not slow to congratulate themselves on the fair and humane nature of their slave laws. Thirty years later, in a report to London, Governor William Bull, son of the man who had come upon the Stono insurgents, favorably mentioned "a particular system of laws adapted to the condition of slaves, called our Negro Act, passed in 1740, calculated to punish offending and to protect abused slaves." Thanks to the "happy temperament of justice and mercy in our Negro Acts, and the general humanity of the masters, the state of slavery is as comfortable in this province as such a state can be." Admittedly, "monsters of cruelty sometimes appear," but these were "punished and abhorred." Bull gave no examples of this happening, nor did he mention that since slaves could not testify in court against whites, the only way to convict an owner of abusing a slave was for one of his overseers, or one of his neighbors, to give evidence against him, hardly something likely to happen.

GEORGIA

Another result of the Stono Insurrection was to confirm General Oglethorpe in his determination to keep Georgia free of Negro slaves. The only colony to be supported financially by the British government, Georgia was to be a charity venture where debtors and other "miserable wretches lately relieved out of jail" could make a new start in life. New settlers were given a grant of land, but they would have to clear and work it themselves, or with the help of indentured white servants or transported white convicts. But no slaves, because, as Oglethorpe explained, "wherever Negroes are, though never so few, the white men grow idle." Moreover, "it would be impossible to prevent them deserting to the Spaniards, our near neighbours, who give freedom, land and protection to all runaway Negroes." And even if they didn't desert "the great number of Negroes, near forty thousand in Carolina, would be either an assistance to the invader or a prize worth near eight hundred thousand Pounds Sterling." Also, as a humanitarian, he deplored the fact that introducing slavery would "occasion the misery of thousands in

Africa, by setting men upon using arts to buy and bring into perpetual slavery the poor people who now live free there."

But although the Scots who settled at Darien, and the German Pietists at Ebenezer, proved by their example that white people could cultivate the land despite the hot climate, that was not what others, especially the speculators, wanted to believe; and in August, 1735, Patrick Tailfer and several other malcontents bypassed Oglethorpe and addressed this petition to the Trustees in London:

"Honoured Sirs: We whose names are underwritten beg leave to lay the ensuing particulars before you: We, all having land in your colony of Georgia and having come here chiefly with a design to settle upon and improve our land, find that it is next to an impossibility to do it without the use of Negroes. For in the first place, most part of our white servants not being used to so hot a climate can't bear the scorching rays of the sun in the summer when they are at work in the woods without falling into distempers which render them useless for almost one half of the year. Secondly, there is a great deal of difference betwixt the expense of white servants and of Negroes, for Negroes can endure this climate almost without any clothes, only a cap, jacket, and pair of trousers made of some coarse woolen stuff in the winter, and one pair of shoes; whereas white men must be clothed as Europeans and proportionable to the season all the year throughout. And then as to their diet, the charge of maintaining Negroes is much less than of white men, for the first live in good plight and health upon salt, Indian corn and potatoes, which they raise themselves with no expense to the master but the seed, and have nothing to drink but water; whereas white men must be fed with flesh meat, bread and other victuals suitable to the European diet which they have been used to and bred up with from their infancy, and must likewise have beer or other strong liquors in due quantities for their drink, otherwise they turn feeble and languid and are not capable to perform their work . . ."

Convicted felons, who were transported for life to Georgia rather than be hanged in England, were of little help, being "hardened abandoned wretches, perfectly skilled in all manner of villainy . . . continually

James Oglethorpe, the strong-willed English general who was the first governor of Georgia. For the new colony to succeed as a refuge for the "worthy [white] poor," Oglethorpe banned strong drink and slavery; the first ban broke down almost at once, and the second soon after his return to England in 1743.

stealing and embezzling our goods and, which is of worse consequence, forming plots and treasonable designs." Also, it was easy for them to run way and pass for free whites, "whereas Negroes would always be known and taken into custody."

Tailfer and the petitioners were also careful to explain that they did not propose employing Negroes in any of the skilled trades, which would be reserved for white artisans, "but only in cutting down trees and stumps, hoeing, trenching and fencing the ground and all other ways of clearing the land, making turpentine and tar, beating of rice &c."

When this petition was rejected, Tailfer and his faction appealed directly to Parliament: "It is experience, seven long years' experience, that has confirmed us of the impossibility of white men being able to work here and live. Consider the difference of the climate, think how unfit a British constitution is to undergo hard labor in a country twenty-three Degrees to the South of England . . . How shocking must it be even to a person of the least humanity, to see his own countrymen, perhaps his own townsmen, laboring in the corn or rice field, broiling in the sun, pale and fainting under the excessive heat, and instances there have been of their dying on the spot! How terrible must such a sight be to any man who has the least grain of compassion within him! How must it make his heart flow with sorrow to see the misery of his fellow creatures!"

But now let the reader of the petition "turn his eyes round to the Negroes in the same fields. There he will see the reverse. He will see the utmost vigours exerted in every act. They go through their work with pleasure. They welcome the rising sun with their songs and when in his meridian their spirits are at their highest. They are far more happy here than in their own country. There they are abject slaves, their lives and whatever else they have are every hour in the hands of some petty tyrant. Here, it is true, they are the property of particular men, but their lives are in no danger. They are sure of being fed and clothed, it being in their master's interest to take the utmost care of them . . ."

So long as Oglethorpe was in charge, there was no slavery in Georgia, but he returned to England for good in 1743, and by 1750 the ban had been revoked. Before leaving, he took advantage of the War of Jenkins' Ear to launch an attack on Fort Mose, the small but heavily fortified village near St. Augustine which was home to about a hundred former slaves who had escaped from South Carolina. More formally known as the Pueblo de Gracia Real de Santa Teresa de Mose, the fort was a strategic outpost where the Spanish governor had invited them to settle, rightly calculating that if the English were ever to attack, the runaways could be counted on to fight to the last, not out of gratitude but to avoid being re-enslaved. Father de Leon, a Spanish Franciscan, was chaplain and Captain Francisco Menendez, a Mandingo, was military commander. When Oglethorpe attacked he greatly outnumbered the garrison, who then retreated to St. Augustine. During the siege that followed a joint force of Spanish soldiers, Indian allies and free blacks commanded by Captain Menendez sallied forth and made a surprise counter-attack on Mose, now occupied by Oglethorpe's troops, killing seventy-five of them in hand to hand fighting. This action contributed greatly to Oglethorpe's decision to abandon the whole campaign. In his official report, Governor Montiano particularly commended the "patriotism, courage and steadiness of the troops, militia, and free Negroes."

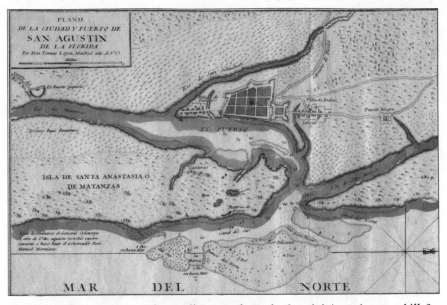

Fort Mose (Fuerte Negro, the small rectangle to the far right), a city on a hill for fugitive slaves who managed to reach Spanish Florida, where slavery had long been banned. On arrival they were recruited into the Spanish army and stationed at this fort near St. Augustine. When Oglethorpe attacked Florida in 1740 some of his heaviest losses came at Fort Mose where Captain Menendez, a former slave from Angola, and his black soldiers repulsed a large force of British regulars.

The following summer it was Governor Montiano's turn to attack the English colonies. His force, wrote Oglethorpe, included "a regiment of Negroes. The Negro commanders were clothed in lace, bore the same rank as the white officers, and with equal freedom and familiarity walked and conversed with their comrades and chief. Such an example might justly have alarmed Carolina." Even more alarming was the Spanish plan to "send out Negroes of all languages to recruit the slaves of the English plantation and offer them freedom and land in the territory of Florida under the protection of the laws of the King of Spain." This time, however, it was the Spanish who were repulsed, and not long afterward the war petered out.

Lord Dunmore, Virginia's last royal governor and author of this country's first emancipation proclamation. Issued in November, 1775, and offering freedom to slaves who enlisted under the royal banner, the proclamation shocked and alienated Loyalists as well as Patriots—a major contribution to the American cause. About a thousand slaves enlisted in the "Ethiopian Regiment" and bore the insignia "Liberty to Slaves." Some were killed at the Battle of Great Bridge; some deserted; many died of smallpox while on board ships evacuating them to New York; and some eventually went with Dunmore to the Bahamas, where it appears that most were re-enslaved.

CHAPTER 6

THE REVOLUTION

IN 1770, WRITING TO LORD HILLSBOROUGH, THE MINISTER RESPONSIBLE for Britain's colonies, Governor William Bull painted a rosy picture of how things were going in South Carolina. "Agriculture is in a very prosperous state," he wrote. "The introducing rice hath proved a very fortunate circumstance to this province as it is a grain which yields the most plentiful harvest when the ground is overflowed with water. Many large swamps, otherwise useless and affording inaccessible shelter for deserting slaves and wild beasts, have been drained and cultivated." Indigo, hemp, flour and tobacco were also doing well. "The number of dwelling-houses in town [Charleston] taken this summer was one thousand two hundred and ninety-two, and the white inhabitants five thousand and thirty, and the black five thousand and eight hundred and thirty-one, employed as domestic servants and mechanics [workmen]." Trade was brisk. "We employ near five hundred sail of vessels to carry off the superfluous produce and import supplies for the wants of the province. Though by the annual importation of three or four thousand Negroes the balance of trade may be against us, yet we cannot be considered in debt as the Negroes remain part of our stock and are the means of increasing our riches." Their number now totaled seventy-five thousand, one hundred and seventy-eight.

The fact that blacks slightly outnumbered whites in Charleston, and greatly outnumbered them in the rest of the colony, did not create a security problem. "The defense of our province as far as our own power can avail is provided for by our militia against foreign, and patrols against domestic enemies." In times of great danger the militia was to be reinforced "with a number of trusty Negroes (and we have many such) not exceeding one-third of the corps they are to join."

Five years later, the next—and last—royal governor of South Carolina was also writing a report. This was Lord William Campbell, who had arrived at Charleston on board the *Scorpion* in June, 1775. By then fighting had broken out in New England, and the government of South Carolina was in the hands of the Committee and Council of Safety, headed by the merchant and slave-trader Henry Laurens. The topic of Lord Campbell's letter to Lord Dartmouth was "the accursed politics of this country" and "the dreadful tragedy acted here on Friday the 18th of this month [August, 1775]."

As Dartmouth must already know, "numberless arts have been used and the most notorious falsehoods propagated to work up the people in every part of America to that pitch of madness and fury to which they are arrived." These falsehoods included a letter "from a Mr. Lee in London to a leading man in this place in which he boldly asserted the ministry had in agitation not only to bring down the Indians on the inhabitants of this province, but also to instigate and encourage an insurrection amongst their slaves. It was also reported, and universally believed, that to effect this plan 14,000 stand of arms were actually on board the *Scorpion*, the sloop of war I came out in. Words, I am told, cannot express the flame that this occasioned amongst all ranks and degrees; the cruelty and savage barbarity of the scheme was the conversation of all companies."

It was true that a few people in London had toyed with the idea of recruiting various Indian tribes, but so half-hearted was the British conduct of the war that little was actually done. As to encouraging a slave insurrection, this was hardly likely to be even considered by George III's aristocratic ministers, several of whom were absentee owners of sugar plantations in the West Indies. However, according to Campbell, it was not long before someone claimed to have overheard some slaves talking about why the militia was drilling so often, whereupon "several of those poor ignorant creatures [were] taken up, who, terrified at the recollection of former cruelties, were easily induced to accuse themselves and others to escape punishment. Among the rest one Thomas Jeremiah, a free black commonly called Jerry, was taken into custody on the accusation of one of those wretches. This unfortunate man, my lord, has by his industry acquired a property of upwards of £1000 sterling, was in a very thriving situation, had several slaves of his own who he employed in fishing, and was one of the best pilots in the harbour . . . It was needless to urge the improbability of a fellow in affluent circumstances who was universally acknowledged to be remarkably sensible and sagacious, possessed of slaves of his own, entering into so wild a scheme as to instigate an insurrection without support, without encouragement (for happily not a shadow of evidence appeared that any white man was concerned)—it was needless to urge this or any other argument in his favour. To trial he was brought a few days after my arrival before two justices and five freeholders according to the Negro Act, and after sitting a week and taking uncommon pains to get evidence, no proof could be produced to convict him or give sufficient grounds to believe any attempt of the kind they pretended to fear was ever intended." But instead of being released "Jerry was ordered to be remanded to prison, and his trial resumed two months afterwards, by which time they hoped to procure more evidence. It is with horror, my lord, I relate the remainder of the story. On Friday the 11th of this month this unhappy man was brought to trial, if such a process deserved that name, and was sentenced to be hanged and afterwards burned."

Campbell demanded to see the trial record and "I assure you, my lord, my blood run cold when I read on what grounds they had doomed a fellow creature to death." He then, as governor, proposed clemency, but this "raised such a clamour amongst the people as is incredible, and they openly and loudly declared if I granted the man a pardon they would hang him at my door." The Rev. Mr. Smith, a Patriot clergyman, visited Jerry several times in prison and came away convinced of his innocence. The "wretched slave" who had been the main witness against him retracted his testimony. But although Jerry himself "was perfectly resigned to his unhappy, his undeserved fate," Campbell "determined on one more effort" and appealed to Henry Laurens, the chairman of the Committee and Council of Safety, which had more or less taken over the government. But Laurens, who disliked Jerry, calling him "puffed up by prosperity" and "grown to an amazing pitch of vanity and ambition," refused to interfere; and so, "to conclude this heartrending story, the man was murdered, I can call it nothing else."

Jerry was not the only black troublemaker Laurens had to deal with. In March of 1776 he received a letter from Colonel Stephen Bull about the situation in Savannah, where an English attack was expected and where some two hundred escaped slaves had taken refuge on nearby

Tybee Island. In a postscript which he asked Laurens to keep confidential, Bull wrote: "The matter is this: It is far better for the public and the owners if the deserted Negroes on Tybee Island . . .be shot, if they cannot be taken." But rather than use his own troops for this purpose, Bull recommended that the runaways "had better be shot by the Creek Indians, as it perhaps may deter other Negroes from deserting, and will establish a hatred or aversion between the Indians and the Negroes." He did not, however, want to take sole responsibility for the proposed massacre, and asked for the Council's backing. In their reply Laurens and the others agreed on the need "to destroy all those rebellious Negroes" and "if Indians are the most proper hands, let them be employed on this Service."

Virginia also had a Scottish lord for its last royal governor. This was John Murray, Earl of Dunmore, reviled by Patriots for his notorious Proclamation of November 7, 1775, issued, he claimed, with great reluctance but forced into it "by a body of men unlawfully assembled and . . . now on its march to attack His Majesty's troops, and destroy the well-disposed of this colony. To defeat such treasonable purposes," he was not only declaring martial law but also requiring "every person capable of bearing arms to resort to His Majesty's standard or be looked upon as traitors to His Majesty's crown and government, and thereby become liable to the penalty the law inflicts upon such offenses, such as forfeiture of life, confiscation of lands, etc." This was bad enough, but worse was to come: "And I do hereby further declare all indented servants, Negroes, or others (appertaining to rebels) free, that are able and willing to bear arms, they joining His Majesty's troops as soon as may be, for the more speedily reducing this colony to a proper sense of their duty to His Majesty's crown and dignity."

Naturally, there was a counter-proclamation, this one issued by the Virginia Convention on January 25, 1776: "Whereas Lord Dunmore . . . hath offered freedom to such able-bodied slaves as are willing to join him, and take up arms against the good people of this colony, giving thereby encouragement to a general insurrection, which may induce a necessity of inflicting the severest punishments upon those unhappy people already deluded by his base and insidious arts; and whereas by an act of the general assembly now in force in this colony it is enacted that all Negro, or other slaves, conspiring to rebel or make insurrection, shall suffer death . . ." nevertheless, as yet another example of "the favorable and kind dispositions shewn by the convention and the natives of this colony," it was resolved that "to the end that all such who have taken this unlawful and wicked step may return in safety to their duty and escape the punishment due to their crimes, we hereby promise pardon to them, they surrendering themselves to Colonel William Woodford or any other commander of our troops, and not appearing in arms after the publication hereof. And we do further earnestly recommend it to all humane and benevolent persons in this colony to explain and make known this our offer of mercy to those unfortunate people."

Reporting back to London, Dunmore was pleased with how things were going. "There are between two and three hundred come in, and those I form into corps as they come in, giving them white officers and non-commissioners in proportion." The unit was called Lord Dunmore's Ethiopian Regiment and their flag bore the motto "Liberty to Slaves." Among those who enlisted were several slaves belonging to Colonel Landon Carter, the perpetually disgruntled lord of Sabine Hall, passages from whose diary appeared earlier. Since then things had continued to get worse.

"June 26 [1776]. Last night after going to bed, Moses, my son's man, Joe, Billy, Postillion John, Mulatto Peter, Tom, Panticove, Manuel and Lancaster Sam, ran away, to be sure, to Lord Dunmore, for they got privately into Beale's room before dark and took away my son's gun and one I had there, took out of his drawer in my passage all his ammunition furniture, Landon's bag of bullets and all the Powder, and went off in my Petty Auger [canoe] new trimmed, and it is supposed that Mr. Robinson's People are gone with them, for a skow they came down in is, it seems, at my Landing. These accursed villains have stolen Landon's silver buckles, George's shirts, Tom Parker's new waistcoat and breeches.

"June 29. At 7 in the morning after their departure some minute men at Mousquito Point saw the Petty Auger with ten stout men in her going very fast on the Middlesex shore. They pursued and fired at them, whereupon the Negroes left the boat and took to the shore where they were followed by the minute men.

"**July 3.** Monday at Court we heard that the King and Queen [counties] men below had killed a mulatto and two of the blacks out of the 8 of my people who ran away, and the remaining 5 surrendered; how true it is I don't know." And indeed news was hard to come by. Six days later a shopkeeper "who I have a long time known to be an egregious liar," reported "that some runaways told him they saw some slaves who had run away from Dunmore, who told him that they saw Moses on the Island [Gwynn's Island, Dunmore's base in Chesapeake Bay;] who swore to them if he could get back he would return to his master; for Dunmore had deceived all the poor slaves and he never met so barbarous or so vile a fellow in all his life." Beale, Carter's steward, also reported that a militia captain had told him that "the slaves were returning daily, most miserably."

Following Beale's report, Carter had this consoling dream:

"**July 25.** A strange dream this day about these runaway people. One of them I dreamt awakened me, and appeared most wretchedly meager and wan. He told me of their great sorrow, that all of them had been wounded by the minutemen, had hid themselves in a cave they had dug and lived ever since on what roots they could grabble, and he had come to ask if I would endeavour to get them pardoned, should they come in, for they knew they should be hanged for what they had done."

A year later he made this final diary entry on the subject: "July 10. [1777.] I am glad when I reflect on my own conduct to Moses and his gang of runaways that I have no kind of severity in the least to accuse myself of to one of them; but on the contrary a behaviour on my part that should have taught them gratitude if there ever was a virtue of the sort in such creatures." He then lists some of the benefits that, thanks largely to his knowledge of medicine, he had conferred on these ungrateful wretches:

"1st, Mr. Moses, before I lent him to my son, was so very subject to worms as to be at times almost in the jaws of death. And yet by God's blessing my care constantly saved him. 2nd, Mr. Manuel I really obliged by bringing Suky, his wife; he then took a fancy from a distant quarter. And at last I purchased the rascal's life condemned by the law, and at the expense of £16. 3rd, Mr. Panticove run a sharpened tobacco stick at his calf almost into his body, and he, to the astonishment of Dr. Jones, I saved by God's permission." (Mrs. Panticove, by the way, was "a jade so fiery in her temper and her lusts that the children are oft left by her whilst she is running about to satiate her desires.") "4th, Mr. Peter was so accustomed to bleed at the nose that though often given over by the doctors I entirely cured, by the favour of heaven. 5th, Mr. Joe to appearance struck dead with lightning for some days, and yet by God's grace I alone saved and restored him. 6th, Mr. Sam, a sheep stealer under a process below which never reached him. I endeavoured to protect him. 7th, Mr. Tom I ever used with the greatest respect." (This although Mr. Tom was "a rogue that sold everything," and "too impudent and, saucy to follow orders.") "8th, Mr. Billy, a fellow too honest and mild in temper, who would not have gone away but to please his father Manuel, who ever was a villain."

Things did not go well for Dunmore's Ethiopian Regiment. As was often to happen to black troops, their lives were thrown away in a suicidal frontal assault, this one at the battle of Long Bridge. Those survivors who did not then die of dysentery and fever were transferred to pioneer units. But the real effect of Dunmore's Proclamation was political rather than military. "Hell itself could not have vomited any thing more black than his design of emancipating our slaves," wrote an outraged Philadelphian. In the opinion of Edward Rutledge, nothing did more "to work an eternal separation between Great Britain and the Colonies." The Continental Congress described it as "tearing up the foundations of civil authority and government." Also, as a letter writer to the *Virginia Gazettte,* pointed out, "to none is freedom promised but to such as are able to do Lord Dunmore's service. The aged, the infirm, the women and children, are still to remain the property of their masters, of masters who will be provoked to severity should part of their slaves desert them . . . But should there be any amongst the Negroes weak enough to believe that Lord Dunmore intends to do them a kindness, and wicked enough to provoke the fury of the Americans against their defenseless fathers and mothers, their wives, their women and children, let them only consider the difficulty of effecting their escape, and what they must expect to suffer if they fall into the hands of the Americans. Let them farther consider what must be their fate should the English prove conquerors in this dispute. If we can judge of the future from the past, it will not be much mended. Long have the Americans, moved by compassion, and actuated by sound policy, endeavoured to stop the progress of slavery. Our assemblies have repeatedly passed acts laying heavy duties upon imported Negroes, by which they meant altogether to prevent the horrid traffick; but their humane intentions have been as often frustrated by the cruelty and covetousness of a set of English merchants who prevailed upon the king to repeal our kind and merciful acts, little indeed to the credit of his humanity. Can it then be supposed that the Negroes will be better used by the English, who have always encouraged and upheld this slavery, than by their present masters, who pity their condition, who wish in general to make it as easy and comfortable as possible, and who would willingly, were it in their power, or were they permitted, not only prevent any more Negroes from losing their freedom, but restore it to such as have already unhappily lost it? No, the ends of Lord Dunmore and his party being answered, they will either give up the offending Negroes to the rigour of the laws they have broken, or sell them in the West Indies, where every year they sell many thousands of their miserable brethren, to perish either by the inclemency of the weather, or the cruelty of barbarous masters. Be not then, ye Negroes, tempted by this proclamation to ruin yourselves! I have given you a faithful view of what you are to expect; and I declare before God, in doing it, I have considered your welfare, as well as that of the country. Whether you will profit by my advice, I cannot tell; but this I know, that whether we suffer or not, if you desert us, you most certainly will." (These last few sentences seem rather odd, addressed as they are directly to Negro slaves, few of whom can have been regular readers of the *Virginia Gazette*.)

It was true, as the letter-writer claimed, that the London government had vetoed various laws passed by colonial assemblies to restrict the import of slaves, usually by imposing a high duty; but the motive for preventing the "horrid traffick" was not "compassion" but either a temporary, panic-stricken reaction to an uprising such as that at Stono, or a protectionist measure to encourage the market in homegrown slaves. But the idea that slavery was an English invention, forced upon reluctant colonists by greedy traders, was what people wanted to believe, among them

Thomas Jefferson who, in his first draft of the Declaration of Independence, indignantly claimed that George III had "waged cruel war against human nature itself, violating its most sacred rights of life and liberty in the persons of a distant people who never offended him, captivating & carrying them into slavery in another hemisphere, or to incur miserable death in their transportation thither. This piratical warfare, the opprobrium of INFIDEL powers, is the warfare of the CHRISTIAN king of Great Britain." And when colonial legislatures had tried "to prohibit or restrain this execrable commerce," what did he do but have his ministers veto them?! ("Prostituted his negative," to use Jefferson's phrase.) However, as he later explained in his autobiography, this clause "reprobating the enslaving the inhabitants of Africa, was struck out in complaisance to South Carolina and Georgia," who wanted to continue the trade.

Although Dunmore remained convinced that he had hit upon a winning strategy, the aristocratic British generals and admirals had no intention of upsetting the social order by encouraging slaves to rise up against their masters. Instead, of the tens of thousands who escaped to the British lines only some were enrolled as pioneers in labor battalions, or hired as servants to officers. For the most part, the only ones to serve as soldiers were those who enlisted in regiments based in the West Indies, where they would fight the French and help keep the slaves in subjection. Owners who were loyalists, or who had been rebels but then changed sides and taken an oath of allegiance to the king, were allowed by the British to reclaim their slaves.

For their part, the Patriots were also unsure how to exploit black people militarily. Everyone could agree that they should be put to work digging entrenchments, cleaning latrines, working as orderlies, loading and unloading and driving wagons, but should they be allowed to fight in the cause of freedom and independence? Among the many things George Washington found to disapprove of when he arrived in Cambridge to take command in July, 1775—the lack of discipline, the "dirty & nasty people" (i.e. New Englanders) and their "leveling spirit"—was the presence of numerous free black soldiers in the army that was now besieging the British in Boston. Soon an order appeared that "neither Negroes, boys unable to bear arms, nor old men unfit to endure the fatigues of the campaign are to be inlisted." Then, in December, free Negroes were allowed to enlist; then Massachusetts passed a militia act excluding all blacks, slave or free; then Washington changed his mind and approved recruiting "such slaves as should be willing to enter into the service." As a result, when Rhode Island was required to supply two battalions for the continental army, the assembly "voted and resolved that every able-bodied Negro, mulatto or Indian man slave in this state may enlist into either of the said two battalions, to serve during the continuance of the present war with Great Britain; that every slave so enlisting shall be entitled to, and receive, all the bounties, wages, and encouragements allowed by the Continental Congress to any soldier enlisting in their service. It is further voted and resolved that every slave so enlisting shall, upon his passing muster before Col. Christopher Greene, be immediately discharged from the service of his master or mistress, and be absolutely FREE, as though he had never been encumbered with any kind of servitude or slavery . . . And whereas slaves have been, by the laws, deemed the property of their owners, and therefore compensation ought to be made to the owners for the loss of their service, It is further voted and resolved that there be allowed, and paid by this state to the owner, for every such slave so enlisting, a sum according to his worth, at a price not exceeding £120 for the most valuable slave; and in proportion for a slave of less value."

Three years later Baron von Closen, an officer with Rochambeau's French army, met some of these soldiers while on their way down to Yorktown. "Three quarters of the Rhode Island Regiment consists of Negroes," he noted, adding that "the regiment is the most neatly dressed, the best under arms, and the most precise in its maneuvers." The soldiers were "merry, confident and sturdy." Victory at Yorktown was assured when two British redoubts, numbers 9 and 10, were successfully stormed at bayonet point. Redoubt number 9 was attacked by the French, commanded by Lafayette, Redoubt number 10 by the Rhode Island Regiment, commanded on this occasion by Alexander Hamilton and John Laurens. Though Rochambeau's troops were mostly white, many of the French soldiers at Yorktown had recently arrived from the French West Indies, among them the Fontages Legion, composed of Haitians. (One of history's many ironies has been the scant attention paid to the role of black soldiers in winning this country's independence.)

In the meantime, John Laurens, son of Henry Laurens, the Charleston slave merchant now prominent in the Continental Congress, had been keen to have South Carolina and Georgia follow Rhode Island's example, and worked hard to persuade Congress to urge them to raise as many as "three thousand able-bodied Negroes." Owners would be compensated "at a rate not exceeding one thousand dollars for each active able-bodied Negro man of standard size, not exceeding thirty-five years of age." Those enlisted would have "no pay or bounty" but would be "cloathed and subsisted at the expense of the United States." Also "every negro who shall well and faithfully serve as a soldier to the end of the present war, and shall then return in arms," would "be emancipated, and receive the sum of fifty dollars." However, though the Continental Congress approved the measure, it gave "great disgust to the southern colonies," who overwhelmingly voted to reject it, some of the leaders even recommending secession and a separate peace with the British rather than take such a risk.

But there was another way to exploit black manpower: use slaves as bounties to white volunteers. This was the core of South Carolina's Act to Procure Recruits and Prevent Desertion. "As an encouragement to those who are willing to serve their country in the defense of her rights and liberties," the law provided that "every able-bodied [white] recruit between the age of sixteen and forty-five years . . . shall receive for each and every year's service, the bounty of one Negro between the age of ten and forty." If the soldier were killed his heirs would receive the bounty. Slaves to pay the bounty were to come from estates confiscated from loyalists. The system was refined to reflect rank, so that in one cavalry regiment "each colonel to receive three grown Negroes and one small Negro; major to receive three grown Negroes; captain, two grown Negroes; lieutenants one large and one small Negro; the sergeants one and a quarter Negro [i.e. $100, since a full Negro was valued at $400. A half Negro was either under ten or over forty]; each private, one grown Negro."

By then the British also had come up with their own ways for using slaves. Those who enlisted in one of the labor battalions such as the Black Pioneers were given regular pay and promised their freedom. There was also an informal arrangement whereby many slaves and their families abandoned their plantations and attached themselves to Cornwallis' army as it zigzagged northward from victory at Charleston to defeat at Yorktown, fighting and plundering along the way. "As it advanced, the army had increasingly come to look like a wandering Arabian or Tartar horde," wrote the Hessian Captain von Ewald. "Lord Cornwallis had allowed junior officers to provide themselves with two horses and one Negro ser-

vant, captains were allowed four horses and two Negroes, and so on. Even
among our jaegers and rangers some officers had four to six horses, three
or four Negro servants, and often a Negress or two as a cook or mistress.
Even ordinary soldiers had a Negro to carry their bundles.

> "In addition, following the baggage train, came a straggling mass of
> another four thousand or more Negroes of both sexes and of every age.
> Wherever they went the place was picked clean, like a field attacked
> by a swarm of locusts. Adding to the unmilitary appearance of this
> motley horde was the way the Negroes were dressed. Before leaving
> many of them had plundered the wardrobes of their masters and mis-
> tresses and were now wearing bits and pieces of their loot. One Negro
> was just about naked except for a pair of silk breeches, another wore
> a finely colored coat, a third had on a silk waistcoat without sleeves, a
> fourth wore only an elegant shirt, a fifth had on a fine clergyman's hat,
> a sixth was entirely naked except for a white wig. The Negresses also
> were variously tricked out in silk skirts, dresses with long trains, jackets,
> laced bodices, silk corsets, and a variety of hats and bonnets."

So long as the British army was on the move, the Negroes served
some purpose, helping to forage and plunder, driving wagons and performing fatigue duties; and when the army took up position at Yorktown,
they were the ones who threw up the massive defensive earth works. But
after that, with space confined and supplies short, they were a burden.
"On the day that we were first attacked by the enemy, all our black
friends, who had been freed by us and taken away so that they could not
work in their masters' fields, and who had served us well by digging entrenchments, were driven out of our camp and toward the enemy," wrote
Captain von Ewald. "They trembled with fear at the prospect of having
to go back to their former owners. When I went out on night patrol I encountered many of these unhappy people who were desperate from hunger
and were trapped between the lines, exposed to the fire from both sides."

To make matters worse, smallpox had broken out and many Negroes
were infected. "During the siege," wrote the American sergeant, Joseph
Martin, "we saw in the woods herds of Negroes which Lord Cornwallis
. . . had turned adrift, with no other recompense for their confidence in
his humanity than the smallpox for their bounty and starvation and death

for their wages. They might be seen scattered about in every direction, dead and dying, with pieces of ears of burnt Indian corn in the hands and mouths, even of those that were dead."

When the British surrendered, Article IV of the terms of capitulation stated that "any property obviously belonging to the inhabitants of these states, in the possession of the garrison, shall be subject to be reclaimed." Such property might be a horse, but more usually a slave. With mixed feelings, Sergeant Martin took part in the reclamation. "After the siege was ended, many of the owners of these deluded creatures came to our camp and engaged some of our men to take them up, generally offering a guinea a head for them. Some of our Sappers and Miners took up several of them that belonged to a Colonel Banister; when he applied for them they refused to deliver them to him unless he would promise not to punish them. He said he had no intention of punishing them, that he did not blame them at all, the blame lay on Lord Cornwallis. I saw several of those miserable wretches delivered to their master; they came before him under a very powerful fit of the ague [i.e. trembling with fear]. He told them that he gave them the free choice either to go with him or remain where they were, that he would not injure a hair of their heads if they returned with him to their duty. Had the poor souls been reprieved at the gallows they could not have been more overjoyed than they appeared to be at what he promised them; their ague fit soon left them."

Earlier in the war, in an attempt to win hearts and minds, the British had declared that any "rebel" who changed sides and took the oath of allegiance to the king would have his sins forgiven and his property restored. This gave rise to the following episode when General Baron von Riedesel, commander of the Hessian troops, and his wife, Frederika, were about to board ship in British-occupied New York en route for Canada. The story is told by the baroness who, with her three small children, had insisted on accompanying her husband during Burgoyne's disastrous campaign.

> "Just as we were on the eve of embarking, we met with a great vexation. Our faithful Negroes, a man, his wife, and a young kinswoman were reclaimed by their first owner (from whom they had been taken on the grounds that he was a rebel) under the pretense that he had again become a royalist. At the very moment when

the signal was being given for our ship to leave, he arrived with an order that they should be delivered up to him. As they had served us faithfully, and the man was a bad master who had treated them shockingly, great were the shrieks and lamentations of these poor people. The young maiden, Phillis by name, fainted, and when she recovered threw herself at my feet, embracing them so strongly with her clasped hands that they were obliged to tear her away by force . . . Later on this excellent young woman actually begged some other people who were going to Canada to take her with them and bring her to me, promising 'My good lady will be very glad to pay for my passage.' She was quite right, but none of them wanted to take the risk. My husband had enough money on hand for just this one purchase, but her greedy owner refused to sell her separately, and insisted that we should buy all three. This was more than we could afford, so we had to refuse. Later on, however, we regretted, that we had not made the sacrifice, as we found that female domestics in Canada were very ignorant and clumsy."

Similar scenes took place in Charleston when it came time for the British to evacuate that city. Slaves belonging to Loyalists who were leaving for the West Indies or Florida had no choice but to go with their masters. Slaves who had run away from Patriot owners and taken refuge in British-occupied Charleston were returned to their owners, unless they had enlisted under the royal standard and been promised their freedom. Much to the chagrin of Washington, the British were surprisingly firm about honoring this promise, and several thousand former slaves left for England, Nova Scotia, New Brunswick or the West Indies, where many served in the First West India Regiment. According to American propaganda, which may have had some truth in it, several hundred were also clandestinely sold as slaves to West Indian planters by Lt. Col. Moncrieff of the Royal Engineers.

Turning now to George Washington and his views on slavery, a good place to start is his last will and testament, which ran in part:

"Upon the decease of my wife, it is my Will & desire that all the slaves which I hold in my own right shall receive their freedom. To emancipate them during her life would, though earnestly wished by me, be attended with such insuperable difficulties on account of their intermixture by marriages with the Dower Negroes, [i.e. those belonging to his wife] as to excite the most painful sensations, if not disagreeable consequences." On their being freed, those "who from old age or bodily infirmities," could not support themselves were to be "comfortably clothed and fed by my heir while they live." Such children "as have no parents living, or if living are unable, or unwilling, to provide for them, shall be bound by the Court until they shall arrive at the age of twenty-five years . . . The Negroes thus bound, are (by their Masters or Mistresses) to be taught to read and write."

Billy Lee, the manservant who had been at his side throughout the war, was to be given "immediate freedom; or if he should prefer it on account of the accidents which have befallen him, and which have rendered him incapable of walking or of any active employment, to remain in the situation he now is, it shall be optional in him to do so: In either case, however, I allow him an annuity of thirty dollars during his natural life, which shall be independent of the victuals and clothes he has been accustomed to receive, if he chooses the last alternative: but in full with his freedom, if he prefers the first: & this I give him as a testimony of my sense of his attachment to me, and for his faithful services during the Revolutionary War."

On the whole the executors appear to have done as he asked, with two exceptions: the provision that the young slaves should be taught to read and write was set aside, as it violated Virginia's laws. And rather than delay their freedom until she died, Martha decided to free George's slaves a year after his death—not out of kindness, but because she was afraid that in order to hasten the day of their liberation they would poison her.

But it was only towards the end of his life that Washington came to disapprove of slavery. To show how much he changed, here is a letter written when he was thirty-four and dated Mount Vernon, July 2nd, 1766. It was addressed to Captain Thompson, of the *Swift*, a schooner trading between Virginia and the West Indies.

"Sir, With this letter comes a Negro (Tom) which I beg the favour of you to sell in any of the islands you may go to, for whatever he will fetch, & bring me in return for him: One hogshead of best molasses; one ditto of best rum; one barrel of limes—if good & cheap; one pot of tamarinds, containing about 10 lbs; two small ditto of mixed sweetmeats—about 5 lbs each; and the residue, much or little, in good old spirits.

"That this fellow is both a rogue and a runaway . . . I shall not pretend to deny. But that he is exceeding healthy, strong, and good at the hoe, the whole neighborhood can testify, & particularly Mr. Johnson and his son, who have both had him under them as foreman of the gang; which gives me reason to hope he may, with your good management, sell well, if kept clean & trim'd up a little when offered to sale. I shall very chearfully allow you the customary commissions on this affair, and must beg the favour of you, (lest he should attempt his escape) to keep him handcuff'd till you get to sea, or in the bay, after which I doubt not but you may make him very useful to you.

"I wish you a pleasant and prosperous passage, and a safe & speedy return," etc, etc.

The next document, written fifteen years later and in a far less breezy tone, was addressed to his cousin, Lund Washington, who was managing the Mount Vernon estate while George was with the army. Though well-intentioned, Lund was politically insensitive and had mismanaged a situation that was embarrassing enough to begin with. This arose from the British policy of sending frigates and gunboats up America's rivers and into her harbors and then bombarding and setting fire to the buildings which, being made of wood, were easy to destroy. The purpose of these raids was to encourage the rebels to "return to their duty," and no matter how often this did not happen, the British kept them up throughout the war. Thus it happened that in April, 1781, only a few months before Yorktown, Captain Graves of the *Savage* sailed up the Potomac, burning and pillaging mansions on both shores. Mount Vernon was spared, but only because it was on a hill high enough to be out of range of the ships' guns; on the other hand, it was an easy walk downhill for anyone wishing to depart. According to a memorandum by Lund these included: "Peter, an old man. Lewis, an old man. Frank, an old man. Frederick, a man about 45 years old, an overseer and valuable. Gunner, a

Mount Vernon, home to the Father of his Country and point of departure for those of his slaves who could manage to escape—on one notable occasion seventeen of them taking refuge on board a Royal Navy frigate that had sailed up the Potomac. Later in life Washington came to deplore slavery, though largely because of the burden on owners of having to support so many non-working children and old people.

man about 45 years old; valuable, a brick maker. Harry, a man about 40 years old, valuable, a horseler [hostler]. Tom, a man about 20 years old, stout and healthy. Sambo, a man about 20 years old, stout and healthy. Thomas, a lad about 17 years old, house servant. Peter, a lad about 15 years old, very likely. Stephen, a man about 20 years old, a cooper by trade. James, a man about 25 years old, stout and healthy. Watty, a man about 20 years old, by trade a weaver. Daniel, a man about 19 years old, very likely. Lucy, a woman about 20 years old. Esther, a woman about 18 years old. Deborah, a woman about 16 years old."

To have seventeen slaves demonstrate their lack of respect by absconding at the first opportunity was bad enough, but then Lund Washington made things worse by trying to negotiate their return—not with them, but with the ship's commander. First he sent Captain Graves a present of some chickens, and when these were well received he went on board where he and the captain spent "some time in perfect harmony." After this Lund dispatched "sheep, hogs, and an abundant supply of other articles as a present to the frigate," clearly in the hope that Captain

Graves would return the compliment by sending back the runaways. Unfortunately for Lund, news that he was trading with the enemy soon got out, and, as Lafayette put it, "this being done by the gentleman who in some measure represents you at your house will certainly have a bad effect, and contrasts with spirited answers from some neighbours that have had their houses burnt accordingly." Stung by this and other criticisms, Washington berated Lund for "the bad example" he had set—"to go on board their vessels; carry them refreshments, commune with a parcel of plundering scoundrels, and request a favor by asking the surrender of my Negroes was exceedingly ill-judged." In the end the *Savage* sailed away with the escaped slaves still on board, and Lund kept his job.

Peter, Lewis, Frank, Frederick, Harry, and the others who boarded the *Savage* were not the only ones to prefer freedom to service in the Washington household. George and Martha were more or less aware of this, and of the problem they faced when, as the First Family, they went to live in Philadelphia, for a while the nation's capital. Their problem was a recent Pennsylvania law giving freedom to any slave who resided in the state for more than six months. Another problem was the city's large and lively community of free blacks, who, it was feared, would give their slaves the wrong ideas. As president, Washington felt that the Pennsylvania law should not apply to him, but to be on the safe side he decided to rotate his slaves between the city and Mount Vernon so that none stayed longer than half a year. This would be to everyone's advantage: slaves "because the idea of freedom might be too great a temptation for them to resist," although of course they would not "be benefited by the change;" and owners because "it might, if they [the slaves] conceived they had a right to it, make them insolent." When giving instructions to his secretary, Washington wrote that the rotation was to be "accomplished under pretext that may deceive both them, and the public." This pretext would be that Martha wanted to visit Mount Vernon and "would naturally bring her maid and Austin and Hercules under the idea of coming home to cook." But this scheme "must be known to none but yourself and Mrs. Washington."

How could Washington have been so obtuse as not to realize that his household staff knew everything that might affect them? At any rate, Hercules, the cook, soon caught on and, according to Tobias Lear, Washington's secretary, claimed to be "extremely unhappy" at the idea that anyone could think that he would even dream of taking advantage of the six months' residence rule. "He said he was mortified to the last degree to think that a suspicion could be entertained of his fidelity or attachment to you, and so much did the poor fellow's feelings appear to be touched that it left no doubt of his sincerity."

For storytelling purposes, Hercules should have decamped immediately after this protestation of personal loyalty; but instead he stayed on, perhaps because he had family back at Mount Vernon, and perhaps also because he found much to enjoy in Philadelphia, where he had many friends, was lord of the presidential kitchen, and was allowed to sell the leftovers and spend the money on theater tickets and elegant clothes. Nevertheless, just as his master was celebrating his sixty-fifth birthday, Hercules disappeared.

"Although diligent inquiries were made for him, he was never apprehended," wrote Tobias Lear, and "all through that spring and summer Mrs. Washington was without a satisfactory cook." She was also personally offended—"blacks are so bad in their nature that they have not the least gratitude for the kindness that may be showed to them." Her husband, convinced that Hercules had gone to ground in Philadelphia, wrote to his steward urging him "to discover (unexpectedly, so as not to alarm him) where his haunts are." Once located, there was no need for legal niceties: Hercules was to be "apprehended at the moment one of the packets for Alexandria is about to sail," and the steward was to "put him therein, to be conveyed hither."

Hercules made good his escape, but in doing so had to abandon a young daughter at Mount Vernon. Soon after, Prince Louis-Philippe, a future king of France but currently an exile, came to visit, and made this entry in his diary: "The general's cook ran away, being now in Philadelphia, and left a little daughter of six at Mount Vernon. Beaudoin [his manservant], ventured that the little girl must be deeply upset that she would never see her father again; she answered, 'Oh, sir! I am very glad because he is free now.'"

On May 23, 1796, the following advertisement appeared in the *Pennsylvania Gazette*: "Absconded from the household of the President of the United States, ONEY JUDGE, a light mulatto girl, much freckled, with very black eyes and bushy black hair, she is of middle stature, slender, and delicately formed, about 20 years of age." Unlike most run-aways, who were dressed in the patched-up, cheap clothing provided by their owners, Oney had "many changes of good clothes, of all sorts, but they are not sufficiently recollected to be described. As there was no sus-picion of her going off, nor no provocation to do so, it is not easy to con-jecture whither she has gone, or fully, what her design is; but as she may attempt to escape by water, all masters of vessels are cautioned against admitting her in to them, although it is probable she will attempt to pass for a free woman, and has, it is said, wherewithal to pay her passage." The reward offered was $10 if taken in Philadelphia or on board a ship in the harbor "and a reasonable additional sum if apprehended at or brought from a greater distance." The advertisement was signed not by the owner, but by his steward, Frederick Kitt.

Oney's own version of events, given many years later, was that "whilst they were packing up to go to Virginia, I was packing to go. I didn't know where; for I knew that if I went back to Virginia, I should never get my liberty. I had friends among the colored people of Philadelphia, had my things carried there beforehand, and left the Washingtons' house while they were eating dinner." She then went to the docks and boarded a ship bound for Portsmouth, New Hampshire. The captain must surely have suspected she was a runaway, but said nothing.

But perhaps Oney had eloped—"seduced" was the term Washing-ton preferred when, after receiving reports that she had been sighted in Portsmouth, he wrote to Oliver Wolcott Jr., the Secretary of the Treasury. Oney, he explained, "has been the particular attendant on Mrs. Wash-ington since she was ten years old, and was handy and useful to her, being perfect mistress of her needle. We have heard that she was seen in New York by someone who knew her, directly after she went off. And since by Miss Langdon, in Portsmouth; who meeting her one day in the street, and knowing her, was about to stop and speak to her, but she brushed quickly by to avoid it." Insisting that Oney was "simple and inoffensive," and not wanting to believe that she would have had the gumption to go off by herself, Washington decided that her escape had been planned by someone else—"someone who knew what he was about, and had the means to defray the expense and to entice her off." In other words, "a Seducer." However, the main business now was to get her back, and to do so discreetly. So, rather than invoke the Fugitive Slave Act, which he had signed into law a few years earlier but which already had many critics, Washington decided to use the power of the federal government to reclaim his private property: the Secretary of the Treasury was to write to the Collector of Customs at Portsmouth, ordering him to arrange for someone to "seize her and put her on board a vessel bound immediately to this place [Philadelphia] or Alexandria, which I should like better"—as being closer, and also to avoid Pennsylvania's anti-slavery laws. In conclusion, "I am sorry to give you, or any one else, trouble on such a trifling occasion, but the ingratitude of the girl, who was brought up and treated more like a child than a servant (and Mrs. Washington's desire to recover her) ought not to escape with impunity."

Though he must have feared that he was risking his job, Joseph Whipple, the collector of customs, did not seize Oney Judge and bundle her off on the next southbound ship. Instead, he invited her to his house on the pretext that he wanted to interview her as a potential domestic. They talked, and, "after a cautious examination, it appeared to me that she had not been decoyed away, as had been apprehended, but that a thirst for compleat freedom which she was informed would take place on her arrival here & in Boston had been her only motive for absconding." Probably realizing that this was not what Washington wanted to hear, but hoping to smooth things over, Whipple went on: "It gave me much satisfaction to find that when uninfluenced by fear she expressed great affection & reverence for her Master and Mistress, and without hesitation declared her willingness to return & to serve with fidelity during the lives of the President & his Lady if she could be freed on their decease, should she outlive them; but that she should rather suffer death than return to slavery & liable to be sold or given to any other person." ("Given to any other person" referred to Martha's decision to pass Oney along to one of her grandchildren, Eliza, daughter of the spoiled and unpleasant Jacky Custis. Martha, a doting grandmother, assumed that she was doing both women a big favor, but Oney had met Eliza, and knew better.) Whipple continued: "Finding this to be her disposition & conceiving it would be a pleasing circumstance both to the President & his Lady should she go back without compulsion, I prevailed on her to confide in my obtaining for her the freedom she so earnestly wished for."

By now the hand that held Whipple's letter must have been trembling with rage at the impudence of the young runaway presuming to negotiate terms with her master. And Whipple could only have made matters worse by pointing out that "many slaves from the Southern States have come to Massachusetts & some to New Hampshire, either of which states they consider an asylum; the popular opinion here in favor of universal freedom has rendered it difficult to get them back to their masters." Finally, and probably hoping to dodge the whole issue, he concluded by advising the president to contact the U.S. Attorney for New Hampshire and ask him "to adopt such measures for returning her to her master as are authorized by the Constitution of the United States." In other words, use the Fugitive Slave law.

Whipple soon got a reply. After a brief preamble he was told that "to enter into such a compromise with her as she suggested to you, is totally inadmissible." Not only would this be "to reward unfaithfulness with a premature preference," it would also "discontent beforehand the minds of all her fellow-servants, who by their steady attachments are far more deserving than herself of favor." Furthermore, as well as her running away "without the least provocation," it was now clear that Oney was a fallen woman. "There is no doubt in this family of her having been seduced and enticed off by a Frenchman," who used to hang around Mount Vernon "but has never been seen here since the girl decamped. We have indeed lately been informed through other channels that she went to Portsmouth with a Frenchman, who getting tired of her, as is presumed, left her." As a result, Oney was probably "in a state of pregnancy." Nevertheless, "if she will return to her former service without obliging me to use compulsory means to effect it, her late conduct will be forgiven by her Mistress, and she will meet with the same treatment from me that all the rest of her family [i.e. the servants and slaves] shall receive. If she will not, you would oblige me by resorting to such measures as are proper to put her on board a vessel bound either for Alexandria or the Federal City." Once again, discretion was needed: "I do not mean, however, by this request that such violent measures should be used as would excite a mob or riot, which might be the case if she has adherents, or even uneasy sensations in the minds of well-disposed citizens; rather than either of these should happen, I would forgo her services altogether."

But far from being the abandoned and pregnant plaything of a French seducer, Oney very soon married a free black sailor, John Staines, and started a family. But even then Washington, very likely at the prodding of Martha, persevered; and hearing that Martha's nephew, Burwell Bassett Jr., was about to make a business trip to Portsmouth, Washington commissioned him to have another try at bringing her back, but cautioning against anything "unpleasant or troublesome." Bassett duly went to see Oney, urged her to go back and, directly contradicting Washington's instructions, promised that on her return she would be freed. To which Oney replied "I am free now, and choose to remain so." Bassett then went off to have dinner with Senator Langdon (whose daughter had been the one to recognize Oney in the street soon after her arrival). While at table, and perhaps in his cups, Bassett announced that he had "orders to bring her and her infant back by force." It is not clear if he would have been acting on his own initiative, or on secret orders from Washington, or at the behest of Aunt Martha. At any rate, Senator Langdon was so shocked that while Bassett was still at table he sent an urgent message to Oney to leave Portsmouth at once, which she did.

A hard life awaited Oney. Her husband and her three children died, her work as a seamstress was poorly paid, and she ended up as a pauper on parish relief. But when interviewed as an old woman by a local paper, she insisted that she had no regrets. She had learned to read and write, had studied the Scriptures and "grown wise unto Salvation." "Mrs. Washington used to read prayers," she said, "but I don't call that praying." But now "I am free, and have, I trust, been made a child of God."

There is a parallel story to the founding of a free and independent United States, one that is in many ways also its mirror image, though on a vastly smaller scale. It is the story of how Sierra Leone, from being an independent country, became a colony of the British Empire—not for the purpose of laying taxes, but in order to provide a haven for poor blacks living in England and former slaves. How this came about is best told through the *Narrative of the Life of David George*.

"I was born [in 1742] in Essex County, Virginia, about fifty or sixty miles from Williamsburg, on Nottaway River, of parents who were brought from Africa but who had not the fear of God before their eyes. The first work I did was fetching water and carding of cotton, afterwards I was sent into the field to work about the Indian corn and tobacco till I was about nineteen years old. I had four brothers and four sisters who, with myself, were all born in slavery. Our master's name was Chapel—a very bad man to the Negroes. My oldest sister was called Patty; I have seen her several times so whipped that her back has been all corruption, as though it would rot.

"I also have been whipped many a time on my naked skin, and sometimes until the blood has run down over my waistband; but the greatest grief I then had was to see them whip my mother, and to hear her on her knees, begging for mercy. She was master's cook, and if they only thought she might do anything better than she did, instead of speaking to her as to a servant, they would strip her directly and cut away.

"Master's rough and cruel usage was the reason for my running away. I left the plantation about midnight, walked all night, got into Brunswick County, then over Roanoke River, and soon met with some white traveling people, who helped me on to the Peedee River. When I had been at work there two or three weeks, a hue and cry found me out, and the master said to me, 'There are thirty guineas offered for you, but I will have no hand in it. I would advise you to make your way toward Savannah River.'

"As I traveled I came to Okemulgee River, near which the Indians perceived my track. They can tell the black people's tracks from their own, because they are hollowed in the midst of their feet, and the blacks' feet are flatter than theirs. They followed my track down to the river, where I was making a log raft to cross over with. One of these Indians was a king, called Blue Salt; he could talk a little broken English. He took and carried me away seventeen or eighteen miles into the woods to his camp, where they had bear meat, turkeys and wild potatoes. I made fences, dug the ground, planted corn, and worked hard, but the people were kind to me.

"From Virginia, S. Chapel, my master's son, came there for me, I suppose eight hundred miles, and paid King Blue Salt for me in rum, linen, and a gun; but before he could take me out of the Creek nation I escaped and went to the Natchez Indians, and got to live with their king, Jack." Before long, King Jack sold him to George Galphin, an influential Indian trader and merchant who lived on the Savannah River at Silver Bluff, "and was very kind to me. I was with him about four years, I think, before I married. Here I lived a bad life and had no serious thoughts about my soul, but after my wife was delivered of her first child a man of my own colour, named Cyrus, who came from Charleston to Silver Bluff, told me one day in the woods that if I lived so I should never see the face of God in Glory."

He struggled hard to find salvation. It was only when he realized that "I could not be saved by my own doings, but that it must be by God's mercy," that "the Lord took away my distress." Soon after, George Liele, who was later to become founding pastor of the First African Baptist Church, in Savannah, came to Silver Bluff where he preached a sermon on the text "Come unto me all ye that labour, are heavy laden, and I will give you rest." Other itinerant Baptist pastors also came to Silver Bluff, and soon there was a congregation of "eight of us who had found the great blessing and mercy from the Lord, and my wife was one of them." All eight were then baptized in the mill stream. The next step came when "I began to exhort in the church, and learned to sing hymns," after which, although he felt "unfit for all that," he was appointed to the office of Elder.

"I proceeded in this way till the American war was coming on, when the ministers were not allowed to come amongst us lest they should furnish us with too much knowledge. The Black people all around attended with us, and as Brother Palmer must not come, I had the whole management and used to preach among them myself. Then I got a spelling book and began to read. As master was a great man he kept a white schoolmaster to teach the white children to read. I used to go to the little children to teach me A, B, C. They would give me a lesson which I tried to learn, and then I would go to them again, and ask them if it was right. The reading so ran in my mind that I think I learned in my sleep as readily as when I was awake, and I can now read the Bible, so that what I have in my heart I can see again in the Scriptures.

"I continued preaching at Silver Bluff till the Church, constituted with light, increased to thirty or more, and till the British came to the city of Savannah and took it."

For the rest of the war the George family stayed in Savannah, where David worked as a butcher. Then, following the British surrender at Yorktown in 1781, he and his family moved to Charleston, where "Major P., the British commander, was very kind to me. When the English were going to evacuate Charlestown, they advised me to go to Halifax, in Nova Scotia, and gave the few black people, and it may be as many as two hundred white people, their passage for nothing." All in all, about thirty thousand Loyalists went to Nova Scotia, of whom about three thousand were black. Discrimination went with them. Blacks were given the worst land in the remotest places—"small allotments in a soil so overrun with rocks and swamps that some of us have actually perished from hunger" wrote one unhappy settler. "Many of my companions have been obliged to give up our small lots, finding that we could not live upon them, and necessity obliged us to cultivate the lands of white men for half the produce."

After arriving in Nova Scotia, David George went to Shelburne, "but found the white people were against me. I began to sing the first night in the woods at a camp, for there were no houses then built, they were just clearing and preparing to erect a town. The black people came far and near, it was so new to them. I kept on so every night in the week, and appointed a meeting for the first Lord's Day in a valley between two hills, close by the river, and a great number of white and black people came, and I was so overjoyed with having an opportunity once more to preach the Word of God that after I had given out the hymn I could not speak for tears. In the afternoon we met again down the river, in the same place, and I had great liberty from the Lord."

They built a simple church. "The worldly Blacks as well as members of the Church assisted in cutting timber in the woods, and in getting shingles, and we used to give a few coppers to buy nails. We were increasing all the winter, and baptized almost every month, and administered the Lord's Supper." Some white people also attended, but not for long. "Soon after this the persecution increased, and became so great that it did not seem possible to preach, and I thought I must leave Shelburne. Several of the black people had houses on my lot, but forty or fifty disbanded soldiers came with the tackle of ships, and turned my dwelling house, and every one of their houses, quite over." Nevertheless, "I continued preaching till they came one night and stood before the pulpit, and swore how they would treat me if I preached again. But I stayed and preached, and the next day they came and beat me with sticks and drove me into the swamp. I returned in the evening and took my wife and children over the river to Birchtown, where some black people were settled."

Meanwhile, across the Atlantic, Granville Sharp and some other leaders of the British campaign to abolish the slave trade had set up the Committee for the Relief of the Black Poor, later to be known as the St. George's Bay Company, and still later as the Sierra Leone Company. Their plan was to establish a settlement on the west coast of Africa that was to be self-governing, with absolute equality between blacks and whites, as symbolized by a green flag with a black hand and a white hand clasped together. It would also serve as a beach-head for spreading Christianity throughout the continent. Among those recruited to run the operation was Olaudah Equiano, who was appointed Commissary of Provisions and Stores for the Black Poor Going to Sierra Leone. Unfortunately for him, Equiano was too honest and too outspoken for his own good. Outraged by the thefts and "flagrant abuses committed by the agent," a white man called Irwin, he let it be known that he would expose him; whereupon Irwin took the initiative and accused Equiano of the same offenses; and so Equiano was the one who got fired. And though later fully vindicated by an official inquiry, he never again had a chance of getting back to Africa.

This was but one of the many setbacks during the first attempt to establish a settlement in Sierra Leone. Far from being the sturdy pioneering types needed, the first settlers were often weakened by poverty and included a number of English prostitutes, "decrepit with disease and so disguised with filth and dirt that I should never have supposed they were born white," according to the hostile testimony of Anna Maria Falconbridge, the discontented wife of Alexander Falconbridge, the ship's surgeon whose description of the horrors of the Middle Passage appeared earlier. According to Mrs. Falconbridge, these fallen women had been lured by crimps to the docks at Wapping, a London slum, where "they were intoxicated with liquor, then inveigled on board of ship, and married to black men, whom they had never seen before!" Other setbacks included their arrival just at the beginning of the rainy season, the erratic and often drunken behavior of the local ruler, King Jemmy, who on one occasion set fire to much of the town, the presence of a slaving station at nearby Bance Island, and outbreaks of fever that soon took off most of the settlers. Within four years of its founding their number had dwindled from several hundred to sixty-four—very much the same thing that had happened to the Pilgrims during their first year at Plymouth.

But before all this bad news was known, it so happened that an Englishman visiting Nova Scotia was invited to dinner by Governor Parr, and while at table gave a glowing description of the Sierra Leone venture. One of the black servants waiting at the governor's table reported what he had heard to Thomas Peters, a former sergeant in the Black Pioneers. Given the treatment they were receiving in Nova Scotia, and the story about the promised land in Africa, it was not long before Peters had made his way to London and was knocking on Granville Sharp's door; and not very long after that before he was back in Nova Scotia, accompanied by John Clarkson, a naval officer whose task it was to check the *bona fides* of those who wanted to leave, and keep full accounts. Clarkson was also responsible for reading out the Proclamation from the governors of what had recently been re-organized as the Sierra Leone Company. Headed "Free Settlement on the Coast of Africa," the proclamation explained that applicants must be able to produce "satisfactory Testimonials of their Characters, (more particularly as to Honesty, Sobriety, and Industry)," known as Certificates of Approbation. After that, "every Free Black (upon producing such a Certificate) shall have a Grant of not less than TWENTY ACRES of LAND for himself, TEN for his Wife, and FIVE for every Child." In addition, "the civil, military, personal and commercial rights and duties of Blacks and Whites shall be the same."

"The white people of Nova Scotia were very unwilling that we should go, though they had been very cruel to us," wrote David George. "They attempted to persuade us that if we went away we should be slaves again." Nevertheless, "the brethren and sisters all around St. Johns, Halifax, and other places, Mr. Wesley's people [i.e. Methodists] and all, consulted what was best to do, and sent in their names to me, to give to Mr.

Founded as a "Province of Freedom" for "the black poor of London," the settlement at Sierra Leone expanded after the Revolutionary War with the arrival of former Loyalist slaves who had been having a hard time in Nova Scotia. After the British had abolished the slave trade, its capital, Freetown, became the home port for ships of the Royal Navy engaged in suppressing the trade.

Clarkson, and I was to tell him that they were willing." Eventually, and to the great dismay of the whites, who would be losing their servants and hired hands, 1196 signed on, about a third of Nova Scotia's black population (including a former slave called Henry Washington, who had escaped from Mt. Vernon in 1776). The fleet set sail in January, 1792. "Our passage to Sierra Leone was seven weeks stormy weather. Several persons died on the voyage of a catching fever, among whom were three of my Elders." But at last they neared the African coast. "There was a great joy to see the land, the high mountain, at some distance from Freetown, where we now live." Although to most sailors the mountain looked like a lion—hence the name, Sierra Leone—to these pilgrims it "appeared like a cloud to us," a reference to the pillar of cloud that led the Israelites out of Egypt. "I preached the first Lord's Day," wrote David George. "It was a blessed time."

Many disappointments and troubles were in store for the settlers. Newcomers had rights, but were given very little say in how they were governed; the slaving station on nearby Bance Island was a constant menace; the thatched houses easily caught fire; they were attacked by a

French ship, whose crew, a "savage-looking set of Republican raga-muffins," wantonly destroyed many of their buildings. "Burning fevers," wrote Mrs. Falconbridge, led to "five, six and seven dying daily, and buried with as little ceremony as so many dogs or cats." There were also the frequent but unwelcome visits of King Jemmy, who "never returns home until he has drank a sufficient quantity of rum or brandy to kindle his savage nature for any manner of wickedness." Other visitors included armies of cockroaches and ants which "come from their nests in such formidable force as to strike terror wherever they go," and could be repulsed only by being doused with boiling water. Last but not least, "we have been twice visited by some ferocious wild beast, supposed to be a Tyger."

But if ever the settlers thought of giving up, they had only to think back on what they had endured in America, and forward to what they could hope for in Africa. As to the first, here is what a former slave called Warwick Francis told the black Quaker merchant Paul Cuffe during his visit to Sierra Leone in 1812. (Francis' speech, or Cuffe's transcription, is a bit confused, but the meaning is clear enough):

> "Sufferings and usage . . . seen among slaves in America [committed] by Aron Jelot, a doctor. A slave boy tied to a wooden spit so near the fire that it scorch him well, and basted with salt and water, the same as you would a pig.
>
> "I have also seen Joseph Belseford in the same county chain two of his slaves and make them walk on a plank at a mill pond and those two got drowned. And the said Joseph Belseford gave a man 360 lashes, and then wash him down with salt and water and after that took a brand that he branded his cattle with and make the brand red hot and put it on his buttocks, the same as you would brand a creature.
> "John Draten, I have seen him take his slave and put them in a tierce [cask] and nailed spikes in the tierce and roll down a steep hill.
>
> "I have seen them with a thumb screw screwed till the blood gushed out of their nails. This I have seen at Isaac Macpherson's . . . What I have said I am an eye witness to, it is not what I have heard."

As to what they could hope for in Africa, they were now free, and among their freedoms was the right to practice their own forms of religion, a right of which thy took full advantage. "Among the black settlers are seven religious sects," wrote Mrs. Falconbridge, "and each sect has one or more preachers attached to it, who alternately preach throughout the night. Indeed, I never met with, heard, or read of any set of people observing the same appearance of Godliness; for I do not remember, since they first landed here, my ever awaking (and I have awoke at every hour of the night), without hearing preachings from some quarter or another."

Among the stated reasons for founding the colony had been "to civilize and Christianize a great Continent, to bring it out of Darkness, and to abolish the Trade in Men." This was a cause dear to the heart of David George, who for one of his sermons took as his text Exodus 14: 13. ("And Moses said unto the people, Fear ye not, stand still, and see the salvation of the Lord, which he will shew you this day.") Part of his sermon ran:

"We all mind since it was so with us, we was in slavery not many years ago! Some maybe worse oppressed than others, but we was all under the yoke. And what then? God saw our afflictions, and heard our cry, and showed his salvation in delivering us, and bringing us over the mighty waters to this place. Now, stand still and see the salvation of God. God made his salvation go from this city through this heathen land; and as Moses and the children of Israel sung a song when they were delivered and had seen the salvation of God, so I hope to see the heathens about us going through the streets of this city, singing hallelujahs and doxologies to God. I hope to see it . . . Stand still, and see what God is doing for our nation, putting into the hearts of his people to come from a far distant nation, to come over the mighty waters and great deep, to bring the salvation of God to this nation, to Africans. Stand ye still, and let your hearts be lifted up to Him."

Following abolition of the trans-Atlantic slave trade in 1808 there was a sharp and continuing rise in the internal trade: every year thousands of slaves from the "breeding states" (principally Virginia and Maryland) were raised for the sole purpose of being sold to the cotton and rice-growing states. Washington, D. C. was the principal market for this trade—hence the dome of the Capitol in the background. Once sold, slave families were broken up, shackled, formed into coffles, and marched down to the docks at Alexandria for shipment to New Orleans, where they were re-sold.

CHAPTER 7

THE PECULIAR INSTITUTION

THIS WAS A TERM SOUTHERNERS CAME UP WITH WHEN LOOKING FOR A euphemism for slavery, using "peculiar" in the sense of "distinctive" or "special to us." Like many another institution that evolved over a long period of time and in different places, it was complex, often irrational and contradictory, based on powerful economic interests and wishful thinking. As a guide to this ramshackle structure, here is a catalog of some of its parts.

THE CONSTITUTION

There were at least two ways of looking at this document. First there was the "miracle at Philadelphia" school of thought, according to which a handful of exceptionally far-sighted and high-minded statesmen—"an assembly of demi-gods," as Jefferson put it—brought forth the best system of government the world has ever seen. Then there was the "compact with the Devil" view, popular in the nineteenth century with abolitionists and in the twentieth with radicals and communists. To these critics the constitution, for all its talk of rights and liberties, was little more than a conspiracy on the part of property-owners to protect their interests and thwart the will of the people, while also condemning millions of slaves to decades of suffering, and making inevitable a bloody civil war.

How justified was this view? Consider the notorious "three-fifths" provision (Article 1, Section 2, Clause 3), which greatly increased the political power of the slaveholders: "Representatives and direct Taxes shall be apportioned among the several States which may be included within this Union according to their respective Numbers, which shall be determined by adding to the whole Number of free Persons, including those bound to Service for a Term of Years [i.e. white indentured servants], and

excluding Indians not taxed, three fifths of all other Persons [i.e. slaves]."
Then there was Article 1, Section 9, Clause 1, which allowed the slave
trade to continue for another twenty years: "The Migration or Importation of such Persons as any of the States now existing shall think proper
to admit, shall not be prohibited by Congress prior to the Year one thousand eight hundred and eight . . ." Section 4 of Article 4 guaranteed that
the federal government would protect every state against both invasion
and "domestic violence," i.e. a slave insurrection. And Clause 3 of Section 2 of Article 4 stated that "no Person held to Service or Labor in one
State, under the Laws thereof, escaping into another, shall, in Consequence of any Law or Regulation therein, be discharged from such Service or Labor, but shall be delivered up on Claim of the Party to whom
such Service or Labor may be due."

This last clause was followed in 1793 by the Fugitive Slave Act, "an
act respecting fugitives from justice, and persons escaping the service of
their masters." Under this law owners could retrieve slaves who had escaped to a free state by having them arrested, often by professional slave-
catchers, and brought before a judge or local magistrate. There was no
trial by jury, or appeal from the judge's decision. Anyone sheltering a
fugitive slave could be fined the large sum of $500. For the fugitives, this
law meant that so long as they remained anywhere in the United States
they were never free of the threat of being returned to slavery; hence the
exodus to Canada. Owners also were unhappy with the law since the
trouble and expense of capturing fugitives fell upon them, and not upon
officials. Also, many of the free states passed "personal liberty laws"
which increased the slave-owner's burden of proof and allowed for jury
trials and appeals from judges' decisions.

The Constitutional Convention shirked the issue of slavery largely
because of the flat refusal of Georgia and South Carolina to make it a
concern of the national government. They would accept such federal benefits as the three-fifths rule, help in arresting and returning runaways,
and assistance in putting down a slave insurrection, but in all other respects slavery was a matter for the states only; otherwise they would refuse to join the Union. None of the demi-gods called their bluff, despite
the fact that because of its large slave population South Carolina, more
than any other state, needed the support of a strong central government.
Georgia too could hardly have afforded to remain outside the Union,

being, in the words of Washington, "a weak state with powerful tribes of Indians in its rear, and the Spanish on its flank."

Faced with this obduracy, and comforted by the vague hope that slavery would somehow or other just fade away, most members of the convention agreed with Oliver Ellsworth of Connecticut that "the wisdom and morality" of slavery were "considerations belonging to the States themselves." George Mason of Virginia was one of the few to oppose the compromise, warning that "Providence punishes national sins by national calamities," and prophesying that slavery would "bring the judgment of Heaven." In the end, Mason refused to sign, declaring that "he would sooner chop off his right hand than put it to the Constitution as it now stands."

ABOLITION IN THE NORTH

"I wish most sincerely there was not a Slave in the province," wrote Abigail Adams during the Revolutionary War to her husband, John. "It always appear'd a most iniquitous scheme to me—fight ourselfs for what we are daily robbing and plund'ring from those who have as good a right to freedom as we have."

A few years later Abigail got her wish when her husband was elected to the convention that was to draft a new constitution for Massachusetts. The convention began by appointing a committee of thirty, which in turn appointed a sub-committee of three, which then left everything to John Adams, who was happy to oblige. He began, as must all writers of constitutions, with a preamble setting forth a number of general principles, the first of which was that "all men are born equally free and independent." However, the sub-committee and then the full committee modified this so that all men were "born free and equal," which was not quite the same thing, but enough to end slavery in his state.

This principle was enforced a little over a year later when a slave called Quock Walker (Quock probably being a form of the Ghanaian name Kwaku, meaning "boy born on Wednesday") sued for his freedom on the grounds that it had been promised him when he turned 25. The promise had been made by a former owner who had died, and his new owner refused to honor it. The case came to trial in 1781 in Western Massachusetts and concluded with the judge declaring: "As to the doctrine of slavery and the right of Christians to hold Africans in perpetual servitude, and sell and treat them as we do our horses and cattle, that, it is true, has been heretofore countenanced by the Province Laws." But now "a different idea has taken place with the people of America, more favorable to the rights of mankind, and to that natural, innate desire of Liberty, with which Heaven (without regard to color, complexion, or shape of noses) has inspired all the human race. And upon this ground our Constitution of Government . . . sets out with declaring that all men are born free and equal —and that every subject is entitled to liberty, and to have it guarded by the laws, as well as life and property—and in short is totally repugnant to the idea of being born slaves. This being the case, I think the idea of slavery is inconsistent with our own conduct and Constitution; and there can be no such thing as perpetual servitude of a rational creature."

Since fewer than two per cent of its population were slaves, abolition caused no great upheaval in Massachusetts. Vermont, which had almost no slaves, had banned slavery outright as early as 1777. Other northern states followed suit, most of them declaring slavery to be wrong but nevertheless abolishing it only gradually. Pennsylvania, while allowing that slavery was "disgraceful to any people, and more especially to those who have been contending in the great cause of liberty themselves," did not free children born after March 1, 1780, until they reached the age of twenty-eight. (Technically they were indentured servants rather than slaves, but this did not lessen their obligation to their masters.) In 1788 the law was amended to prevent owners from getting around it by moving their pregnant slaves out of the state. It also declared that husbands, wives and children were not to be separated, and imposed a ban on building and supplying slave ships. In Connecticut slave children born after March 1, 1784, were not freed until they were twenty-five, and New York had similar provisions. As a result of this gradualism, in 1810 there were still 27,000 slaves in the North; on the other hand, the number of free blacks had grown from a few hundred at the start of the Revolution to about 100,000.

For the most part, emancipation did not mean full citizenship. Once freed, most slaves went to live in cities, where they were resented by working-class whites, routinely excluded from the better jobs and kept from voting by property qualifications—as de Tocqueville observed, "the prejudice which repels Negroes seems to increase in proportion as they are emancipated." On the positive side, they could no longer be sold, could keep what they earned, start their own small businesses, choose their own names, marry whomever they chose, and establish their own churches and way of life.

THE SOUTH

Here the story was very different. For a while Virginia flirted with the idea of gradual emancipation, but this went nowhere, and in the meantime other states were busy tightening their laws. William Wells Brown summed up the result in *Extracts from the American Slave Code*, which he published as an appendix to his autobiography. "The following are mostly abridged selections from the statutes of the slave states," he wrote. "Most of the important provisions here cited, though placed under the name of only one state, prevail in nearly all the states, with slight variations in language, and some diversity in the penalties." Here are some of the laws he quoted:

> *Louisiana*: "A slave is one who is in the power of his master, to whom he belongs. The master may sell him, dispose of his person, his industry and his labor; he can do nothing, possess nothing, nor acquire anything, but what must belong to his master . . . Slaves are incapable of inheriting or transmitting property . . . No slave can be party in a civil suit, or witness in a civil or criminal matter, against any white person . . . Every slave found on horseback without a written permission from his master shall receive twenty-five lashes . . . It is lawful to fire upon runaway Negroes who are armed, and upon those who, when pursued, refuse to surrender . . . A slave for willfully striking his master or mistress, or the child of either, or his white overseer, so as to cause a bruise or shedding of blood, shall be punished with death . . . Any person cutting or breaking any iron chain or collar used to prevent the escape of slaves, shall be fined not less than two hundred dollars, nor more than one thousand dollars, and be imprisoned not more than two years nor less than six months . . . All slaves sentenced to death or perpetual imprisonment, in virtue of existing laws, shall be paid for out of the public treasury, provided the sum paid shall not exceed $300 for each slave."

Mississippi: "Penalty for any slave or free colored person exercising the functions of a minister of the gospel, thirty-nine lashes; but any master may permit his slave to preach on his own premises, no slaves but his own being permitted to assemble . . . Penalty for teaching a slave to read, imprisonment for one year. For using language having a tendency to promote discontent among free colored people, or insubordination among slaves, imprisonment at hard labor, not less than three, nor more than twenty-one years, or death, at the discretion of the court . . . Every Negro or mulatto found in the state not able to show himself entitled to freedom, may be sold as a slave."

Alabama: "No slave can be emancipated but by a special act of the Legislature."

Georgia: "Penalty for any free person of color (except regularly articled seamen) coming into the state, a fine of one hundred dollars, and on failure of payment to be sold as a slave . . .Penalty for permitting a slave to labor or do business for himself, except on his master's premises, thirty dollars . . . Every colored person is presumed

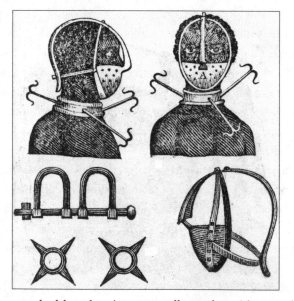

Most southern states had laws barring unusually cruel punishments, but these were rarely enforced since slaves could not testify in court against whites. This left sadistic owners free to come up with devices such as this. The prongs sticking out from the collar were to prevent the wearer from resting his head when lying down.

to be a slave, unless he can prove himself free . . . Any person who sees more than seven men slaves without any white person, in a high road, may whip each slave twenty lashes."

South Carolina: A few additions had been made to the draconian laws passed in the wake of the Stono Insurrection : "A slave endeavoring to entice another slave to run away, if provision be prepared for the purpose of aiding or abetting such endeavor, shall suffer death . . . Meetings for religious worship before sunrise, or after nine o'clock P.M., unless a majority are white persons, are forbidden."

Tennessee: "No slave can be emancipated but on condition of immediately removing from the state, and the person emancipating shall give bond, in a sum equal to the slave's value, to have him removed."

William Wells Brown claimed that these laws cut only one way. "Has the case ever occurred where the slaveholder has been sent to the state's prison, or anything of the kind, for ill-treating or for murdering a slave? No such case is upon record." This was not quite true. For example, in December, 1839, in North Carolina, a man called Hoover was put on trial for the murder of his slave, named Mira. "Through a period of four months, including the latter stages of pregnancy, delivery, and recent recovery therefrom, he beat her with clubs, iron chains and other deadly weapons, time after time; burnt her; inflicted stripes over and often, with scourges, which literally excoriated her whole body; forced her out to work in inclement weather without being duly clad; provided for her insufficient food; exacted labor beyond her strength, and wantonly beat her because she could not comply with his requisitions. These enormities, besides others too disgusting to be particularly designated, without his heart once relenting . . . he did not relax even up to the last hours of his victim's existence." Hoover's excuses were "that she stole his turnips and sold them to the worthless people in the neighborhood, and that she had attempted to burn his barn, and was disobedient and impudent to her mistress." Hoover was convicted but such cases were rare.

PLANTATIONS

Although by the time of the Civil War most owners had fewer than ten slaves—some of whom would have been domestic servants—it was the large plantations that set their stamp on the peculiar institution. Three first-person descriptions of plantation life appear in the next two chapters. In the meantime, here are some features of the system:

> *Overseers:* "On larger estates, employing fifty or a hundred, or perhaps two hundred hands, an overseer is deemed indispensable. These gentlemen ride into the field on horseback, without an exception, to my knowledge, armed with pistol, bowie knife, whip, and accompanied by several dogs. They follow, equipped in this fashion, in rear of the slaves, keeping a sharp lookout upon them all. The requisite qualifications in an overseer are utter heartlessness, brutality and cruelty. It is his business to produce large crops, and if that is accomplished, no matter what amount of suffering it may have cost."
>
> —SOLOMON NORTHUP

Some overseers, like this letter-writer to *De Bow's Review*, prided themselves on the efficiency of their management techniques. For example, slaves should not be allowed to cook for themselves for two reasons. One, "the cooking being done in a hurry, is badly done." Two, "to make one Negro cook for all is a saving of time. If there be but ten hands, and these are allowed two hours at noon, one of which is employed in cooking their dinner," that hour could have been "spent in ploughing or hoeing, and would be equal to ten hours work of one hand."

Overseers should also see to it that the hands got enough sleep. "They are thoughtless, and if allowed to do so will sit up late of nights." The length of daytime rest periods should vary according to the weather; the hotter the day, the longer the rest—in spring "a hand need not be allowed any more time at noon than is sufficient to eat," but "in July and August, three hours rest at noon." Result: "hands have better health, and can do more work," and "will certainly last much longer."

"While at work, they should be brisk. If one is called to you or sent from you, and he does not move briskly, chastise him at once. If this does not answer, repeat the dose and double the quantity. When at work, I have no objection to their whistling or singing some lively tune, but no drawling tunes are allowed in the field, for their motions are almost certain to keep in time with the music." Another point: "Implicit obedience should be required and rigidly enforced. Firmness of manner and promptness to enforce obedience will save much trouble, and be the means of avoiding the necessity for much whipping. The Negro should feel that his master is his law-giver and judge, and yet is his protector and friend, but so far above him as never to be approached save in the most respectful manner."

Drivers. "Besides the overseer, there are drivers under him, the number being in proportion to the number of hands in the field. The drivers are black, who in addition to the performance of their equal share of the work, are compelled to do the whipping of their several gangs. Whips hang around their necks, and if they fail to use them thoroughly, they are whipped themselves."   SOLOMON NORTHUP

The Whip. "The whip used by the overseers on the cotton plantations is different from all other whips that I have ever seen. The staff is about twenty or twenty-two inches in length, with a large and heavy head, which is often loaded with a quarter or half a pound of lead, wrapped in cat-gut . . . The lash is ten feet long, made of small strips of buckskin, tanned so as to be dry and hard, and plaited carefully and closely together, of the thickness, in the largest part, of a man's little finger, but quite small at each extremity. At the farthest end of this thong is attached a cracker, nine inches in length, made of strong sewing silk, twisted and knotted until it feels as firm as the hardest twine. This whip, in an unpractised hand, is a very awkward and inefficient weapon," but "when wielded by an experienced arm, it is one of the keenest instruments of torture ever invented."

—CHARLES BALL

"Husbands always went to the woods when they know the wives was due for a whipping, but in the field they dare not leave. Had to stay there, not daring even look like they didn't like it. Charlie Jones was one slave that had his wife working in the same field with him. Was planting tobacco—he was setting out and she was hilling. Annie was big with child and getting near her time, so one day she made a slip and chopped a young shoot down. Old man Diggs, the overseer, come running up screaming at her and it made her more nervous and she chopped off another one. Old overseer lift up that rawhide and beat Annie cross the back and shoulders till she fell to the ground. And Charlie, he just stood there hearing his wife scream, and a-staring at the sky, not daring to look or even say a word."

—JORDAN JOHNSON

The Paddle. "The paddle is made of a piece of hickory timber, about one inch thick, three inches in width, and about eighteen inches in length. The part which is applied to the flesh is bored full of quarter inch auger holes, and every time this is applied to the flesh of the victim the blood gushes through the holes of the paddle, or a blister makes it appearance. The persons who are thus flogged are always stripped naked, and their hands tied together. They are then bent over double, their knees are forced between their elbows, and a stick is put through between the elbows and the bend of the legs, in order to hold the victim in that position while the paddle is applied."

—HENRY BIBB

Dogs. A typical advertisement:

"The undersigned having an excellent pack of HOUNDS for trailing and catching runaway slaves, informs the public that his prices in future will be as follows for such services:—

"For each day employed in hunting or trailing...................... $2.50
"For catching each slave... $10.00
"For going over ten miles and catching slaves.................... $20.00

If sent for, the above prices will be exacted in cash. The subscriber resides one mile and half south of Dadeville, Ala. September 1, 1852. B. Black.

—HARRIET BEECHER STOWE: *A Key to Uncle Tom's Cabin*

"They had bloodhounds too; they'd run you away in the woods. Send for a man that has hounds to track you if you run away. They'd run you and bay you, and a white man would ride up there and say,

'If you hit one of the hounds I'll blow your brains out.' He'd say, 'Your damn brains.' Them hounds would worry you and bite you and have you bloody as a beef, but you dassent to hit one of them. They would tell you to stand still and put your hands over your privates. I don't guess they'd have killed you, but you believed they would. They wouldn't try to keep the hounds off of you. They would set them on you to see them bite you. Five or six or seven hounds biting you on every side and a man setting on a horse holding a doubled shotgun on you."   —HENRY WALSON

There were several ways to throw dogs off the scent. "I could do it with red pepper," recalled John Warren, who escaped from Mississippi to Canada. "Another way I have practised is to dig into a grave where a man has been buried a long time, get the dust of the man, make it into a paste with water, and put it on the feet, knees, and elbows, or wherever I touched the bushes. The dogs won't follow that." Turpentine and onions were also used. So were Indian turnips, dried, pulverized and tied in bags, around the feet. "No bloodhound could trail a bit further after smelling it," claimed Gus Smith of Missouri.

Patrols. "On Bayou Boeuf there is an organization of patrollers, as they are styled, whose business it is to seize and whip any slave they may find wandering from the plantation. They ride on horseback, headed by a captain, armed, and accompanied by dogs. They have the right, either by law or by general consent, to inflict discretionary chastisement upon a black man caught beyond the boundaries of his master's estate without a pass, and even to shoot him if he attempts to escape. Each company has a certain distance to ride up and down the bayou. They are compensated by the planters, who contribute in proportion to the number of slaves they own. The clatter of their horses' hoofs dashing by can be heard at all hours of the night, and frequently they may be seen driving a slave before them, or leading him by a rope fastened around his neck, to his owner's plantation."
                                                    —SOLOMON NORTHUP

"These are just about the worst fellows that can be found; as bad as any you could pick up on the wharves . . . If a slave don't open his door to them, at any time of night, they break it down. They steal his money, if they can find it, and act just as they please with his wives and daughters. If a husband dares to say a word, or even look as if he wasn't quite satisfied, they tie him up and give him thirty-nine lashes. If there's any likely young girls in a slave's hut, they're mighty apt to have business there . . . Oh how often I've seen the poor girls sob and cry when there's been such goings on! Maybe you think, because they're slaves, they ain't got no feelings and no shame. A woman's being a slave don't stop her genteel ideas; that is, according to their way, and as far as they can. They know they must submit to their masters; besides, their masters, maybe, dress 'em up, and make 'em little presents, and give 'em more privileges, while the whim lasts; but that ain't like having a parcel of low, dirty, swearing, drunk patter rollers let loose among 'em, like so many hogs. This breaks down their spirits dreadfully, and makes 'em wish they were dead."

—LEWIS CLARK

"I remember one time they was a dance at one of the houses in the quarters. All the niggers was a-laughing and a-patting they feet and a-singing . . . The paddyrollers shove the door open and start grabbing us. Uncle Joe's son he decide they was one time to die and he start to fight. He say he tired standing so many beatings, he just can't stand no more. The paddyrollers start beating him and he start fighting. Oh Lordy, it were trouble. They whip him with a cowhide for a long time, then one of them take a stick and hit him over the head, and just bust his head wide open. The poor boy fell on the floor just a-moaning and a-groaning. The paddyrollers just whip about half a dozen other niggers and send 'em home and leave us with the dead boy."

—FANNIE MOORE

Poor Whites. "The institution of slavery has produced not only heathenish, degraded, miserable slaves, but it produces a class of white people who are, by universal admission, more heathenish, degraded and miserable. The institution of slavery has accomplished the double feat, in America, not only of degrading and brutalising her black working classes, but of producing, notwithstanding a fertile soil and abundant room, a poor white population as degraded and brutal as ever existed in any of the most crowded districts of Europe.

"The way it is done can be made apparent in a few words. 1. The distribution of the land into large plantations, and the consequent sparseness of settlement, make any system of common school education impracticable. 2. The same case operates with regard to the preaching of the Gospel. 3. The degradation of the idea of labor, which results inevitably from enslaving the working class, operates to a great extent in preventing respectable working men of the middling classes from settling or remaining in slave States." As a consequence, "without schools or churches, these miserable families grow up heathen on a Christian soil, in idleness, vice, dirt, and discomfort of all sorts. They are the pest of the neighborhood, the scoff and contempt or pity even of the slaves. The expressive phrase, so common in the mouths of the Negroes, of 'poor white trash,' says all for this luckless race of beings that can be said . . . This miserable class of whites form, in all the Southern States, a material for the most horrible and ferocious of mobs. Utterly ignorant, and inconceivably brutal, they are like some blind, savage monster which, when aroused, tramples heedlessly over everything in its way.

"Singular as it may appear, though slavery is the cause of the misery and degradation of this class, yet they are the most vehement and ferocious advocates of slavery. The reason is this: they feel the scorn of the upper classes, and their only means of consolation is in having a class below them, whom they may scorn in turn. To set the negro at liberty would deprive them of this last comfort; and accordingly no class of men advocate slavery with such frantic and unreasoning violence, or hate abolitionists with such demoniac hatred. The leaders of the community, those men who play upon other men with as little care for them as a harper plays on a harp, keep this blind, furious monster of the MOB very much as an overseer keeps his plantation-dogs, as creatures to be set on to any man or thing whom they may choose to have put down. These leading men have used the cry of 'abolitionism' over the mob much as a huntsman uses the 'set on' to his dogs. Whenever they have a purpose to carry, a man to put down, they have only to raise this cry, and the monster is wide awake, ready to spring wherever they shall send him." —*A Key to Uncle Tom's Cabin*

Dueling. Slavery was also responsible for a readiness to settle disputes by violent means. Reports of "affrays, duels, street-fights, shootings, stabbings and assassinations," wrote the visiting traveler, J.S. Buckingham, filled southern newspapers, and were so commonplace as to arouse only passing interest. For example, the day he arrived in Charleston, "there was a duel fought in the public street, and in the presence of many people, none of whom interfered. Two young men from the country were in attendance at the Court of Law then sitting in Charleston, and some angry words having passed between them, there was an immediate challenge given and accepted; when the parties, either having pistols with them, or procuring them very speedily, repaired to the public street, and there, in the middle of the day, and in the presence of several spectators and passers-by, measured off twelve paces and exchanged fire. One of the combatants was shot through the cheek, and disfigured for life, and the other was slightly wounded in the thigh. The parties then withdrew from the combat, but no notice was taken of the affair by the public authorities, and with the community it excited no sensation beyond the passing hour."

In 1839, while residing on her husband's plantation on St. Simon's Island, Fanny Kemble read this story in the *Brunswick Advertiser* about two neighbors who had quarreled about a property line: "It is with pain we lay before our readers an account of a fatal affray which took place in this city on Monday last, between Mr. John A. Wylly and Dr. Thomas F. Hazzard, both of this county . . . They met on the piazza of the Oglethorpe House, and after exchanging a few words, Mr. W. struck Dr. H. with a cane. Judge Henry, who was here holding a term of the Supreme Court, and Col. Du Bignon, happening to be present, immediately interfered and succeeded in separating them. A short time after, Mr. W. again met Dr. H. in the entry of the house and spat in his face, when the latter drew a pistol and fired, the ball of which passed directly through Mr. W.'s heart. He reeled a moment, at the same time striking at the doctor with his cane, then fell and expired instantly."

A few days later, Fanny went to visit some genteel neighbors. They discussed the fight "and both ladies agreed that there was not the slightest chance of Dr. H.'s being punished in any way for the murder he had committed; that shooting down a man who had offended you was part of the morals and manners of the Southern gentry, and that the circumstance was one of quite too frequent occurrence to cause any sensation, even in the small community where it obliterated one of the principal members of the society. If the accounts given by these ladies of the character of the planters in this part of the South may be believed, they must be as idle, arrogant, ignorant, dissolute and ferocious as that medieval chivalry to which they are fond of comparing themselves."

Censorship. This took two forms: self-censorship—widespread, unacknowledged, and highly effective; and imposed censorship, sometimes official, but more often the work of Committees of Vigilance backed by Lynch Law and mobs. Here, from *The Life of Benjamin Lundy,* is one example: "At Charleston, South Carolina, on the 29th of July, [1835] it became known soon after the arrival of the mail from New York, that a large quantity of abolition tracts had come in it. This fact, being published in the *Courier* of the next morning, caused a great excitement. On the succeeding evening, between 10 and 11 o'clock, a number of persons assembled, forcibly entered the post office by wrenching open a window, and carried off the packages containing 'the incendiary matter,' as it was called." Next evening, in accordance with a notice published in the newspapers, "the pamphlets, &c. were burnt at 8 o'clock, P.M., opposite the main guard house, three thousand persons being present." At the same time, William Lloyd Garrison and other abolitionists were burned in effigy.

In August of the same year an unfortunate youth named Amos Dresser, "a former student of Lane [Theological] Seminary and a member of the Anti-Slavery Society established at that institution, was arrested at a Methodist camp-meeting ground near Nashville, Tennessee, on a charge of having in his possession, and distributing, incendiary abolition publications. He had left Cincinnati on the 1st of July, with the 'Cottage Bible' [edited for home study] and some other religious books for sale, and had also taken some Anti-Slavery publications, the most of which he left at Danville, Ky., where an Anti-Slavery Society existed. On his arrival at Nashville, he sent his barouche [carriage] to be repaired, inadvertently leaving in the box some anti-slavery tracts and other pamphlets. The workmen employed on the barouche found and examined the tracts, one of which was a number of the *Anti-Slavery Record*, containing 'a print of a drove of slaves chained, the two foremost having violins on which they were playing—the American flag waving in the center, while the slave-driver with his whip was urging on the rear.' It was then reported that Mr. Dresser had been 'circulating incendiary periodicals among the free colored people, and trying to excite the slaves to insurrection.'" Hauled before "a committee of vigilance consisting of sixty prominent citizens," Dresser denied preaching insurrection, claimed that the offending tract had been nothing more than a wrapper for the Cottage Bible, and while acknowledging "his anti-slavery sentiments, declared that he sought the good both of the master and the slave; contemplated emancipation through persuasion; and that in his few interviews with slaves he had recommended to them quietness, patience, and submission. The committee, having deliberated, found him guilty: 1. Of being a member of the Ohio Anti-Slavery Society. 2. Of having in his possession periodicals published by the American Anti-Slavery Society; and thirdly they declared that they believed he had circulated those periodicals, and advocated the principles inculcated in them. They therefore sentenced him to receive twenty lashes on his bare back, and to leave the place in twenty-four hours. He was then taken to the public square, it being near midnight; and the punishment was inflicted by Mr. Braughton, the principal police officer, with a heavy cow-skin, in the presence of a large circle of spectators."

Censorship was also enforced by state laws. In 1857, Samuel Green, a free Negro of Cambridge, Maryland, was indicted "for having in his possession papers, pamphlets and pictorial representations having a tendency to create discontent, etc, among the people of color in the State." The evidence was collected when "a party of gentlemen from New Market district went at night to Green's house and made search, whereupon was found a volume of *Uncle Tom's Cabin*, a map of Canada, several schedules of routes to the North, and a letter from his son in Canada." There were two trials. The first was "for having in possession the letter, map, and route schedules," but despite the fact that "nine-tenths of the community in which he lived believed that he had a hand in the running away of slaves, it was the opinion

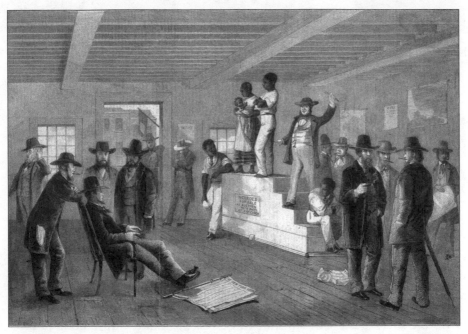

Captioned "A slave auction in Virginia," this picture appeared in The Illustrated London News *in 1861. The Civil War was followed closely in Britain, where opinion was divided. A desire not to offend readers who sympathized with the South may account for the picture's somewhat neutral style.*

of the court that the law under which he was indicted was not applicable to the case." Green was discharged, but was then "immediately arraigned upon another indictment, for having in possession *Uncle Tom's Cabin.*" This time there were no legal quibbles, and he was "found guilty by the court, and sentenced to the penitentiary for the term of ten years."

THE INTERNAL SLAVE TRADE

During the first sixty years of the nineteenth century some one million slaves were transferred from the east to the newly acquired territories in the southwest, there to work on the sugar and cotton plantations. The principal slave-exporting states were Maryland, Virginia, Kentucky, North Carolina, Tennessee, and Missouri; these were known as "breeding states." Traders would travel from plantation to plantation, or market to market, steadily adding to their stock. The slaves traveled in coffles, the men roped or chained together, the women and children unfettered. Sometimes they were shipped south by boat, but more usually they went on foot. Journeys were usually made in winter, when there was less work to be done.

Ten years seems to have been the lowest age at which slaves were bought or sold without their parents. "I wish to purchase immediately, for the South, any number of Negroes from 10 to 30 years of age, for which I will pay the very highest cash prices," ran an advertisement in the *Alexandria Gazette*. And from the *Lynchburg Virginian*: "The subscriber . . . is giving the highest cash prices for negroes between the ages of 10 and 30 years." But there were many exceptions, as in this from the *New Orleans Bulletin*: "Negros for Sale.—A negro woman 21 years of age, and has two children, one eight and the other three years. Said negroes will be sold separately or together as desired. She will be sold for cash, or exchanged for groceries." And from the *Milledgeville Journal*: "Executor's Sale. Agreeable to an order of the court of Wilkinson County, will be sold on the first Tuesday in April next, before the Court-house door in the town of Irwinton, one negro girl, about two years old, named Rachel, belonging to the estate of William Chambers dec'd."

Almost always, being sold meant separation for life. There was no exchange of letters, since parents did not know where their children had gone; also, most slaves were illiterate, and none were allowed to use the mails. Contemporary estimates of the numbers sold varied greatly. In 1836 the *Virginia Times* put the figure from that state at forty thousand a year. In 1837, the Rev. Dr. Graham of North Carolina stated that "there were nearly seven thousand slaves offered in New Orleans market last winter. From Virginia alone six thousand were annually sent to the South, and from Virginia and North Carolina there had gone to the South, in the last twenty years, three hundred thousand slaves." Many whites felt it to be a shameful business, not at all in harmony with the "benevolent patriarch" image they liked to cherish. "How can an honourable mind," asked Thomas Jefferson Randolph of Virginia, "a patriot, and a lover of his country, bear to see this Ancient Dominion, rendered illustrious by the noble devotion and patriotism of her sons in the cause of liberty, converted into one grand menagerie, where men are to be reared for the market, like oxen for the shambles [slaughterhouse]."

"Never knew who Marsa done sold," recalled Nancy Williams, of Virginia, in her old age. "Remember one morning old whiteman ride up in a buggy and stop plumb by a gal named Lucy that was working in the yard. He say, 'Come on, get in this buggy. I bought you this morning.' Then she beg him to let her go tell her baby and husband goodbye, but he say, 'Naw! Get in this buggy! Ain't got no time for crying and carrying on.' I started crying myself, 'cause I'se so scared he gonna take me too. But old aunt Crissy, whose child it was, went to Marsa and told him he was a mean dirty nigger-trader. Old Marsa got sore, but ain't never said nothing to Aunt Crissy. Then Hendley, what was next to the youngest of her seven chillun got sick and died. Aunt Crissy ain't sorrowed much. She went straight up to old Marsa and shouted in his face, 'Praise God, praise God! My little chile is gone to Jesus. That's one chile of mine you never gonna sell."

And there was this from Sis Shackelford: "Had a slave-jail built at the cross-roads with iron bars cross the windows. Soon's the coffle get there, they bring all the slaves from the jail, two at a time, and string them along the chain back of the other poor slaves. Everybody in the village come out, specially the wives and sweethearts and mothers, to see their sold-off chillun for the last time. And when they start the chains a-clanking and step off down the line, they all just sing and shout and make all the noise they can, trying to hide the sorrow in their hearts and cover up the cries and moanings of them they's leaving behind."

Upbringing. "The Virginians," wrote the visiting German naturalist, Johann Schoepf, "are an indolent, haughty people whose thoughts and designs are directed solely towards playing the lord, owning great tracts of land and numerous troops of slaves . . . They pass the greatest part of the summer on soft pallets, attended by one or several Negroes to ward off the flies, light pipes, and proffer punch, sangry, toddy or julep." The young people "grow up without much literary instruction, which they either have small occasion for or hold to be superfluous. A Virginia youth of 15 years is already such a man as he will be at twice that age. At 15 his father gives him a horse and a Negro, with which he riots about the country, attends every fox-hunt, horse-race, and cock-fight, and does nothing else whatever."

"The whole commerce between master and slave," wrote Jefferson in *Notes on Virginia*, "is a perpetual exercise of the most boisterous passions, the most unremitting despotism on one part, and degrading submissions on the other. Our children see this, and learn to imitate it . . . The parent storms, the child looks on, catches the lineaments of wrath, puts on the same airs in the circle of smaller slaves, gives a loose to his worst of passions; and thus nursed, educated, and daily exercised in tyranny, cannot but be stamped by it with odious peculiarities. The man must be a prodigy who can retain his manners and morals undepraved by such circumstances."

As an example of the truth of this observation, here is part of a letter to the abolitionist Theodore Weld, dated January 3, 1839, and written by John Nelson: "I was born and raised in Augusta County, Virginia. My father was an elder in the Presbyterian church, and owner of about twenty slaves . . . When I was quite a child, I recollect it grieved me very much to see one tied up to a tree to be whipped, and I used to intercede with tears in their behalf, and mingle my cries with theirs, and feel almost willing to take part of the punishment. I have been severely rebuked by my father for this kind of sympathy. Yet, such is the hardening effect of such scenes, that from this kind of commiseration for the suffering slave I became so blunted that I could not only witness their stripes with composure, but myself inflict them, and that without remorse. One case I have often looked back to with sorrow and contrition, particularly since I have been convinced that Negroes are men. When I was perhaps fourteen or fifteen years of age, I undertook to correct a young fellow named Ned for some supposed offense—I think it was leaving a bridle out of its proper place. He, being larger and stronger than myself, took hold of my arms and held me, in order to prevent my striking him. This I considered the height of insolence, and cried for help, when my father and mother both came running to my rescue. My father stripped and tied him, and took him into the orchard, where switches were plenty, and directed me to whip him. When one switch wore out, he supplied me with others. After I had whipped him a while, he fell on his knees to implore forgiveness, and I kicked him in the face. My father said, 'Don't kick him, but whip him.' This I did until his back was literally covered with welts. I know I have repented, and trust I have obtained pardon for these things."

Cotton. From being a minor business at the end of the eighteenth century, cotton became the country's most important export—two million bales in 1791; ten years later, following the introduction of Eli Whitney's cotton gin, which increased productivity by a factor of fifty, exports were eighty million bales; in 1831 they were three hundred and fifty-four million; in 1851, seven hundred and fifty-seven million; and on the eve of the Civil War, one billion, three hundred and ninety million bales—two thirds of all the cotton grown in the world.

Most of the exports went to Great Britain, then the world's leading industrialized country. By 1850 more than half of all British exports consisted of cotton goods. The price of raw cotton varied, but the general trend was upward, and between leaving the plantation and ending up as someone's clothes, cotton employed a vast network of middlemen—bankers, brokers, insurers, shippers, spinners, distributors, retailers. Because demand kept growing, there was a constant push to acquire new land suitable for cotton; and because a principal requirement was a climate that provided two hundred days free of frost, this push led to the Seminole Wars in Florida, the annexation of Texas, the war with Mexico, various one-sided treaties with Indian tribes, and plans to take over Cuba and Nicaragua.

The demand for slaves also kept rising, pushing up prices—in 1800 the cost of a young man on the New Orleans market was $500, in 1860 it was $1800. Women slaves known to be good "breeders" also fetched a high price; as Jefferson wrote in 1820 to his son-in-law, John Epps, "A woman who brings a child every two years is more valuable than the best man on the farm."

It was axiomatic among growers that cotton plantations could be worked only with slave labor. As the *American Cotton Planter* put it, in 1853: "The slave labor of the United States has hitherto conferred, and is still conferring, inappreciable blessings on mankind. If these blessings continue, slave labor must also continue, for it is idle to talk of producing Cotton for the world's supply with free labor."

Another popular opinion was expressed by David Christy in his 1860 book, *Cotton is King*: "By the industry, skill and enterprise employed in the manufacture of cotton, mankind are better clothed; their comfort better promoted; general industry more highly stimulated; commerce more widely extended; and civilization more rapidly advanced than in any preceding age."

Religion. Out of the more than three quarters of a million words in the Bible, Christian slaveholders—and, if asked, most slaveholders would have defined themselves as Christian—had two favorites texts, one from the beginning of the Old Testament and the other from the end of the New Testament. In the words of the King James Bible, which was the version then current, these were, first, Genesis IX, 18–27:

> "And the sons of Noah that went forth from the ark were Shem, Ham, and Japheth: and Ham is the father of Canaan. These are the three sons of Noah: and of them was the whole world overspread. And Noah began to be an husbandman, and he planted a vineyard: and he drank of the wine, and was drunken; and he was uncovered within his tent. And Ham, the father of Canaan, saw the nakedness of his father, and told his two brethren without. And Shem and Japheth took a garment, and laid it upon both their shoulders, and went backward, and covered the nakedness of their father; and their faces were backward, and they saw not their father's nakedness. And Noah awoke from his wine, and knew what his younger son had done unto him. And he said, Cursed be Canaan; a servant of servants shall he be unto his brethren. And he said, Blessed be the Lord God of Shem; and Canaan shall be his servant. God shall enlarge Japheth, and he shall dwell in the tents of Shem; and Canaan shall be his servant. And Noah lived after the flood three hundred and fifty years."

Despite some problems with this story—What was so terrible about seeing Noah drunk? Why curse Canaan rather than Ham? How long was the servitude to last? Surely Ham would have been the same color as his brothers?—it eventually became the foundational text for those who wanted to justify slavery on Biblical grounds. In its boiled-down, popular version, known as "The Curse of Ham," Canaan was dropped from the story, Ham was made black, and his descendants were made Africans.

The other favorite came from the Apostle Paul's Epistle to the Ephesians, VI, 5-7: "Servants, be obedient to them that are your masters according to the flesh, with fear and trembling, in singleness of your heart, as unto Christ; not with eye-service, as men-pleasers; but as the servants of Christ, doing the will of God from the heart; with good will doing service, as to the Lord, and not to men: knowing that whatsoever good thing any man doeth, the same shall he receive of the Lord, whether he be bond or free." (Paul repeated himself, almost word for word, in the third chapter of his Epistle to the Colossians.)

The rest of the Old Testament was often mined by pro-slavery polemicists for examples proving that slavery was common among the Israelites. The New Testament was largely ignored, except in the negative sense of pointing out that nowhere did Jesus condemn slavery, although the story of Philemon, the runaway who St. Paul returned to his master, was often quoted. It was also generally accepted that the Latin word *servus*, usually translated as servant, really meant slave.

As the daughter, sister and mother of ministers, and wife of a theologian, Harriet Beecher Stowe was unlikely to have underestimated the importance of the clergy. "There is no country in the world where the religious influence has a greater ascendancy than in America," she wrote. "No country where the clergy are more powerful"—so powerful in fact "that no statesman would ever undertake to carry a measure against which all the clergy of the country should unite." What effect, then, did the clergy have "on this great question of slavery?" Denomination by denomination, she reviewed their record.

"The Methodist Society especially, as organized by John Wesley, was an anti-slavery society, and the *Book of Discipline* contained the most positive statutes against slave-holding. In 1780, before the church was regularly organized in the United States, they resolved as follows: 'The conference acknowledges that slavery is contrary to the laws of God, man, and nature, and hurtful to society; contrary to the dictates of conscience and true religion; and doing what we would not others should do unto us.'" In 1801 it was declared "that we are more than ever convinced of the great evil of African slavery, which still exists in these United States." Members were urged to collect signatures for petitions asking legislatures to end slavery. But then, "in 1836, let us notice the change. The General Conference held its annual session in Cincinnati, and resolved as follows: 'That they are decidedly opposed to modern abolitionism, and wholly disclaim any right, wish, or intention to interfere in the civil and political relation between master and slave.'" The same year "the New York Annual Conference voted that no one should be elected a deacon or elder in the church unless he would give a pledge to the church that he would refrain from discussing the subject." In 1847, after the Methodists had split North and South, the Philadelphia Annual Conference reminded its members of "the question that we have been accustomed, for a few years past, to put to candidates for admission among us, namely, 'Are you an abolitionist?' And without each one answered in the negative, he was not received."

(It was the opinion of the abolitionist Stephen Symonds Foster, author of *The Brotherhood of Thieves: or, A True Picture of the American Church and Clergy* "that the Methodist-Episcopal Church was more corrupt and profligate than any house of ill fame in New York—that the Southern ministers of that body were desirous of perpetuating slavery for the purpose of supplying themselves with concubines—that many of our clergymen were guilty of enormities that would disgrace an Algerine pirate . . .")

Mrs. Stowe then considered the Presbyterians. In 1818 their Assembly declared that "it is manifestly the duty of all Christians . . . to use honest, earnest, unwearied endeavors to correct the errors of former times, and as speedily as possible to efface this blot on our holy religion, and to obtain the complete abolition of slavery throughout Christendom and throughout the world." Less than twenty years later, hoping to avoid a north-south schism, the Assembly resolved "that this whole subject be indefinitely postponed." Southern Presbyterians, however, were less willing to compromise and the Harmony Presbytery, of South Carolina, passed this resolution: "That as the kingdom of our Lord is not of this world, His church, as such, has no right to abolish, alter, or affect any institution or ordinance of men, political or civil. That slavery has existed from the days of those good old slave-holders and patriarchs, Abraham, Isaac and Jacob (who are now in the kingdom of heaven), to the time when the Apostle Paul sent a runaway home to his master, Philemon. That . . . the existence of slavery itself is not opposed to the will of God." In 1843 the Assembly resolved that they did "not think it fit for the edification of the church for this body to take any action on this subject." And when the 1850 Fugitive Slave Act was passed, "What," asked Mrs. Beecher, "said the Presbyterian Church?" Answer: "She said *nothing*!"

Next, the Baptists. In 1835 the Charleston Baptist Association declared that the question of slavery was neither moral nor religious. It was "a question purely of political economy. It amounts in effect to this: Whether the operatives of a country shall be bought and sold, and themselves become property, as in this state; or whether they shall be hirelings, and their labor only become property, as in some other states." And so, since slavery was "a question purely of political economy," and not of morality, it followed that "the State of South Carolina alone has the right to regulate the existence and condition of slavery within her territorial limits." And in the meantime, "the right of masters to dispose of the time of their slaves has been distinctly recognized by the Creator."

Mrs. Stowe also explained why the northern clergy, who generally disapproved of slavery, were so ineffective. "The slave power has been a united, steady, uncompromising principle. The resisting element has been, for many years wavering, self-contradictory, compromising. There has been, it is true, a deep and ever-increasing hostility to slavery in a decided majority of ministers and Church-members in the free States, taken as individuals." But faced with "the perfect inflexibility of the slave system, and its absolute refusal to allow any discussion of the subject," they had retreated. When they met in convention, instead of confronting the great moral issue of their time, they debated such matters as "whether a man might lawfully marry his deceased wife's sister," and whether "promiscuous dancing"—i.e. men dancing with women—should be allowed. (The Presbyterians' answer to the second question was No—such dancing was "entirely unscriptural" and "wholly inconsistent with the spirit of Christ.")

But perhaps there would be a place for slaves in the newly formed Mormon Church? At first it seemed that this might be possible, for did not the Second Book of Nephi, Chapter 26, Verse 33, say that the Lord God "denieth none that come unto him, black and white, bond and free, male and female?" And had not Joseph Smith himself, soon after translating the mystical golden plates, ordained Elijah Abel, a former slave, and Walker Lewis, a free black? On the other hand there was the story in the Book of Mormon of how the Lamanites, who had once been "white, and exceedingly fair and delightsome," had "hardened their hearts against Him," and as a punishment "the Lord God did cause a skin of blackness to come upon them. And thus saith the Lord God: I will cause that they shall be loathsome unto thy people." (2 Nephi 5: 21, 22.) And, following the trek out to Utah, Brigham Young declared that "The Lord had cursed Cain's seed with blackness and prohibited them the Priesthood."

As to other religions, Quakers did not allow their members to own slaves, but did little to persuade others to follow suit. Catholics were still only a minor presence in this country. And finally, when it came to Episcopalians, Mrs. Stowe dismissed them out of hand. "As to the Episcopal Church, it has never done anything but comply, either North or South."

This was a bit unfair, as ever since its founding one of the functions of the Church of England, the parent of the Episcopal Church, had been to support the established order. To comply was not a failure; it was an obligation. An example of how this worked in practice comes from Harriet Jacobs, who was a household slave living with a doctor's family in Edenton, North Carolina.

> "After the alarm caused by Nat Turner's insurrection had subsided, the slaveholders came to the conclusion that it would be well to give the slaves enough of religious instruction to keep them from murdering their masters. The Episcopal clergyman offered to hold a separate service on Sundays for their benefit." The meetings were held not in the church, but in the house of a free black.
>
> "When the Rev. Mr. Pike came, there were some twenty persons present. The reverend gentleman knelt in prayer, then seated himself and requested all present who could read to open their books, while he gave out the portions he wished them to repeat or respond to. His text was, 'Servants, be obedient to them that are your masters according to the flesh, with fear and trembling, in singleness of your heart, as unto Christ.'
>
> "Pious Mr. Pike brushed up his hair till it stood upright, and in deep, solemn tones began: 'Hearken, ye servants! Give strict heed unto my words. You are rebellious sinners. Your hearts are filled with all manner of evil. 'Tis the devil who tempts you. God is angry with you, and will surely punish you if you don't forsake your wicked ways. You that live in town are eye-servants behind your master's back [i.e. you work only when watched]. Instead of

serving your masters faithfully, which is pleasing in the sight of your heavenly Master, you are idle, and shirk your work. God sees you. You tell lies. God hears you. Instead of being engaged in worshiping Him, you are hidden away somewhere, feasting on your master's substance, tossing coffee-grounds with some wicked fortune-teller, or cutting cards with another old hag. Your masters may not find you out, but God sees you, and will punish you. Oh, the depravity of your hearts! When your master's work is done, are you quietly together, thinking of the goodness of God to such sinful creatures? No; you are quarreling, and tying up little bags of root to bury under the door-steps to poison each other with. God sees you. You men steal away to every grog shop to sell your master's corn, that you may buy rum to drink. God sees you. You sneak into the back streets, or among the bushes, to pitch coppers. Although your masters may not find you out, God sees you, and He will punish you. You must forsake your sinful ways, and be faithful servants . . . If you disobey your earthly master, you offend your heavenly Master. You must obey God's commandments. When you go from here, don't stop at the corners of the streets to talk, but go directly home, and let your master and mistress see that you have come.'"

Another Episcopalian, Bishop William Meade of Virginia, also delivered a sermon addressed to slaves. After reviewing the duties they owed to their masters, he urged them to

"take care that you do not fret or murmur, grumble or repine at your condition; for this will not only make your life uneasy, but will greatly offend Almighty God. Consider that it is not yourselves, it is not the people that you belong to, it is not the men that have brought you to it, but it is the will of God who hath, by His providence, made you servants, because, no doubt, He knew that condition would be best for you in this world, and help you the better towards heaven, if you would but do your duty in it."

Even apparent abuses, when looked at in the right light, worked out for the best. Suppose, for example, that you have been punished for something you did not do, "is it not possible you may have done some other bad thing which was never discovered and that Almighty God, who saw you doing it, would not let you escape without punishment one time or another? And ought you not in such a case to give glory to Him, and be thankful that He would rather punish you in this life for your wickedness than destroy your souls for it in the next life? But suppose that even this was not the case—a case hardly to be imagined—and that you have by no means, known or unknown, deserved the correction you suffered; there is this great comfort in it, that if you bear it patiently, and leave your cause in the hands of God, He will reward you for it in heaven, and the punishment you suffer unjustly here shall turn to your exceeding great glory hereafter."

Bishop Stephen Elliott, of Georgia, also knew how to look on the bright side. Critics of slavery should "consider whether, by their interference with this institution, they may not be checking and impeding a work which is manifestly Providential. For nearly a hundred years the English and American Churches have been striving to civilize and Christianize Western Africa, and with what result? Around Sierra Leone, and in the neighborhood of Cape Palmas, a few natives have been made Christians, and some nations have been partially civilized; but what a small number in comparison with the thousands, nay, I may say millions, who have learned the way to Heaven and who have been made to know their Savior through the means of African slavery! At this very moment there are from three to four millions of Africans, educating for earth and for Heaven in the so vilified Southern States—learning the very best lessons for a semi-barbarous people—lessons of self-control, of obedience, of perseverance, of adaptation of means to ends; learning, above all, where their weakness lies, and how they may acquire strength for the battle of life. These considerations satisfy me with their condition, and assure me that it is the best relation they can, for the present, be made to occupy."

Reviewing the work of the white churches, Frederick Douglass had this to say: "Between the Christianity of this land and the Christianity of Christ, I recognize the widest possible difference—so wide that to receive the one as good, pure, and holy, is of necessity to reject the other as bad, corrupt, and wicked. To be the friend of the one is of necessity to be the enemy of the other. I love the pure, peaceable, and impartial Christianity of Christ; I therefore hate the corrupt, slave-holding, women-whipping, cradle-plundering, partial and hypocritical Christianity of this land. Indeed, I can see no reason but the most deceitful one for calling the religion of this land Christianity . . ."

Eng.^d by A.H.Ritchie.

Later in life, Harriet Beecher Stowe explained why she wrote Uncle Tom's Cabin: *"Because as a woman, as a mother, I was oppressed and broken-hearted with the sorrows and injustice I saw; because as a Christian I felt the dishonor to Christianity; because as a lover of my country I trembled at the coming day of wrath." The book sold over 300,000 copies in its first year, quite a few of which were publicly burned in the South, where several "anti-Tom" novels soon appeared, e.g.* Little Eva: The Flower of the South. *To rebut criticism that her book was mere fiction, Mrs. Stowe also published* A Key to Uncle Tom's Cabin: Facts and Documents upon which the Story is Founded.

CHAPTER 8

WHITE TESTIMONY

PERHAPS BECAUSE THE UNITED STATES HAD NOT YET BECOME THE DOMINANT power in the world, Americans of the nineteenth century cared a good deal more than they do now about what people from European countries thought of them. As Wendell Phillips, the Boston brahmin turned abolitionist, put it, "the heart of every man is constantly asking the question, 'What do they say of us in England?' Europe is the great tribunal for whose decision American sensitiveness always stands waiting in awe."

This interest was reciprocated. Even before the Napoleonic Wars came to an end in 1815, visitors were arriving armed with notebooks and sketch-pads, confident of a welcome on their arrival and a publishing contract on their return home. Most were sympathetic but critical. Topics were obvious—the abundance, the opportunities, the mobility, the vulgarity, the equality, the democracy and, of course, the slavery. For example, the English merchant and Quaker, Robert Sutcliff, wrote in *Travels in North America 1804-1806*:

> "There is a very striking contrast between the appearance of the horses or teams in Pennsylvania and those in the Southern States, where slaves are kept. In Pennsylvania we meet with a great number of wagons, drawn by four or more fine fat horses, the carriages firm and well-made, and covered with stout good linen, bleached almost white; and it is not uncommon to see ten or fifteen together, traveling cheerfully along the road, the driver riding on one of his horses. Many of these come more than three hundred miles to Philadelphia, from the Ohio, Pittsburgh, and other places.
>
> "The appearance of things in the slave States is quite the reverse of this. We sometimes meet a ragged black boy or girl driving

a team consisting of a lean cow or a mule, sometimes a lean bull, or an ox and a mule; and I have seen a mule, a bull, and a cow, each miserable in its appearance, composing one team, with a half-naked black slave or two, riding or driving, as occasion suited. The carriage or wagon, if it may be called such, appeared in as wretched a condition as the team and its driver."

Thirty years later, and far to the west, Alexis de Tocqueville made a similar comment in the notebook he kept when researching *Democracy in America*: "Ohio offers a striking example of the effects slavery and freedom have on society. The state of Ohio is separated from Kentucky only by a river; on either side the soil is fertile and conditions favorable, but the difference is great. On one side the people are feverishly active, doing whatever they can to make money; they may not appear to be prosperous, for they work with their hands, but that work is making them wealthy. On the other side of the river the people are lethargic and unenterprising. On one side work is honored and rewarded, on the other work is despised as being the mark of servitude. The population of Kentucky, which has been settled for nearly a century, grows slowly. Ohio, which joined the Union only thirty years ago, already has a million inhabitants. These differences have only one cause: slavery. It degrades the black people and enervates the white. Its harmful effects are acknowledged but nothing is done about it and it will last for a long time to come. It is deeply embedded in the white Kentuckian's habits, customs and prejudices and threatens not only his own future but that of the entire country. "The comparison between these two states clearly demonstrates that prosperity depends more on the institutions of society and the will of the people than on external conditions. Man is not made for slavery—a fact proved as much by its effect on the master as on the slave."

Another visitor was James Silk Buckingham, an outspoken English journalist who had already traveled much of the world, especially India and the Middle East, and was now to be found with his wife in a horse-drawn coach lumbering through the night over bad roads on their way to Columbia, S. C. A few years earlier, Buckingham, a Liberal Member of Parliament, had promoted the 1833 law which abolished slavery throughout the British Empire, a fact which did not make him popular with his Southern fellow-passengers, one of whom claimed that the British had only done this "for the sake of encouraging a Negro revolt in the southern states, and thus revenging yourselves on America." This was just the kind of remark Buckingham was sure to note, as he took particular interest in the stultifying effect of slavery on the minds of its supporters. And he would find other examples as their coach rolled on.

"At the earliest dawn of day, soon after four o'clock, we met many of the field-Negroes going to their work. All of them were wretchedly clad, in tattered and ragged fragments of garments hanging in shreds around their bodies; and when, at the sight of their miserable condition, Mrs. Buckingham involuntarily sighed, and said in a scarcely audible whisper, 'Poor creatures!' three or four voices immediately and impatiently exclaimed, 'Ah! Madam, they are among the happiest of human beings; for when their work is over, they have no cares, as everything they need is provided for them.' It has been often remarked that the constant representation of a falsehood ultimately occasions even its utterers to believe it to be true. This often-repeated falsehood of 'the Negroes having everything they need provided for them,' must be of this class." (Perhaps rather tactlessly, Buckingham pointed out that if to have one's basic needs taken care of was the key to happiness, then who so fortunate as "the inmates of State prisons and penitentiaries?") "Persons brought up in slave countries, and accustomed from their cradles to regard the institution of slavery as one of mercy instead of injustice, and to repeat every day of their lives that 'slaves are the happiest of human beings,' are impervious to reason on this subject . . . Throughout the South, slavery is a topic upon which no man and, above all, a foreigner, can open his lips without imminent personal danger, unless it is to defend and uphold the system. Then, indeed, he may speak as freely as he pleases."

This was also true of southern publications. "There is not one that ever ventures to speak of slavery as an institution to be condemned, or even regretted. They are all either indulgent towards, or openly advocates of, this state of bondage." Such conformism inevitably led to mediocrity. Consider, for example, a recent issue of *The Southern Literary Journal*, one of the best of its kind. This contained a "puerile" anti-abolition letter; an editorial rejecting out of hand the "ruinous and degrading" idea of compensated emancipation"; an article by a college president that began "I do not know a more bold, a more impudent, a more unprincipled, unblushing falsehood than to say that slavery is inconsistent with the laws of God . . ."; a round-up of several recent pro-slavery publications, and an excerpt from Judge Harper's address to the South Carolina Society for the Advancement of Learning. This, too, was about the "cherished institution" and why it was bound to endure: "'Our proudest feelings—our most essential interests—our humanity and consideration for the slaves themselves—nay, almost physical impossibility, forbid that this [abolition] should be done by our own act; and, thank God! we, the slave-holding communities of the South, are too strong, and on this subject too united, to admit the thought that it can be effected by external force.'"

Summing up, Buckingham wrote: "When such influential persons as editors of quarterly journals and daily newspapers, presidents of colleges, and judges on the bench, maintain and propagate such views as these, it is certainly not to be wondered at that the youths of Carolina, educated at home, and hearing scarcely any other view of slavery expressed but such as I have quoted, should grow up in the belief that they are just and sound, and receive them as the maxims of wisdom from the lips and pens which are guided by age and experience."

While traveling by boat along the Ashley River, he had a conversation with some southerners and "could not help observing that the testimonies of the same persons differed very much according to the turn which the conversation took. When they spoke of the coercion employed towards the Negroes, and endeavored to justify the necessity of it, they were represented as 'an indolent, worthless and ungrateful race, wholly incompetent to arouse themselves to voluntary labor.'" But when Buckingham suggested that their condition might be improved, "it was replied that 'they were already as happy as persons could be, that they were perfectly contented with their condition, and . . . were now faithful, kindhearted and attached to their masters, whereas education would destroy all their natural virtues.' Such were the contradictory statements which I heard, not from different persons, but from the same individuals."

Then there was the "question of the false economy of employing slave-labor in the cultivation of the land. Everything I heard and saw confirmed me in the opinion that it was most injurious to the interests of the planters; and that none would benefit more by a system of free labor than

the very landowners themselves. At present, if a planter wishes to purchase an estate for cultivation, he can get 1,000 acres of land for $10,000;
and if he could obtain free labor to till the land, hiring it by the day, and
paying for such labor as he required and no more, $5,000 would be
ample for a reserved capital by which to procure his seed, labor, and
stock. But as he must, according to the present system, buy his slaves as
well as his land, it will require at last $500 for each working Negro that
he may need; and supposing only one hundred Negroes to be purchased,
this would require $50,000 to be laid out in the purchase of prospective
labor, paying for it before he receives the slightest benefit, and under all
the risks of sickness, desertion, and death. In this manner, according to
the statement of Mr. Clay in his Anti-abolition speech in Congress, there
is locked up, of dead capital, in the purchase and cost of the Negro slaves
in the United States, the enormous sum of $1,200,000,000! Now, if slav-
ery had never been permitted to exist here, and labor could have been
hired by the day, or week, or year, as in other free countries, this enormous amount of capital would have been available to devote to other
purposes; and the whole country would have been advanced at least a
century beyond its present condition."

When Buckingham asked why owners did not therefore free their
slaves, he was answered that "up to a very recent period the feeling was
almost universal in Kentucky that it would be better to do so, especially
as the neighboring State of Ohio, without slaves, was making so much
more rapid strides in prosperity than Kentucky with them; and that probably in a few years their emancipation would have been agreed upon; but
that the proceedings of the Abolitionists in the North wounded their
pride, and they determined that they would not submit to interference or
dictation in the regulation of their 'domestic institution.'"

Buckingham let this pass without comment.

Another English witness to the mentally and morally warping effect of
slavery on owners was the acerbic Mrs. Trollope, whose 1832 book,
Domestic Manners of the Americans, was a lengthy catalog of this country's failings.

"Among the poorer classes of landholders, who are often as profoundly ignorant as the Negroes they own, the effect of this plenary power over males and females is most demoralizing [i.e. lowering moral standards]; and the kind of coarse, not to say brutal, authority which is exercised, furnishes the most disgusting moral spectacle I ever witnessed. In all ranks, however, it appeared to me that the greatest and best feelings of the human heart were paralyzed by the relative positions of slave and owner. The characters, the hearts, of children, are irretrievably injured by it.

"In Virginia we boarded for some time in a family consisting of a widow and her four daughters, and I there witnessed a scene strongly indicative of the effect I have mentioned. A young female slave, about eight years of age, had found on the shelf of a cupboard a biscuit, temptingly buttered, of which she had eaten a considerable portion before she was observed. The butter had been copiously sprinkled with arsenic for the destruction of rats, and had been thus most incautiously placed by one of the young ladies of the family. As soon as the circumstance was known, the lady of the house came to consult me as to what had best be done for the poor child; I immediately mixed a large cup of mustard and water (the most rapid of all emetics) and got the little girl to swallow it. The desired effect was instantly produced, but the poor child, partly from nausea, and partly from the terror of hearing her death proclaimed by half a dozen voices round her, trembled so violently that I thought she would fall. I sat down in the court where we were standing and, as a matter of course, took the little sufferer in my lap. I observed a general titter among the white members of the family . . . The youngest of the family, a little girl about the age of the young slave, after gazing at me for a few moments in utter astonishment, exclaimed, 'My! If Mrs. Trollope has not taken her in her lap, and wiped her nasty mouth! Why, I would not have touched her mouth for two hundred dollars!'

"The little slave was laid on a bed, and I returned to my own apartments; some time afterwards I sent to enquire for her, and learnt that she was in great pain. I immediately went myself to enquire farther, when another young lady of the family, the one by whose imprudence the accident had occurred, met my anxious enquiries with ill-suppressed mirth—told me they had sent for the doctor—and then burst into uncontrollable laughter. The idea of really sympathizing in the sufferings of a slave appeared to them as absurd as weeping over a calf that had been slaughtered by the butcher. The daughters of my hostess were as lovely as features and complexion could make them; but the neutralizing effect of this total want of feeling upon youth and beauty must be witnessed to be conceived."

However, there really were good masters—probably not all that many, and even the best of them necessarily despotic. Of these benevolent patriarchs an outstanding example was Colonel Thomas Dabney, whose life and good deeds were fondly recalled by his daughter, Susan Dabney Smedes, in *Memorials of a Southern Planter*, published toward the end of the nineteenth century. It begins with a description of life on an estate called Elmington, in Gloucester County, "often called the garden-spot of Virginia."

"The house was of red brick, quaint and old-fashioned in design. It was built very near the water's edge. The lapping of the waves of the incoming tide was a sweet lullaby to the quiet scene, as the eye rested on the greensward of the lawn, or took in the bend of the river that made a broad sweep just below the Elmington garden. The North River is half a mile wide. On the other shore could be seen the groves and fields and gardens of the neighboring country seats. The low grounds on the rivershore extend back a distance of a mile and three quarters, and lie like a green carpet, dotted here and there with grand old forest trees, and corn, wheat, rye and tobacco fields." This part of Virginia "had been settled by the best class of English people who came to this country, the youngest sons of noble houses, and other men of standing," with the result that "courtesy and good breeding seemed inherent in the men and women in Gloucester society."

Idyllic, but also an expensive place to live, what with all the open-handed entertaining and, in Dabney's case, a growing family; also, after some two centuries of growing tobacco the soil was becoming exhausted. And so, in 1835, like many others, he decided to move to the southwest. After a careful search, he bought four thousand acres in Hinds County, Mississippi. He then had to decide which of his slaves would go with him to the new plantation, which he called Burleigh. "The family servants, inherited for generations, had come to be regarded with great affection, and this feeling was warmly returned by the Negroes. The bond between master and servant was, in many cases, felt to be as sacred and close as the tie of blood.

> "During the course of years many of the Elmington Negroes had intermarried with the Negroes on neighboring estates. When the southern move was decided on, Thomas called his servants together and announced to them his intention to remove, with his family, to Mississippi. He further went on to say that he did not mean to take one unwilling servant with him. His plan was to offer to buy all husbands and wives who were connected with his Negroes, at the owners' price, or he should, if his people preferred, sell those whom he owned to any master or mistress whom they might choose. No money difficulty should stand in the way. Everything should be made to yield to the important consideration of keeping families together. Without an exception, the Negroes determined to follow their beloved master and mistress."

As she often did, Mrs. Smedes quotes "my dear old black mammy," whose name was Harriet. "Marster was good all de time. He do all he could to comfort he people. When he was gittin' ready to move to Mississippi, he call 'em all up, an' tell 'em dat he did not want anybody to foller him who was not willin'. He say, all could stay in Figinny, an' dey could choose dey own marsters to stay wid. Ebery one o' he own, and all who b'long to de odder members o' de fambly who was wid him, say dey want to foller him 'ceptin' 'twas two ole people, ole gray-headed people, who was too ole to trabble. An' dey was de onliest ones leff behind on dat plantation, an' dey did cry so much I did feel so sorry for dem. I couldn't help cryin', I feel so sorry. Our people say, 'Ef you got a husband or a wife who won't go to Mississippi, leff dat one behind. Ef you got a good marster, foller him.' My husband b'long to Cappen Edward Tabb, an' marster went dyar twice to try to buy him. But Cappen Tabb say dat no money couldn't buy him from him. Den Mrs. Tabb say dat she would buy me, an' two odder people dyar wanted to buy me too. But I say, 'No, indeed! Go 'long! I shall foller my marster.'" Mammy Harriet's sister also decided to abandon her husband in order follow her master.

The journey took over two months. Members of the Dabney family traveled in carriages, the baggage went in wagons, Dabney himself rode a horse, and most of the slaves walked. "The white families were quartered at night, if practicable, in the houses that they found along the way. Tents were provided for the Negroes. The master himself, during the entire journey, did not sleep under a roof . . . He wrapped himself in his greatcoat, with sometimes the addition of a blanket, and slept all night in their midst, under one of the traveling wagons."

Mammy Harriet recalled that "marster do eberything on dat journey dat was for our good." For example, "Marster gib we all new fryin'-pans an' buckets for de journey," but to her annoyance some of the others used her bucket to bring water to the horses and mules. "I say, 'Who got my bucket?' Eberybody say, 'I dunno.' So I say, 'Lem my bucket 'lone; marster done gib it to me . . . Ef he want it he ken hab it, but nobody else.'" The overseer took the matter up with Dabney himself, who declared, "You let Harriet alone; let her bucket alone, everyone of you."

"When we fust come out to dis country, Mississippi, marster made de ploughers tik out de muels at eleven o'clock. An' he didn't 'low 'em to put 'em back 'fore three o'clock, an' nobody worked in dem hours. I s'pose dat was to get us used to de new country. Oh no, we was neber hurried. Marster neber once said, 'Get up an' go to work,' and no overseer eber said it, neither. Ef some on 'em did not git up when de odders went out to work, marster neber said a word." Also unlike other plantations, "Marster would neber hab no horn to wake us up. When one oberseer come dyar wid de horn, marster soon put a stop to dat. He said 'I do not keep hounds to be called up with horns.'"

On the Fourth of July there was "a plenty o' holiday—a beef kilt, a mutton, hogs, salt and pepper, an' eberything. He had a great trench dug, an' a whole load o' wood put in an' burned down to coals. Den dey put wooden spits across, an' dey had spoons an' basted de meat, an' he did not miss givin' us whiskey to drink—a plenty of it, too. An' we 'vite all de cullud people aroun', an' dey come, an' we had fine times. Our people was so good, and dey had so much. Dyar warn't no sich people nowhyar. Marster mus'n't be named de same day as odder people." Also: "Marster 'lowed us to hab meetin', just as much meetin' as we choose. A heap o' people didn't let dey people hab meetin'; didn't like for dem to visit an' see odder people. Marster warn't dat way. We went 'bout."

Mammy Harriet also recalled the death of her aged aunt, known as Grannie Harriet.

> "I was settin' wid her, and she was on de bed, an' she look mighty strange all on a sudden. I thought she was dyin'. I run to de house to missis. Marster was out in de fiel'. I tell missis dat I thought Grannie Harriet was dyin'. Missis she put on her bonnet an' went to her jes' as fast as she could. When Grannie see her she could not speak, but she hold out both arms to her. Missis run into her arms an' bust out cryin'. She put her arms roun' Grannie's neck, and Grannie could not speak, but de big tears roll down her cheeks. An' so she die."

Mrs. Smedes was still a child when she attended Grannie Harriet's night-time funeral. "I remember well the death of this aged servant. The master himself led the funeral procession, and all his children followed the coffin as mourners. He ordered out the whole plantation, everyone who could walk, and every man, woman and child carried a torch. The sound of the mournful funeral hymn, and the blazing of the many torches, as we wound down the road to the dark shades of the burying-ground, made a painful impression on me as a child, and caused many a secret tear. I wished much to be excused from going to the funeral; but the master seemed unapproachable in his grief, and I was afraid of incurring his displeasure if he should discover that I was unwilling to pay what he considered fitting respect to the memory of this trusted friend."

Dabney's plantation "was considered a model one, and was visited by planters anxious to learn his methods. He was asked how he made his Negroes do good work. His answer was that a laboring man could do more and better work in five and a half days than in six. He used to give the half of Saturdays to his Negroes, unless there was a great press of work; but a system of rewards was more efficacious than any other method. He distributed prizes of money among his cotton-pickers every week during the season, which lasted four or five months. One dollar was the first prize, a Mexican coin valued at eighty-seven and a half cents the second, seventy-five cents the third, and so on, down to the smallest prize, a small Mexican coin called a picayune, which was valued at six and a half cents . . . The master gave money to all who worked well for the prizes, whether they won them or not. When one person picked six hundred pounds in a day, a five-dollar gold piece was the reward. On most other plantations four hundred pounds, or three hundred and fifty, or three hundred was considered a good day's work, but on the Burleigh place many picked five hundred pounds." The champion picker was "a very tall and lithe young woman" who "picked two rows at a time, going down the middle with both arms extended and grasping the cotton-bolls with each hand.

"On wedding occasions, in addition to the materials for a cake, the bride always expected a good many gifts, and some of the master's family to be present. The mistress's big prayer-book was taken over, and the marriage service read by one of the young masters." Recalling her own wedding Mammy Harriet said "Your pa gib me a head weddin'—kilt a mutton—a round o' beef—tukkeys—cakes, one on t'other—trifle. I had all de chany off de sideboard, cups an' saucers, de table, de white table-cloth. I had on your pa's wife's weddin' gloves and slippers an' veil. De slippers was too small, but I put my toes in. Miss Mary had a mighty neat foot. Marster brought out a milk-pail o' toddy an' more in bottles . . . I had a tearin'-down weddin', to be sure."

Mrs. Smedes also had a happy memory. "When we children were allowed to go to see some of the servants, they delighted in setting out a little feast . . . Once, at Christmas, Mammy Harriet gave a 'high tea' to us children. I was at that time about fourteen years of age, the oldest of the invited. A friend of my own age, Arabella Foote, the youngest daughter of Henry S. Foote (Governor and United States Senator), was spending her Christmas holidays with me. Mammy felt some modesty about inviting the young lady into her house, but I took Arabella, and she enjoyed it as much as any of us. Mammy had made a nice cake and hot biscuits and tea for the occasion, set out in her choicest cups, some of rare old china, and with sugar in the sugar-bowl that she had inherited from her mother. She gave us, besides, sweetmeats, nuts, raisins, fruits of several kinds—indeed, a delightful tea. And she stood behind us waiting on the table, her bright bandana handkerchief towering aloft on her head, and she looking so pleased."

And now, a jump to the eve of the Civil War. Opposing secession, and correctly foreseeing that "whether conquered or victorious, the South would be ruined," Dabney decided to sell up and move to England. "'Yes, my dear, but what will you do with Abby?'" his wife replied when told of this decision. "'What will you do with Maria, with Harriet, with their children and husbands?'" There was not enough money to set them all free and "make them comfortable" and still be able to move to England. "That question of my good mother's settled forever his mind and the destiny of the house. Thomas Dabney and his wife deliberately chose to go down with their country. Has not their daughter, then, the right to say . . . that the tie between this master and his slaves was as sacred and binding, if not as near, as the tie of blood?"

Pierce Butler also thought of himself as a good master, but few people can have been so ill-prepared to confront the realities of slavery as his wife, the beautiful and passionate young English actress, Fanny Kemble. A member of a famous acting family, she had been educated at private schools in London and Paris, and at the age of twenty had made a brilliant stage debut in the part of Juliet. Soon after that came a successful tour in this country, during which she met and married Butler, the handsome, enamored and very rich grandson of one of the Founding Fathers— also called Pierce Butler, of South Carolina, the man who introduced the Fugitive Slave Clause into the Constitution. Once married, Fanny gave up her career, and for several years the Butlers enjoyed a comfortable life in Philadelphia; but then, in 1839, Pierce decided that he should visit some of the Georgia sea islands plantations he had inherited, and made the mistake of bringing his family with him. Fanny already knew in the abstract that slavery was wrong, but had no idea of its reality. After a long and horrible journey by stage coach and primitive trains they transferred to a sloop for the last part of the journey, and after sailing down the Altamaha River arrived to an enthusiastic, almost rapturous welcome—not insincere, but nevertheless a standard part of the slaves' repertoire of accommodating devices.

"We now approached the low, reedy bank of Butler Island, and passed the rice mill and buildings surrounding it, all of which, it being Sunday, were closed. As we neared the bank, the steersman

Fanny Kemble, the beautiful English actress who while on a tour of the United States met and married Pierce Butler, grandson of the man who introduced the Fugitive Slave Clause into the Constitution. Shocked by what she saw while on a visit to the Butler plantation, she poured her indignation into a series of vivid letters, later published as Journal of a Residence on a Georgian Plantation.

took up a huge conch, and in the barbaric manner of early times in the Highlands, sounded out our approach." Very soon, the wharf "began to be crowded with Negroes, jumping, dancing, shouting, laughing and clapping their hands, and using the most extravagant and ludicrous gesticulations to express their ecstasy at our arrival.

"On our landing from the boat, the crowd thronged about us like a swarm of bees; we were seized, pulled, pushed, carried, dragged and all but lifted in the air by the clamorous multitude . . . They seized our clothes, kissed them—then our hands, and almost wrung them off. One tall, gaunt Negress flew to us, parting the throng on either side, and embraced us in her arms. I believe I was almost frightened, and it was not until we were safely housed, and the door shut upon our riotous escort, that we indulged in a fit of laughing, quite as full on my part of nervousness as of amusement."

Once the Butlers had settled in, Fanny began looking about her. In a series of letters to her New England friend, Elizabeth Sedgwick, she wrote of her shock at the squalor she found in the slave quarters—"such of these dwellings as I visited today were filthy and wretched in the extreme." Even worse was the apathy of the inhabitants. "Instead of the order, neatness, and ingenuity which might convert even these miserable hovels into tolerable residences, there was the careless, reckless, filthy indolence which even the brutes do not exhibit in their lairs." Wood shavings, dirt, dust and scraps of moss littered the floors, "while the back door of the huts, opening upon a most unsightly ditch, was left open for the fowls and ducks, which they are allowed to raise, to travel in and out, increasing the filth of the cabin."

As a woman of independent mind, Fanny did not hesitate to seize a broom and demonstrate how to put it to use, but "sighing as I went over the futility of my own exertions, for how can slaves be improved?" If only, "instead of beginning at the end, I could but begin at the beginning of my task. If the mind and soul were awakened . . . the physical good would result and the great curse would vanish away."

Next she visited the infirmary, a two-story wooden building with four large rooms. Only half the windows had glass, "and these were obscured with dirt." The other windows were "darkened by dingy shutters which the shivering inmates had fastened in order to protect themselves from the cold. In the enormous chimney glimmered the powerless embers of a few sticks of wood, round which, however, as many of the sick women as could approach were cowering, some on wooden settles, most of them on the ground, excluding those who were too ill to rise; and these last poor wretches lay prostrate on the floor without bed, mattress, or pillow, buried in tattered filthy blankets . . . I stood in the midst of them, perfectly unable to speak, the tears pouring from my eyes at this sad spectacle of their misery, myself and my emotion alike strange and incomprehensible to them. Here lay women expecting every hour the terrors and agonies of childbirth, others who had just brought their doomed offspring into the world, others who were groaning over the anguish and bitter disappointment of miscarriages—here lay some burning with fever, others chilled with cold and aching with rheumatism, upon the hard, cold ground, the drafts and dampness of the atmosphere increasing their sufferings, and dirt, noise and stench, and every aggravation of which sickness is capable, combined in their condition . . . Now pray take notice that this is the hospital of an estate where the owners are supposed to be humane, the overseer efficient and kind, and the Negroes remarkably well cared for."

Toward the end of her letter, Fanny wrote: "I forgot to tell you that in the hospital were several sick babies, whose mothers were permitted to suspend their field labor in order to nurse them. Upon addressing some remonstrances to one of these [Harriet] who, besides having a sick child was ill herself, about the horribly dirty condition of her baby, she assured me that it was impossible for them to keep their children clean; that they went out to work at daybreak, and did not get their tasks done till evening, and that then they were were too tired and worn out to do anything but throw themselves down and sleep. This statement of hers I mentioned on my return from the hospital, and the overseer [Mr. Oden] appeared extremely annoyed by it, and assured me repeatedly that it was not true."

Next day: "This morning I paid my second visit to the infirmary and found there had been some faint attempt at sweeping and cleaning, in compliance with my entreaties," but Harriet "was crying bitterly. I asked her what ailed her when, more by signs and dumb show, she and old Rose [the midwife] informed that Mr. Oden had flogged her that morning for having told me that the women had not time to keep the children clean . . . I again and again made her repeat her story, and she again and again affirmed that she had been flogged for what she told me, none of the whole company in the room denying it or contradicting her. I left the room because I was so disgusted and indignant that I could hardly restrain my feelings."

Later that day, "I told Mr. Butler, with much indignation, of poor Harriet's flogging . . . He said he would ask Mr. Oden about it, assuring me, at the same time, that it was impossible to believe a single word any of these people said. At dinner, accordingly, the inquiry was made as to the cause of her punishment, and Mr. Oden then said it was not at all for what she had told me that he had flogged her, but for having answered him impertinently; that he had ordered her into the field, whereupon she had said that she was ill and could not work; that he retorted he knew better, and bade her get up and go to work; she replied, 'Very well, I'll go, but I shall just come back again,' meaning that when in the field she would be unable to work, and obliged to return to the hospital. 'For this reply,' Mr. Oden said, 'I gave her a good lashing. It was her business to have gone into the field without answering me.'"

Ironically, that very day Fanny had been given proof that "it was impossible to believe a single word any of these people said"—though not in the way Mr. Butler intended. A young slave named Jack had been assigned to accompany Fanny "in my roamings about the island and rowing expeditions on the river." Jack was bright and inquisitive. "His questions, like those of an intelligent child, are absolutely inexhaustible; his curiosity about all things beyond this island, the prison house of his existence, is perfectly intense . . . Today, in the midst of his torrent of inquires about places and things, I suddenly asked him if he would like to be free. A gleam of light absolutely shot over his whole countenance, like vivid and instantaneous lightning. He stammered, hesitated, became excessively confused, and at length replied, 'Free, missis? What for me wish to be free? Oh no, missis, me no wish to be free . . .' The fear of offending by uttering that forbidden wish—the dread of admitting, by its expression, the slightest discontent with his present situation—the desire to conciliate my favor, even at the expense of strangling the intense natural longing that absolutely glowed in his every feature—it was a sad spectacle, and I repented my question."

Fanny's outspoken sympathy for the slaves eventually got her in trouble with her husband. As was normal for those times, she spoke of him as "Mr. Butler," and thought of herself as "belonging" to him and owing him obedience. "I have had a most painful conversation with Mr. Butler, who has declined receiving any of the people's petitions through me," she wrote to Elizabeth Sedgwick. "'Why do you listen to such stuff?'" he had asked. "'Why do you believe such trash? Don't you know the niggers are all d—d liars?'" In future she was "to bring him no more complaints or requests of any sort." She thought of returning to the North—"this is no place for me, since I was not born among slaves and cannot bear to live among them." But to leave would be a drastic step; instead there was "the blessed refuge of abundant tears," and the reflection that "God will provide. He has not forgotten, nor will He forsake these His poor children."

In the meantime the list of sufferers grew longer: Charlotte and Judy, who had been forced to return to work in the field three weeks after giving birth; Louisa, who had run away and hidden in a rattlesnake-infested swamp to escape a flogging and had returned almost dead with hunger; Fanny, "who has had six children, all dead but one," and asked to have her work load lightened; Sarah, who "had had four miscarriages, had brought seven children into the world, five of whom were dead, and was again with child. She complained of dreadful pains in the back, and an internal tumor which swells with the exertion of working in the fields; probably, I think, she is ruptured." Sarah also had bouts of insanity. So did Judy, who had run away but was caught, "brought back, and punished by being made to sit, day after day, for hours in the stocks—a severe punishment for a man, but for a woman perfectly barbarous." Judy's first-born was the child of the former overseer, Mr. King, "who had forced her, flogged her severely for having resisted him, and then sent her off, as a further punishment, to Five Pound—a horrible swamp in a remote corner of the estate, to which the slaves are sometimes banished." Then there was "a poor woman called Mile, who could hardly stand for pain and swelling in her limbs; she had had fifteen children and two miscarriages; nine of her children had died; for the last three years she had become almost a cripple with chronic rheumatism, yet she is driven every day to work in the field." And there was Die. "She had had sixteen children, fourteen of whom were dead; she had had four miscarriages; one had been caused with falling down with a very heavy burden on her head, and one from having her arms strained up to be lashed."

"And to all this I listen," wrote Fanny. "I, an Englishwoman, the wife of the man who owns these wretches, and I cannot say, 'That thing shall not be done again; that cruel shame and villainy shall never be known here again.'" All she could do was give small presents of rice, sugar or flannel cloth, and remain "choking with indignation and grief . . . And never forget that the people on this plantation are well off, and consider themselves well off, in comparison with the slaves on some of the neighboring estates."

One particular incident occurred quite early in their visit, when Fanny was still in her husband's good graces. It concerned a young house slave called Psyche, notable for "the perfect sweetness of her expression" and for the fact that she was always "sad and silent," with "an air of melancholy and timidity." Eventually Psyche revealed what was troubling her: she was not sure who owned her and her two small children. She knew that at one time they had been the property of Mr. King, the former overseer, who was there on a visit, but were they still? King had recently bought a plantation of his own in Alabama, and Psyche feared that they might have to go there, which would mean being separated from her husband Joe, "a fine, intelligent, active, excellent young man." Joe belonged to Mr. Butler, so now Psyche asked Fanny to ask him to buy her too. "Now, Elizabeth," wrote Fanny, "just conceive for one moment the state of mind of this woman, believing herself to belong to a man who in a few days was going down to one of those abhorred and dreaded Southwestern states, and who would then compel her, with her poor little children, to leave her husband and the only home she had ever known, and all the ties of affection, relationship, and association of her former life . . . Do you think I wondered any more at the woebegone expression of her countenance?"

Before she had a chance to talk with her husband, Fanny met Mr. Oden, the current overseer. "I asked him about Psyche, and who was her proprietor when, to my infinite surprise, he told me that he had bought her and her children from Mr. King, who had offered them to him saying that they would be rather troublesome to him than otherwise down where he was going. 'And so,' said Mr. Oden, 'as I had no objection to investing a little money that way, I bought them.' With a heart much lightened, I flew to tell poor Psyche the news so that, at any rate, she might be relieved from the dread of any immediate separation from her husband." But that was not the end of the story.

> "Early the next morning, while I was still dressing, I was suddenly startled by hearing voices in loud tones in Mr. Butler's dressing room, which adjoins my bedroom, the noise increasing until there was an absolute cry of despair uttered by some man. I could restrain myself no longer, but opened the door of communication and saw Joe, the young man, poor Psyche's husband, raving almost in a state of frenzy, and in a voice broken with sobs and almost inarticulate with passion, reiterating his determination never to leave this plantation, never to go to Alabama, never to leave his old father and mother, his poor wife and children, and dashing his hat, which he had been

wringing like a cloth in his hands, upon the ground, he declared he would kill himself if he was compelled to follow Mr. King. I glanced from the poor wretch to Mr. Butler, who was standing leaning against a table with his arms folded, occasionally uttering a few words of counsel to his slave to be quiet and not fret, and not make a fuss about what there was no help for." Withdrawing from the scene, Fanny went to find Mr. Oden and asked him if he knew the cause of Joe's distress. "He then told me that Mr. Butler, who is highly pleased with Mr. King's past administration of his property, wished, on his departure for his newly acquired slave plantation, to give him some token of his satisfaction, and had made him a present of the man Joe, who had just received the intelligence that he was to go down to Alabama with his new owner the next day, leaving father, mother, wife and children behind."

As soon as she met up with her husband, Fanny "appealed to him, for his own soul's sake, not to commit so great cruelty—how I cried, and how I adjured, and how all my sense of justice and of mercy, and of pity for the poor wretch, and of wretchedness at finding myself implicated in such a state of things, broke in torrents of words from my lips and tears from my eyes! God knows such a sorrow at seeing anyone I belonged to commit such an act was indeed a new and terrible experience to me, and it seemed to me that I was imploring Mr. Butler to save himself more than to spare these wretches."

Her husband gave "no answer whatever," but later that evening Mr. Oden came into the living room and sat down to look over some accounts. Fanny asked him if he had seen Joe recently. "'Yes, ma'am,' he replied. 'He is a great deal happier than he was this morning.'

"'Why, how is that?' asked I eagerly.

"'Oh, he is not going to Alabama. Mr. King heard that he had kicked up such a fuss about it'—being in despair at being torn from one's wife and children is called kicking up a fuss; this is a sample of overseer appreciation of human feelings—'and said that if the fellow wasn't willing to go with him, he did not wish to be bothered with any niggers down there who were to be troublesome, so he might stay behind.'

"'And does Psyche know this?'

"'Yes, ma'am, I suppose so.'

"I drew a long breath . . ." But there remained the matter of securing Psyche's future. The next evening Fanny, who had some money of her own from her days as an actress, being once again alone with the overseer, said, "Mr. Oden, I have a particular favor to beg of you. Promise me that you will never sell Psyche and her children without first letting me know of your intention to do so, and giving me the option of buying them."

Mr. Oden, "a remarkably deliberate man," put down the book he was reading and replied, "Dear me, ma'am, I am very sorry—I have sold them."

> "My mouth opened wide, but I could utter no sound, I was so dismayed and surprised; and he deliberately proceeded, 'I didn't know, ma'am, you see, at all, that you entertained any idea of making an investment of that nature; for I'm sure, if I had, I would willingly have sold the woman to you; but I sold her and her children this morning to Mr. Butler.'
>
> "I jumped up and left Mr. Oden still speaking, and ran to find Mr. Butler, to thank him for what he had done, and with that will now bid you good-bye. Think, Elizabeth, how it fares with slaves on plantations where there is no crazy Englishwoman to weep, and entreat, and implore, and upbraid for them, and no master willing to listen to such appeals."

So Psyche and Joe were saved, at least until 1859, when Pierce Butler, deeply in debt, sold 429 slaves at the largest such sale ever held in the United States. Butler pocketed some three hundred thousand dollars, out of which he personally gave one dollar to every slave sold. By then, after ten years of legal wrangling, he and Fanny were divorced and she had returned to the stage, giving immensely popular readings from Shakespeare. She did not publish her memoirs until 1863 and did so primarily to influence public opinion in England where the Tory government, in the hope that a divided America would be less of a challenge to the British Empire, was showing signs of coming out in support of the Confederacy.

"The Father of American Landscape Architecture," Frederick Law Olmsted *was also well-known for* The Cotton Kingdom, *about his travels in the South. Unlike the highly emotional works of many abolitionists, Olmsted's style was calm and objective, condemning slavery by implication rather than exclamation.*

Much of the best reporting on slavery and the South was written by Frederick Law Olmsted, a man of many talents. As well as being a farmer, journalist, conservationist, traveler, and organizer of medical services during the Civil War, he was famous for his work as a landscape architect—Brooklyn's Prospect Park and New York's Central Park are among his masterpieces. No less famous in its day was his book, *The Cotton Kingdom*, published in 1861 and remarkable for its objectivity at a time when passions and tempers were running high.

On the train to Richmond. Dec 16, 1852. "Seeing a lady entering the car at a way-station with a family behind her, and that she was looking about to find a place where they could be seated together, I rose and offered her my seat, which had several vacancies round it. She accepted it, without thanking me, and immediately installed in it a stout Negro woman; took the adjoining seat herself, and seated the rest of the party before her. It consisted of a white girl, probably her daughter, and a bright and very pretty mulatto girl. They all talked and laughed together; and the girls munched confectionery out of the same paper, with a familiarity and closeness of intimacy that would have been noticed with astonishment, if not with manifest displeasure, in almost any chance company at the North. When the Negro is definitely a slave, it would seem that the alleged natural antipathy of the white race to associate with him is lost.

On arrival. "Richmond, at a glance from adjacent high ground, through a dull cloud of bituminous smoke, upon a lowering winter's day, has a very picturesque appearance . . . But the moment it is examined at all in detail, there is but one spot in the whole picture upon which the eye is at all attracted to rest. This is the Capitol, a Grecian edifice, standing alone and finely placed on open and elevated ground, in the center of the town. It was built soon after the Revolution, and the model was obtained by Mr. Jefferson, the Minister to France, from the Maison Carrée." However, on closer inspection, it turned out that thanks to "a parsimonious pretense of dignity," rather than being built of marble, it was built of wood painted to look like marble, and was "nothing but a cheap stuccoed building." (Symbolic, according to some, of Southern culture as a whole.)

Sunday street scene in Richmond. "In what I suppose to be the fashionable streets there were many more well-dressed and highly-dressed colored people than white; and among this dark gentry the finest French cloths, embroidered waistcoats, patent-leather shoes, resplendent brooches, silk hats, kid gloves, and *eau de mille fleurs*, were quite common. Nor was the fairer, or rather the softer sex, at all left in the shade of this splendor. Many of the colored ladies were dressed not only expensively, but with good taste and effect, after the latest Parisian mode. Some of them were very attractive in appearance, and would have produced a decided sensation in any European drawing-room.

"There was no indication of their belonging to a subject race, except that they invariably gave way to the white people they met. Once, when two of them, engaged in conversation and looking at each other, had not noticed his approach, I saw a Virginian gentleman lift his walking-stick and push a woman aside with it. In the evening I saw three rowdies, arm-in-arm, taking the whole of the sidewalk, hustle a black man off it, giving him a blow as they passed that sent him staggering into the middle of the street. As he recovered himself he began to call out to, and threaten, them. Perhaps he saw me stop, and thought I should support him, as I was certainly inclined to: 'Can't you find anything else to do than to be knockin' quiet people round! You jus' come back here, will you? Here, you! Don't care if you is white. You jus' come back here, and I'll teach you how to behave—knockin' people round!—don't care if I does hab to go to der watch-house.' They passed on without noticing him further, only laughing jeeringly—and he continued: 'You come back here, and I'll make you laugh. You is just three white nigger cowards, dat's what you be.'

Another street scene. "Yesterday morning, during a cold, sleety storm, against which I was struggling, with my umbrella, to the post-office, I met a comfortably-dressed Negro leading three others by a rope; the first was a middle-aged man; the second a girl of perhaps twenty; and the last a boy, considerably younger. The arms of all three were secured before them with hand-cuffs, and the rope by which they were led passed from one to another, being made fast at each pair of hand-cuffs. They were thinly clad, the girl especially so, having only an old ragged handkerchief round her neck, over a common calico dress, and another handkerchief twisted around her head. They were dripping wet, and icicles were forming at the time on the awning bars. The boy looked most dolefully, and the girl was turning around with a very angry face, and shouting, 'O pshaw! Shut up!'

"'What are they?' said I, to a white man who had also stopped for a moment to look at them. 'What's he going to do with them?'

"'Come in a canal boat, I reckon; sent down here to be sold. That ar's a likely girl.'

"Nearly opposite the post-office was another singular group of Negroes. They consisted of men and boys, and each carried a coarse white blanket, drawn together at the corners so as to hold some articles; probably extra clothes. They stood in a row, in lounging attitudes, and some of them were quarreling or reproving one another. A villainous-looking white man stood in front of them. Presently, a stout, respectable-looking white man, dressed in black according to the custom, and without any overcoat or umbrella, but with a large gold-headed walking-stick, came out of the door of an office, and without saying a word walked briskly up the street; the Negroes immediately followed in file; the other white man bringing up the rear. They were slaves that had been sent into the town to be hired out as servants or factory hands. The gentleman in black was probably the broker in the business."

The help. "A Southern lady, of an old and wealthy family," was complaining about her servants. "If I order a room to be cleaned, or a fire to be made in a distant chamber, I can never be sure I am obeyed unless I go there and see for myself. If I send a girl out to get anything I want for preparing the dinner, she is as likely to forget what is wanted, and not to come back till after the time at which dinner should be ready. The parade of a military company has sometimes entirely prevented me from having any dinner cooked; and when the servants standing in the square looking at the soldiers see my husband coming after them, they only laugh, and run away to the other side, like playful children. And when I reprimand them they only say they don't mean to do anything wrong, or they won't do it again, all the time laughing as though it was a joke. They don't mind it at all. They are just as playful and careless as any willful child; and they never will do any work if you don't compel them."

Church Service in New Orleans. "Walking this morning through a rather mean neighborhood I was attracted, by a loud chorus of singing, to the open door of a chapel, or small church. I found a large congregation of Negroes within, and the singing being just then concluded, and a Negro preacher commencing a sermon, I entered an empty pew near the entrance. I had no sooner taken a seat than a Negro usher came to me, and in the most polite manner, whispered, 'Won't you please to let me give you a seat higher up, master, 'long o' tudder white folks?'

"I followed him to the uppermost seat, facing the pulpit, where there were three other white persons. One of them was a woman—old, very plain, and not as well dressed as many of the Negroes; another looked like a ship's officer, and was probably a member of the police force in undress [i.e. out of uniform; as in many other southern states, the law required that at least one white man be present at a Negro service]. Both of these remained diligently and gravely attentive during the service. The third was a foreign-looking person, very flashily dressed and sporting a yellow-headed walking stick and much cheap jewelry.

"The preacher was nearly black, with close woolly hair. His figure was slight, he seemed to be about thirty years of age, and the expression on his face indicated a refined and delicately sensitive nature. His eye was very fine, bright, deep, and clear; his voice and manner generally quiet and impressive. The text was, 'I have fought the good fight, I have kept the faith; henceforth there is laid up for me a crown of glory'; and the sermon was an appropriate and generally correct explanation of the customs of the Olympian games, and a proper and often eloquent application of the figure to the Christian course of life. Much of the language was highly metaphorical; the figures long, strange and complicated, yet sometimes, however, beautiful.

"As soon as I had taken my seat, my attention was attracted by an old Negro near me, whom I supposed for some time to be suffering under some nervous complaint; he trembled, his teeth chattered, and his face, at intervals, was convulsed. He soon began to respond aloud to the sentiments of the preacher in such words as these: 'Oh, yes!' 'That's it, that's it!' 'Yes, yes—glory—yes!' and similar expressions could be heard from all parts of the house whenever the speaker's voice was unusually solemn, or his language and manner eloquent or excited. Sometimes the outcries and responses were not confined to ejaculations of this kind, but shouts, and groans, terrific shrieks, and indescribable expressions of ecstasy—of pleasure or agony—and even stamping, jumping and clapping of hands were added. The tumult often resembled that of an excited political meeting; and I was once surprised to find my own muscles all stretched, as if ready for a struggle—my face glowing and my feet stamping—having been infected unconsciously, as men often are, with instinctive bodily sympathy with the excitement of the crowd.

"I took notes as well as I could of a single passage of the sermon. The preacher, having said that among the games of the arena were 'raaslin' (wrestling) and boxing, and described how a combatant, determined to win the prize, would come boldly up to his adversary and stand square before him, looking him straight in the eyes, and while he guarded himself with one hand, would give him a 'lick' with the other, continued in these words: 'Then would he stop, and turn away his face, and let the adversary hit back? No, my brethren, no, no! He'd follow up his advantage, and give him another lick; and if he fell back, he'd keep close after him, and not stop!—and not faint!—not be content with merely driving him back—but he'd persevere! (Yes, glory!) and hit him again! (That's it! Hit him again! Hit him again! Oh, glory! Hi! Hi! Glory!) and drive him into the corner! And never, never stop till he had him down! (Glory! Glory! Glory!) And he had got his foot on his neck, and the crown of wild olive leaves was placed upon his head by the lord of the games. (Ha! Ha! Glory to the Lord! etc.) It was the custom of the Olympian games, my brethren, for the victor to be crowned with a crown of wild olive leaves; but sometimes, after all, it wouldn't be awarded right, because the lord of the games was a poor, frail, erroneous man, and maybe he couldn't see right, or maybe he wasn't an honest man, and would have his favorites among the combatants, and if his favorite was beaten, he would not allow it, but would declare that he was the victor, and the crown would descend on his head. (Glory!) But there ain't no danger of that with our fight with the world, for our Lord is throned in justice. (Glory!—Oh, yes! Yes!—Sweet Lord! Sweet Lord!) He seeth in secret, and he knoweth all things, and there's no chance for a mistake, and if we only will just persevere and conquer, and conquer and persevere (Yes, sir! Oh, Lord, yes!) and persevere—not for a year, or for two year, or ten year, nor for seventy year, perhaps; but if we persevere—(Yes! Yes!)—if we persevere—(Oh, Lord! Help us!)—if we persevere unto the end—(Oh! Oh! Glory! Glory! Glory!)—until he calls us home! (Frantic shouting.) Henceforth there is laid up for us a crown of immortal glory—(Ha! Ha! Ha!)—not a crown of wild olive leaves that begin to droop as soon as they touch our brow, (Oh! Oh! Oh!) but a crown of immortal glory! That fadeth not away! Never begins to droop! But is immortal in the heavens!' (Tremendous uproar, many of the congregation on their feet, uttering cries and shrieks impossible to be expressed in letters. The shabby gentleman by my side, who had been asleep, suddenly awakened, dropped his stick, and shouted with all his might, 'Glory to the Lord!')

"The preacher was drawing his sermon to a close and offering some sensible and pertinent advice, soberly and calmly, and the congregation was attentive and comparatively quiet, when a small old woman, perfectly black, among those in the gallery, suddenly rose and began dancing and clapping her hands; at first with a slow and measured movement, and then with increasing rapidity, at the same time beginning to shout 'Ha! Ha!' The women about her arose also and tried to hold her, as there appeared great danger that she would fall out of the gallery, and those below left their pews that she might not fall on them.

"The preacher continued his remarks—much the best part of his sermon—but it was plain that they were wasted; everyone was looking at the dancing woman in the gallery, and many were shouting and laughing aloud (in joyful sympathy, I suppose.) His eye flashed as he glanced anxiously from the woman to the people, and then stopping in the middle of a sentence, a sad smile came over his face; he closed his book and bowed his head upon his hands to the desk. A voice in the congregation struck into a tune, and the whole congregation rose and joined in a roaring song. The woman was still shouting and dancing, her head thrown back and rolling from one side to another. Gradually her shout became indistinct, she threw her arms wildly about instead of clapping her hands, fell back into the arms of her companions, then threw herself forward and embraced those before her, then tossed herself from side to side, gasping, and finally sank to the floor, where she remained at the end of the song, kicking, as if acting a death struggle."

This was followed by another sermon by a different preacher, mostly against drinking rum, and then by a hymn, many of the congregation keeping time with their feet, "and swinging their bodies." After some announcements, the service ended with the Apostles' blessing, "and the congregation slowly passed out, chatting and saluting one another politely as they went."

Alabama. After a week in Montgomery, Olmsted "left for Mobile, on the steamboat *Fashion*, a clean and well-ordered boat, with polite and obliging officers." The crew "was composed partly of Irishmen and partly of Negroes; the latter were slaves and were hired of their owners at $40 a month—the same wages paid to the Irishmen. A dollar of their wages was given to the Negroes themselves for each Sunday they were on the passage. So far as convenient, they were kept at work separately from the white hands; they were also messed separately.

"We were two days and a half making the passage, the boat stopping at almost every bluff and landing to take on cotton, until she had a freight of nineteen hundred bales, which was built up on the guards, seven or eight tiers in height, and until it reached the hurricane deck. The boat was thus brought so deep that her guards were in the water, and the ripple of the river constantly washed over them. There are two hundred landings on the Alabama River, and three hundred on the Bigby [Tombigbee] at which the boats advertise to call, if required, for passengers or freight."

These landings were little more than stopping places, without docks or wharves, where the boats tied up to a tree at the river's edge. At one of them, called Claiborne, where they stopped one night, there was a village "situated upon a bluff, a hundred and fifty feet high, with a nearly perpendicular bank. The boat came to the shore at the foot of a plank slide-way, down which cotton was sent to it from a warehouse at the top.

"There was something truly Western in the direct, reckless way in which the boat was loaded. A strong gang-plank being placed at right angles to the slide-way, a bale of cotton was let slide from the top, coming down with fearful velocity. On striking the gang-plank, it would rebound up and out on to the boat, against a barricade of bales previously arranged to receive it. The moment it struck this barricade it would be dashed at by two or three men and jerked out of the way, and others would roll it to its place for the voyage on the tiers aft. The mate, standing near the bottom of the slide, as soon as the men had removed one bale to what he thought a safe distance, would shout to those aloft, and down would come another. Not unfrequently a bale would not strike fairly on its end, and would rebound off, diagonally, overboard; or would be thrown up with such force as to go over the barricade, breaking stanchions and railings, and scattering the passengers on the berth deck. Negro hands were sent to the top of the bank to roll the bales to the slide, and Irishmen were kept below to remove them and stow them. On asking the mate the reason of this arrangement, he said, 'The niggers are worth too much to be risked here; if the Paddies are knocked overboard, or get their backs broke, nobody loses anything.'"

Organization of labor. At a long-established plantation that had been in the same family for generations, Olmsted witnessed slavery "under its most favorable aspects," softened by "the ties of long family association, common traditions, common memories and, if ever, common interests between the slaves and their rulers." The field-hands were divided "into four classes, according to their physical capacities. The children beginning as 'quarter hands,' advancing to 'half-hands,' and then to 'three quarter hands'; and finally, when mature and able-bodied, healthy and strong, to 'full hands.' As they decline in strength, from age, sickness or other cause, they retrograde in the scale, and proportionately less labor is required of them.

Amalgamation. This was the euphemism for sex between blacks and whites—usually a matter of a white man forcing himself on a black woman, but there were also long-standing arrangements whereby a wealthy white man kept his wife and official family in one household, and his colored mistress and their offspring in another. Either way, in the opinion of a certain Mrs. Douglass, who had been sent to jail for teaching slaves to read, and from there had written a letter that Olmsted quoted, amalgamation was "one great evil hanging over the Southern Slave States, destroying domestic happiness and the peace of thousands . . . The white mothers and daughters of the South have suffered under it for years—have seen their dearest affections trampled upon—their hopes of domestic happiness destroyed, and their future lives embittered, even to agony, by those who should be all in all to them, as husbands, sons and brothers."

Pursuing this topic, Olmsted wrote: "A Negress was hung this year in Alabama for the murder of her child. At her trial she confessed her guilt. She said her owner was the father of the child, and that her mistress knew it, and treated it so cruelly in consequence, that she had killed it to save it from further suffering." Also: "A large planter told, as a reason for sending his boys to the North to be educated, that there was no possibility of their being brought up in decency at home. Another planter told me that he was intending to move to a free country on this account. He said that the practice was not occasional or general, it was universal. 'There is not,' he said, 'a likely-looking black girl in this State that is not the concubine of a white man. There is not an old plantation in which the grandchildren of the owner are not whipped in the field by his overseer.'"

Sugar plantation. From New Orleans, Olmsted went by steamboat up the Mississippi to the large sugar plantation owned by "Mr. R."—actually Richard Taylor, son of President Zachary Taylor and future Confederate general. Mr. R. was "a man of more than usual precision of mind, energetic and humane; and while his Negroes seemed to be better disciplined than any others I had seen, they evidently regarded him with affection and pride." The plantation had about nine hundred acres of well-tilled land, drained by two canals. A large and comfortable mansion stood close to the river, with gardens in front and numerous outbuildings in the back. The Negroes' houses were "as neat and well-made externally as the cottages usually provided by large manufacturing companies in New England," and food, clothing, coffee and tobacco were generously supplied. Nursing mothers were allowed to be with their children for two hours at noon and to leave work an hour early. Labor was most intensive during the grinding season, which began in October and lasted two or three months. "Mr. R. assured me that during the last grinding season nearly every man, woman and child on his plantation, including the overseer and himself, were on duty fully eighteen hours a day. From the moment the grinding first commences until the end of the season, it is never discontinued: the fires under the boiler never go out, and the Negroes only rest six hours in the twenty-four, by relays." Yet despite the hard work "Mr. R. said that his Negroes were as glad as he was himself to have the time for grinding arrive, and they worked with greater cheerfulness than at any other season." Why was this so? Answer: incentives—"they are then better paid; they have better and more varied food and stimulants than usual, but especially they have a degree of freedom and of social pleasure, and a variety of occupation which brings recreation of the mind ... Men of sense have discovered that when they desire to get extraordinary exertions from their slaves, it is better to offer them rewards than to whip them."

Poor whites. "At one corner of Mr. R.'s plantation there was a hamlet consisting of about a dozen small houses or huts, built of wood or clay, in the old French peasant style. The residents owned small farms on which they raised a little corn and rice; but Mr. R. described them as lazy vagabonds, doing but little work, and spending much time in shooting, fishing and play. He wanted much to buy all their land, and get them to move away. He was willing to pay two or three times as much as the property was actually worth to get them to move off. As fast as he got possession he destroyed their houses and gardens, removed their fences and trees, and brought all their land into his cane-plantation.

> "Why did he so dislike to have these poor people living near him, I asked? Because, he straightway answered, they demoralized his Negroes. Seeing them live in apparent comfort, without much property and without steady labor, the slaves could not help thinking that it was unnecessary for men to work so hard as they themselves were obliged to, and that if they were free they would not work."
>
> "[Mr. R.] acknowledged slavery to be a very great evil, morally and economically. It was a curse upon the South; he had no doubt at all about it: nothing would be more desirable than its removal, if it were possible to be accomplished. But he did not think it could be abolished without instituting greater evils than those sought to be remedied. Its influence on the character of the whites was what was most deplorable. He was sorry to think that his children would have to be subject to it. He thought that eventually, if he were able to afford it, he should free his slaves and send them to Africa."

Three observations: "It is difficult to handle simply as property a creature possessing human passions and human feelings, however debased and torpid the condition of that creature may be; while, on the other hand, the absolute necessity of dealing with property as a thing greatly embarrasses a man in any attempt to treat it as a person. And it is the natural result of this complicated state of things that the system of slave management is irregular, ambiguous, and contradictory; that it is never either constantly humane or consistently economical.

"As a general rule, the larger the body of Negroes on a plantation or estate, the more completely are they treated as mere property.

"Throughout the South-west the Negroes, as a rule, appear to be worked much harder than in the Eastern and Northern Slave States. I do not think they accomplish as much as agricultural laborers at the North usually do, but they certainly labor much harder, and more unremittingly."

Life on a large plantation. One of the last places Olmsted visited was a very large cotton plantation on the Mississippi—so large that it employed four overseers as well as a manager, "a gentleman of good education, generous and poetic in temperament," while "the overseers were superior to most of their class." All were well paid. "These five men, each living more than a mile distant from either of the others, were the only white men on the estate." As to the slaves, who numbered several hundred, they "appeared to be well taken care of and abundantly supplied with the necessaries of vigorous physical existence."

The estate was divided into four plantations, and "each overseer regulated the hours of work on his own plantation. I saw the Negroes at work before sunrise and after sunset. At about eight o'clock they were allowed to stop for breakfast, and again, about noon, to dine. The length of these rests was at the discretion of the overseers or drivers, usually, I should say, from half an hour to an hour. There was no rule. The number of hands directed by each overseer was considerably over one hundred. The ploughs at work, both with single and double mule teams, were generally held by women, and very well held, too . . . Twenty of them were ploughing together, with double teams and heavy ploughs. They were superintended by a Negro man who carried a whip, which he frequently cracked at them, permitting no dawdling or delay at the turning; and they twitched their ploughs around on the head-land, jerking their reins and yelling to their mules, with apparent ease, energy and rapidity."

As to the other field-hands, "they are constantly and steadily driven up to their work, and the stupid, plodding and machine-like manner in which they labor is painful to witness. This was especially the case with the hoe-gangs. One of them numbered nearly two hundred hands (for the force of two plantations was working together), moving across the field in parallel lines with a considerable degree of precision. I repeatedly rode through the lines at a canter, with other horsemen, often coming upon them suddenly, without producing the smallest change or interruption in the dogged action of the laborers or causing one of them, so far as I could see, to lift an eye from the ground. I had noticed the same thing with smaller numbers before, but here, considering that I was a stranger, and that strangers could but very rarely visit the plantation, it amazed me very much. I think it told a more painful story than any I had ever heard of the cruelty of slavery. It was emphasized by a tall and powerful Negro who walked to and fro in the rear of the line, frequently cracking his whip, and calling out in the surliest manner, to one and another, 'Shove your hoe there! Shove your hoe!'"

Shortly afterward "I happened to see the severest corporeal punishment of a Negro that I witnessed at the South." Olmsted had just met up with one of the overseers "and he was showing me his plantation. In going from one side of it to the other we had twice crossed a deep gully, at the bottom of which was a thick covert of brushwood. We were crossing it a third time, and had nearly passed through the brush, when the overseer suddenly stopped his horse, exclaiming, 'What's that? Hallo! Who are you, there?'

"It was a girl lying at full length on the ground at the bottom of the gully, evidently intending to hide herself from us in the bushes.

"'Who are you, there?'

"'Sam's Sall, sir.'

"'What are you skulking there for?' The girl half rose, but gave no answer. 'Have you been here all day?'

"'No, sir.'

"'How did you get here?' The girl made no reply. 'Where have you been all day?' The answer was unintelligible. After some further questioning, she said her father accidentally locked her in when he went out in the morning.

"'How did you manage to get out?'

"'Pushed a plank off, sir, and crawled out.'

"The overseer was silent for a moment, looking at the girl, and then said, 'That won't do; come out here.' The girl arose at once and walked towards him. She was about eighteen years of age. A bunch of keys hung at her waist, which the overseer espied. He said, 'Your father locked you in; but you have got the keys.' After a little hesitation, she replied that these were the keys of some other locks; her father had the door-key."

Whether her story was true or false could have been ascertained in two minutes by riding to the gang with which her father was at work; but the overseer had made up his mind. "That won't do,' said he; 'get down.' The girl knelt on the ground; he got off his horse, and holding him with his left hand, struck her thirty or forty blows across the shoulders with his tough, flexible raw-hide whip (a terrible instrument for the purpose). They were well laid on, at arm's length, but with no appearance of angry excitement on the part of the overseer. At every stroke the girl winced and exclaimed, 'Yes, sir!' or 'Ah, sir!' or 'Please, sir!' not groaning or screaming. At length he stopped and said, 'Now tell me the truth.' The girl repeated the same story. 'You have not got enough yet,' said he. 'Pull up your clothes—lie down.' The girl without any hesitation, without a word or look of remonstrance or entreaty, drew closely all her garments under her shoulders, and lay down upon the ground with her face toward the overseer, who continued to flog her with the raw-hide across her naked loins and thighs, with as much strength as before. She now shrunk away from him, not rising, but writhing, grovelling and screaming, 'Oh don't, sir! Oh, please stop, master! Please, sir! Please, sir! Oh, that's enough, master! Oh, Lord! Oh, master, master! Oh, God, master, do stop! Oh, God, master! Oh, God, master!'

"A young gentleman of fifteen was with us; he had ridden in front and now, turning on his horse, looked back with an expression only of impatience at the delay. It was the first time I had ever seen a woman flogged. I had seen a man cudgelled and beaten in the heat of passion, but never flogged with a hundredth part of the severity used in this case. I glanced again at the perfectly passionless but, rather grim business-like face of the overseer, and again at the young gentleman, who had turned away; if not indifferent, he had evidently not the faintest sympathy with my emotion. Only my horse chafed. I gave him rein and spur and we plunged into the bushes and scrambled fiercely up the steep acclivity. The screaming, yells and the whip strokes had ceased when I reached the top of the bank. Choking, sobbing, spasmodic groans only were heard. I rode on to where the road, coming diagonally up the ravine, ran out upon the cotton-field. My young companion met me there, and immediately afterward the overseer. He laughed as he joined us, and said: 'She meant to cheat me out of a day's work, and she has done it, too.'

"'Did you succeed in getting another story from her?' I asked, as soon as I could trust myself to speak.

"'No; she stuck to it.'

"'Was it not perhaps true?'

"'Oh no, sir; she slipped out of the gang when they were going to work, and she's been dodging about all day, going from one place to another as she saw me coming.'

"'Was it necessary to punish her so severely?'

"'Oh yes, sir,' (laughing again). 'If I hadn't, she would have done the same thing again to-morrow, and half the people on the plantation would have followed her example. Oh, you've no idea how lazy these niggers are. You Northern people don't know anything about it. They'd never do any work at all if they were not afraid of being whipped.'"

Another white witness to American slavery was the upper-class and middle-aged Swedish novelist, Fredrika Bremer. A moderate feminist and Christian socialist, she was also a bold traveler, who spent two years—1849-1851—in this country, taking notes as she went. Here she is in New Orleans in mid-winter, attending a slave auction with a medical friend.

"Dr. D. and I entered a large and somewhat cold and dirty hall, on the basement story of a house, and where a great number of people were assembled. About twenty gentlemanlike men stood in a half circle around a dirty wooden platform, which for the moment was unoccupied. On each side, by the wall, stood a number of black men and women, silent and serious. The whole assembly was silent, and it seemed to me as if a heavy gray cloud rested upon it. One heard through the open door the rain falling heavily in the street. The gentlemen looked askance at me with a gloomy expression, and probably wished that they could send me to the North Pole.

"Two gentlemen hastily entered; one of them a tall, stout man, with a gay and good-tempered aspect, evidently a *bon vivant*, ascended the auction platform . . . He came apparently from a good breakfast, and he seemed to be actively employed in swallowing his last mouthful. He took the auctioneer's hammer in his hand, and addressed the assembly much as follows:

"'The slaves which I have now to sell, for what price I can get, are a few home-slaves, all the property of one master. This gentleman having given his bond for a friend who afterward became bankrupt, has been obliged to meet his responsibilities by parting with his faithful servants. These slaves are thus sold, not in consequence of any faults which they possess, or for any deficiencies. They are all faithful and excellent servants, and nothing but hard necessity would have compelled their master to part with them. They are worth the highest price, and he who purchases them may be sure that he increases the prosperity of his family.'

"After this he beckoned to a woman among the blacks to come forward, and he gave her his hand to mount upon the platform, where she remained standing beside him. She was a tall, well-grown mulatto, with a handsome but sorrowful countenance, and a remarkably modest, noble demeanor. She bore on her arm a young sleeping child, upon which, during the whole auction ceremonial, she kept her eyes immovably riveted, with her head cast down. She wore a gray dress made to the throat, and a pale yellow handkerchief, checked with brown, was tied round her head.

"The auctioneer now began to laud this woman's good qualities, her skill, and her abilities, to the assembly. He praised her character, her good disposition, order, fidelity; her uncommon qualifications for taking care of a house; her piety, her talents, and remarked that the child which she bore at her breast, and which was to be sold with her, also increased her value. After this he shouted with a loud voice, 'Now, gentlemen, how much for this very superior woman, this remarkable, &c., &c., and her child?'

"He pointed with his outstretched arm and fore-finger from one to another of the gentlemen who stood around, and first one and then another replied to his appeal with a short silent nod, and all the while he continued in this style:

"'Do you offer me five hundred dollars? Gentlemen, I am offered five hundred dollars for this superior woman and her child. It is a sum not to be thought of! She, with her child, is worth double that money. Five hundred and fifty, six hundred, six hundred and fifty, six hundred and sixty, six hundred and seventy. My good gentlemen, why do you not at once say seven hundred dollars for this uncommonly superior woman and her child? Seven hundred dollars—it is downright robbery! She would never have been sold at that price if her master had not been so unfortunate,'" &c.,&c.

"The hammer fell heavily; the woman and her child were sold for seven hundred dollars to one of those dark, silent figures before her. Who he was; whether he was good or bad; whether he would lead her into tolerable or intolerable slavery—of all this, the bought and sold woman and mother knew as little as I did, neither to what part of the world he would take her. And the father of the child—where was he?

"With eyes still riveted upon that sleeping child, with dejected but submissive mien, the handsome mulatto stepped down from the auction-platform to take her stand beside the wall, but on the opposite side of the room.

"Next, a very dark young negro girl stepped upon the platform. She wore a bright yellow handkerchief tied very daintily round her head, so that the two ends stood out like little wings, one on each side. Her figure was remarkably trim and neat, and her eyes glanced round the assembly both boldly and inquiringly. The auctioneer exalted her merits likewise, and then he exclaimed, 'How much for this very likely young girl?' She was soon sold, and, if I recollect rightly, for three hundred and fifty dollars.

"After her a young man took his place on the platform. He was a mulatto, and had a remarkably good countenance, expressive of gentleness and refinement. He had been a servant in his former, master's family, had been brought up by him, was greatly beloved by him, and deserved to be so—'a most excellent young man!' He sold for six hundred dollars.

"After this came an elderly woman, who had also one of those good-natured, excellent countenances so common among the black population and whose demeanor and general appearance showed that she too had been in the service of a good master, and, having been accustomed to gentle treatment, had become gentle and happy. All these slaves, as well as the young girl, who looked pert rather than good, bore the impression of having been accustomed to an affectionate family life.

"And now, what was to be their future fate? How bitterly, if they fell into the hands of the wicked, would they feel the difference between then and now—horrible would be their lot! The mother in particular, whose whole soul was centered in her child, and who, perhaps, would have soon to see that child sold away, far away from her—what would then be her state of mind?"

Many of slavery's defenders were ready to admit that there were cruel masters, but claimed that these were exceptions to an otherwise benevolent institution; as one popular argument ran, just because some husbands murdered their wives, and some wives their husbands, it did not follow that marriage should be abolished. It was also claimed that most cases of brutality were the work of overzealous drivers, who were themselves Negro slaves, or of owners belonging to the lower levels of white society. On the other hand, to be a servant in the household of a well-to-do family that spent half the year on a plantation and half in town, was to enjoy a carefree life of easy duties and mutual affection.

Unfortunately for this comforting belief, two sisters, Sarah and Angelina Grimké, knew better, and felt morally obliged to say so out loud; and since they were the daughters of Judge Grimké of the Supreme Court of South Carolina, and a leading member of Charleston society, their testimony carried weight. For their boldness the two sisters were ostracized and had to move to Philadelphia, where Angelina married the abolitionist Theodore Dwight Weld, with whom she wrote and edited *American Slavery As It Is*. Sarah was the first to publish, which she did in 1830:

> "As I left my native state on account of slavery, and deserted the home of my fathers to escape the sound of the lash and the shrieks of the tortured victims, I would gladly bury in oblivion the recollection of those scenes with which I have been familiar; but this may not, cannot be; they come over my memory like gory specters, and implore me with resistless power, in the name of a God of mercy, in the name of a crucified Savior, in the name of humanity; for the sake of the slaveholder as well as the slave, to bear witness to the horrors of the southern prison house." Of particular impor-

Unlike Fanny Kemble in appearance, but no less passionate in her condemnation of slavery, Sarah Grimké, and her sister Angelina, gave up comfortable lives as members of Charleston's upper class in order to devote themselves to the causes of abolition and women's rights. Both were persuasive writers, whose works were often confiscated by southern postmasters.

tance was the fact that "the actors in these tragedies were all men and women of the highest respectability, and of the first families in South Carolina, and, with one exception, citizens of Charleston; and that their cruelties did not in the slightest degree affect their standing in society.

"A handsome mulatto woman, about 18 or 20 years of age, whose independent spirit could not brook the degradation of slavery, was in the habit of running away: for this offense she had been re-peatedly sent by her master and mistress to be whipped by the keeper of the Charleston work-house. This had been done with such inhuman severity as to lacerate her back in the most shocking manner; a finger could not be laid between the cuts. But the love of liberty was too strong to be annihilated by torture; and, as a last resort, she was whipped at several different times and kept close prisoner. A heavy iron collar, with three long prongs projecting from it, was placed round her neck, and a strong and sound front tooth was extracted, to serve as a mark to describe her, in case of escape . . . These outrages were committed in a family where the mistress daily read the Scriptures, and assembled her children for family worship. She was accounted, and was really, so far as alms-giving was concerned, a charitable woman, and tender-hearted to the poor; and yet this suffering slave, who was the seamstress of the family, was continually in her presence, sitting in her chamber to sew, or engaged in her other household work, with her lacerated and bleeding back, her mutilated mouth, and heavy iron collar, without, so far as appeared, exciting any feelings of compassion.

"A punishment dreaded more by the slaves than whipping, unless it is unusually severe, is one which was invented by a female acquaintance of mine in Charleston—I heard her say so with much satisfaction. It is standing on one foot, and holding the other in the hand. Afterwards it was improved upon, and a strap was contrived to fasten around the ankle and pass around the neck; so that the least weight of the foot resting on the strap would choke the person. The pain occasioned by this unnatural position was great; and when continued, as it sometimes was, for an hour or more, produced intense agony. I heard this same woman say that she had the ears of of her waiting maid slit for some petty theft. This she told me in the presence of the girl, who was standing in the room. She often had the helpless victims of her cruelty severely whipped, not scrupling herself to wield the instrument of torture, and with her own hands inflict severe chastisement." This lady and her husband "were of one of the first families on Charleston."

Sarah's sister, Angelina, also had some stories to tell. One was about "the woman of the highest respectability—one who was foremost in every benevolent enterprise, and stood for many years, I may say, at the head of the fashionable élite of the city of Charleston, and afterwards at the head of the moral and religious female society there . . . This lady used to keep cowhides, or small paddles (called 'pancake sticks,') in four different apartments of her house; so that when she wished to punish, or

have punished, any of her slaves, she might not have the trouble of sending for an instrument of torture. For many years, one or other, and often
more, of her slaves were flogged every day; particularly the young slaves
about the house, whose faces were slapped, or their hands beat with the
'pancake stick' for every trifling offence—and often for no fault at all.
But the floggings were not all; the scoldings and abuse daily heaped upon
them were worse: 'fools' and 'liars,' 'sluts' and 'husseys,' 'hypocrites' and
'good-for-nothing creatures,' were the common epithets with which her
mouth was filled when addressing her slaves, adults as well as children.
Very often she would take a position at her window, in an upper story,
and scold at her slaves while working in the garden, at some distance
from the house (a large yard intervening), and occasionally order a flogging. I have known her thus on the watch, scolding for more than an
hour at a time, in so loud a voice that the whole neighborhood could
hear her; and this without the least apparent feeling of shame. Indeed, it
was no disgrace among the slaveholders, and did not in the least injure
her standing, either as a lady or a Christian, in the aristocratic circle in
which she moved.

"Persons who own plantations and yet live in cities often take children from their parents as soon as they are weaned and send them
into the country, because they do not want the time of the mother
taken up by attendance upon her own children, it being too valuable
to the mistress. As a *favor*, she is in some cases permitted to go to
see them once a year. So, on the other hand, if field slaves happen
to have children of an age suitable to the convenience of the master,
they are taken from their parents and brought to the city. Parents
are almost never consulted as to the disposition to be made of their
children; they have as little control over them as have domestic animals over the disposal of their young.

"Every thing cruel and revolting is carefully concealed from
strangers, especially those from the North. Take an instance. I have
known the master and mistress of a family send to their friends to
borrow servants to wait on company because their own slaves had
been so cruelly flogged in the Work House that they could not walk
without limping at every step, and their putrified flesh emitted such
an intolerable smell that they were not fit to be in the presence of

company. How can Northerners know these things when they are hospitably received at Southern tables and firesides? I repeat it, no one who has not been an integral part of a slave-holding community can have any idea of its abominations."

Finally, this story from the memoirs of Boston-born Mary Livermore, who was serving as a governess to the family of a southern planter when she witnessed this scene: "Caroline, a pretty and graceful mulatto, was a servant in the dining room. One morning, when passing a cup of coffee to Mr.——, her master and owner, by an unlucky movement of his hand he knocked it from the tray on which she served it, to his knees. It was warm weather; he was attired in linen, and the hot coffee scalded him. Jumping up with an oath, he raised his chair and felled the girl to the floor, striking her two or three times after she had fallen. She was carried to the cottage of 'Aunt Aggy,' her mother, who had witnessed the scene from an adjoining room—stunned, bruised, bleeding and unconscious. I left the table and withdrew to my own apartment, shocked beyond expression.

"Later in the day Aunt Aggy came to my room on some household errand, when I expressed my indignation at the brutal treatment her daughter had received, uttering myself with the frankness of a New England girl of nineteen who had been trained to be true to her convictions. I was astonished at the change that came over the taciturn and dignified woman. Turning squarely about and facing me, with her large, lustrous eyes blazing with excitement, she spoke in a tone and manner that would have befitted a seer uttering a prophecy:—

"'Thar's a day a-comin'! Thar's a day a-comin'!' she said, with her right hand uplifted. 'I hear the rumblin' of the chariots! I see the flashin' of the guns! White folks' blood is a-runnin' on the ground like a river, and the dead's heaped up that high,' measuring to the level of her shoulder. 'Oh, Lord! hasten the day when the blows, and the bruises, and the aches, and the pains shall come to the white folks, and the buzzards shall eat them as they is dead in the streets. Oh Lord! roll on the chariots, and give the black people rest and peace. Oh, Lord! give me the pleasure of livin' till that day, when I shall see white folks shot down like the wolves when they come hungry out of the woods.'

"And without another word she walked from the room."

SOLOMON IN HIS PLANTATION SUIT.

Portrait of Solomon Northup from the frontispiece of Twelve Years a Slave. *Although he may have had some editorial help, the book was clearly written by Northup himself—hence the signature written with such a confident flourish. The condescending tone of the caption, using his first name only—"Solomon in his plantation suit"—is typical of well-meaning but often prejudiced Northerners. The clean white "plantation suit" is misleading since field slaves were given only the cheapest and coarsest of clothing. And his relaxed posture, sitting comfortably with folded hands, his broom set aside, does little to prepare the reader for the horror story he had to tell.*

CHAPTER 9

BLACK EXPERIENCE

THIS STORY WAS TOLD BY HENRIETTA KING, OF VIRGINIA, TO AN INTERVIEWER for the Federal Writers' Project and later included in the multi-volume series known as *Slave Narratives*. The interviews were conducted in the late nineteen-thirties, when she was probably in her mid-eighties.

"See this face? See this mouth all twisted over here so I can't shut it? See that eye? All red, ain't it? Been that way for eighty-some years now. Guess it gonna stay that way till I die. Well, old Missus made this face this way."

This happened when Henrietta, then aged about eight, was a house servant whose duties included emptying the washbasin in the owners' bedroom. One day she found a piece of peppermint candy on the washstand.

"I seed that peppermint stick laying there, and I ain't dared go near it 'cause I knew old Missus just waiting for me to take it. Then one morning I so hungry that I can't resist. I went straight in there and grab that stick of candy and stuffed it in my mouth and chew it down quick so old Missus never find me with it.

"Next morning old Missus say, 'Henrietta, you take that piece of candy out my room?' 'No mam, ain't seed no candy.' 'Chile, you lying to me. You took that candy.' 'Deed, Missus, I tell the truth. Ain't seed no candy.' 'You lying and I'm gonna whip you. Come here.' She got her rawhide down from the nail by the fireplace, and she grabbed me by the arm and she try to turn me cross her knees whilst she sat in the rocker so's she could hold me. I twisted and turned till finally she called her daughter. The gal come in and took that strap like her mother told her and commence to lay it on real hard whilst Missus hold me. I twisted away so there warn't no chance of her getting in no solid lick. Then old Missus lift me up by the legs, and she stuck my head under the bottom of the rocker, and she rock forward so as to hold my head and whip me some more. I guess they must have whipped me near an hour with that rocker leg a-pressing down on my head.

"Next thing I knew the old doctor was there, and I was lying on my pallet in the hall, and he was a-pushing and digging at my face, but he couldn't do nothing at all with it. Seem like that rocker pressing on my young bones had crushed them all into soft pulp. The next day I couldn't open my mouth, and I feel it and they weren't no bone in the left side at all. And my mouth kept a-slipping over to the right side and I couldn't chew nothing, only drink milk. Well, old Missus must have got kind of sorry 'cause she gets the doctor to come regular and pry at my mouth. He gets it afterwhile so as it open and I could move my lips, but it kept moving over to the right, and he couldn't stop that. After a while it was over just where it is now. And I ain't never growed no more teeth on that side. Ain't never been able to chew nothing good since. Don't even remember what it is to chew.

"Here, put your hand on my face—right here on this left cheek—that's what slave days was like."

The *Slave Narratives* were the last of a large number of first-person accounts by those who had actually experienced slavery in this country. For a long time these had been few in number, but as the nineteenth century progressed, and the crisis of disunion drew closer, there was a growing—though not overwhelming—demand in the North for such works. Because of the laws in the South against teaching slaves to read and write, and because free blacks in the North were often denied an education, many of these narratives were dictated to or written up by sympathetic white editors; this accounts for the often formal style, but does not affect the truth of their stories.

One of the best-known of these accounts was *Twelve Years a Slave*, by Solomon Northup, a free black who had been living in upper New York State, happily married and doing quite well, when he was tricked into going to Washington, D. C. by two men who promised him a well-paying job as a musician for a circus. Once there he was drugged, kidnapped and, since he was in the South, and was black, and was therefore presumed to be a slave, he was easily sold in a local market. From Washington he was sent to New Orleans for re-sale. After working for a kindly planter named Ford, and a brutal carpenter named Tibeats, he was sold yet again to Edwin Epps, who had a cotton plantation on Bayou Boeuf, "a sluggish, winding stream—one of those stagnant bodies of water common in that region, setting back from Red River . . . Large cotton and sugar plantations line each shore, extending back to the borders of interminable swamps. It is alive with alligators."

Epps, his new owner, was "a large, portly, heavy-bodied man with light hair, high cheek bones, and a Roman nose." His eyes were blue, he had a "sharp, inquisitive expression," and his manners and speech were "repulsive and coarse." When drunk he "was a roystering, blustering, noisy fellow whose chief delight was in dancing with 'niggers,' or lashing them about the yard with his long whip, just for the pleasure of hearing them screech and scream." When sober, "he was silent, reserved and cunning." In his youth he had been a driver and overseer, and was proud of his reputation as a "nigger-breaker." He now managed a cotton plantation that he leased from his wife's uncle.

After a detailed explanation of the laborious and complicated business of raising cotton, Northup goes on:

"The hands are required to be in the cotton fields as soon as it is light in the morning, and, with the exception of ten or fifteen minutes which is given to them at noon to swallow their allowance of cold bacon, they are not permitted to be a moment idle until it is too dark to see; and when the moon is full they often times labor till the middle of the night. They do not dare to stop even at dinner time, nor return to the quarters, however late it be, until the order to halt is given by the driver.

"The day's work over in the field, the baskets are 'toted,' or in other words, carried to the gin-house, where the cotton is weighed. No matter how fatigued and weary he may be—no matter how much he longs for sleep and rest—a slave never approaches the gin-house with his basket of cotton but with fear. If it falls short in weight—if he has not performed the full task appointed him, he knows that he must suffer. And if he has exceeded it by ten or twenty pounds, in all probability his master will measure the next day's task accordingly. After weighing, follow the whippings; and then the baskets are carried to the cotton house, and their contents stored away.

"This done, the labor of the day is not yet ended, by any means. Each one must then attend to his respective chores. One feeds the mules, another the swine—another cuts the wood, and so forth; besides, the packing is all done by candle-light. Finally, at a late hour, they reach the quarters, sleepy and overcome with the long day's toil. Then a fire must be kindled in the cabin, the corn ground in the small hand-mill, and supper, and dinner for the next day, prepared. All that is allowed them is corn and bacon, which is given out at the corn-crib and smoke-house every Sunday morning. Each one receives, as his weekly allowance, three and a half pounds of bacon, and corn enough to make a peck of meal. That is all."

Solomon's bed was "a plank twelve inches wide and ten feet long. My pillow was a stick of wood. The bedding was a coarse blanket, and not a rag or shred beside." His cabin was "constructed of logs, without floor or window." When it rained, the water was driven in through the crevices, "rendering it comfortless and extremely disagreeable.

"An hour before day-light the horn is blown. Then the slaves arouse, prepare their breakfast, fill a gourd with water, and in another deposit their dinner of cold bacon and corn cake, and hurry out to the field again. It is an offense invariably followed by a flogging to be found at the quarters after day-break. Then the fears and labors of another day begin; and until its close there is no such thing as rest. He fears he will be caught lagging through the day; he fears to approach the gin-house with his basket-load of cotton at night; he fears, when he lies down, that he will oversleep himself in the morning."

At least once a fortnight Epps would come home drunk after attending shooting matches at the nearby town of Holmesville. "At such times he was boisterous and half-crazy. Often he would break the dishes, chairs and whatever furniture he could lay his hands on. When satisfied with his amusement in the house, he would seize the whip and walk forth into the yard. Then it behooved the slaves to be watchful and exceeding wary. The first one who came within reach felt the smart of his lash. Sometimes for hours he would keep them running in all directions, dodging around the corners of the cabins. Occasionally he would come upon one unawares, and if he succeeded in inflicting a fair, round blow, it was a feat that much delighted him. The younger children, and the aged who had become inactive, suffered then. In the midst of the confusion he would slily take his stand behind a cabin, waiting with raised whip, to dash it into the first black face that peeped cautiously around the corner.

"At other times he would come home in a less brutal humor. Then there must be merry-making." Solomon would be ordered to fetch the violin that Mrs. Epps, who was "passionately fond of music," had induced her husband to buy for him, and everyone assembled in the living room of "the great house," as it was called. "No matter how worn out and tired we were, there must be a general dance. When properly stationed on the floor, I would strike up a tune. 'Dance, you d—d niggers, dance!' Epps would shout. Then there must be no halting, no delay, no slow or languid movements; all must be brisk, and lively, and alert. 'Up and down, heel and toe, and away we go,' was the order of the hour. Epps' portly form mingled with those of his dusky slaves, moving rapidly through all the mazes of the dance. Usually his whip was in his hand, ready to fall about the ears of the presumptuous thrall who dared to rest a moment, or even stop to catch his breath. When he was himself exhausted there would be a brief cessation, but it would be very brief. With a slash, and crack, and flourish of the whip, he would shout again, 'Dance, niggers, dance!' and away they would go once more." Despite being kept up most of the night, the hands still had to be in the field as soon as it was light, and "the whippings were just as severe . . . Indeed, after such frantic revels, he was always more sour and savage than before."

Epps had two sons, the older "an intelligent lad of ten or twelve years of age. It is pitiable sometimes to see him chastising, for instance, the venerable Uncle Abram. He will call the old man to account, and if in his childish judgment it is necessary, sentence him to a certain number of lashes, which he proceeds to inflict with much gravity and deliberation. Mounted on his pony he often rides into the field with his whip, playing the overseer, greatly to his father's delight. At such times he applies the rawhide, urging the slaves forward with shouts, and occasional expressions of profanity, while the old man laughs."

Among the other slaves at Bayou Boeuf was one called Patsey, whose parents had been brought from Africa to Cuba and then smuggled into America. Patsey was twenty-three, "slim and straight," and "with an air of loftiness in her movement that neither labor, nor weariness, nor punishment could destroy." In cotton-picking time she "was queen of the field," flying along the rows and gathering the bolls "with both hands and with such surprising rapidity that five hundred pounds a day was not unusual for her." By temperament she "was a joyous creature, a laughing, light-hearted girl, rejoicing in the mere sense of existence.

> "Yet Patsey wept oftener, and suffered more, than any of her com-
> panions. She had been literally excoriated. Her back bore the scars
> of a thousand stripes; not because she was backward in her work, nor
> because she was of an unmindful and rebellious spirit, but because it
> had fallen her lot to be the slave of a licentious master and a jealous
> mistress. She shrank before the lustful eye of the one, and was in dan-
> ger even of her life at the hands of the other, and between the two she
> was indeed accursed. In the great house, for days together, there were
> high and angry words, poutings and estrangement, whereof she was
> the innocent cause. Nothing delighted the mistress so much as to see
> her suffer, and more than once, when Epps refused to sell her, has she
> tempted me with bribes to put her secretly to death, and bury her
> body in some lonely place in the margin of the swamp."

Sometimes when he returned from a shooting-match in Holmesville, Epps would stumble out into the field where the hands were hoeing and beckon to Patsey, "motioning and grimacing, as was his habit when half-intoxicated. Aware of his lewd intentions, Patsey began to cry." At other times when he had been drinking Epps would beat her, claiming that it was to please his wife. Ironically, when a child Patsey had been Mrs. Epps' favorite—"petted and admired for her uncommon sprightliness and pleasant disposition." Mrs. Epps would give her treats and "fondle her as she would a playful kitten." But now "only black and angry fiends ministered in the temple of her heart, until she could look on Patsey with concentrated venom.

> "It is a mistaken opinion that the slave does not understand the idea of
> freedom. Even on Bayou Boeuf, where I conceive slavery exists in its
> most abject and cruel form, the most ignorant of them generally know
> full well its meaning . . . Patsey's life, especially after her whipping, was

one long dream of liberty. Far away, to her fancy an immeasurable distance, she knew there was a land of freedom. A thousand times she had heard that somewhere in the distant North, there were no slaves—no masters. In her imagination it was an enchanted region, the Paradise of the earth. To dwell where the black man may work for himself—live in his own cabin—till his own soil, was a blissful dream of Patsey's—a dream, alas! the fulfillment of which she can never realize."

After twelve years as a slave, Northup succeeded in regaining his freedom. With the help of a sympathetic carpenter, he smuggled a letter to friends in the North, telling what had happened to him. His case clearly came under the 1840 New York law, "An act more effectually to protect the free citizens of this state from being kidnapped or reduced to slavery." The governor "took a lively interest in the matter" and before long an official agent was sent to Bayou Boeuf to obtain his release. After various legal formalities had been completed, the moment came for Solomon to depart. Mrs. Epps was "affected to tears," Mr. Epps cursed him "in a surly, malicious manner," and Patsey, "tears streaming down her face," exclaimed "You're goin' to be free—you're goin' way off yonder, where we'll nebber see ye any more . . . I'm glad you're goin' to be free—but oh! de Lord! de Lord! What'll become of me?"

Few slave narratives were more popular in their day than *The Life of Josiah Henson,* the man who claimed to have been the original for the saintly Uncle Tom in Harriet Beecher Stowe's novel. Born the youngest of six children in 1789 in Maryland on a farm belonging to Francis Newman, Henson had a rough start in life. His first memory "was the appearance of my father one day, with his head bloody and his back lacerated . . . His right ear had been cut off close to his head, and he had received a hundred lashes on his back. He had beaten the overseer for a brutal assault on my mother, and this was his punishment. Furious at such treatment, my father became a different man, and was so morose, disobedient and intractable that Mr. Newman determined to sell him." The buyer was Newman's son, who lived in Alabama, "and neither my mother nor I ever heard of him again."

Soon after, Josiah and his mother were sold to a Dr. McPherson, "a man of good natural impulses, kind-hearted, liberal, and jovial. The latter quality was so much developed as to be his great failing," and one evening "the doctor was riding home from one of his scenes of riotous excess when, falling from his horse in crossing a little run not a foot deep, he was unable to save himself from drowning.

"In consequence of his decease it became necessary to sell the estate and the slaves in order to divide up the property among the heirs; and we were all put up at auction and sold to the highest bidder, and scattered over various parts of the country. My brother and sisters were bid off one by one, while my mother, holding my hand, looked on in an agony of grief, the cause of which I but ill understood at first, but which dawned on my mind with dreadful clearness as the sale proceeded. My mother was then separated from me and put up in her turn. She was bought by a man named Isaac Riley, residing in Montgomery County, and then I was offered to the assembled purchasers. My mother, half distracted with the parting forever from all her children, pushed through the crowd while the bidding was going on to the spot where Riley was standing. She fell at his feet and clung to his knees, entreating him in tones that a mother only could command, to buy her baby as well as herself, and spare to her one of her little ones at least. Will it, can it, be believed that this man, thus appealed to, was capable not merely of turning a deaf ear to her supplication, but of disengaging himself from her with such violent blows and kicks as to reduce her to the necessity of creeping out of his reach, and mingling the groan of bodily suffering with the sob of a breaking heart?"

Josiah was sold to a different buyer, but by a piece of what might be called slave's luck, he fell so seriously ill that his new owner offered to sell him to Riley "at such a trifling rate that it could not be refused. I was thus providentially restored to my mother; and under her care I recovered my health and grew up to be an uncommonly vigorous and healthy boy and man."

Captioned "Mother being separated from her baby," this naive woodcut had an impact that in a more visually sophisticated age may be hard to appreciate, but was powerful at the time. The heartbreak caused by separating families was one of the abolitionists' most compelling themes.

When he was eighteen, he went to hear a lay preacher—"a baker, whose character was that of an upright, benevolent Christian man," and who was "noted especially for his detestation of slavery." Until then "I had never heard a sermon, nor any discourse or conversation whatever upon religious topics, except what had been impressed upon me by my mother of the responsibility of all to a Supreme Being. When I arrived at the place of meeting the speaker was just beginning his discourse, from the text Hebrews ii. 9: 'That he, by the grace of God, should taste of death for every man.' This was the first text of the Bible to which I had ever listened, knowing it to be such. I have never forgotten it, and scarce a day has passed since in which I have not recalled it, and the sermon that was preached from it. The divine character of Jesus Christ, his life and teachings, his sacrifice of himself for others, his death and resurrection were all alluded to, and some of the points were dwelt upon with great power—great at least to me, who heard of these things for the first time of my life. I was wonderfully impressed too with the use which the preacher made of the last words of the text—'for every man.' He said the death of Christ was not designed for the benefit of a select few only, but for the salvation of the world, for the bond as well as the free; and he dwelt on the glad tidings of the Gospel to the poor, the persecuted, and the distressed, its deliverance to the captive, and the liberty wherewith Christ has made us free, till my heart burned within me and I was in a state of the greatest excitement."

Looking back, Josiah dated "my conversion and my awakening to a new life from this day, so memorable to me. I used every means and opportunity of inquiry into religious matters; and so deep was my conviction of their superior importance to everything else, so clear my perception of my own faults, and so undoubting my observation of the sin and darkness that surrounded me, that I could not help talking much on these subjects with those about me; and it was not long before I began to pray with them, and exhort them, and to impart to the poor slaves those little glimmerings of light from another world which had reached my own eye. In a few years I became quite an esteemed preacher among them, and I will not believe it is vanity which leads me to think that I was useful to some."

His calling as a preacher did not interfere with his other duties. These included acting as bodyguard to Riley, who was "coarse and vulgar in his habits, unprincipled and cruel in his general deportment, and especially addicted to the vice of licentiousness." On weekends, Riley would get together with other planters at the local tavern and "gamble, run horses or fight gamecocks, discuss politics, and drink whiskey, and brandy and water, all day long. Perfectly aware that they would not be able to find their own way home at night, each one ordered a slave, his particular attendant, to come after him and help him home. I was chosen for this confidential duty by my master, and many is the time I have held him on his horse when he could not hold himself in the saddle, and walked by his side in the darkness and mud from the tavern to his house." Tavern fights often broke out, "and whenever they became especially dangerous, and glasses were thrown, dirks drawn and pistols fired, it was the duty of the slaves to rush in, and each one was to drag his master from the fight and carry him home."

Josiah also acted as overseer on the farm and was responsible for selling its products—wheat, oats, hay, fruit and butter—in the local markets, always keeping scrupulous accounts. When he was twenty-two he "married a very efficient and, for a slave, a very well-taught girl belonging to a neighboring family, reputed to be pious and kind, whom I first met at the chapel I attended; and during nearly forty years that have since elapsed I have had no reason to regret the connection." At the time of writing, his wife had borne twelve children.

"Things remained in this condition for a considerable period," and then Riley got involved in a lawsuit. To dodge his creditors, he decided to move all his slaves from Maryland to his brother's property in Kentucky. Josiah was made to promise that he would escort them there, Riley "well knowing from his past experience of my character that I should hold myself bound by such promise to do all that it implied." They set off in February, 1825. "There were eighteen Negroes besides my wife, two children and myself, to transport nearly a thousand miles through a country I knew nothing about, and in winter time. My master . . . furnished me with a small sum of money and some provisions, and I bought a one-horse wagon to carry them, and to give the women and children a lift now and then; the rest of us were to trudge on foot."

At Wheeling he sold the wagon and bought a boat in which they sailed down the river. Everything went well except for "one source of anxiety." This came when, "passing along the State of Ohio, we were frequently told that we were free, if we chose to be so. At Cincinnati especially the colored people gathered round us and urged us with much importunity to remain with them; told us it was folly to go on; and in short used all the arguments now so familiar to induce slaves to quit their masters." Josiah admitted that he was tempted—"from my earliest recollection freedom had been the object of my ambition"—but his "sense of honor on the subject" led him to believe that the only way to gain his freedom was to buy it. As to those in his charge, to let them escape "would have been a retribution which might be called righteous," but "it was a punishment which it was not for me to inflict. I had promised that man to take his property to Kentucky and deposit it with his brother; and this, and this only, I resolved to do."

Four years later he was again on a riverboat, this time heading for New Orleans. In the meantime he had remained in Kentucky, working for Riley's brother, Amos, and also serving as a part-time itinerant preacher; by concluding his sermons with appeals for financial help, he had managed to accumulate 350 of the 450 dollars Riley had agreed to take for his freedom. On a visit back to Maryland, he handed over the $350, gave a note for the rest, and received his manumission papers; but before returning to Kentucky, Riley persuaded him that it would be safer to mail the precious papers to his brother Amos, rather than carry them with him. This seemed a sensible idea, but on his return Amos Riley told him that he would not be given the papers until he had made up the full purchase price; and this, said Amos, was $1000, rather than $450. Unable to prove otherwise, Josiah "set about my work again, with as quiet a mind as I could command, resolved to trust in God, and never despair."

But worse was to come, for Riley, desperate for money, wrote to Amos to send Josiah to New Orleans, and there sell him. Josiah got wind of the plan, "and my heart sunk within me"; but he felt there was nothing he could do. Amos Riley told him that he was to go down-river on a flat boat, along with son, also called Amos, a crew of three, and a load of farm produce.

"My wife and children accompanied me to the landing, where I bade them an adieu which might be for life, and then stepped into the boat. The load consisted of beef-cattle, pigs, poultry, corn whiskey and other articles from the farm which were to be sold as we dropped down the river." Everyone had to take a turn at the helm, and "as I was the only Negro on the boat I was made to stand at least three tricks to any other person's one; so that from being much with the captain, and frequently thrown upon my own exertions, I learned the art of steering and managing the boat far better than the rest. I watched the maneuvers necessary to shoot by a sawyer, to land on a bank, or avoid a snag or a steamboat in the rapid current of the Mississippi." Josiah often also had to keep watch when they tied up at night, "to prevent depredations by Negroes on shore, who used frequently to attack boats such as ours. As I paced backwards and forwards on the deck during my watch, it may well be believed I revolved many a painful and passionate thought." The more he dwelt on the cruel injustice being done him, the "more ferocious" he became, until he was in the grip of an "almost uncontrollable fury." At length, "blinded by passion and stung to madness," he "resolved to kill my four companions, take what money there was in the boat, then to scuttle the craft and escape to the north.

"One dark, rainy night, within a few days of New Orleans, my hour seemed to have come. I was alone on deck; Mr. Amos and the hands were all asleep below. I crept down noiselessly, got hold of an axe, and looking by the aid of the dim light there for my victims, my eye fell upon Master Amos, who was nearest to me. My hand slid along the axe handle. I raised it to strike the fatal blow—when suddenly the thought came to me, 'What! Commit murder? And you a Christian?' I had not called it murder before. It was self-defense—it was preventing others from murdering me—it was justifiable—it was even praiseworthy. But now all at once the truth burst upon me that it was a crime. I was going to kill a young man who had done nothing to injure me but obey commands which he could not resist; I was about to lose the fruit of all my efforts at self-improvement, the character I had acquired, and the peace of mind which had never deserted me. All this came upon me instantly, and with a distinctness which made me almost think I heard it whispered in my ear; and I believe I even turned my head to listen. I shrank back, laid down the axe, crept up on deck again, and thanked God, as I have done every day since, that I had not committed murder."

Apart from those who wondered how it was possible to have below-deck cabins on a flat-bottomed boat, or whether he would really have been able to murder four able-bodied men one after the other, few questioned this story of Christian redemption. It was what people wanted to hear, and Josiah emerged the hero of his own tale. And after his escape to Canada, he did his best to help things along, remembering further details for later editions; and when Mrs. Stowe's novel appeared, letting it be known that he was the model for Uncle Tom—a claim she neither confirmed or denied, but tactfully let pass. Josiah also became pastor and leader of a community of former slaves who had settled in Canada at a place called Dawn; and while on a fund-raising trip to England met not only the Archbishop of Canterbury but also Queen Victoria, who graciously presented him with a photograph of herself.

Delia Garlic was an old woman living in Montgomery, Alabama, when she told her story to an interviewer for the Federal Writers' Project:

"I was born in Powhatan, Virginia, and was the youngest of thirteen chillen. I never seed none of my brothers and sisters 'cept brother William. Him and my mother and me was brought in a speculator's drove to Richmond and put in a warehouse with a drove of other niggers. Then we was all put on a block and sold to the highest bidder. Never seed brother William again.

"Mammy and me was sold to a man by the name of Carter, who was the sheriff of the county. They wasn't no good times at his house. He was a widower and his daughter kept house for him. I nursed for her and one day I was playing with the baby. It hurt its little hand and commenced to cry, and she whirl on me, pick up a hot iron and run it all down my arm and hand. It took off the flesh when she done it.

"After a while master married again, but things weren't no better. I seed his wife blacking her eyebrows with smut one day, so I thought I'd black mine just for fun. I rubbed some smut on my eyebrows and forgot to rub it off, and she catched me. She was powerful mad and yelled, 'You black devil, I'll show you to mock your betters.' Then she pick up a stick of stovewood and flails it against my head. I didn't know nothing more till I come to, lying on the floor. I heard the mistress say to one of the girls, 'I thought her thick skull and cap of wool could take it better than that.'

"I kept on staying there, and one night the master come in drunk and set at the table with his head lolling around. I was waiting on the table, and he look up and see me. I was scared, and that made him awful mad. He called an overseer and told him, 'Take her out and beat some sense in her.' I begin to cry and run and run in the night, but finally I run back by the quarters and heard Mammy calling me. I went in, and right away they come for me. A horse was standing in front of the house, and I was took that very night to Richmond and sold to a speculator again. I never seed my Mammy anymore.

"I has thought many times through all these years how Mammy looked that night. She pressed my hand in both of hers and said, 'Be good, and trust in the Lord.' Trusting was the only hope of the poor black critters in them days. Us just prayed for strength to endure it to the end. We didn't 'spect nothing but to stay in bondage till we died."

Though born into slavery, Thomas Jones was lucky enough to have had an easy-going and kindly master, Owen Holmes, who "did more for me than my own father could have done." Mr. Holmes had a house and business in Wilmington, N. C., and an estate in the country. When in town, Jones hired himself out as a dock-worker, but during the summers he accompanied the Holmes family as a general servant, and was allowed to range about the countryside preaching and holding camp meetings. One of these took place at the estate belonging to a Mr. Blackman Crumpling, whose family were all Methodists. The meeting was probably held outdoors or in a barn, rather than in a church; blacks and whites attended in about equal numbers and on equal terms; the "anxious" were those teetering on the edge of giving themselves to God; exhorters were assistant ministers who uttered encouraging cries and exclamations.

"My remarks at this meeting were based upon the Scripture, 'O Lord, revive thy work.' And the Lord did revive it in mighty power. Large numbers of both white and colored persons were stricken down and led to cry for mercy at God's hand. I observed that during the sermon Mr. Crumpling was very much affected. I afterwards learned the cause: he was burdened for a neighbor who was present. When I gave the usual invitations for the anxious to come forward for prayer, this neighbor was one of the first to come. Mr. Crumpling immediately stepped to his side, and putting his arm around his neck, exclaimed, 'Thank God! My prayers are answered!' We continued the meeting to a very late hour in the evening. Many were converted and returned to their homes shouting the praises of God. One of Mr. Crumpling's daughters exhorted and shouted praises until her strength gave way and she fell to the ground in a dead faint. It was one of the best meetings I ever attended.

"There is one incident of which I would like to speak just here. One day my master sent me to do an errand at Mr. Crumpling's. When I reached the house I found the family at dinner, and to my great surprise I observed that the slaves were eating at the same table with the white people. I had never beheld the like before." Clearly, "what I beheld at Mr. Crumpling's was due to the grace of God," which "makes all one, regardless of color or condition."

At his next meeting the congregation was once again composed of blacks and whites. "All of a sudden, in the midst of the sermon, an old class-leader named Sampson White sprang from his seat, ran up the aisle to the altar, and shouted, 'My God! Preach the truth, brother, preach the truth!' Soon after he sat down, an old colored sister arose and exclaimed, 'Lord Jesus, let it come, let the power come!' Next came a white brother with an occasional 'Amen,' and they were the longest Amens that I ever heard from human lips. But none of these things moved me, except to push me right along in the good work. I never in all my life have felt more the power of God upon me than I did that day. At the close of the sermon we held a prayer-meeting. As many as could be accommodated came and knelt at the altar, and the season of prayer that followed was one never to be forgotten. There was a perfect Babel of sound. Everybody was engaged in prayer, either for themselves or someone else. Whites prayed for blacks, and blacks for whites. All distinctions as between the different races seemed to have disappeared . . . I let the meeting continue in this way for a short time, and then I called the brethren and sisters to order. Several persons still remained prostrate on the floor, too much exhausted to rise. I addressed a few words to such as could give me their attention, asking any who felt that they had been blessed that day to bear testimony to the fact. The first one to rise was a young lad of about sixteen years of age. He shouted at the top of his voice, 'Glory to God! Jesus has blessed my soul!' He then commenced shaking hands with those who stood near him. Thirteen others also testified to having obtained a hope in Christ."

As the summer drew to an end, Mr. Holmes and the family prepared to return to Wilmington. "It took two days for the journey. The first day we went as far as Little Washington, where we put up for the night. Before retiring, my master told me to have the horses fed and groomed, and ready for an early start the next morning. Accordingly I arose about three o'clock. As I stepped out of doors I discovered that the stars were falling in all directions. I ran to the kitchen and shouted to the cook that the heavens were all on fire. I then ran to the great house and awoke my master. He came out doors, looked at the heavens for a few moments, and then asked me what I thought it was. 'I don't know,' I replied, 'unless it is the Day of Judgment.' He soon returned to his room and awoke the other members of his family. I turned to go back to the kitchen. As I did so I saw the cook standing outside the door, swinging her arms and shouting at the top of her voice, 'Glory to God! Glory to God!' supposing that the end of the world had come. By this time the whole plantation was awake and everybody was out gazing, some in fear and some in joy at the strange appearance of the heavens. The tavern-keeper came out and asked if I could not stop the cook making so much noise. I got a man to help me, and we carried her into the kitchen. We could not stop her shouting. She begged us to let her go out again; she wanted to see the Savior when he came. I went back to the tavern-keeper and told him we could do nothing with her. 'Well, let her alone, then,' he replied. As day began to dawn the fiery red of the heavens began to disappear, and at sunrise it was all gone. I went to my master and told him the horses were ready for a start at any moment."

What Jones—and almost everybody else in the country—had witnessed was the great Leonids Meteor Storm of 1833, the most spectacular on record, with meteors falling at the rate of over one hundred thousand an hour. Like the cook, a great many people took it as a sign that the Second Coming was imminent—see Mark XIII: 24-26: "The sun shall be darkened, and the moon shall not give her light, and the stars of heaven shall fall . . . And then shall they see the Son of Man coming in the clouds with great power and glory." The event soon became known as The Night the Stars Fell.

Interviewed in her old age, Rose Williams looked back on her life as a slave:

"I's born in Bell County, right here in Texas, and am owned by Massa William Black. He owns Mammy and Pappy too. Massa Black has a big plantation, but he has more niggers than he needs for work on that place, 'cause he am a nigger trader. He trade and buy and sell all the time. Massa Black am awful cruel, and Mammy and Pappy powerful glad to get sold, and they and I is put on the block with 'bout ten other niggers. One man shows the interest in Pappy. Him named Hawkins. He talk to Pappy, and Pappy talk to him and say, 'Them my woman and childs. Please buy all of us and have mercy on we-uns.' Massa Hawkins say, 'That gal am a likely-looking nigger; she am portly and strong. But three am more than I wants, I guesses.'

"The sale start, and 'fore long Pappy am put on the block. Massa Hawkins wins the bid for Pappy, and when Mammy am put on the block, he wins the bid for her. Then there am three or four other niggers sold before my time comes. Then Massa Black calls me to the block, and the auction man say, 'What am I offer for this portly, strong young wench? She's never been 'bused and will make a good breeder.'

"I wants to hear Massa Hawkins bid, but him say nothing. Two other men am bidding 'gainst each other, and I sure has the worriment. There am tears coming down my cheeks 'cause I's being sold to some man that would make separation from my Mammy. One man bids $500, and the auction man ask, 'Do I hear more? She am gwine at $500.' Then someone say '$525,' and the auction man say, 'She am sold for $525 to Massa Hawkins.' Am I glad and 'cited! Why, I's quivering all over.

"Massa Hawkins takes we-uns to his place, and it am a nice plantation. Lots better than Massa Black's. There is 'bout fifty niggers what is growed and lots of chillen. The first thing Massa do when we-uns gets home am give we-uns rations and a cabin. You must believe this nigger when I say them rations a feast for us. There plenty meat and tea and coffee and white flour. The quarters am pretty good. There am twelve cabins all made from logs, and a table and some benches and bunks for sleeping, and a fireplace for cooking and the heat.

"Massa Hawkins am good to he niggers," but there was on thing he did "what I can't shunt from my mind. After I been at he place 'bout a year, the Massa come to me and say, 'You gwine live with Rufus in that cabin over yonder. Go fix it for living.' I's 'bout sixteen years old and has no larning, and I's just ignomus child. I's thought that him mean for me to tend the cabin for Rufus and some other niggers. Well, that am start the pestigation for me.

"I's took charge of the cabin after work am done and fixes supper. Now, I don't like that Rufus, 'cause he a bully. He am big and 'cause he so he think everybody do what him say. We-uns has supper, then I goes here and there talking till I's ready for sleep, and then I gets in the bunk. After I's in, that nigger come and crawl in the bunk with me 'fore I knows it. I says, 'What you means, you fool nigger?' He say for me to hush the mouth. 'This am my bunk too,' he say. 'You's teched in the head, get out,' I's told him, and I puts the feet 'gainst him and give him a shove, and out he go on the floor 'fore he knows what I's doing. That nigger jump up and he mad. He look like the wild bear. He starts for the bunk, and I jumps quick for the poker. It am 'bout three feet long, and when he comes at me I lets him have it over the head. Did that nigger stop in he tracks? I's say he did. He looks at me steady for a minute, and you could tell he thinking hard. Then he go and set on the bench and say, 'Just wait. You thinks it am smart, but you am foolish in the head. They's gwine larn you something.'

"The next day I goes to the Missy and tells her what Rufus wants, and Missy say that am the Massa's wishes. She say, 'You am the portly gal, and Rufus am the portly man. The massa wants you-uns for to bring forth portly chillen.'

"I's thinking 'bout what the Missy say, but say to myself, 'I's not gwine live with that Rufus.' That night when him come in the cabin, I grabs the poker and sits on the bench and says, 'Get 'way from me, nigger, 'fore I bust your brains out and stomp on them.' He say nothing and get out.

"The next day the Massa call me and tell me, 'Woman, I's pay big money for you, and I's done that for the cause I wants you to raise me chillens. I's put you to live with Rufus for that purpose. Now, if you doesn't want whipping at the stake, you do what I wants.'

"I thinks 'bout Massa buying me offen the block and saving me from being separated from my folks, and 'bout being whipped at the stake. There it am. What am I's to do? So I decides to do as the Massa wish, and so I yields.

"When we-uns am given freedom, Massa Hawkins tells us we can stay and work for wages or share-crop the land. I stays with my folks till they dies. I never marries, 'cause one 'sperience am 'nough for this nigger. After what I does for the Massa, I's never wants no truck with any man. The Lord forgive this colored woman, but he have to 'scuse me and look for some others for to 'plenish the earth."

Like Col. Landon Carter, lord of Sabine Hall and owner of large plantations in Virginia (who appears in an earlier chapter), William Johnson also kept a diary with many entries about the misdeeds of his troublesome slaves. Like most masters—and indeed like most parents of the time—both men believed in the whip, though Johnson's punishments were a far cry from the savage floggings common on plantations. Unlike the colonel, Johnson had to work for a living, which he did by running a successful barber shop in Natchez. Another difference between Carter and Johnson was that Johnson did his best to teach his slaves to read and write. Yet another was that Johnson was a free black.

His diary began when he was about twenty-six, and eventually ran to several hundred pages. From the thousands of entries here are some of those concerning his "boys"—most of them slaves, but some of them free blacks—who worked in his barbershop and lodged with him:

1835. October 25: "William & John Stayed Out until after ten Oclock. I beat them Both with my stick when they came home. They were both doun at Mr Parkers kitchen"—i.e. at the Mississippi Hotel, owned by Mr. Parker. November 3:"Find William at Mr Parkers Kitchen with his Girls. Struck him with the whip 1st and then with the stick. He ran home and I followed him there and whiped him well for it, having often told him about going Down there." December 17: "William & John & Bill Nix staid out untill ½ 10 O'clock at night. When they came they knocked so Loud at the Door and made so much noise that I came Out with my stick and pounded both of them."

1836. August 6: "Bill Nix Commences in the spelling Book to Read for he failed in Reading." September 1: Steven, a slave who was addicted to drink, had been hired out. He was supposed to hand his wages over to Johnson, but it was now "three weeks since since I Received any wages from Steven. I found Out this Evening by whiping him prety severely that he had Received his wages from Messrs. Spraigue & Howll, and had made away with the whole of it. On the Back of which old Mr Christopher Miller comes and complained of Steven Coming Out to his House after his girl &c." October 13: "I sent Steven Out to Col. Bingamans to work in the Cotton field." November 29: "Col. Bingaman Sent Steven in town to me to day and instead of coming in he went under the Hill and got Drunk."

1837. March 21: "Mr Thom Evans Came up to my shop to tell French William that he must not Let him find Him coming about his primices again. French had been peeping through his fence at One of his Girls on Sunday Last." July 23: "I herd to day that my Negro man Walker had ran away On Bourd of Some Steam Boat that Left here on Friday Evening, 21st inst." July 24: "I was writing and Flying around as Buisy as you please in search of Walker, that ranaway from me. I Sent a Letter by Mr Birk to be handed to the Sheriff of Louisville with a Discription of the thief and the Negro—and I also Sent an advertizement to the office of the Courrier to be published in the daily." September 19: "This morning Little Hastings was making some remarks in the presence of several gentleman about Mrs Horn . . . and it happened that Mr Horn was present and Hastings did not know him—he Just Caught Hastings by the nose and pulled his nose for him then Kicked his back sides."

1838. March 19: "Steven got drunk Last night and went of and remained all night and was not here this morning to go to Market. I sent Bill Nix to the Jail to see if He was there and He was not there. I then sent Him out to Dr. Ogdons and in going there He found Him and brought Him Down and Left Him in the gate, and he [Steven] Jumped over the Fence and went threw Judge Montgomery's yard. Bill He ran around the Corner and found him and brought him Home after a while and I went to the stable and gave him a pretty severe thrashing with the Cow hide—then he was perfectly Calm and Quiet and could then do his work. Tis singular how much good it does some people to get whiped." March 22: "I wrote the following Lines and gave them to Mr. Umphrys: 'Ranaway from the subscriber in Natchez on the 21st July, 1837, a negro man by the name of Walker. He is about forty years of age—very black Complection, smiles when spoken to and shows his teeth which are very sound and white tho he chews tobacco to Excess.'" The reward offered was $200 if Walker was taken in Natchez, and $300 if in Ohio. March 27: "Steven ran off last Night and God Only Knows where he has gone to." March 31: "I got on my Horse Early this morning and wrode Out to Washington in search of Steven but Could not find Him at all. I also went out again in the afternoon to Becon Landing but could not hear of Him. During the time that I was in search of him He sent me word that if I would Only Let him off without whiping him that he would never runaway again Durring His Life." November 16: "This morning quite Early I Came Down in my shop and found that the Boys had Just been smoking some of my Cegars which they Denied. I Listened a while and was satisfied that they had stolen them. I then Boxed Bills Jaws and Kicked his Back Side and I slaped Charles along side of the head several times."

1839. June 18: "I find by being absent for a few minutes that as I returned Bill and Charles had a Black Girl at the Shop Door. Oh how they were Shaking Hands and Cutting up in Greate Friendship—Oh what Puppys. Fondling—beneath a Levell—Low minded Creatures. I look on them as Soft."

1840. Many entries about Steven, ranging from January 10: "Steven ranaway yesterday—He got Drunk as usual and then ranaway." through December 1: "Steven Ranaway."

1841. More of the same—March 6: "When I got up this morning I found that Steven had not fed the Horses nor gone to work—After Breakfast I found Him in the Guard House—Had been taken up during the night and put in thare—I had him Flogged and then turned Him Out and sent Him down to work . . . " April 4: "I Kept the Boys Home to day until Dinner time at there Books." April 5: "Theater and Circus and several other shows are in operation to day—I, Bill & Charles were all down at the Animall Show." May 14: "I wrode out this afternoon to the Forks of the Road to try and swop Steven off for Some One Else, but could find no one that I would Like." July 24: "Large Company of Our Citizens went out to day in the Bayous in search of Runaway Negroes. Mr R finds a fire Burning in the woods—Jo Mesho finds a Bucket of meat in a tree where the Runaways has been tho there was no Negroes Caught." August 22: "To day I wrode down into the Swamp and took Steven with me and Left him at Mr Gregorys to work at the rate of 20 dollars per month." September 12: "I understood this morning Early that Steven was in town and I Knew if he was in town that he must have runaway from Mr Gregory where I had hired him to haul wood in the swamp." He was soon caught, whipped, and returned to Mr. Gregory. November 8: "I Gave Lucinda a Good Floging this Evening for her Conduct on yesterday. She asked Leave to go to Church yesterday and in place of going to Church and remaining she went off in some private Room, the Little Strumpet." November 24: "Steven got up very Early this morning and ranaway."

1843. More entries about Steven getting drunk and running away, including this for September 24: "Near 11 Oclock to day Phill Came down Main St. Leading Steven who had gone up the Street and had got drunk, very drunk. I was Buisy at the time and could not get out to see him. He managed to Slip away from Phill and . . . ran off arround the Corner and the Boys took after him and I followed but Could not See him. They however Caught him Some where up town and brot him down. When he found that I was not thare he cut up Greate Shines, got in a fight with one of the men, an Italian that Lives in a part of my House, Antonio Lynch is his name. He bit the Italians hand a Little and the fellow made more talk about it than Enough—All this was done whilst I was up the street and when I Came down they had put him in the Guard House." September 25: "I went to the Guard House this morning after Breakfast and took Steven Out, tho not until Capt. Hanstable had given him thirty nine Lashes with a whip which the Italian said he was satisfied. He is Jailed up in my Corn Cribb. I intend to send him to New Orleans Soon." December 19: "Steven is drunk to day and is on the town but I herd of him around at Mr Brovert Butlers and I sent arround thare and had him brot Home and I have him now up in the garret fast and I will Sell him if I Can get Six Hundred Dollars for Him. I was offered 550 to day for him but would not take it. He must go for he will drink." December 30: "I Expect from what past between Mr Cannon [a broker] and myself that he will take Steven On Monday if Nothing happens—And what is the Cause of my parting with him, why it is nothing more but Liquor, Liquor, His fondness for it. Nothing more, Poor Fellow. There are many worse fellows than poor Steven is, God Bless Him. Tis his

Own fault." December 31: "To day has been to me a very Sad Day; many tears was in my Eyes On acct. of my Selling poor Steven."

1844. January 1: "I got up this morning Early and took Steven with me down to the Ferry Boat and gave him up to the Overseer of Young & Cannon. I gave Steven a pair of Suspenders and a pr of Socks and 2 Cigars. Shook hands with him and see him go On Bourd for the Last time. I felt hurt but Liquor is the Cause of his troubles; I would not have parted with Him if he had Only have Let Liquor alone but he cannot do it I believe. I received a check from Mr Cannon to day On Mr Britton & Co for four Hundred dollars and a demand note or due bill for two Hundred more."

Before becoming an outstanding leader and speaker in the abolition movement, Frederick Douglass had to endure many hardships, as described in the first of his autobiographical works, *Narrative of the Life of Frederick Douglass,* published in 1845.

"I was born in Tuckahoe, near Hillsborough, and about twelve miles from Easton, in Talbot County, Maryland. I have no accurate knowledge of my age, never having been given any authentic record containing it. By far the larger part of the slaves know as little of their ages as horses know of theirs, and it is the wish of most masters within my knowledge to keep their slaves thus ignorant. I do not remember ever to have met a slave who could tell of his birthday.

"My mother was named Harriet Bailey. She was the daughter of Isaac and Betsey Bailey, both colored, and quite dark. My mother was of a darker complexion than either my grandmother or grandfather. My father was a white man. He was admitted to be such by all I ever heard speak of my parentage. The opinion was also whispered that my master was my father; but of the correctness of this opinion, I know nothing; the means of knowing was withheld from me. My mother and I were separated when I was but an infant—before I knew her as my mother. It is a common custom, in the part of Maryland from which I ran away, to part children from their mothers at a very early age. Frequently, before the child has reached its twelfth month, its mother is taken from it and hired out on some farm a considerable distance off, and the child is placed under the care of an old woman, too old for field labor. For what this separation is done, I do not know, unless it be to hinder the development of the child's affection toward its mother, and to blunt and destroy the natural affection of the mother for the child. This is the inevitable result.

"I never saw my mother, to know her as such, more than four or five times in my life; and each of these times was very short in duration, and at night. She was hired by a Mr. Stewart, who lived about twelve miles from my home. She made the journeys to see me in the night, travelling the whole distance on foot, after the performance of her day's work. She was a field hand, and a whipping is the penalty for not being in the field at sunrise, unless a slave has special permission from his or her master . . . I do not recollect of ever seeing my mother by the light of day. She was with me in the night. She would lie down with me, and get me to sleep, but long before I waked she was gone. Very little communication took place between us. Death soon ended what little we could have while she lived, and with it her hardship and suffering. She died when I was about seven years old, on one of my master's farms, near Lee's Mill. I was not allowed to be present during her illness, at her death, or burial. She was gone long before I knew anything about it."

Douglass' master, Captain Anthony, was clerk and superintendent to a very rich plantation owner called Colonel Lloyd, who was said to own a thousand slaves.

"Colonel Lloyd owned so many that he did not know them when he saw them; nor did all the slaves of the out-farms know him. It is reported of him that, while riding along the road one day, he met a colored man, and addressed him in the usual manner of speaking to colored people on the public highways in the South: 'Well, boy, whom do you belong to?' 'To Colonel Lloyd,' replied the slave. 'Well, does the colonel treat you well?' 'No, sir,' was the ready reply. 'What, does he work you too hard?' 'Yes, sir.' 'Well, don't he give you enough to eat?' 'Yes, sir, he gives me enough, such as it is.'

"The colonel, after ascertaining where the slave belonged, rode on; the man also went about his business, not dreaming that he had been conversing with his master. He thought, said, and heard nothing more of the matter, until two or three weeks afterwards. The poor man was then informed by his overseer that, for having found fault with his master, he was now to be sold to a Georgia trader. He was immediately chained and handcuffed; and thus, without a moment's warning, he was snatched away, and forever sundered from his family and friends, by a hand more unrelenting than death. This is the penalty of telling the truth, of telling the simple truth, in answer to a series of plain questions. It is partly in consequence of such facts that slaves, when inquired of as to their condition and the character of their masters, almost universally say they are contented, and that their masters are kind.

"I was seldom whipped by my old master, and suffered little from anything else than hunger and cold. I suffered much from hunger, but much more from cold. In hottest summer and coldest winter I was kept almost naked—no shoes, no stockings, no jacket, no trousers, nothing on but a coarse tow linen shirt, reaching only to my knees. I had no bed. I must have perished with cold but that, the coldest nights, I used to steal a bag which was used for carrying corn to the mill. I would crawl into this bag, and there sleep on the cold, damp, clay floor, with my head in and my feet out. My feet have been so cracked with the frost that the pen with which I am writing might be laid in the gashes.

"Our food was coarse corn meal boiled. This was called mush. It was put into a large wooden tray or trough, and set down upon the ground. The children were then called, like so many pigs, and like so many pigs they would come and devour the mush; some with oyster-shells, others with pieces of shingle, some with naked hands, and none with spoons. He that ate fastest got most; he that was strongest secured the best place; and few left the trough satisfied.

"I was probably seven or eight years old when I left Colonel Lloyd's plantation. I left it with joy. I shall never forget the ecstasy with which I received the intelligence that my old master (Captain Anthony) had determined to let me go to Baltimore, to live with Mr. Hugh Auld, brother to my old master's son-in-law, Captain Thomas Auld. I received this information about three days before my departure. They were three of the happiest days I ever enjoyed. I spent the most part of all these three days in the creek, washing off the plantation scurf, and preparing myself for my departure."

He made the journey by boat, and arrived in Baltimore early on a Sunday morning. "Mr. and Mrs. Auld were both at home, and met me at the door with their little son Thomas, to take care of whom I had been given. And here I saw what I had never seen before: it was a white face beaming with the most kindly emotions. It was the face of my new mistress, Sophia Auld. I wish I could describe the rapture that flashed through my soul as I beheld it.

"My new mistress proved to be all she appeared when I first met her at her door—a woman of the kindest heart and finest feelings. She had never had a slave under her control previously to myself, and prior to her marriage she had been dependent upon her own industry for a living. She was by trade a weaver; and by constant application to her business she had been in a good degree preserved from the blighting and dehumanizing effects of slavery. I was utterly astonished at her goodness.

"Very soon after I went to live with Mr. and Mrs. Auld she very kindly commenced to teach me the A, B, C. After I had learned this, she assisted me in learning to spell words of three or four letters. Just at this point of my progress, Mr. Auld found out what was going on, and at once forbade Mrs. Auld to instruct me further, telling her, among other things, that it was unlawful, as well as unsafe, to teach a slave to read. To use his own words, further, he said, 'If you give a nigger an inch, he will take an ell. A nigger should know nothing but to obey his master—to do as he is told to do. Learning would spoil the best nigger in the world . . . It would forever unfit him to be a slave . . .' These words sank deep into my heart."

The lessons with Mrs. Auld ended, but Douglass did not give up. "I had resided but a short time in Baltimore before I observed a marked difference in the treatment of slaves from that which I had witnessed in the country. A city slave is almost a freeman." He soon put this relative freedom to good use. "The plan which I adopted, and the one by which I was most successful, was that of making friends of all the little white boys whom I met in the street. As many of these as I could I converted into teachers." Douglass would fill his pockets with bread, of which there was always plenty in the Auld household, and "this bread I used to bestow upon the hungry little urchins, who in return would give me that more valuable bread of knowledge."

In 1832, Frederick's owner died, and after living seven years in Baltimore he was sent to live on a farm with another member of the family, the mean-spirited and brutal Thomas Auld. "He found me unsuitable to his purpose. My city life, he said, had had a very pernicious effect upon me." After a few months, Thomas Auld "resolved to put me out, as he said, to be broken; and, for this purpose, he let me for one year to a man named Edward Covey," a class leader in the Methodist church and well-known as a "nigger-breaker."

"I left Master Thomas's house, and went to live with Mr. Covey on the 1st of January, 1833. I was now, for the first time in my life, a field hand. In my new employment I found myself even more awkward than a country boy appeared to be in a large city. I had been at my new home but one week before Mr. Covey gave me a very severe whipping, cutting my back, causing the blood to run, and raising ridges on my flesh as large as my little finger."

The reason given was Douglass's failure to control a team of unbroken oxen that had damaged a cart by running it against a gate-post. Covey said "he would teach me how to trifle away my time and break gates."

"I lived with Mr. Covey one year. During the first six months of that year scarce a week passed without his whipping me . . . We were worked in all weathers. It was never too hot or too cold; it could never rain, blow, hail or snow too hard for us to work in the field. Work, work, work, was scarcely more the order of the day than of the night. The longest days were too short for him, and the shortest nights too long for him. I was somewhat unmanageable when I first went there, but a few months of this discipline tamed me. Mr. Covey succeeded in breaking me. I was broken in body, soul, and spirit. My natural elasticity was crushed, my intellect languished, the disposition to read departed, the cheerful spark that lingered about my eye died; the dark night of slavery closed in upon me; and behold a man transformed into a brute!"

But not forever. "You have seen how a man was made a slave; you shall see how a slave was made a man." This happened "on one of the hottest days of the month of August, 1833." While fanning grain, Douglass had collapsed from heat and overwork. Covey beat him savagely, and Douglass ran off, but returned two days later, on a Sunday. "Upon entering the yard gate, out came Mr. Covey on his way to meeting. He spoke to me very kindly, bade me drive the pigs from a lot nearby, and passed on towards the church." However, on Monday morning, while Douglass was in the stable throwing down some hay from the loft, "Mr. Covey entered the stable with a long rope; and just as I was half out of the loft, he caught hold of my legs, and was about tying me. As soon as I found what he was up to, I gave a sudden spring, and as I did so, he holding my legs, I was brought sprawling on the stable floor. Mr. Covey seemed now to think he had me, and could do what he pleased; but at this moment—from whence came the spirit I don't know—I resolved to fight." And fight they did, Douglass seizing Covey by the throat, and giving a man who came to help Covey "a heavy kick close under the ribs." Covey called on another hand to help him, but the man replied that "his master hired him out to work, not to help to whip me." Off and on, the fight lasted two hours, with Douglass the victor; and "the whole six months afterwards that I spent with Mr. Covey, he never laid the weight of his finger on me.

"This battle with Mr. Covey was the turning point in my career as a slave. It rekindled the few expiring embers of freedom, and revived within me a sense of my own manhood . . . I now resolved that however long I might remain a slave in form, the day had passed forever when I could be a slave in fact." As for Mr. Covey, Douglass at first wondered why he did not "have me taken by the constable to the whipping-post, and there regularly whipped for the crime of raising my hand against a white man." The only possible answer was that "Mr. Covey enjoyed the most unbounded reputation for being a first-rate overseer and negro-breaker. It was of considerable importance to him. That reputation was at stake; and had he sent me—a boy about sixteen years old—to the public whipping post, his reputation would have been lost."

Soon after he was sent back to the household of Hugh Auld.

"In a few weeks after I went to Baltimore, Master Hugh hired me to Mr. William Gardner, an extensive ship-builder, on Fell's Point. I was put there to learn how to caulk. It, however, proved a very unfavorable place for the accomplishment of this object. Mr. Gardner was engaged that spring in building two large man-of-war brigs, professedly for the Mexican government. The vessels were to be launched in July of that year, and in failure thereof Mr. Gardner was to lose a considerable sum; so that when I entered, all was hurry. There was no time to learn anything. Every man had to do that which he knew how to do.

"In entering the ship-yard, my orders from Mr. Gardner were to do whatever the carpenters commanded me to do. This was placing me at the beck and call of about seventy-five men. I was to regard all these as masters. Their word was to be my law. My situation was a most trying one. At times I needed a dozen pair of hands. I was called a dozen ways in the space of a single minute. Three or four voices would strike my ear at the same moment. It was—'Fred, come help me to cant this timber here.'—'Fred, come carry this timber yonder.'—'Fred, bring that roller here.'—'Fred, go get a fresh can of water.'—'Fred, come help saw off the end of this timber.'—'Fred, go quick, and get the crowbar.'—'Fred, hold on the end of this fall.'—'Fred, go to the blacksmith's shop and get a new punch.'—'Hurra, Fred! run and bring me a cold chisel.'—'I say, Fred, bear a hand, and get up a fire as quick as lightning under that steam-box.'—'Halloo, nigger! Come, turn this grindstone.'—'Come, come! Move, move, and bowse this timber forward.'—'I say, darky, blast your eyes, why don't you heat up some pitch?'—'Halloo! Halloo! Halloo!' (Three voices at the same time.) 'Come here!—Go there!—Hold on where you are!—Damn you, if you move, I'll knock your brains out!'

"This was my school for eight months; and I might have remained there longer, but for a most horrid fight I had with four of the white apprentices, in which my left eye was nearly knocked out, and I was horribly mangled in other respects. The facts in the case were these: until a very little while after I went there, white and black ship-carpenters worked side by side, and no one seemed to see any impropriety in it. All hands seemed to be very well satisfied. Many of the black carpenters were freemen. Things seemed to be going on very well. All at once, the white carpenters knocked off, and said they would not work with free colored workmen. Their reason for this, as alleged, was that if free carpenters were encouraged, they would soon take the trade into their own hands, and poor white men would be thrown out of employment. They therefore felt called upon at once to put a stop to it. And, taking advantage of Mr. Gardner's necessities, they broke off, swearing they would work no longer, unless he would discharge his black carpenters.

"Now, though this did not extend to me in form, it did reach me in fact. My fellow-apprentices very soon began to feel it degrading to them to work with me. They began to put on airs, and talk about the 'niggers' taking the country, saying we all ought to be killed; and, being encouraged by the journeymen, they commenced making my condition as hard as they could, by hectoring me around, and sometimes striking me. I, of course . . . struck back again, regardless of consequences; and while I kept them from combining, I succeeded very well; for I could whip the whole of them, taking them separately. They, however, at length combined, and came upon me armed with sticks, stones, and heavy handspikes. One came in front with a half brick. There was one at each side of me, and one behind me. While I was attending to those in front, and on either side, the one behind ran up with the handspike and struck me a heavy blow upon the head. It stunned me. I fell, and with this they all ran upon me and fell to beating me with their fists. I let them lay on for a while, gathering strength. In an instant, I gave a sudden surge and rose to my hands and knees. Just as I did that, one of their number gave me, with his heavy boot, a powerful kick in the left eye. My eyeball seemed to have burst. When they saw my eye closed and badly swollen, they left me. With this I seized the handspike and for a time pursued them. But here the carpenters interfered, and I thought I might as well give it up. It was impossible to stand my hand against so many.

"All this took place in sight of not less than fifty white ship-carpenters, and not one interposed a friendly word; but some cried, 'Kill the damned nigger! Kill him! Kill him! He struck a white person!' I found my only chance for life was in flight. I succeeded in getting away without an additional blow, and barely so; for to strike a white man is death by Lynch law—and that was the law in Mr. Gardner's ship-yard; nor is there much of any other out of Mr. Gardner's ship-yard."

Though often overshadowed by the charismatic Frederick Douglass, William Wells Brown was also prominent in his day as an abolitionist lecturer and writer; he was also well-known as a novelist, playwright and historian. Born in Kentucky, Brown escaped to freedom when he was barely twenty. Before that he spent some time working in the internal slave trade, having been "hired out" in St. Louis to a Mr. Walker, "a Negro speculator, or a 'soul-driver,' as they are generally called." Brown was hired because he had worked as a steward on a Mississippi river-boat, and Walker had a gang of slaves he wanted to ship down to the market in New Orleans, the largest in the country.

> "There was on the boat a large room on the lower deck in which the slaves were kept, men and women, promiscuously—all chained two and two, and a strict watch kept that they did not get loose; for cases have occurred in which slaves have got off their chains and made their escape at landing-places, while the boats were taking in wood. And with all our care we lost one woman who had been taken from her husband and children, and having no desire to live without them, in the agony of her soul jumped overboard, and drowned herself."

After selling several of the slaves during a stop-over at Natchez, they reached New Orleans. "Here the slaves were placed in a Negro-pen, where those who wished to purchase could call and examine them. The Negro-pen is a small yard surrounded by buildings, from fifteen to twenty feet wide, with the exception of a large gate with iron bars. The slaves are kept in the building during the night, and turned out in the yard during the day. After the best of the stock was sold at private sale at the pen, the balance were taken to the Exchange Coffee-House Auction Room, and sold at public auction."

Nine weeks after their return to St. Louis, Mr. Walker had another "cargo of human flesh made up. There was in this lot a number of old men and women, some of them with gray locks. We left St. Louis in the steamboat *Carlton*, bound for New Orleans. On our way down, and before we reached Rodney, the place where we made our first stop, I had to prepare the old slaves for market. I was ordered to have the old men's whiskers shaved off, and the gray hairs plucked out where they were not too numerous, in which case he had a preparation of blacking to color it, and with a blacking brush we would put it on. This was new business to me and was performed in a room where the passengers could not see us. These slaves were also taught how old they were by Mr. Walker, and after going through the blacking process they looked ten or fifteen years younger.

"We proceeded to New Orleans and put the gang in the same Negro-pen which we occupied before. In a short time the planters came flocking to the pen to purchase slaves. Before the slaves were exhibited for sale, they were dressed and driven out into the yard. Some were set to dancing, some to jumping, some to singing, and some to playing cards. This was done to make them appear cheerful and happy. My business was to see that they were placed in those situations before the arrival of the purchasers, and I have often set them to dancing when their cheeks were wet with tears. As slaves were in good demand at that time, they were all soon disposed of, and we again set out for St. Louis."

When traveling on land, Mr. Walker "always put up at the best hotel, and kept his wines in his room, for the accommodation of those who came to negotiate with him for the purchase of slaves. One day, while we were at Vicksburg, several gentlemen came to see him for that purpose, and as usual the wine was called for. I took the tray and started round with it, and having accidentally filled some of the glasses too full, the gentlemen spilled the wine on their clothes as they went to drink. Mr. Walker apologized to them for my carelessness, but looked at me as though he would see me again on the subject.

"The next morning he gave me a note to carry to the jailer, and a dollar in money to give him. I suspected that all was not right, so I went down near the landing where I met a sailor, and, walking up to him, asked if he would be so kind as to read the note for me." The sailor did so, and said, "This is a note to have you whipped, and says that you have a dollar to pay for it." The sailor left and, uncertain what to do, Brown "went up to the jail, took a look at it, and walked off again."

"While meditating on the subject, I saw a colored man about my size walk up, and the thought struck me in a moment to send him with my note. I walked up to him, and asked him who he belonged to. He said he was a free man, and had been in the city but a short time. I told him I had a note to go into the jail, and get a trunk to carry to one of the steamboats; but was so busily engaged that I could not do it, although I had a dollar to pay for it. He asked me if I would not give him the job. I handed him the note and the dollar, and off he started for the jail.

"I watched to see that he went in, and as soon as I saw the door close behind him, I walked around the corner and took my station, intending to see how my friend looked when he came out." After a while, "the young man made his appearance and looked around for me." Seeing Brown, he began "complaining bitterly, saying that I had played a trick upon him. I denied any knowledge of what the note contained, and asked him what they had done to him." He replied that "'they whipped me and took my dollar, and gave me this note.'"

"He showed me the note which the jailer had given him, telling him to give it to his master. I told him I would give him fifty cents for it—that being all the money I had. He gave it to me and took his money. He had received twenty lashes on his bare back with the Negro-whip." Brown went back to the hotel where he asked a stranger to read the note to him. It ran: "'Dear Sir: By your direction I have given your boy twenty lashes. He is a very saucy boy, and tried to make me believe that he did not belong to you, and I put it on him well for lying to me.'"

In retrospect, Brown was sorry for what he had done. "Had I entertained the same views of right and wrong which I now do, I am sure I should never have practiced the deception upon that poor fellow. I know of no act committed by me while in slavery which I have regretted more than that."

For their third trip Brown and Mr. Walker "took the steamboat and went to Jefferson City, a town on the Missouri River. Here we landed and took a stage for the interior of the state. He bought a number of slaves as he passed the different farms and villages. After getting twenty-two or twenty-three men and women, we arrived at St. Charles, a village on the banks of the Missouri. Here he purchased a woman who had a child in her arms, appearing four or five weeks old.

> "Soon after we left St. Charles the young child grew very cross and kept up a noise during the greater part of the day. Mr. Walker complained of its crying several times, and told the mother to stop the child's d—d noise, or he would. The woman tried to keep the child from crying, but could not. We put up at night with an acquaintance of Mr. Walker, and in the morning, just as we were about to start, the child again commenced crying. Walker stepped up to her [the mother], and told her to give the child to him. The mother tremblingly obeyed. He took the child by one arm, as you would a cat by the leg, walked into the house, and said to the lady, 'Madam, I will make you a present of this little nigger; it keeps such a noise that I can't bear it.'
>
> "'Thank you, sir,' said the lady.
>
> "The mother, as soon as she saw that her child was to be left, ran up to Mr. Walker, and falling upon her knees begged him to let her have her child; she clung around his legs and cried, 'Oh, my child! My child! Master, do let me have my child! Oh, do, do, do! I will stop its crying if you will only let me have it again.' Mr. Walker commanded her to return into the ranks with the other slaves. Women who had children were not chained, but those that had none were. As soon as her child was disposed of she was chained in the gang."

They arrived once again in New Orleans, where, while still on board the riverboat, Brown witnessed this incident: "In the evening, between seven and eight o'clock, a slave came running down the levee, followed by several men and boys. The whites were crying out, 'Stop that nigger! Stop that nigger!' while the poor panting slave, in almost breathless accents, was repeating, 'I did not steal the meat! I did not steal the meat!' The poor man at last took refuge in the river. The whites who were in pursuit of him ran on board one of the boats to see if they could discover him. They finally espied him under the bow of the steamboat *Trenton*. They got a pike-pole and tried to drive him from his hiding place. When they would strike at him he would dive under the water. The water was so cold that it soon became evident that he must come out or be drowned.

"While they were trying to drive him from under the bow of the boat or drown him, he would, in broken and imploring accents, say, 'I did not steal the meat! I did not steal the meat! My master lives up the river. I want to see my master. I did not steal the meat. Do let me go home to master.' After punching him, and striking him over the head for some time, he at last sank in the water, to rise no more alive.

"On the end of the pike-pole with which they were striking him was a hook, which caught in his clothing, and they hauled him up on the bow of the boat. Some said he was dead; others said he was 'playing possum;' while others kicked him to make him get up. But it was of no use—he was dead.

"As soon as they became satisfied of this they commenced leaving, one after another. One of the hands on the boat informed the captain that they had killed the man, and that the dead body was lying on deck. The captain came on deck and said to those who were remaining, 'You have killed this nigger; now take him off my boat.' The dead body was dragged on shore and left there. I went on the boat where our gang of slaves were, and during the whole night my mind was occupied with what I had seen. Early in the morning I went on shore to see if the dead body remained there. I found it in the same position that it was left the night before. I watched to see what they would do with it. It was left there until between eight and nine o'clock when a cart which takes up the trash out of the streets came along, and the body was thrown in, and in a few minutes more was covered with dirt which they were removing from the streets."

Mary Reynolds, born in Louisiana, claimed to be one hundred years old when she told the story of her life to a Federal Writers' interviewer:

"My paw's name was Tom Vaughn, and he was from the North, born free man and lived and died free to the end of his days. He wasn't no educated man, but he was what he calls himself a piano man. He told me once he lived in New York and Chicago and he built the insides of pianos and knew how to make them play in tune. He said some white folks from the South told he if he'd come with them to the South he'd find a lot of work to do with pianos in them parts, and he come off with them.

"He saw my maw on the Kilpatrick place and her man was dead. He told Dr. Kilpatrick, my massa, he'd buy my maw and her three children with all the money he had, iffen he'd sell her. But Massa was never one to sell any but the old niggers who was past working in the fields and past their breeding times. So my paw married my maw and works the field, same as any other nigger.

"I was born the same time as Miss Sara Kilpatrick. Dr. Kilpatrick's first wife and my maw come to their time right together. Miss Sara's maw died, and they brung Miss Sara to suck with me. It's a thing we ain't never forgot. My maw's name was Sallie, and Miss Sara always looked with kindness on my maw. We sucked till we was a fair size and played together, which wasn't no common thing. None the other little niggers played with the white children. But Miss Sara loved me so good.

"I was just about big enough to start playing with a broom to go about sweeping up and not even half doing it when Dr. Kilpatrick sold me. They was a old white man at Trinity, and his wife died and he didn't have chick or child or slave or nothing. Massa sold me cheap, 'cause he didn't want Miss Sara to play with no nigger young-un. That old man bought me a big doll and went off and left me all day, with the door open. I just sat on the floor and played with that doll. I used to cry. He'd come home and give me something to eat and then go to bed, and I slept on the foot of the bed with him. I was scared all the time in the dark. He never did close the door.

"Miss Sara pined and sickened. Massa done what he could, but they wasn't no pertness in her. She got sicker and sicker, and Massa brung another doctor. He say, 'You little gal is grieving the life out of her body, and she sure gwine die iffen you don't do something about it.' Miss Sara says over and over, 'I wants Mary.' Massa say to the doctor, 'That a little nigger young-un I done sold.' The doctor tells him he better get me back iffen he wants to save the life of his child. Massa has to give a big plenty more to get me back than what he sold me for, but Miss Sara plumps up right off and grows into fine health.

"Then Massa marries a rich lady from Mississippi, and they has chillen for company to Miss Sara, and seems like for a time she forgets me.

"Massa Kilpatrick wasn't no piddling man. He was a man of plenty. He had a big house with no more style to it than a crib, but it could room plenty people. He was a medicine doctor, and they was rooms in the second story for sick folks what come to lay in. It would take two days to go over all the land he owned. He had cattle and stock and sheep and more'n a hundred slaves and more besides. He bought the best of niggers near every time the speculators came that way. He'd make a swap of the old ones and give money for young ones what could work.

"Slavery was the worst days was ever seed in the world. They was things past telling, but I got the scars on my old body to show to this day. I seed worse than what happened to me. I seed them put the men and women in the stock with they hands screwed down through holes in the board and they feets tied together and they naked behinds to the world. Solomon the overseer beat them with a big whip and Massa look on. The niggers better not stop in the fields when they hear them yelling. They cut the flesh 'most to the bones, and when they taken some of them out of the stock and put them on the beds, they never got up again.

"The conch shell blowed afore daylight, and all hands better get out for roll call, or Solomon bust the door down and get them out. It was work, get beatings, and half-fed. They brung the victuals and water to the fields on a slide pulled by a old mule. Plenty times they was only a half barrel water, and it stale and hot, for all us niggers on the hottest days. Mostly we ate pickled pork and corn bread and peas and beans and 'taters. They never was as much as we needed.

"The times I hated most was picking cotton when the frost was on the bolls. My hands get sore and crack open and bleed. We'd have a little fire in the fields, and iffen the ones with tender hands couldn't stand it no longer we run and warm our hands a little bit. When I could steal a 'tater, I used to slip it in the ashes, and when I'd run to the fire I'd take it out and eat it on the sly.

"In the cabins it was nice and warm. They was built of pine boarding, and they was one long row of them up the hill back of the big house. Near one side of the cabins was a fireplace. They'd bring in two, three big logs and put on the fire, and they'd last near a week. The beds was made out of puncheons fitted in holes bored in the wall, and planks laid 'cross them poles. We had ticking mattresses filled with corn chucks. Sometimes the men build chairs at night. We didn't know much 'bout having nothing, though.

"Sometimes Massa let niggers have a little patch. They'd raise 'taters or goobers. They liked to have them to help fill out on the victuals. 'Taters roasted in the ashes was the best-tasting eating I ever had. I could die better satisfied to have just one more 'tater roasted in hot ashes. The niggers had to work the patches at night, and dig the 'taters and goobers at night. Then if they wanted to sell any in town, they'd have to get a pass to go."

"On Saturday evenings the niggers which sold they goobers and 'taters brung fiddles and guitars and come out and play. The others clap they hands and stomp they feet and we young-uns cut a step round. I was plenty biggity and liked to cut a step.

"We was scared of Solomon and his whip, though, and he didn't like frolicking. He didn't like for us niggers to pray, either. We never heard of no church, but us have praying in the cabins. We'd set on the floor and pray with our heads down low and sing low, but if Solomon heared he'd come and beat on the wall with the stock of his whip. He'd say, 'I'll come in there and tear the hide off you backs.' But some the old niggers tell us we got to pray to God, that He don't think different of the blacks and the whites. I know that Solomon is burning in hell today, and it pleasures me to know it.

"Once my maw and paw taken me and Katherine after night to slip to another place to a praying and singing. A nigger man with white beard told us a day am coming when niggers only be slaves of God. We prays for the end of tribulation and the end of beatings and for shoes that fit our feet. We prayed that us niggers could have all we wanted to eat, and special for fresh meat. Some the old ones say we have to bear all, 'cause that all we can do. Some say they was glad to the time they's dead, 'cause they'd rather rot in the ground than have the beatings.

"In them days I weared shirts, like all the young-uns. They had collars and come below the knees and was split up the sides. That's all we weared in hot weather. The men weared jeans and the women gingham. Shoes was the worstest trouble. We weared rough russets when it got cold, and it seem powerful strange they'd never get them to fit. Once when I was a young gal they got me a new pair and all brass studs in the toes. They was too little for me, but I had to wear them. The brass trimmings cut into my ankles and them places got miserable bad. I rubs tallow in them sore places and wraps rags round them, and my sores got worser and worser. The scars are there to this day . . .

"I wasn't sick much, though. Some niggers had chills and fevers a lot, but they hadn't discovered so many diseases then as now. Dr. Kilpatrick give sick niggers ipecac and asafetida and oil and turpentine and black fever pills.

"Once Massa goes to Baton Rouge and brung back a yaller gal dressed in fine style. She was a seamster nigger. He builds her a house 'way from the quarters, and she done fine sewing for the whites. Us niggers knowed the doctor took a black woman quick as he did a white, and took any on his place he wanted, and he took them often. But mostly the chillen born on the place looked like niggers. Aunt Cheney always say four of hers was Massa's, but he didn't give them no mind. But this yaller gal breeds so fast and gets a mess of white young-uns. She learned them fine manners and combs out they hair.

"Once two of them goes down the hill to the dollhouse, where the Kilpatrick children am playing. They wants to go in the dollhouse and one the Kilpatrick boys says, 'That's for white chillen.' They say, 'We ain't no niggers, 'cause we got the same daddy you has, and he comes to see us near every day and fetches us clothes and things from town.' They is fussing, and Missy Kilpatrick is listening out her chamber window. She hears them white niggers say,

Under the watchful but seemingly benign eye of the white master a black preacher exhorts his slave listeners. The picture was drawn by the visiting English artist, Frank Vizitelly, at the time of the Civil War.

'He is our daddy and we call him daddy when he comes to our house to see our mamma.'

"When Massa come home that evening, his wife hardly say nothing to him, and he ask her what the matter, and she tells him, 'Since you asks me, I'm studying in my mind 'bout them white young-uns of that yaller nigger wench from Baton Rouge.' He say, 'Now, honey, I fetches that gal just for you, 'cause she a fine seamster.' She say, 'It look kind of funny they got the same kind of hair and eyes as my children, and they got a nose look like yours.' He say, 'Honey, you just paying 'tention to talk of little chillen that ain't got no mind to what they say.' She say, 'Over in Mississippi I got a home and plenty with my daddy, and I got that in my mind.'

"Well, she didn't never leave, and Massa bought her a fine new span of surrey hosses. But she don't never have no more children, and she ain't so cordial with the Massa. That yaller gal has more white young-uns, but they don't never go down the hill no more to the big house.

"Massa used to hire out his niggers for wage hands. One time he hired me and a nigger boy, Turner, to work for some ornery white trash name of Kidd. One day Turner goes off and don't come back. Old Man Kidd say I knowed 'bout it, and he tied my wrists together and stripped me. He hanged me by the wrists from a limb on a tree and spraddled my legs round the trunk and tied my feet together. Then he beat me. He beat me worser than I ever been been beat before, and I faints dead away. When I come to I'm in bed. I didn't care so much iffen I died.

"I didn't know 'bout the passing of time, but Miss Sara come to see me. Some white folks done get word to her. Mr. Kidd tries to talk hisself out of it, but Miss Sara fetches me home when I'm well 'nough to move. She took me in a cart and my maw takes care of me. Massa looks me over good and says I'll get well, but I'm ruined for breeding children."

After the war Mary Reynolds and her family moved to Texas.

"Mammy gets to Galveston and dies there. My husband and me farmed round for times, and then I done housework and cooking for many years. My husband died years ago. I guess Miss Sara been dead these long years.

"I been blind and almost helpless for five years. I'm getting mighty enfeebling, and I ain't walked outside the door for a long time back. I sets and remembers the times in the world. I remembers now clear as yesterday things I forgot for a long time. I remembers about the days of slavery, and I don't believe they ever gwine have slaves no more on this earth. I think God done took that burden offen his black children, and I'm aiming to praise Him for it to His face in the days of glory what ain't so far off."

Many other slaves had a strong religious faith, despite the fact that until after the Civil War there were few black churches outside the cities. Most owners allowed only those preachers who toed the official line. "The niggers didn't go to the church building," recalled Lucretia Alexander, a former slave. "The preacher came and preached to them in their quarters. He'd just say, 'Serve your masters. Don't steal your master's turkey. Don't steal your master's chickens. Don't steal your master's hogs. Don't steal your master's meat. Do whatsomever your master tells you to do.' Same old thing all the time."

"You ought to heard that preaching," recalled Wes Brady. "Obey your massa and missy, don't steal chickens and eggs and meat, but nary a word about having a soul to save." "All that preacher talked about was for us slaves to obey our masters and not to lie and steal," said another. "Nothing about Jesus was ever said." Tom Hawkins remembered that when he was a boy on a plantation near Marshall, Texas, "us niggers on the Poore plantation went to church with our white folks. Couldn't none of us read no Bible. The preacher preached to the white folks first, and then when he preached to the niggers all he ever said was: 'It's a sin to steal. Don't steal Master and Mistress's chickens and hogs, and such like. How could anyone be converted on that kind of preaching? And besides, it never helped none to listen to that sort of preaching, 'cause the stealing kept going right on every night."

Carey Davenport, who later became a Methodist minister, told of three distinct forms of worship on the Texas plantation where he had been born in 1855. First there were Sunday prayers in the big house, conducted by the master, who was "'ligious." However "I could never understand his 'ligion 'cause sometimes he get up off his knees, and before we get out of the house he cusses us out." Then there were the occasions when "the white Methodist circuit riders come round on horseback and preach. There was a big box house for a church house, and the cullud folks sit off in one corner of the church." And third, "sometimes the cullud folks go down in dugouts and hollows and hold they own service, and they used to sing songs what come a-gushing up from the heart."

Richard Carruthers, of Bastrop County, Texas, had a similar experience. "When the white preacher come he preach and pick up his Bible and claim he getting the text right out from the Good Book, and he preach: 'The Lord say, don't you niggers steal chickens from your missus. Don't you steal your master's hogs.' That would be all he preach." But then "us niggers used to have a prayin' ground down in the hollow, and sometimes we come out of the field between eleven and twelve at night, scorchin' and burnin' up with nothin' to eat, and we wants to ask the good Lord to have mercy. We puts grease in a snuff pan or bottle, and make a lamp. We takes a pine torch, too, and goes down to the hollow to pray. Some gets so joyous they starts to holler loud and we has to stop up they mouth. I see niggers get so full of the Lord and so happy they drop unconscious."

Mrs. Sutton told of a common aid to privacy. "White people wouldn't let them have meetings, but they would get a big old wash kettle and put it right outside the door, and turn it bottom upwards to get the sound, then they would go in the house and sing and pray, and the kettle would catch the sound."

Among the many failings for which they were reproached by the Rev. Mr. Pike, as narrated earlier by Harriet Jacobs, were "tossing coffee grounds with some wicked fortune teller . . . cutting cards with an old hag . . . tying up little bags of roots to bury under the door-steps to poison each other." Generally known as "conjuring," some of these practices could be traced back to Africa, while others seem to have been home-grown. "They powder up the rattle offen the snake and tie it up in the little old rag bag, and they do devilment with it," reported Rosanha Frazier. "They get old scorpion and make bad medicine. They get dirt out of the graveyard, and that dirt, after they speak on it, would make you go crazy. When they wants to conjure you they sneak round and get the hair combing or the finger or toenail, or anything natural about your body and works the hoodoo on it. They make the straw man or the clay man and they puts the pin in he leg, and you leg gwineter get hurt or sore jus' where they puts the pin. Iffen they puts the pin through the heart, you gwineter die."

In her old age, May Satterfield also recalled some folk remedies and superstitions: "If you wants to have good luck, get some rat veins, wild cherry blossom, and bile them together with whiskey and make some bitters. Put the bitters in a demijohn and keep it in a dark place. Every now and then take a good slug of them bitters, and you ain't never gonna be sick a day in your life." Also: "Ain't no use of nobody killing no hogs on the dark of the moon, 'cause all the meat'll draw up and there won't be nothing but grease. Kill hogs on the light moon. Ain't nothing gonna mount to nothing on the dark moon except Irish taters . . . If you sprinkle a little salt all round the house, nothing can bother you. The spirits can't get to you . . . If you want a job with a certain person there is a root that you can chew, and then you go to the person, spit round them, and you'll get the job . . . I knows too about Old Christmas night that come just before Christmas. Ain't many now knows about Old Christmas. On that night I done seen the chickens flap they wings, the cows get down in their stall and pray, the horses neigh, and the trees swing this way and that. All these and many more dumb beasts give thanks to God on Old Christmas night. I've seen this with these two eyes."

Other slaves also had miraculous experiences, among them Ophelia Jemison:

> "When I was seeking the Lord, before I converted, he place me in Hell to convince me. I stay down there mos' a hour. Hell one terrible place. The fire down there is a big pit of brimstone a-roaring and a-roaring. It bigger than Charleston, it seem like. I see the souls boiling in the pit of brimstone. Oh! God have mercy on my soul!
>
> "When I been converted, I went to heaven in the spirit and see with the eye of faith. I done been there. Heaven is white as snow. God and the Holy Ghost, they is one and sat at a big table with the book stretched out before them. God's two eyes just like two big suns shining, and his hair like lamb's wool. I walk in there and look over his shoulder. He had a long gold pen and writ down the names of the people down on the earth yet, and when he call the roll up there in his own time, he know them.
>
> "Oh, I 'joicing! I 'joicing! Never the like before. An angel take me and show me the stars, how they hang up there by a silver cord, and the moon just a ball of blood, but I ain't know how it hold up, and the sun on the rim of all these, going round and round, and Christ setting in a rocking chair over the sun. Gabriel and Michael was with him, one on this side, and one on the other, holding the laws. I see everything just like I say. Sweet Jesus, I hope I reach that place I see."

Harriet Tubman (1823 – 1913)
nurse, spy and scout

The "Moses of her People" poses for a studio photograph when aged about fifty—like so many others born into slavery, Harriet Tubman did not know the date of her birth. The caption "Nurse, spy and scout," tells only part of her story, ignoring the many hazardous trips she made to bring slaves to freedom. Nor does the portrait convey the fact that she was barely five feet tall but as strong in body as she was in spirit. Also not shown is the loaded pistol she carried when on a mission in case anyone wanted to back out, thereby endangering the other fugitives. As she put it, "Dead men tell no tales."

CHAPTER 10

FUGITIVES

A NAGGING PROBLEM FOR MANY LATTER-DAY SLAVE-OWNERS WAS THIS: IF, as everyone had now come to acknowledge, slavery was as beneficial to the slaves as it was to the owners, then why did so many of them keep running away? Ingratitude was one ostensible reason; childish willfulness was another; and then there were the lies and propaganda of the fanatical abolitionists. These explained a lot, but was there something else, some other motive that made slaves behave in a manner so contrary to their best interests?

One possible answer—but not one the owners wanted to hear—lay in the pages of *American Slavery As It Is: Testimony of a Thousand Witnesses*, published in 1839, and edited by Theodore Dwight Weld and Sarah and Angelina Grimké. In their "Advertisement to the Reader," the editors explained that rather than rely on the denunciations of their fellow-abolitionists, the "majority of facts and testimony contained in this work rests upon the authority of slaveholders, whose names and addresses are given to the public, to vouch for the truth of their statements . . . Their testimony is taken, mainly, from recent newspapers, published in the slave states." The Introduction began: "Reader, you are empaneled as a juror to try a plain case and bring in an honest verdict. The question at issue is not one of law, but of fact: What is the actual condition of the slaves in the United States? A plainer case never went to a jury. Look at it . . ."

Among the vast amount of evidence produced by Weld and the Grimké sisters were hundreds of newspaper advertisements for runaways—"testimony of the slaveholders themselves, and in their own chosen words." The book was densely printed, and to save space the editors used only extracts from the advertisements; to save even more space, the names and addresses of the advertisers have now also been dropped. Here, under the heading *Floggings*, are some of the reasons why slaves ran away:

The Standard of Union, Milledgeville, Ga. Oct 2, 1838. "Ranaway, a negro woman named Maria, some scars on her back occasioned by the whip." *The Sentinel*, Vicksburg, Miss. Aug 22, 1837. "Ranaway, a negro fellow named Dick—has many scars on his back from being whipped." *The Chronicle and Sentinel*, Augusta, Ga. Oct 18, 1838. "Ranaway, a negro man named Johnson—he has a great many marks of the whip on his back." *The Baltimore Republican*, Md. Jan 13, 1838. "Ranaway, Bill—has several large scars on his back from a severe whipping in early life." *The Bulletin*, New Orleans. August 11, 1838. "Ranaway, the mulatto boy Quash—considerably marked on the back and other places with the lash." *The St. Francisville Journal*, La. July 6, 1837. "Committed to jail, a negro boy named John, about 17 years old—his back is badly marked with the whip, his upper lip and chin severely bruised." Nineteen other such notices appear in the book, all within a period of not much more than one year—"mere samples," says Weld "of the hundreds of similar ones published during the same period."

The next section was titled *Tortures by Iron Collars, Chains, Fetters, Handcuffs, &c.*

The Spectator, Staunton, Va. Sept 27, 1838. "Ranaway, a negro named David—with some iron hobbles around each ankle." *Grand Gulf Advertiser*, Washington, Mi. Aug 29, 1838. "Ranaway, a black woman, Betsey—had an iron bar on her right leg." *The New Orleans Bee*, June 20, 1837. "Ranaway, the negro Manuel, much marked with irons." *The New Orleans Bee*, Aug 11, 1838. "Ranaway, the negress Fanny—had on an iron band about her neck." *The Memphis Enquirer*, June 7, 1837. "Absconded, a colored boy named Peter— had an iron round his neck when he went away." *The Mobile Chronicle*, Ala. June 15, 1838. "Ranaway, a negro boy about twelve years old—had round his neck a chain dog-collar." *The New Orleans Bee*, July 2, 1838. "Ranaway, the negro Hown—has a ring of iron on his left foot. Also, Grisce, his wife, having a ring and chain on the left leg." *The New Orleans Bee*, June 9, 1838. "Detained at the police station, the negro wench Myra—has several marks of lashing, and has irons on her feet." *The New Orleans Bee*, Aug 11, 1837. "Ranaway, Betsey—when she left she had on her neck an iron collar."

From *Branding, Maiming, Gun-shot Wounds, &c.* here are eighteen of the more than one hundred examples, almost all from a period of a mere eighteen months:

The Raleigh Standard, July 18, 1838. "Ranaway, a negro woman and two children; a few days before she went off I burnt her with a hot iron on the left side of her face. I tried to make the letter M." *The New Orleans Bee*, Dec. 21, 1838. "Ranaway, a negro woman named Rachel, has lost all her toes except the large one." *The Georgia Journal*, March 27, 1837. "Twenty-five dollars reward for my man Isaac. He has a scar on his forehead caused by a blow, and one on his back made by a shot from a pistol." *The Natchez Courier*, Aug. 24, 1838. "Ranaway, a negro girl called Mary, has a small scar over her eye, a good many teeth missing, the letter A is branded on her cheek and forehead." (The letter A would have stood for Ashford, the owner's name.) *The Southern Sun*, Columbus, Ga. Aug 7, 1838. "Ranaway, a negro boy named Mose, he has a wound in the right shoulder near the back bone, which was occasioned by a rifle shot." *The Milledgeville Union*, Nov 7, 1837. "Ranaway, negro boy Ellic, has a scar on one of his arms from the bite of a dog." *The New Orleans Bee*, Aug 27, 1837. "Fifty dollars reward for the negro Jim Blake— has a piece cut out of each ear, and the middle finger of the left hand cut off to the second joint." *The Georgia Messenger*, July 27, 1837. "Ranaway, my man Fountain—has holes in his ears, a scar on the right side of his forehead—has been shot in the hind parts of his legs— is marked on the back with the whip." *The Commercial Register*, Mobile, Ala. Oct 27, 1837. "Ranaway, the slave Ellis—he has lost one of his ears." *The Knoxville Register*, June 6, 1838. "Ranaway, a black girl named Mary—she has a scar on her cheek, and the end of one of her toes cut off." *The Winchester Virginian*, July 11, 1837. "Ranaway, a mulatto man named Joe—his fingers on the left hand are partly amputated." *The New Orleans Commercial Bulletin*, July 21, 1837. "Ranaway, Bill—has a scar over one eye, also one on his leg from the bite of a dog—has a burn on his buttock from a piece of hot iron in the shape of a T." *The Commercial Bulletin*, New Orleans, Sept 18, 1838. "Ranaway a negro named David Drier—has two toes cut." *The Columbus Enquirer*, Ga. Jan 18, 1838. "Ranaway, a negro boy twelve or thirteen years old—has a scar on his left cheek from the bite of a dog." *The New Orleans Bee*, Feb 19, 1838. "Ranaway, the negro Patrick—has his little finger of the right hand cut close to the hand." *The Mercury*, Charleston, S.C. Nov 27, 837. "Ranaway, Dick—has lost the little toe of one of his feet." *The Natchez Courier*, Aug 17, 1838. "Ranaway, a negro man named Jerry, has a small piece cut out of the top of each ear." *The Alexandria Gazette*, Md. Feb 6, 1838. "Ranaway, negro Phil, scar through the right eyebrow, part of the middle toe on the right foot cut off."

"Another method of marking slaves," wrote Weld, "is by drawing out or breaking off one or two front teeth—commonly the upper ones, as the mark in that case would be the more obvious." He then cites twenty-four advertisements for runaways with missing teeth, adding that "were it necessary we might easily add to the preceding list hundreds. The reader will remark that all the slaves whose ages are given are young—not one has arrived at middle age; consequently it can hardly be supposed that they have lost their teeth either from age or decay. The probability that their teeth were taken out by force is increased by the fact of their being front teeth in almost every case, and . . . it is well known that the front teeth are not generally the first to fail."

American Slavery As It Is sold well. So did first-person stories by fugitive slaves. A notable example was the *Narrative* of William Wells Brown, whose experiences working for a trader taking slaves to the New Orleans market appeared earlier. From an early age "the love of liberty had been burning in my bosom," but family ties held him back. Then, when he was barely twenty, and living in St. Louis, he learned that his beloved sister was about to be sold to a man in Natchez, who wanted her as his concubine. There was nothing he could do to prevent this, and his parting from her in the jail where she was being held was painful. "She was seated with her face toward the door where I entered, yet she did not look up until I walked up to her. As soon as she observed me, she sprung up, threw her arms around my neck, leaned her head upon my breast and, without uttering a word, burst into tears. As soon as she recovered herself sufficiently to speak, she advised me to take mother and try to get out of slavery. She said there was no hope for herself, that she must live and die a slave. After giving her some advice, and taking from my finger a ring and placing it upon hers, I bade her farewell forever and returned to my mother, and then and there made up my mind to leave for Canada as soon as possible."

His mother, who had several other children, all in slavery, wanted to stay in St. Louis, and tried to persuade him to go off by himself, but "I could not bear the idea of leaving her among those pirates, when there was a prospect of being able to get away from them. After much persuasion I succeeded in inducing her to make the attempt." The first step, crossing the Ohio River, was easy enough. "We left the city just as the clock struck nine. We proceeded to the upper part of the city, where I had been two or three times during the day, and selected a skiff to carry us across the river.

> "We were soon upon the Illinois shore, and leaping from the boat, turned it adrift. We took the main road to Alton, and passed through just at daylight, when we made for the woods, where we remained during the day. As soon as darkness overshadowed the earth we started again on our gloomy way, having no guide but the North Star. We continued to travel by night, and secrete ourselves in the woods by day.
>
> "On the eighth day of our journey we had a very heavy rain, and in a few hours after it commenced we had not a dry thread upon our bodies. This made our journey still more unpleasant. On the tenth day we found ourselves entirely destitute of provisions, and how to obtain any we could not tell. We finally resolved to stop at some farmhouse, and try to get something to eat. We had no sooner determined to do this than we went to a house, and asked them for some food. We were treated with great kindness, and they not only gave us something to eat, but gave us provisions to carry with us.

Finding ourselves about one hundred and fifty miles from St. Louis, we concluded that it would be safe to travel by daylight, and did not leave the house until the next morning.

"I had just been telling my mother how I should try to get employment as soon as we reached Canada, and how I intended to purchase us a little farm, and how I would earn money enough to buy sister and brothers, and how happy we would be in our own free home—when three men came up on horseback, and ordered us to stop. I turned to the one who appeared to be the principal man, and asked him what he wanted. He said he had a warrant to take us up. The three immediately dismounted, and one took from his pocket a handbill advertising us as runaways, and offering a reward of two hundred dollars for our apprehension and delivery in the city of St. Louis.

"While they were reading the advertisement, mother looked me in the face and burst into tears. A cold chill ran over me, and such a sensation I never experienced before, and I hope never to again. They took out a rope and tied me, and we were taken back about six miles to the house of the individual who appeared to be the leader. We reached there about seven o'clock in the evening, had supper, and were separated for the night. Before the family retired to rest, they were all called together to attend prayers. The man who but a few hours before had bound my hands together with a strong cord, read a chapter from the Bible, and then offered up a prayer, just as though God had sanctioned the act he had just committed upon a poor, panting, fugitive slave.

"The next morning a blacksmith came in and put a pair of handcuffs on me, and we started on our journey back to the land of whips, chains and Bibles. Mother was not tied, but was closely watched at night. We were carried back in a wagon, and after four days' travel we came in sight of St. Louis. I cannot describe my feelings upon approaching the city."

After a short spell in jail, Brown was returned to his master, who sent him to work in the fields where he "was closely watched by the overseer during the day, and locked up at night. The overseer gave me a severe whipping on the second day that I was in the field." Not long after, his owner sold him to a merchant tailor called Samuel Willi, who "soon de-

cided to hire me out; and as I had been accustomed to service in steamboats, he gave me the privilege of finding such employment. I soon secured a situation aboard the steamer, *Otto*, Capt. J. B. Hill, which sailed
from St. Louis to Independence, Missouri. My former master, Dr. Young,
did not let Mr. Willi know that I had run away, or he would not have
permitted me to go on board a steamboat. The boat was not quite ready
to commence running, and therefore I had to remain with Mr. Willi. But
during this time I had to undergo a trial for which I was entirely unpre-
pared." This was to say good-bye to his mother, who had been kept in
jail since her arrest and was now about to be shipped down to the New
Orleans slave market.

"At about ten o'clock in the morning I went on board of the boat,
and found her there in company with fifty or sixty other slaves. She
was chained to another woman. On seeing me, she immediately
dropped her head upon her heaving bosom. She moved not, neither
did she weep. Her emotions were too deep for tears. I approached,
threw my arms around her neck, kissed her, and fell upon my knees,
begging her forgiveness, for I thought myself to blame for her sad
condition; for if I had not persuaded her to accompany me, she
would not then have been in chains.

"She finally raised her head, looked me in the face, (and such a
look none but an angel can give!) and said, 'My dear son, you are not
to blame for my being here. You have done nothing more nor less than
your duty. Do not, I pray you, weep for me. I cannot last long upon a
cotton plantation. I feel that my heavenly Master will soon call me
home, and then I shall be out of the hands of the slave-owners!'

"I could bear no more—my heart struggled to free itself from
the human form. In a moment she saw Mr. Mansfield [her owner]
coming toward that part of the boat, and she whispered in my ear,
'My child, we must soon part to meet no more this side of the grave.
You have ever said that you would not die a slave; that you would
be a free man. Now try to get your liberty! You will soon have no
one to look after but yourself!' And just as she whispered the last
sentence into my ear, Mansfield came up to me, and with an oath
said, 'Leave here this instant! You have been the means of my losing
one hundred dollars to get this wench back'—at the same time kick-

ing me with a heavy pair of boots. As I left her, she gave one shriek, saying, 'God be with you!' It was the last time that I saw her, and the last word I heard her utter."

A few months later Brown got his chance to escape. This came when his steamboat took on a cargo to be delivered to Cincinnati. "The first place in which we landed in a free state was Cairo, a small village at the mouth of the Ohio River. We remained here but a few hours, when we proceeded to Louisville. After unloading some of the cargo, the boat started on her upward trip. The next day was the first of January. I had looked forward to New Year's Day as the commencement of a new era in the history of my life." Soon after, "the boat landed at a point which appeared to me the place of all others to start from. When the boat was discharging her cargo, and the passengers engaged carrying their baggage on and off shore, I improved the opportunity to convey myself with my little effects on land. Taking up a trunk, I went up the wharf, and was soon out of the crowd. I made directly for the woods, where I remained until night, knowing well that I could not travel, even in the state of Ohio, during the day, without danger of being arrested.

"I had long since made up my mind that I would not trust myself in the hands of any man, white or colored. The slave is brought up to look upon every white man as an enemy to him and his race; and twenty-one years of slavery had taught me that there were traitors, even among the colored people. After dark I emerged from the woods into a narrow path, which led me into the main travelled road. But I knew not which way to go. I did not know north from south, east from west. I looked in vain for the North Star; a heavy cloud hid it from my view. I walked up and down the road until near midnight, when the clouds disappeared, and I welcomed the sight of my friend—truly the slave's friend—the North Star!

"As soon as I saw it I knew my course, and before daylight I travelled twenty or twenty-five miles. It being in the winter, I suffered intensely from the cold, being without an overcoat, and my other clothes rather thin for the season. I was provided with a tinder-box, so that I could make up a fire when necessary. And but for this I should certainly have frozen to death.

The future abolitionist, William Wells Brown, fails in his first attempt to escape as bloodhounds pick up his scent. Keeping hounds was a well-established business, with rates on a sliding scale according to the distance traveled. On being returned to his owner, Brown was first whipped and then "smoked"—exposed to the thick and choking fumes of a fire of tobacco stems.

"On the fourth day my provisions gave out, and then what to do I could not tell. Have something to eat I must; but how to get it was the question! On the first night after my food was gone, I went to a barn on the road-side and there found some ears of corn. I took ten or twelve of them, and kept on my journey. During the next day, while in the woods, I roasted my corn and feasted upon it, thanking God that I was so well provided for.

"On the fifth or sixth day it rained very fast, and froze about as fast as it fell, so that my clothes were one glare of ice. I travelled on at night until I became so chilled and benumbed—the wind blowing into my face—that I found it impossible to go any further, and accordingly took shelter in a barn, where I was obliged to walk about to keep from freezing. I have ever looked upon that night as the most eventful part of my escape from slavery. Nothing but the providence of God, and that old barn, saved me from freezing to death."

But his luck soon changed for the better. Reversing his decision not to ask for help, he went out on to the road and soon encountered "an old man walking towards me, leading a white horse. He had on a broad-brimmed hat and a very long coat"—evidently a Quaker—and "as soon as I saw him, and observed his dress, I thought to myself, 'You are the man that I have been looking for!'" And so indeed he was, for Wells Brown, the Quaker, took the frost-bitten fugitive home, where he and his elderly wife fed and housed him. They also looked after him when he succumbed to a fever, "treating me as kindly as if I had been one of their own children. I remained with them twelve or fifteen days, during which time they made me some clothing, and the old gentleman purchased me a pair of boots."

As a final act of kindness Wells Brown invited him to share his name. This was a matter of great importance to the narrator who, while still a boy, had been ordered to give up the name William when his owner's nephew, also called William, came to live at the plantation. "This, at the time, I thought to be one of the most cruel acts that could be committed upon my rights; and I received several very severe whippings for telling people that my name was William, after orders were given to change it." He also refused to take the last name of any of his owners "for I always detested the idea of being called by the name of either of my masters."

Hence this parting scene:

"Before leaving this good Quaker friend, he inquired what my name was besides William. I told him that I had no other name. 'Well,' said he, 'thee must have another name. Since thee has got out of slavery, thee has become a man, and men always have two names.'

"I told him that he was the first man to extend the hand of friendship to me, and I would give him the privilege of naming me.

"'If I name thee,' said he, 'I shall call thee Wells Brown, after myself.'

"'But,' said I, 'I am not willing to lose my name of William. As it was taken from me once against my will, I am not willing to part with it again upon any terms.'

"'Then,' said he, 'I will call thee William Wells Brown.'

"'So be it,' said I; and I have been known by that name ever since I left the house of my first white friend."

Brown's story was famous in his time, but nowhere near so famous as this one: its young and attractive heroine, Eliza Harris, with her four-year-old son, Harry, in her arms, has just reached the Kentucky side of the ice-choked Ohio River. On the other side lies Indiana and freedom, behind her the slave-catchers are drawing near—"right on behind her they came; and, nerved with strength such as God gives only to the desperate, with one wild cry and flying leap, she vaulted sheer over the turbid current by the shore, on to the raft of ice beyond. It was a desperate leap—impossible to anything but madness and despair . . . The huge green fragment of ice on which she alighted pitched and creaked as her weight came on it, but she stayed there not a moment. With wild cries and desperate energy she leaped to another and still another cake—stumbling—leaping—slipping—springing upwards again! Her shoes are gone—her stockings cut from her feet—while blood marked every step; but she saw nothing, felt nothing, till dimly, as in a dream, she saw the Ohio side, and a man helping her up the bank . . ."

This of course is one of the many high points in *Uncle Tom's Cabin*, Harriet Beecher Stowe's hugely successful novel—three hundred thousand copies sold in just one year (1852). But though a novel, it was not, Mrs. Stowe insisted, primarily a work of fiction: many of the characters and incidents were based on real people and real events, and as proof she wrote and published *A Key to Uncle Tom's Cabin*, citing her sources. Among these was Levi Coffin, the original for Simeon Halliday, the Quaker at whose house Eliza was made welcome soon after her arrival in Indiana. Like Josiah Henson, who was not slow to declare himself the real-life model for Uncle Tom, Coffin was more than willing to have lived up to his fictional counterpart. Here he is explaining how his house in Newport, Indiana, came to be known as "The Grand Central Station of the Underground Railroad."

"In the winter of 1826–27, fugitives began to come to our house, and as it became more widely known on different routes that the slaves fleeing from bondage would find a welcome and shelter at our house, and be forwarded safely on their journey, the number increased. Friends [i.e. Quakers] in the neighborhood, who had formerly stood aloof from the work, fearful of the penalty of the law, were encouraged to engage in it when they saw the fearless manner in which I acted, and the success that attended my efforts. They would contribute to clothe the fugitives, and would aid in forwarding them on their way, but were timid about sheltering them under their roof; so that part of the work devolved on us." Many of these Friends "tried to discourage me, and dissuade me from running such risks . . . telling me that such a course of action would injure my business and perhaps ruin me; that I ought to consider the welfare of my family; and warning me that my life was in danger, as there were many threats made against me by the slave-hunters.

"After listening quietly to these counselors," Coffin loftily rebuked them. "If by doing my duty and endeavoring to fulfill the injunctions of the Bible, I injured my business, then let my business go. As to my safety, my life was in the hands of my Divine Master, and I felt that I had His approval." In the meantime "I soon became extensively known to the friends of the slaves, at different points on the Ohio River, where fugitives generally crossed . . . Seldom a week passed without our receiving passengers by this mysterious road. We knew not what night or what hour of the night we would be roused from slumber by a gentle rap at the door. That was the signal announcing the arrival of a train . . . I have often been awakened by this signal, and sprang out of bed in the dark and opened the door. Outside, in the cold or rain, there would be a two-horse wagon loaded with fugitives, perhaps the greater part of them women and children. I would invite them, in a low tone, to come in, and they would follow me into the darkened house without a word, for we knew not who might be watching and listening. When they were all safely inside and the door fastened, I would cover the windows, strike a light and build a good fire. By this time my wife would be up and preparing victuals for them, and in a short time the cold and hungry fugitives would be made comfortable. I would accompany the conductor of the train to the stables, and care for the horses, that had, perhaps, been driven twenty-five or thirty miles that night through the cold and rain . . . This work was kept up during the time we lived at Newport, a period of more than twenty years. The number of fugitives varied considerably in different years, but the annual average was more than one hundred."

Most stories about the Underground Railroad were written well after the Civil War by white people keen to have played a heroic part.

The railroad certainly did exist, but was most active in the free states; the closer fugitives got to Canada, and the less they needed help, the more it was available. Levi Coffin no doubt helped a number of fugitives, but fewer than the thousands he claimed, and surely sometimes without the clichés that larded his account—the gentle rap at the door in the dark of night, the wagon loaded with rain-soaked fugitives, the precautions against prying eyes, the noble disregard of his own interests.

Another white man who claimed to have done valuable and dangerous work for the Underground Railroad was Dr. Alexander Ross, a Canadian who long after the Civil War described this incident in Delaware in the summer of 1859. A good-looking young slave woman was about to be sent for sale to New Orleans "where prices ranged in proportion to the beauty and personal charms possessed by the victims of man's inhumanity." Determined to save her from this fate, Ross obtained a horse and light carriage and arranged to meet her outside her owner's house. The hour was midnight.

> "She was standing near a fence, well shaded from the light of the moon. I drove near the sidewalk, and taking her into the carriage drove rapidly away on the road to Kennett Square, Pennsylvania. I kept the horse at a rapid gait until I got out of sight of Wilmington. After four o'clock in the morning I heard the sound of a carriage rapidly following me. Upon reaching the top of a small hill I looked back and saw a horse coming at full gallop—behind him a buggy with two men in it. I directed the girl to crouch down in the bottom of the vehicle. I then put the horse to its utmost speed, hoping to cross the Pennsylvania line before the pursuers came up to me.

> "The piteous sobs and stifled cries of the poor slave at my feet made me resolve to defend her to the last extremity. I had two good navy revolvers with me, and got them ready for action. Looking back I saw that my pursuers were gaining upon me. They were not more than two hundred yards distant, and I could hear shouts for me to stop; but the more vigorously I urged on my horse. In another moment I heard the report of fire-arms, and the whizzing sound of a bullet near my head. I then drew a revolver, and fired four times in quick succession at my pursuer's horse. I saw their horse stagger and fall to the ground. One of my pursuers

then fired several times at me without effect. I was soon out of danger from them, and safe with my charge at the house of kind Hannah Cox."

An exciting story, to be sure, but, apart from the fact that there really was a Quaker abolitionist called Hannah Cox, almost certainly untrue. As with his other accounts of his heroic deeds, not only did Dr. Ross fail to provide any corroboration—not even the name of the young woman he says he rescued—but how likely is it that he would have managed to disable one of his pursuers with a pistol shot fired in the dark at a distance of some two hundred yards while also driving a galloping horse? Similar doubts have been cast on his stories of foiling a Confederate plot to invade Maine from New Brunswick during the Civil War, and of his several meetings with John Brown, an event never mentioned in Brown's voluminous papers. But it is not so much Ross's boasts that are offensive as his depiction of runaway slaves as the passive objects of the white man's charity, courage and leadership—the whimpering young woman cowering in the bottom of the carriage while he whips on the horses and guns down the pursuers.

Levi Coffin and Alexander Ross had the advantage of writing their own versions of events, but the most intrepid of the railroad conductors, Harriet Tubman, was illiterate, and most of what we know of her comes from the pen of her friend Sarah Bradford, a genteel New England writer. Her book, written in a style typical of that period, was published in 1886. Here is how it begins:

> "On a hot summer's day, perhaps sixty years ago, a group of merry little darkies were rolling and tumbling in the sand in front of the large house of a Southern planter. Their shining skins gleamed in the sun as they rolled over each other in their play, and their voices, as they chattered together or shouted in glee, reached even to the cabins of the negro quarter, where the old people groaned in spirit as they thought of the future of those unconscious young revelers; and their cry went up, 'O Lord, how long!'

"Apart from the rest of the children, on the top rail of a fence, holding tight on to the tall gate post, sat a little girl of perhaps thirteen years of age; darker than any of the others, and with a more decided woolliness in the hair; a pure unmitigated African. She was not so entirely in a state of nature as the rollers in the dust beneath her; but her only garment was a short woolen skirt, which was tied around her waist, and reached about to her knees. She seemed a dazed and stupid child, and as her head hung upon her breast, she looked up with dull blood-shot eyes towards her young brothers and sisters without seeming to see them. Bye and bye the eyes closed, and still clinging to the post, she slept. The other children looked up and said to each other, 'Look at Hatt, she's done gone off agin!' Tired of their present play-ground they trooped off in another direction, but the girl slept on heavily, never losing her hold on the post, or her seat on her perch. Behold here, in the stupid little Negro girl, the future deliverer of hundreds of her people; the spy and scout of the Union armies; the devoted hospital nurse; the protector of hunted fugitives; the eloquent speaker in public meetings; the cunning eluder of pursuing man-hunters; the heaven-guided pioneer through dangers seen and unseen; in short, as she has been well called, 'The Moses of her People.'

"Here in her thirteenth year she is just recovering from the first terrible effects of an injury inflicted by her master, who in an ungovernable fit of rage threw a heavy weight at the unoffending child, breaking in her skull and causing a pressure upon her brain, from which in her old age she is suffering still. This pressure it was which caused the fits of somnolency so frequently to come upon her, and which gave her the appearance of being stupid and half-witted in those early years. But that brain which seemed so dull was full of busy thoughts, and her life problem was already trying to work itself out there.

"She had heard the shrieks and cries of women who were being flogged in the Negro quarter; she had listened to the groaned-out prayer, 'Oh, Lord, have mercy!' She had already seen two older sisters taken away as part of a chain gang, and they had gone no one knew whither; she had seen the agonized expression on their faces as they turned to take a last look at their 'Old Cabin Home;' and had watched from the top of the fence as they went off weeping and lamenting, till they were hidden from her sight forever. She saw the hopeless grief of the poor old mother and the silent despair of the aged father, and already she began to revolve in her mind the question, 'Why should such things be?' 'Is there no deliverance for my people?'"

For a while Harriet was hired out as a maid of all work to a local lady, who was quick to whip her for any perceived shortcoming—"that poor neck is even now covered with the scars which sixty years of life have not been able to efface." Eventually she was returned to her owner, "a poor, scarred wreck, nothing but skin and bone, with the words that 'She wasn't worth a sixpence.' The poor old mother nursed her back to life, and her naturally good constitution asserted itself," but "as soon as she was strong enough for work she was hired out to a man whose tyranny was worse, if possible, than that of the woman she had left. Now it was out-of-door drudgery which was put upon her. The labor of the horse and the ox, the lifting of barrels of flour and other heavy weights were given to her; and powerful men often stood astonished to see this woman perform feats of strength from which they shrank incapable." But "still the pressure upon the brain continued, and with the weight half lifted she would drop off into a state of insensibility from which even the lash in the hand of a strong man could not rouse her." And so once again she was returned, sick and exhausted, to her owner, who decided to sell her.

Throughout her life Harriet was guided by her religious beliefs. "Brought up by parents possessed of strong faith in God, she had never known the time when she did not trust Him, and cling to Him, with an all-abiding confidence. She seemed ever to feel the Divine Presence near, and she talked with God 'as a man talketh with his friend.' Hers was not the religion of a morning and evening prayer at stated times, but when she felt a need she simply told God of it, and trusted Him to set the matter right. 'And so,' she said to me [the author, Sarah Bradford], 'as I lay so sick on my bed, from Christmas till March, I was always praying for poor ole master. 'Pears like I didn't do nothing but pray for ole master. "Oh, Lord, convert ole master—Oh, dear Lord, change that man's heart and make him a Christian." And all the time he was bringing men to look at me, and they stood there saying what they would give, and what they would take, and all I could say was, "Oh, Lord, convert ole master!" Then I heard that as soon as I was able to move I was to be sent with my brothers in the chain-gang to the far South. Then I changed my prayer, and I said, "Lord, if you ain't never going to change that man's heart, kill him, Lord, and take him out of the way, so he won't do no more mischief." Next thing I heard, ole master was dead; and he died just as he had lived, a wicked, bad man.'"

A few years later, when Harriet was in her early twenties, she was warned that her new owner was planning to sell her and two of her brothers. She immediately decided they should escape to the north. They set off, but her brothers soon lost heart and turned back; but not Harriet. "After watching the retreating forms of her brothers, she turned her face toward the north, and fixing her eyes on the guiding star, and committing her way unto the Lord, she started again upon her long, lonely journey.

"After many long and weary days of travel, she found that she had passed the magic line which then divided the land of bondage from the land of freedom . . . No one could take her now, and she would never call any man 'Master' more. 'I looked at my hands,' she said, 'to see if I was the same person now I was free. There was such a glory over everything, the sun came like gold through the trees and over the fields, and I felt like I was in heaven.'

"But then came the bitter drop in the cup of joy. She was alone, and her kindred were in slavery . . . 'I had crossed the line of which I had so long been dreaming. I was free, but there was no one to welcome me to the land of freedom. I was a stranger in a strange land, and my home after all was down in the old cabin quarter, with the old folks, and my brothers and sisters. But to this solemn resolution I came: I was free, and they should be free also. I would make a home for them in the North, and the Lord helping me, I would bring them all there. Oh, how I prayed then, lying all alone on the cold, damp ground! 'Oh, dear Lord,' I said, 'I ain't got no friend but you. Come to my help, Lord, for I'm in trouble!'

"It would be impossible here to give a detailed account of the journeys and labors of this intrepid woman for the redemption of her kindred and friends during the years that followed. Those years were spent in work, almost by night and day, with the one object of the rescue of her people from slavery. All her wages were laid away with this sole purpose, and as soon as a sufficient amount was secured, she disappeared from her Northern home, and as suddenly and mysteriously she appeared some dark night at the door of one of the cabins on a plantation, where a trembling band of fugitives, forewarned as to time and place, were anxiously awaiting their deliverer. Then she piloted them North, traveling by night, hiding by day, scaling the mountains, fording the rivers, threading the forests, lying concealed as the pursuers passed them, she carrying the babies, drugged with paregoric, in a basket on her arm. So she went nineteen times, and so she brought away over three hundred pieces of living and breathing 'property,' with God-given souls."

As well as providing herself with opium to drug babies into silence, Harriet also carried a loaded pistol. This was for those occasions when some of the men "would drop on the ground, groaning that they could not take another step. They would lie there and die, or, if their strength came back, they would return on their steps and seek their old homes again. Then the revolver carried by this bold and daring pioneer would come out, and while pointing it at their heads she would say 'Dead niggers tell no tales. You go on or die!' And by this heroic treatment she compelled them to drag their weary limbs along on their northward journey."

For the first few years, Harriet's destination was New York State, where she had established a home for her parents and relatives after helping them escape. But then, as part of the Compromise of 1850, Congress passed the Fugitive Slave Act, which greatly strengthened the hand of the slave-catchers. Under the earlier law, passed in 1793, owners could retrieve slaves who had escaped to a free state by having them arrested, usually by slave-catchers, and brought before a local magistrate; by affidavit or in person, the master would then assert his ownership and ask the court to restore his property. But from the owners' viewpoint this law was inadequate: it was they who had to bear the trouble and expense of recapturing the runaways. Also, "personal liberty laws" passed by many states made the hearings less arbitrary and often required trial by jury, with the consequent risk of coming before justices or jurors with abolitionist sympathies. So, in 1850, Congress decided that it would be "desirable for the peace, concord and harmony of the Union of these States, to settle and adjust amicably all existing questions of controversy between them arising out of the institution of slavery upon a fair, equitable and just basis." To achieve these desirable ends, resolutions were passed admitting California as a free state to the Union, settling the boundaries of Texas and New Mexico, and discontinuing the slave trade (but not slavery itself) in the District of Columbia. Congress also resolved to make "more effectual provision . . . for the restitution and delivery of persons bound to service or labor in any State who may escape into any other State or Territory in the Union."

In essence, the Fugitive Slave Act forced everyone in the free states to assist in the arrest and return of runaways. Officials executing warrants of arrest were authorized to "summon and call to their aid the bystanders, or *posse comitatus* of the proper county . . . and all good citizens are hereby commanded to aid and assist in the prompt and efficient execution of this law whenever their services may be required." Special commissioners were appointed to hear cases, with fees of $5 if the accused was released, and $10 if convicted. Moreover "in no trial or hearing under this act shall the testimony of such alleged fugitive be admitted in evidence." Also "any persons who shall knowingly and willingly obstruct, hinder or prevent" the execution of this law, or "shall aid, abet or assist" a fugitive to escape, or "shall harbor or conceal such fugitive," would be liable to "a fine not exceeding one thousand dollars, and imprisonment not exceeding six months."

As a sop to the slaveholders, the law was a success. As a gift to the abolitionists, it was an even greater success. "The Fugitive Slave Bill," wrote Frederick Douglass, "has especially been of positive service to the anti-slavery movement," revealing "the horrible character of slavery" and "the arrogant and overbearing spirit of the slave States towards the free States." As a means of recapturing fugitives it was not very effective, accounting for fewer than three hundred, though it did increase the number of those who went to "shake the paw of the British lion"—that is, flee to Canada. Another consequence was to set off some first-class riots, such as this one reported by the *Troy Whig* on April 28, 1859:

> "Yesterday afternoon the streets of this city and West Troy were made the scenes of unexampled excitement. For the first time since the passage of the Fugitive Slave Act, an attempt was made here to carry its provisions into execution, and the result was a terrific encounter between the officers and the prisoner's friends, the triumph

of mob law, and the final rescue of the fugitive." This was Charles Nalle, "about thirty years of age, tall, quite light-complexioned and good-looking." Nalle had been a slave in Virginia, but had escaped and come to live near Troy, where he was employed as a coachman. He had been spotted by an informer, who denounced him to his owner, who "sent on an agent, by whom the necessary papers were got out to arrest the fugitive.

"Yesterday morning about 11 o'clock, Charles Nalle was sent to procure some bread for the family by whom he was employed. He failed to return. At the baker's he was arrested by Deputy United States Marshal J. W. Holmes, and immediately taken before United States Commissioner Miles Beach. The son of Mr. Gilbert, [Nalle's employer] thinking it strange that he did not come back, sent to the house of William Henry on Division Street where he boarded, and his whereabouts was discovered.

"The examination before Commissioner Beach was quite brief. The evidence of the agent was taken, and the Commissioner decided to remand Nalle to Virginia. The necessary papers were made out and given to the Marshal.

"By this time it was two o'clock, and the fact began to be noised abroad that there was a fugitive slave in Mr. Beach's office, corner of State and First Streets. People in knots of ten or twelve collected near the entrance, looking at Nalle, who could be seen at an upper window. William Henry, a colored man with whom Nalle boarded, commenced talking from the curb-stone in a loud voice to the crowd. He uttered such sentences as, 'There is a fugitive slave in that office—pretty soon you will see him come forth. He is going to be taken down South . . .' A number of women kept shouting, crying, and by loud appeals excited the colored persons assembled.

"Still the crowd grew in numbers. Wagons halted in front of the locality and were soon piled with spectators. An alarm of fire was sounded, and hose carriages dashed through the ranks of men, women, and boys; but they closed again, and kept looking with expectant eyes at the window where the Negro was visible. Meanwhile, angry discussions commenced. Some persons agitated a rescue, and others favored law and order. Mr. Brockway, a lawyer, had his coat torn for expressing his sentiments, and other *melees* kept the interest alive.

"All at once there was a wild halloo, and every eye was turned up to see the legs and part of the body of the prisoner protruding from the second story window, at which he was endeavoring to escape. Then arose a shout—'Drop him!' 'Catch him!' 'Hurrah!' But the attempt was a fruitless one, for somebody in the office pulled Nalle back again, amid the shouts of a hundred pairs of lungs. The crowd at this time numbered nearly a thousand persons. Many of them were black, and a good share were of the female sex. They blocked up State Street from First Street to the alley, and kept surging to and fro."

In the meantime Martin Townsend, an anti-slavery lawyer, had gone to Judge Gould of the State Supreme Court and obtained a writ of *habeas corpus* on Nalle's behalf, "returnable immediately." This in effect meant that Nalle had to be taken from Commissioner Beach's office to Judge Gould's office, only two blocks away, but those two blocks were filled with "an excited, unreasonable crowd." As soon as the prisoner appeared in the doorway, escorted by four policemen, "the crowd made one grand charge, and those nearest the prisoner seized him violently, with the intention of pulling him away from the officers, but they were foiled; and down First Street to Congress Street, and up the latter in front of Judge Gould's chambers, went the surging mass. Exactly what did go on in the crowd it is impossible to say, but the pulling, hauling, mauling and shouting gave evidences of frantic efforts on the part of the rescuers, and a stern resistance from the conservators of the law . . . A number in the crowd were more or less hurt, and it is a wonder that these were not badly injured, as pistols were drawn and chisels used.

"The battle had raged as far as the corner of Dock and Congress Streets, and the victory remained with the rescuers at last. The officers were completely worn out with their exertions, and it was impossible to continue their hold upon him any longer. Nalle was at liberty. His friends rushed him down Dock Street to the lower ferry, where there was a skiff lying ready to start. The fugitive was put in, the ferryman rowed off, and amid the shouts of hundreds who lined the banks of the river, Nalle was carried into Albany County." There was a good deal more, but the last line of the story runs: "He has since arrived safely in Canada."

A familiar figure was in the thick of the fight to rescue Nalle. According to Martin Townsend, the lawyer who obtained the writ of *habeas corpus,* "when Nalle was brought from Commissioner Beach's office into the street, Harriet Tubman, who had been standing with the excited crowd, rushed amongst the foremost to Nalle, and running one of her arms around his manacled arm, held on to him without ever loosening her hold through the more than half-hour's struggle to Judge Gould's office, and from Judge Gould's office to the dock, where Nalle's liberation was accomplished. In the *melee* she was repeatedly beaten over the head with policemen's clubs, but she never for a moment released her hold, but cheered Nalle and his friends with her voice, and struggled with the officers until they were literally worn out with their exertions, and Nalle was separated from them."

Writing in 1868 to Sarah Bradford, Tubman's biographer, Thomas Garrett, a Quaker abolitionist and shoe-maker who lived in Wilmington, Delaware, had this to say:

"In truth I never met with any person, of any color, who had more confidence in the voice of God, as spoken direct to her soul. She has frequently told me that she talked with God, and he talked with her every day of her life; and she has declared to me that she felt no more fear of being arrested by her former master, or any other person, when in his immediate neighborhood, than she did in the State of New York, or Canada, for she said she ventured only where God sent her, and her faith in the Supreme Power was truly great.

"No slave who placed himself under her care was ever arrested that I have heard of. She mostly had her regular stopping places on her route, but in one instance when she had several stout men with her, she said that God told her to stop, which she did, and then asked him what she must do. He told her to leave the road, and turn to the left; she obeyed and came to a small stream of tide water. There was no boat, no bridge. She again inquired of her Guide what she was to do. She was told to go through. It was cold, in the month of March, but having confidence in her Guide she went in; the water came up to her armpits; the men refused to follow until they saw her safe on the opposite shore. They then followed, and, if I mistake not, she had soon to wade another stream; soon after which she came to a cabin of colored people, who took them all in, put them to bed, and dried their clothes, ready to proceed next night on their journey."

On another occasion Harriet went into Garrett's shoe shop and said, "'God tells me you have money for me.' I asked 'if God never deceived her?' She said, 'No!' 'Well! How much does thee want?' After studying a moment, she said, 'About twenty-three dollars.' I then gave her twenty-four dollars and some odd cents, the net proceeds of five pounds sterling received through Eliza Wigham, of Scotland, for her. I had given some account of Harriet's labor to the Anti-Slavery Society of Edinburgh, of which Eliza Wigham was secretary." Members had contributed, and Miss Wigham had sent the money to Garrett to give to her. In those days a pound was worth just under five dollars, so five pounds yielded slightly more than the amount God had told Harriet to expect.

Harriet never kept count of the slaves she helped to freedom. Sarah Bradford estimated the number at "somewhat over three hundred," but her estimate did not include the many runaways she helped during the Civil War. Long after that war ended, Harriet wrote to Frederick Douglass for an endorsement of the book she and Sarah Bradford had written. Here is part of what he wrote in reply:

"You ask for what you do not need when you call upon me for a word of commendation. I need such words from you far more than you can need them from me, especially where your superior labors and devotion to the cause of the lately enslaved of our land are known as I know them. The difference between us is very marked. Most of what I have done and suffered in the service of our cause has been in public, and I have received much encouragement at every step of the way. You, on the other hand, have labored in a private way. I have wrought in the day—you in the night. I have had the applause of the crowd and the satisfaction that comes of being approved by the multitude, while the most that you have done has been witnessed by a few trembling, scared, and foot-sore bondmen and women, whom you have led out of the house of bondage, and whose heartfelt '*God bless you*' has been your only reward."

Like Thomas Garrett, who had spoken to the Anti-Slavery Society of Edinburgh about Harriet Tubman, many other abolitionists went on speaking tours of Great Britain to raise money and to be buoyed up by popular support. Among them was James Pennington, author of *The Fugitive Blacksmith*, first published in 1849 in London where he was attending the Second World Conference on Slavery. By then he was an ordained minister, popular speaker on the abolitionist circuit, and author of *The Origin and History of the Colored People*. From London he would go on to Germany to visit the University of Heidelberg, where he was honored with the degree of Doctor of Divinity. This was a very far cry from his situation twenty-two years earlier when he had been an illiterate slave working as a blacksmith on a plantation near Hagerstown, in Maryland. It was an embittering experience, marked by hunger, fear, ignorance, neglect by his overworked parents, "the tyranny of the master's children" and "the abuse of the overseers." This went on until Pennington was nineteen, when he decided to escape.

The immediate causes of this decision began on a Monday morning when, hearing of the late return of some of his slaves from a weekend visit to a neighboring plantation, "my master [Frisby Tilghman] was greatly irritated, and resolved to have, as he said, 'a general whipping-match among them.' Preparatory to this, he had a rope in his pocket and a cowhide in his hand, walking about the premises and speaking to every-one he met in a very insolent manner, and finding fault with some without just cause." Encountering Pennington's father, he complained about the absentees and swore "By the Eternal, I'll make them know their hour! The fact is, I have too many of you; my people are getting to be the most careless, lazy and worthless in the country."

> "'Master,' said my father, 'I am always at my post. Monday morning never finds me off the plantation.'
>
> "'Hush, Bazil! I shall have to sell some of you, and then the rest will have enough to do. I have not work enough to keep you all tightly employed. I have too many of you.'
>
> "All this was said in an angry, threatening and exceedingly insulting tone. My father was a high-spirited man, and feeling deeply the insult, replied to the last expression, 'If I am one too many, sir, give me a chance to get a purchaser, and I am willing to be sold when it may suit you.'
>
> "'Bazil, I told you to hush!' and suiting the action to the word, he drew forth the cowhide from under his arm, fell upon him with most

savage cruelty, and inflicted fifteen or twenty severe stripes with all his strength, over his shoulders and the small of his back. As he raised himself upon his toes, and gave the last stripe, he said, 'By the *** I will make you know that I am master of your tongue as well as of your time!'

Pennington "was near enough to hear the insolent words that were spoken to my father, and to hear, see, and even count the savage stripes inflicted upon him. Let me ask any one of Anglo-Saxon blood and spirit, how would you expect a son to feel at such a sight? This act created an open rupture with our family—each member felt the deep insult that had been inflicted upon our head; the spirit of the whole family was roused . . . Although it was some time after this event before I took the decisive step, yet in my mind and spirit I never was a slave after it."

Soon after, the master found a pretext to whip James—"about a dozen severe blows, so that my limbs and flesh were sore for several weeks. This affair my mother saw from her cottage, which was near; I being one of the eldest sons of my parents, our family was now mortified to the lowest degree." From then on "I thought of nothing but the family disgrace under which we were smarting, and how to get out of it."

He decided to escape to Pennsylvania, which in terms of distance was not far off, but for that very reason hazardous to reach because the roads were closely watched. He left in November, on a Sunday, "the holy day which God in his infinite wisdom gave for the rest of both man and beast." All he had with him was a small bundle of clothing and a piece of corn bread. He had decided not to tell his family of his plans, nor even to say good-bye to them, for fear that doing so might lessen his determination. Once he had set out, "my only guide was the north star."

Three days later, tired and weakened by hunger, he was walking along a minor road when he came to a tavern—"a dangerous place to pass, much less to stop at. I was therefore passing it as quietly and as rapidly as possible when from the lot just opposite the house I heard a coarse, stern voice cry, 'Halloo!'

"I turned my face to the left, the direction from which the voice came, and observed that it proceeded from a man who was digging potatoes. I answered him politely, when the following occurred: 'Who do you belong to?'

"'I am free, sir.'

"'Have you got papers?'

"'No, sir.' "

"'Well, you must stop here.'

"By this time he had got astride the fence, making his way into the road. I said, 'My business is onward, sir, and I do not wish to stop.'

"'I will see then if you don't stop, you black rascal.' He was now in the middle of the road, making after me in a brisk walk. I saw that a crisis was at hand. I had no weapons of any kind, not even a pocketknife, but I asked myself, Shall I surrender without a struggle? The instinctive answer was, No. What will you do? Continue to walk. If he runs after you, run. Get him as far from the house as you can, then turn suddenly and smite him on the knee with a stone. That will render him, at least, unable to pursue you.

"This was a desperate scheme, but I could think of no other, and my habits as a blacksmith had given my eye and hand such mechanical skill that I felt quite sure that if I could only get a stone in my hand, and have time to wield it, I should not miss his knee-pan.

"I had just begun to glance my eye about for a stone to grasp, when he made a tiger-like leap at me. This of course brought us to running. At this moment he yelled out 'Jake Shouster!' and at the next moment the door of a small house standing to the left was opened, and out jumped a shoemaker girded up in his leather apron, with his knife in his hand. He sprang forward and seized me by the collar, while the other seized my arms behind. I was now in the grasp of two men, either of whom was larger bodied than myself, and one of them was armed with a dangerous weapon. Standing in the door of the shoemaker's shop was a third man; and in the potato lot I had passed was still a fourth man. Thus surrounded by superior physical force, the fortune of the day it seemed to me was gone. My heart melted away. I sank resistlessly into the hands of my captors, who dragged me immediately into the tavern which was near."

Having gone to such trouble to capture Pennington, the locals soon lost interest. They tried to haul him before a magistrate, but the magistrate was not in; they talked of collecting a reward of $200, but also half-believed his story that he was free; when he made a break they quickly re-captured him, but then left him in the custody of a nine-year-old boy; most of them then drifted away; and in the evening, while the few that remained were busy putting horses in the barn, Pennington had no trouble at all in sprinting across a field and into a nearby wood, with no one in pursuit.

After a rainy night scrabbling his way through a thick wood, he came upon a road which he hoped led north. "The day dawned upon me when I was near a small house and barn, situate close to the road-side. The barn was too near the road, and too small to afford secure shelter for the day; but as I cast my eye round by the dim light, I could see no wood, and no larger barn." Rather than contain hay, "the barn was filled with corn fodder, newly cured and lately got in." Unable not to make a noise as he crawled in among the corn cobs "I had the misfortune to attract the notice of a little house-dog, such as we call in that part of the world a 'fice,' on account of its being not only the smallest species of the canine race, but also the most saucy, noisy and teasing of all dogs. The little creature commenced a fierce barking. I had at once great fears that the mischievous little thing would betray me. I fully apprehended that as soon as the man of the house arose, he would come and make search in the barn."

But that did not happen. After pottering about in the yard, the man of the house spent the day afield. After he had gone "my unwelcome little annoyer" returned "and continued with occasional intermissions through the day. He made regular sallies from the house to the barn, and after smelling about would fly back to the house, barking furiously. I cannot now, with pen or tongue, give a correct idea of the feeling of wretchedness I experienced." In the afternoon he heard horsemen passing by on the road, and "from a word which I now and then overheard, I had not a shadow of doubt that they were in search of me." But they rode on without looking in the barn, and when the man of the house returned at the end of the day he paid no attention to the renewed barking of the fice. Then the horsemen returned and Pennington heard them ask, "Have you seen a runaway nigger pass here today?" After mentioning that "a stiff reward is out for him—two hundred dollars," they rode away, the man went into the house and "hope seemed to dawn for me once more."

As soon as it was dark he left the barn—the fice still yapping shrilly at him—and after "beating my way across marshy fields" and through "woods and thickets where there were no paths" he found his way back to the road. Passing by a cornfield he got an ear and then, to escape the bitter cold, crept inside a corn shock where, overcome with exhaustion, he fell asleep. "When I awoke the sun was shining around. I started with alarm, but it was too late to think of seeking any other shelter. I therefore nestled myself down, and concealed myself as best I could from the light of day. After recovering a little from my fright, I commenced again eating my whole corn. Grain by grain I worked away at it; when my jaws grew tired, as they often did, I would rest, and then begin afresh. Thus, although I began an early breakfast, I was nearly the whole of the forenoon before I had done.

"Nothing of importance occurred during the day until about the middle of the afternoon, when I was thrown into a panic by the appearance of a party of gunners, who passed near me with their dogs. After shooting one or two birds, however, and passing within a few rods of my frail covering, they went on, and left me once more in hope." Next day "I continued my flight on the public road; and a little after the sun rose, I came in sight of a toll gate." The gate-keeper was "an elderly woman, who I afterwards learned was a widow, and an excellent Christian woman. I asked her if I was in Pennsylvania. On being informed that I was, I asked her if she knew where I could get employ? She said she did not; but advised me to go W. W. [William Wright], a Quaker, who lived about three miles from her, whom I would find to take an interest in me. She gave me directions which way to take; I thanked her, and bade her good morning, and was very careful to follow her directions.

"In about half an hour I stood trembling at the door of William Wright. After knocking, the door opened upon a comfortably spread table, the sight of which seemed at once to increase my hunger sevenfold. Not daring to enter, I said I had been sent to him in search of employ. 'Well,' said he, 'come in and take thy breakfast, and get warm, and we will talk about it; thee must be cold without any coat.' *'Come in and take thy breakfast and get warm!'* These words spoken by a stranger, but with such an air of simple sincerity and fatherly kindness, made an overwhelming impression upon my mind. They made me feel, in spite of all my fear and timidity, that I had, in the providence of God, found a friend and a home." And so indeed he had—just like William Wells Brown, who had also had the good fortune to meet a benevolent Quaker. But Pennington was even more fortunate, for while Wells Brown was willing to share his name, William Wright had once been a schoolteacher and offered to teach Pennington to read and write. This had long been one of his dearest wishes.

In exchange for his lessons, he worked on the Wright farm for the next six months; but then word of his presence got around, and to avoid being taken by slave-catchers he went to live with another Quaker family, near Philadelphia. From there he moved to New York so he could continue his studies, and then it was on to Yale Divinity School, where he was allowed to attend lectures but "my voice was not to be heard in the classroom asking or answering a question. I could not get a book out of the library, and my name was never to appear on the catalogue." Nor, unlike the University of Heidelberg, did Yale give him a degree. In spite of that he was ordained a minister, and it was he who performed the marriage ceremony between Anna Murray and his fellow fugitive, Frederick Douglass.

Like James Pennington and William Wells Brown, most fugitives headed north to a free state, or, particularly after the passage of the Fugitive Slave Act, to Canada. But there were also many who headed south. Until its acquisition by the United States and the wars that led to the expulsion of the Seminoles, Florida had been a popular destination. Mexico, which had abolished slavery in 1829, was another place of refuge. When traveling through Texas in the 1850s Frederick Law Olmsted reported on three episodes concerning runaways.

The first happened soon after he arrived at a town called Victoria. Here Olmsted overheard some men discussing a slave who had recently escaped after attacking his owner, a local judge—"cut the judge right bad. Like to have killed the judge. Cut his young master too."

"Reckon, if they caught him, 'twould go rather hard with him."

"Reckon 'twould. We caught him once, but he got away from us again. We was just tying his feet together, and he give me a kick in the face, and broke. I had my six-shooter handy, and I tried to shoot him, but every barrel missed fire. Been loaded a week. We shot at him three times with rifles, but he'd got too far off, and we didn't hit, but we must have shaved him close. We chased him, and my dog got close to him once. If he'd gripped him, we should have got him, but he had a dog himself, and just as my dog got within about a yard of him, his dog turned and fit my dog, and he hurt him so bad we

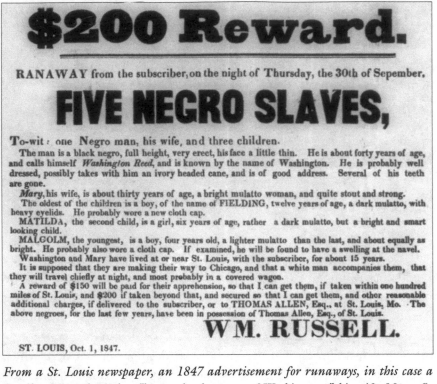

$200 Reward.

RANAWAY from the subscriber, on the night of Thursday, the 30th of Sepember.

FIVE NEGRO SLAVES,

To-wit: one Negro man, his wife, and three children.

The man is a black negro, full height, very erect, his face a little thin. He is about forty years of age, and calls himself *Washington Reed*, and is known by the name of Washington. He is probably well dressed, possibly takes with him an ivory headed cane, and is of good address. Several of his teeth are gone.

Mary, his wife, is about thirty years of age, a bright mulatto woman, and quite stout and strong.

The oldest of the children is a boy, of the name of FIELDING, twelve years of age, a dark mulatto, with heavy eyelids. He probably wore a new cloth cap.

MATILDA, the second child, is a girl, six years of age, rather a dark mulatto, but a bright and smart looking child.

MALCOLM, the youngest, is a boy, four years old, a lighter mulatto than the last, and about equally as bright. He probably also wore a cloth cap. If examined, he will be found to have a swelling at the navel.

Washington and Mary have lived at or near St. Louis, with the subscriber, for about 15 years.

It is supposed that they are making their way to Chicago, and that a white man accompanies them, that they will travel chiefly at night, and most probably in a covered wagon.

A reward of $150 will be paid for their apprehension, so that I can get them, if taken within one hundred miles of St. Louis, and $200 if taken beyond that, and secured so that I can get them, and other reasonable additional charges, if delivered to the subscriber, or to THOMAS ALLEN, Esq., at St. Louis, Mo. The above negroes, for the last few years, have been in possession of Thomas Allen, Esq., of St. Louis.

WM. RUSSELL.

ST. LOUIS, Oct. 1, 1847.

From a St. Louis newspaper, an 1847 advertisement for runaways, in this case a family of five: the father "known by the name of Washington," his wife, Mary, "a bright mulatto woman," and three children, aged twelve, six and four. The reward was $150 "if taken within 100 miles of St. Louis, and $200 if taken beyond that, and secured so that I can get them."

couldn't get him to run again. We run him close, though, I tell you. Run him out of his coat, and his boots, and a pistol he'd got. But 'twas getting towards dark, and he got into them bayous, and kept swimming from one side to another."

"If he's got across the river, he'd get to the Mexicans in two days, and there he'd be safe. The Mexicans'd take care of him."

Olmsted's second report came after he and some companions had crossed the Rio Grande into Mexico at Piedras Negras, where the people were "lounging outside their doors, chatting cheerfully, laughing, and singing a great deal, nearly all smoking."

"As we turned a corner near the bank we came suddenly upon two Negroes as they were crossing the street. One of them was startled, and looking ashamed and confounded, turned hesitatingly and walked away from us; whereat some Mexican children laughed, and the other Negro, looking at us, grinned impudently, expressing plainly enough, 'I am not afraid of you.' He touched his hat, however, when I nodded to him and then, putting his hands in his pockets, as if he hadn't meant to, stepped up on one of the sand-bank caverns, whistling. Thither, wishing to have some conversation with him, I followed. He very civilly informed me, in answer to inquiries, that he was born in Virginia, and had been brought south by a trader and sold to a gentleman who had brought him to Texas, from whom he had run away four or five years ago. He would like right well to see old Virginia again, that he would—if he could be free. He was a mechanic, and could earn a dollar very easily by his trade every day. He could speak Spanish fluently and had traveled extensively in Mexico, sometimes on his own business, and sometimes as a servant or muleteer. Once he had been beyond Durango, or nearly to the Pacific; and northward to Chihuahua, and he professed to be competent as a guide to any part of Northern Mexico. He had joined the Catholic True Church, he said, and he was very well satisfied with the country.

"Runaways were constantly arriving here; two had got over, as I had previously been informed, the night before. He could not guess how many came in a year, but he could count forty that he had known of in the last three months. At other points, further down the river, a great many more came than here. He supposed a good many got lost and starved to death, or were killed on the way, between the settlements and the river. Most of them brought with them money, which they had earned and hoarded for the purpose, or some small articles which they had stolen from their masters. They had never been used to taking care of themselves, and when they first got here were so excited with being free, and with being made so much of by these Mexican women, that they spent all they brought very soon; generally they gave it all away to the women, and in a short time they had nothing to live upon, and not knowing the language of the country they couldn't find any work to do, and often they were very poor and miserable. But after they had learned the language, which did not generally take them long if they chose to be industrious, they could live very comfortably. Wages were low, but they had all they earned for their own, and a man's living didn't cost him much here. Colored men who were industrious and saving always did well; they could make money faster than Mexicans themselves because they had more sense. The Mexican Government was very just to them, they could always have their rights as fully protected as if they were Mexicans born. He mentioned to me several Negroes whom he had seen, in different parts of the country, who had acquired wealth and positions of honor. Some of them had connected themselves by marriage with rich old Spanish families who thought as much of themselves as the best white people in Virginia. In fact, a colored man, if he could behave himself decently, had rather an advantage over a white American, he thought. The people generally liked them better. These Texas folks were too rough to suit them."

According to Olmsted, these statements were confirmed "in all essential particulars, by every foreigner I saw who had lived or traveled in this part of Mexico, as well as by Mexicans themselves." Indeed, back in the American South, "it is repeated as a standing joke—I suppose I have heard it fifty times in the Texas taverns, and always to the great amusement of the company—that a nigger in Mexico is just as good as a white man."

Olmsted was impressed by the courage of the escaping slaves. "There is a permanent reward offered by the state [of Texas] for their recovery, and a considerable number of men make a business of hunting them"—including the so-called "filibusters" who made illegal raids across the border. "Most of the frontier rangers are ready at any time to make a couple of hundred dollars by taking them up, if they come in their way . . . If they escape immediate capture by dogs or men, there is then the great dry desert country to be crossed, with the danger of falling in with savages, or of being attacked by panthers or wolves, or of being bitten or stung by the numerous reptiles that abound in it; of drowning miserably at the last of the fords; in winter of freezing in a norther, and, at all seasons, of famishing in the wilderness for want of means to procure food. Brave Negro! say I."

His third story was copied from the *West Feliciana Whig:*

"On Saturday last, a runaway Negro was killed in the parish of East
Baton Rouge, just below the line of this parish, under the following circumstances: Two citizens of Port Hudson, learning that a Negro was
at work on a flat boat, loading with sand, just below that place, who
was suspected of being a runaway, went down in a skiff for the purpose
of arresting him. Having seized him and put him into the skiff they
started back, but had not proceeded far when the Negro, who had been
at the oars, seized a hatchet and assaulted one of them, wounding him
very seriously. A scuffle ensued, in which both parties fell overboard.
They were both rescued by the citizen pulling to them with the skiff.
Finding him so unmanageable, the Negro was put ashore, and the parties returned to Port Hudson for arms and a pack of Negro dogs, and
started again with the intention to capture him. They soon got on his
trail, and when found again he was standing at bay upon the outer edge
of a large raft of drift wood, armed with a club and pistol.

"In this position he bade defiance to men and dogs—knocking
the latter into the water with his club, and resolutely threatening death
to any man who approached him. Finding him obstinately determined
not to surrender, one of his pursuers shot him. He fell at the third fire,
and so determined was he not to be captured, that when an effort was
made to rescue him from drowning he made battle with his club, and
sunk waving his weapon in angry defiance at his pursuers."

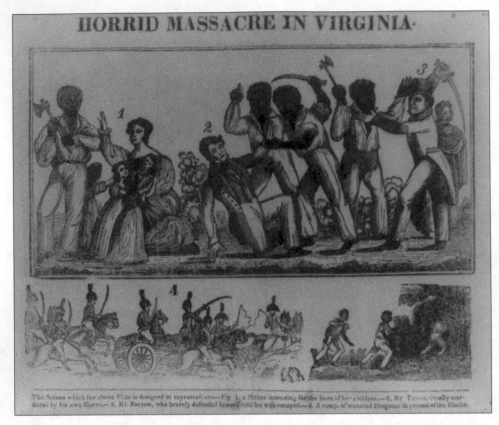

A contemporary woodcut published shortly after Nat Turner's Rebellion. The text
below reads: "The Scenes which the above Plate is designed to represent are: Fig 1. A
Mother intreating for the lives of her children.—2. Mr. Travis cruelly murdered by
his own Slaves.—3. Mr. Barrow, who bravely defended himself until his wife escaped.—
4. A company of mounted Dragoons in pursuit of the Blacks." Turner's 1831 rebellion
was the country's bloodiest slave uprising.

CHAPTER 11

RESISTANCE

THE NINETEENTH CENTURY GOT OFF TO A BAD START FOR THE MASTER CLASS: 1800 was the year that Denmark Vesey, having won $1500 in a state lottery, bought his freedom; that Nat Turner and John Brown were born; and that Richmond, Virginia, was thrown into a panic by an aborted uprising led by a young blacksmith called Gabriel Prosser.

But even before the century began, great alarm was caused in this country by events in Haiti, then a French colony and called Saint Domingue, or St. Domingo. Known as "the pearl of the West Indies," its coffee and sugar plantations produced fabulous amounts of money for their aristocratic owners who—or at least until the outbreak of the French Revolution in 1789—spent most of it on high living in Paris. This absenteeism was one of the features that differentiated Saint Domingue from the American South. Another was the existence of a large class of free blacks and mulattoes known as *gens de couleur*, who aspired to equality with whites. Yet another was the ratio of slaves to whites—about five hundred thousand to fifty thousand, or ten to one. On paper, the slaves were protected by the laws of the *Code Noir*, but for the most part these were a dead letter, and there were many reports of insanely brutal tortures carried out by owners, such as slaves being buried alive, or staked out on their backs so that birds could pick out their eyes, or scalded to death by having boiling sugar poured over them. Also unlike American slavery was the French obsession with parsing negritude, so that there were, at least in theory, no fewer than 128 categories, starting with full blacks, and following with mulattoes, who were half white, quadroons, who were a quarter white, octoroons, an eighth, *marabous, griffes, sacatras* and so on, and not forgetting the *sang-mêlés*, who were 127 parts white and one part black. To add to the social divisions, there were deep political rifts caused by the French Revolution, most notably those between royalists and republicans.

Despite these special circumstances, what happened in Haiti shocked slave-owners everywhere. Bryan Edwards, a naturalist and historian who lived in the British West Indies, gives this account:

> "In the month of September, 1791, when I was at Spanish Town in Jamaica, two French gentlemen were introduced to me who were just arrived from St. Domingo, with information that the Negro slaves belonging to the French part of that island, to the number, as was believed, of 100,000 and upwards had revolted, and were spreading death and desolation over the whole of the northern province. They reported that the governor-general, considering the situation of the colony as a common cause among the white inhabitants of all nations in the West Indies, had dispatched commissioners to the neighbouring islands, as well as to the States of North America, to request immediate assistance."

Although Britain and France were traditional enemies, the appeal to white solidarity hit home. Two Royal Navy frigates and a sloop of war were made ready, military supplies were loaded, the French commissioners went on board, and "I was easily persuaded to accompany them."

"We arrived in the harbour of Cape François in the evening of the 26th of September, and the first object which arrested our attention as we approached was a dreadful scene of devastation by fire. The noble plain adjoining the Cape was covered with ashes, and the surrounding hills, as far as the eye could reach, everywhere presented to us ruins still smoking, and houses and plantations at that moment in flames. It was a sight more terrible than the mind of any man, unaccustomed to such a scene, can easily conceive."

Edwards summarized what he had been told.

> "It was on the morning of the 23rd of August, just before day, that a general alarm and consternation spread throughout the towns of the Cape. The inhabitants were called from their beds by persons who reported that all the Negro slaves in the several neighbouring parishes had revolted, and were at that moment carrying death and

desolation over the adjoining large and beautiful plain to the north-east. The governor and most of the military officers on duty assembled together, but the reports were so confused and contradictory as to gain but little credit; when, as day-light began to break, the sudden and successive arrival, with ghastly countenances, of persons who had with difficulty escaped the massacre and flown to the town for protection, brought a dreadful confirmation of the fatal tidings.

"The approach of day-light served only to discover sights of horror. It was now apparent that the Negroes on all the estates of the plain acted in concert, and a general massacre of the whites took place in every quarter. On some few estates, indeed, the lives of the women were spared, but they were reserved only to gratify the brutal appetites of the ruffians; and it is shocking to relate that many of them suffered violation on the dead bodies of their husbands and fathers!"

There were many other such horror stories. "The largest sugar-plantation on the plain was that of Mons. Gallifet, situated about eight miles from the town, the Negroes belonging to which had always been treated with much kindness and liberality." But when the overseer went to see what was happening "to his surprise and grief he found all the Negroes in arms on the side of the rebels, and (horrid to tell!) their standard was the body of a white infant which they had recently impaled on a stake!" The overseer was killed but others escaped "and conveyed the dreadful tidings to the inhabitants of the town." Meanwhile "the ruffians exchanged the sword for the torch. The buildings and cane-fields were everywhere set on fire; and the conflagrations, which were visible from the town, in a thousand different quarters, furnished a prospect more shocking, and reflections more dismal, than fancy can paint or the powers of man describe. Consternation and terror now took possession of every mind: and the screams of the women and children running from door to door heightened the horrors of the scene."

"[The country was] wholly abandoned to the ravages of the enemy . . . All the white, and even the mulatto children whose fathers had not joined in the revolt, were murdered without exception, frequently before the eyes, or clinging to the bosoms, of their mothers. Young women of all ranks were first violated by a whole troop of barbarians, and then generally put to death . . . In the parish of Limbé, at a place called the Great Ravine, a venerable planter, the father of two beautiful young ladies, was tied down by a savage ringleader of a band, who ravished the eldest daughter in his presence, and delivered over the youngest to one of his followers. Their passion being satisfied, they slaughtered both the father and the daughters."

In assigning blame for these events, Edwards, while offering some mild reprimands on the conduct of the owners, came down hard on the French reformers called *Les Amis des Noirs* and the British Association for the Abolition of the Slave Trade, led by William Wilberforce— "pestilent reformers" whose "vile machinations" and "pretences to philanthropy were as gross a mockery of human reason as their conduct was an outrage on all the feelings of our nature." Among other activities "they distributed at a prodigious expense throughout the colonies tracts and pamphlets without number, the direct tendency of which was to render the white inhabitants odious and contemptible in the eyes of their own slaves, and excite in the latter such ideas of their natural rights and equality of condition as should lead them to a general struggle for freedom through rebellion and bloodshed. In many of those writings, arguments are expressly adduced, in language which cannot be misunderstood, to urge the Negroes to rise up and murder their masters without mercy . . ."

Many of the whites who survived the massacres came to live in the South, where they kept their stories alive. To them, and to American slaveholders, the lessons of Haiti were obvious: with a few exceptions, Negro slaves were essentially savages, thirsting for blood and lusting after white women; kindness was wasted on people who did not know the meaning of gratitude; beware of outside agitators distributing subversive tracts; and never let down your guard. In the meantime they had to watch incredulously as first a British army of some 15,000 men lost more than half its number in a failed attempt to conquer the island, and then as an even larger French army suffered the same fate. To be sure, these defeats were largely due to the yellow fever, but the result, after many more years of strife and bloodshed, was the establishment, just a few hundred miles from the coast of the United States, of an independent, self-governing, and seemingly impregnable republic of former slaves—an abomination for owners, "a city upon a hill" for black people, slave or free.

Meanwhile, back in this country, Gabriel Prosser was planning his own uprising. An imposing figure, well over six feet tall, very dark and with a "bony face," Gabriel would also have developed powerful arms and shoulders from his trade as a blacksmith. To add to his formidable appearance, two of his front teeth were missing, he had scars on his head and he was known to be a ferocious fighter—when caught by his overseer stealing a pig, Gabriel attacked him with such ferocity that he bit off most of the white man's ear. Normally this would have caused him to be hanged, but he got off with branding on his left hand and a month in jail. This leniency was probably due to the intercession of his owner, Thomas Prosser, for Gabriel was a skilled worker and was usually hired out for good wages (which his owner of course kept), to one of the iron foundries in Richmond. Like other members of the conspiracy, he was literate, and often quoted the Bible—indeed one of their meetings began with a sermon before getting down to more sanguinary matters.

According to the testimony of another of Prosser's slaves, Ben Woolfolk, who had been pardoned on condition that he testify against the others, after the sermon Gabriel said he wanted "to bring on the business as soon as possible," while it was still late summer. His brother, Martin, said "there was this expression in the Bible, delay breeds danger"; also that "five of you shall conquer an hundred, and a hundred a thousand of our enemies."

Also according to Woolfolk, "The plan was to be as follows: we were all to meet at the briery spot on the Brook; one hundred men were to stand at the Brook bridge; Gabriel was to take a hundred more and go to Gregory's tavern and take the arms which were there; fifty more were to be sent to Rocketts [a riverside district of Richmond] to set that on fire, in order to alarm the upper part of the town and induce the people to go down there; while they were employed in extinguishing the fire Gabriel and the other officers and soldiers were to take the Capitol, seize all the arms they could find and be ready to slaughter the people on their return from Rocketts. Sam Bird was to have a pass as a free man and was to go to the nation of Indians called Catawbas to persuade them to join the Negroes to fight the white people. As far as I understood, all the whites were to be massacred, except the Quakers, the Methodists and the Frenchmen, and they were to be spared on account as they conceived of their being friendly to liberty . . . They intended also to spare all the poor white women who had no slaves." Another witness for the prosecution (there were none for the defense) declared that after the massacre they would "take the treasury and divide the money."

Other testimony raises the question of whether the plot was much more than wishful thinking and wild talk—there are several mentions of "money to buy liquor" and meeting "to drink grog," and when arrested a slave called Isaac was said to be "much intoxicated." There were also weird statements like Ben Woolfolk's testimony that following the massacre, "if the white people agreed to their freedom they would then hoist a white flag, and he [Gabriel] would dine and drink with the merchants of the city." Then there was the matter of weaponry. Again according to Woolfolk, they would "commence the fight with scythe blades until they could procure arms from the white people," and when arrested, Gabriel was armed only with a bayonet fixed on a stick. But if their weapons were few, their numbers were supposed to be enormous. "Gabriel said he had nearly ten thousand men; he had one thousand in Richmond, about six hundred in Caroline, and nearly five hundred at the coal pits, besides others at different places, and that he expected the poor white people would also join him."

But before anything could happen, the alarm was given when two slaves warned their masters, who in turn warned the governor, James Monroe. The militia was called out and cannon were posted in the streets. More importantly, "that very evening, just about sunset, there came on the most terrible thunder accompanied with an enormous rain, that I ever witnessed in this State. Between Prosser's and Richmond there is a place called Brook Swamp which runs across the high road, and over which there was a bridge. By this the Africans were of necessity to pass, and the rain had made the passage impracticable." (The journalist James Callender to Thomas Jefferson.) The trials that followed were exceptionally hasty—seven men were condemned on a

Thursday and hanged on Friday. All in all, about thirty-five were condemned to death, and many others banished. Gabriel himself escaped but was soon captured, tried, convicted and hanged. Monroe interviewed him before his execution but got little out of him. "He seemed to have made up his mind to die, and to have resolved to say but little on the subject of the conspiracy."

Chronologically, the next instance of organized armed resistance came in 1816 and took place outside the then borders of the United States, in Florida. Ever since 1704, when Governor Zuniga y Cera had proclaimed that "any Negro of Carolina, Christian or not, free or slave, who wishes to come fugitive, will be given complete liberty," that colony had been a thorn in the side of American slave-owners. During the War of 1812, the British had established a fort on a cliff above the Apalachicola River, fifteen miles from its mouth, and a mere sixty miles from the American border. When the war ended, probably looking to make trouble for the victorious Americans, the British stocked the fort with a large supply of guns and ammunition, and then handed it over to a force of several hundred fugitive slaves and their Choctaw allies. It then became known as the Negro Fort.

In June, 1816, the *Georgia Journal* summarized the situation: "It was not to be expected that an establishment so pernicious to the Southern States, holding out to a part of their population temptations to insubordination, would have been suffered to exist after the close of the war. In the course of the last winter several slaves from this neighborhood fled to that fort; others have lately gone from Tennessee and the Mississippi Territory. How long shall this evil, requiring immediate remedy, be permitted to exist?"

The fact that Florida was a Spanish colony, and Spain and the United States were at peace, was not a consideration of much importance to General Andrew Jackson, who ordered General Gaines to destroy the Negro Fort. General Gaines passed the order on to Colonel Clinch, and on August 2, 1816, Colonel Clinch submitted his report, part of which ran:

"On the 17th [July] I left this place [Camp Crawford in Georgia]] with one hundred and sixteen chosen men, in boats, and commenced descending the river. On the same evening I was joined by Major M'Intosh, with one hundred and fifty Indians, and on the 18th by an old chief called Captain Isaacs, and the celebrated chief Koteha-haigo (or Mad Tiger,) at the head of a large body of Indians. Their object was to capture the Negroes within the fort and restore them [i.e. sell them back] to their proper owners. We held a council, and an agreement was entered into. I ordered the chiefs to keep parties in advance, and to secure every Negro they fell in with, and to join me near the fort."

The fort "was situated on a beautiful and commanding bluff"—sometimes known as Prospect Bluff, and sometimes as Bloody Bluff—"with the river in front, a large creek just below, a swamp in the rear, and a small creek just above." On arrival Colonel Clinch landed his force in a nearby wood and waited for his artillery to come up. Meanwhile, his Indian allies surrounded the fort and kept up an irregular fire. "In the evening a deputation of chiefs went into the fort and demanded its surrender; but they were abused and treated with the utmost contempt. The black chief heaped much abuse on the Americans, and said he had been left in command of the fort by the British government, and that he would sink any American vessels that should attempt to pass it; and would blow up the fort if he could not defend it. The chiefs also informed me that the Negroes had hoisted a red flag, and that the English jack was flying over it."

Early the next morning the riverboats carrying the artillery "came up in handsome style, and made fast along side of the intended battery. In a few minutes we received a shot from a 32 pounder, which was returned in a gallant manner. The contest was momentary. The fifth discharge (a hot shot) from gun vessel No. 154, commanded by Sailing Master Bassett, entered the magazine, and blew up the fort. The explosion"—which was said to have been heard in Pensacola, a hundred miles away—"was awful, and the scene horrible beyond description.

"Our first care, on arriving at the scene of destruction, was to rescue and relieve the unfortunate beings that survived the explosion. The war yells of the Indians, the cries and lamentations of the wounded, compelled the soldier to pause in the midst of victory to drop a tear for the sufferings of his fellow beings, and to acknowledge that the great Ruler of the Universe must have used us as his instruments in chastising the blood-thirsty and murderous wretches that defended the fort." Following this pious observation, Colonel Clinch reverted to facts and figures. "The fort contained about one hundred effective men, including twenty-five Choctaws, and about two hundred women and children, not more than one sixth of which number were saved. The greater part of the Negroes belonged to the Spanish and Indians. The American Negroes had principally settled on the river, and a number of them had left their fields and gone over to the Seminoles on hearing of our approach. Their corn fields extended nearly fifty miles up the river, and their numbers were daily increasing. The chiefs passed sentence of death on the outlawed Choctaw chief and the black commandant (Garson), for the murder of the four Americans, and the sentence was immediately carried into execution. The Spanish Negroes were delivered to Mr. Hambly, agent for the house of Messrs. Forbes & Co., and the American Negroes are confined at this post."

This was the beginning of the long and bloody Seminole Wars, which were waged as much against the fugitive slaves as against the Indians—"this is a Negro, not an Indian war," wrote General Thomas Jesup, in 1836. In the end, both groups were forced out, the Seminoles winding up in Oklahoma, and many of the blacks eventually finding refuge in Mexico.

The next major domestic conspiracy was that of Denmark Vesey in 1822. Most of what is known about it comes from *An Official Report of the Trials of Sundry Negroes Charged in an Attempt to Raise an Insurrection in the State of South Carolina,* written by Lionel Kennedy and Thomas Parker, judges who had presided at the trials. Though biased, it is the principal account of the insurrection, since by tacit consent the Charleston papers mostly suppressed the story. Here is some of the report:

"At the head of this conspiracy stood Denmark Vesey, a free Negro; with him the idea undoubtedly originated. For several years before he disclosed his intentions to anyone he appears to have been constantly and assiduously engaged in endeavoring to embitter the minds of the colored population against the white. He rendered himself perfectly familiar with all those parts of the Scriptures which he thought he could pervert to his purpose, and would readily quote them to prove that slavery was contrary to the laws of God, that slaves were bound to attempt their emancipation, however shocking and bloody might be the consequences, and that such efforts would not only be pleasing to the Almighty, but were absolutely enjoined, and their success predicted in the Scriptures."

Along with perverting the Scriptures, Vesey was accused of distributing "inflammatory pamphlets on slavery brought into Charleston from some of our sister states within the last four years," and of spreading reports of "the speeches in Congress of those opposed to the admission of Missouri [as a slave state] into the Union." Nor was that all.

"Even whilst walking through the streets in company with another he was not idle; for if his companion bowed to a white person he would rebuke him, and observe that all men were born equal, and that he was surprised that anyone would degrade himself by such conduct, that he would never cringe to the whites, nor ought anyone else who had the feelings of a man. When answered, 'We are slaves,' he would sarcastically and indignantly reply, 'You deserve to remain slaves.' And if he were further asked, 'What can we do?' he would remark, 'Go and buy a spelling book and read the fable of Hercules and the Wagoner,' which he would then repeat, and apply it to their situation." [In the fable, Hercules comes across a wagoner praying for divine help in getting his wagon out of a rut; Hercules tells him to stop praying and put his shoulder to the wheel.] "He also sought every opportunity of entering into conversation with white persons when they could be overheard by Negroes nearby, especially in grog shops, during which conversation he would artfully introduce some bold remark on slavery; and sometimes, when from the character he was conversing with he found he might be still bolder, he would go so far that had not his declarations in such situations been clearly proved, they would scarcely have been credited."

When he was about thirty, Vesey had won $1500 in a city lottery and used $600 of it to buy his freedom, but for some reason was unable to do the same for his wife and children. He set up a carpentry shop and prospered, but was said to have been embittered by the fate of his family. In 1817 he helped found a local branch of the African Methodist Episcopal Church, which was repeatedly closed down by the white authorities. As a class leader, Denmark taught a small group of believers at his home, focusing on the Book of Exodus and claiming that slaves were the New Israelites who would one day be freed from their bondage, and that God was on their side. (This was the sort of thing the official report had in mind when it spoke of his attempts "to embitter the minds of the colored population" and "pervert" the Scriptures to his purpose.)

Denmark's next step was to recruit an inner circle: Rolla and Ned, slaves belonging to Governor Bennett, Peter Poyas, Gullah Jack, also known as Cooter Jack, and Monday Gell. With their help "he engaged great numbers to join in the intended insurrection. He also at his house held nocturnal meetings for the purpose of interchanging opinions, maturing the plan, and collecting and giving information, at which meetings numbers of the insurgents, both from country and town attended, and where collections were made for the purpose of providing arms and ammunition." Also, "In order to induce the colored population to join them, every principle which could operate on the mind of man was artfully employed: religion, hope, fear and deception were resorted to as occasion required. All were told, and many believed, that God approved of their design; those whose fears would have restrained them were forced to yield by threats of death; those whose prudence and foresight induced them to pause were cheered with the assurance that assistance from Santo Domingo and Africa were at hand." Also, "vast numbers firmly believed that Gullah Jack was a sorcerer; that he could neither be killed nor taken; and that whilst they retained the charms which he had distributed they would themselves be invulnerable." ("A little man, a Gullah Negro, with small hands and feet," who was also "artful, cruel, bloody," Jack distributed crab-claws to the insurrectionists, telling them to keep them in their mouths "and you can't then be wounded.")

> "In enlisting men the great caution observed by the leaders was re-markable. Few if any domestic servants were spoken to, as they were distrusted, and all who were consulted were told that death would certainly await them if they informed . . . The enlistments appear to have been principally confined to Negroes hired or working out, such as carters, draymen, sawyers, porters, laborers, stevedores, mechan-ics, those employed in lumber yards, and, in short, to those who had certain allotted hours at their own disposal."

It was also noted that "This was about the time that the African Congregation was formed, and their church built." All the ringleaders were members and some were class leaders. Meetings were held at night "avowedly for religious instruction and worship" but in fact to propa-gate "inflammatory and insurrectionary doctrines." The meetings were also "rallying points for communicating to all the exact night and hour on which the first blow was to be struck."

This was to be "at twelve o'clock on the night of Saturday the 16th of June, at which hour everyone was to move, and the attack at every point to be made at the same moment. Peter was to lead a party which was to assemble on South Bay, and to be joined by a force from James' Island; he was then to march up and seize the Arsenal and Guard House opposite St. Michael's Church and secure the arms." Other arsenals and gun-shops were to be raided, and "arms thus being provided from these different sources, the city was to have been fired, and an indiscriminate slaughter of the whites to commence, and also those of their own color who had not joined them, or did not immediately do so." Plans for what would happen after the insurgents had taken Charleston were vague, though some said that "Vesey, after robbing the banks of specie and plun-dering the city of all that was most valuable, intended to sail for Santo Domingo with his principal adherents."

But before any of that could happen the plot was "crushed in the bud." On May 30, the Intendant, or mayor, received an urgent message from "a gentleman of great respectability who that morning had returned from the country. This gentleman stated 'that a favorite and confidential slave of his had communicated to him, on his arrival in town, a conversation which had taken place at the market on the Saturday preceding between himself and a black man, which afforded strong reasons for believing that a revolt and insurrection were in contemplation.'"

Soon after, the Intendant received a visit from another gentleman, "advantageously known in the community," who reported that "a faithful slave belonging to his family" had told him that another slave, who was a friend, had been told by yet another slave, "who had been trusted by the conspirators with the secret," that an insurrection was to take place on Sunday the 16th; and since this day was Friday the 14th, "not a moment should be lost." As a result, "such measures were taken by his Excellency the Governor as the occasion required," and "on the night appointed for the attack, the insurgents found a very strong guard on duty, and by ten o'clock the whole town was surrounded by the most vigilant patrols."

But although the uprising was prevented, "so true were they in observing their pledge of secrecy to each other" that it took a while to round up the leading conspirators. However, some were less true than others, notably Charles Drayton, who after being sentenced to hang was "overwhelmed with terror and guilt," and let it be known that he was "prepared to make the most ample declarations." Monday Gell also turned state's evidence after being sentenced, and it was largely on the basis of their testimony that 131 people were arrested. Of these 67 were convicted and 35 were hanged—22 of them on the same day and at the same place. Those convicted but not hanged were sent "out of the limits of the United States," which probably meant being sold to one of the West Indies. As a reward for their testimony, Charles Drayton and Monday Gell, were pardoned but also sent out of the country.

For the authors of the official report, a striking and perplexing feature of the plot was that "the character and condition of most of the insurgents were such as rendered them objects the least liable to suspicion. It is a melancholy truth that the general good conduct of all the leaders, except Gullah Jack, had secured them not only the unlimited confidence of their owners, but they had been indulged in every comfort, and allowed every privilege compatible with their situation in the community; and although Gullah Jack was not remarkable for the correctness of his deportment, he by no means sustained a bad character. Vesey himself was free, and had amassed a considerable estate for one of his color." Another conspirator, Rolla, "was the confidential servant of his master." Peter Poyas "possessed the confidence of his master in a remarkable degree, and had been treated with indulgence, liberality and kindness." Monday Gell "was much indulged and trusted by his master; his time and a large proportion of the profits of his labor were at his own disposal."

After passing sentence of death on ten of the accused who had been convicted in a joint trial, the judges also condemned them to this tongue lashing: "Your conduct, on the present occasion, exhibits a degree of depravity rarely paralleled . . . In addition to the crime of treason, you have on the present occasion displayed the vilest ingratitude. It is a melancholy truth that those servants in whom was reposed the most unlimited confidence have been the principal actors in this wicked scheme . . . You have moreover committed the grossest impiety: you have perverted the sacred words of God, and attempted to torture them into a sanction for crimes at the bare imagination of which humanity shudders." If only they had searched the Scriptures "in the spirit of truth, you would have discovered instructions peculiarly applicable to yourselves—'Servants (says St. Paul) be obedient to them that are your masters according to the flesh, with fear and trembling, in singleness of your heart, as unto Christ; not with eye-service as men-pleasers, but as the servants of Christ, doing the will of God from the heart.' Had you listened with sincerity to such doctrines, you would not have been arrested by an ignominious death.

> "Your days on earth are near their close and you now stand upon the confines of eternity. While you linger on this side of the grave, permit me to exhort you, in the name of the everliving God, whose holy ordinances you have violated, to devote most earnestly the remnant of your days in penitence and preparation for that tribunal whose sentence, whether pronounced in anger or in mercy, is eternal."

Great umbrage was taken by the members of the court when the editor of the *Charleston Courier* published a letter headed *Melancholy Effect of Popular Excitement*, by William Johnson, a Charlestonian and

associate justice of the Supreme Court. As well as containing "an insin-
uation that the Court, under the influence of popular prejudice, was capable of committing perjury," the letter impugned the "purity of their
motives" and included such terms as "injustice," "precipitation," and
"legal murder." For this libel Johnson was rebuked by the court, while
the editor apologized for publishing the letter. But writing privately to
his friend Thomas Jefferson, Johnson spoke of the "shame and anguish"
he felt at having "lived to see what I really never believed it possible I
should see—courts held with closed doors, and men dying by scores who
had never seen the faces nor heard the voices of their accusers." As to
the plot itself, it had been "infinitely exaggerated."

Johnson may well have been right, but most Charlestonians were determined to have had a narrow escape; and when casting about for people
to blame, they came up with the usual suspects: outside agitators, and
the enemy within. According to *A Refutation of the Calumnies Circulated Against the Southern and Western States* a "swarm of Missionar-
ies, white and black, that are perpetually visiting us, who, with the
Sacred Volume of God in one hand, breathing peace to the whole family
of man, scatter at the same time with the other the fire-brands of discord
and destruction, and secretly disperse among our Negro population the
seeds of discontent and sedition." These "apostolic vagabonds," had
been distributing "religious magazines, newspaper paragraphs and in-
sulated [i.e. out of context] texts of Scripture, all throwing such a delu-
sive light upon their condition as was calculated to bewilder and deceive,
and finally to precipitate them into ruin. Religion was stripped of her
pure and spotless robe, and . . . her voice was heard instigating the midnight ruffian and coward to creep silently to the pillow of his unsuspect-
ing master, and at one fell swoop to murder him in the unconscious hour
of sleep, prostitute the partner of his bosom, violate the child of his affections, and dash out the brains of his innocent and unoffending infant." There was more, but "such are a few of the barbarities to which
we would have been exposed had the late intended Insurrection been
crowned with success."

As to the enemy within, "we look upon the existence of our Free
Blacks among us as the greatest and most deplorable evil with which we
are unhappily afflicted. They are, generally speaking, an idle, lazy, inso-

402 | THE GREAT STAIN

lent set of vagabonds, who live by theft or gambling, or other means equally vicious and demoralizing. And who, from their general carriage and insolent behavior in the community, are a perpetual source of irritation to ourselves, and a fruitful cause of dissatisfaction to our slaves." A petition to the South Carolina House of Representatives to "send out of our State, never again to return, all the free persons of color," explained that "the superior condition of the free persons of color excites discontent among our slaves, who continually have before their eyes persons of the same color—freed from the control of masters, working where they please, going whither they please, and expending their money how they please. The slave, seeing this, finds his labor irksome; he becomes dissatisfied with his state, he pants after liberty!" And "let it not be forgotten that Denmark Vesey was a free person."

Seven years later, in September, 1829, southern readers of northern publications had their worst suspicions about outside agitators confirmed with the appearance of a pamphlet written by David Walker, a young black Bostonian, and titled, *Appeal in Four Articles, together with a Preamble, to the Colored Citizens of the World, but in particular and very expressly to those of the United States of America*. Walker made his living by selling second-hand clothes, and although, or perhaps because, he lacked a formal education, as a writer he could strike off some memorable phrases—"There are indeed more ways to kill a dog besides choking it to death with butter," and "Many of our children . . . leave school knowing but a little more about the grammar of their language than a horse does about handling a musket." He also knew how to grab his readers' attention:

> "Dearly beloved Brethren and Fellow Citizens," he wrote, "Having travelled over a considerable portion of these United States, and having, in the course of my travels taken the most accurate observations of things as they exist—the result of my observations has warranted the full and unshaken conviction that we—colored people of these United States—are the most degraded, wretched, and abject set of beings that ever lived since the world began."

Walker had two targets: whites who enslaved blacks, and blacks who allowed themselves to be enslaved. Both greatly offended God and would pay a price, especially the whites—"an unjust, jealous, unmerciful, avaricious and blood-thirsty set of beings, always seeking after power and authority." But at the same time "the man who would not fight under our Lord and Master Jesus Christ in the glorious and heavenly cause of freedom and of God—to be delivered from the most wretched, abject and servile slavery that ever a people was afflicted with since the foundation of the world to the present day—ought to be kept with all of his children or family in slavery, or in chains, to be butchered by his cruel enemies."

If only blacks would rise up and fight, they would be sure to win. "I give it as a fact, let twelve black men get well armed for battle and they will kill and put to flight fifty whites." That being so, Walker was particularly enraged by "servile submission"—black people who collaborated with owners. "To show the force of degraded ignorance and deceit among us" he then quoted a recent story from the *Columbian Centinel* datelined "Portsmouth, (Ohio) August 22, 1829."

"A most shocking outrage was committed in Kentucky about eight miles from this place, on the 14th inst. A negro driver, by the name of Gordon, who had purchased in Maryland about sixty negroes, was taking them, assisted by an associate named Allen and the wagoner who conveyed the baggage, to the Mississippi. The men were hand-cuffed and chained together in the usual manner for driving these poor wretches, while the women and children were suffered to proceed without incumbrance. It appears that by means of a file the negroes unobserved had succeeded in separating the irons which bound their hands, in such a way as to be able to throw them off at any moment. About 8 o'clock in the morning, while proceeding on the state road leading from Greenup to Vanceburg, two of them dropped their shackles and commenced a fight, when the wagoner (Petit) rushed in with his whip to compel them to desist. At this moment, every negro was found to be perfectly at liberty; and one of them seizing a club, gave Petit a violent blow on the head and laid him dead at his feet; and Allen, who came to his assistance, met a similar fate from the contents of a pistol fired by another of the

gang. Gordon was then attacked, seized and held by one of the negroes, whilst another fired twice at him with a pistol, the ball of
which each time grazed his head, but not proving effectual, he was
beaten with clubs and left for dead. They then commenced pillaging
the wagon and with an axe split open the trunk of Gordon and rifled
it of the money, about $2,490. Sixteen of the negroes then took to
the woods. Gordon, in the meantime, not being materially injured,
was enabled by the assistance of one of the women to mount his
horse and flee, pursued, however, by one of the gang on another
horse, with a drawn pistol; fortunately he escaped with his life,
barely arriving at a plantation as the negro came in sight; who then
turned about and retreated. The neighborhood was immediately rallied, and a hot pursuit given—which, we understand, has resulted
in the capture of the whole gang and the recovery of the greatest
part of the money."

David Walker then comments on this story:

"Here, my brethren, I want you to notice particularly in the above
article the ignorant and deceitful actions of this colored woman. I
beg you to view it carefully, as for ETERNITY!!! Here a notorious
wretch, with two other confederates had SIXTY of them in a gang,
driving them like brutes—the men all in chains and hand-cuffs, and
by the help of God they got their chains and hand-cuffs thrown off
and caught two of the wretches and put them to death, and beat the
other until they thought he was dead, and left him for dead; however, he deceived them, and rising from the ground this servile
woman helped him upon his horse and he made his escape.
Brethren, what do you think of this? Was it, the natural fine feelings
of this woman to save such a wretch alive? . . . For my own part, I
cannot think it was anything but servile deceit, combined with the
most gross ignorance: for we must remember that humanity, kindness
and the fear of the Lord does not consist in protecting devils . . . Are
they not the Lord's enemies? Ought they not to be destroyed? Any
person who will save such wretches from destruction, is fighting
against the Lord!"

Such talk was shocking to most white readers, including "moral suasion" abolitionists. "Believing, as we do, that men should never do evil that good may come," wrote William Lloyd Garrison, in *The Liberator*; "that a good end does not justify wicked means in the accomplishment of it, and that we ought to suffer, as did our Lord and his Apostles, unresistingly . . . we deprecate the spirit and tendency of this Appeal." And Benjamin Lundy, the Quaker pacifist, calling it an "attempt to rouse the worst passions of human nature,"declared that "I can do no less than set the broadest seal of condemnation on it."

Meanwhile the unrepentant Walker managed to have some copies of his *Appeal* smuggled into Charleston and Savannah by black sailors who sewed them inside their jackets. In response, the mayor of Savannah asked the mayor of Boston to arrest Walker, and the Georgia legislature offered a reward of $10,000 if he were delivered to their state alive, and $1,000 if dead. However, before anything could happen, Walker died. Many suspected that he had been poisoned, but it is probable that he died of tuberculosis, the same disease that had killed his daughter a week earlier.

A little over one year after Walker's death, Nat Turner led his famous uprising in Southampton County, Virginia. Unlike Gabriel Prosser's insurrection, which was washed out before it could get started, and Denmark Vesey's, whose leaders were all arrested before they could act, Turner's Revolt was the real thing, causing widespread bloodshed and terror. It differed also in that it took place in the country rather than in a town, and in that the best account was given by the leader himself— although some allowance should be made for the fact that Nat Turner's famous *Confession* was written up, and doubtless somewhat edited, by Thomas Gray, a lawyer who visited him in prison shortly after he had been captured.

Gray described Turner as "a complete fanatic" with "an uncommon share of intelligence" and "a mind capable of attaining anything, but warped and perverted by the influence of early impressions. He is below the ordinary stature, though strong and active, having the true Negro face, every feature of which is strongly marked . . . The calm, deliberate composure with which he spoke of his late deeds and intentions; the expression of his fiend-like face when excited by enthusiasm, still bearing the stains of the blood of helpless innocence about him; clothed with rags and covered with chains, yet daring to raise his manacled hands to heaven; with a spirit soaring above the attributes of man—I looked on him, and my blood curdled in my veins."

Turner spoke freely, ranging back to his childhood and his first awareness that he had been singled out by God for a special destiny. "Being at play with other children, when three or four years old, I was telling them something which my mother overhearing, said it had happened before I was born." This was confirmed by others "and caused them to say, in my hearing, I surely would be a prophet, as the Lord had shown me things that had happened before my birth. And my father and mother strengthened me in this, my first impression, saying in my presence I was intended for some great purpose, which they had always thought from certain marks on my head and breast."

Also significant was "the manner in which I learned to read and write." Although he "had no recollection whatever of learning the alphabet," yet "to the astonishment of the family, one day when a book was shown to me to keep me from crying, I began spelling the names of the different objects. This was a source of wonder to all in the neighborhood, particularly the blacks." As he grew up he spent much time in fasting and prayer and reading the Scriptures, with growing "confidence in my superior judgment." And then, "as I was praying one day at my plough, the Spirit spoke to me, saying: 'Seek ye the kingdom of heaven, and all things shall be added unto you.' And I was greatly astonished, and for two years prayed continually, whenever my duty would permit; and then, again, I had the same revelation, which fully confirmed me in the impression that I was ordained for some great purpose in the hands of the Almighty.

"Several years rolled round in which many events occurred to strengthen me in this, my belief," and then he had another vision. "And I saw white spirits and black spirits engaged in battle, and the sun was darkened—the thunder rolled in the heavens, and blood flowed in streams—and I heard a voice saying, 'Such is your luck, such you are called to see, and let it come rough or smooth, you must surely bear it.'" Following this revelation he isolated himself as much as he could and "sought more than ever to obtain true holiness before the great day of judgment should appear; and then I began to receive the true knowledge of faith. And from the first steps of righteousness until the last was I made perfect, and the Holy Ghost was with me and said, 'Behold me as I stand in the heavens'; and I looked and saw the forms of men in different attitudes, and there were lights in the sky to which the children of darkness gave other names than what they really were, for they were the lights of the Saviour's hands, stretched forth from east to west, even as they were extended on the cross on Calvary for the redemption of sinners. And I wondered greatly at these miracles, and prayed to be informed of a certainty of the meaning thereof, and shortly afterwards, while laboring in the field, I discovered drops of blood on the corn, as though it were dew from heaven, and I communicated it to many, both black and white, in the neighborhood; and I then found on the leaves in the woods hieroglyphic characters and numbers, with the forms of men in different attitudes, portrayed in blood, and representing the figures I had seen before in the heavens. And now the Holy Ghost had revealed itself to me, and made plain the miracles it had shown me, for as the blood of Christ had been shed on this earth, and had ascended to heaven for the salvation of sinners, and was now returning to earth again in the form of dew; and as the leaves on the trees bore the impression of the figures I had seen in the heavens, it was plain to me that the Saviour was about to lay down the yoke he had borne for the sins of men, and the great day of judgment was at hand."

One last vision: "And on the 12th of May, 1828, I heard a loud noise in the heavens, and the Spirit instantly appeared to me and said the Serpent was loosened, and Christ had laid down the yoke he had borne for the sins of men, and that I should take it on and fight against the Serpent, for the time was fast approaching when the first should be last and the last should be first." But "until the first sign appeared I should conceal it from the knowledge of men." This did not happen until early 1831, when there was a solar eclipse. "And immediately on the sign appearing in the heavens, the seal was removed from my lips, and I communicated the great work laid out for me to do to four in whom I had the greatest confidence (Henry, Hark, Nelson, and Sam). It was intended by us to have begun the work of death of the 4th of July," but then Turner fell sick and the work was postponed until August 20.

They agreed that they would begin at the house belonging to Mr. Travis, Turner's owner and "a kind master." When they got there, "Hark went to the door with an axe for the purpose of breaking it open, as we knew we were strong enough to murder the family if they were awaked by the noise; but reflecting that it might create an alarm in the neighborhood, we determined to enter the house secretly and murder them whilst sleeping. Hark got a ladder and set it against the chimney, on which I ascended, and hoisting a window, entered and came down stairs, unbarred the door, and removed the guns from their places. It was then observed that I must spill the first blood, on which, armed with a hatchet and accompanied by Will, I entered my master's chamber. It being dark I could not give a death blow; the hatchet glanced from his head; he sprang from the bed and called his wife; it was his last word; Will laid him dead with a blow of his axe, and Mrs. Travis shared the same fate as she lay in bed. The murder of this family, five in number, was the work of a moment, not one of them awoke. There was a little infant sleeping in a cradle that was forgotten until we had left the house and gone some distance, when Henry and Will returned and killed it."

Their next target was the house belonging to Mr. Salathul Francis, "about six hundred yards distant. Sam and Will went to the door and knocked. Mr. Francis asked who was there. Sam replied it was him, and he had a letter for him; on which he got up and came to the door. They immediately seized him, and dragging him out a little from the door, he was dispatched by repeated blows on the head. There was no other white person in the family. We started from there for Mrs. Reese's, maintaining the most perfect silence on our march, where, finding the door unlocked, we entered and murdered Mrs. Reese in her bed while sleeping. Her son awoke but . . . he had only time to say Who is that? and he was no more. From Mrs. Reese's we went to Mrs. Turner's, a mile distant, which we reached about sunrise on Monday morning. Henry, Austin and Sam went to the still, where, finding Mr. Peebles, Austin shot him, and the rest of us went to the house. As we approached, the family discovered us and shut the door. Vain hope! Will, with one stroke of his axe opened it, and we entered and found Mrs. Turner and Mrs. Newsome in the middle of the room, almost frightened to death. Will immediately killed Mrs. Turner with one blow of his axe. I took Mrs. Newsome by the hand, and with the sword I had when I was apprehended, I struck her several blows over the head, but not being able to kill her, as the sword was dull, Will, turning round and discovering it, despatched her also. A general destruction of property and search for money and ammunition always succeeded the murders."

Their number having now grown to twenty-four, they divided into two groups and headed for the Whitehead house by different routes. On the way Turner's group met Mr. Whitehead "standing in the cotton patch near the lane fence. We called him over," and Will killed him with his axe. By the time they got to the house the others had already arrived and "all the family were already murdered but Mrs. Whitehead and her daughter Margaret. As I came round to the door I saw Will pulling Mrs. Whitehead out of the house, and at the step he nearly severed her head from her body with his broad axe. Miss Margaret, when I discovered her, had concealed herself in the corner formed by the projection of the cellar cap from the house. On my approach she fled, but was soon overtaken, and after repeated blows with the sword, I killed her by a blow on the head with a fence rail."

It was now after nine o'clock in the morning. From twenty-four their number had grown to about forty "all mounted and armed with guns, axes, swords and clubs," and carrying "terror and devastation wherever we went . . . Having murdered Mrs. Waller and ten children, [gathered there for school] we started for Mr. William Williams', having killed him and two little boys that were there. While engaged in this, Mrs. Williams fled and got some distance from the house, but she was pursued, overtaken, and compelled to get up behind one of the company, who brought her back, and after showing her the mangled body of her lifeless husband, she was told to get down and lay by his side, where she was shot dead. I then started for Mr. Jacob Williams', where the family was murdered. Here we found a young man named Drury, who had come on business with Mr. Williams; he was pursued, overtaken, and shot. Mrs. Vaughan's was the next place we visited and, after murdering the family there, I determined on starting for Jerusalem [a nearby town]. Our number now amounted to fifty or sixty."

By now the militia had turned out and regular troops were on the way. After the first skirmishes Turner's men went from sixty to forty and then twenty. The next day, "coming in sight of Captain Harris', where we had been the day before, we discovered a party of white men at the house, on which all deserted me but two." By Wednesday evening Turner found himself alone in the woods dodging mounted patrols. He then "gave up all hope for the present, and on Thursday night, after having supplied myself with provisions from Mr. Travis', I scratched a hole under a pile of fence rails in a field, where I concealed myself for six weeks."

At first he left his hiding place only very briefly and at night to fetch water; then, growing more confident, "I began to go about in the night and eavesdrop the houses in the neighborhood." This led to his capture, for one night while he was out a dog crawled into his hiding place and stole some meat. "A few nights later, two Negroes having started to go hunting with the same dog, and passed that way, the dog came again to the place, and having just gone out to walk about, discovered me and barked, on which, thinking myself discovered, I spoke to them to beg concealment. On making myself known, they fled from me. Knowing then they would betray me, I immediately left my hiding place, and was pursued almost incessantly until I was taken a fortnight afterwards by Mr. Benjamin Phipps, in a little hole I had dug out with my sword, for the purpose of concealment, under the top of a fallen tree. On Mr. Phipps' discovering the place of my concealment, he cocked his gun and aimed at me. I requested him not to shoot, and I would give up, upon which he demanded my sword. I delivered it to him and he brought me to prison."

By the time the rampage ended, some sixty whites, many of them children, had been murdered. The number would have been higher but for some of the domestic slaves. Thus "Miss Whitehead concealed herself between the bed and the mat that supported it, while they murdered her sister in the same room without discovering her. She was afterwards carried off and concealed for protection by a slave of the family, who gave evidence against several of them on their trial." Also, as the rebels approached the house of John Barrow, he told his wife to make her escape while he held them off. "As directed by him, she attempted to escape through the garden, when she was caught and held by one of her servant girls, but another coming to her rescue, she fled to the woods and concealed herself."

Turner was hanged on November 11, 1831. Fifty-four others were also executed, and many more were banished. As the panic spread, wrote Henry "Box" Brown, slaves were "whipped, hung, and cut down with swords in the streets [of Richmond], and some that were found away from their quarters after dark were shot. The whole city was in the utmost excitement, and the whites seemed terrified beyond measure. Great numbers of slaves were loaded with irons; some were 'half-hung,' as it was termed: that is, they were suspended from some tree with a rope around their necks, so adjusted as not quite to strangle them, and then they were pelted by men and boys with rotten eggs."

Dramatic events such as plots and insurrections, with their court trials and public executions, naturally tended to overshadow acts of individual defiance. Of these some were recorded in the personal narratives of former slaves, such as the Rev. G. W. Offley, who told this story about a slave called Praying Jacob:

"Jacob's rule was to pray three times a day, at just such an hour of the day; no matter what his work was, or where he might be, he would stop and go and pray. His master has been to him and pointed his gun at him, and told him if he did not cease praying he would blow out his brains. Jacob would finish his prayer and then tell his master to shoot and welcome—your loss will be my gain—I have two masters, one on earth and one in heaven—master Jesus in heaven and master Saunders on earth. This man [Saunders] said in private conversation that several times he went home and drank an unusual quantity of brandy to harden his heart that he might kill him; but he never had power to strike or shoot him."

At the opposite end of the spiritual spectrum was J. D. Green, who was born in 1813 and as a boy worked as a servant in the household of Judge Charles Earle in Maryland. Green was not one to leave scores unsettled, so when a white boy stole his marbles he fought to get them back. "I had him on the ground when Mr. Burney came up. He kicked me away from the white boy, saying if I belonged to him he would cut off my hands for *daring* to strike a white boy."

So now Green had another score to settle, and soon got his chance to do so. "At this time my master's wife had two lovers, this same Burney and one Rogers. Master's wife seemed to favor Burney most, who was a great smoker, and she provided him with a large pipe with a German silver bowl, which screwed on the top; this pipe she usually kept on the mantel piece, ready filled with tobacco. One morning I was dusting and sweeping out the dining-room, and saw the pipe on the mantelpiece. I took it down, and went to my young master William's [gun] powder closet and took out his powder horn, and after taking half the tobacco out of the pipe filled it nearly full with powder, and covered it over with tobacco to make it appear as usual, replaced it, and left. Rogers came in about eight o'clock in the morning, and remained until eleven, when Mr. Burney came, and in about an hour I saw a great number running about from all parts of the plantation. I left the barn where I was thrashing buck-wheat and followed the rest to the house, where I saw Mr. Burney lying back in the arm chair in a state of insensibility, his mouth bleeding profusely, and from particulars given it appeared he took the pipe as usual, and lighted it, and had just got it to his mouth when the powder exploded. The party suspected was Rogers, who had been there immediately preceding; and Burney's son went to Rogers and they fought about the matter. Law ensued, which cost Rogers $800, Burney $600 and his face disfigured; and my master's wife came in for a deal of scandal, which caused further proceedings at law, costing the master $1400, and I was never once suspected."

Many other stories have come down to us orally, most notably those included in the *Slave Narratives*. Here are a few examples:

ELLEN CRAGIN, OF LITTLE ROCK, ARKANSAS, told this story about her mother: "She didn't work in the field, she worked at a loom. She worked so long and so often that once she went to sleep at the loom. Her master's boy saw her and told his mother. His mother told him to take a whip and wear her out. He took a stick and went to beat her awake. When she woke up she took a pole out of the loom and beat him nearly to death with it. He hollered, 'Don't beat me no more, and I won't let 'em whip you.' She said, 'I'm going to kill you. These black titties sucked you, and then you come out here to beat me.' And when she left him he wasn't able to walk. And that was the last I seen of her until after freedom. She went out and got on an old cow that she used to milk—Dolly, she called it. She rode away from the plantation because she knew they would kill her if she stayed."

LEONARD FRANKLIN, OF WARREN, ARKANSAS, recalled this of his mother: "There wasn't many men could class up with her when it come to working. She could do more work than any two men. There wasn't no use for no one man to try to do nothing with her. No overseer never downed her . . . Her boss [a man called Pennington] went off deer hunting once for a few weeks. While he was gone the overseer tried to whip her. She knocked him down and tore his face up so that the doctor had to tend to him. When Pennington came back, he noticed his face all patched up and asked him what was the matter with it. The overseer told him that he went down in the field to whip the hands, and that he just thought he would hit Lucy a few licks to show the slaves that he was impartial, but she jumped on him and like to tore him up. Old Pennington said to him, 'Well, if that is the best you could do with her, damned if you won't just have to take it.'"

JOHN HENRY KEMP, OF DAYTONA BEACH, FLORIDA: "One day when an old woman was plowing in the field an overseer came by and reprimanded her for being so slow. She gave him some back talk, he took out a long closely woven whip and lashed her severely. The woman became sore and took her hoe and chopped him right across his head, and, child, you should have seen how she chopped this man to a bloody death."

WEST TURNER, OF WHALEYVILLE, VIRGINIA, on what happened when Aunt Sallie, who had been nurse to the white children in the "big house," was put to work in the field as a punishment after her mistress had complained about her: "Aunt Sallie ain't said nothing but the next morning she ain't nowhere about. Finally Marsa come down to the quarters and get my pa and ask him where was Aunt Sallie. Pa says he don't know nothing about her. Marsa didn't do nothing to pa, but he knowed pa was lying 'cause he done heard that pa had been feeding Aunt Sallie in the night time. Well, pa used to put food in a pan 'neath the wash bench outside the cabin, and it was so dark Aunt Sallie come on inside to eat it.

"I was lying on the pallet listening to her and pa whispering and just then there came a banging on the door. It was wedged shut and there was old Marsa banging. 'Come on out there, Sallie,' he yelled. 'I know you is in there.' Didn't nobody say nothing. Then I heard old Marsa yelling for all the niggers and telling them to come there and catch Sallie else he going to whip them all. They all come, too, and gather round the door. Pa didn't know what to do. But Aunt Sallie ain't catched yet. She grabbed up a scythe knife from the corner and she pulled the chock out that door and come out a-swinging. And those niggers was glad 'cause they didn't want to catch her. And Marsa didn't dare touch her.

"She cut her way out, then turned round and backed off into the woods, and old Marsa was just screaming and cussing and telling her one minute what he's gonna do when he catch her, and the next minute saying he gonna take her back in the big house if she stay. I was peeking out of the slip of window, and the last I see was Aunt Sallie going into the bushes still swinging that scythe. Didn't no one follow her neither."

AN ANONYMOUS FORMER SLAVE, POSSIBLY CHARLIE CRAWLEY OF VIRGINIA: "Old Saunders was the meanest poor white devil that ever drawed breath. Had beat and beat us till we made up our mind not to stand it no longer. One bright moonlight night Marsa told the overseer to put all the slaves out in the planting patch for to clean it up and get it in order for planting the next day. We had already worked all day so we decided we was gonna fix old Saunders that night.

"Marsa went on in and went to bed and we went out to the field and started raking up the brush. The overseer told some of us to pile the tree limbs and brush in the middle of the patch so's he could set fire to it. When there was a right big pile that old devil struck a match to it and soon it blazed up. Just then someone yelled, 'Look, what a big fire we got.' That was the signal. Old overseer was standing near the blaze with his hands behind him, and some of the slaves crept up behind and all at once pushed him over in the fire. Down he went on his face in the middle of the pile, and all of us just kept piling brush on top of him.

"The next morning there wasn't no overseer to call us out at sun up, and everybody stood round making believe they was waiting for him. Bye and bye Marsa come out and ask where Saunders was. For a long time nobody said nothing. At last someone said, 'Marsa, when I seed him last he was standing out in the middle of the field burning the brush. Didn't see him no more after we finish clearing up last night.'

"Marsa went out in the field and call and call the overseer, but didn't get no answer. Then he got some more white men and they went on a hunt, beating through the bushes round the field, but they didn't find him. Finally someone got to poking round the ashes of the fire with a stick, and poked out something, then yelled for the others. It was the overseer's heart. You know the heart don't burn. They talked out there for a long time, and we stood round the edge of the field watching them. Finally, Marsa come and told us to go clear another field. He say he guess Saunders had got sick while standing there and fell over in the brush and got burnt up."

WILLIAM MOORE, OF DALLAS, TEXAS: "Marse Tom had a fine, big house painted white and a big prairie field in front his house and two, three farms and orchards. He had five hundred head of sheep, and I spent most my time being a shepherd boy. Marse Tom been dead long time now. I believe he's in hell. Seem like that where he belong. He was a terrible mean man and had a indifferent mean wife. But he had the finest, sweetest chillen the Lord ever let live and breathe on this earth. They's so kind and sorrowing over us slaves. Some them chillen used to read us little things out of papers and books.

"One day I'm down in the hog pen and hears a loud agony screaming up to the house. When I got up close I see Marse Tom got mammy tied to a tree with her clothes pulled down, and he's laying it on her with the bullwhip, and the blood am running down her eyes and off her back. I goes crazy. I say, 'Stop, Marse Tom,' and he swings the whip and don't reach me good, but it cuts just the same. I sees Miss Mary standing in the cookhouse door. I runs round crazy like and sees a big rock, and I takes it and throws it, and it catches Marse Tom in the skull and he goes down like a poled ox. Miss Mary comes out and lifts her pa and helps him in the house and then comes and helps me undo Mammy. Mammy and me takes to the woods for two, three months, I guess. My sisters meets us and grease Mammy's back and brings us victuals. Pretty soon they say it am safe to for us to come in the cabin and eat at night and they watch for Marse Tom."

After a while "we sees Sam and Billie, and they tell us they am fighting over us niggers. Then they done told us the niggers declared to Marse Tom they ain't gwine be no more beatings and we could come up and stay in our cabin and they'd see Marse Tom didn't do nothing. And that's what Mammy and me did. Sam and Billie was the two biggest niggers on the place, and they done got the shotguns out of the house some way or another.

"One day Marse Tom am in a rocker on the porch and Sam and Billie am standing by with the guns. We all seen five white men riding up. When they gets near, Sam say to Marse Tom, 'First white man sets his self inside that rail fence gets it from the gun.' Marse Tom waves the white men to go back, but they gallops right up to the fence and swings off they hosses. Marse Tom say, 'Stay outside, gentlemen, please do. I done change my mind.' They say, 'What's the matter here? We come to whip you niggers like you done hire us to.' Marse Tom say, 'I done change my mind, but if you stay outside I'll bring you the money.' They argues to come in, but Marse Tom outtalk them and they say they'll go if he brings them they three dollars apiece. He takes them the money and they goes away."

DELICIA PATTERSON, BORN IN ST. LOUIS IN 1845: "When I was fifteen years old, I was brought to the courthouse, put up on the auction block to be sold. Old Judge Miller from my county was there. I knew him well because he was one of the wealthiest slave owners in the county, and the meanest one. He was so cruel all the slaves and many owners hated him because of it. He saw me on the block for sale, and he knew I was a good worker. So, when he bid for me,

I spoke right out on the auction block and told him: 'Old Judge Miller, don't you bid for me, 'cause if you do I would not live on your plantation. I will take a knife and cut my own throat from ear to ear before I would be owned by you.' So he stepped back and let someone else bid for me. My own father knew I was to be for sale, so he brought his owner to the sale for him to buy me, so we could be together. But when father's owner heard what I said to Judge Miller, he told my father that he would not buy me because I was sassy, and he never owned a sassy nigger and did not want one that was sassy. That broke my father's heart, but I couldn't help that."

GUS FEASTER told this story of when he was a very young boy on the plantation of Thomas Anderson Carlisle, near the town of Union, S. C. Evans was the overseer; "old" in "old lady" means adult; John was another small boy.

"Old man Wash Evans was a wicked man. He take vantage of all the slaves when he get half chance. He was a great source of worriment to my mammy, old lady Lucy Price, and another woman, old lady Lucy Charles. My mammy and old lady Lucy was religious womens. That didn't make no difference with wicked old man Evans.

"One day Missus sent my mammy and the other old lady, Lucy, to fetch her some blackberries by dinner. Me and John was with them a-picking and filling of the big buckets from the little buckets when old man Evans came riding up. He argued with both mammy and old lady Lucy, and they kept telling him that the Missus want her blackberries and that they was religious womens anyhow and didn't practice no life of sin and vile wickedness. Finally he got down offen his horse and pull out his whip and allow if they didn't submit to him he gwine to beat them half to death. At that me and John took off to the woods. My mammy and old lady Lucy start to crying and axing him not to whip them.

"Finally they act like they gwine to indulge in the wickedness with that old man. But when he tuck off his whip and some other garments, my mammy and old lady Lucy grab him by his goatee and further down and hist [hoist] him over in the middle of the blackberry bushes. With that they call me and John. Us grab all the buckets and us all put out for the big house fast as our legs could carry us, old man Evans just a-hollering and a-cussing down in them briars. Quick as us get to the big house us run in the kitchen. Cilla [the cook] calls Missus. She come and ax what ailing us and why we is so ashy looking. Well, my mammy and old lady Lucy tell her the whole story of they humiliations down on the creek.

"Missus allowed that it didn't make no difference if Marse was in Union, [the local town] she gwine to act prompt. So she sent for Mr. Evans, and he took real long to get there, but when he do come, Missus she allow 'Mr. Evans, us does not need yo' services on the plantation no more, sir!' He allow Marse ain't here. Missus allow 'I doesn't want to argue the point with ye, Mr. Evans, for yo' services has come to an end on this plantation.' With that, old man Evans go off with his head a-hanging in shame."

FANNIE BERRY, OF VIRGINIA, told a similar story about a fellow slave called Sukie: "She was a big strapping nigger gal that never had nothing to say much. She used to cook for Miss Sarah Ann, but old Marsa was always trying to make Sukie his gal. One day Sukie was in the kitchen making soap. Had three great big pots of lye just coming to a boil in the fireplace when old Marsa come in for to get after her about something. He lay into her, but she ain't answer him a word. Then he tell Sukie to take off her dress. She told him no. Then he grabbed her and pull it down offen her shoulders and try to pull her down on the floor. Then that black gal got mad. She took and punch old Marsa and made him break loose, and then she gave him a shove and push his hind parts down in the hot pot of soap. Soap was near to boiling, and it burnt him near to death. He got up holding his hind parts and ran from the kitchen, not daring yell, 'cause he didn't want Miss Sarah Ann to know 'bout it."

Finally, an event that was more than a spontaneous act of individual defiance and less than an insurrection. Sometimes known as The Christiana Riot, sometimes as The Christiana Tragedy, and also as The Awful Affair at Christiana, it took place in Lancaster County, Pennsylvania, on

Armed fugitives firing on their owner, Edward Gorsuch, and the sheriff's posse that had come to reclaim them. The white man on horseback was later tried for refusing to assist the sheriff. Gorsuch was killed, two other whites were wounded, and most of the fugitives escaped to Canada. The 1851 event, which took place in Pennsylvania, was known as The Christiana Riot.

September 10th, 1851—a year after the passage of the Fugitive Slave Act and a time when feelings were running high. Very early in the morning of that day, a small posse of slave-catchers, led by Deputy Federal Marshal Henry Kline, approached a two-story stone house in the village of Christiana. Their mission was to recapture four—some say six—slaves who had run away from their owner, Edward Gorsuch, who owned a plantation in Maryland. Gorsuch accompanied the posse, as did several family members.

> "We came to the house about daylight," wrote Deputy Marshal Kline in his official statement. "Before reaching the house we came to the orchard, where we saw a negro who espied us and ran back to the house; he was a short, thick-set, chestnut-colored fellow, with a dark spot under his chin. The door was open—the fellow ran up stairs—I walked into the house—I went to the door of the stairway and halloed up to know who was the man that kept the house, I wished him to come, I wanted to speak to him. I then heard them

loading their guns. I told them there was no necessity for that, I did not wish to harm anybody, I merely wished two persons that were in the house. They said they would not come down. The old gentleman [Edward Gorsuch] then came to the door and called them by name, and said if they would come down he would take them along and treat them kindly, and he would forgive them all. He called Nelson by name—he saw one of them and knew him. He then went out of the door and looked up at the window and called there, as he thought he could call them better that way, and they fired right on him. He kind of dodged. They threw an axe out, and then I fired my revolver at them . . . I read the warrants three different times, and called to them that the owner of the house would be responsible for harboring them. I then gave them ten minutes to consider.

"In the mean time a white man came up on a sorrel horse with a white face. I asked him if he lived in that neighborhood, he said it was none of my business. I have since found out that his name is Castner Hanway"—a local miller and anti-slavery man. "I told him the reason why I asked that question. I showed him my papers, and he read them, and I called upon him to assist me in the name of the United States. He said he would not, he did not care for any Act of Congress, or anything else. By this time up came another man, as I have since been told by the name of Lewis; he asked me my authority and I handed him my papers, and he read them and handed them to the man on the horse, and he handed them back to me, and then Lewis replied that the Negroes had a right to defend themselves. I then called upon him to assist, and he refused. I asked him his name, and he said it was none of my business. I then asked them both where they lived, he (Hanway) said that I would have to find that out. I then told them what the Act of Congress was, and that by their aid these Negroes would escape. Then came the Negroes, about fifteen or twenty, with guns, and they came in the direction that the white men came from. The first party of Negroes came with their guns pointed towards me, and ready cocked—one yellow-looking fellow came up with a kind of corn-cutter in one hand and a revolver in the other. Doctor Pierce"—a nephew of the owner, Edward Gorsuch—"was present when I read the warrants. When the Negroes came I told these two white men for God Almighty's sake to keep them from firing on us, I would withdraw my men and leave the Negroes go. Hanway said the Negroes had a right to defend themselves, and he would not interfere, and I replied that they were not good citizens to let the law be put in defiance by the Negroes. Doctor Pierce then remarked, all they wanted was their own property, they did not wish to hurt a hair of their heads. Lewis replied that 'Negroes were no property' and then walked away. I then saw another gang of Negroes come with guns and clubs, and Hanway rode towards them and said something, and then our men run and the Negroes fired from every direction."

Summoned by a horn blown from an upper window, other groups of armed blacks kept appearing. Then Edward Gorsuch, who had remained near the house, still trying to persuade his slaves to return, was shot. "The son ran to his assistance, and he was shot; and when I saw the old gentleman afterwards, about two hours, he was dead." A member of the posse was badly wounded in the head, "and Dr. Pierce was also shot at, and hit." ("Some twenty or thirty holes in my clothes, a buckshot passed through my hat." A shot also entered his side, another hit his shoulder blade, and "I was struck by a missile thrown also from the window.") "Dickerson Gorsuch, the son, was dangerously wounded. I also was shot at, but not wounded. Among the Negroes that were armed and who shot was an Indian-looking fellow with long-looking and bushy hair, curious look out of his eyes; another Negro about 30 years old, very dark, big whiskers, a good-sized man; another Negro about 18 years of age, swelled face, yellow color, a light mulatto, round full face, with straw hat on; another black-looking fellow with blue nankeen pants, straw hat on; another yellow-looking fellow with military-cut whiskers, in shirt sleeves; he had likewise a shot-bag over his shoulders. They all had guns, excepting the black good-looking Negro with whiskers; he had a club. I do not know their names. The keeper of the house [William Parker] was a rather tall mulatto. He said we would have to walk over their dead bodies."

In the end, a much larger force succeeded in putting down the riot. Several of the leaders, including William Parker, escaped to Canada. At the urging of Secretary of State Daniel Webster, one of the architects of the Compromise of 1850, and with the approval of President Fillmore, thirty-six blacks and five whites were charged with treason—"levying war against the United States." Castner Hanway, the uncooperative miller, was tried first, with the idea that once he had been found guilty then the other cases would follow suit—except that Hanway was easily acquitted, even the judge complaining that the charge of treason was excessive. (It helped that Anthony Roberts, the U.S. Marshal for Eastern Pennsylvania, was an anti-slavery man who packed the jury with sympathizers. Also, two key prosecution witnesses he had in custody disappeared before the trial.)

Long before any verdicts were reached the case was judged in the press, in a manner indicating how deep the divisions had become. To Frederick Douglass, who had abandoned the Garrisonian doctrine of non-resistance and "moral suasion," the conflict provided a lesson "which even the most obtuse may understand, namely, that all Negroes are not such fools and dastards as to cling to life when it is coupled with chains and slavery. This lesson, though most dearly bought, is quite worth the price paid . . . For never were there, never can there be more sacred rights to defend than were menaced on this occasion. Life and liberty are the most sacred of all man's rights. If these be invaded with impunity, all others may be, for they comprehend all others . . ."

Many abolitionists compared the fight with the hallowed events of the Revolution. "Men who reverence our fathers for throwing British tea into Boston harbor, and shooting to death British soldiers at Lexington and Bunker Hill, cannot fail to do honor to Negroes who repel violence by violence," declared the Boston clergyman, Theodore Parker. "I say, I rejoice that a negro shot a kidnapper. Black men may now hold up their heads before those haughty Caucasians and say, 'You see we also can fight!'" The name of Crispus Attucks, the black man who was shot by the British redcoats in the Boston Massacre of 1770, was often invoked.

The southern press saw things in a different light, as did some northern papers, among them the *Rochester Advertiser* which declared that the issue was "whether the white races are to maintain their rights and their position, or whether negro mob law is to govern and ride rampant over our laws, constitution and liberties." If Negroes "wish to provoke a war of the races by re-enacting the bloody scenes at Christiana, they will find our civil and military authorities, and our citizens at large, prepared to defend themselves, and to put down their murderous assaults with an avenging arm that will carry retributive justice home to such vile traitors and assassins."

And the *Saturday Express*, of Lancaster, Pennsylvania, ran this headline: "Civil War—The First Blow Struck!"

Called the "cast-iron man" because of his refusal to bend or compromise, John C. Calhoun was a dominant political figure from 1825, when he became vice president, to his death in 1850. A "fire-eating" defender of states' rights, it was he who declared that slavery "is, instead of an evil, a good—a positive good." To prove his point, he thought it fair to compare the condition of the rural American slave with that of the unemployed factory worker in England—"look at the old and the infirm slave on one hand, in the midst of his family and friends, under the kind superintending care of his master and mistress, and compare it with the wretched condition of the pauper in the poorhouse."

CHAPTER 12

THE POSITIVE GOOD

BETWEEN THE TURN OF THE NINETEENTH CENTURY AND THE OUTBREAK OF THE Civil War, slavery went from being spoken of in the South as "a necessary evil" to what John C. Calhoun called "a positive good," and others "a great moral, social and political blessing—a blessing to the slave and a blessing to the master." This did not of course mean that there had been any improvement in the lives of the slaves; the change was solely a matter of perception—of people convincing themselves of what it was in their interest to believe and seeing what they wanted to see (and not seeing what they did not want to see). Here are some examples of the process at work:

As his paddle-ship steamed up the Savannah River in the late fall of 1853, the Rev. Nehemiah Adams knew what to expect: "There was one thing which I felt sure I should see on landing, viz., the whole black population cowed down . . . 'I am a slave,' will be indented on the faces, limbs and actions of the bondmen. Hopeless woe, entreating yet despairing, will frequently greet me. How could it be otherwise if slavery be such as our books, and sermons, and lectures, and newspaper articles represent?"

A Harvard graduate, and pastor of the Union Congregational Church in Boston, Adams' anti-slavery credentials were impeccable—it was he who only recently had drawn up *The Remonstrance of New England Clergymen against the Extension of Slavery into the Contemplated Territories of Nebraska and Kansas.* His reason for coming to Georgia for a three month visit was not to investigate slavery on the spot, but to recuperate from an unspecified sickness.

"The steam boat reached the landing, and the slaves were all about us. One thing immediately surprised me; they were all in good humor, and some of them in a broad laugh. The delivery of every trunk from the tug to the wharf was the occasion of some hit, or repartee, and every burden was borne with a jolly word." Delighted by these cheerful and colorfully-dressed slaves and their infectious good humor, "I began to laugh with them. It was irresistible. Who could have convinced me, an hour before, that slaves could have any other effect upon me than to make me feel sad?" This first impression was soon confirmed. "Let anyone at the North afflicted with depression of spirits drop down among these Negroes, walk these streets, form a passing acquaintance with some of them, and unless he is a hopeless case he will find himself in moods of cheerfulness never awakened surely by the countenances of the whites in any strange place."

Having thus begun to clear his mind of northern preconceptions, "I shall now relate the impressions which were involuntarily made upon me while residing in some of the slave states." Among them:

Good Order.

"The streets of southern cities and towns immediately struck me as being remarkably quiet in the evening and at night. 'What is the cause of so much quiet?' I said to a friend. 'Our colored people are mostly at home. After eight o'clock they cannot be abroad [outdoors] without a written pass, which they must show on being challenged, or go to the guard house.'" At first this struck Nehemiah as "interference with the personal liberty of the colored people," but on reflection "it was easy to see that to keep such a part of the population out of the streets after a reasonable hour at night, preventing their unrestrained, promiscuous roving, is a great protection to them, as well as to the public peace." Naturally, "if attending evening worship, a written pass is freely given." Such restrictions worked to the advantage of "the moral and religious character of the colored people at the South," and it was to be regretted that there were not similar laws in Boston "forbidding certain youths to be in the streets after a certain hour without a pass from their employers."

Dress.

"Coming out of church the first Sabbath which I spent in a country village, I saw a group of colored men standing under the trees around the house, waiting for the rest of the people to pass out. I could not be mistaken in my impression from their looks that they were Christian men. Their countenances were intelligent and happy." Even more convincing was the way they were dressed. "To see slaves with broadcloth suits, well-fitting and nicely-ironed fine shirts, polished boots, gloves, umbrellas for sunshades, the best of hats... as respectable in their attire as any who that day went to the house of God, was more than I was prepared to see." Had he not been in the company of other whites, Nehemiah "would have followed my impulse to shake hands with the whole of them, as a vent to my pleasure in seeing slaves with all the bearing of respectable, dignified Christian gentlemen. As it was, I involuntarily lifted my hat to them, which was responded to by them with smiles, uncovering of the head, and graceful salutations."

Absence of Popular Delusions.

"Another striking peculiarity of southern society which is attributable to slavery" was that "while the colored people are superstitious and excitable, popular delusions and fanaticisms do not prevail among them . . . Second-adventism, Mormonism, and the whole spawn of errors which infest us, do not find subjects at the South. There is far more faith in the South, taken as a whole, than with us."

Absence of Pauperism.

"Every slave has an inalienable claim in law upon his owner for support for the whole of his life. He cannot be thrust into an almshouse, he cannot become a vagrant, he cannot beg his living, he cannot be wholly neglected when he is old and decrepit." For example: "Going into the office of a physician and surgeon, I accidentally saw the leg of a black man which had just been amputated for an ulcer. The patient will be a charge upon his owner for life. An action at law may be brought against one who does not provide a comfortable support for his servants." As a result, there were almost no paupers in the South, and no need for those "large State workhouses, which we so patiently build for the dregs of the foreign population" (e.g. Irish immigrants fleeing the Great Famine.) Nehemiah also cited the case of the washerwoman who had saved enough to buy her freedom, but refused to do so. Why not? Because if she did, "she would have no one to take care of her for the rest of her life. Now her master is responsible for her support. She has no care about the future." In fact "her only trouble is that her master may die before her; then she will 'have to be free.'"

Religious Instruction.

"When religious instruction, the pure, simple gospel of Jesus Christ, is extended to our laboring classes generally, adults and children, as fully as it is enjoyed by the slaves in such parts of the South as I visited, an object will be gained of far more intrinsic importance to our national prosperity than all questions relating to slavery. Probably, in very many places at the South, a larger proportion of the slaves than of the whites have given evidence of being the children of God." Nehemiah went to some of their services and heard such "beautiful and affecting" prayers as these: "'O Lord, we prostrate ourselves before thee on the sinful hands and knees of our poor miserable bodies and souls.' 'O Lord, may our hearts all be set right to-night.' 'Bless our dear masters and brothers, who come here to read the Bible to us, and pay so much attention to us.'" Laws against teaching slaves to read did not mean that they were deprived of the Bible, for there were plenty of pious whites willing to read it to them. "How often at the north can we find a scene like this?—a Christian master, surrounded every morning by fifty laborers in his employ hearing the Bible read, repeating passages which were given out the preceding day, singing and praying, and then going forth to their labor." To sum up: "of all the situations in which human beings can be placed favorable to the salvation of the soul . . . it is difficult to conceive of one better suited to this end, and in fact more successful, than the relation of these slaves to their Christian masters."

Slave Auctions.

"Passing up the steps of a court-house in a southern town with some gentlemen, I saw a man sitting on the steps with a colored infant wrapped in a coverlet, its face visible, and the child asleep." The sight "seemed out of place and strange. 'Is the child sick?' I said to the man, as I was going up the steps.

"'No, master. She is going to be sold.'

"'Sold! Where is her mother?'

"'At home, master.'

"'How old is the child?'

"'She is about a year, master.'

"It is hardly necessary to say that my heart died within me. Now I had found slavery in its most awful feature—the separation of a child from its mother!" Unwilling to witness such a distressing scene, Nehemiah "walked into a friend's law office, and looked at his books. I heard the sheriff's voice, the 'public outcry' as the vendue [auction] is called, but did not go out, partly because I would not betray the feelings which I knew would be awakened."

On leaving the office he was told that the child had been sold for $140.

"I could take this case, so far as I have described it, go into any pulpit or upon any platform at the North, and awaken the deepest emotions known to the human heart, harrow up the feelings of every father and mother, and make them pass a resolution surcharged with all the righteous indignation which language can express . . ." But wait! Soon afterward "three or four estimable gentlemen," feeling "that such a transaction needed to be explained and justified," told him what had really happened: "The mother of the infant belonged to a man who had become embarrassed in his circumstances, in consequence of which the mother was sold to another family in the same place, before the birth of the child; but the first owner still laid claim to the child, and there was some legal doubt with regard to his claim." To dispose of the first owner's claim, a distinguished lawyer had come up with a legal maneuver whereby "through an old execution the child should be levied upon, be sold at auction, and thus removed from him. The plan succeeded. The child was attached, advertised, and offered for sale. The mother's master bought it, at more than double the ratable price, and the child went to its mother."

This revelation provided food for reflection. "Had I not known the sequel to this story, what a thrilling, effective appeal could I have made at the North by the help of this incident! Then what injustice I should have inflicted upon the people of that place! . . . How might I have helped on the dissolution of the Union, how have led half our tribes to swear that they would have war with the rest forever, when in truth the men and women who had done this thing had performed one of the most tender and humane actions."

And this story was by no means unique. "Very many of the slave auctions advertised with full descriptions, looking like invitations to buy, are merely legal appointments to determine claims, settle estates, without any purpose to let the persons offered for sale pass from families to which they belong." In fact, when "settling estates, good men exercise as much care with regard to the disposition of slaves as though they were providing homes for white orphan children."

Approaches to Emancipation.

After quoting from the resolution on slavery adopted by the General Assembly of the Presbyterian Church in 1818—"We consider the voluntary enslaving of one part of the human race by another as . . . utterly inconsistent with the law of God, which requires us to love our neighbor as ourselves"—Nehemiah wondered what had happened to the anti-slavery sentiment once so common in the South. "This was not a mere ecclesiastical movement," but widespread "public sentiment." But then "a great change very soon came over the South. Remonstrances from among themselves, legislative measures, free, earnest discussions of slavery, all tending to its removal as soon as the best method could be determined, were suddenly hushed."

Was this, as widely supposed in the North, due to the "astounding revelations of the profitableness of cotton?" To believe this was not only absurd, it was to slander "the Christian character of a community distinguished for intellectual and moral excellence." No, the real reason for the sudden hush was "the din and clamor of northern invectives against slavery . . . Abolition societies were formed to effect the immediate emancipation of the slaves. Publications were scattered through the South whose direct tendency was to stir up insurrection among the colored people. A traveling agent of a northern society was arrested, and on searching his trunk there were found some prints which might well have wrought, as they did, upon the feelings of the southern people. These prints were pictorial illustrations of the natural equality before God of all men, without distinction of color, and setting forth the happy fruits of this truth by exhibiting a white woman in no equivocal relations to a colored man." Along with these obscene pictures, "incendiary sentiments" were printed on handkerchiefs to be distributed in the South, and "the old-fashioned, blue-paper wrappers of chocolate had within them some eminently suggestive emblems. When these amalgamation [blacks with whites] pictures were discovered, husbands and fathers at the south considered that whatever might be true of slavery as a system, self-defense, the protection of their households against a servile insurrection, was their first duty. Who can wonder that they broke into the post-office, and seized and burned abolition papers? Indeed, no excesses are surprising in view of the perils to which they saw themselves exposed. Then ensued those more stringent laws, so general now throughout the slave-holding States, forbidding the slaves to be publicly instructed." And then also ensued the general embargo on even discussing the issue of slavery. "Nothing forces itself more constantly upon the thoughts of a northerner at the South, who looks into the history and present state of slavery, than the vast injury which has resulted from northern interference."

A Final Thought.

"Instead of regarding the South as holding their fellow-men in cruel bondage, let us consider whether we may not think of them as guardians, educators, and saviors of the African race in this country . . . The South is competent to manage this subject without our help."

Six years after the publication of the *Communist Manifesto*, George Fitzhugh, of Virginia, also addressed the topics of class warfare, but with a solution that would have startled Karl Marx had *Sociology for the South* been published in Germany: slavery, not communism, was the only way to "place labor and capital in harmonious or friendly relations." But though coming to different conclusions, the two men had much in common, particularly their outrage at the exploitation and injustice that characterized the free enterprise system. "The bestowing upon men of rights is but giving license to the strong to oppress the weak," wrote Fitzhugh. "Liberty and equality throw the whole weight of society on its weakest members. The employer cheapens their wages, and the retailer takes advantage of their ignorance...They are the producers and artificers of all the necessaries, the comforts, the luxuries, the pomp and splendor of he world; they create it all, and enjoy none of it; they are at constant war with those above them, asking higher wages but getting lower; for they are also at war with each other, underbidding to get employment. This process of underbidding never ceases so long as employers want profits or laborers want employment. It ends, when wages are reduced too low to afford subsistence, in filling poor-houses, and jails, and graves. It has reached that point already in France, England and Ireland. A half million died in one year in Ireland," died during the Great Famine because they were free, whereas "had they been vassals or serfs" they would have been fed. "Slaves never die of hunger."

Then there was the "moral effect of free society," which was "to banish Christian virtue, that virtue which bids us love our neighbor as ourself, and to substitute the very equivocal virtues proceeding from mere selfishness. The intense struggle to better one's pecuniary condition, the rivalries, the jealousies, the hostilities which it begets, leave neither time nor inclination to cultivate the heart or the head . . . What makes money, and what costs money, are alone desired. Temperance, frugality, thrift, attention to business, industry, and skill in making bargains are virtues in high repute, because they enable us to supplant others and increase our own wealth. The character of our Northern brethren is proof enough of the justice of these reflections." By contrast, "domestic slavery in the Southern states has produced the same results in elevating the character of the master that it did in Greece and Rome. He is lofty and independent in his sentiments, generous, affectionate, brave and eloquent; he is superior to the Northerner in everything but the arts of thrift. History proves this.

> "But the chief and far most important inquiry is, how does slavery affect the condition of the slave? One of the wildest sects of Communists in France proposes not only to hold all property in common, but to divide the profits not according to each man's input and labor, but according to each man's wants. Now this is precisely the system

of domestic slavery with us. We provide for each slave in old age and infancy, in sickness and in health, not according to his labor but according to his wants. The master's wants are more costly and refined, and he therefore gets a larger share of the profits. A Southern farm is the *beau ideal* of Communism; it is a joint concern in which the slave consumes more than the master of the coarse products, and is far happier, because although the concern may fail, he is always sure of a support; he is only transferred to another master to participate in the profits of another concern; he marries when he pleases, because he knows he will have to work no more with a family than without one, and whether he live or die that family will be taken care of; he exhibits all the pride of ownership, boasts of 'our crops, horses, fields and cattle;' and is as happy as a human being can be.

"There is no rivalry, no competition to get employment among slaves, as among free laborers. Nor is there a war between master and slave. The master's interest prevents his reducing the slave's allowance or wages in infancy and sickness, for he might lose the slave by doing so. His feelings for his slave never permits him to stint him in old age." Indeed, the benign influence of the peculiar institution "gives full development and full play to the affections. Free society chills, stints and eradicates them . . . We are better husbands, better fathers, better friends and better neighbors than our Northern brethren. Love for others is the organic law of our society, as self-love is of theirs. At the slave-holding South all is peace, quiet, plenty, and contentment. We have no mobs, no trades unions, no strikes for higher wages . . . Wealth is more equally distributed than at the North, where a few millionaires own most of the property of the country. These millionaires are men of cold hearts and weak minds; they know how to make money, but not how to use it, either for the benefit of themselves or of others. High intellectual and moral attainments, refinement of the head and heart, give standing to a man in the South, however poor he may be.

"Until the last fifteen years our great error was to imitate Northern habits, customs and institutions . . . We distrusted our social system. We thought slavery morally wrong, we thought it would not last, we thought it unprofitable. The Abolitionists assailed us; we looked more closely into our circumstances; became satisfied that slavery is morally right, that it would continue ever to exist, that it was as profitable as it was humane. This begat self-confidence, self-reliance. Since then our improvement has been rapid. Now we may safely say that we are the happiest, most contented and prosperous people on earth. The inter-meddling of foreign pseudo-philanthropists in our affairs, though it has occasioned great irritation and indignation, has been of inestimable advantage in teaching us to form a right estimate of our condition."

Fitzhugh's claim that "high intellectual and moral attainments, refinement of head and heart, give standing to a man in the South," touched on the belief, often asserted though never fully substantiated, that there had evolved in the South a degree of civilization not seen since the days of ancient Greece. This topic was taken up by the South Carolina politician and lawyer, William Harper, in his 1838 *Memoir on Slavery*:

"President Dew [of the College of William and Mary] has shown that the institution of slavery is a principal cause of civilization. Perhaps nothing can be more evident than that it is the *sole* cause. If anything can be predicated as universally true of uncultivated man, it is that he will not labor beyond what is absolutely necessary to maintain his existence . . . The coercion of slavery alone is adequate to form man to habits of labor. Without it there can be no accumulation of property, no providence for the future, no tastes for comfort or elegancies which are the characteristics and essentials of civilization. He who has obtained the command of another man's labor, first begins to accumulate and provide for the future, and the foundations of civilization are laid.

"There seems to be something in this subject that blunts the perceptions, and darkens the understanding and moral feelings of men. Tell them that, of necessity, in every civilized society there must be an infinite variety of conditions and employments, from the most eminent and intellectual to the most servile and laborious; that the Negro race, from their temperament and capacity, are peculiarly suited to the situation which they occupy, and not less happy in it than any corresponding class to be found in the world; prove incontestably that no scheme of emancipation could be carried into effect without the most intolerable mischiefs and calamities to both master and slave—and you have done nothing . . . They repeat, as the fundamental maxim of our civil policy, that all men are born free and equal, and quote from our Declaration of Independence 'that men are endowed by their Creator with certain inalienable *rights*, among which are life, liberty, and the pursuit of happiness.'

"It is not the first time that I have had occasion to observe that men may repeat with the utmost confidence some maxim or sentimental phrase as a self-evident or admitted truth which is either palpably false, or to which, upon examination, it will be found they attach no definite idea." We should respect the Declaration, but not those parts which are "false, sophistical or unmeaning. *All men are born free and equal.* Is it not palpably nearer the truth to say that no man was ever born free, and that no two men were ever born equal?" And not just at birth, but throughout life "wealth and poverty, fame or obscurity, strength or weakness, knowledge or ignorance, ease or labor, power or subjection, mark the endless diversity in the condition of men.

"What is the foundation of the bold dogma so confidently announced? Females are human and rational beings. They may be found of better faculties, and better qualified to exercise political privileges, and to attain the distinctions of society, than many men; yet who complains of the order of society by which they are excluded from them?" To give women political rights would be to "desecrate them; do violence to the nature which their Creator has impressed upon them; drag them from the position which they necessarily occupy for the existence of civilized society, and in which they constitute its blessing and ornament—the only position which they have ever occupied in any human society—to place them in a situation in which they would be alike miserable and degraded." Enough then of this "well-sounding but unmeaning verbiage of natural equality and inalienable rights." It is the law of nature that "the strong and the wise should control the weak and the ignorant."

Harper also posed the question, "Is it not better that the character and intellect of the individual should be suited to the station which he is to occupy? If there are sordid, servile and laborious offices to be performed, is it not better that there should be sordid, servile and laborious beings to perform them?"

This question was taken up by another leading politician, James Henry Hammond, twice governor of South Carolina, twice a Congressman, and twice a U.S. Senator. A hard-liner who agreed with Harper in repudiating as "ridiculously absurd that much-lauded but nowhere accredited dogma of Mr. Jefferson that 'all men are born equal,'" Hammond delivered his notorious Mudsill speech in March, 1858, in the Senate during a debate on the admission of Kansas as a free state. While boasting that "Cotton is King," Hammond nevertheless claimed that the greatest strength of the South came not from its wealth but from "the harmony of her political and social institutions." The key to this harmony was recognition of the fact that "in all social systems there must be a class to do the menial duties, to perform the drudgery of life. That is, a class requiring but a low order of intellect and but little skill. Its requisites are vigor, docility, fidelity. Such a class you must have, or you would not have that other class which leads progress, civilization and refinement. It constitutes the very mud-sill of society and of political government; and you might as well attempt to build a house in the air as to build either the one or the other, except on this mud-sill. [The term refers to the lowest foundation of a building.] Fortunately for the South, she found a race adapted to that purpose to her hand. A race inferior to her own, but eminently qualified in temper, in vigor, in docility, in capacity to stand the climate, to answer all her purposes. We use them for our purpose, and call them slaves." But although inferior, "the status in which we have placed them is an elevation. They are elevated from the condition in which God first created them, by being made our slaves. None of that race on the whole face of the globe can be compared with the slaves of the South. They are happy, content, unaspiring and utterly incapable, from intellectual weakness, ever to give us any trouble by their aspirations."

Hammond also took pains to refute the assertion made by the English abolitionist, Thomas Clarkson, "that licentiousness in intercourse between the sexes is a prominent trait of our social system." This absurd charge had become "a favorite theme of abolitionists," especially "learned old maids" who dwelt on the subject with "insatiable relish." Surely "such rage without betrays the fires within." Still, he would set the record straight.

It was true that "some intercourse of the sort does take place. Its character and extent, however, are grossly and atrociously exaggerated." Also, nearly all such "irregularities" took place in the cities, many of whose white inhabitants were "natives of the North, or foreigners." Among the southern gentry such conduct was "highly disreputable. If carried on habitually, it seriously affects a man's standing, so far as it is known; and he who takes a colored mistress—with rare and extraordinary exceptions—loses caste at once." The fact was that "a people whose men are proverbially brave, intellectual and hospitable, and whose women are unaffectedly chaste, devoted to domestic life, and happy in it, can neither be degraded nor demoralized."

Unfortunately for his future reputation, Hammond kept a plantation journal in which he recorded his January, 1839, purchase for $900 of Sally Johnson, aged eighteen, and her daughter, Louisa, aged one. Though he set them up in a separate establishment, the situation was so blatant that his downtrodden wife—whom he had married for her fortune—left him. Over the years Sally produced a number of mulatto children, and when Louisa reached the age of twelve she too became Hammond's mistress and the mother of several children. (Hammond also kept a diary in which he recorded his "wanton toying" with his four "lovely and luscious" teenage nieces. But it wasn't his fault—the girls had thrown themselves at him "rushing on every occasion into my arms and covering me with kisses, lolling on my lap, pressing their bodies almost into mine, wreathing their limbs with mine . . .")

Although his father had been a New England laborer, Hammond warmly endorsed the idea that masters were like the patriarchs of the Old Testament, a status "well calculated to awaken the higher and finer feelings of our nature." Here was the master, "beloved and honored," and here were the "faithful and admiring" slaves who had "served his father, and rocked his cradle—who have been through life the props of his fortune and the objects of his care—who have partaken of his griefs, and looked to him for comfort in their own—whose sickness he has so frequently watched over and relieved—whose holidays he has so often made joyous by his bounties and his presence—whose hearty and affectionate greetings never fail to welcome him home. In this cold, calculating, ambitious world of ours, there are few ties more heartfelt, or of more benignant influence, than those which mutually bind the master

How the South liked to see itself: a top-hatted patriarch and his lady look on with benevolent eye as members of his "family" cut loose in a "plantation frolic."

and the slave, under our ancient system, handed down from the Father of Israel."

There were many other expressions of this kindly patriarch/faithful slave myth. "The Southern Gentleman entertains more real love for his 'human chattels' than all the hare-brained abolitionists the world ever saw," wrote Daniel Hundley in *Social Relations in our Southern States*. "The proof of their well-fed condition is strikingly observable in their sleek skins, full cheeks and general plumpness . . . They are nearly always jovial and smiling, indulging all the time in snatches of song, and giving vent to the most stunning peals of laughter."

And there was this anecdote told by the journalist Edward Pollard in *Black Diamonds Gathered in Darkey Homes of the South:* "On the morning following my return home after years of absence, I was told that Uncle George, who was too decrepit from age to come up to the house, wanted me to come to the negro quarter to see him . . . I found the old fellow very comfortably situated. He had grown old gently; he had never seen any hard service; and now in his old age was he not only not required to do any work, but, with that regard commonly exhibited toward the slave when stricken with age, he had every attention paid him in the evening of his life. His meals were sent out to him from our own table. There was one little consideration that touched me. His passion for gardening, which had been the whole occupation of his life, had been gratified by giving him a little patch of ground in front of his cabin, where he might amuse himself at his own option.

> "I found Uncle George in his miniature garden. The old fellow staggered up to see me, and, suddenly dropping, clasped me around the knees. This poor old man was 'a slave,' and yet he had a place in my heart, and I was not ashamed to meet him with tears in my eyes. Miserable abolitionists! You prate of brotherly love and humanity. If you or any man had dared to hurt a hair of this slave, I would have trampled you into the dust!"

Pollard was also the author of *The Lost Cause*, published just after the Civil War. In it he explained that the "sectional animosity" between North and South was not really about slavery; rather it was a conflict that "went deeper to the very elements of the civilization of each," between "the Puritan exiles who established themselves upon the cold and rugged and cheerless soil of New England, and the Cavaliers who sought the brighter climes of the South." The first were characterized by "intolerance . . . painful thrift . . . external forms of piety . . . jaundiced legislation . . . convenient morals . . . and their unremitting hunt after selfish aggrandizement." By contrast, "the colonists of Virginia and the Carolinas were from the first distinguished by their polite manners, their fine sentiments, their attachment to a sort of feudal life, their landed gentry, their love of field sports and dangerous adventure." They lived in "baronial halls" and were famous for "their constant rounds of hospitality and gaiety." The Northerner might have more money, but he was "coarse and inferior in comparison with the aristocracy and chivalry of the South." In sum, "Slavery established in the South a peculiar and noble type of civilization. It was not without attendant vices; but the virtues which followed in its train were numerous . . . It afforded opportunity for extraordinary culture, elevated the standards of scholarship in the South, enlarged and emancipated social intercourse, and established schools of individual refinement." (Pollard seems to have felt that these assertions were so obviously true that there was no need to provide substantiating examples.)

Was slavery a sin—"a great sin, nay the greatest of sins that exist in the nation?" If yes, then "it behooves all Christians who are involved in the sin to repent in dust and ashes, and wash their hands of it." But how can we know if something is a sin? Because God tells us, "either by preceptive prohibition ['Thou shalt not . . .']; by principles of moral fitness; or examples of inspired men contained in the Sacred Volume." But if the way to discover the truth is so clear, why do the North and South differ so profoundly? The answer was that while men of the South were "cleaving to the Bible, and taking all our decisions about this matter from its inspired pages," men of the North displayed "a palpable ignorance of the Divine Will in reference to the institution of slavery. I have seen but few who made the Bible their study."

After this preamble to his popular booklet *The Bible Argument, or, Slavery in the Light of Divine Revelation,* the Rev. Thornton Stringfellow continued, "I propose therefore to examine the Sacred Volume briefly, and, if I am not greatly mistaken, I shall be able to make it appear that the institution of slavery has received:

> "First. The sanction of the Almighty in the Patriarchal Age," (i.e. "that portion of time stretching from Noah until the Law was given to Abraham's posterity at Mount Sinai.")

> "Second. That it was incorporated into the only National Constitution which ever emanated from God.

> "Third. That its legality was recognized, and its relative duties regulated, by Jesus Christ in his kingdom."

After explaining that the word "servant" as used by translators of the Bible really meant "slave," Stringfellow launches into an extensive history, beginning with Genesis and the famous "Cursed be Canaan . . . a servant of servants shall he be to his brethren"; then dilating upon Abraham, "a man that is held up as a model to all," who not only owned hundreds of slaves but used one of them, Hagar, as "a secondary wife." And when Hagar ran away, hoping to get back to Egypt, did not God send an angel in pursuit who ordered the fugitive "Return unto thy mistress, and submit thyself under her hands"? (Gen. xvi: 9.)

"The next notice we have of servants as property is from God himself, when clothed with all the visible tokens of his presence and glory, on the top of Sinai, he proclaimed his law to the millions that surrounded the base: 'Thou shalt not covet thy neighbor's house, thou shalt not covet thy neighbor's wife, nor his man-servant, nor his maid-servant, nor his ox, nor his ass, nor any thing that is thy neighbor's." (Ex. xx. 17.) "Here," as Stringfellow points out, "is a patriarchal catalog of property having God for its author."

As to "the only National Constitution which ever emanated from God," this referred to the various laws which regulated the conduct of the Jewish people; and here again there is ample proof that God approved slavery. For example, here is Leviticus xxv. 44, 45, 46: "'Thy bond-men and thy bond-maids which thou shalt have, shall be of the heathen that are round about you; of them shall ye buy bond-men and bond-maids. Moreover, of the children of strangers that do sojourn among you, of them shall ye buy, and of their families that are with you, which they begat in your land. And they shall be your possession . . . they shall be your bond-men forever.' I ask any candid man if the words of this institution could be more explicit? It is from God himself."

Now all that remained was "to show that Jesus Christ recognized this institution as one that was lawful among men." This was easy enough. First, and most significant, "he has not abolished slavery by a prohibitory commandment." Second, "he has introduced no new moral principles which can work its destruction." Also, "in all the Roman provinces where churches were planted by the Apostles, hereditary slavery existed, as it did among the Jews, and as it does now among us; and in instructing such churches the Holy Ghost, by the Apostles, has recognized the institution as one legally existing among them." And remember what St. Paul said: "Servants, obey in all things your masters, according to the flesh; not with eye-service as men-pleasers, but in singleness of heart fearing God . . ." This applies even if "a Christian slave have an unbelieving master, who acknowledges no allegiance to Christ."

"But, say the abolitionists, he has introduced new moral principles which will extinguish it as an unavoidable consequence without a direct prohibitory command. What are they? 'Do to others as you would they should do to you.'" But these moral principles were not new at all; they were no different from "these words of Moses, (Levit. xix: 18.) 'Thou shalt love thy neighbor as thyself.'" In other words, "Jesus has added no new moral principles above those in the law of Moses to prohibit slavery."

Some of the confusion concerning the legitimacy of slavery arose from the little-known fact that even in the Early Church "there were abolition teachers among them," perverters of the truth "who taught that godliness abolished slavery." Then and now, such men were, in the words of the Apostle Timothy, bringers of "envy, strife, railings, evil surmisings, perverse disputings . . . men of corrupt minds and destitute of the truth. From such withdraw thyself." (1 Tim. vi: 4, 5.) "Such were the bitter fruits which abolition sentiments produced in the Apostolic day, and such precisely are the fruits they produce now."

As a polemicist, Stringfellow was unusual in that he appealed not only to the Bible but also to that other great—though more recent—authority: statistics. These were in abundant supply, particularly following the census of 1850, which had been a good deal more extensive than its predecessors. In the introduction to his paper, *Statistical Views in Favor of Slavery*, Stringfellow explained that he was addressing those "who admit the legality of slavery in the sight of God," but question its "expediency." Hitherto, "the non-slaveholding States affirmed, and the slaveholding States tacitly admitted, that by this test the slaveholding States must suffer in comparison." But was this really the case? Did "unquestionable facts and experience warrant the conclusion that while slavery is lawful, yet its continuance or expansion among us is inexpedient?" Thanks to the 1850 census "the facts which belong to the subject are now before the world."

He began by comparing the six states of New England and the five old slave states, from Maryland to Georgia. "I select these States not because they are the richest (for they are not,) but because they all lie on the Atlantic side of the Union—because they were settled at or near the same time—because they have (within a fraction) an equal free population—and because it has been constantly affirmed, and almost universally admitted, that the advantages of freedom and the disadvantages of slavery, have been more perfectly developed in these two sections than they have been anywhere else in the United States.

"The first facts I shall examine are those which throw light on the progress made in each of these two localities in religion. Of all the evils ascribed to slavery by free men of the North, none equals, in their estimation, its deleterious tendency upon religion and morals." And what can we learn from the census? With a white population that was almost identical (2,728,000 for the six Northern states, and 2,730,000 for the five slave states) we find that "New England has erected 4607 churches," and the five slave states "have erected 8081 churches. These New England churches will accommodate 1,893,450 hearers; the churches of the five slave states will accommodate 2,896,472 hearers. Thus we see that these slave States, with an equal free population, have erected nearly double the number of churches, and furnished accommodation for upwards of a million more persons."

Moving on:

"It is assumed in the North that slavery tends to produce social, moral and religious evils. This assumption is flatly contradicted by the facts of the census." Thus "New England has 518,532 families, and 447,789 dwellings. The five slave states have 506,968 families, and 496,369 dwellings. Here we see the astonishing fact that with an equal population, New England has 11,564 more families than these five states, and that these five states have 48,580 more dwellings than New England—so that New England actually has 70,743 families without a home . . . It is truly painful to think of the effects upon morals and virtue which must flow from this state of things; and it is a pleasure to a philanthropic heart to think of the superior condition of the slave-holding people, who generally have homes where parents can throw the shield of protection around their offspring, and guard them against the dangers and demoralizing tendencies of an unprotected condition."

Turning now to economics:

"It is the settled conviction of the non-slaveholding states that investments in slave labor, for agricultural purposes, is the worst of all investments, and tends greatly to lessen its profits. This has been proclaimed to the South so long by our Northern neighbors that many have been brought to believe it." But what does the census say? "New England, with a population now numbering 2,728,016, with all the advantages of a commercial and manufacturing investment, and with the most energetic and enterprising free men on earth to give that investment its greatest productiveness, has accumulated wealth, in something over two hundred years to the amount of $1,003,466,181; while these five slave states, with an equal population, have, in the same time, accumulated wealth to the amount of $1,420,989,573." Put another way, "the property belonging to New England, if equally divided, would give to each citizen but $367, while that belonging to the slave States, if equally divided, would give to each citizen the sum of $520."

One consequence of this prosperity is that southern slavery "has been, and now is, a blessing to this race of people in all the essentials of human happiness and comfort. Our slaves all have homes, are bountifully provided for in health, cared for and kindly nursed in childhood, sickness, and old age; multiply faster, live longer, are free from all the corroding ills of poverty and anxious care, labor moderately, enjoy the blessings of the gospel and, let alone by wicked men, are contented and happy." Indeed, "slavery is becoming, to this people, so manifestly a blessing that fugitives from labor are constantly returning to their masters again, after tasting the blessings, or rather the awful curse to them, of freedom in non-slaveholding States.

"The South did not seek or desire the responsibility and the onerous burden of civilizing and Christianizing these degraded savages; but God, in his mysterious providence, brought it about. He allowed England and her Puritan sons at the North, from the love of gain, to become the willing instruments to force African slaves upon the Cavaliers of the South. These Cavaliers were a noble race of men.

They remonstrated against this outrage to the last . . . But God intended, as we now see, to bless these savages by forcing us, against our wills, to become their masters and guardians; and He has abundantly blessed us also, as we now see, for allowing his Word to be our counselor in this relation."

To conclude the statistical argument, here are some facts quoted by David Christy in his book *Cotton is King*. The figures are for the year ending June 30, 1859:

Exports of the North: $45,305,541

Exports of the South: $193,399,618

The largest items of the North were "Animals and their products" ($15,262,769) and "Wheat and wheat flour" ($15,113,455). For the South the largest were "Tobacco, in leaf," ($21,074,038) and "Cotton" ($161,434,923).

That remark by Stringfellow about fugitives "constantly returning to their masters again, after tasting the blessings, or rather the awful curse to them, of freedom in non-slaveholding states," refers to one of the South's most cherished and oft-repeated anecdotes. It had many versions; the one that follows is told by an English lady of noble birth, the Honourable Amelia Murray, who after touring Canada was now favoring this country with a visit:

"New Orleans, March 31, 1855. Last night, conversing with a very intelligent gentleman who has traveled in Canada, I remarked that the free Negroes there were in a much more degraded, suffering and irreligious state than any slaves I have seen; and that they often reproach the whites with having by false pretenses, inveigled them to their destruction. He said, 'I will tell you a circumstance which occurred relative to that matter. A confidential black, who was treated with the greatest kindness by his master, took it into his head one day to run away, with the idea of establishing himself in Canada. When in that country I accidentally fell in with him, acting as a waiter in a hotel. We immediately recognized each other, and, with tears in his eyes, he said, "Oh, sir! Tell of the family. How is this one, how is that?" I answered his inquiries, and then asked how he got on. "I get on in the season pretty well; I make some money, but very bad in the winter. Oh sir! Beg my dear master for me; beg him to forgive, and take me back again.'" And I [that is, the Honourable Amelia Murray] feel sure that those Negroes who are not so far gone in drunkenness and profligacy as to have lost all self-respect, would generally make the same request."

A popular argument among slave-owners was "show us some country in which slavery has been abolished, and we will abide by the experiment." The recent history of Haiti, once "the pearl of the West Indies," but now impoverished and turbulent, was one example. Another came when the British government abolished slavery throughout the empire. £20,000,000 was to be paid as compensation to the owners, and all slaves over the age of six were to become free on August 1, 1834. There would then be a four-to-six-year period of compulsory "apprenticeship," but this proved hard to enforce, and was soon dropped.

Less than twenty years later, the *Southern Quarterly* published a review of two recent books on the topic of West Indian emancipation. "Immediately upon its passage," wrote the reviewer, "this act was heralded to the world as the great event of the times. The British nation signalized itself in the eyes of the world by its self-gratulations and boastings upon the passage of this act, as illustrating its wisdom, justice and humanity. Brilliant results were anticipated for it; and a new era in the prosperity of her West Indian Islands, it was thought, was about to be inaugurated." But "alas for the short-sightedness of human wisdom!" After eighteen years, all "those bright anticipations" must give way to the "melancholy realities of degradation and ruin caused by this act of folly." The reviewer paid particular attention to the book titled *Jamaica in 1850* since its author, John Bigelow, a New York lawyer and journalist, was known to be an abolitionist, and "it is natural to suppose he would be inclined to give the most favorable accounts of the results of the experiment of freedom."

And here is some of what Bigelow found: "It is difficult to exaggerate, and yet more difficult to define, the poverty and industrial prostration of Jamaica." The soil was so fertile that no one starved, but ever since "the Emancipation Act was passed, the real estate of the island has been rapidly depreciating in value . . . Out of the 653 sugar estates then in cultivation more than 150 have been abandoned, and the works broken up. This has thrown out of cultivation over 200,000 acres of rich land, which in 1832 gave employment to about 30,000 laborers . . . During the last three years the island has exported less than half the sugar, rum or ginger; less than one third the coffee; less than one tenth the molasses; and nearly two million pounds less of pimento, than during the three years which preceded the Emancipation Act." Property values had plunged—"the Spring Valley estate in the parish of St. Mary's, embracing 1,244 acres, had been sold once for £18,000 sterling. In 1842 it was abandoned, and in 1845 the freehold, including works, machinery, plantation utensils and water power, was sold for £1,000. The Tremoles estate, of 1,450 acres, once worth £68,265 sterling, has since been sold for £8,400, and would not now bring half that sum." Towns such as Kingston were also in decline: "In the busiest parts of the city, and on every block, may be seen vacant lots, on which are crumbling the foundation walls of houses long in ruins . . . Though Kingston is the principal port of the island, one looks and listens in vain for the noise of carts and the bustle of busy men; no one seems to be in a hurry, but few are doing anything, while the mass of the population are lounging about in idleness and rags . . . I could not perceive that sixteen years of freedom had advanced the dignity of labor, or of the laboring classes, one particle."

And it wasn't just Jamaica. "The other British West India islands have all been visited by equally serious, if not the same, prostrating influences, and all consider themselves ruined and helpless."

The *Southern Quarterly* reviewer drew the obvious conclusions: to have expected that a race "whose natural disposition is to avoid all manner of effort or action would have been capable of appreciating" freedom, was to hope "against all reason, and in the face of all experience. The truth is, that owing to its natural inferiority, the Negro race is incapable of attaining the same high degree of civilization which belongs to the white, and can only be made to reach that lower grade of which it is capable by that process known as slavery." Emancipation was therefore "the very worst thing for the future welfare of the Negro race. As well as causing the entire destruction of the prosperity of these islands, it removed the wholesome restraints of a civilization which had been imposed by the whites, took from it the only efficient stimulus to effort—that of compulsion—and left it abandoned to all its natural impulses and habits of idleness, soon to relapse into a condition of complete degradation.

> "The results of this experiment are of the greatest importance as teaching fundamental truth upon the whole subject of Negro slavery; and to the South, of vital value as justifying and confirming the policy she has hitherto maintained, and in the future should maintain, in the government of this race. It holds up to view the picture which her condition would present under a similar experiment. She cannot therefore be too vigilant or too careful in guarding against all the insidious approaches of abolitionism."

And then there was the appeal to science. In May, 1851, the *New Orleans Medical and Surgical Journal* printed a *Report on the Diseases and Physical Peculiarities of the Negro Race*, by Dr. Samuel Cartwright. As a medical student, Cartwright had studied under Dr. Benjamin Rush, a fervent abolitionist; but Cartwright was a man who thought for himself, and eventually came to a number of conclusions based on "observation in the field of experience." Here are some of them:

> "It is commonly taken for granted that the color of the skin constitutes the main and essential difference between the black and the white race; but there are other differences more deep, durable and indelible, in their anatomy and physiology, than that of mere color." There were differences "in the membranes, the muscles, the tendons and in all fluids and secretions. Even the Negro's brain and nerves . . . are tinctured with a shade of the prevailing darkness. His bile is of a deeper color and his blood is blacker than the white man's." On the other hand "his bones are whiter and harder than those of the white race, owing to their containing more phosphate of lime . . . His brain is a ninth or tenth less than in other races of men." However, "the Negro's hearing is better, his sight is stronger, and he seldom needs spectacles.

"The profuse distribution of nervous matter to the stomach, liver and genital organs would make the Ethiopian race entirely unmanageable if it were not that this excessive development is associated with a deficiency of red blood in the pulmonary and arterial systems, from a defective atmospherization or arterialization of the blood in the lungs," i.e. they did not breathe in as much oxygen as white people. This, along with "a deficiency of cerebral matter in the cranium, and an excess of nervous matter distributed to the organs of sensation," was "the true cause of that debasement of mind which has rendered the people of Africa unable to take care of themselves. It is the true cause of their indolence and apathy, and why they have chosen, through countless ages, idleness, misery and barbarism to industry and frugality." This was also why "they always prefer the same kind of government, which we call slavery, but which is actually an improvement on the government of their forefathers, as it gives them more tranquility and sensual enjoyment." And even if they did not prefer slavery, "yet their organization of mind is such that if they had their liberty, they have not the industry, the moral virtue, the courage and vigilance to maintain it, but would relapse into barbarism or into slavery, as they have done in Haiti. The reason for this is found in unalterable physiological laws. Under the compulsive power of the white man they are made to labor and exercise, which makes the lungs perform the duty of vitalizing the blood more perfectly than is done when they are left free to indulge in idleness. It is the red, vital blood sent to the brain that liberates their mind when under the white man's control; and it is the want of a sufficiency of red, vital blood that chains their mind to ignorance and barbarism when in freedom." In sum: "Anatomy and physiology have been interrogated, and the response is that the Ethiopian, or Canaanite, is unfitted . . . for the responsible duties of a free man, but, like a child, is only fitted for a state of dependence and subordination."

Dr. Cartwright's best-known contribution to medical science was to identify and diagnose two ailments peculiar to the Negro. The first of these was *Drapetomania*, "the disease causing slaves to run away." (Cartwright invented the term himself, the first part coming from the Greek word *drapetes*, meaning a runaway slave.) "The cause, in the most of cases, that induces the Negro to run away from service is as much a disease of the mind as any other species of mental alienation, and much more curable." The disease had two causes. Either the white man "attempts to oppose the Deity's will by trying to make the Negro anything else than the submissive knee-bender, (which the Almighty declared he should be,) by trying to raise him to a level with himself." Or the white man "abuses the power which God has given him over his fellow-man, by being cruel to him or punishing him in anger." If a Negro becomes "sulky and dissatisfied" it is a symptom of the onset of *drapetomania*. Inquiries should be made, and if there are legitimate grounds for the sulkiness they should be removed. If there are no such ground then he prescribed "whipping them out of it, as a preventive measure against absconding or other bad conduct."

Cartwright's other breakthrough was to define *Dysaesthesia Aethiopis*, or "hebetude of mind and obtuse sensibility of body." Its main symptoms are "stupidness of mind and insensibility of the nerves." These cause those infected to "break, waste and destroy everything they handle . . . tear, burn or rend their own clothing . . . steal to replace what they have destroyed . . . wander about at night and keep in a half-nodding sleep during the day . . . slight their work . . . cut up corn, cane, cotton or tobacco when hoeing, as if for pure mischief . . . raise disturbances with their overseers and fellow servants without cause." Doctors in the North "have noticed the symptoms, but not the disease from which they spring. They ignorantly attribute the symptoms to the debasing influence of slavery on the mind," whereas quite the opposite was the case, for "the disease is the natural offspring of Negro liberty—the liberty to be idle."

Fortunately, "the complaint is easily curable, if treated on sound physiological principles." The first step was "to stimulate the skin" by having the patient "well washed with warm water and soap, then to anoint him all over with oil, and to slap the oil in with a broad leather strap; then to put the patient to some kind of hard work in the open air and sunshine that will compel him to expand his lungs, as chopping wood, splitting rails, or sawing." This would "vitalize the impure circulating blood by introducing oxygen and expelling carbon." Patients should take frequent rests and "drink freely of cold water or some cooling beverage, as lemonade, or alternated with pepper tea sweetened with molasses." Food should be wholesome, and bedding clean and warm. Every morning more oil should be slapped in. The result of this course of treatment "is

often like enchantment. The Negro seems to be awakened to a new existence, and to look grateful and thankful to the white man whose compulsory power, by making him inhale vital air, has restored his sensation and
dispelled the mist that clouded his intellect. His intelligence restored and
his sensations awakened, he is no longer the *bipedum nequissimus*, or ar-
rant rascal, he was supposed to be, but a good Negro that can hoe or plow
and handle things with as much care as his other fellow-servants."

A final thought: "*Dysaesthesia Aethiopis* adds another to the many
ten thousand evidences of the fallacy of the dogma that abolitionism is
built on; for here, in a country where two races of men dwell together,
born on the same soil, breathing the same air, and surrounded by the
same external agents—liberty, which is elevating the one race of people
above all other nations, sinks the other into beastly sloth and torpidity;
and slavery, which the one would prefer death rather than endure, im-
proves the other in body, mind and morals; thus establishing the truth
that there is a radical, internal or physical difference between the two
races, so great in kind as to make what is wholesome and beneficial for
the white man, as liberty, republican or free institutions, etc., not only
unsuitable to the Negro race, but actually poisonous to its happiness."

Thanks to the three-fifths rule, northern sympathizers, and its extension
to the new states in the southwest, the slave interest was more than able
to hold its own in national politics, where its cardinal principle was that
slavery was a matter reserved exclusively to the states. It was, as the fire-
brand John C. Calhoun of South Carolina put it, "beyond the jurisdiction of Congress—they have no right to touch it in any shape or form."
There could be no yielding on this matter. "If we concede an inch, concession would follow concession—compromise would follow compromise until our ranks would be so broken that effectual resistance would
be impossible. We must meet the enemy on the frontier." The root of
the problem was the "incendiary spirit" of northern fanatics. "Unless it
be speedily stopped, it will spread and work upwards till it brings the
two great sections of the Union into deadly conflict . . . Abolition and
Union cannot co-exist. As the friend of the Union I openly proclaim it—
and the sooner it is known, the better . . . We of the South will not, can-

not surrender our institutions. To maintain the existing relationship between the two races inhabiting that section of the Union is indispensable to the peace and happiness of both. It cannot be subverted without drenching the country in blood, and extirpating one or the other of the races. Be it good or bad, it has grown up with our society and institutions, and is so interwoven with them, that to destroy it would be to destroy us as a people.

> "But let me not be understood as admitting, even by implication, that the existing relation between the two races in the slave-holding States is an evil. Far otherwise, I hold it to be a good, as it has thus far proved to be to both, and will continue to prove so if not disturbed by the fell spirit of abolition. I appeal to facts. Never before has the black race of Central Africa, from the dawn of history to the present day, attained a condition so civilized and so improved, not only physically, but morally and intellectually. It came among us in a low, degraded and savage condition, and in the course of a few generations it has grown under the fostering care of our institutions, reviled as they have been, to its present comparatively civilized condition. This, with the rapid increase in numbers, is conclusive proof of the general happiness of the race, in spite of all the exaggerated reports to the contrary." Far, then, from being "an evil," slavery was "a good—a positive good."

Words were not the only weapons used in Congress. "Within the last three years," wrote Theodore Dwight Weld in 1839, "some of the most prominent slave-holding members of the House, and among them the late Speaker, have struck and kicked, and throttled, and seized each other by the hair, and with their fists pummeled each others' faces, on the floor of the Congress . . . During the session of the last Congress, Mr. Wise of Virginia and Mr. Bynum of North Carolina, after having called each other 'liars, villains' and 'damned rascals,' sprang from their seats, both sufficiently armed for any desperate, purpose, cursing each other as they rushed together, and would doubtless have butchered each other on the floor of Congress if both had not been seized and held by their friends."

The abolitionist Senator Charles Sumner of Massachusetts, holding in his right hand a quill pen (perhaps a symbol of non-violent eloquence) is brutally thrashed by Preston Brooks of South Carolina. Some of the senators in the background—presumably southerners—seem to be enjoying the show.

At the close of the 1838 session there was "another brutal and bloody row. It occurred on Sunday morning, immediately at the moment of adjournment, between Messrs. Campbell and Maury, both of Tennessee. He [Maury] took offense at some remarks made to him by his colleague, Mr. Campbell, and the fight followed." According to the *Huntville (Ala.) Democrat*, "Mr. Maury is said to be badly hurt. He was near losing his life by being knocked through the window; but his adversary, it is said, saved him by clutching the hair of his head with his left hand, while he struck him with his right." The same paper gave the particulars of a fist-fight on the floor of the House "between Mr. Bell, the late Speaker, and Mr. Turney of Tennessee." Bell had called Turney "the fool of fools," and soon "both gentlemen were perceived in personal conflict, and blows with the fist were aimed by each at the other. Several members interfered and suppressed the personal violence; others called 'Order! Order!'" Three such fights took place in one month, and "at the same session Messrs. Peyton of Tennessee and Wise of Virginia went armed with pistols and dirks to the meeting of a committee of Congress, and threatened to shoot a witness while giving his testimony."

The most notorious instance of this "ruffianism" occurred in May, 1856, after Senator Charles Sumner of Massachusetts, the leader of the Radical Republicans, had delivered a lengthy and at times sarcastic speech called *The Crime Against Kansas*. As he rambled along, one of his colleagues, Senator Stephen Douglas, of Illinois (Lincoln's future debating opponent), said to another, "This damn fool Sumner is going to get himself shot by some other damn fool!"

What prompted Douglas' remark was Sumner's comments on the character of the elderly Senator Andrew Butler, of South Carolina, one of the sponsors of the Kansas-Nebraska Act, which opened the door to slavery in those territories. (Douglas was the other sponsor.) Butler was not present, so missed hearing Sumner describe the Act as if it were one of sexual assault. "Rape . . . lust . . . hateful embrace . . . depraved desire" were some of the terms he used. Next he compared Butler to Don Quixote and the short and portly Douglas to Sancho Panza, figures of fun "who sally forth together in the same adventure." Then he focused on Butler: "The Senator from South Carolina has read many books of chivalry, and believes himself a chivalrous knight with sentiments of honor and courage. Of course, he has chosen a mistress to whom he has made his vows, and who, though ugly to others, is always lovely to him; though polluted in the sight of the world, is chaste to his sight—I mean the harlot, Slavery!" And now Butler was trying to force this polluted harlot into the arms of the good people of Kansas and Nebraska! And if he fails to do so "the chivalric Senator will conduct the State of South Carolina out of the Union. Heroic knight! Excellent Senator! A second Moses come to a second Exodus!"

Now it happened that Senator Butler had a young nephew, Preston Brooks, also of South Carolina and currently a member of the House. Two days later, while Sumner was sitting at his desk in the Senate, conning over the printed text of his speech, young Brooks approached. "Mr. Sumner," he said. "I have read your speech twice over carefully. It is a libel on South Carolina and Mr. Butler, who is a relative of mine." Thereupon he began to thrash Sumner with a gold-knobbed gutta-percha cane, first beating him over the head so that he was soon blinded by blood. Sumner, who was tall and strong, tried to rise, but was trapped by his desk which was bolted to the floor. When nearby members tried to intervene, Brooks's friend, Laurence Keitt, pulled out a revolver and cried "Let them be!" Eventually Brooks's cane broke, after which he left. (Brooks thrashed Sumner rather than challenge him to a duel because he did not consider Sumner to be a gentleman.)

Reaction to the episode revealed how far apart North and South had become. "The South cannot tolerate freedom of speech anywhere," wrote the *Cincinnati Gazette*, "and would stifle it in Washington with the bludgeon and the bowie knife, as they are now trying to stifle it in Kansas by massacre, rapine and murder." "I do not see how a barbarous community and a civilized community can continue one state," wrote Emerson. "I think we must get rid of slavery, or we must get rid of freedom."

In the South matters were viewed differently. Hundreds of canes were sent to Preston Brooks, some with the message "Hit him again!" The *Richmond Enquirer* was of the opinion that "these vulgar abolitionists must be lashed into submission." A motion to expel Brooks from the House failed; he then resigned, but was re-elected. His gun-wielding friend, Keitt, also resigned and was also re-elected, and two years later set off a brawl in the House by calling Galusha Grow of Pennsylvania a "black Republican puppy," and then, when Grow called him "a Negro driver," trying to choke him.

Any hope that the law might help the cause of emancipation ended with the 1857 case of Dred Scott vs. John Sandford. The events leading up to it began in 1834 when Scott, a slave, was taken by his master from Missouri to Illinois, a free state, and then to the Wisconsin Territory, where slavery was also illegal. In 1846, after being brought back to Missouri, he sued for his freedom on the grounds that he had become free when taken to a free territory. Eleven years later, after various trials and appeals, the case ended up in the Supreme Court, which was presided over by Chief Justice Roger Taney, then aged eighty. Many years earlier Taney had freed the slaves on his Maryland plantation and called slavery "a blot on our national character." Since then his attitude had, as a contemporary put it, "hardened."

Two main questions had to be answered by the court: was Scott a citizen of Missouri, and therefore entitled to bring a case in federal court; and had his residence in Illinois and Wisconsin made him free? (The case was tried in federal court because the two parties resided in different states.) Here are some of Taney's decisions:

"The question is simply this: Can a Negro, whose ancestors were imported into this country and sold as slaves, become a member of the political community formed and brought into existence by the Constitution of the United States, and as such become entitled to all the rights, and privileges, and immunities guaranteed by that instrument to the citizen?"

To this the short answer was No—"they are not included, and were not intended to be included, under the word 'citizens' in the Constitution, and can therefore claim none of the rights and privileges which that instrument provides for and secures to the citizens of the United States. On the contrary, they were at that time considered as a subordinate and inferior class of beings, who had been subjugated by the dominant race, and whether emancipated or not, yet remained subject to their authority, and had no rights or privileges but such as those who held the power and the government might choose to grant them."

Next, an important distinction: "We must not confound the rights of citizenship which a State may confer within its own limits and the rights of citizenship as a member of the Union. It does not by any means follow, because he has all the rights and privileges of a citizen of a State, that he must be a citizen of the United States . . . The question then arises, whether the provisions of the Constitution, in relation to the personal rights and privileges to which the citizen of a State should be entitled, embraced the Negro African race at that time in this country, or who might afterward be imported, who had then or should afterward be made free in any State; and to put it in the power of a single State to make him a citizen of the United States, and endue him with the full rights of citizenship in every other State."

Once again the answer was No—or rather, "the court thinks the affirmative of these propositions cannot be maintained. And if it cannot, the plaintiff in error [Dred Scott] could not be a citizen of the State of Missouri, within the meaning of the Constitution of the United States, and consequently was not entitled to sue in its courts."

That could have been the end of the matter, but Taney still had a lot more to say. "In the opinion of the court, the legislation and histories of the time, and the language used in the Declaration of Independence, show that neither the class of persons who had been imported as slaves, nor their descendants, whether they had become free or not, were then acknowledged as a part of the people, nor intended to be included in the general words used in that memorable instrument . . . They had for more than a century been regarded as beings of an inferior order, and altogether unfit to associate with the white race, either in social or political relations; and so far inferior that they had no rights which the white man was bound to respect . . ."

After this history lesson, Taney went on for another fifty pages of opinion and precedents, including the declaration that the Missouri Compromise of 1820 was invalid, since Congress had no right to ban slavery anywhere. Six of the judges concurred, two dissented, one of whom, Benjamin Curtis, also resigned from the court.

Reaction to the decision was as might be expected. "The opinion of Chief Justice Taney in the case of Dred Scott was more thoroughly abominable than anything of the kind in the history of the courts," wrote Senator Sumner. "Judicial baseness reached its lowest point."

To others the verdict was a triumph. "This decision, except the Declaration of National Independence in 1776, is the most momentous event that has ever occurred on this continent," wrote Dr. Van Evrie in his introduction to a mass-market pamphlet on the case. "The relations of citizenship—the rights of the individual—in short, the status of the dominant race is thus defined and fixed for ever." All "doubts and uncertainties" were now at an end "and the Supreme Court, in the Dred Scott decision, has defined the relations, and fixed the status of the subordinate race forever. This decision must be accepted and sustained by the northern masses, or there must be a disunion and dismemberment of the Union."

The great orator, author and abolitionist, Frederick Douglass, as he approached old age. Although the fight against slavery and racism was his main concern, Douglass also supported free public education, an end to capital punishment, temperance, land reform, Home Rule for Ireland and women's suffrage—he was present at the famous Seneca Falls Convention of 1848, and died while attending the National Council of Women in Washington, D. C. in 1895. For good reason, his newspaper, The North Star, *had as its motto: "Right is of no sex, Truth is of no color, God is the Father of us all, and we are all Brethren."*

CHAPTER 13

THE ABOLITIONISTS

APART FROM THE SLAVES THEMSELVES, WHO IT MAY BE ASSUMED WERE ALL abolitionists but were denied a voice, there had always been a few people in this country who were outspoken in their condemnation of slavery— Samuel Sewall, Benjamin Lay, Benjamin Franklin, Anthony Benezet. But these individuals did not constitute a movement. That did not appear until well into the nineteenth century, starting on a very small scale and characterized by pacifism and non-resistance, and ending with the long and bloody Civil War.

A good way to begin that story is to turn to *The Life, Travels and Opinions of Benjamin Lundy,* written by Thomas Earle, and published in 1847.

> "Directly after the adoption of the Constitution, petitions were sent to Congress by the Pennsylvania Society and others, asking that body to exert its full constitutional power for the abolition of slavery. These petitions were referred to a committee who reported that the national government had no power to interfere for the extinction of slavery within the limits of any state within the confederacy [i.e. the Union]. The report to this effect was adopted with unanimity. From that time the energy of anti-slavery action evidently declined . . . insomuch that in the year 1810 there were scarcely any abolition societies still in existence.
>
> "The lethargy into which the nation had sunk in reference to the great question of slavery was at length dissipated by a renewed agitation, in which Benjamin Lundy, the subject of this memoir, may be justly considered the pioneer, as well as one of the more energetic, indefatigable and self-sacrificing actors."

Much of *The Life, Travels and Opinions* was in Lundy's own words. Earle, who seems to have known him well, described him as "slightly under the middle size, of a slender form, light and rather sandy complexion and hair, a sanguine temperament, and a cheerful and sprightly disposition. His manners were gentle and very unassuming." Born of Quaker parents in New Jersey in 1789, Lundy had little education but "an unquenchable thirst for knowledge." When he was nineteen he moved to Wheeling, Virginia, where he was apprenticed to a saddler; briefly led astray by "wild, fashionable youths," he soon sobered up, "kept on my plain dress, attended regularly the meetings of our religious Society, shunned every species of gambling and frolicking, and spent most of my leisure time in reading instructive books. It was in this situation that I first became acquainted with the wrongs of the slave. Wheeling was a great thoroughfare for the traffickers in human flesh. Their coffles passed through the place frequently. My heart was deeply grieved at the gross abomination; and the question, 'What can I do?' was the continual response to the impulses of my heart. As I enjoyed no peace of mind, I at length concluded that I must act. I called a few friends together and unbosomed my feelings to them. The result was the organization of an anti-slavery association, called the Union Humane Society. The first meeting, which was held at my own house, consisted of but five or six persons. In a few months afterwards, the Society contained nearly five hundred members, among whom were most of the influential preachers and lawyers, and many respectable citizens of several counties in that section of the state." (By now he had moved to Ohio.)

This was in 1815, when Lundy was twenty-six. Invited to contribute to the *Philanthropist*, an anti-slavery paper, he soon became the editor, and when that paper folded in 1821 he gave up his leather-working business and started his own weekly publication, the *Genius of Universal Emancipation* ("genius" in the sense of "guiding spirit"). "I had my printing done at Steubenville, Ohio, a distance of twenty miles. I went to and fro on foot, carrying my papers, when printed, on my back. I had begun the work without a dollar of funds, trusting for success to the sacredness of the cause; nor was I disappointed. In four months from the commencement, my subscription list had become quite large."

By 1824 he had moved once again, to Tennessee, and his paper had "obtained a pretty wide circulation in the United States. As it was the only anti-slavery paper in America, I concluded to attempt the transfer of its publication to one of the Atlantic cities, hoping thereby to extend its influence." The place he settled on was Baltimore. He made the entire journey from Tennessee on foot, proselytizing as he went. "At one time I went to the raising of a house, and lectured to the persons who were there assembled. At another I called a meeting at a place where there was to be a militia muster. The captain and some of his men attended, as did also a number of Friends." Afterward, "an anti-slavery society, consisting of fourteen members, was formed. The captain of militia was chosen president, and a member of the Society of Friends, secretary . . . Before I left the State there were some twelve or fourteen anti-slavery societies organized."

In January, 1827, Lundy was assaulted by the Baltimore slave-trader, Austin Woolfolk. This incident began when Lundy, following what was then standard journalistic practice, reprinted in the *Genius* an article from another paper, the *Christian Inquirer*, about "the execution, at New York, of William Bowser, a slave, for the murder of the captain and mate of the *Decatur*, a vessel engaged in transporting some of Woolfolk's slaves to Georgia. The slaves, twenty-nine in number, had risen for their liberty when a few days out from Baltimore, taken possession of the vessel, thrown the captain and mate overboard, and given the command to one of the crew, a white man, upon his promising to carry them to Hayti: but as he knew not how to manage the vessel, she was some days afterwards fallen in with by another vessel, which took her to New York, where the slaves escaped; but Bowser was afterwards apprehended at West Chester, New York, brought to New York City, convicted, and on December 15th, 1826, executed." But first, again according to standard practice, Bowser was allowed to address the spectators who had come to watch him being hanged, and "as Woolfolk was present, he particularly addressed his discourse to him, saying he could forgive him all the injuries he had done him, and hoped they might meet in Heaven. But this unfeeling soul-seller, with a brutality which becomes his business, told him, with an oath (not to be named,) that he was now going to have what he deserved, and he was glad of it, or words to that effect. He would probably have continued his abusive language to this unfortunate man had he not been stopped by some of the spectators, who were shocked at this unfeeling, profane, and brutal conduct.

"Lundy, in remarking on the above, strongly cautioned the colored people against attempting to obtain their rights by violent measures and urged upon them 'a spirit of forbearance, forgiveness, and charitable brotherly kindness.' He added: 'The citizens of Baltimore have now a clue to unravel the character of that monster in human shape, the Ishmaelite, Woolfolk. The adamantine-hearted creature, knowing himself to be the cause of the death of the captain and mate of the *Decatur*, and also of the poor unfortunate Bowser, could, with a fiend-like assurance, insult him with his outrageous profanity when he was just about to be launched into eternity . . .!'"

As it happened, the *Christian Inquirer* had got it wrong, and Woolfolk had not been present at Bowser's execution. Soon after, encountering Lundy in the street, he accused him of libel. But Lundy was not inclined to apologize, and tried to move away. Woolfolk stepped up to him "stripped off his coat, gave it to one of the by-standers, and took hold of my collar. Being much stronger than myself, and as I resolved to make no resistance, he found it an easy matter to prostrate my body on the pavement. Then with a brutal ferocity that is perfectly in character with his business, he choked me until my breath was nearly gone, and stamped me in the head and face with the fury of a very demon." Some by-standers intervened and Lundy, when he had recovered from his wounds, sued Woolfolk. He won his case but the fine imposed by Judge Brice was the token sum of one dollar. The judge also told Lundy "that 'I got nothing more than I deserved.'"

"In 1828 I made a journey to the middle and eastern States for the purpose of lecturing and obtaining subscriptions to *The Genius*." He also visited Philadelphia, New York and Boston where he met William Lloyd Garrison, who "had not then turned his attention to the anti-slavery question. I also visited New Hampshire, Maine and New York, after which I returned home, having, during my tour, considerably increased my subscription list and, as I have since learned, scattered the seed of anti-slavery in strong and luxuriant soil."

"In the spring of 1829 William Lloyd Garrison joined me at Baltimore in the editorship of the *Genius*. I then set out again on a tour to lecture, but I was soon obliged to return on account of the imprisonment of Garrison, for writings published in the paper," he "being less guarded in his language than myself." (After a trial before the prejudiced Judge Brice, Garrison had been found guilty of libel and, unable to pay the fine of fifty dollars, had been sentenced to six months in prison. Happily, the warden took a liking to him, provided him with a desk in the family's parlor and invited him to share their meals. "I am as snug as a robin in his cage," he wrote to a friend. After he had been there six weeks, the rich anti-slavery philanthropist, Arthur Tappan, paid his fine, and Garrison was released and went back to Boston.)

Following Nat Turner's insurrection in 1831 "the southern papers attributed the origin of the plots to the *Genius* and the *Liberator*, especially the latter, which it was said had been circulated in the South in large numbers. It is probable, however, that the conspiracies were instigated chiefly by the pamphlet of David Walker [*Appeal to the Colored Citizens*], if in fact they owed their origin to any publication whatever. From the time that these events occurred, Anti-Slavery Societies in the South ceased almost entirely to be formed, and those previously established soon sank into disuse."

The *Genius* for 1834 contained reports of riots "directed against abolitionists which took place in New York City on the nights of the 9th and 10th of July. The mob broke the doors and windows of the house of Lewis Tappan at midnight of the 9th and carried his furniture into the street and set fire to it . . . The doors and windows of Dr. Cox's Presbyterian church were broken; also the windows of Zion's church, belonging to a colored Methodist society; those of an African Baptist church in Division Street; the doors and windows of Dr. Ludlow's house; and the doors, windows and furniture of Dr. Ludlow's church in Spring Street. St. Phillip's African Episcopal church was nearly destroyed, including a fine organ. An African school house in Orange Street was destroyed; and a number of dwelling houses inhabited by colored people were totally destroyed, and a number [of people] greatly injured." The *Genius* also reported that "on the night of the 13th of August, 1834, a series of anti-abolition riots, which lasted three nights, commenced at Philadelphia, in the southern suburbs of the city. They were principally directed against the colored people, and the houses occupied by them, or in which they worshiped . . . The colored people were pursued and beaten, one of them to death, and another lost his life in attempting to swim the Schuylkill in order to escape his pursuers.

"Numerous petitions for the abolition of slavery in the District of Columbia having been presented to Congress, that body, on motion of Mr. Pinckney of South Carolina made February 8th, 1836, resolved by a vote of 201 to 7 that 'Congress possesses no constitutional authority to interfere in any way with the institution of slavery in any of the States.'" In May, the House adopted 117 to 68 a resolution "that all petitions, memorials, resolutions and propositions relating in any way, or to any extent whatever to the subject of slavery, shall, without being either printed or referred, be laid on the table, and that no further action whatever shall be had thereon." (Known as the "gag rule," this was rescinded eight years later.)

Though moribund in the South, the Anti-Slavery Society grew rapidly elsewhere, and in May, 1836, it reported that there were now "five hundred and twenty-six anti-slavery societies known to exist, of which three hundred and twenty-eight had been formed during the preceding year. The Society had expended, during the year, $25,866, being an increase of 150 per cent on the preceding year. It had employed thirteen lecturing agents during a good portion of the time, and had printed upwards of one million of copies of various tracts."

Meanwhile, acts of violence against abolitionists grew. On July 22, 1836, in Cincinnati, "a large meeting was held at the lower market house, at which resolutions were passed threatening violence if the publication of the *Philanthropist* was not discontinued, and a committee was appointed to wait upon Mr. Birney [the editor] and his associates, and request them to desist from the publication of their paper, and to warn them that if they persisted the meeting could not hold themselves responsible for the consequences. Mr. Birney and the Executive Committee of the Ohio [Anti-Slavery] Society, having declined to comply with the request, a large mob assembled on the evening of July 31st, proceeded to the office, broke the windows and furniture, scattered the papers and books, and burned many of them, and took out the press, drew it down to the river, broke it to pieces and threw it into the stream. They then went to the houses of Birney and his friend, Donaldson, with a view, apparently, of personal violence; but finding neither of them at home, they proceeded to several houses inhabited by colored people, and tore them down."

In November, 1837, a mob in Alton, Illinois, murdered the abolitionist editor, Elijah Lovejoy, while also destroying his presses. In 1838, "the Pennsylvania Hall, which had been built at Philadelphia by abolitionists and others, was opened on the 14th of May, and various free discussions and public meetings, among which was that of an Anti-Slavery Convention of American Women, were held during that and the two succeeding days. A great and constantly increasing excitement prevailed in the city during this period," leading the mayor to ask the building's managers to cancel the meeting scheduled for the evening of the 17th, which they did. Nevertheless a large mob assembled, the doors were forced, "and the Hall was set on fire, with little apparent resistance from the police. The fire engines of the city repaired to the spot, and by their efforts protected the surrounding buildings. Many of the firemen were not disposed to extinguish the fire in the Hall, and some who attempted it were deterred by threats of violence. The Hall, which had cost upward of thirty thousand dollars, was consequently consumed—the wall only being left standing."

Also suffering great loss was Benjamin Lundy, who was about to set out on a tour in the West, and had "collected the little property that he possessed, and placed it one of the rooms of the Hall, then occupied as the Anti-Slavery Office. It was there consumed in the flames." Lundy took this loss with his usual disregard for material things: "'Well,'" he wrote to a friend, "'My papers, books, clothes—everything of value (except my journal in Mexico, &c.) are all, all gone—a total sacrifice on the altar of Universal Emancipation. They have not yet got my *conscience*, they have not taken my *heart*, and until they rob me of these, they cannot prevent me from pleading the cause of the suffering slave . . . I am not disheartened, though everything of earthly value (in the shape of property) is lost. Let us persevere in the good cause. We shall assuredly "triumph yet."

Lundy died the following year, but already he had been superseded as abolition's spokesman by William Lloyd Garrison, an "intelligent and remarkably pure-minded man," in the opinion of the Boston reformer and novelist, Lydia Maria Child, "whose only fault is that he cannot be moderate on a subject which it is exceedingly difficult for an honest mind to examine with calmness." Garrison's lack of moderation applied only to his language; like Lundy, he believed in non-violence, passive resistance and "moral suasion," rather than political or direct action. To his enemies an "officious and pestiferous fanatic," a "mawkish sentimentalist" who, like an "antiquated spinster," wept over the "imaginary sufferings" of slaves, to Frederick Douglass and to many others his words seemed to "glow with holy fire," and the man himself was "a Moses raised up by God to deliver his modern Israel from bondage." Soon after his return to Boston from Baltimore, he began publishing *The Liberator*, with himself as compositor, printer, reporter, publisher and editor. "Of all despicable and degraded beings, a time-serving, shuffling, truckling editor has no parallel," he had written earlier, and the first issue of his paper, which appeared on January 1, 1831, made it clear that he meant what he said.

He began, as was then not unusual, with some verses that he had written himself—*My name is LIBERATOR! I propose/ To hurl my shafts at freedom's deadliest foes! . . .*" Then he explained why he was publishing in Boston rather than Washington: it was New England, rather than the South, that needed a "revolution in public sentiment." In New England he had "found contempt more bitter, opposition more active, detraction more relentless, prejudice more stubborn, and apathy more frozen than among slave owners themselves." This was why he had "determined, at every hazard, to lift up the standard of emancipation in the eyes of the nation, *within sight of Bunker Hill, and in the birthplace of liberty.* That standard is now unfurled; and long may it float, unhurt by the spoliations of time or the missiles of a desperate foe—yea, till every chain be broken, and every bondman set free! Let southern oppressors tremble—let their secret abettors tremble—let their northern apologists tremble—let all the enemies of the persecuted blacks tremble . . ." After quoting from the Declaration of Independence to the effect that all men are created equal, and apologizing for having earlier endorsed the "popular but pernicious doctrine of *gradual* abolition," he continued: "I am aware that many object to the severity of my language; but is there not cause for severity? I *will* be as harsh as truth, and as uncompromising as justice. On this subject I do not wish to think, or speak, or write, with moderation. No! No! Tell a man whose house is on fire to give a moderate alarm; tell him to moderately rescue his wife from

William Lloyd Garrison at the age of thirty, and looking unusually dapper. Though mild in manner and a believer in non-violence, Garrison's intemperate editorials in The Liberator *and rallying cry "No Union with Slavery!" made him a byword in the South for abolitionist "fanaticism."*

the hand of the ravisher; tell the mother gradually to extricate her babe from the fire into which it has fallen;—but urge me not to use moderation in a cause like the present. I am in earnest—I will not equivocate—I will not excuse—I will not retreat a single inch—AND I WILL BE HEARD. The apathy of the people is enough to make every statue leap from its pedestal, and to hasten the resurrection of the dead . . ." Finally, another piece of verse: "Oppression! I have seen thee face to face,/ And met thy cruel eye and cloudy brow;/ But thy soul-withering glance I fear not now . . ."

In December, 1833, Garrison drew up the *Declaration of Sentiments* for the American Anti-Slavery Society's first convention, in Philadelphia: "More than fifty-seven years have elapsed since a band of patriots convened in this place to devise measures for the deliverance of this country from a foreign yoke. The cornerstone upon which they founded the Temple of Freedom was broadly this—'that all men are

created equal; that they are endowed by their Creator with certain inalienable rights; that among these are life, LIBERTY, and the pursuit of
happiness.' At the sound of their trumpet-call three millions of people
rose up as from the sleep of death, and rushed to the strife of blood;
deeming it more glorious to die instantly as freemen than desirable to
live one hour as slaves. They were few in number—poor in resources;
but the honest conviction that Truth, Justice and Right were on their
side, made them invincible.

> "Their principles led them to wage war against their oppressors, and
> to spill human blood like water, in order to be free. Ours forbid the
> doing of evil that good may come, and lead us to reject, and to en-
> treat the oppressed to reject, the use of all carnal [i.e. physical]
> weapons for deliverance from bondage; relying solely upon those
> which are spiritual, and mighty through God, to the pulling down
> of strongholds. Their methods were physical resistance—the mar-
> shaling in arms—the hostile array—the mortal encounter. Ours shall
> be such only as the opposition of moral purity to moral corruption—
> the destruction of error by the potency of truth—the overthrow of
> prejudice by the power of love—and the abolition of slavery by the
> spirit of repentance."

To bring this about "we shall organize Anti-Slavery Societies, if possible, in every city, town and village in our land—We shall send forth
agents to lift up the voice of remonstrance, of warning, of entreaty and of
rebuke—We shall circulate, unsparingly and extensively, anti-slavery tracts
and periodicals—We shall enlist the pulpit and the press in the cause of
the suffering and the dumb—We shall aim at a purification of the churches
from all participation in the guilt of slavery—We shall encourage the labor
of freemen rather than that of slaves, by giving preference to their pro-
ductions; and—We shall spare no exertions nor means to bring the whole
nation to speedy repentance. Our trust for victory is solely in God. We
may be personally defeated, but our principles never! Truth, Justice, Reason, Humanity, must and will gloriously triumph . . ."

Though eschewing active measures, this challenge to the established
order, and to the many profitable businesses based on slavery, alarmed
northern "gentlemen of property and standing," and in 1835, while ad-

dressing a meeting of the Boston Female Anti-Slavery Society, Garrison was seized by a mob of respectable citizens, who hustled him out of the building with cries of "Lynch him!" and "Turn him right nigger color with tar!" Though his life was in danger, Garrison stuck to his principles of Christian meekness and did not fight back; however, luckily for him, two workmen, Daniel and Buff Cooley, uninhibited by principles of non-resistance, waded into the crowd, grabbed the about-to-be martyr and hauled him off to safety. The incident took place very near the site of the notorious Boston Massacre of 1770, when the redcoats shot and killed five colonists.

Not until its rather hasty sanctification as the Civil War drew near, was the idea of the Union as something almost holy generally accepted in the North. The idea of secession, though more popular in the South, also had many supporters in the North. As early as 1845, convinced that the constitution was the great barrier to abolition, and that because of the two-thirds requirement it could never be amended, the American Anti-Slavery Society had adopted the slogan "No Union with Slaveholders!" This was in the wake of the annexation of Texas, in Garrison's opinion "the greatest crime of the age," and the occasion for this editorial in *The Liberator* of January 10, 1845, addressed to the "Tyrants of the world!"

"Proclaim not to your vassals that the American Union is an experiment in Freedom which, if it fail, will forever demonstrate the necessity of whips for the backs, and chains for the limbs of the people. Know that its subversion is essential in the triumph of justice, the deliverance of the oppressed, the vindication of the Brotherhood of the Race. It was conceived in sin, and brought forth in iniquity; and its career has been marked by unparalleled hypocrisy, by high-handed tyranny, by a bold defiance of the omniscience and omnipotence of God . . . To say that this Covenant with Death shall not be annulled—that this Agreement with Hell shall continue to stand—that this Refuge of Lies shall not be swept away—is to hurl defiance at the eternal throne, and to give the lie to Him who sits thereon."

Therefore—

"Accursed be the American Union, as a stupendous republican imposture! Accursed be it, as the most frightful despotism, with regard to three millions of the people, ever exercised over any portion of the human family! Accursed be it, as stained with human blood, and supported by human sacrifices! Accursed be it, for the terrible evils it has inflicted on Africa, by burning her villages, ravaging her coast, and kidnapping her children, at an enormous expense of human life, and for a diabolical purpose! Accursed be it for its hypocrisy, its falsehood, its impudence, its lust, its cruelty, its oppression! Accursed be it, from the foundation to the roof, and may there soon not be left one stone upon another that shall not be thrown down! Henceforth, the watchword of every uncompromising abolitionist, of every friend of God and liberty, must be, both in a religious and political sense—*No Union With Slaveholders!*"

By then, Garrison had been joined by another outstanding orator. "In the month of August, 1841," he later wrote, "I attended an anti-slavery convention in Nantucket"—long a Quaker stronghold—"at which it was my happiness to become acquainted with Frederick Douglass." Since his escape from slavery in Maryland a few years earlier, Douglass had been living in New Bedford, where he worked in the ship-yards and was moderately involved in anti-slavery activities. To reach Nantucket he traveled by steamship and soon after disembarking was buttonholed by William Coffin, a Friend and one of the organizers, who urged him—if moved by the spirit—to "testify." Douglass did so, though he later claimed that he was so nervous that he spoke haltingly and could "not remember a single connected sentence." Others, however, were riveted.

"I shall never forget his first speech at the convention," wrote Garrison. "The extraordinary emotion it excited in my own mind—the powerful impression it created upon a crowded auditory, completely taken by surprise—the applause which followed from the beginning to the end of his felicitous remarks . . . There stood one, in physical proportion and stature commanding and exact—in intellect richly endowed—in natural eloquence a prodigy—in soul manifestly 'created but a little lower than the angels'—yet a slave, aye, a fugitive slave!"

The moment Douglass finished speaking, Garrison, "filled with hope and admiration, rose and declared that Patrick Henry, of revolutionary fame, never made a speech more eloquent in the cause of liberty than the one we had just listened to from the lips of that hunted fugitive . . . I reminded the audience of the peril which surrounded this self-emancipated young man at the North—even in Massachusetts, on the soil of the Pilgrim Fathers, among the descendants of revolutionary sires; and I appealed to them, whether they would ever allow him to be carried back into slavery—law or no law, constitution or no constitution. The response was unanimous and in thunder-tones— 'NO!' 'Will you succor and protect him as a brother-man—a resident of the old Bay State?' 'Yes!' shouted the whole mass, with an energy so startling that the ruthless tyrants of Mason and Dixon's line might almost have heard the mighty burst of feeling, and recognized it as the pledge of an invincible determination."

To complete the triumph, Douglass was recruited on the spot "to consecrate his time and talents to the promotion of the anti-slavery enterprise" as a paid agent and lecturer, "a powerful impetus" to the cause, wrote Garrison, and "a stunning blow at . . . northern prejudice against a colored complexion."

Over the years, many others were to bear witness to the power of Douglass' oratory—what a reporter for the *Christian Recorder* called "the magnetism and melody of his wonderfully elastic voice . . . No printed sentences can convey any adequate idea of the manner, the tone of voice, the gesticulation, the action, the round, soft, swelling pronunciation with which Frederick Douglass spoke, and which no orator we have ever heard can use with such grace, eloquence and effect." According to another witness, "flinty hearts were pierced, and cold ones melted by his eloquence." His physical presence was as impressive as his oratory. "He was more than six feet in height, and his majestic form, as he rose to speak, straight as an arrow, muscular, yet lithe and graceful, his flashing eye, and, more than all, his voice, that rivaled Webster's in its richness and in the depth and sonorousness of its cadences, made up such an ideal of an orator as the listeners never forgot." Many years later, Elizabeth Cady Stanton recalled hearing him at a Boston anti-slavery meeting. She had been "spellbound" by his "burning eloquence." In comparison, "all the other speakers seemed tame," whereas Douglass had "stood there like an African prince, majestic in his wrath."

His skill as a speaker was no accident. When he was about twelve, and still in Baltimore, he "got hold of a book entitled *The Columbian Orator [The Columbian Orator: Containing a Variety of Original and Selected Pieces, Together with Rules which are Calculated to Improve Youth and Others in the Ornamental and Useful Art of Eloquence]*. Every opportunity I got I used to read this book . . . These were choice documents to me. I read them over and over again with unabated interest. They gave tongue to interesting thoughts of my own soul which had frequently flashed through my mind, and died away for want of utterance."

Among the *Columbian Orator's* guidelines was this: "It is not of so much moment what our compositions are, as how they are pronounced; since it is the manner of delivery by which the audience is moved." A good example of how he "pronounced" his speeches is the one delivered at Rochester in 1852: "The Meaning of July Fourth for the Negro," more generally known as "What to the Slave is the Fourth of July?" The speech is very long, even by nineteenth-century standards—only Lincoln seems to have known how to be brief, and that not often—but it was a technical masterpiece, using almost every rhetorical device in the book. For example, although since Nantucket he had been a professional public lecturer for the Anti-Slavery Society, he began with a humble apology for his lack of skill as a speaker: "He who could address this audience without a quailing sensation, has stronger nerves than I have. I do not remember ever to have appeared as a speaker before any assembly more shrinkingly, nor with greater distrust of my ability, than I do this day . . . The little experience I have had in addressing public meetings"—eleven years!—"avails me nothing on the present occasion." Perhaps sensing how insincere this might have sounded, he added: "Should I seem at ease, my appearance would much misrepresent me."

Next, he reminds his largely white audience of his most important credential: he is an escaped slave, and "you will not therefore be surprised if in what I have to say I evince no elaborate preparation, nor grace my speech with any high-sounding *exordium*"—Latin for the introduction to an oration. After a few more disclaimers he gets down to business: "This, for the purpose of this celebration, is the Fourth of July. It is the birth day of your National Independence, and your political freedom. This, to you, is what the Passover was to the emancipated people of God . . ." One can only imagine the subtly changing emphasis with which, during the lengthy summary of the Revolution that followed, Douglass used the words "you" and "your," rather than "we" and "our." At the same time, throughout the history lesson, he kept hinting that the cause of abolition, without once mentioning the word, was much the same as the cause of the Revolution—"to side with the right against the wrong, with the weak against the strong, and the oppressed against the oppressor! Here lies the merit, and the one which of all others seems unfashionable in our day. The cause of liberty may be stabbed by the men who glory in the deeds of your fathers!"

But let there be no misunderstanding: "Fellow Citizens, I am not wanting in respect for the fathers of this republic. The signers of the Declaration of Independence were brave men. They were great men too— great enough to give frame to a great age. It does not often happen to a nation to raise, at one time, such a number of truly great men. The point from which I am compelled to view them is not, certainly, the most favorable; and yet I cannot contemplate their great deeds with less than admiration. They were statesmen, patriots, and heroes, and for the good they did, and the principles they contended for, I will unite with you to honor their memory."

Having paid his unavoidable dues to the Founders, he moved on— "my business, if I have any here today, is with the present. The accepted time with God and His cause is the ever-living now." He also changed his tone. "Fellow-citizens, pardon me, allow me to ask, why am I called upon to speak here today? What have I, or those I represent to do with your national independence? Are the great principles of political freedom and natural justice, embodied in that Declaration of Independence, extended to us? . . . Such is not the state of the case . . . This Fourth July is yours, not mine. You may rejoice, I must mourn . . . Above your national, tumultuous joy, I hear the mournful wail of millions whose chains, heavy and grievous yesterday, are today rendered more intolerable by the jubilee shouts that reach them."

And so—"What, to the American slave, is your Fourth of July? I answer, a day that reveals to him, more than all other days in the year, the gross injustice and cruelty to which he is the constant victim. To him, your celebration is a sham; your boasted liberty, an unholy license; your national greatness, swelling vanity; your sounds of rejoicing are empty and heartless; your denunciation of tyrants, brass-fronted impudence; your shouts of liberty and equality, hollow mockery; your prayers and hymns, your sermons and thanksgivings, with all your religious parade and solemnity, are, to him, mere bombast, fraud, deception, impiety and hypocrisy—a thin veil to cover up crimes which would disgrace a nation of savages. There is not a nation on the earth guilty of practices more shocking and bloody than are the people of the United States, at this very hour."

There was a good deal more—indeed Douglass at this point was only halfway through: bitter sarcasm, harrowing descriptions of the internal slave trade ("in the solitude of my spirit I see clouds of dust raised on the highways of the South; I see the bleeding footsteps; I hear the doleful wail of fettered humanity on the way to the slave markets . . ."); denunciation of the recently-passed Fugitive Slave Act ("one of the grossest infringements of Christian Liberty, and if the churches and ministers of our country were not stupidly blind, or most wickedly indifferent, they, too, would so regard it . . ."); denial that the constitution enshrined slavery; and finally, a brighter note: "Allow me to say, in conclusion, notwithstanding the dark picture I have this day presented of the state of the nation, I do not despair of this country. There are forces in operation which must inevitably work the downfall of slavery. 'The arm of the Lord is not shortened,' and the doom of slavery is certain. I therefore leave off where I began, with hope."

His final words were a quotation from a poem, or at any rate a piece of verse, by William Lloyd Garrison ("*God speed the year of jubilee/ The wide world o'er!/ When from the galling chains set free,/ Th'oppressed shall vilely bend the knee,/ And wear the yoke of tyranny/ Like brutes no more!*") Given the popular taste of that time, this was not the anti-climax that it may seem now. It may also have served as a peace-offering to its author, for by the time he gave his July Fourth speech, Douglass, who had earlier called Garrison "the Moses raised up by God to deliver his modern Israel from bondage," was barely on speaking terms with him. This was in part due to Douglass' need to strike out on his own—moving to Rochester, founding his own paper, *The North Star*—as well differences in age, personality and policy. In particular, as he insisted in his Rochester speech, Douglass disagreed with the Garrisonian doctrine that slavery was "guaranteed and sanctioned by the Constitution of the United States." This, he said, was a "slander" on the Founders; indeed "there is no matter in respect to which the people of the North have allowed themselves to be so ruinously imposed upon as that of the pro-slavery character of the Constitution. In that instrument I hold that there is neither warrant, license, nor sanction of the hateful thing; but interpreted as it ought to be interpreted, the Constitution is a glorious liberty document." Douglass managed to come to this conclusion by insisting that the Declaration of Independence was an integral part of the constitution, in which case slavery could be fought by political action. Also, it must have been almost impossible for a man of such forceful spirit to espouse the meek Garrisonian doctrine of "moral suasion" and passive resistance.

Six weeks before Douglass gave his Fourth of July speech, this advertisement appeared in the *New York Independent*:

UNCLE TOM'S CABIN.
50,000 COPIES IN EIGHT WEEKS !

"A SALE unprecedented in the history of book-selling in America. On the 20th of March the first sale was made of the unparalleled book, and in *sixty days*, 50,000 copies, making

100,000 Volumes, have been sold.

"Editors of Newspapers, Magazines, and even the staid Quarterlies, have vied with each other in their eulogistic notices. The ordinary style of book notices has been laid aside, and instead of puffs of half a finger's length, the press has sent forth column after column—literally hundreds of columns—of stronger and heartier commendations than were ever bestowed upon one book; and with well-nigh one voice, it has been pronounced to be:

The Greatest Book of its Kind

ever issued from the American Press. In thrilling delineation of character, and power of description, it is without a rival; and will be read and re-read in every intelligent family in America, and produce an impression never yet made by any similar work.

"From a thousand notes we cull a line each from a few:

"We know of no publication which promises to be more effective in the service of a holy but perilous work than this." *Christian Examiner*. "A book over which 20,000 families are alternately crying and laughing." *Unitarian Magazine*. "The greatest work of its kind which has appeared in half a century." *Providence Mirror*. "These volumes will be read South as well as North, and find response in every honest heart." *Albany Spectator*. "Will be read by almost everybody." *Puritan Recorder*. "We welcome the work as amongst the most powerful agents that human genius has yet produced for the removal of the one fearful curse that rests upon our country." *Christian Register*. "We look upon the writing of this book as providential, and as the best missionary God has yet sent into the field." *Congregationalist*. (Not reviewed by these worthy publications were the immensely popular "Tom Shows," which quickly sprang up and added such features as banjo-playing minstrels and slavering bloodhounds pursuing Eliza as she crossed the ice-choked Ohio River.)

The following year Mrs. Stowe published *A Key to Uncle Tom's Cabin: Presenting the Original Facts and Documents upon which the Story is Founded*. She makes her purpose clear in her opening lines: "At different times, doubt has been expressed whether the representations of *Uncle Tom's Cabin* are a fair representation of slavery as it at present exists. This work, more, perhaps, than any other work of fiction that ever was written, has been a collection and arrangement of real incidents—of actions really performed, of words and expressions really uttered." As well as thoroughly researching her subject, Mrs. Stowe later claimed that she had had a co-author. This was none other than God himself, who had dictated the text which she then wrote down.

Reaction in the South was twofold. First, there were the "anti-Tom" novels, such as *Aunt Phillis's Cabin, or, Southern Life As It Is* by Mary H. Eastman. This included scenes that "would have softened the heart of the sternest hater of Southern institutions." For example: "It was just sundown, but the servants were all at home after their day's work, and they too were enjoying the pleasant evening time. Some were seated at the doors of their cabins, others lounging on the grass, all at ease and without care. Many of their comfortable cabins had been recently white-washed, and were adorned with little gardens in front; over the one nearest the house a multiflora rose was creeping in full bloom. Singularly musical voices were heard at intervals, singing snatches of songs, of a style in which the servants of the South especially delight . . ."

Then there were the reviews of *Uncle Tom's Cabin*, among them this one from the *Southern Literary Messenger,* written by George Holmes, a Virginia professor, at the invitation of the editor, John Thompson. "I would have the review as hot as hell fire," Thompson told him, "blasting and searing the reputation of the vile wretch in petticoats who could write such a volume . . ." Holmes was happy to oblige.

He began by adopting the pose of the chivalrous southern cavalier for whom womanhood—or at any rate upper-class white womanhood—was sacred. Thus it was "with peculiar sensations of both reluctance and repugnance" that he approached his task, since the work in question was "the effusion of one of that sex whose natural position entitles them to all forbearance and courtesy, and which, in all ordinary cases, should be shielded from even just severity by that protecting mantle which the name and thought of woman cast over even the erring and offending members of the sex." The next word had to be—and was—"But..." "But higher interests are involved; the rule that everyone bearing the name and appearance of a lady should receive the delicate gallantry and considerate tenderness which are due to a lady, is not absolutely without exception. If she deliberately steps beyond the hallowed precincts—the enchanted circle—which encompasses her as with the halo of divinity, she has wantonly forfeited her privilege of immunity... We cannot accord the termagant virago or the foul-mouthed hag the same deference that is rightfully due to the maiden purity of untainted innocence." Nevertheless, he would not "take the critical lash into our hands." Instead, he would try to forget that the author was a woman and would "concentrate our attention and our reprehension on her book."

Then he got to work. "*Uncle Tom's Cabin* is a fiction. It is a fiction not for the sake of more effectually communicating the truth, but for the purpose of more effectually disseminating a slander . . . Every fact is distorted, every incident discolored, in order to awaken rancorous hatred and malignant jealousies between the citizens of the same republic, the fellow countrymen whose interests and happiness are linked with the perpetuity of a common union, and with the prosperity of a common government."

Yes, of course abuses occurred under the slave system, but had there ever been a form of society without them? "In all periods of history...instances of misery and barbarity equal to any depicted in this atrocious fiction have been of constant recurrence, and whatever changes may hereafter take place, unless the nature of man be also changed, they must continually recur until the very end of time."

Another error in these "dangerous and dirty little volumes" was to ignore the fact that "what might be grievous misery to the white man, is none to the differently tempered black . . . The joys and sorrows of the slave are in harmony with his position, and are entirely dissimilar from what would make the happiness or misery of another class." In fact, the effect of slavery was not to increase but "to diminish the amount of individual misery in the servile classes; to mitigate and alleviate all the ordinary sorrows of life; to protect the slaves against want as well as against material and mental suffering; to prevent the separation and dispersion of families." Also, "the communities where it prevails exhibit the only existing instance of a modern civilized society in which the interests of the laborer and the employer of labor are absolutely identical." In conclusion, "the average condition of the slave at the South is infinitely superior, morally and materially, in all respects, to that of the laboring class under any other circumstances in any other part of the world."

Another high-minded lady who rallied to the cause was Fanny Wright. The nineteenth century was the great age of utopian communities and Fanny was just the right person to lead one, having a strong character, a magnetic presence, firmly-held progressive opinions (atheism, free love, birth control, racial equality), and plenty of money. She was also tall, handsome, a self-confident member of the Anglo-Scottish gentry, and a close friend—and reputed lover—of the Marquis de Lafayette, whom she accompanied on his triumphant return visit to this country in 1824. While here she also delivered lectures on her advanced ideas to packed theaters, holding the audiences spellbound (except for a few heckling rowdies up in the galleries, who had to be forcibly ejected).

While still a young girl living in Scotland, Fanny had convinced herself that America was "a country dedicated to freedom," that slavery—

"the most atrocious of all the sins"—had been forced upon it by English traders, and that most slaveholders wanted to free their slaves but did not know where to begin. Hence *A Plan for the Gradual Abolition of Slavery in the United States, Without Danger or Loss to the Citizens of the South*, published while touring the country with Lafayette. At the heart of the plan was an educational, self-supporting commune where, under the supervision of qualified whites, some fifty to a hundred slaves and their families would learn how to cope with the challenges of being free. During this "apprenticeship," which would last five years, the ex-slaves would continue to work, part of the money being used to compensate their former owners, part to support the commune. There would be no overseers or drivers, since the inmates would know that "their labor was for their personal redemption, the relief of the race, and the practical education of their children." To accelerate the improvement of the children, they would be separated from their parents and brought up by experts. There would be no religious services; instead there would be evening lectures by Fanny and her sister, Camilla. Interracial sex was authorized, provided it was consensual. Management would be in the hands of ten trustees, all of them white. Once this prototype had proved its success, thousands of others would spring up everywhere, and before long slavery would be no more.

The first step was to set up the commune, called Nashoba, which Fanny did in October, 1825, buying with her own money over a thousand acres of swampy woodland on the Wolf River, in Tennessee—a site recommended to her by Andrew Jackson who, a few years earlier, had driven out the Chickasaw Indians. (Nashoba is Chickasaw for wolf.) Next, since no one offered to donate his slaves, she had to buy ten of them, and their families, at an auction in Nashville, paying between $400 and $500 each. Clearing the land went slowly since the "apprentices," skeptical of their new owner's intentions, worked at the sluggish pace typical of slave labor everywhere. Raising buildings also went slowly, and the swampy surroundings proved to be so unhealthy that after living there for a few months Fanny fell sick. Though her enthusiasm remained high, it was decided that for the sake of her health she should spend some time in Italy. Her sister, Camilla, and another trustee called James Richardson, a Scotsman, would remain in charge.

On July 28, 1827, the day after Fanny landed at Le Havre, Benjamin Lundy's abolitionist paper, the *Genius of Universal Emancipation*, published what the editor, in his innocence, must have thought would be a puff piece about Nashoba. It was written by James Richardson, and included several entries from the log book he had been keeping. For example:

> "*May 6*. Agreed that if any of the slaves neglect their duty, and thus retard the object of the plan, we will exclude such slaves from the benefit of the plan, and will treat them according to the slave system, until it shall appear that their habits are changed for the better.

> "*May 20*. Camilla Wright informed [the slaves] that to-morrow the children Delila, Lucy, Julia and Alfred, will be taken altogether from under the management of their parents, and will be placed, until our school is organized, under the management of Mamselle Lolotte [a free black]; that all communication between the parents and children shall in future be prevented, except such as may take place by permission, and in the presence of the manager of the children.

> "*May 26*. Agreed that the slaves shall not be allowed to receive money, clothing, food, or indeed any thing whatever from any person . . . Agreed that the slaves shall not be permitted to eat elsewhere than at the public meals.

> "*June 1*. Isabel had laid a complaint against Redrick for coming during the night to her bedroom, uninvited, and endeavoring, without her consent, to take liberties with her person. Our views of the sexual relationship had been repeatedly given to the slaves; Camilla Wright again stated it, and informed the slaves that, as the conduct of Redrick, which he did not deny, was a gross infringement of that view, a repetition of such conduct ought to be punished by flogging.

> "*June 17*. James Richardson informed that last night Mamselle Josephine [daughter of Mamselle Lolotte] and he began to live together; and he took this occasion of repeating to them our views on color, and on the sexual relation." ("All colors are equal in rank," and sex was to be based on "the unconstrained and unrestrained choice of *both* parties.")

Although he did not include two other entries for the month of May—"Reprimanded Dilly for having given bread and meat to one of her own children," and "Two women slaves tied up and flogged by James Richardson in presence of Camilla and the slaves. Two dozen and one dozen on the bare back with a cowskin"—Richardson could hardly have done more damage to Nashoba had he deliberately set out to sabotage it. As one outraged subscriber wrote to the editor of the *Genius*, such "indecent" and "libidinous" activities were "repugnant to the safe and honest maxims of Christian life . . . Who can read without disgust that an accomplished young English woman apparently concurs in giving a sanction to the formation of illicit sexual connections without the obligations of marriage?" Nashoba was nothing but "one great brothel, disgraceful to its institutors, and most reprehensible." (As tactless as ever, when rebutting this charge, Richardson wrote to the editor that "I have seen a brothel, and I never knew a place so unlike it as Nashoba . . .")

On her return from Italy, Fanny tried to re-establish her interracial utopia, but as an instrument for ending slavery it was finished. To find a home for the former slaves she personally escorted them to Haiti, where President Boyer, probably as dazzled by her as had been Lafayette and Andrew Jackson, promised to take good care of them. On her return to this country she resumed her career as a public speaker, adored by some—"a brilliant woman," wrote Walt Whitman, "who was never satisfied unless she was busy doing good—public good, private good"; but to Catharine Beecher (Harriet Stowe's sister), "intolerably offensive and disgusting." And to others "the petticoated politician" or "the Red Harlot of Infidelity."

A powerful but often muted argument against slavery was the sexual exploitation of black women by their white masters. Though this was often talked about quite freely in private, social conventions demanded that public discussion be rare and unspecific. However, in 1852, Julia Tyler of Virginia, wife of President John Tyler, published a defense of slavery in which she asserted, among other things, that slaves were "sold only under very peculiar circumstances." In response, Harriet Jacobs, who before escaping to freedom had spent many years in Edenton, N. C., as a slave in the household of Dr. Norcom, wrote this letter giving an example of what "very peculiar circumstances" really meant: "My mother was held as property by a maiden lady. When she married, my younger sister was in her fourteenth year . . . as gentle as she was beautiful . . . innocent and guileless . . . the light of our desolate hearth! But oh, my heart bleeds to tell you of the misery and degradation she was forced to suffer in slavery. The monster who owned her had no humanity in his soul and every stratagem was used to seduce my sister. Mortified and tormented beyond endurance, this child came and threw herself on her mother's bosom . . . with bitter tears she told her troubles, and entreated her mother to save her. And oh, Christian mothers! you that have daughters of your own, can you think of your sable sisters without offering a prayer to that God who created all in their behalf? My poor mother . . . sought her master, entreating him to spare her child. Nothing could exceed his rage at this, what he called impertinence. My mother was dragged to jail," where she was put up for sale and "my sister was told that she must yield, or never expect to see her mother again. There were three younger children; on no other condition could she be restored to them . . . That child gave herself up to her master's bidding, to save one that was dearer to her than life itself. Can you, Christian, find it in your heart to despise her?"

And there was more: "At fifteen, my sister held to her bosom an innocent offspring of her guilt and misery. In this way she dragged a miserable existence of two years, between the fires of her mistress's jealousy and her master's brutal passion. At seventeen she gave birth to another helpless infant . . ." At twenty-one "sorrow and suffering had made its ravages upon her—she was less the object to be desired by the fiend who had crushed her to the earth." Also, "as her children grew, they bore too strong a resemblance to him who desired to give them no other inheritance save Chains and Handcuffs." And so, "in the dead hour of the night, when this young, deserted mother lay with her little ones clinging around her," they were seized and carried off, "and when the sun rose on God's beautiful earth, that heart-broken mother was far on her way to the capital of Virginia," there to be sold. "And where she now is God only knows."

There was yet another reason why that mother and her children were sold. This was "to make room for another sister, who was now the age of that mother when she entered the family"—i.e. fourteen. "And such are the 'peculiar circumstances' of American Slavery—of all the evils in God's sight, the most to be abhorred."

Thanks to Article 1, Section 2, of the Constitution, which dealt with the apportionment of taxes and representatives, what was then called an enumeration but is now known as a census has been held—with a few exceptions—every ten years, starting in 1790. As with many another government program, once started it did not stop growing, and by 1850 the scope of inquiry had expanded from a simple head count to an elaborate compilation of statistics about such matters as property values, manufacturing, agriculture, crime, pauperism and mortality rates. Once published, the results were seized upon by opposing polemicists to prove their arguments conclusively, Thornton Stringfellow bringing out *Statistical Views in Favor of Slavery* (mentioned in the previous chapter) in 1856, and Hinton Rowan Helper *The Impending Crisis of the South* in 1857.

Helper began by making it clear that he was not one of those Northern fanatics but "as proud as any Southerner—the South being my birthplace and my home, and my ancestry having resided there for more than a century." Nor was it "part of my purpose to cast unmerited opprobrium on slaveholders, or to display any special friendliness or sympathy for the blacks. I have considered my subject more particularly with reference to its economic aspects as regards the whites—not with reference, except in a very slight degree, to its humanitarian or religious aspects." Northern writers, including "Yankee wives," [e.g. Mrs. Stowe], had written about these aspects of slavery, often "in the form of novels . . . Against this I have nothing to say; it is all well enough for women to give the fictions of slavery; men should give the facts." Using information from past censuses, he would "take a survey of the relative position and importance of the several states, and when, of two sections of the country starting under the same auspices, and with equal natural advantages, we find the one rising to a degree of almost unexampled power and eminence, and the other sinking into a state of comparative imbecility and obscurity, it is our determination to trace out the causes which have led to the elevation of the former, and the depression of the latter." The results, he forewarned, could not but be painful to "a true-hearted Southerner."

Getting down to facts and figures: "In 1790, when the first census was taken, New York contained 340,120 inhabitants; at the same time the population of Virginia was 748,308, being more than twice the number of New York. Just sixty years afterward, as we learn from the census of 1850, New York had a population of 3,097,394; while that of Virginia was only 1,421,661, being less than half the number of New York! In 1791 the exports of New York amounted to $2,505,465; the exports of Virginia amounted to $3,130,865. In 1852 the exports of New York amounted to $87,484,456; the exports of Virginia during the same year amounted to only $2,724,657."

Next he compared Massachusetts and North Carolina, and here the story was much the same: "In 1790, Massachusetts contained 378,717 inhabitants; in the same year North Carolina contained 393,751; in 1850 the population of Massachusetts was 994,514, all freemen; while that of North Carolina was only 869,039, of whom 288,548 were slaves.

"In 1850, the products of manufacture, mining and the mechanic arts in Massachusetts amounted to $151,137,145; those of North Carolina to only $9,111,245. In 1850, the cash value of all the farms, farming implements and machinery in Massachusetts was $112,285,931; the value of the same in North Carolina was only $71,823,298."

A comparison between Pennsylvania and South Carolina produced much the same results. "In Pennsylvania, in 1850, the annual income of public schools amounted to $1,348,249; the same in South Carolina, in the same year, amounted to only $200,600; in the former state there were 393 libraries other than private, in the latter only 26; in Pennsylvania 310 newspapers and periodicals were published, circulating 84,898,672 copies annually; in South Carolina only 46 newspapers and periodicals were published, circulating but 7,145,930 copies per annum."

As a result of these disparities "we are compelled to go to the North for almost every article of utility and adornment, from matches, shoepegs and paintings up to cotton mills, steamships and statuary . . . We want Bibles, brooms, buckets and books, and we go to the North; we want pens, ink, paper, wafers and envelopes, and we go to the North; we want shoes, hats, handkerchiefs, umbrellas and pocket knives, and we go to the North; we want toys, primers, school books, fashionable apparel, machinery, medicines, tombstones, and a thousand other things, and we go to the North for them all. Instead of keeping our money in circulation at home, by patronizing our own mechanics, manufacturers and laborers, we send it all away to the North, and there it remains; it never falls into our hands again."

And what caused this "unmanly dependence," this "contemptible insignificance," this "galling poverty and ignorance?" The answer lay in one word, "the most hateful and horrible word that was ever incorporated into the vocabulary of human economy—*Slavery!*"

Although he did mention "the sin and shame" of slavery, calling it "a great moral evil," Helper's main objection was "that slavery, and nothing but slavery, has retarded the progress and prosperity of our portion of the Union; made us tributary to the North, and reduced us to the humiliating condition of mere provincial subjects in fact, though not in name. We believe, moreover, that every patriotic Southerner thus convinced will feel it a duty he owes to himself, to his country, and to his God, to become a thorough, inflexible, practical abolitionist."

Next, Helper set out "to open the eyes of the non-slaveholders of the South to the system of deception that has so long been practiced upon them" by the selfish manipulations of the planter aristocracy—these "august knights of the whip and the lash," these "haughty cavaliers of shackles and handcuffs." Although "the white non-slaveholders of the South are in the majority, as five to one, they have never yet had any part or lot in framing the laws under which they live. There is no legislation except for the benefit of slavery and slaveholders." Thanks to the "demagogical manoeuverings of the oligarchy," poor whites were led to believe that "slavery is the very bulwark of our liberties, and the foundation of American independence." But in truth they were reduced to a state whose "freedom is merely nominal, and whose unparalleled illiteracy and degradation is purposely and fiendishly perpetuated. How little the 'poor white trash', the great majority of the southern people, know of the real condition of the country is, indeed, sadly astonishing." In sum: "Never were the poorer classes of a people, and those classes so largely in the majority, and all inhabiting the same country, so basely duped, so adroitly swindled, or so damnably outraged."

Another point: "slavery is the parent of ignorance, and ignorance begets a whole brood of follies and of vices . . . A free press is an institution almost unknown at the South. Free speech is considered as treason against slavery; and when people dare neither speak nor print their thoughts, free thought itself is well nigh extinguished. All that can be said in defense of human bondage may be spoken freely; but question either its morality or its policy, and the terrors of lynch law are at once invoked to put down the pestilent heresy . . . Slavery tolerates no freedom of the press—no freedom of speech—no freedom of opinion . . . Where free thought is treason, the masses will not long take the trouble of thinking at all."

Well reviewed in the North, *The Impending Crisis* was reviled in the South. In the Senate, Asa Biggs of North Carolina denounced Helper as "dishonest, degraded and disgraced . . . an apostate son catering to a diseased appetite at the North." In response, Helper armed himself with a revolver and a bowie knife—he was, after all, and as he kept insisting, a true son of the South—and rushed to the Capitol to avenge himself. Not finding Senator Biggs, he instead attacked a Congressman who he believed had also slandered him, but was pulled off before he could do serious harm. Meanwhile his book sold very nicely, some fourteen thousand copies in the first year alone, and ten times that number in a special abbreviated edition; several hundred copies were also burned at public bonfires throughout the South.

Another way to end slavery was to subvert its economic underpinnings—depose King Cotton, and those he held in bondage would be freed. Cotton itself could not of course be done away with, but what if it were raised in some other part of the world, and under different conditions? This possibility was the subject of an 1839 letter from Wendell Phillips to the English radical, George Thompson. "I am rejoiced to hear of your new movement in regard to India," he wrote. "It seals the fate of the slave system in America. The industry of the pagan [i.e. Hindus and Muslims] shall yet wring from Christian hands the prey they would not yield to the commands of conscience or the claims of religion."

Known as "Abolition's Golden Trumpet" for his skill as an orator, Phillips had once been an exemplar of the Boston brahmin—a Mayflower descendant and Harvard-educated lawyer, he was wealthy, dignified and aloof—until, at the age of twenty-four, after witnessing a mob of respectable Bostonians trying to lynch William Lloyd Garrison, he underwent a sudden conversion to radical abolitionism. While he was about it, he also advocated disunion, temperance, universal suffrage, including votes for women, animal magnetism and phrenology. Alarmed at such deviant behavior, his family tried to restrain him but failed, and so now here he was in London in 1840 attending the world's first anti-slavery convention, held under the patronage of Queen Victoria's high-minded Prince Consort, "Albert the Good." While there, Phillips was invited to address the mildly progressive British India Society, and chose for his topic the scheme that would seal the fate of slavery in America.

Briefly, the plan was to grow cotton in India, then largely run by the East India Company, and grow it in such vast quantities as to put slave-grown American cotton out of business. "If it is a fact that there are 24,000,000 acres within the reach of the Ganges, upon which cotton can be grown, now lying waste; if it is true that there are 54,000,000 men anxious for labor, and that their services can be had for a penny or two pence a day; if they can bring their cotton to Liverpool at four pence per pound—how can slavery stand against it?" Nor was it merely a matter of money. "It is one of the most immutable of truths, that the moment a free hand touches an article, that moment it falls from the hand of the slave . . . No article can be grown and manufactured at the same time by both free and slave labor. Slavery can only be maintained by monopoly; the moment she comes into competition with free labor, she dies. Cotton is the corner-stone of slavery in America; remove it, and slavery receives its mortal blow. [Cries of "Hear! Hear!" from the audience.] You may think it strange for an American to speak thus of a system that is to make bankrupt one half of his country, and paralyze the other; but though I love my country, I love my countrymen more, and these countrymen are the colored men of America. [Cheers.] For their sakes I say, welcome the bolt that smites our commerce to the dust, if with it, by the blessing of God, it will strike off the fetters of the slave! [Cheers.]"

One wonders: was Phillips listening to what he was saying? Were there really 24,000,000 acres lying fallow on the banks of the Ganges, and 54,000,000 unemployed Indians available for hire—and at a wage of a penny or two a day? Since when had it been true that no article could be grown or made at the same time by free and slave labor? And did he really love "the colored men of America" more than he loved his country?

At any rate, news of the Indian cotton-growing scheme caused some real anxiety in the South. "Little, perhaps, thought those young planters and overseers, when they consented to go to India, that they were to be used as tools in the unholy hands of the abolitionists!" wrote the *Natchez*

Free Trader about some Americans who had recently been recruited by the East India Company. "England is arraying its vast moral, commercial, and political power against us" with "the express purpose of rendering the labor of three millions of black slaves in America unproductive and of no value. All India will, in a year or two, teem like a vast beehive with the cotton enterprise, cheered on by the fratricide abolitionists and mock philanthropists of the Northern States . . ."

But the alarm, though real, was not that serious. Cotton had been grown in India since prehistoric times, and crops would greatly increase during the second half of the nineteenth century, but in the meantime the quantity was nowhere near enough to supply the Lancashire mills. Also, it was slow and expensive to transport—unlike American cotton, which could easily be carried in bales to the landing stage of some nearby river, Indian cotton had to be loaded on to bullock carts for the long journey to some seaport and then shipped to England via the Cape of Good Hope. This would change when railroads had been built and the Suez Canal dug, but neither happened until after the Civil War.

The English also tried to encourage cotton-growing in West Africa, which would have had the added benefit of helping to suppress the slave trade, now illegal but still active: local rulers, realizing that more money was to be made by putting their people to work raising cotton, would stop selling them. But it took a while for that scheme to get going. In 1858, on the eve of the Civil War, cotton exports from West Africa amounted to some two thousand bales, while exports from America were well over three million.

Angelina Grimké, the renegade member of Charleston's upper class who with her husband Theodore Weld edited *American Slavery As It Is*, was also the author of *An Appeal to the Christian Women of the South*, published in 1836. As she told her readers, what prompted her to write was her "deep and tender interest in your present and eternal welfare"—eternal because slavery was a sin, and its punishment was everlasting damnation. She acknowledged that most of her readers would at first think that "I had been most strangely deceived," but asked them "for the sake of former confidence and former friendship, to read the following pages in the spirit of calm investigation and fervent prayer."

Much of her argument was based on the Bible, "my ultimate appeal in all matters of faith and practice, and it is to this test I am anxious to bring the subject at issue between us. Let us then begin with Adam . . ." After proving—which was not difficult—that there had been no slavery in the Garden of Eden, she dealt with "the curse pronounced upon Canaan, by which his posterity was consigned to servitude." But this was only a prophecy, and "prophecy does not tell us what ought to be, but what actually does take place . . . Prophecy has often been urged as an excuse for slavery, but be not deceived, the fulfillment of prophecy will not cover one sin in the awful day of account."

Next to be refuted was the argument that "the patriarchs held slaves, and therefore slavery is right. Do you really believe that patriarchal servitude was like American slavery? Can you believe it? If so, read the history of these primitive fathers of the church, and be undeceived. Look at Abraham, though so great a man, going to the herd himself and fetching a calf from thence and serving it up with his own hands, for the entertainment of his guests. Look at Sarah, that princess as her name signifies, baking cakes upon the hearth. If the servants they had were like Southern slaves, would they have performed such comparatively menial offices for themselves?"

Numerous chapters and verses were then quoted to prove that servitude among the ancient Israelites was limited in duration, restrained by numerous laws, and not inheritable—"in studying the subject I have been struck with wonder and admiration at perceiving how carefully the servant was guarded from violence, injustice and wrong." For example, "servants were set free at the death of their masters and did not descend to their heirs"; every fiftieth year was "a year of Jubilee, when all servants were set at liberty"; and "to protect servants from violence, it was ordained that if a master struck out the tooth or destroyed the eye of a servant, that servant immediately became free." And so, "where then, I would ask, is the warrant, the justification, or the palliation of American slavery from Hebrew servitude? How many of the southern slaves would now be in bondage according to the laws of Moses? Not one!"

Turning to the New Testament, "some have even said that Jesus Christ did not condemn slavery." But in fact he did. "Let us examine some of his precepts. 'Whatsoever ye would that men should do to you, do ye even so to them.' Let every slaveholder apply these queries to his own heart: Am I willing to be a slave—am I willing to see my mother a slave, or my father, my sister or my brother? If not, then in holding others as slaves, I am doing what I would not wish to be done to me or any relative I have; and thus have I broken this Golden Rule which was given to me to walk by."

After establishing that there was no religious justification for slavery, Angelina asked: "But perhaps you will be ready to query, why appeal to *women* on this subject? *We* do not make the laws which perpetuate slavery. No legislative power is vested in us. We can do nothing to overthrow the system, even if we wished to do so. To this I reply, I know you do not make the laws, but I also know that you are the wives and mothers, the sisters and daughters of those who do; and if you really suppose you can do nothing to overthrow slavery, you are greatly mistaken. You can do much in every way: four things I will name. 1st. You can read on this subject. 2nd. You can pray over this subject. 3rd. You can speak on this subject. 4th. You can act on this subject."

To elaborate:

1. "Search the Scriptures daily, whether the things I have told you are true. Other books and papers might be a great help to you in this investigation, but they are not necessary, and it is hardly probable that your Committees of Vigilance will allow you to have any other."

2. "Pray also for that poor slave, that he may be kept patient and submissive under his hard lot, until God is pleased to open the door of freedom to him without violence or bloodshed. Pray too for the master that his heart may be softened."

Numbers three and four—speaking and acting on the subject—would be harder. "You will perhaps say, such a course of conduct would inevitably expose us to great suffering. Yes! My Christian friends, I believe it would, but this will not excuse you or anyone else for the neglect of duty. If Prophets and Apostles, Martyrs and Reformers had not been willing to suffer for truth's sake, where would the world have been now?"

Her readers should also take courage from the example of their sisters in the North who "have engaged in this work from a sense of religious duty, and nothing will ever induce them to take their hands from it until it is fully accomplished. They feel no hostility to you, no bitterness or wrath; they rather sympathize in your trials and difficulties; but they well know that the first thing to be done to help you is to pour in the light of truth on your minds, to urge you to reflect on, and pray over the subject. This is all they can do for you. You must work out your own deliverance with fear and trembling, and with the direction and blessing of God, you can do it . . . It is manifest to every reflecting mind that slavery must be abolished; the era in which we live, and the light which is overspreading the whole world on this subject, clearly show that the time cannot be distant when it will be done. Now, there are only two ways in which it can be effected: by moral power or physical force, and it is for you to choose which of these you prefer."

As she drew near the end of her nonfiction work, *A Key to Uncle Tom's Cabin*, Harriet Beecher Stowe also called for self-sacrifice. "Brethren in the South, there are many of you who are truly convinced that slavery is a sin, a tremendous wrong; but, if you confess your sentiments, and endeavor to propagate your opinions, you think that persecution, affliction, and even death await you. How can we ask you, then, to come forward? *We* do not ask it. Ourselves weak, irresolute and worldly, shall we ask you to do what perhaps we ourselves should not dare? But we will beseech Him to speak to you, who dared and endured more than this for your sake, and who can strengthen you to dare and endure for His. He can raise you above all temporary and worldly considerations. He can inspire you with that love to himself which will make you willing to leave father and mother, and wife and child, yea, to give up life itself, for His sake . . ."

In 1854, to please the South and the railroad interests, Congress passed the Kansas-Nebraska Act, another long step on the road to war. Under the seemingly democratic principle of "popular sovereignty," the act left it up to the settlers themselves to decide whether the future states to be formed out of the territory should be slave or free. Almost immediately, large numbers of pro-slavery "border ruffians" accepted this invitation to mayhem and crossed over from Missouri, sometimes staying just long enough to vote—in one election 6000 votes were cast out of a qualified electorate of 1500—sometimes settling down in new homes from which they could intimidate the free-state settlers, many of whom had been sponsored by the New England Emigrant Aid Company. The resulting conflict, dubbed

"Bleeding Kansas" by Horace Greeley of the *New-York Tribune*, was seen by many Northerners as nothing less than a clash between good and evil. As *The Gun and the Gospel,* by the Rev. H. D. Fisher, put it, "Robbery, murder and arson marked the march of . . . the border ruffians who invaded Kansas, while free-state men had come as came the Pilgrims from across the ocean, with wives and children, Bibles and hymn-books, school books and teachers—to establish a kind of Christian civilization superior to any yet developed on the American continent. It was with this last-named band that John Brown had become identified with all the zeal and enthusiasm of his rugged and devout nature. Struggling against mighty odds, this purposeful people had written on high their legend, 'Resistance to tyranny is obedience to God!'"

Before long Kansas had competing constitutions and capitals, Lecompton for the pro-slavery faction, and Lawrence for the free-staters. Two newspapers, the *Kansas Free State* and the *Herald of Freedom*, were published in Lawrence, and the New England Emigrant Aid Company had its headquarters there in the Free State Hotel. On May 21, 1856—one day before Preston Brooks viciously beat Charles Sumner in the chamber of the U. S. Senate—a pro-slavery sheriff's posse attacked the town, beginning with a raid on the Free State Hotel's wine cellar. After disposing of the cellar's contents, they burned down the hotel, smashed up the newspaper presses and threw the type into the river, burned down two houses, had one of their men killed by falling masonry; and then departed. This, to the anti-slavery people, at once became known as the "Sack of Lawrence," and was spoken of as if the whole town had been reduced to smoldering rubble. Still, it was a serious matter and, as Captain Brown put it, "something must be done to show these barbarians that we too have rights." Many years later, James Townsley, at that time a young man who had recently settled at Pottawatomie, not far from Lawrence, told an interviewer how "something" was indeed done.

"I joined the Pottawatomie Rifle Company at its re-organization in May, 1856." When news came of the impending attack on Lawrence, "the company was hastily called together, and a forced march to aid in its defense immediately determined upon." But before they could arrive, the town had been attacked, so they halted at Ottawa Creek, where "we remained in camp undecided over night, and until noon the next day. About this time, Owen Brown, and a little later old John Brown himself, came to me and said information had just been received that trouble was expected on the Pottawatomie. The old man asked me if I would go with my team and take him and his boys down there, so that they could watch what was going on. I replied that I would do so, my reason being that my family was then living on the Pottawatomie, in Anderson County. Making ready for the trip as quickly as possible, we started about two o'clock in the afternoon. The party consisted of old John Brown and four of his sons—Frederick, Oliver, Owen and Watson—Henry Thompson and his son-in-law, Mr. Winer, and myself. Winer rode a pony; all the rest rode in the wagon with me. We camped that night between two deep ravines about one mile above Dutch Henry's crossing.

"After supper, John Brown first revealed to me the purpose of the expedition. He said it was to sweep the Pottawatomie of all pro-slavery men living on it. To this end he desired me to guide the company some five or six miles up to the forks of the creek, into the neighborhood where I lived, and point out to him on the way up the residences of all the pro-slavery men, so that on the way down he might carry out his designs. Horrified at his purpose, I positively refused to comply with his request, saying that I could not take men out of their beds and kill them in that way. Brown said, 'Why don't you fight your enemies?' To which I replied, 'I have no enemies I can kill in that way.' Failing to prevail upon me, he decided to postpone the expedition until the following night when they would go, as the old man himself said, where they knew pro-slavery men to be. I then proposed to him that he take his things out of my wagon and allow me to go home; to which he replied that 'I could not go, that I must stay with them; there was no other way of getting along.' We remained in camp that night and all the next day. During the morning of this day, the 24th, I tried to dissuade him and his boys from carrying out the expedition, and to this end talked a great deal. Brown said it was necessary to 'strike terror into the hearts of the pro-slavery party,' and taking out his revolver, said to me, 'Shut up! You are trying to discourage my boys. Dead men tell no tales.' From the last remark, I inferred that I must henceforth keep still or suffer the consequences.

"Some time after dark we were ordered to march, and went northward, crossing Mosquito Creek above the residence of the Doyles. Soon after crossing the creek, one of the party knocked at the door of a cabin, but received no reply. I do not know whose cabin it was. We next came to the residence of the Doyles. John Brown, three of his sons and son-in-law went to the door, leaving Frederick Brown, Winer, and myself a short distance away.

"The old man Doyle and his sons were ordered to come out. This order they did not immediately obey, the old man being heard instead to call for his gun. At this moment, Henry Thompson threw into the house some rolls or balls of hay in which during the day wet gunpowder had been mixed, setting fire to them as he threw them in. This stratagem had the desired effect. The old man and his sons came out, and were marched one quarter of a mile in the road toward Dutch Henry's crossing, where a halt was made. Here old John Brown drew his revolver and shot old man Doyle in the forehead, killing him instantly; and Brown's two youngest sons immediately fell upon the younger Doyles with their short two-edged swords. One of the young Doyles was quickly dispatched; the other, attempting to escape, was pursued a short distance and cut down also. We then went down Mosquito Creek, to the house of Allen Wilkinson. Here, as at the Doyle residence, old John Brown, three sons and son-in-law went to the door and ordered Wilkinson out, leaving Frederick Brown, Winer and myself in the road a little distance east of the house. Wilkinson was marched a short distance south and killed by one of the young Browns with his short sword, after which his body was dragged to one side and left lying by the side of the road.

"We then crossed the Pottawatomie and went to Dutch Henry's house. Here, as at the other two houses, Frederick Brown, Winer and myself were left outside a short distance from the door, while old man Brown, three sons and son-in-law went into the house and brought out one or two persons with them. After talking with them some time they took them back into the house, and brought out William Sherman, Dutch Henry's brother, and marched him down into Pottawatomie Creek, where John Brown's two youngest sons slew him with their short swords, as in the former instances, and left his body lying in the creek.

Unlike Garrison, John Brown believed in deeds rather than words, as when killing "border ruffians" during the Pottawatomie Massacre of 1856 or raiding Harper's Ferry three years later. In his own opinion, and that of many others, his death by hanging made him a martyr— as Ralph Waldo Emerson put it, his execution made "the gallows glorious like the Cross."

"The killing was done with swords in order to avoid alarming the neighborhood by the discharge of fire-arms. Soon after midnight we went back to where my team and the other things had been left, and remained there in camp until the next afternoon. Just before daylight, Owen Brown came to me and said, 'There shall be no more such work as that.'

"I did not then approve of the killing of those men, but Brown said it must be done for the protection of the Free-state settlers . . . I told him I was willing to go to Lecompton and attack the leaders, or to fight the enemy anywhere in open field, but that I could not kill men in that way. The deeds of that night are indelibly stamped upon my memory.

"In after years my opinion changed as to the wisdom of the massacre. I became, and am, satisfied that it resulted in the good to the Free-state cause, and was especially beneficial to the Free-state settlers on Pottawatomie Creek. The pro-slavery men were dreadfully terrified, and large numbers of them soon left the Territory."

As for John Brown, his belief that his actions were justified never wavered. "Time and the honest verdict of posterity will approve of every act of mine," he said, while waiting to be hanged after Harper's Ferry.

Meanwhile, back in the East, lawlessness was also becoming more common. In Boston there had been a great—but not complete—change in public opinion since the well-dressed mob had tried to lynch William Lloyd Garrison; now the violence was often exercised on behalf of the fugitive slave. This happened on three notable occasions.

First, there was the case of Shadrach Minkins. Although for a brief period he was one of the best-known men in America, very little is known about him. He was born a slave in Norfolk, Virginia, but whether his last name was Minkins or Jenkins or Wilkins remains uncertain. Thanks to an advertisement in the Norfolk *American Beacon*, we know that he was sold at public auction on July 23, 1849, to pay the debts of his owner; we also know that he escaped the following year, perhaps by bribing the captain of a ship, or perhaps by stowing away.

Having arrived in Boston, he was hired as a waiter at Taft's Cornhill Coffee House, an elegant establishment in the center of town, and it was there that in February, 1851, he was arrested on a warrant issued under the recently-passed Fugitive Slave Law. This was the first time that the law was about to be enforced in Boston, whose bustling black community included several hundred fugitive slaves. Hitherto, thanks to the state's personal freedom laws, they had felt fairly secure; but now, if Shadrach could be seized under the new law, so could other fugitives. And those blacks who had always been free were not inclined to sit back and do nothing while one their neighbors was hauled off. So, in a very short time, a large and almost entirely black crowd gathered at the Court House to which Shadrach had been taken.

Many years later, the radical abolitionist Thomas Wentworth Higginson wrote in his memoirs of the "skill and daring" of "a colored man of great energy and character"—probably Lewis Hayden, a leader in the black community—who worked nearby and "strolled into the Court House. Many colored men were at the door and had been excluded; but he, being known and trusted, was admitted, and the others, making a rush, followed in behind him with a hubbub of joking and laughter. There were but a few constables on duty, and it suddenly struck this leader, as he and his followers passed near the man under arrest, that they might as well keep on and pass out the other door, taking among them the man under arrest, who was not handcuffed. After a moment's beckoning the prisoner saw his opportunity, fell in with the jubilant procession, and amid continued uproar was got outside the Court House, when the crowd scattered in all directions."

Richard Henry Dana, author of *Two Years Before the Mast* and now a lawyer preparing to work on Shadrach's behalf, was in his office nearby when "we heard a shout from the Court House, continued into a yell of triumph, & in an instant after, down the steps came two huge Negroes, bearing the prisoner between them, with his clothes half torn off, & so stupefied by the sudden rescue and the violence of his dragging off, that he sat almost down, & I thought had fainted; but the men seized him, & being powerful fellows, hurried him through the Square into Court St., where he found the use of his feet, & and they went off toward Cambridge, like a black squall, the crowd driving along with them & cheering as they went. It was all done in an instant, too quick to be believed, & so successful was it that not only was no Negro arrested, but no attempt was made at pursuit."

From other sources we know that Shadrach was put into a cab, hurried out of town, passed on from one sympathizer to another until—like several thousand others fugitives—he reached safety in Canada. There he settled for the rest of his life, working first in a restaurant in Montreal and then as a barber, marrying an Irish girl with whom he had four children, and returning, probably with relief, to the obscurity from which he had so dramatically emerged.

In the meantime, back in the United States, there was a great deal of outrage. Henry Clay, one of the architects of the Compromise of 1850, was particularly angry that the rescue had been carried out "by Negroes; by African descendants; by people who possess no part, as I contend, in our political system." Daniel Webster, another architect of the Compromise, which he hoped would carry him into the White House at the next election, declared that Shadrach's rescue was nothing less than "an act of treason . . . levying war against the Union." President Fillmore issued a proclamation in which, among other things, he said, "I do especially direct that prosecutions be commenced against all persons who have made themselves aides or abettors in this flagitious offense." The conservative, pro-Compromise Boston papers—the so-called "Cotton Press"—chimed in. "One of the most lawless and atrocious acts that ever blackened the character of any community," wrote the *Boston Daily Times*, which also deplored "the predominancy of Negrodom in the Athens of America." As for the Southern press, a fairly typical example was the opinion of the *Savannah Republican* that "The city of Boston is a black speck on the map, disgraced by the lowest, the meanest, the BLACKEST kind of NULLIFICATION!!" Several of those who had taken part in the rescue were arrested and put on trial, but the evidence against them was so weak and the prosecution so incompetent that all the cases were dismissed.

The Shadrach case made southern owners all the more determined to assert their rights in the heartland of abolitionism. Their chance came a few months later when a youth named Thomas Sims, who had escaped from Savannah, was positively identified, arrested, and taken to the same Court House where Shadrach had been held. His lawyers did their best to slow down the peremptory legal proceedings. For example, was Sims really Sims? But of this there could be no doubt, one of the witnesses who had come up from Georgia testifying that he had "known the prisoner for the last ten months in Savannah, under the name of Thomas Sims; that he worked as a bricklayer on the same scaffolding with him in August and September last; that he once asked the prisoner if he was a slave, and he replied that he was, and that he belonged to James Potter, a rice planter, who lives ten or twelve miles from Savannah, and that he had to pay his wages to Mr. Potter monthly, to the amount of about $10 a month.

> "The other witness, Bacon, is the agent of Mr. Potter, who came here to make the arrest. He testifies that he has known the prisoner as the property of Mr. Potter for fifteen years, that he last saw him in Savannah on the 22nd of February; that during the last ten years the prisoner has generally lived with his mother, in Savannah, accounting to Mr. Potter for his wages; that he knew the prisoner did so account for his wages from being present both when they were paid to Mr. Potter by

the mother and by the prisoner, and from repeatedly seeing his mother go after him for his wages, and that there is not a shadow of doubt with reference to his identity. He [Bacon] also testifies that the last thing the mother said to him on the eve of his departure, was to beg him, whether her son was in a free state or a slave state, for God's sake to bring him back again."

Meanwhile, the Boston Vigilance Committee, formed in the wake of the Shadrach affair and composed largely of well-intentioned whites, met to consult. According to Thomas Wentworth Higginson, who prided himself on being a man of action, it was "impossible to conceive a set of men, personally admirable, yet less fitted on the whole than this committee to undertake any positive action in the direction of forcible resistance to authorities. In the first place, half of them were non-resistants, as was their great leader, Garrison, who stood composedly at his desk preparing his next week's editorial . . ." Black members were demoralized and weakened by the new Fugitive Slave Law—in the first month after its passage an estimated two thousand blacks had left the North for Canada. One of their leaders, Lewis Hayden, told Higginson that "we do not wish anyone to know how really weak we are. Practically, there are no colored men in Boston; the Shadrach prosecutions have scattered them all. What is to be done must be done without them."

"The next day showed that absolutely nothing could be accomplished in the court-room. There were one or two hundred armed policemen in and around the Court-house. Six men were at the door of the court-room. The prisoner, a slender boy of seventeen, sat with two strong men on either side and five men in the seat behind him, while none but his counsel could approach in front." When not in court, Sims was held a prisoner on the third floor of the Court-house building. "It was evident that if anything was done, it must be done by a very few."

A plan was soon made. "The room where Sims was confined, being safe by reason of its height from the ground, had no gratings at the windows. The colored clergyman of Boston, Mr. Grimes, who alone had the opportunity to visit Sims, agreed to arrange with him that at a specified hour that evening he should go to a certain window, as if for air, and should spring out on mattresses which we were to bring from a lawyer's office across the way; we also providing a carriage in which to place him.

All was arranged—the message sent, the mattresses ready, the carriage engaged as if for an ordinary purpose; and behold! in the dusk of that evening, two of us, strolling through Court Square, saw men busily at work fitting iron bars across this safe third-story window. Whether we had been betrayed, or whether it was a bit of extraordinary precaution, we never knew." (Or perhaps Sims himself, having worked on a scaffold in Savannah and thus well aware how dangerous a drop from a third floor could be, had asked for the bars to be installed, choosing rather to go back to mother and Mr. Potter than risk breaking his neck by jumping on to a pile of mattresses which, coming from a lawyer's office, cannot have been that many and would also, like most mattresses in those days, have been thin, without springs, and stuffed with horsehair.)

At any rate, to the shame of the city and the delight of the South, Sims was taken under military escort to the Long Wharf where a ship provided by the government was waiting to take him back to Savannah. Twelve years later, during the Civil War, he escaped once again and returned to Boston, just in time to watch the famous black 54th Massachusetts Regiment parade through the streets he had once traveled under heavy escort as they embarked for the campaign in the South.

The third case was that of Anthony Burns, who was arrested by federal marshals on May 24, 1854, on the charge of being a fugitive from the "service and labor" of Charles F. Suttle, a merchant of Alexandria, Virginia. After the arrest, which was made very discreetly, "he was escorted to an upper room in the Court House where, under a strong guard of officers, he was kept for the night, and the intelligence of his arrest did not transpire until the following morning." (This account comes from *Boston Slave Riot and Trial of Anthony Burns*, a quickie book composed mostly of edited newspaper accounts.)

> "Burns, who is about thirty years old, has for some time been in the employ of Coffin Pitts, clothing dealer, No. 36 Brattle Street. He is a shrewd fellow and his story of the manner of his leaving Alexandria is curious. After acquitting his master of all suspicion of cruelty, he stated that leaving him was the result of an accident—that one day, while

tired, he laid down on board a vessel to rest, got asleep, and during his slumbers the vessel sailed! Burns, at one time after his arrest, expressed a willingness to return with his master, but he was induced by his advisers to make his claimants show their authority for his return." (Other accounts, such as that by Richard Henry Dana, his lawyer, say nothing about falling asleep or being willing to return.)

When he was brought before Commissioner Loring, Burns was identified by a friend of the owner and was then held prisoner—like Sims—in an upstairs room at the Court House, under heavy guard. Soon after, this notice "appeared in all the papers and was placarded throughout the city: 'A Man Kidnapped!—A Public Meeting will be held at Faneuil Hall this (Friday) evening, May 26, at 7 o'clock, to secure justice for a man claimed as a slave by a Virginia kidnapper, and imprisoned in Boston Court House, in defiance of the laws of Massachusetts. Shall he be plunged into the hell of Virginia slavery by a Massachusetts Judge of Probate?"

As expected, the meeting at Faneuil Hall was crowded, noisy and disputatious. "On taking the chair, Judge Russell said he had once thought that a fugitive could never be taken from Boston. But he had been mistaken! One [Sims] had been taken from among us, and another lies in peril of his liberty. The boast of the slave holder is that he will catch his slaves under the shadow of Bunker Hill. We have made compromises until we find that compromise is concession, and concession is degradation. (Applause.)

"Dr. S. G. Howe then presented a series of resolutions which set forth that the trial on Saturday was an outrage not to be sanctioned, or tamely submitted to—That as the South has decreed, in the late passage of the Nebraska Bill, that no faith is to be kept with freedom; so, in the name of the living God, and on the part of the North, we declare that henceforth and forever, no compromises should be made with slavery. That . . . it is the will of God that every man should be free; we will as God wills; God's will be done!"

Wendell Phillips said, among other things, that the question to be settled was "whether we shall adhere to the result of the case of Shadrach or the case of Sims. Will you adhere to the case of Sims and see this man carried down State Street between two hundred men? (No!)" Theodore Parker also spoke, and "after some fiery remarks" said that when the meeting adjourned it should re-convene "in Court Square tomorrow morning at 9 o'clock. A hundred voices cried out, 'No, to-night!' 'Let us take him out!' 'Let us go now!' 'Come on!'" This was followed by a good deal of shouting, confusion and indecision—"the scene was tumultuous in the extreme." Then, just as things were quietening down, "a man at the lower end of hall cried out, 'Mr. Chairman, I am just informed that a mob of Negroes is in Court Square, attempting to rescue Burns! I move we adjourn to Court Square.' The audience immediately began rapidly to leave the hall, and most of them wended their way to Court Square."

"At the Court House the crowd halted on the east side and endeavored to force the door on that part of the building, but failing in their attempt they ran round to the door on the west side, opposite the Railroad Exchange, with loud cries that the fugitive was in that wing of the building, and there proceeded with a long plank which they used as a battering ram, and two axes, to break in and force an entrance . . . The battering ram was manned by a dozen or fourteen men, white and colored, who plunged it against the door until it was stove in. Meantime, several brickbats had been thrown at the windows, and the glass rattled in all directions. The leaders, or those who appeared to act as ringleaders in the melee, continually shouted, 'Rescue him!' 'Bring him out!' 'Where is he?' &c. &c. The Court House bell rung an alarm at half past nine o'clock. At this point reports of pistols were heard in the crowd, and firearms, we understand, were used by those within the building." Large numbers of Boston policemen now appeared, headed by Chief Taylor who "pressed through the excited multitude and, with great heroism, seized several men with axes in their hands.

"At the time the mob beat down the westerly door of the Court House, several men employed as United States officers were in the passage-way, using their endeavors to prevent the ingress of the crowd, and among the number was Mr. James Batchelder, a truckman in the employ of Colonel Peter Dunbar, who, almost at the instant of the forcing of the door, received a pistol shot in the abdomen. Mr. Batchelder uttered the exclamation, 'I'm stabbed!' and falling backwards into the arms of watchman Isaac Jones, expired almost immediately."

News of the murder had a sobering effect on the crowd, so did the arrival of more police "fully armed for any emergency." Several arrests were made—"A. G. Brown, Jr., American, 23 years of age, riotous conduct; John J. Roberts, American, 25 years of age, breaking a gas lamp in the square; Walter Phinney, colored, 36, and John Wesley, colored, 26, riotous conduct . . ." Two companies of artillery also arrived, whose "presence served to restore quiet, and Court House Square was soon deserted by the rioters. At half past twelve o'clock the square was deserted." To be on the safe side, a steamship was dispatched to Fort Independence "where she took on board a corps of the United States Marines." Also, "during the tumult, a number of our most respectable citizens called at the police office and tendered their services to assist in maintaining peace and order. Their offer was accepted."

The next day, Saturday, the crowd reassembled in Court Square while "the body of the unfortunate officer Batchelder, who fell a victim to the unrestrained passions of the mob last night, was removed by order of Coroner Smith to his late residence in Charlestown. As the coffin was being placed in the covered carriage which conveyed it out of the Square, the noisy outcries of the assembled multitude were hushed." Mayor Smith and High Sheriff Eveleth then appeared on the court house steps and warned the crowd "that a sufficient force was in readiness to preserve the public peace; and that, at all hazards, the laws of the city, the laws of the State, and the laws of the United States SHALL be maintained. (Applause.) Just as the mayor closed his remarks, a colored man made some demonstration of disrespect, and he was immediately arrested."

Meanwhile, inside the court house the examination of Burns was in progress. Under the Fugitive Slave Act there was no jury, no *habeas corpus* and no right of appeal, but Burns was allowed to have a lawyer, and Richard Henry Dana volunteered to serve. Dana did his best to cast doubt on the legality of the Fugitive Slave Law, and on whether Burns really was the man Charles Suttle, the owner, said he was. But the first objection was dismissed, and as to the second, Burns was his own worst enemy: soon after his arrest, when Suttle visited him in jail, Burns' first words, in front of witnesses, were "How do you do, Master Charles?"

THE ESCAPE ON SHIPBOARD.

ARREST IN BOSTON.

DEPARTURE FROM BOSTON.

THE SALE.

THE ADDRESS.

The most famous victim of the notorious Fugitive Slave Law, Anthony Burns' arrest in Boston, trial and return to slavery did much to radicalize the people of New England—"We went to bed one night old-fashioned, conservative, Compromise Union Whigs," wrote one prominent merchant, "and waked up stark mad Abolitionists."

(Burns, who seems to have been something of an innocent, had given himself away by writing a letter to his brother, also owned by Suttle, telling him where he was. "And as is the custom at the South, when letters are received directed to slaves, they are delivered to the owner of such

slaves, who opens them and examines their contents.") Suttle apparently
was not a hard master, and in the conversation that followed Burns readily admitted that he had never been whipped, had been allowed to choose
who he would work for when hired out, and was well looked after when
sick. Burns also confirmed the story that he had not intended to run away,
but had taken a nap while on board a ship docked in Alexandria, and
was still asleep when the ship set sail.

One solution would have been to buy Burns his freedom. Suttle at
first agreed to this, and named $1,200 as his price, a sum which was
soon raised, mostly from the black community; but then he decided not
to sell until he had proved his point by winning his case. This was done
in a few days. Only by disregarding his oath of office and embracing the
abolitionists' "higher law" could Commissioner Loring have come to
any other decision than the one he did: "On the law and facts of the
case, I consider the claimant entitled to the certificate from me which
he claims."

"As soon as the decision was rendered, the court room was cleared
of all spectators, to allow the necessary preparations to be made for the
sending back of the fugitive. Court Square was also cleared of the crowds
which thronged it. Every window overlooking the square was filled with
at least a dozen heads of persons anxious to witness the poor fugitive
when he should be brought out. The shutters of the stores on State Street
were closed and business was completely suspended. At ten o'clock a detachment of the Dragoons passed up Court Street, and were received with
groans and hisses, and cries of 'Shame! Shame!' &c."

As well as the dragoons "a detachment of the 4th Regiment U. S.
Artillery, having previously been to the Navy Yard and received a field
piece, marched up State Street. The cannon was drawn by a pair of
horses, and it was planted in Court Square a little south of the easterly
entrance of the Court House, and pointing towards Court Street"—
almost exactly the same thing had been done by British redcoats at the
time of the Boston Massacre. Along with the artillery, there were U. S.
Marines, "some 1500 or 1800 men of the Volunteer Militias, all with
their guns loaded," and hundreds of police and special officers. The side
streets were roped off, and orders were given to shoot anyone who
crossed a police line. The troops then formed a square, and Burns was
brought out of the Court House and placed in the middle of the square,

which then headed for Long Wharf. Probably feeling overwhelmed, "Burns appeared as indifferent as the most uninterested spectator, and the cries of 'Shame! Shame!' the hisses, groans and other demonstrations which greeted his appearance did not seem in the least to excite him."

Many of the buildings on Court Street were draped as if for a funeral. One owner "displayed heavy folds of black cambric from each of the three windows of his office," and several others had "their awnings hung with festoons of black. The *Commonwealth* office presented three American flags dressed in mourning, and lines of crepe were stretched across the street." Soon after, "a coffin was lowered out of one of the windows with the inscription 'Liberty' on it."

At length prisoner and escort arrived at Long Wharf where "the steamer *John Taylor* was lying. Burns was marched directly aboard and taken to the cabin out of sight of the crowd. The wharves and vessels in the vicinity were crowded with thousands of persons gathered to witness the embarkation." At last "the word to cast off was given," and "at precisely twenty minutes after three the steamer swung from the wharf and proceeded down the harbor."

On his return to Virginia, Burns spent some in prison in Richmond before being sold by Suttle to a North Carolina speculator called Mc Daniel for $905—almost three hundred dollars less than the offer he had refused on principle in Boston. McDaniel then turned around and sold him to some members of Boston's black community, led by the Rev. Leonard Grimes, for $1300—a quick profit of nearly fifty per cent. Once free, Burns paid a return visit to Boston and then moved on to Oberlin College, Ohio, the first college to admit women and blacks. After that he settled in Upper Canada, where he became a non-ordained Baptist minister and died of tuberculosis in 1862, aged twenty-eight. (The cause of the non-ordination may have been this: soon after being freed, Burns applied to the Baptist church that he had belonged to in Virginia for "a letter of dismission in fellowship and of recommendation to another church." In reply, he was informed that he had been unanimously excommunicated on the grounds that he had "absconded from the service of his master, and refused to return voluntarily, thereby disobeying both the laws of God and man.")

A few weeks after Burns was returned to Virginia, several hundred Bostonians gathered for a July 4 picnic in a grove of oak trees near Framingham. The event was sponsored by the Massachusetts Anti-Slavery Society and the day was to be observed not as a celebration but as one of "humiliation and sorrow." Banners depicted Virginia triumphant and Massachusetts downtrodden. The American flag was hung upside down and trimmed with black crepe. Among the speakers were Henry Thoreau, Wendell Phillips, Lucy Stone, Sojourner Truth, and, most notably, William Lloyd Garrison, whose newspaper, *The Liberator*, had already denounced the Burns case with headlines reading:

"SLAVE HUNTING DEFENDED AT THE POINT OF THE BAYONET—CIVIL LIBERTY PROSTRATE BEFORE MILITARY DESPOTISM—MASSACHUSETTS IN CHAINS AND HER SUBJUGATION ABSOLUTE!"

In a gesture that would have reminded his Protestant listeners of Martin Luther publicly burning the papal bull of excommunication—an act that many consider the start of the Reformation—Garrison, after describing the Constitution as being, among other things, "most bloody and heaven-daring . . . a system of the most atrocious villainy . . . the source and parent of the other atrocities . . . a covenant with death and an agreement with hell," held up a copy of that document, struck a match and set it on fire, exclaiming "So perish all compromises with tyranny! And let all the people say, Amen!"

The 54th Massachusetts Regiment assaulting the formidable defense works of Fort Wagner during the siege of Charleston. The regiment, composed of black troops and white officers, all of them volunteers, launched their attack at dusk after a day-long bombardment which was believed to have knocked out the fort's artillery; instead, as they closed in, "the fort became a mound of fire from which poured a stream of shot and shell." The picture shows the moment when Colonel Shaw was killed while a color sergeant holds high the Union flag. The attack failed to take the fort, but succeeded in demonstrating to skeptics that black soldiers would fight just as bravely as whites.

CHAPTER 14

THE CIVIL WAR

INTERVIEWED WHEN HE WAS A VERY OLD MAN, SAM WORD RECALLED THE TIME when he was a very young boy and the Union troops arrived at the Arkansas plantation where he had been born into slavery. "Mother had lots of nice things, quilts and things, and kept 'em in a chest in her little old shack. One day a Yankee soldier climbed in the back window and took some of the quilts. He rolled 'em up and was walking out of the yard when mother saw him and said, 'Why you nasty, stinkin' rascal! You say you come down here to fight for the niggers, and now you're stealin' from me!' He said, 'You're a Goddam liar! I'm fightin' for $14 a month and the Union.'"

Many others in the North would have agreed with the thieving Yankee that the aim of the war was to save the Union, not to end slavery. At the same time, many in the South had no doubt that they were fighting to preserve slavery. Mississippi's Declaration of Secession, of January 9, 1861, offered an explanation of "the prominent reasons which have induced our course."

> "Our position is thoroughly identified with the institution of slavery." A blow at slavery was not only a blow at "the greatest material interest in the world," it was a blow at "civilization. That blow has been long aimed at the institution, and was at the point of reaching its consummation. There was no choice left us but submission to the mandates of abolition, or a dissolution of the Union, whose principles had been subverted to work out our ruin. That we do not overstate the dangers to our institution, a reference to a few facts will sufficiently prove." Among these facts were the "hostility to the institution" displayed ever since the North West Ordinance of 1787;

the reluctance to admit "new slave States into the Union" and the attempt to confine slavery "within its present limits, denying the power of expansion." Then there was the way the North "has nullified the Fugitive Slave Law in almost every free State in the Union" and "advocates negro equality, socially and politically, and promotes insurrection and incendiarism in our midst. It has enlisted its press, its pulpit and its schools against us, until the whole popular mind of the North is excited and inflamed with prejudice." To remain in the Union would bring "utter subjugation."

Can the author of the Mississippi Declaration—Lucius Quintus Cincinnatus Lamar II—have read the text of the Republican platform adopted in 1860? Here, for example, is Clause 4: "Resolved, That the maintenance inviolate of the rights of the States, and especially the right of each State to order and control its own domestic institutions according to its own judgment exclusively, is essential to that balance of powers on which the perfection and endurance of our political fabric depend." John Brown's raid on Harper's Ferry was condemned—"We denounce the lawless invasion by armed force of the soil of any State or territory, no matter under what pretext, as among the gravest of crimes." To be sure, Clause Eight denied "the authority of Congress, of a territorial legislature, or of any individuals, to give legal existence to slavery in any territory of the United States"; but to oppose slavery's extension to the as yet unformed states was a far cry from proposing its extinction in states where it was already established.

In his debates with Stephen Douglas, and in his many speeches, Lincoln had also made his stance quite clear. Personally, "I have always hated slavery, I think, as much as any Abolitionist." It was a "monstrous injustice," but politically "we must not interfere with the institution of slavery where it exists, because the Constitution forbids it." However, when it came to the *extension* of slavery into the Territories, especially Kansas and Nebraska, he was "inflexible." These future states must be reserved "for poor"—and implicitly white—"people to go to and better their condition. This they cannot do, to any considerable extent, if slavery shall be planted within them." As to civil rights, "There is no reason in the world why the Negro is not entitled to all the natural rights enumerated in the Declaration of Independence—the right to life, liberty and the pursuit of happiness." On the other hand, "I am not, nor ever have been, in favor of bringing about in any way the social and political equality of the white and black races." He did not "favor making voters or jurors of Negroes, nor of qualifying them for holding office, nor to intermarry with white people; and I will say in addition to this that there is a physical difference between the white and black races which I believe will for ever forbid the two races living together on terms of social and political equality."

In March, 1861, in his first inaugural address, Lincoln re-affirmed his position: "I have no purpose, directly or indirectly, to interfere with the institution of slavery in the States where it exists." In August, 1862, writing to Horace Greeley, editor of the *New-York Tribune,* he declared, "My paramount object in this struggle is to save the Union, and is not either to save or to destroy Slavery. If I could save the Union without freeing any slave, I would do it, and if I could save it by freeing all the slaves, I would do it; and if I could save it by freeing some and leaving others alone, I would also do that. What I do about Slavery, and the colored race, I do because I believe it helps to save this Union."

This was made clear in the Emancipation Proclamation. Hedged about with qualifications—only the slaves in certain designated states were freed—the Proclamation was presented primarily as a "necessary war measure . . . warranted by the Constitution upon military necessity." However, as often happens in wartime, intentions were overtaken by events, and the document was taken to mean more than it said.

So, was the Great Emancipator a racist? Here is what Frederick Douglass had to say on April 14, 1876—the eleventh anniversary of Lincoln's assassination—at the ceremony unveiling the Freedmen's Monument in Washington, D. C.: "He was preeminently the white man's President, entirely devoted to the welfare of white men. He was ready and willing at any time during the first years of his administration to deny, postpone, and sacrifice the rights of humanity in the colored people."

Nevertheless, Lincoln should be judged not by his attitudes but by what he achieved. "His great mission was to accomplish two things: first, to save his country from dismemberment and ruin; and second to free his country from the great crime of slavery. To do one or the other, or both, he must have the earnest sympathy and the powerful cooperation of his loyal fellow-countrymen. Without this primary and essential condition to success his efforts must have been vain and utterly fruitless. Had he put the abolition of slavery before the salvation of the Union, he would have inevitably driven from him a powerful class of the American people and rendered resistance to the rebellion impossible. Viewed from the genuine abolition ground, Mr. Lincoln seemed tardy, cold, dull, and indifferent; but measuring him by the sentiment of his country, a sentiment he was bound as a statesman to consult, he was swift, zealous, radical and determined. Though Mr. Lincoln shared the prejudices of his white fellow countrymen against the Negro, it is hardly necessary to say that in his heart of hearts he loathed and hated slavery."

By the time the war ended, some 180,000 black soldiers had served in the Union army. Of these, about one in five came from the free states; one quarter, mostly slaves, from the border states; and the rest, the so-called "contrabands," were slaves who escaped from the Confederate states. At first these were enlisted as cooks, servants, teamsters and laborers, thus freeing up white men to do the fighting; not until the middle of the war were they allowed to serve as fighting soldiers.

In the meantime, there were many who did not wait for permission to act. Among these was William Tillman, whose story was written up by William Wells Brown, the prominent abolitionist.

"In the month of June, 1861, the schooner *S. J. Waring*, from New York, bound to South America, was captured on the passage by the rebel privateer *Jeff. Davis*, a prize-crew put on board, consisting of a captain, mate, and four seamen; and the vessel set sail for the port of Charleston, S. C. Three of the original crew were retained on board, a German as steersman, a Yankee who was put in irons, and a black man named William Tillman, the steward and cook of the schooner. The latter was put to work at his usual business, and told that he was henceforth the property of the Confederate States, and would be sold, on his arrival at Charleston, as a slave.

"Night comes on; darkness covers the sea; the vessel is gliding swiftly towards the South; the rebels, one after another, retire to their berths; the hour of midnight approaches; all is silent in the cabin; the captain is asleep; the mate, who has charge of the watch, takes his brandy toddy and reclines upon the quarter deck. The Negro thinks of home and all its endearments; he sees in the dim future chains and slavery.

"He resolves, and determines to put the resolution into practice upon the instant. Armed with a heavy club, he proceeds to the captain's room. He strikes the fatal blow; he feels the pulse, and all is still. He next goes to the adjoining room; another blow is struck, and the black man is master of the cabin. Cautiously he ascends to the deck, strikes the mate; the officer is wounded, but not killed. He draws his revolver, and calls of help. The crew are aroused; they are hastening to aid their commander. The Negro repeats his blow with the heavy club; the rebel falls dead at Tillman's feet. The African seizes the revolver, drives the crew below deck, orders the release of the Yankee, puts the enemy in irons, and proclaims himself master of the vessel. The *Waring's* head is turned towards New York, with the stars and stripes flying . . ."

On arrival, Tillman was hailed as a hero, even by "those who are usually awkward in any other vernacular than derision of the colored man." The *New-York Tribune* declared that "to this colored man was the nation indebted for the first vindication of its honor on the sea." At Barnum's Museum, which also featured "Tom Shows" (minstrel shows based on *Uncle Tom's Cabin*), "he was the center of attractive gaze to daily increasing thousands." Even better, "the Federal Government awarded to Tillman the sum of six thousand dollars as prize-money for the capture of the schooner."

Even more popular was the exploit of Robert Smalls, whose story was told in an official Congressional report: "On May 13, 1862, the Confederate steamboat *Planter*, the special dispatch boat of General Ripley, the Confederate post commander at Charleston, S. C., was taken by Robert Smalls under the following circumstances from the wharf at which she was lying, carried safely out of Charleston Harbor, and delivered to one of the vessels of the Federal fleet then blockading that port.

"On the day previous, May 12, the *Planter*, which had for two weeks been engaged in removing guns from Coles Island to James Island, returned to Charleston. That night all the officers went ashore and slept in the city, leaving on board a crew of eight men, all colored. Among them was Robert Smalls, who was virtually the pilot of the boat, although he was only called a wheelman, because at that time no colored man could have, in fact, been made a pilot. For some time previous he had been watching for an opportunity to carry into execution a plan he had conceived to take the *Planter* to the Federal fleet. This, he saw, was about as good a chance as he would ever have to do so, and therefore he determined not to lose it. Consulting with the balance of the crew, Smalls found that they were willing to cooperate with him, although two of them afterwards concluded to remain behind. The design was hazardous in the extreme. The boat would have to pass beneath the guns of the forts in the harbor. Failure and detection would have been certain death. Fearful was the venture, but it was made. The daring resolution had been formed, and under the command of Robert Smalls wood was taken aboard, steam was put on, and with her valuable cargo of guns and ammunition intended for Fort Ripley, a new fortification just constructed in the harbor, about two o'clock in the morning the *Planter* silently moved off from the dock, steamed up to North Atlantic Wharf, where Smalls' wife and two children, together with four other women and one other child, and also three men, were waiting to embark. All these were taken on board, and then, at 3.25 a.m., May 13, the *Planter* started on her perilous adventure, carrying nine men, five women, and three children. Passing Fort Johnson, the *Planter's* steam whistle blew the usual salute and she proceeded down the bay. Approaching Fort Sumter, Smalls stood in the pilot house leaning out of the window, with his arms folded across his breast after the manner of Captain Relay, the commander of the boat, and his head covered with the huge straw hat which Captain Relay commonly wore on such occasions.

"The signal required to be given by all steamers passing out was blown as coolly as if General Ripley was on board, going out on a tour of inspection. Sumter answered by signal, 'All right,' and the *Planter* headed toward Morris Island, then occupied by Hatch's light artillery, and passed beyond the range of Sumter's guns before anyone suspected that anything was wrong. When at last the *Planter* was obviously going toward the Federal fleet off the bar, Sumter signaled toward Morris

Hero of one of the most daring exploits of the war, Robert Smalls stole the Confederate gunboat Planter *out from under the guns defending Charleston and handed her over to the Union fleet blockading that city. After very active service during the war, he returned to Charleston in April, 1865, to witness the raising of the Union flag over Fort Sumter.*

Island to stop her. But it was too late. As the *Planter* approached the Federal fleet, a white flag was displayed, but this was not at first discovered, and the Federal steamers, supposing the Confederate rams were coming to attack them, stood out to deep water. But the ship *Onward*, Captain Nichols, which was not a steamer, remained, opened her [gun] ports, and was about to fire into the *Planter* when she noticed the flag of truce. As soon as the vessels came within hailing distance of each other, the *Planter's* errand was explained. Captain Nichols then boarded her, and Smalls delivered the *Planter* to him."

Smalls' exploit deservedly made him a hero overnight, and he and the *Planter* later played an important part in the river campaigns of the famous First Regiment of South Carolina Volunteers. Less distinguished, but easier to sympathize with, were the wartime experiences of Thomas Cole, aged eighteen when the fighting started. For most of his life, Thomas had been relatively fortunate. His owner, "Massa Dr. Cole," was "a smart man and a good man with it. He had respect for the slave's feelings and didn't treat them like dumb brutes, and allowed them more privileges than any other slaveholder round there. He was one of the best men I ever knows in my whole life, and his wife was just like him. Massa

Cole allow us to read the Bible. He awful good about that. Most of the slave-owners wouldn't allow no such." Thomas' mother was the family cook and "we lived in one room of the big house, and always had a good bed to sleep in and good things to eat at the same table, after the white folks get through." But then "Massa get sick and the next summer he die. Missy Cole, she move to Huntsville, Alabama, but she leaves me on the plantation 'cause I'm big and stout then. She takes my mother to cook, and that's the last time I ever seed my mother." An overseer called Anderson, known for his brutality, was hired to run the plantation. "I thinks to myself, that Mr. Anderson, the overseer, he'll give me that cat-o-nine-tails the first chance he gets, but make up my mind he won't get the chance 'cause I's gwine run off the first chance I gets."

Soon after, food being in short supply, he and some others were sent into the woods to hunt for deer or wild hogs. "This the chance I been wanting, so when we gets to the hunting ground the leader says to scatter out, and I tells him me and 'nother man goes north and make the circle round the river and meet 'bout sundown. I crosses the river and goes north. I's gwine to the free country, where they ain't no slaves. I travels all that day and night up the river and follows the north star. Several times I thunk the bloodhounds am trailing me, and I gets in the big hurry."

He spent the next day hiding in a big thicket and then, "along evening, I hears guns shooting. I sure am scared this time, sure 'nough. I's scared to come in and scared to go out, and while I's standing there I hears two men say, 'Stick your hands up, boy. What you doing?' I says, 'Uh-uh-uh, I dunno. You ain't gwine take me back to the plantation, is you?' They says, 'No. Does you want to fight for the North?' I says I will, 'cause they talks like Northern men. Us walk night and day and gets in General Rosecrans' camp, and they thunk I's the spy from the South. They asks me all sorts of questions and says they'll whip me if I don't tell them what I's spying 'bout. Finally they 'lieves me and puts me to work helping with the cannons. I feels 'portant then, but I didn't know what was in front of me, or I 'spects I'd run off 'gain.

"I helps set them cannons on this Chickamauga Mountain, in hiding places. I has to go with a man and wait on him and that cannon. First thing I knows—Bang! Bang! Boom!—things has started, and guns am shooting faster than you can think, and I looks round for the way to run. But them guns am shooting down the hill in front of me, and shooting at me, and over me, and on both sides of me. I tries to dig me a hole and get in it. All this happens right now, and first thing I knows the man am kicking me and wanting me to help him keep that cannon loaded. Man, I didn't want no cannon, but I has to help anyway. We fit till dark, and the Rebels got more men than us, so General Rosecrans sends the message to General Woods to come help us out. When the messenger slips off I sure wish it am me slipping off, but I didn't want to see no General Woods, I just wants to get back to that old plantation and pick more cotton. I'd been willing to do 'most anything to get out of that mess, but I done told General Rosecrans I wants to fight the Rebels, and he sure was letting me do it. He wasn't just letting me do it, he was making me do it. I done got in there, and he wouldn't let me out.

"There was men laying wanting help, wanting water, with blood running out of them and the top or sides of their heads gone, great big holes in them. I just promises the good Lord if He just let me get out that mess I wouldn't run off no more, but I didn't know then He wasn't gwine let me out with just that battle. He gwine give me plenty more, but that battle ain't over yet, for next morning the Rebels 'gin shooting and killing lots of our men, and General Woods ain't come, so General Rosecrans orders us to 'treat, and didn't have to tell me what he said neither. The Rebels comes after us, shooting, and we runs off and leaves that cannon what I was with setting on the hill, and I didn't want that thing, nohow.

"We kept hotfooting it till we gets to Chattanooga, and there is where we stops. Here comes one of them Rebel generals with the big bunch of men and gets right on top of Lookout Mountain, right close to Chattanooga, and wouldn't let us out. I don't know just how long, but a long time. Lots our hosses and mules starves to death, and we eats some of the hosses. We all like to starve to death ourselves. Chattanooga is in the bend of the Tennessee River, and on Lookout Mountain, on the east, am them Rebels and they could keep up with everything we done. After a long time General Thomas gets in some way. He finds the rough trail or wagon road round the mountain 'long the river, and supplies and men comes by boat up the river to this place and comes on into Chattanooga. More Union men kept coming, and I guess maybe six or eight generals, and they gets ready to fight.

"They starts climbing this steep mountain, and when us gets three-fourths the way up it am foggy, and you couldn't see no place. Everything wet, and the rocks am slick, and they 'gins fighting. I 'spects some shoots their own men, 'cause you couldn't see nothing, just men running and the guns roaring. Finally them Rebels fled, and we gets on Lookout Mountain, and takes it.

"There a long range of hills leading 'way from Lookout Mountain, nearly to Missionary Ridge. This ridge 'longside the Chickamauga River, what am the Indian name meaning 'River of Death.' They fights the Rebels on Orchard Knob Hill, and I wasn't in that, but I's in the Missionary Ridge battle. We has to come out the timber and run 'cross a strip or opening up the hill. They sure killed lots our men when we runs 'cross that opening. We runs for all we's worth and uses guns or anything we could. The Rebels turns and runs off, and our soldiers turned the cannons round what we's captured and killed some the Rebels with their own guns.

"I never did get to where I wasn't scared when we goes into the battle. This the last one I's in, and I's sure glad, for I never seed the like of dead and wounded men. We picks them up, the Rebels like the Unions, and doctors them the best we could. When I seed all that suffering, I hope I never lives to see 'nother war. I sure wished lots of times I never run off from the plantation. I begs the General not to send me on any more battles, and he says I's the coward and sympathizes with the South. But I tells him I just couldn't stand to see all them men lying there dying and hollering and begging for help and a drink of water, and blood everywhere you looks." After that "when they wants to battle, General Thomas always leaves me in camp to tend to supplies. He calls me a coward, and I sure glad he thunk I was. I wasn't no coward, I just couldn't stand to see to all them people tore to pieces."

During the first part of the war, many Union generals were opposed to recruiting or even freeing slaves. "Any attempt at insurrection," McClellan told Unionist slaveholders in West Virginia, would be crushed "with an iron hand." In Florida, General Slemmer shackled runaways before returning them. In St. Louis, in November, 1861, General Halleck issued Order No. 3 directing that no fugitive "be hereafter permitted to enter the lines of any camp or of any forces on the march, and that any now within such lines be immediately excluded therefrom."

But others took a different line. General Fremont, who commanded in the West, proclaimed that "the property, real and personal, of all persons in the State of Missouri, who shall take up arms against the United States . . . is declared to be confiscated to the public use, and their slaves, if any they have, are hereby declared free men." The following year, 1862, General Hunter, in the South, proclaimed that all persons in "Georgia, Florida and South Carolina, heretofore held as slaves, are therefore declared forever free." However, both proclamations were canceled by Lincoln, who was anxious not to offend slave-owners in the border states which had sided with the Union. Also, such powers "I reserve to myself." In the meantime, however, Congress had passed two Confiscation Acts allowing the seizure of property, including slaves, of those in rebellion.

Soon after declaring that all slaves in his command were free, General Hunter decided to recruit a regiment from among them. When Lincoln countermanded Hunter's proclamation, most of the recruits were discharged. Then there was a change of policy, and those who remained became the nucleus of the First Regiment of South Carolina Volunteers. Their camp was an abandoned plantation near Beaufort. As usual, all the officers were white. Their colonel was Thomas Wentworth Higginson, a longtime abolitionist and one of the leaders in the attempt to free Thomas Sims from prison in Boston. In February he reported to General Saxton on a raid up the St. Mary's River, "the most dangerous in the department," carried out by two and hundred and fifty of his troops on board the *John Adams*, an armor-plated riverboat:

> "The stream is narrow, swift, winding, and bordered at many places with high bluffs, which blazed with rifle shots. With our glasses, as we approached these points, we could see mounted men by the hundreds galloping through the woods, from point to point, to await us; and though fearful of our shot and shell, they were so daring against musketry that one rebel actually sprang from the shore upon the large boat which was towed at our stern, where he was shot down by one of my

sergeants. We could see our shells scatter the rebels as they fell among them, and some terrible execution must have been done; but not a man of this regiment was killed or wounded, though the steamer is covered with bullet-marks . . . The secret of our safety was in keeping the regiment below, except the gunners; but this required the utmost energy of the officers, as the men were wild to come on deck, and even implored to be landed on shore and charge on the enemy. Nobody knows anything about these men who has not seen them in battle. I find that I myself knew nothing. There is a fiery energy about them beyond any thing of which I have ever read . . . During our first attack on the river, before I got them all penned below, they crowded at the open end of the steamer, loading and firing with inconceivable rapidity, and shouting to each other, 'Never give it up!' When collected in the hold they actually fought each other for places at the few port-holes from which they could fire on the enemy." In conclusion: "No officer in this regiment now doubts that the key to the successful prosecution of this war lies in the unlimited employment of black troops."

In July, 1863, another expedition took the regiment up the Edisto River to destroy a railroad bridge and bring back slaves. This was a hard assignment. "After the capture of Port Royal, the outlying plantations along the whole southern coast were abandoned, and the slaves withdrawn into the interior. It was necessary to ascend some river for thirty miles in order to reach the black population at all. This ascent could only be made by night, as it was a slow process, and the smoke of a steamboat could be seen for a great distance. The streams were usually shallow, winding, and muddy, and the difficulties of navigation were such as to require a full moon and a flood tide." There was also reported to be a battery of artillery at Wiltown Bluff, and wooden barricades across some parts of the river.

"In former narrations I have sufficiently described the charm of a moonlight ascent into a hostile country, upon an unknown stream, the dark and silent banks, the rippling water, the wail of the reed-birds, the anxious watch, the breathless listening, the veiled lights, the whispered orders." At four in the morning they reached Wiltown Bluff where they quickly knocked out the battery. "As the firing ceased and the smoke cleared away, I looked across the rice fields which lay beneath the bluff. The first sunbeams glowed upon their emerald levels and on the blossoming hedges along the rectangular dikes. What were those black dots which everywhere appeared? Those moist meadows had become alive with human heads, and along each narrow path came a straggling file of men and women, all on a run for the river-side . . . Presently they began to come from the houses also, with their little bundles on their heads; then with larger bundles. Old women, trotting on the narrow paths, would kneel to pray a little prayer, still balancing the bundle; and then would suddenly spring up, urged by the accumulating procession behind, and would move on till irresistibly compelled by thankfulness to dip down for another invocation. Reaching us, every human being must grasp our hands, amid exclamations of 'Bless you, master!' and 'Bless the Lord!' . . . Women brought children on their shoulders; small black boys carried on their back little brothers equally inky and, gravely depositing them, shook hands."

The rest of the expedition did not go so smoothly; the railroad bridge was too heavily defended to be destroyed, the boats had to fight their way back down river, and there were several casualties, including Higginson who was wounded. But, as he later wrote, "Before the war, how great a thing seemed the rescue of even one man from slavery; and since the war has emancipated all, how little seems the liberation of two hundred! But no one then knew how the contest might end; and when I think of that morning sunlight, those emerald fields, those thronging numbers, the old women with their prayers, and the little boys with their living burdens, I know that the day was worth all it cost, and more."

Of all black regiments the most famous was the Massachusetts 54th, whose history was told by one of its white officers, Captain Luis Emilio, in his book, *A Brave Black Regiment*:

"At the close of the year 1862, the military situation was discouraging to the supporters of the Federal Government. We had been repulsed at Fredericksburg and at Vicksburg, and at tremendous cost had fought the battle of Stone River. Some sixty-five thousand troops would be discharged during the ensuing summer and fall. Volunteering was at a standstill. On the other hand, the Confederates, having filled their ranks, were never better fitted for conflict.

"In consequence of the situation, the arming of Negroes, first determined upon in October, 1862, was fully adopted as a military measure; and President Lincoln, on Jan. 1, 1863, issued the Emancipation Proclamation. In September, 1862, General Butler began organizing the Louisiana Native Guards from free Negroes. General Saxton, in the Department of the South, formed the First South Carolina from contrabands in October of the same year. Col. James Williams, in the summer of 1862, recruited the First Kansas Colored. After these regiments next came, in order of organization, the Fifty-fourth Massachusetts, which was the first raised in the Northern States east of the Mississippi River. Thenceforward the recruiting of colored troops, North and South, was rapidly pushed. As a result of the measure, 167 organizations of all arms, embracing 186,097 enlisted men of African descent were mustered into the United States service."

John Andrew, the governor of Massachusetts, had long been an advocate of black enlistment. Shortly after the Emancipation Proclamation he went down to Washington and extracted from the Secretary of War, Edwin Stanton, a letter authorizing him to raise a regiment of volunteers that "may include persons of African descent, organized into special corps." Andrew's next step was to recruit officers who would be "gentlemen of the highest tone and honor" from the "circles of educated anti-slavery society." Robert Gould Shaw, of a prominent abolitionist family, would be the colonel.

"At the time a strong prejudice existed against arming the blacks and those who dared to command them. The sentiment of the country and of the army was opposed to the measure. It was asserted that they would not fight, that their employment would prolong the war, and that white troops would refuse to serve with them. Besides the moral courage required to accept commissions in the Fifty-fourth at the time it was organizing, physical courage was also necessary, for the Confederate Congress, on May 1, 1863, passed an act, a portion of which read as follows: 'Every white person being a commissioned officer, or acting as such, who, during the present war, shall command Negroes or mulattoes in arms against the Confederate States . . . shall be deemed as inciting servile insurrection, and shall, if captured, be put to death.'" (In December, 1862, Jefferson Davis had already issued a "proclamation of outlawry" ordering that "all negro slaves captured in arms be at once delivered over to the executive authorities of the respective States to which they belong, to be dealt with according to the laws of said States" i.e. be executed. In May, 1863, this was extended to all blacks and mulattoes, free or slave, "who gave aid or comfort to the enemies of the Confederacy.")

Although the rate of volunteering among free blacks was much higher than among whites, there were not enough of them in Massachusetts to fill the regiment, so recruiters spread out across the free states. A powerful assist came from Rochester, New York, with some splendid rhetoric in the form of the broadside "Men of Color, to Arms!" "When first the rebel cannon shattered the walls of Sumter and drove away its starving garrison, I predicted that the war then and there inaugurated would not be fought out entirely by white men," wrote Frederick Douglass. "A war undertaken and brazenly carried on for the perpetual enslavement of colored men calls logically and loudly for colored men to help suppress it." And now, at last, this call was being heeded. "From East to West, from North to South, the sky is written all over, 'Now or never!' Liberty won by white men would lose half its luster. 'Who would be free, themselves must strike the blow.' 'Better even die free, than to live slaves.' This is the sentiment of every brave colored man among us . . . By every consideration which binds you to your enslaved fellow-countrymen, and the peace and welfare of your country; by every aspiration which you cherish for the freedom and equality of yourselves and your children; by all the ties of blood and identity which make us one with the brave black men now fighting our battles in Louisiana and South Carolina, I urge you to fly to arms, and smite with death the power that would bury the government and your liberty in the same hopeless grave." Although New York had not yet decided to raise a regiment, "we can get at the throat of treason and slavery through the State of Massachusetts," which "now welcomes you to arms as soldiers. She has but a small colored population from which to recruit, so "go quickly and help fill up the first colored regiment from the North . . . Do not hesitate . . . Do not doubt. The day dawns; the morning star is bright upon the horizon! The iron gate of our prison stands half open. One gallant rush from the North will fling it wide open, while four millions of our brothers and sisters shall march out into liberty . . . This is our golden opportunity. Let us accept it, and forever wipe out the dark reproaches unsparingly hurled against us by our enemies. Let us win for ourselves the gratitude of our country, and the blessings of our posterity . . ."

The first intake, which included several former slaves, arrived at Camp Meigs, Readville, near Boston, in February, and by mid-May the regiment was completed. Recruitment for another, the 55th, began at once. Soon after, Governor Andrew and other dignitaries attended a parade at Readville at which he presented four flags, "brilliant in color and of the finest texture, fluttering in the fresh breeze." These were "a national flag, a State color, an emblematic banner of white silk with the figure of the Goddess of Liberty, and the motto 'Liberty, Loyalty, and Unity,' and another with a cross upon a blue shield, and the motto, *In Hoc Signo Vinces*. (In this sign, conquer!) After presenting them, Governor Andrew delivered a high-flown speech, whose peroration ran: "I know not, Mr. Commander, when, in all human history, to any given thousand men in arms there has been committed a work at once so proud, so precious, so full of hope and glory as the work committed to you. And may the infinite mercy of Almighty God attend you every hour of every day through all the experiences and vicissitudes of that dangerous life in which you have embarked; may the God of our fathers cover your heads in the day of battle; may He shield you with the arms of everlasting power; may He hold you always—most of all, first of all, and last of all—up to the highest and holiest conception of duty, so that if, on the field of stricken fight, your souls shall be delivered from the thraldom of the flesh, your spirits shall go home to God, bearing aloft the exulting thought of duty well performed, of glory and reward won, even at the hands of the angels who shall watch over you from above!"

At the request of General David Hunter, commander of the Department of the South and a keen abolitionist, the regiment was ordered to the Sea Islands, to take part in the siege of Charleston. On the morning of May 28, the regiment arrived at Boston railroad station and then, bands playing, marched through the city's streets on their way to the docks. "All along the route the sidewalks, windows, and balconies were thronged with spectators, and the appearance of the regiment caused repeated cheers and waving of flags and handkerchiefs. The national colors were displayed everywhere . . . Entering State Street, the band played the stirring music of John Brown's hymn, while passing over ground moistened by the blood of Crispus Attucks [killed by the redcoats in the Boston Massacre of 1770], and over which Anthony Burns and Thomas Sims had been carried back to bondage. It is a curious fact that Sims himself witnessed the march of the 54th. All along this street the reception accorded was most hearty; and from the steps of the Exchange, crowded with business men, the appearance of the regimental colors was the signal for repeated and rousing cheers."

Upon arriving at Battery Wharf the regiment embarked on the steamer *De Molay*, and at four o'clock "the lines were cast off and the vessel slowly moved from the wharf, where friendly and loving hands waved adieus, to which those on board responded."

Two months later, the regiment was drawn up on the sandy beach of low-lying Morris Island preparatory to an assault on Fort Wagner, one of the strongholds defending Charleston harbor, heavily defended by artillery and some seventeen hundred Confederate troops. After a day-long bombardment by Union gunboats the fort had fallen silent, and "the belief was general that the enemy had been driven from his shelter, and the armament of Wagner rendered harmless." Unaware that in fact only eight rebels had been killed and twenty wounded, General Gilmore decided on a frontal assault. Colonel Gould requested the "post of honor"—leading the attack—for the Fifty-fourth. Gould must have known how hazardous this would be: the soldiers, already tired from long marches, would have to advance three quarters of a mile through heavy sand and without any cover towards "the strongest single earthwork known in the history of warfare." Daylight was fading, and the incoming tide narrowed the beach, forcing the exposed attackers to bunch up or wade knee-deep through the water. But, like most of his comrades, Gould was anxious to prove that "the Negro would fight." As Captain Emilio put it: "The whole question of employing three hundred thousand colored soldiers hung in the balance. But few, however, doubted the result. Wherever a white officer led that night, even to the gun-muzzles and bayonet points, there, by his side, were black men as brave and steadfast as himself.

"Away over the sea to the eastward the heavy sea-fog was gathering, the western sky bright with the reflected light, for the sun had set. Far away thunder mingled with the occasional boom of cannon. The gathering host all about, the silent lines stretching away to the rear, the passing of a horseman now and then carrying orders—all was ominous of the impending onslaught. Far and indistinct in front was the now silent earthwork, seamed, scarred, and ploughed with shot, its flag still waving in defiance.

"It was about 7.45 pm, with darkness coming on rapidly, when the Fifty-fourth moved." Guns from Fort Sumter and Sullivan's Island fired on the regiment, but Fort Wagner remained largely silent. Gould and the color sergeant led the attack, and "with eyes strained upon the colonel and the flag," the soldiers "pressed on toward the work, now only two hundred yards away.

"At that moment Wagner became a mound of fire, from which poured a stream of shot and shell. Just a brief lull, and the deafening explosions of cannon were renewed, mingled with the crash and rattle of musketry. A sheet of flame, followed by a running fire, like electric sparks, swept along the parapet . . . When this tempest of war came, before which men fell in numbers on every side, the only response the 54th made to the deadly challenge was to change step to the double-quick, that it might the sooner close with the foe . . . As the swifter pace was taken, and officers sprang to the fore with waving swords barely seen in the darkness, the men closed the gaps, and with set jaws, panting breath, and bowed heads, charged on." They reached the ditch in front of the fort's wall. "Down into this they went, through the two or three feet of water therein, and mounted the slope beyond in the teeth of the enemy, some of whom, standing on the crest, fired down on them . . . Both flags were planted on the parapet . . . Colonel Shaw had led his regiment from first to last. Gaining the rampart, he stood there for a moment with uplifted sword, shouting, 'Forward, Fifty-fourth!' and then fell dead, shot through the heart."

There was savage hand-to-hand fighting, but so great were their losses that "numbers soon told against the 54th, for it was tens against hundreds. Outlined against the sky, they were a fair mark for the foe. Men fell every moment . . . The garrison was stronger than had been supposed, and brave in defending the work. The first rush had failed . . . and the supports were not at hand to take full advantage of their first fierce attack. Repulsed from the crest after the short hand-to-hand struggle, the assailants fell back," and then withdrew completely.

So many officers were killed or wounded that the narrator, Luis Emilio, the regiment's junior captain, became its temporary commanding officer. Further attempts to storm the fort by other regiments also failed, with heavy losses and with Union soldiers firing on each other in the darkness and confusion. Soon after the attack Lt. Iredell Jones of the C. S. A. visited Fort Wagner and reported that "the dead and wounded were piled up in a ditch together, sometimes fifty in a heap, and they were strewn all over the plain for a distance of three fourths of a mile . . . Numbers of both white and black were killed on top of our breastworks as well as inside. The Negroes fought gallantly, and were headed by as brave a colonel as ever lived. He mounted the breastworks waving his sword, and at the head of his regiment, and he and a Negro orderly sergeant fell dead over the inner crest of the works. The Negroes were as fine-looking a set as I ever saw."

Later that year Fort Wagner was taken with little loss of life by laying siege to it in the classic manner—sapping, mining and digging trenches that zig-zagged closer and closer until huge amounts of gunpowder could be buried under the outer walls, and then blowing everything up (except that the defenders abandoned the fort before that could happen). But if it could be taken that simply, why sacrifice so many in a frontal assault? The answer was that the purpose of the attack was not so much to capture the fort as to demonstrate the valor of black soldiers. This they certainly did, and were acknowledged at the time to have done so. Fort Wagner, said the *New-York Tribune*, would be to black Americans what Bunker Hill was to white Americans. "Through the cannon smoke of that dark night," wrote the *Atlantic Monthly*, "the manhood of the colored race shines before many eyes that would not see." The *Boston Commonwealth* quoted a white soldier as saying "We don't know any black men here, they're all soldiers." However, as it turned out, one such battle was not enough, and throughout the war they had to prove themselves again and again—and indeed in subsequent wars too.

Fort Wagner also demonstrated the attitude of many white officers toward black soldiers. In testimony before a War Department commission, the journalist Nathaniel Paige reported that when planning the attack General Gilmore, "who ridiculed negro troops," asked his subordinate, General Seymour, how he intended to organize his command. "Gen. Seymour answered, 'Well, I guess we will let [Brigadier] Strong lead and put those d—d niggers from Massachusetts in the advance; we may as well get rid of them one time as another.' General Gilmore laughed, but ordered the movement to take place."

Brigadier Strong was among those killed in the battle. However, according to Paige, "Gen. Seymour was not in the advance at Fort Wagner, but early in the action received a very slight wound in his heel, not drawing blood, immediately after which he retired to the south end of Morris Island, and remained there all night. Next morning . . . he charged the failure of the assault upon the d—d negroes from Massachusetts." In the Florida campaign that followed Fort Wagner, Seymour more than once withdrew white troops from the line without informing the 54th, leaving it dangerously exposed. He was also known for ordering the summary execution—later commuted—of black soldiers for such offenses as stealing a chicken or accidentally firing a musket.

Another such officer was General Dwight, whose "antecedents with regard to the rights of the Negro and his ability to fight were not of the most favorable character." In spite of this, Dwight was put in command of the colored brigade for the battle at Port Hudson, a Confederate stronghold on the Mississippi. It was fought on May 26, 1863, a day that was as hot "as an overheated oven." One of the regiments was the First Louisiana, formerly known as the Native Guard, a long-established militia unit based in New Orleans with officers drawn from that city's free black elite. As was expected of such a unit, their colonel "petitioned their commander to allow them to occupy the post of danger in the battle," a request General Dwight was only too willing to grant.

"At last the welcome word was given, and our men started. The enemy opened a blistering fire of shell, canister, grape and musketry. The first shell thrown by the enemy killed and wounded a number of the blacks; but on they went. 'Charge!' was the word. At every pace the column was thinned by the falling dead and wounded. The blacks closed up steadily as their comrades fell, and advanced within fifty paces of where the rebels were working a masked battery, situated on a bluff where the guns could sweep the whole field over which the troops must charge . . . No matter how gallantly the men behaved, no matter how bravely they were led, it was not in the course of things that this gallant brigade should take these works by charge. Yet charge after charge was ordered and carried out under all these disasters with Spartan firmness. Six charges in all were made. Col. Nelson reported to Gen. Dwight the fearful odds he had to contend with. Says Gen. Dwight in reply, 'Tell Col. Nelson I shall consider that he has accomplished nothing unless he takes those guns.' Humanity will never forgive Gen. Dwight for this last order; for he certainly saw that he was only throwing away the lives of his men. But what were his men? 'Only niggers.'" (Throughout the battle, Dwight remained well to the rear, drinking heavily.)

According to the *New York Herald*, "The First Regiment Louisiana Native Guard, Col. Nelson, were in this charge. They went on the advance, and, when they came out, six hundred out of nine hundred men could not be accounted for. It is said on every side that they fought with the desperation of tigers. One negro was observed with a rebel soldier in his grasp, tearing the flesh from his face with his teeth, other weapons having failed him. There are other incidents connected with the conduct of this regiment that have raised them very much in my opinion as soldiers. After firing one volley they did not deign to load again, but went in with bayonets; and wherever they had a chance, it was all up with the rebels."

And there was this from the *New-York Tribune*: "Nobly done, First Regiment of Louisiana Native Guards! Though you failed to carry the rebel works against overwhelming numbers, you did not charge and fight and fall in vain. That heap of six hundred corpses lying there stark and grim and silent before and within the rebel works is a better proclamation of freedom than even President Lincoln's. A race ready to die thus was never yet retained in bondage, and never can be."

A final word from William Wells Brown, who wrote much of the above account: "At the surrender of Port Hudson, not a single colored man could be found alive, although thirty-five were known to have been taken prisoners during the siege. All had been murdered."

Throughout the war there were many other incidents of black prisoners being murdered after they had surrendered. In July, 1864, Sergeant Samuel Johnson, of the 2nd U.S. Colored Cavalry, had been on a recruiting mission to Plymouth, N. C. when it was suddenly attacked and captured by rebel forces. "When I found that the city was being surrendered I pulled off my uniform and found a suit of citizen's clothes which I put on, and when captured I was supposed and believed by the Rebels to be a citizen." This subterfuge saved his life. "All the Negroes found in blue uniform or with any outward marks of a Union soldier upon him was killed. I saw some taken into the woods and hung. Others I saw stripped of all their clothing, and they stood upon the bank of the river with their faces riverwards and then they were shot. Still others were killed by having their brains beaten out by the butt end of the muskets in the hands of the Rebels. All were not killed the day of the capture. Those that were not were placed in a room with their officers, they (the officers) having previously been dragged through the town with ropes around their necks, where they were kept confined until the following morning when the remainder of the black soldiers were killed."

The most notorious of such incidents took place at Fort Pillow, an earthwork fortification on a bluff above the Mississippi, fifty miles north of Memphis. Its garrison was composed of some 300 white troops and the same number of black soldiers, most of them former slaves. A Union gunboat was moored in the river at the foot of the bluff, and at the time of the attack other gunboats were on their way bringing reinforcements.

Early in April, 1864, Fort Pillow became the target of the Confederate cavalry leader Nathan Bedford Forrest, former slave trader and future founder of the Ku Klux Klan. After surrounding the fort with a force that outnumbered the garrison by more than two to one, Forrest summoned it to surrender. While Major Bradford, the fort's commander, decided on his response, there was a truce during which troops were supposed to hold their fire and keep their positions; instead, the rebels crept forward on all sides until they were at the foot of the fort's embankments. As soon as Major Bradford rejected the summons, "the rebels made a rush from the positions they had so treacherously gained, and obtained possession of the fort, raising the cry 'No quarter!' But little opportunity was allowed for resistance. Our troops, white and black, threw down their arms and sought to escape by running down the steep bluff near the fort and secreting themselves behind trees and logs, in the bushes, and under the brush; some even jumping into the river, leaving only their heads above the water as they crouched down under the bank. Then followed a scene of cruelty and murder without parallel in civilized warfare. . ." (This text is from the report of a sub-committee of the Congressional Joint Committee on the Conduct of the War, which held an inquiry at the site shortly after the massacre.)

"Numbers of our men were collected together in lines or groups, and deliberately shot. Some were shot while in the river, while others on the bank were shot and their bodies kicked into the water, many of them still living but unable to make exertions to save themselves from drowning. Some of the rebels stood on the top of the hill, or a short distance from its side, and called to our soldiers to come up to them, and, as they approached, shot them down in cold blood; and if their guns or pistols missed fire, forced them to stand there until they were again prepared to fire. All around were heard cries of 'No quarter! No quarter! Kill the damned niggers! Shoot them down!'

"The huts and tents in which many of the wounded sought shelter were set on fire . . . One man was deliberately fastened down to the floor of a tent, face upwards, by means of nail driven through his clothing and into the boards under him, so that he could not possibly escape; and then the tent was set on fire. Another was nailed to the side of a building outside of the fort, and then the building was set on fire and burned. The charred remains of five or six bodies were afterwards found, all but one so disfigured and consumed by the flames that they could not be identified. These deeds of murder and cruelty closed when night came on, only to be renewed the next morning, when the demons carefully sought among the dead lying about in all directions for any other wounded yet alive, and those they found were deliberately shot.

"The rebels themselves had made a pretense of burying a great many of their victims; but they had merely thrown them, without the least regard to care or decency in the trenches and ditches about the fort, or the little hollows and ravines on the hillside, covering them but partially with earth." When the Congressional sub-committee visited Fort Pillow, "we could still see the faces, hands and feet of men, white and black, protruding out of the ground."

Another massacre occurred in October, 1864, when a Union force largely composed of black troops moved into a mountainous part of western Virginia with the aim of attacking Saltville and destroying the salt works there. These were defended by a Confederate force which, though smaller, had a strong tactical position up in the surrounding hills, where they were also protected by "rifle pits made of logs and stones to the height of three feet." (This is from the official report by Union Colonel James Brisbin.) "All being in readiness the Brigade moved to the attack. The Rebels opened upon them a terrific fire but the line pressed steadily forward up the steep side of the mountain until they found themselves within fifty yards of the enemy. Here Col. Wade ordered his force to charge, and the Negroes rushed upon the works with a yell, and after a desperate charge carried the entire line, killing and wounding a large number of the enemy and capturing some prisoners. There were four hundred black soldiers engaged in the battle" and "out of the four hundred engaged, one hundred and fourteen men and four officers fell killed or wounded. Of this fight I can only say that men could not have behaved more bravely. I have seen white troops fight in twenty-seven battles and I never saw any fight better." At the end of the day, however, the Union troops were in a weak position and had to be withdrawn.

Colonel Brisbin also mentioned in his report that on their march up to the front "the colored soldiers as well as their white officers were made the subject of much ridicule and many insulting remarks by the white troops, and in some instances petty outrages such as the pulling off the caps of the colored soldiers, stealing their horses, etc, was practiced by the white soldiers. These insults, as well as the jeers and taunts that they would not fight, were borne by the colored soldiers patiently—in no instance did I hear colored soldiers make any reply to insulting language." After the battle, "on the return of the forces, those who had scoffed at the colored troops on the march out were silent."

The colonel also included this terse sentence: "Such of the colored troops as fell into the hands of the enemy during the battle were brutally murdered." So too were the wounded who had been left behind on the battlefield. In his memoirs, *Kentucky Cavaliers in Dixie*, George Mosgrove, who served with a Confederate cavalry regiment, told what happened: "I awoke at the first faint light of the dawn and saw that, as usual, a dense fog enveloped mountain and valley. All was quiet and impenetrably dark in front. Presently I heard a shot, then another and another . . . It seemed to indicate that the enemy were still near our front." Mosgrove mounted his horse and rode forward through the fog to the site of the battle, and there "the desultory firing was at once explained—the Tennesseans were killing Negroes. Dead Federals, whites and Negroes, were lying all about me. Of course, many of the Negroes had been killed in battle, but many of them had been killed after the battle, that morning. Hearing more firing in front, I cautiously rode forward and came upon a squad of Tennesseans, mad and excited to the highest degree. They were shooting every wounded Negro they could find. Hearing firing on other parts of the field, I knew that the same awful work was going on all about me. It was horrible, most horrible," wrote Mosgrove, who "pitied them from the bottom of my heart, and would have interposed in their behalf had I not known that any effort on my part to save them would be futile." Soon after, "Entering a little log cabin, I paused at the threshold when I saw seven or eight slightly wounded Negroes standing with their backs against the walls. I had scarcely been there a minute when a pistol-shot from the door caused me to turn and observe a boy, not more than sixteen years old, with a pistol in each hand. I stepped back, telling him to hold on until I could get out of the way. In less time than I can write it, the boy had shot every Negro in the room."

Killing black prisoners was a matter of official policy as well as battlefield ferocity. In November, 1862, Colonel Tattnall, commander of an Alabama regiment, reported that a number of black Union troops had been taken prisoner after fighting "shoulder to shoulder with the [white] abolition soldiers." The latter were being held prisoner, but "I have given orders to shoot, wherever & whenever captured, all Negroes found armed & acting in concert with the abolition troops." Acknowledging this report, General Forney ordered that in future Colonel Tattnall should "hang instead of shooting any Negroes caught bearing arms"—hanging being generally considered a more ignominious way of being put to death. That same month James Seddon, the Confederate Secretary of War, after consulting with Jefferson Davis, ruled that slaves taken "in flagrant rebellion are subject to death by the laws of every slave-holding State," and "cannot be recognized in any way as soldiers subject to the rules of war." In some cases, instead of being executed, black prisoners were sold into slavery.

In September, 1863, not long after his regiment's heroic assault on Fort Wagner, Corporal Gooding of the 54th Massachusetts wrote to the president:

"Your Excellency will pardon the presumption of an humble individual like myself in addressing you, but the earnest Solicitations of my Comrades in Arms beside the genuine interest felt by myself in the matter is my excuse for placing before the Executive head of the Nation our Common Grievance.

On the 6th of the last month, the Paymaster of the department informed us that, if we would receive the sum of $10 (ten dollars) per month, he would come and pay us that sum, but that on the sitting of Congress the Reg't would, in his opinion, be allowed the other 3. He did not give us any guarantee that this would be as he hoped; certainly he had no authority for making any such guarantee.

Now the main question is, Are we Soldiers, or are we Labourers? We are fully armed and equipped, have done all the various Duties pertaining to a Soldier's life, have conducted ourselves to the complete satisfaction of General Officers, who were, if anything, prejudiced against us but who now accord us all the encouragement and honour due us; have shared the perils and labour of Reducing the first stronghold that flaunted a Traitor Flag; and more, Mr. President. Today the Anglo-Saxon Mother, Wife, or Sister are not alone in tears for departed Sons, Husbands and Brothers. The patient, trusting Descendants of Afric's Clime have dyed the ground with blood in defense of the Union and Democracy . . .

Now, your Excellency, we have done a Soldier's Duty. Why can't we have a Soldier's pay?"

When he enlisted, Corporal Gooding had relied on the word of Governor Andrew of Massachusetts that the regiment would be paid at the same rate as white soldiers: $10 a month, plus a clothing allowance of $3. In promising this, Andrew had relied on the direct assurance of Secretary of War Stanton. However, Congress had passed two separate laws concerning soldiers' pay. Under the 1862 Militia Act, so-called contrabands—slaves who had escaped to Union lines and been recruited as noncombat workers—were to be paid $10 a month, less $3 to be deducted for clothing. Under the 1863 Enrollment Act, black soldiers in combat regiments would be paid the same as whites. This seems clear enough, but slothful bureaucrats and prejudiced lawyers managed to con-

Contrabands—fugitive slaves who had been recruited to serve the Union, either as soldiers or workers—posing for a photograph during the Peninsular Campaign of 1862. The picture was taken by James F. Gibson, for a while partner of the legendary Civil War photographer Matthew Brady.

clude that the 54th was covered by the first law, not the second. Considering this a humiliation, many soldiers refused to accept any pay at all. Governor Andrew tried to patch things up by getting the state legislature to vote the funds to make up the difference, but this offer was rejected with indignation. "We did not come to fight for money," said one soldier of the 55th. "We came not only to make men of ourselves, but of our other colored brothers at home . . . It is the principle, the one that made us men when we enlisted." (As to Corporal Gooding's letter, it is not known if it ever reached the president; however, when Frederick Douglass brought the matter up with him, Lincoln replied that "the employment of colored troops at all was a great gain to the colored people—that the measure could not have been successfully adopted at the beginning of the war—that the fact that they were not to receive the same pay as white soldiers seemed a necessary concession to smooth the way to their employment at all as soldiers, but that ultimately they would receive the same.")

In the meantime, the pay dispute led some soldiers to mutiny.

> "Sgt. William Walker, of Company A, Third South-Carolina Colored troops was yesterday killed, in accordance with the sentence of a court-martial. He had declared he would no longer remain a soldier for seven dollars per month, and had brought his company to stack their arms before their captain's tent, refusing to do duty until they should be paid thirteen dollars a month, as had been agreed when they were enlisted by Col. Saxton. He was a smart soldier and an able man . . . The execution took place at Jacksonville, Fla., in the presence of the regiments there in garrison. He met his death unflinchingly. Out of eleven shots first fired, but one struck him. A reserve firing party had been provided, and by these he was shot to death. The mutiny for which this man suffered death arose entirely out of the inconsistent and contradictory orders of the Paymaster and the Treasury Department at Washington."   —*Beaufort (S. C.) Tribune*.

Only towards the end of the war were the black troops fairly paid. In the meantime, to add to the injustice, many worried about the effect on their families. "How our families are to live and pay house-rent I know not," wrote one soldier of the 55th. And money was only one of their worries. "My dear husband," wrote one wife from Missouri, one of the states exempt from the Emancipation Proclamation. "I rec'd your letter dated Jan'y 9th also one dated Jan'y 1st but have got no one till now to write for me. You do not know how bad I am treated. They are treating me worse and worse every day. Our child cries for you. Send me some money as soon as you can for me and my child are almost naked . . . . . Your affectionate wife, Ann. P. S. Send our little girl a string of beads in your next letter to remember you by."

Many other black soldiers must have been tormented by news from home telling of hardships they could do nothing to alleviate. Here, for example, is another letter from Missouri, this one dated December 30, 1863:

My Dear Husband,

I have received your last kind letter a few days ago and was much pleased to hear from you once more. It seems like a long time since you left me. I have had nothing but trouble since you left. You recollect what I told you how they would do after you was gone. They abuse me because you went & they say you will not take care of our children & do nothing but quarrel with me all the time and beat me scandalously the day before yesterday—Oh I never thought you would give me so much trouble as I have got to bear now. You ought not to left me in the fix I am in & all these little helpless children to take care of . . . The children talk about you all the time. I wish you could get a furlough & come to see us once more. We want to see you worse than we ever did before. Remember all I told you about how they would do me after you left—for they do worse than they ever did & I do not know what will become of me & my poor little children. Oh I wish you had staid with me & not gone till I could go with you for I do nothing but grieve all the time about you . . . Write to me & do not forget me & my children—farewell my dear husband from your wife.

Martha

And here, datelined Camp Nelson, Kentucky, March 25, 1865, is the affidavit made before a notary public by Patsey Leach, "is a woman of color, who being duly sworn according to law doth depose and say:

"I am a widow and belonged to Warren Wiley of Woodford County, Ky. My husband Julius Leach was a member of Co. D. 5th U. S. Colored Cavalry and was killed at the Salt Works, Va., about six months ago. He had only been about a month in the service when he was killed. I was living with aforesaid Wiley when he died. He knew of my husband's enlisting before I did, but never said anything to me about it. From that time he treated me more cruelly than ever, whipping me frequently without any cause and insulting me on every occasion. About three weeks after my husband enlisted a company of colored soldiers passed our house, and I was there in the garden and looked at them as they passed. My master had been watching me, and when the soldiers had gone I went into the kitchen. My master followed and knocked me to the floor senseless, saying as he did so, 'You have been looking at them darned nigger soldiers.' When I recovered my senses he beat me with a cowhide. When my husband was killed my master whipped me severely, saying my husband had gone into the army to fight against white folks and he, my master, would let me know that I was foolish to let my husband go, he would 'take it out on my back,' he would 'kill me by piecemeal,' and he hoped 'that the last one of the nigger soldiers would be killed.' He whipped me twice after that using similar expressions. The last whipping he gave me he took me into the kitchen, tied my hands, tore all my clothes off until I was entirely naked, bent me down, placed my head between his knees, then whipped me most unmercifully until my back was lacerated all over, the blood oozing out in several places so that I could not wear my underclothes without their becoming saturated with blood. The marks are still visible on my back. On this and other occasions my master whipped me for no other cause than my husband having enlisted."

To preserve them from such treatment many soldiers were allowed to bring their families with them to camp; but this was no favor if the officer in charge was high-handed or prejudiced, or both. This was the case at Camp Nelson, Ky., where some four hundred members of soldiers' families were living in tents and makeshift huts. On the grounds that this was bad for military discipline, the commandant suddenly decided to expel them. In a sworn affidavit, Private Joseph Miller, of the 124th U. S. Colored Infantry, told what happened to his family on November 22, 1864, when, without forewarning, "a mounted guard gave my wife notice that she and her children must leave Camp before morning. This was about six o'clock at night. My little boy about seven years of age had been very sick and was slowly recovering. My wife had no place to go and so remained until morning. About eight o'clock Wednesday morning November 23rd a mounted guard came to my tent and ordered my wife and children out of Camp. The morning was bitter cold. It was freezing hard. I was certain it would kill my sick child to take him out in the cold. I told the man in charge that it would be the death of my boy. I told him that my wife and children had no place to go and I told him that I was a soldier of the United States. He told me that it did not make any difference, he had orders to take all out of the Camp. He told my wife and family that if they did not get up into the wagon which he had he would shoot the last one of them. On being thus threatened my wife and children went into the wagon. My wife carried her sick child in her arms. When they left the tent the wind was blowing hard and cold, and having had to leave much of our clothing when we left our master, my wife with her little one was poorly clad. I followed them as far as the lines. I had no knowledge where they were taking them. At night I went in search of my family. I found them at Nicholasville about six miles from Camp. They were in an old meeting house belonging to the colored people. The building was very cold, having only one fire. My wife and children could not get near the fire, because of the number of colored people huddled together by the soldiers. I found my wife and children shivering with cold and famished with hunger. They had not received a morsel of food during the whole day. My boy was dead. He died directly after getting down from the wagon. I know he was killed by exposure to the inclement weather. I had to return to Camp that night so I left my family in the meeting house and walked back. I had walked there. I traveled in all twelve miles. Next morning I walked to Nicholasville. I dug a grave myself and buried my own child. I left my family in the meeting house, where they still remain."

Another hardship for black soldiers was the poor quality of many of their officers, all of whom, until near the end of the war, were white. In elite regiments such as the Massachusetts 54th, great care was taken to appoint only well-qualified officers who were sympathetic to abolition—though even then their colonel, Robert Gould Shaw, routinely wrote of his soldiers as "niggers." Thanks largely to Colonel Higginson, the First South-Carolina Volunteers was also well officered. But this was not always the case. For many whites, to take a commission in a black regiment was to lose caste. Also, many of the black contraband regiments were assigned to labor rather than to combat, a prospect not likely to attract officers of high quality. Hence some of what follows:

> From a letter approved by forty-five members of a labor battalion at Bermuda Hundreds, Va, September, 1864: "No one knows the injustice practiced on the Negroes at Roanoke. Our gardens are plundered by the white soldiers. What we raise is stolen from us, and if we say anything about it we are sent to the guard house. Rations that the government allows the contrabands are sold to the white secesh citizens, and got out the way at night. It's no uncommon thing to see women and children crying for something to eat. Old clothes sent to the Island from the North for contrabands are sold to the white secesh citizens."
>
> From an anonymous letter to the Secretary of War, datelined Lexington, Ky, October 22, 1865, when the fighting was over: "We haven't had six days furlough to see our wives and we have been in the army fourteen months . . . When our wives come to the camp to see us they are not allowed to come in camp and we are not allowed to go and see them. They are drummed off and the officers say, Go, you damned bitches . . . If we say anything we are put in jail and two or three months pay docked from us . . . Shame, shame, shame how we are treated."

Black troops suffered from many other forms of discrimination. If they were quartered with a white regiment, most of the fatigue duty fell to them. Even after Fort Wagner the Massachusetts 54th was not exempt. "For four months," wrote an anonymous soldier, "we have been steadily working night and day under fire. And such work! Up to our knees in mud half the time, causing the tearing and wearing out of more than the volunteers' yearly allowance of clothing, denied time to repair and wash, denied time to drill and perfect ourselves in soldierly qualities, denied the privilege of burying our dead decently. All this we've born patiently . . ."

And there was this unsigned letter, dated August, 1864, addressed to President Lincoln and sent from Camp Parpit in Louisiana: "My Dear

Friend and x Pre. I take up my Pen to Address you a few simpels And facts. We so-called the 20th U.S. Colored troops, we was got up in the state of New York so said by a grant of the President. We . . . are treated in a Different manner to what other Rigiments is, both Northern men or southern raised Rigiment. Instead of the musket it is the spad and the Wheelbarrow and the Axe, cutting in one of the most horable swamps in Louisiana, stinking and misery . . . The Colored man is like a lost sheep. Many of them old and young was Brave and Active, but has been hurrided by and ignominious Death into Eternity. But I hope God will presearve the rest now in existence to get Justice and Rights. We have to do our Duty or Die and no help for us." Also "We haven't received a cent of Pay since we bin in the field," and "we are cut short of our Ration in A most shocking maner . . . sum times No meat for 2 days. It is a hard thing to be Keept in such a state of misery Continuly. Remember we are men standing in Readiness to face thous vile traitors and Rebels who are trying to Bring your Peaceable homes to Destruction. And how can we stand them in A weak and starving Condition?" And here the letter ends, unsigned and most likely unacknowledged.

There was also the matter of medical care. For all soldiers this was rudimentary, but it was worse for blacks than for whites. About one in twelve white soldiers died of sickness or disease, but blacks died at the rate of one in five. In part this was due to the effects of slavery, in part to the poor food, harsh conditions and overwork in the labor battalions in which so many served, and in part to medical neglect, as described in this report from Lorenzo Thomas, the Adjutant General of the Army, to the Assistant Surgeon General, datelined Nashville, Tenn. January 16, 1865.

> "Sir: A complaint having been made by a Captain of Colored Troops that the wounded soldiers of his company in Hospital were neglected, I made an inspection of Hospital No. 16., containing a large number of sick and wounded of the Colored Troops.
>
> "I have inspected many Hospitals but have never seen one that was not in good order, except this one. The building was unsuitable,

but that, I judge, was unavoidable... What I complained of were the filthy conditions of the wounded, and the bedding. Words of mine cannot describe the utter filthiness of what I saw. I will instance one or two cases:—A soldier wounded Dec. 15, with leg amputated, was on a bed the clothing of which had not been changed up to yesterday, and he was still in the dress in which he was carried from the battle-field, everything saturated with blood—and he complained that the lice were eating him up. Another was shirtless, having discarded his shirt ten days previous on account of its filthy condition. Other in-stances could be given, but let this suffice.

"Had these men been white soldiers, think you this would have been their condition? No! And yet the Black fell side by side of the White with their faces to the Foe . . ."

Finally, there was this question, posed by William Wells Brown, the prominent abolitionist speaker and former slave: "In the struggle between the Federal government and the rebels, the colored men asked the ques-tion, 'Why should we fight?' The question was a legitimate one, at least for those residing in the Northern States, and especially in those States where there were any considerable number of colored people. In every State north of Mason and Dixon's Line, except Massachusetts and Rhode Island, which attempted to raise a regiment of colored men, the blacks are disfranchised, excluded from the jury-box, and in most of them from the public schools. The iron hand of prejudice in the Northern States is as circumscribing and unyielding upon him as the manacles that fettered the slave of the South."

Consider, for example, the New York Riots of July, 1863, that fol-lowed passage of the Conscription Act. "The mob was composed of the lowest and most degraded of the foreign population (mainly Irish), raked from the filthy cellars and dens of the city, steeped in crimes of the deepest dye, and ready for any act, no matter how dark and damnable; together with the worst type of our native criminals . . . ever on the hunt for some deed of robbery or murder."

While the police stood by, "murder, arson, robbery and cruelty reigned triumphant throughout the city, day and night, for more than a week. Breaking into stores, hotels and saloons, and helping themselves to strong drink *ad libitum*, they became inebriated, and marched through every part of the city. Calling at places where large bodies of men were at work, and pressing them in, their numbers rapidly increased to thousands, and their fiendish depredations had no bounds. Having been taught by the leaders of the Democratic party to hate the Negro, and having but a few weeks previous seen regiments of colored volunteers pass through New York on their way South, this infuriated band of drunken men, women and children paid special visits to all localities inhabited by the blacks, and murdered all they could lay their hands on, without regard to age or sex. Every place known to employ Negroes was searched. Steamboats leaving the city, and railroad depots, were watched lest some should escape their vengeance."

The Orphan Asylum for Colored Children, located on Fifth Avenue between 43rd and 44th Street, was a particular target. Though none of the children was killed, the building was ransacked—including "even the little garments for the orphans, which were contributed by the benevolent ladies of the city." The building was then set on fire and "there is now scarcely one brick left on another." Meanwhile "blacks were chased to the docks, thrown into the river, and drowned; while some, after being murdered, were hung to lamp-posts. Between forty and fifty colored persons were killed, and nearly as many maimed for life."

Others put the figure ten times higher—about as many as the black losses in the assault on Fort Wagner, which took place that same week.

But the obvious answer to Brown's question, "Why should we fight?" was that black soldiers were fighting for freedom, a motive that led to many acts of bravery and sacrifice in battle after battle. One of these took place in November, 1864, at Honey Hill, S. C. where a large Confederate force was entrenched behind earthworks that overlooked a swamp crossed by a road. Four black regiments, including the 54th and 55th Massachusetts, composed the main attacking force. According to an account published in the *Savannah Republican*, "The Negroes as usual formed the advance, and had nearly reached the creek when our batteries opened upon them down the road with a terrible volley of spherical case [grapeshot]. This threw them into temporary confusion;

A supply depot on the Mississippi for Grant's army besieging Vicksburg, Milliken's Bend was defended by about a thousand troops, mostly black and recently recruited, when it was attacked on June 7, 1863. After vicious hand-to-hand fighting the Confederates were beaten back, though with very heavy Union losses, and the Vicksburg siege continued.

but the entire force, estimated at five thousand, was quickly restored to order and thrown into a line of battle parallel with our own, up and down the margin of the swamp. Thus the battle raged from eleven in the morning until dark . . . The center and left of the enemy fought with a desperate earnestness. Several attempts were made to charge our batteries, and many of them got nearly across the swamp, but were in every instance forced back by the galling fire poured into them from our lines. We made a visit to the field the day following, and found the road literally strewn with their dead. Some eight or ten bodies were floating in the water where the road crosses; and in a ditch on the roadside, just beyond, we saw six Negroes piled one on top of the other . . . We counted some sixty or seventy bodies in the space of about an acre, many of which were horribly mutilated by shells; some with half their heads shot off, and others completely disemboweled. The artillery was served with great accuracy, and we doubt if any battle-field of the war presents such havoc . . ."

Another battle took place at Milliken's Bend, a Union outpost on the Mississippi above Vicksburg. It began when about five hundred black and two hundred white troops were surprised in camp by a rebel force of about two thousand. At first, wrote an anonymous witness, "the rebels drove our forces towards the gun-boats, taking colored men prisoners and murdering them. This so enraged them that they rallied, and charged the enemy more heroically and desperately than has been recorded during the war. It was a genuine bayonet-charge, a hand-to-hand fight . . . Upon both sides men were killed with the butts of muskets. White and black men were lying side by side, pierced by bayonets, and in some instances transfixed to the earth. In one instance two men—one white and the other black—were found dead, side by side, each having the other's bayonet through his body . . . Broken limbs, broken heads, the mangling of bodies, all prove that this was a contest between enraged men: on the one side from hatred to a race; and on the other desire for self-preservation, revenge for past grievances and the inhuman murder of their comrades." Early in the battle, the rebels had cried, "No quarter!" and indeed "no Negro was ever found alive that was taken a prisoner by the rebels in this fight."

In a letter written very soon after the battle, Captain Miller, company commander in the Ninth Louisiana (Colored) Regiment, described Milliken's Bend as "a horrible fight, the worst I was ever engaged in—not even excepting Shiloh. We went into the fight with thirty-three men. I had sixteen killed, eleven badly wounded, and four slightly . . . I never felt more grieved and sick at heart than when I saw how my brave soldiers had been slaughtered—one with six wounds, all the rest with two or three, none less than two wounds. Two of my colored sergeants were killed; both brave, noble men, always prompt, vigilant, and ready for the fray. I never more wish to hear the expression, 'The niggers won't fight.' Come with me, a hundred yards from where I sit, and I can show you the wounds that cover the bodies of sixteen as brave, loyal and patriotic soldiers as ever drew bead on a rebel."

The Union government was not alone in realizing that if it wanted to win the war it must recruit blacks.

"We must either employ the negroes ourselves, or the enemy will employ them against us," ran an editorial in the *Mississippian* in September, 1863. "Let them be declared free, placed in the ranks, and told to fight for their homes and country." Doing so "would show that although slavery is one of the principles that we started to fight for, yet it falls far short of being the chief one; that, for the sake of our liberty, we are capable of any personal sacrifice; that we regard the emancipation of slaves, and the consequent loss of property, as an evil infinitely less than the subjugation and enslavement of ourselves; that it is not a war exclusively for the privilege of holding negroes in bondage. It would prove to our soldiers, three-fourths of whom never owned a negro, that it is not 'the rich man's war and the poor man's fight,' but a war for the most sacred of all principles, for the dearest of all rights—the right to govern ourselves."

To be sure, from the very first, there had been a place for slaves in the C. S. A., most notably as faithful body-servants to young massa, and many were the tales of their selfless devotion. Such was "The Touching Story of Old Gabe, Who Saved his Wounded Master from Drowning, and Who Sleeps Beside Him in the Family Cemetery," first published in 1897 in *The Sunny South*. The story took place at Clarksville, Tennessee, just before Grant's assault on Fort Donelson. The narrator's family lived close by, so when his father, Col. Mills, was badly wounded he was put on a litter to be carried to a riverboat for the short journey that would bring him home. But to reach the boat the orderlies had to paddle out into the river in a canoe, and "as he was being lifted from the canoe the frail craft tottered, and he dropped into the water among the blocks of floating ice. He was too badly wounded to make any effort to save or help himself, and sank immediately. But his faithful old body servant had never left him, and as soon as he saw what had happened he leaped into the water and fought his way amid the floating ice to where my father was sinking. He caught him with one strong arm, and with the other swam back to the boat, where he and my father were taken on board." Col. Mills died soon after being brought home, but it was to Old Gabe's "faithfulness and bravery that mother and I are indebted for the fact that my father is sleeping in the churchyard, rather than beneath the waters of the Cumberland." After the war, "old Uncle Gabe never left us. He lived for several years after my father's death and served us faithfully to the last, and when he died he was laid by his master's side. A marble tombstone was placed at the head of his grave upon which we inscribed the simple words, 'He was faithful to the end.'"

And then there was the story of Levi Miller, who had been a servant for Capt. McBride and Capt. Anderson (the narrator), of Company C, Fifth Texas Regiment. When Capt. McBride was wounded in the Battle of Manassas, Levi "nursed the captain until he recovered, and both rejoined the company in time for the Fredericksburg fight." Later, during the Pennsylvania campaign, he "met several negroes whom he knew and who had run away from Virginia. They tried to get Levi to desert, but he would not." In 1864, at the Battle of the Wilderness, Levi "brought to me a haversack of rations. In order to get to me in our little temporary ditch and breastworks he had to cross an open field of about 200 yards, and as he came across the field in full run the enemy's sharpshooters clipped the dirt all around him. I told him he could not go back until night as those sharpshooters would get him," but before then "I saw from the maneuvers of the enemy in our front that they were fixing to charge us." Levi then "asked for a gun and ammunition. We had several extra guns in our ditch and the men gave him a gun and ammunition. About 4 p.m. the enemy made a rushing charge. Levi Miller stood by my side and man never fought harder and better than he did; and when the enemy tried to cross our little breastworks and we clubbed and bayoneted them off, no one used his bayonet with more skill and effect than Levi Miller. During the fight the shout of my men was 'Give 'em hell, Lee!' After the fight was over, one of the men made a motion that Levi Miller be enrolled as a full member of the company. I put the motion and of course it passed unanimously, and I immediately enrolled his name as a full member of the company." To conclude: "No better servant was in General Lee's army."

For those slaves not fortunate enough to be officers' servants, there was always service in labor battalions. As early as June, 1861, the Tennessee legislature had voted to enlist black males between the ages of fifteen and fifty, and soon after the *Memphis Avalanche* reported on "a procession of several hundred stout negro men" marching through that city "in military order, under command of Confederate officers." Instead of weapons they carried "shovels, axes, blankets, &c . . . A merrier set were never seen. They were brimful of patriotism, shouting for Jeff Davis and singing war songs"—no doubt under the watchful eyes of their Confederate officers.

For a long time there was no question of enlisting blacks as soldiers in the C .S. A. But as the war went on and on, the South kept having to extend the range of enlistment. In April, 1862, it ran from eighteen to thirty-five; five months later it went from eighteen to forty-five; in February, 1864, it went from seventeen to fifty; and finally from sixteen to sixty. Among those who faced the obvious fact that this shortage of manpower could lead to defeat was Patrick Cleburne, an Irish immigrant who had enlisted as a private and risen to the rank of major general. Early in 1864, he drew up a plan which he addressed to his commander, General Joseph Johnston:

> "We have now been fighting for nearly three years, have spilled much of our best blood, and lost, consumed or thrown to the flames a vast amount of property," wrote Cleburne; and yet "the fruits of our struggle and sacrifices have invariably slipped away from us and left us nothing but long lists of dead and mangled . . . Our soldiers can see no end to this state of affairs except in our own exhaustion; hence, instead of rising to the occasion, they are sinking into a fatal apathy." Desertion was growing, "our supplies failing, our finances in ruin. If this state of things continues much longer we must be subjugated."

Another hard fact:

> "Slavery, from being one of the chief sources of strength at the commencement of the war, has now become, in a military point of view, one of our chief sources of weakness." Slaves absconded to join the Union army and were "an omnipresent spy system, revealing our positions, purposes and resources." As a consequence, the choice was "between the loss of independence and the loss of slavery. We assume that every patriot will freely give up the latter—give up the negro slave rather than be a slave himself." Emancipation would also induce England and France to end their neutrality and provide "both

moral support and material aid." It would "leave the enemy's negro army no motive to fight for," and would "probably cause much of it to desert over to us."

Perhaps because he had not been raised in the South, Cleburne next uttered the heretical opinion that rather than being happy in his lot, the Negro longed for freedom—"the paradise of his hopes. To attain it he will tempt dangers and difficulties not exceeded by the bravest in the field . . . When we make soldiers of them we must make freemen of them beyond all question, and thus enlist their sympathies also. We can do this more effectually than the North can now do, for we can give the negro not only his own freedom, but that of his wife and child, and secure it to him in his old home."

Finally, "Will the slaves fight?" Of course they would. "The negro slaves of St. Domingo, fighting for freedom, defeated their white masters and the French troops sent against them." And more recently "half-trained negroes have fought as bravely as many other half-trained Yankees."

Thirteen other field officers signed on to Cleburne's proposal, which was then sent to General Joseph Johnston, who refused to forward it to the Confederate War Department on the grounds that it was "more political than military." A copy did, however, reach Jefferson Davis, who deemed "it inexpedient, at this time, to give publicity to this paper, and request that it be suppressed."

Nevertheless, the plan somehow became known and stirred strong opinions, especially among other generals. "A monstrous proposition," wrote General Patton Anderson, "revolting to Southern sentiment, Southern pride, and Southern honor." General Beauregard deplored the idea of enlisting "a merciless servile race as soldiers." "The most pernicious idea that has been suggested since the war began," wrote General Howell Cobb. "You cannot make soldiers of slaves, nor slaves of soldiers . . . If slaves will make good soldiers, our whole theory of slavery is wrong."

Many civilians felt the same. A letter writer to the *Richmond Whig*, after reminding his readers of "the opinion held by the whole South... that servitude is a divinely appointed condition for the highest good of the slave," concluded that "if the slave must fight, he should fight for the blessings he enjoys as a slave, and not for the miseries that would attend him if freed." "Q" in the *Macon Telegraph*, January, 1865, asserted that "every life that has been lost in this struggle was an offering upon the altar of African Slavery," and that to arm and emancipate slaves "would be a foul wrong to our departed heroes who have fallen in its defense." Representative Henry Chambers of Mississippi declared that "victory itself would be robbed of its glory if shared with slaves." "Independence without slavery would be valueless," wrote a Texan. And an editorial in the *Richmond Dispatch* insisted that "we have no occasion to resort to any such extreme measure. Our affairs are in a better condition, and our prospects brighter, than they ever have been since the commencement of the war." (This was published on November 9, 1864, the day after Lincoln's re-election and just as General Sherman, having destroyed Atlanta, was setting off on his devastating March to the Sea.)

But the opinion that really mattered was that of Robert E. Lee. In January, 1865, he wrote "We must decide whether slavery shall be extinguished by our enemies, and the slaves used against us, or use them ourselves . . . My own opinion is that we should employ them without delay." In February, Jefferson Davis declared that "it is now becoming daily more evident to all reflecting persons that we are reduced to choosing whether the negroes shall fight for us or against us." In March the Confederate Congress voted that the President is "hereby authorized to ask for, and accept from the owners of slaves, the services of such numbers of able-bodied negro men as he may deem expedient for and during the war to perform military service. The enlistment will be for the war"— which ended on April 9, less than three weeks later, with Lee's surrender at Appomattox.

While the South debated whether to enlist slaves, the armies of the North were setting them free. Here are some accounts of how that happened, drawn from the *Slave Narrative* interviews conducted many years later. First, Katie Rowe, of Arkansas, who grew up on a plantation owned by Dr. Isaac Jones, who lived in a nearby town.

"He get boiling mad when the Yankees have that big battle at Pea Ridge and scatter the 'Federates all down through our country, all bleeding and tied up and hungry, and he just mount on his hoss and ride out to the plantation where we all hoeing corn. He ride up and tell old man Saunders—that the overseer—to bunch us all up round the lead row man—that my own uncle, Sandy—and then he tell us the law: 'You niggers been seeing the 'Federate soldiers coming by here looking pretty raggedy and hurt and wore out,' he say, 'but that no sign they licked! Them Yankees ain't gwine get this far, but iffen they do, you all ain't gwine get free by 'em, 'cause I gwine free you before that. When they get here they gwine find you already free, 'cause I gwine line you up on the bank of Bois d'Arc Creek and free you with my shotgun! Anybody miss just one lick with the hoe, or one step in the line, or one clap of that bell, or one toot of the horn, and he gwine be free and talking to the Devil long before he ever see a pair of blue britches!' That the way he talk to us, and that the way he act with us all the time."

But not for much longer, for just as the rural South was losing to the industrially advanced North, so Dr. Jones was to fall victim to a piece of modern technology—a steam-powered threshing machine, known as "the gin."

"Next fall, after he ride out and tell us he gwine shoot us before he let us free, he come out to see how his steam gin doing. The gin box was a little old thing, 'bout as big as a bedstead, with a long belt running through the side of the gin house out to the engine and boiler in the yard. The boiler burn cord wood, and it have a little crack in it where the nigger ginner been trying to fix it.

"Old Master come out, hopping mad 'cause the gin shut down, and asked the ginner, Old Brown, what the matter. Old Brown say the boiler weak and it liable to bust, but Old Master jump down offen his hoss and go round to the boiler and say, 'Cuss fire to your black heart! That boiler all right! Throw on some cord wood, cuss fire to your heart!'

"Old Brown start to the wood pile grumbling to hisself, and Old Master stoop down to look at the boiler again, and it blow right up, and him standing right there! Old Master was blowed all to pieces, and they just find little bitsy chunks of his clothes and parts of him to bury. The woodpile blow down, and Old Brown land way off in the woods, but he wasn't killed. Two wagons of cotton blowed over, and the mules ran away, and all the niggers was scared nearly to death 'cause we knowed the overseer gwine be a lot worse now that Old Master was gone.

"Old Man Saunders was the hardest overseer of anybody. He would get mad and give a whipping some time, and the slave wouldn't even know what it was about. Later on, in the War, the Yankees come in all around us and camp, and the overseer get sweet as honey in the comb. Nobody get a whipping all the time the Yankees there.

"I never forget the day we was set free. That morning we all go to the cotton field early, and then a house nigger come out from Old Mistress on a hoss and say she want the overseer to come into town, and he leave and go in. After while, the old horn blow up at the overseer's house, and we all stop and listen, 'cause it the wrong time of day for the horn.

"We start chopping again, and there go the horn again. The lead row nigger holler, 'Hold up!' And we all stop again. 'We better go in. That our horn.' When we get to the quarters we see all the old ones and the children up in the overseer's yard, so we go on up there.

"Sitting on the gallery in a hide-bottom chair was a man we never see before. He had on a big broad black hat like the Yankees wore, but it didn't have no yellow string on it like most the Yankees had, and he was in store clothes that wasn't homespun or jeans, and they was black. His hair was plumb gray and so was his beard, and it come way down here on his chest.

"The man say, 'You darkies know what day this is?' He talk kind, and smile.

"We all don't know, of course, and we just stand there and grin. Pretty soon he ask again and the head man say, 'No, we don't know.'

"'Well, this the fourth day of June, and this is 1865, and I want you all to 'member this date, 'cause you always going 'member the day. Today you is free, just like I is, and Mr. Saunders, and your mistress and all us white people. I come to tell you, and I wants you to be sure you all understand, 'cause you don't have to get up and go by the horn no more. You is your own bosses now, and you don't have to have no passes to go and come.' We never did have no passes, nohow, but we knowed lots of other niggers on other plantations got 'em. 'I wants to bless you and hope you always is happy, and tell you you got all the right that any white people got,' the man say, and then he get up on his hoss and ride off.

"Old Mistress never get well after she lose all her niggers, and one day the white boss tell us she just drop over dead sitting in her chair, and we know her heart just broke. Next year the chillun sell off most the place and we scatter off, and I and Mammy go into Little Rock and do work in the town.

"Lots of old people like me say that they was happy in slavery, and that they had the worst tribulations after freedom, but I knows they didn't have no white master and overseer like we all had on our place. They both dead now, and they no use talking about the dead, but I know I been long gone by now iffen that white man Saunders didn't lose his hold on me.

"It was the fourth day of June in 1865 I begins to live, and I gwine take the picture of that old man in the big black hat and long whiskers, sitting on the gallery and talking kind to us, clean into my grave with me."

Eda Harper, Pine Bluff, Ark.:

"When the war ended, white man come into the field and tell my mother-in-law she free as he is. She dropped her hoe and danced up to the turn road and danced right up into Old Master's parlor. She went so fast a bird could have sat on her dress tail. That was in June. That night she sent and got all her neighbors, and they danced all night long."

Margaret Hughes, of Columbia, S. C.:

"My old aunty was glad to hear 'bout the Yankees coming. She just set and talk 'bout what a good time we was going to have after the Yankees come. She'd say, 'Child, we going to have such a good time a-setting at the white folks' table, a-eating off the white folks table, and a-rocking in the big rocking chair.'

"Something awful happen to one of the slaves though when the Yankees did come. One of the young gals tell the Yankees where missus had her silver, money, and jewelry hid, and they got it all. What do you think happened to the poor gal? After the Yankees had gone, the missus and massa had the poor gal hung till she die. It was something awful to see.

"When the slaves were freed the most of them didn't had nowhere to go, so we just stayed with the massa and missus. I wishes sometimes I was a slave again, 'cause I likes being a slave, didn't have nothing to worry 'bout then."

Cheney Cross was a young house slave on a prosperous plantation in Alabama when the war came. Her mistress was Mary Fields—"Miss Mary"—and "I was brung up in the house with my white folks. I slept on the little trundler bed what pushed under the big bed during the day. I watched over them chillun day and night. I washed 'em, and fed 'em, and played with 'em."

When news came that Union soldiers were expected to raid that part of Alabama, "my mistress took me down to the spring at the back of the house. Down there was a hollow tree stump, taller than you is. She tell me to climb up to the top of that hollow tree, then she hand me a big heavy bundle, all wrapped up and tied tight. It sure was heavy! Then she say, 'Drop it in, Cheney.' I didn't know what she's up to, but that was the silver and jewelry she was hiding?

The day the soldiers arrived, "I's sitting there in the loom room, and Mr. Thad Watt's little girl, Louise, she's standing at the window. She say, 'O-o-h! Nannie! Just look down yonder!' 'Baby, what is that?' I says. 'Them's the Yankees coming!' 'God help us!' I says, and before I can catch my breath the place is covered. When they pass on by me, they nigh shook me out of my skin. 'Where's the mens?' they say, and shake me up. 'Where's the arms?' They shake me till my eyeballs loosen up. 'Where's the silver?' Lord! Was my teeths dropping out? They didn't give me time to catch my breath. All the time, Miss Mary just look 'em in the eye and say nothing.

"They took them Enfield rifles, half as long as that door, and bust in the smokehouse window. They jack me up offen my feet and drag me up the ladder and say, 'Get that meat out.' I kept on throwing out Miss Mary's hams and sausages till they holler, 'Stop.' I come backing down that ladder like a squirrel, and I ain't stopped backing till I reach Miss Mary.

"Yes, Lord! Them Yankees loaded up a wagon full of meat and took the whole barrel of 'lasses. Taking that 'lasses killed us children, our mainest amusement was making 'lasses candy—then us cakewalk round it. Now that was all gone. Look like them soldiers had to sharpen their swords on everything in sight. The big crepe mullen bush by the parlor window was blooming so pink and pretty, and they just stood there and whack off them blooms like folks' heads dropping on the ground.

"I seed the sergeant when he run his bayonet clean through Miss Mary's bestest feather bed and rip it slam open. With that, a wind blowed up and took them feathers every whichaway for Sunday. You couldn't see where you's at. The sergeant, he just throwed back his head and laugh fit to kill hisself. Then first thing next, he done suck a feather down his windpipe. Lord, honey, that white man sure struggled! Them soldiers throwed water in his face. They shook him and beat him and roll him over, and all the time he's getting limberer and bluerer. Then they jack him up by his feets and stand him on his head. Then they pump him up and down. Then they shook him till he spit. Then he come to.

"They didn't cut no more mattresses. And they didn't cut nothing much up in the parlor, but when they left the next day, the whole place was strewed with mutilation."

Sarah Debro, who had been "born some time back in the fifties," had been a privileged young house servant at the start of the war, living with the rich Cain family of Orange County, North Carolina. "Marse Cain was good to his niggers. He didn't whip them like some owners did, but if they done mean, he sold them. They knew this so they minded him."

Mrs. Cain was generally spoken of as Miss Polly.

"Whenever she seed a child down in the quarters that she wanted to raise by hand, she took them up to the big house and trained them. I was to be a housemaid. The day she took me, my mammy cried, 'cause she knew I would never be allowed to live at the cabin with her no more. Miss Polly was big and fat and she made us niggers mind, and we had to keep clean. My dresses and aprons was starched stiff. I had a clean apron everyday. We had white sheets on the beds, and we niggers had plenty to eat too, even ham. When Miss Polly went to ride, she took me in the carriage with her. The driver set way up high, and me and Miss Polly set way down low. They was two hosses with shiny harness. I toted Miss Polly's bags and bundles, and if she dropped her handkerchief, I picked it up. I loved Miss Polly and loved staying at the big house.

"The first cannon I heard scared me near about to death. We could hear them going Boom! Boom! I thought it was thunder, then Miss Polly say, 'Listen, Sarah. Hear them cannons? They's killing our mens.' Then she began to cry. I run in the kitchen where Aunt Charity was cooking and told her Miss Polly was crying. She said, 'She ain't crying 'cause the Yankees killing the mens. She's doing all that crying 'cause she scared we's going to be set free.' Then I got mad and told her Miss Polly wasn't like that.

"I remember when Wheeler's Cavalry come through. They was 'Federates, but they was mean as the Yankees. They stole everything they could find and killed a pile of niggers. They come around checking. They asked the niggers if they wanted to be free. If they say yes, then they shot them down, but if they say no, they let them alone. They took three of my uncles out in the woods and shot they faces off.

"I remember the first time the Yankees come. They come galloping down the road, jumping over the palings, trompling down the rose bushes and messing up the flower beds. They stomped all over the house, in the kitchen, pantries, smokehouse and everywhere, but they didn't find much, 'cause near about everything done been hid. I was setting on the steps when a big Yankee come up. He had on a cap, and his eyes was mean. 'Where did they hide the gold and silver, nigger?' he yelled at me.

"I was scared, and my hands was ashy, but I told him I didn't know nothing about nothing; that if anybody done hid things, they hid it while I was asleep.

"When the war was over, the Yankees was all around the place, telling the niggers what to do. They told them they was free, that they didn't have to slave for the white folks no more. My folks all left Marse Cain and went to live in houses that the Yankees built. They was like poor white folks' houses, little shacks made out of sticks and mud, with sticks-and-mud chimneys. They wasn't like

Marse Cain's cabins, planked up and warm.

"One day my mammy come to the big house after me. I didn't want to go. I wanted to stay with Miss Polly. I begun to cry, and Mammy caught hold of me. I grabbed Miss Polly and held on so tight that I tore her skirt binding loose. 'Let her stay with me,' Miss Polly said to Mammy.

"But Mammy shook her head. 'You took her away from me and didn't pay no mind to my crying, so now I's taking her back home. We's free now, Miss Polly, we ain't going to be slaves no more to nobody.' She dragged me away. I can see how Miss Polly looked now. She didn't say nothing, but she looked hard at mammy, and her face was white.

"I looks back and thinks. I ain't never forgot them slavery days, and I ain't never forgot Miss Polly and my white starched aprons."

Martha Colquist, of Athens, Georgia:

"My grandma was a powerful Christian woman, and she did love to sing and shout. That's how come Marse Billy had her locked up in the loom room when the Yankee mens come to our plantation. Grandma would get to shouting so loud she would make so much fuss nobody in the church could hear the preacher, and she would wander off from the gallery and go downstairs and try to go down the white folks' aisle to get to the altar where the preacher was, and they was always locking her up for 'sturbing worship, but they never could break her from that shouting.

"Them Yankee soldiers rode up in the big house yard and 'gun to ask me questions about where Marse Billy was and where everything on the place was kept, but I was too scared to say nothing. Everything was quiet and still as could be, 'cept for Grandma a-singing and shouting up in the loom house all by herself. One of them Yankees tried the door, and he asked me how come it was locked. I told him it was 'cause Grandma had 'sturbed the Baptist meeting with her shouting. Them mens grabbed the axe from the woodpile and busted the door down. They went in and got Grandma. They asked her about how come she was locked up, and she told 'em the same thing I had told 'em. They asked if she was hungry, and she said she was. They took Grandma to the kitchen and told Ma to give her some of the white folks' dinner. Ma said, 'But the white folkses ain't ate yet.' 'Go right on,' the Yankees said, 'and give it to her, the best in the pot, and if they's anything left when she gets through, maybe us will let the white folkses have some of it.'

After the Yankees was done gone off, Grandma 'gun to fuss: 'Now, them soldiers was telling us what ain't so, 'cause ain't nobody got no right to take what belongs to Master and Mistress.' And Ma joined in: 'Sure it ain't no truth in what them Yankees was a-saying,' and us went right on living just like us always done till Marse Billy called us together and told us the war was over and us was free."

William Colbert, of Georgia:

"Massa had three boys to go to war, but there wasn't one to come home. All the chillun he had was killed. Massa, he lost all his money and the house soon begin droppin' away to nothin'. Us niggers one by one left the old place, and the last time I seed the home plantation I was a-standing on a hill. I looked back on it for the last time through a patch of scrub pines and it look so lonely. There wasn't but one person in sight, the massa. He was a-setting in a wicker chair in the yard lookin' out over a small field of cotton and corn. There was four crosses in the graveyard in the side lawn where he was a-settin'—the fourth one was his wife."

As a boy, Primus Smith, of Virginia, had served in the household of Robert E. Lee, "swishing the flies off the table with a brush" while his master was "eating dinner and talking about how some day it looked like the South was going to have to go to war against the North." By the time that war came, he had a different master, who went off to fight, leaving "us darkies in charge of an overseer. This overseer's name was John Ashby, and he had a terrible temper. One day us darkies was cuttin' cane and Ashby got mad at my uncle and gave him a flogging 'til the blood run down his back. My uncle said, 'Some day I will get free, and some day I will get you for this, John Ashby.'

"Well, sir, years later me and my uncle were free, and we were a-settin' on the river bank talking. This same John Ashby came ridin' by on a horse, and he recognized us. He got off his horse, and came over like he wanted to be friendly. My uncle didn't say a word, but he picked up John Ashby and threw him out in the river. Every time John Ashby would start to crawl up on the bank, my uncle would hit him on the head with a stick and throw him back in the river. Finally he drowned. It was kind of wicked, but I saw it with my own eyes."

In her *Reminiscences*, Annie Burton, who had been born into slavery, recalled this anecdote from her childhood in Clayton, Alabama. The war had recently ended, bringing "a sad, sad change on the old plantation; and the beautiful, proud Sunny South, with its masters and mistresses, was bowed beneath the sin brought about by slavery." After a long separation, the family had just been reunited and "my mother had got settled in her hut, with her little brood hovered around her, from which she had been so long absent." The brood was composed of five small children, and the hut, made of logs, "had one door, and an opening in one wall, with an inside shutter, was the only window. The door was fastened with a latch. Our beds were some straw.

"The first day in the hut was a rainy day, and as night drew near it grew more fierce, and we children had gathered some little fagots to make a fire by the time mother came home with something for us to eat. It was only corn meal and pease and ham-bone and skins. She started a little fire, and swung the pot over the fire, and filled it with the pease and ham-bone and skins. Then she seated her little brood around the fire on pieces of blanket, where we watched with all our eyes. She took down an old broken earthen bowl, and tossed into it the little meal she had brought, stirring it up with water, making a hoe cake." Then "all at once there came a knock at the door. My mother answered the knock. When she opened the door, there stood a white woman and three little children, all dripping with the rain. My mother said, 'In the name of the Lord, where are you going on such a night with these children?' The woman said, 'Auntie, I am traveling. Will you please let me stop here tonight, out of the rain, with my children?' My mother said, 'Yes, honey. I ain't got much, but what I have got I will share with you.' 'God bless you!' They all came in. We children looked in wonder at what had come, but my mother scattered her own little brood and made a place for the forlorn wanderers. She said, 'Wait, honey, let me turn over that hoe cake.' Then the two women fell to talking, each telling a tale of woe.

"My mother said to the woman, 'Honey, ain't you got no husband?' She said, 'No, my husband got killed in the war.' My mother replied, 'Well, my husband died right after the war. But with God's help, I can get along.'" They talked, and the white woman explained that she was on her way to her kinsfolk, who lived about fifty miles away, "'up in the country. I am on my way there now.'

"We hoped the talk was most ended, for we were anxiously watching that pot. Pretty soon my mother exclaimed, 'My Lord! I suppose the little children are nearly starved. Are those pease done, young ones?' She turned and said to the white woman, 'Have you-all had anything to eat?' 'We stopped at a house about dinner time, but the woman didn't have anything but some bread and buttermilk.' My mother said, 'Well, honey, I ain't got but a little, but I will divide with you.' The woman said, 'Thank you, Auntie. You just give my children a little; I can do without it.'

"Then came the dividing. We all watched with all our eyes to see what the shares would be. My mother broke a mouthful of bread and put it on each of the tin plates. Then she took the old spoon and equally divided the pea soup. We children were seated round the fire, with some little wooden spoons. But the wooden spoons didn't quite go round, and some of us had to eat with our fingers. Our share of the meal was so small that we were as hungry when we finished as when we began."

After supper "my mother said 'One of you go and pull that straw out of the corner and get ready to go to bed.' We all lay down on the straw, the white children with us, and my mother covered us with the blanket. We were soon in 'the Land of Nod', forgetting our empty stomachs. The two mothers still continued to talk, sitting down on the only seats.

"Bright and early in the morning we were called up, and the rest of the hoe cake was eaten for breakfast. The little wanderers and their mother shared our meal and then they started again on their journey towards their home among their kinsfolk, and we never saw them again. My mother said, 'God bless you! I wish you all good luck. I hope you will reach your home safely.'"

With the war's end, regiments disbanded. In September, 1865, the *New-York Tribune* ran this story:

"The Fifty-fourth Regiment of Massachusetts Volunteers was welcomed back to Boston on Saturday. There was a public reception, a review by the Governor and Council at the State House, another on the Common by the Mayor, an address to his officers and men by Colonel Hallowell; and then the regiment was disbanded. The demonstrations of respect were rather more than have usually been awarded to returning regiments, even in Massachusetts, which cherishes her soldiers with an unforgetting affection. They were so honored in this case, we presume, because the regiment is a representative one. There were regiments from that State which had seen more fighting than this, though none which had done any better fighting when occasion offered; none which had a higher reputation for discipline, patient endurance, and impetuous valor. But the true reason why Massachusetts singled out this regiment for peculiar honor is because this was the first colored regiment organized in the North, and was that one on whose good conduct depended for a long time the success of the whole experiment of arming black citizens in defense of the Republic. It is not too much to say that if this Massachusetts Fifty-fourth had faltered when its trial came, two hundred thousand colored troops for whom it was a pioneer would never have been put into the field . . . But it did not falter. It made Fort Wagner such a name to the colored race as Bunker Hill has been for ninety years to the white Yankees.

"To this Massachusetts Fifty-fourth was set the stupendous task to convince the white race that colored troops would fight— and not only that they would fight, but that they could be made, in every sense of the word, soldiers. It is not easy to recall at this day the state of public opinion on that point—the contemptuous disbelief in the courage of an enslaved race, or rather of a race with a colored skin. Nobody pretends now that the Negro won't fight."

In February, 1866, Lt. Col. Christopher Trowbridge, who had succeeded Higginson as commander of the First South Carolina Volunteers, bade his troops farewell. The first all-slave regiment in the U. S. Army, it had been formed by General Hunter, then partially disbanded, then reconstituted as the 33rd U. S. C. T.; but the soldiers still thought of themselves as the First South Carolina Volunteers. This final parade was held on Morris Island, within sight of Fort Wagner.

"Comrades: The hour is at hand when we must separate for ever. Nothing can take from us the pride we feel when we look upon the history of the First South Carolina Volunteers, the first black regiment that ever bore arms in defense of freedom on the continent of America. On the 9th day of May, 1862, at which time there were nearly four millions of your race in bondage, sanctioned by the laws of the land and protected by our flag—on that day, in the face of the floods of prejudice that well-nigh deluged every avenue to manhood and true liberty, you came forth to do battle for your country and kindred.

"For long and weary months, without pay or even the privilege of being recognized as soldiers, you labored on, only to be disbanded and sent to your homes without even a hope of reward; and when our country, necessitated by the deadly struggle with armed traitors, finally granted you the opportunity again to come forth in defense of the nation's life, the alacrity with which you responded to the call gave abundant evidence of your readiness to strike a manly blow for the liberty of your race. And from that little band of hopeful, trusting, and brave men who gathered at Camp Saxton, on Port Royal Island, in the fall of '62, amidst the terrible prejudices that surrounded us, has grown an army of a hundred and forty thousand black soldiers, whose valor and heroism have won for your race a name which will live as long as the undying pages of history shall endure; and by whose efforts, united with those of the white man, armed rebellion has been conquered, the millions of bondsmen have been emancipated, and the fundamental law of the land has been so altered as to remove forever the possibility of human slavery being established within the borders of redeemed America. The flag of our fathers, restored to its rightful significance, now floats over every foot of our territory, from Maine to California, and beholds only free men!"

Following the war, three amendments to the Constitution were passed:

Article XIII. December, 1865. Section 1. "Neither slavery nor involuntary servitude, except as a punishment for crime whereof the party shall have been duly convicted, shall exist within the United States, or any place subject to their jurisdiction."

Article XIV. July, 1868. Section 1. "All persons born or naturalized in the United States, and subject to the jurisdiction thereof, are citizens of the United States and of the State wherein they reside. No State shall make or enforce any law which shall abridge the privileges or immunities of citizens of the United States; nor shall any State deprive any person of life, liberty, or property, without due process of law; nor deny to any person within its jurisdiction the equal protection of the laws."

Article XV. March, 1870. Section 1. "The right of citizens of the United States to vote shall not be denied or abridged by the United States or by any State on account of race, color, or previous condition of servitude."

Finally, here are some passages from three speeches by Frederick Douglass, which reflect the hopes, fears and disappointments that followed Emancipation and Reconstruction.

The first was given on December 28, 1862, at the African Methodist Episcopal Zion Church in Rochester, on the eve of the promulgation of the Emancipation Proclamation, "a moment for joy, thanksgiving and Praise." Though the Proclamation did not cover the whole country, it was clear that "slavery once abolished in the rebel states, will give the death wound to slavery in the border states. When Arkansas is a free state, Missouri cannot be a slave state." But this was "no time for the friends of freedom to fold their hands and consider their work at an end. Slavery has existed in this country too long, and has stamped its character too deeply and indelibly, to be blotted out in a day or a year, or even a generation. Law and the sword can and will in the end abolish slavery. But law and the sword cannot abolish the malignant slave-holding sentiment which has kept the slave system alive in this country during two centuries. Pride of race, prejudice against color, will raise their hateful clamor for oppression of the Negro as heretofore. The slave having ceased to be the abject slave of a single master, his enemies will endeavor to make him the slave of society at large."

Next, a passage from Douglass' speech at a ceremony unveiling the Freedmen's Monument in memory of Abraham Lincoln. The event took place in Washington, D. C., on April 14, 1876, when there was still some hope that Reconstruction would be a success:

> "Few facts could better illustrate the vast and wonderful change which has taken place in our condition as a people than the fact of our assembling here to-day for the purpose which has called us together. Harmless, beautiful, proper and praiseworthy as this demonstration is, I cannot forget that no such demonstration would have been tolerated here twenty years ago. The spirit of slavery and barbarism which, in some dark and distant parts of our country, still lingers to blight and to destroy, would have made our assembling here the signal and excuse for opening upon us all the flood-gates of wrath and violence. That we are here in peace to-day is a compliment and a credit to American civilization, and a prophecy of still greater national enlightenment and progress in the future. I refer to the past not in malice, for this is no day for malice, but simply to place more distinctly in front the gratifying and glorious change which has come both to our white fellow-citizens and to ourselves, and to congratulate all upon the contrast between now and then—between the new dispensation of freedom with its thousand blessings to both races, and the old dispensation of slavery with its ten thousand evils to both races, white and black."

And finally, here are parts of his speech at a rally held in Elmira, N.Y. on August 1, 1880, to celebrate the anniversary of West Indian emancipation. Reconstruction had collapsed, but Douglass did his best to find a silver lining:

"We are sometimes asked why we American citizens annually celebrate West India emancipation when we might celebrate American emancipation. Why go abroad, say they, when we might as well stay at home? The answer is easily given. Human liberty excludes all idea of home and abroad. It is universal and spurns localization. The cause of human liberty is one the whole world over. The downfall of slavery under British power meant the downfall of slavery, ultimately, under American power, and the downfall of Negro slavery everywhere.

"The abolitionists of this country have been charged with bringing on the war between the North and South, and in one sense this is true. Had there been no anti-slavery agitation at the North, there would have been no active anti-slavery agitation anywhere to resist the demands of the slave power at the South, and where there is no resistance there can be no war. Slavery would then have been nationalized, and the whole country would then have been subjected to its power. Resistance to slavery, and the extension of slavery, invited and provoked secession and war."

But now, "How stands the case with the recently emancipated millions of colored people in our own country? What is their condition today? By law, by the constitution of the United States, slavery has no existence in our country. The legal form has been abolished. By the law and the constitution, the Negro is a man and a citizen, and has all the rights and liberties guaranteed to any other variety of the human family residing in the United States. He has a country, a flag, and a government, and may legally claim full and complete protection under the laws. This is our legal and theoretical condition. This is our condition on paper and parchment.

"It is a great thing to have the supreme law of the land on the side of justice and liberty. It is the line up to which the nation is destined to march—the law to which the nation's life must ultimately conform. It is a great principle, up to which we may educate the people, and to this extent its value exceeds all speech.

"But to-day, in most of the Southern States, the fourteenth and fifteenth amendments are virtually nullified. The rights which they were intended to guarantee are denied and held in contempt. The citizenship granted in the fourteenth amendment is practically a mockery, and the right to vote, provided for in the fifteenth amendment, is literally stamped out in face of government. The old master class is to-day triumphant, and the newly enfranchised class in a condition but little above that in which they were found before the rebellion.

"Do you ask me how, after all that has been done, this state of things has been made possible? I will tell you. Our reconstruction measures were radically defective. They left the former slave completely in the power of the old master, the loyal citizen in the hands of the disloyal rebel against the government. Wise, grand, and comprehensive in scope and design as were the reconstruction measures, high and honorable as were the intentions of the statesmen by whom they were framed and adopted, time and experience, which try all things, have demonstrated that they did not successfully meet the case.

"History does not furnish an example of emancipation under conditions less friendly to the emancipated class than this American example. The very manner of their emancipation invited to the heads of the freedmen the bitterest hostility of race and class. They were hated because they had been slaves, hated because they were now free, and hated because of those who had freed them. Nothing was to be expected other than what has happened, and he is a poor student of the human heart who does not see that the old master class would naturally employ every power and means in their reach to make the great measure of emancipation unsuccessful and utterly odious. It was born in the tempest and whirlwind of war, and has lived in a storm of violence and blood. When the Hebrews were emancipated, they were told to take spoil from the Egyptians. When the serfs of Russia were emancipated, they were given three acres of ground upon which they could live and make a living. But not so when our slaves were emancipated. They were sent away empty-handed, without money, without friends, and without a foot of land to stand upon. The wonder is, not that the colored people of the South have done so little in the way of acquiring a comfortable living, but that they live at all.

"Taking all the circumstances into consideration, the colored people have no reason to despair. We still live, and while there is life there is hope. The fact that we have endured wrongs and hardships which would have destroyed any other race, and have increased in numbers and public consideration, ought to strengthen our faith in ourselves and our future. Let us then, wherever we are, whether at the North or at the South, resolutely struggle on in the belief that there is a better day coming, and that we by patience, industry, uprightness, and economy may hasten that better day.

"Greatness does not come to any people on flowery beds of ease. We must fight to win the prize."

ACKNOWLEDGMENTS

Many thanks to my agent, Bill Hanna; to my editor, Adam O'Brien; and to my wife, Linda, for her great help with the index and illustrations, and to my son, Alexander.

NOTES

CHAPTER I: For Ibn Battuta and other travelers see *The Travels of Ibn Battuta*, translated by the Rev. Samuel Lee, The Oriental Translation Committee, London, 1829; also, *Corpus of Early Arabic Sources for West African History*, translated by J. F. P. Hopkins, edited and annotated by N. Levtzion, Cambridge University Press, Cambridge, U. K., 1981; for the Portuguese see *The Chronicle of the Discovery and Conquest of Guinea, written by Gomes Eannes de Azurara; now first done into English by Charles Raymond Beazley and Edgar Prestage*, The Hakluyt Society, London, 1886; for Cadamosto and Barros see *The Voyages of Cadamosto, and other Documents on Western Africa in the Second Half of the Fifteenth Century*, translated and edited by G. R. Crone, The Hakluyt Society, London, 1937; for Columbus and the Spanish see *The Letter of Columbus to Luis de Sant Angel, 1493*, edited by Albert B. Hart and Edward Channing, American History Leaflets No. 1, Parker P. Simmons, Cambridge, 1913; also, *The Devastation of the Indies: A Brief Account* by Bartolomeo de las Casas, The Seabury Press, New York, 1974; for Sir John Hawkins see *Voyages and Travels Mainly During the 16th and 17th Centuries*, edited by Charles Raymond Beazley, reissued by Cooper Square Publishers, New York, 1964.

CHAPTER 2: For Captain Phillips see *Journal of his Voyage from England to Cape Monseradoe in Africa*, in Awnsham Churchill's *A Collection of Voyages and Travels*, Vol 6, London, 1732; for Silas Told see *An Account of the Life and Dealings of God with Silas Told*, printed by R.W.Cowdroy, London, 1805; for John Newton see *Thoughts Upon the African Slave Trade*, J. Buckland, London, 1788; for John Barbot see *Description of the Coasts of Nigritia*, in Awnsham Churchill's *A Collection of Voyages and Travels*, Vol 5, London, 1732; for David van Nyendael see *A Description of the Kingdom of Benin* in *A New and Accurate Description of the Coast of Guinea* by William Bosman, London, 1705; for Alexander Falconbridge see *An Account of the Slave Trade on the Coast of Africa*, J. Phillips, London, 1788; for Olaudah Equiano see *The Interesting Narrative of the Life of Olaudah Equiano, or Gustavus Vassa, the African, Written by Himself*, edited by Vincent Carretta, Penguin Books, New York, 1995; for Francis Moore see *Travels into the Inland Parts of Africa* in Awnsham Churchill's *A New Collection of Voyages, Discoveries and Travels*, Vol. 6, London, 1767; for William Snelgrave see *A New Account of Some Parts of Guinea, and the Slave Trade*, Frank Cass, London, 1971.

CHAPTER 3. For the anonymous friend of Charles Ball see *Fifty Years in Chains* by Charles Ball, Dover Publications, New York, 1970; for Job Ben Solomon see *Some Memoirs of the Life of Job, the Son of Solomon, the High Priest of Boonda in Africa,* by Thomas Bluett, Richard Ford, London, 1784; also see Francis Moore, above; for Louis Asa-Asa see *Narrative of Louis Asa-Asa, A Captured African* in *Six Women's Slave Narratives,* edited by William L. Andrews, Oxford University Press, Oxford, 1988; for the story of Nealee see *Travels in the Interior Districts of Africa* by Mungo Park, Wordsworth Classics, Hertfordshire, U.K., 2002; for Olaudah Equiano, see above.

CHAPTER 4. For Captain Phillips see above; for Philip Drake see *Revelations of a Slave Smuggler* Metro Books, New York, 1972; for Alexander Falconbridge see above; for William Snelgrave see above; for Olaudah Equiano see above.

CHAPTER 5. For Massachusetts court cases see *Judicial Cases Concerning American Slavery and the Negro* edited by Helen T. Catterall, Carnegie Institution, Washington, D.C., 1926; for advertisements see *Documents Illustrative of the History of the Slave Trade to America,* edited by Elizabeth Donnan, Carnegie Institution, Washington, D.C., 1931; for Mr. Maverick's Negro woman see *An Account of Two Voyages to New-England,* by John Josselyn, University Press of New England, Hanover and London, 1988; for Cotton Mather see *Diary of Cotton Mather, 1681-1724,* Frederick Ungar Publishing, New York, 1957; for Tituba see *More Wonders of the Invisible World* by Robert Calef, printed by Nathaniel Hillar, London, 1700; also *Transcripts of Tituba's Confessions, Appendix C,* in *Tituba, Reluctant Witch of Salem,* by Elaine G. Breslaw, New York University Press, New York and London, 1996; *The Selling of Joseph* by Samuel Sewall was printed by Bartholomew Green and John Allen, Boston, 1700; *The Negro Christianized* by Cotton Mather was printed by Bartholomew Green, Boston, 1706; Phillis Wheatley's *Complete Writings,* edited by Vincent Carretta, was published by Penguin Classics, New York, 2001; *A Journal of the Proceedings etc,* by Daniel Horsmanden was printed by James Parker, New York, 1744; for Governor Hunter's report on the 1712 conspiracy see *Documents Relative to the Colonial History of the State of New York,* 5:341-42, Weed, Parsons & Co, Albany, 1855; for Benjamin Franklin see *The First American* by H. W. Brands, Doubleday, NewYork, 2000; also Franklin's *Autobiography and Other Writings,* Oxford University Press, New York. 2009; for Benjamin Lay see *Memoirs of the Lives of Benjamin Lay and Ralph Sandiford* by Robert Vaux, Solomon W. Conrad, Philadelphia, 1815; for Anthony Benezet see *The Complete Antislavery Writings of Anthony Benezet 1754-1783,* edited by David L. Crosby, Louisiana State University Press, Baton Rouge, 2014; for Charity Dallen see *The Old Dominion in the Seventeenth Century* edited by Warren M. Billings, University of North Carolina Press, Charlotte, 2007; for Carib slaves see *Judicial Cases, etc.,* above; for laws on slavery see *A Documentary History of Slavery in North America* edited by Willie Lee Rose, Oxford University Press, New York, 1976; for

Mary Williamson see *The Old Dominion, etc,* above; for William Byrd see *Documents Illustrative,* etc., above; for William Strickland see *Journal of a Tour in the United States of America 1794-1795,* New York Historical Society, New York, 1971; for Landon Carter see *The Diary of Colonel Landon Carter of Sabine Hall 1752-1778,* University Press of Virginia, Charlottesville, 1965; for runaway advertisements see *A Documentary History of Slavery* above; also *American Negro Slavery, A Documentatry History* edited by Michael Mullin, University of South Carolina Press, Columbia, 1976; for William Gooch, same source; for Oglethorpe's letter and Stono account see *A Documentary History of Slavery in North America* above; for story in *Boston Weekly Newsletter* see *American Negro Slave Revolts* by Herbert Aptheker, Columbia University Press, New York, 1943; for the *Clare* galley, John Major and Guinea-man see *Black Majority* by Peter H. Wood, W. W. Norton, New York, 1974; for Le Jau see *The Carolina Chronicle of Dr. Francis Le Jau* edited by Frank J. Klingberg, University of California Press, Berkeley and Los Angeles, 1956; for Charles Wesley see *The Journal of Charles Wesley,* Baker Books House, Grand Rapids, 1980; for Olaudah Equiano see above; for South Carolina laws see *The Statutes at large of South Carolina* edited by Thomas Cooper and J. McCord, Columbia, 1840; for Oglethorpe and petitioners see *General Oglethorpe's Georgia* edited by Mills Lane, Beehive Press, Savannah, 1975.

CHAPTER 6. For William Bull, Lord Campbell and Henry Laurens see *Documents of the American Revolution* edited by K. G. Davies, Irish University Press, Shannon, 1976; for Dunmore's Proclamation and the counter-proclamation see *Chronicles of the American Revolution* by Hezekiah Niles and Alden T. Vaughan, Grosset and Dunlap, New York, 1956; for the Virginia Convention see previous entry; for Landon Carter see above; the letter to the *Virginia Gazette* was published on November 24, 1775; for deletions to the Declaration of Independence see *The Autobiography of Thomas Jefferson,* Library of America, New York, 1984; for the Rhode Island Regiment see *The American Revolution: A Bicentennial Collection* by Richard B. Morris, Harper and Row, New York, 1970; for *An Act to Procure Recruits, etc.* see *The Statutes at Large of South Carolina, 1752-1786,* Columbia, 1838; for Captain von Ewald see *Diary of the American War: A Hessian Journal,* edited by Joseph P. Tustin, Yale University Press, New Haven, 1979; for Joseph Martin see *A Narrative of Some of the Adventures, Dangers etc.* by, Joseph P. Martin, Arno Press, New York, 1962; for Baroness von Riedesel see her *Journal,* Omohundro Institute, Williamsburg, 2012; for George Washington see *George Washington and Slavery: A Documentary Portrayal by* Fritz Hirschfeld, Missouri University Press, Columbia, 1997; also *An Imperfect God* by Henry Wiencek, Farrar, Straus, New York, 2003; for Oney Judge see previous entry, also *Washington's Runaway Slave* in *The Granite Freeman,* Concord, New Hampshire, 1845; also *Slave Testimony, etc.* edited by John W. Blassingame, Louisiana State University Press, Baton Rouge, 1977; for David George and Sierra Leone see *An Account of the Life of Mr. David George, given by himself etc.,* Annual Baptist Register, Birmingham, U.K., 1793; for Olaudah Equiano see above; for Anna

Maria Falconbridge see *Narrative of Two Voyages to the River Sierra Leone, etc.* L. Higham, London, 1802; for Warwick Francis see *Memoir of Paul Cuffe*, Edmund Fry, London, 1840.

CHAPTER 7. For the Constitution, the Northwest Ordinance, and the Fugitive Slave Act see *Documents of American History* edited by Henry Steele Commager, Appleton-Century-Crofts, New York,1958; for Quock Walker see *History of Slavery in Massachusetts* on Wikipedia; for William Wells Brown see *Narrative of William Wells Brown, A Fugitive Slave,* The Anti-Slavery Office, Boston,1848; also his *The Black Man: His Antecedents, His Genius, and His Accomplishments,* James Redpath, Boston, 1863; also his *The Negro in the American Rebellion,* Lee & Shepard, Boston, 1867; for overseers see *Twelve Years a Slave* by Solomon Northup, above; also, for article in *South Carolinian* see *The Cotton Kingdom* by Frederick Law Olmsted, The Modern Library, New York, 1984; also, *How to Manage Negroes* in *Debow's Review,* New Orleans, March, 1851; for *The Whip* see *Fifty Years in Chains* by Charles Ball, Dover Publications, New York, 1970; for *The Paddle* see *Narrative of the Life and Adventures of Henry Bibb, an American Slave, Written by Himself,* Dover Publications, New York, 2005; for *Dogs* see *A Key to Uncle Tom's Cabin* by Harriet Beecher Stowe, John J. Jewett & Co., Boston, 1858; for Solomon Northup see above; for Francis Henderson see *The Refugee: a North-Side View of Slavery* by Benjamin Drew, in *Four Fugitive Slave Narratives* edited by Tilden G. Edelstein, Addison-Wesley, Reading, 1969; for Lewis Clark see *Witness to Freedom* by Peter C. Porter, University of North Carolina Press, Chapel Hill, 1993; for Fannie Moore see *The American Slave,* edited by George P. Rawick, Greenwood, Westport, 1972; for poor whites see *A Key to Uncle Tom's Cabin* above; for dueling see *The Slave States of America* by James Silk Buckingham, Fisher Son & Co., London, 1842; also *Journal of a Residence on a Georgia Plantation in 1838-1839* by Frances Anne Kemble, University of Georgia Press, Athens, 1984; for *Censorship* see *The Life of Benjamin Lundy* above; for Samuel Green see *The Underground Railroad* by William Still, Dover Publications, New York, 2007; for *Upbringing* see *Travels in the Confederation 1783-4* by Johan Schoepf, Burt Franklin, New York, 1968; for Jefferson see *Notes on Virginia,* Library of America, New York, 2003; for John Nelson see *American Slavery As It Is* by Theodore Dwight Weld, Arno Press, New York, 1968; for Harriet Beecher Stowe on religion see above; for Harriet Jacobs see *Incidents in the Life of a Slave Girl,* Harvard University Press, Cambridge, 1987; for Bishop Meade see Harriet Beecher Stowe above; for Bishop Elliott see *Letters from the United States* by Amelia Murray, G. P. Putnam & Co, New York, 1856; for the Mormons see *The Book of Mormon, Translated by Joseph Smith, Jr.* The Church of Jesus Christ of Latter-Day Saints, Salt Lake City, 1981; for Frederick Douglass see Appendix to *Narrative of the Life of Frederick Douglass,* Dover Publications, New York, 1996.

CHAPTER 8. For Robert Sutcliff see *Travels in Some Parts of North America in the Years 1804, 1805 & 1806,* W. Alexander, York, 1814; for Alexis de Tocqueville see *Democracy in America*, Alfred A. Knopf, New York, 1945; for James Silk Buckingham see *The Slave States of America,* above; Mrs. Trollope's *Domestic Manners of the Americans,* edited by Donald Smalley, was reissued by Vintage Books, New York, in 1944; Susan Dabney Smedes' *Memorials of a Southern Planter* was reissued by Alfred A. Knopf, New York, in 1965; for Fanny Kemble see above; for Frederick Law Olmsted see above; for Fredrika Bremer see *The Homes of the New World,* Negro Universities Press, Westport, 1968; for Sarah Grimké see *American Slavery As It Is* above; for Mary Livermore see *My Story of the War,* Da Capo Press, New York, 1998.

CHAPTER 9. For Solomon Northup see *Twelve Years a Slave* above; for Josiah Henson see *The Life of Josiah Henson, Formerly a Slave,* Applewood Books, Carlisle, 2003; also *An Autobiography of the Rev. Josiah Henson ("Uncle Tom"),* Schuyler Smith & Co. London, Ontario, 1881; for Delia Garlic see *Born in Slavery: Slave Narratives from the Federal Writers' Project 1936-1938,* Library of Congress Digital Collection; for Thomas Jones see *The Experience of Thomas H. Jones,* E. Anthony & Sons, New Bedford, 1885; for Rose Williams see *Born in Slavery* above; for William Johnson see *William Johnson's Natchez: The Ante-bellum Diary of a Free Negro,* Louisiana State University Press, Baton Rouge, 1951; for *Narrative of the Life of Frederick Douglass* see above; for *Narrative of William Wells Brown* see above; for Mary Reynolds, Lucretia Alexander, Wes Brady, Carey Davenport, Richard Carruthers, Mrs. Sutton and May Satterfield see *Born in Slavery* above; for Harriet Jacobs see *Incidents in the Life of a Slave Girl* above; for Ophelia Jemison and Henrietta King see *Born in Slavery* above.

CHAPTER 10. For Theodore Dwight Weld's *American Slavery As It Is* see above; for William Wells Brown's *Narrative* see above; *Uncle Tom's Cabin* was first published in book form by John P. Jewett & Co, of Boston in 1852; for *A Key to Uncle Tom's Cabin* by Harriet Beecher Stowe see above; for Levi Coffin see *Reminiscences of Levi Coffin,* Forgotten Books, London, 2013; for Alexander Ross see *Recollections and Experiences of an Abolitionist,* Leopold Classic Library, London, 2015; for Harriet Tubman see *Harriet Tubman, the Moses of her People* by Sarah Bradford, Applewood Books, Carlisle, MA., 1993; for *Troy Whig,* Martin Townsend and Thomas Garrett see Appendix to *Harriet Tubman,* above; for James Pennington see *The Fugitive Blacksmith* in *Great Slave Narratives* edited by Arne Bontemps, Beacon Press, Boston, 1969; for Frederick Law Olmsted's *Cotton Kingdom* see above.

CHAPTER 11. For Bryan Edwards see *The History, Civil and Commercial, of the British West Indies,* AMS Press, New York, 1966; for Gabriel Prosser see *American Negro Slave Revolts* by Herbert Aptheker, International Publishers, New York, 2013; also *A Documentary History of Slavery* edited by Willie Lee Rose, see above; for the Negro Fort story see Colonel Clinch's report in Appendix to *Sketches, Historical and Topographical, of the Floridas* by James Grant Forbes, University of Florida Press, Gainesville, 1964; for Denmark Vesey see *The Trial*

Record of Denmark Vesey edited by John Oliver Killens, Beacon Press, Boston, 1970; also *Denmark Vesey: The Slave Conspiracy of 1822* edited Robert S. Starobin, Prentice-Hall, Englewood Cliffs, N. J., 1970; for David Walker see *Walker's Appeal in Four Articles,* Ayer Company, Boston, 1848; for Nat Turner's *Confession* see *A Documentary History of Slavery in North America* edited by Willie Lee Rose, above; for J. D. Green see *Narrative of the Life of J. D. Green, A Runaway Slave,* Henry Fielding, Huddersfield (U. K.), 1864; for the story of Praying Jacob see *A Narrative of the Life and Labors of the Rev. G. W. Offley,* Hartford, 1859; for Ellen Cragin, Leonard Franklin, John Henry Kemp, Wes Turner, Charlie Crawley, Delicia Patterson, Fanny Cannaday, Gus Feaster see Library of Congress *Slave Narratives* above; for Christiana story see *A Full and Correct Report of the Christiana Tragedy* compiled by J. Franklin Reigart, printed by John W. Pearson, Lancaster, PA, 1851; for Frederick Douglass see *Freedom's Battle at Christiana* in *Frederick Douglass' Paper,* Rochester, 1851; for Theodore Parker, the Rochester *Advertiser* and Lancaster *Saturday Express* see *Resistance at Christiana* by Jonathan Katz, Thomas Y. Crowell, New York, 1974.

CHAPTER 12. For the Rev. Adams see *A Southside View of Slavery* by Nehemiah Adams, T. R. Marvin, Boston, 1854; for George Fitzhugh see *Sociology for the South* A. Morris, Richmond,1854; for Chancellor Harper see *Cotton is King, and Pro-Slavery Arguments* edited by E. N. Elliott, Pritchard, Abbott, and Loomis, Augusta, 1860; for Hammond's "Mud-sill" speech see his *Speech on the Admission of Kansas* U. S. Senate, March 4, 1858; see also his *Slavery in the Light of Political Science* in *Cotton is King,* above; see also *Secret and Sacred, The Diaries of John Hammond,* edited by Carol Blessed, Oxford University Press, New York, 1988; *Black Diamonds Gathered in Darkey Homes* by Edward Pollard was published by Pudney & Russell, New York, 1859, and his *The Lost Cause* by G. W. Carleton, New York, 1868; for the Rev. Thornton Stringfellow see *Cotton is King* above; for Stringfellow's *Statistical Views in Favor of Slavery* see *Cotton is King* above; for Amelia Murray see *Letters from the United States, Cuba and Canada,* G. P. Putnam & Co, New York, 1856; for John Bigelow see *Jamaica in 1850,* George P. Putnam, New York, 1851; also *The Southern Quarterly Review, Vol 7,* Columbia, S. C., 1854; for Dr. Cartwright see *Report on the Diseases and Physical Peculiarities of the Negro Race,* The New Orleans Medical and Surgical Journal, New Orleans, 1851;for Calhoun see *U. S. Senate, February 6, 1837. Works, II,* D. Appleton, New York, 1856; for Professor Dew see *Review of the Debates in the Virginia Legislature,* T. W. White, Richmond, 1832; for Theodore Weld and the *Huntsville Democrat* see *American Slavery As It Is,* above; for Dred Scott see *Documents of American History,* edited by Henry Steele Commager, above; see also *Battle Cry of Freedom* by James McPherson, Oxford University Press, New York, 1988; for Dr. J. H. Van Evrie see *The Dred Scott Decision,* Books on Demand, 2014.

CHAPTER 13. For Lundy see *The Life, Travels and Opinions of Benjamin Lundy* by Thomas Earle, Augustus M. Kelley, New York, 1971; for William

Lloyd Garrison's *Declaration of Sentiments* of 1833 see *The Abolitionists* by Louis Ruchames, Capricorn Books, New York, 1963; also *All on Fire* by Henry Mayer, W. W. Norton, New York, 1998; for Frederick Douglass see *The Complete Autobiographies of Frederick Douglass,* Wilder Publications, Radford, VA., 2008; also *Frederick Douglass* by William S. McFeely, W. W. Norton, New York, 1991; for *American Slavery As It Is* by Theodore Dwight Weld see above; for *Uncle Tom's Cabin* see above; for *A Key to Uncle Tom's Cabin* see above; *Aunt Phillis's Cabin* by Mary H. Eastman was published by Lippincott, Grambo & Co, Philadelphia, 1852; for the review of *Uncle Tom's Cabin* by George Frederick Holmes see *Southern Literary Messenger,* Richmond, VA., 1852; Fanny Wright's *Plan for the Gradual Abolition of Slavery* was published in the *Genius of Universal Emancipation* in 1825; for Harriet Jacobs see *Incidents in the Life of a Slave Girl* above; Hinton Rowan Helper's *The Impending Crisis of the South* was published by Burdick Brothers, New York, in 1857; for Wendell Phillips see his *Speeches, Lectures and Letters* Lee and Shepard, Boston, 1896; Angelina Grimké's *Appeal* was published by the American Anti-Slavery Society, New York, in 1836; *The Gun and the Gospel* by the Rev. H. D. Fisher was published by the Library of Congress in 1897; for James Townsley see *History of the State of Kansas* by William G. Cutler, Atchison County Historical Society, Atchison, 1976; for Shadrach see *Shadrach Minkins* by Gary Collinson, Harvard University Press, Cambridge, 1997; also *Cheerful Yesterdays* by Thomas Wentworth Higginson, Houghton Mifflin, Boston, 1898; also *The Journal of Richard Henry Dana,* Harvard University Press, Cambridge, 1968; for Thomas Sims see *The Trial of Thomas Sims on an Issue of Personal Liberty,* Library of Congress, 1851; also Thomas Wentworth Higginson above, and his *Letters and Journals,* Houghton Mifflin, Boston, 1921; for Anthony Burns see *Trial of Anthony Burns, the Alleged Fugitive,* Fetridge & Co., Boston, 1854; for Burns' correspondence with the Baptist church see *Front Royal Gazette,* Nov. 8. 1855; for William Lloyd Garrison see *The Liberator,* above.

CHAPTER 14. For Sam Word see *Slave Narratives,* Library of Congress, above; for the Mississippi Declaration see University of Tennessee Microfilm Collection; for Republican platform see *Documents of American History,* by Henry Steele Commager, above; for Abraham Lincoln see *Speeches, Letters, Miscellaneous Writings, etc.,* Library of America, New York, 1989; also *"What Shall We Do with the Negro?"* by Paul Escott, University of Virginia Press, Charlottesville, 2009; for the Emancipation Proclamation see *Documents of American History,* by Henry Steele Commager, above; for Frederick Douglass see *The Complete Autobiographies* above; for William Tillman see *The Negro in the American Rebellion* by William Wells Brown, Lee & Shepard, Boston, 1867; for Robert Smalls see *House Report No. 3505, Forty-Ninth Congress, Second Session;* also *The Negro in the American Rebellion* by William Wells Brown, above; for Thomas Cole see *Slave Narratives,* Library of Congress, above; for Union generals see *The Negro in the American Rebellion* by William Wells Brown, above; for Thomas Wentworth Higginson see *Army Life in a Black Regiment,* W. W.

Norton, New York, 1984; for the Massachusetts 54th, see *A Brave Black Regiment,* by Luis F. Emilio, Da Capo Press, New York, 1995; see also *Freedom's Soldiers* by Ira Berlin, Joseph Reidy and Leslie Rowland, Cambridge University Press, Cambridge, 1998; for Port Hudson see *Black Soldiers in Blue* by John David Smith, University of North Carolina Press, Chapel Hill, 2002; also *The Negro in the American Rebellion,* by William Wells Brown, above; for Sergeant Johnson see *Freedom's Soldiers* by Ira Berlin, Joseph Reidy and Leslie Rowland, above; for Fort Pillow see *House of Representatives 38th Congress, 1st Session, Report Numbers 65 and 67, Fort Pillow Massacre and Returned Prisoners,* Johnson Reprint Corp. New York, 1970; also *The Negro in the American Rebellion* by William Wells Brown, above; for Battle of Saltville see *Freedom's Soldiers* by Ira Berlin et al., above; also *The Saltville Massacre* by Thomas D. Mays, McWhiney Foundation Press, Abilene, 1998; also *Kentucky Cavaliers in Dixie* by George Dallas Mosgrove, University of Nebraska Press, Lincoln, 1999; for Colonel Tattnall see *Freedom's Soldiers* by Ira Berlin et al., above; for Corporal Gooding see *On the Altar of Freedom* edited by Virginia A. Adams, University of Massachusetts Press, Amherst, 1991; for Sergeant Walker see *The Negro in the American Rebellion* by William Wells Brown, above; for wives' letters see *Families and Freedom* by Ira Berlin, The New Press, New York, 1997; also *Freedom's Soldiers,* by Ira Berlin, above; also *Autobiography of a People* by Herb Boyd, Doubleday, New York, 2000; for anonymous soldier of the 54th see *A Brave Black Regiment* by Luis F. Emilio, above; for the unsigned letter to Lincoln and for the report by the Adjutant General see *Freedom's Soldiers* by Ira Berlin, above; for the New York Riots and the battles at Honey Hill and Milliken's Bend see *The Negro in the American Rebellion* by William Wells Brown, above; for the editorial in the *Mississippian* see the Montgomery *Weekly Mail,* September 9, 1863; for the stories of Old Gabe, Levi Miller, black labor battalion, and General Cleburne's plan see *Black Southerners in Confederate Armies* by J. H. Segars and Charles Kelley Barrow, Pelican Publishers, Gretna, LA, 2007; also *"What Shall We Do with the Negro?"* by Paul D. Escott, above; for Katie Rowe, Eda Harper, Cheney Cross, Margaret Hughes, Sarah Debro, Martha Colquist, William Colbert and Primus Smith see *Slave Narratives,* Library of Congress, above; for Annie Burton see *Memoirs of Childhood's Slavery Days* in *Six Women's Slave Narratives,* edited by William Andrews, Oxford University Press, New York, 1988; for the 54th Massachusetts Regiment see *A Brave Black Regiment* by Luis F. Emilio, above; for the 1st South Carolina Volunteers see *A Black Woman's Civil War Memories* by Susie King Taylor, Markus Wiener Publishers, Princeton, 1988; for the constitutional amendments see *Documents of American History* edited by Henry Steele Commager, above; for Frederick Douglass see *The Complete Autobiographies of Frederick Douglass,* above.

BIBLIOGRAPHY

Aptheker, Herbert, *A Documentary History of the Negro People in the United States*, Citadel Press, New York, 1990. Also, *American Negro Slave Revolts*, International Publishers, New York, 1963.

Astley, Thomas, *A New Collection of Voyages and Travels, Four Volumes*, Frank Cass & Co., London, 1968.

Austen, Ralph A., *Trans-Saharan Africa in World History*, Oxford University Press, New York, 2010.

Baptist, Edward E, *The Half Has Never Been Told*, Basic Books, New York, 2014.

Beckert, Sven, *Empire of Cotton*, Alfred A. Knopf, New York, 2014.

Berlin, Ira, *Many Thousands Gone*, Harvard University Press, Cambridge, 1998; also *Freedom: A Documentary History of Emancipation, 1861-1867*, Cambridge University Press, Cambridge, U.K., 1982; also *Freedom's Soldiers*, Cambridge University Press, Cambridge, U.K., 1998; also *Generations of Captivity*, Harvard University Press, Cambridge, 2003; also *Families and Freedom*, The New Press, New York, 1997.

Billings, Warren, *The Old Dominion in the Seventeenth Century*, University of North Carolina Press, Charlotte, 2007.

Blassingame, John, *Slave Testimony*, Louisiana State University, Baton Rouge, 1977.

Blockson, Charles, *The Underground Railroad*, Berkeley Books, New York, 1987.

Breen, T.H. and Stephen Innes, *"Myne Owne Ground," Race and Freedom on Virginia's Eastern Shore*, Oxford University Press, New York, 1980.

Collins, Robert O., *Documents of the African Past*, Markus Wiener, Princeton, 2001.

Collinson, Gary, *Shadrach Minkins*, Harvard University Press, Cambridge, 1997.

Commager, Henry Steele, *Documents of American History*, Appleton-Century-Crofts, New York, 1958.

Cornish, Dudley Taylor, *The Sable Arm: Black Troops in the Union Army*, University Press of Kansas, Lawrence, 1987.

Curtin, Philip D., *The Atlantic Slave Trade: A Census*, University of Wisconsin Press, Madison, 1969.

Davidson, Basil, *The African Slave Trade*, Atlantic Monthly Press, Boston, 1980.

Davies, K. G., *The Royal African Company*, Longman's, Green & Co. London, 1957.

Davis, David Brion, *Inhuman Bondage*, Oxford University Press, New York, 2006; also *The Problem of Slavery in Western Culture*, Cornell University

Press, Ithaca, 1966; also *Slavery and Human Bondage,* Oxford University Press, New York, 1984.

Deyle, Stephen, *Carry Me Back: The Domestic Slave Trade in American Life,* Oxford University Press, New York, 2005.

Donnan, Elizabeth, *Documents Illustrative of the History of the Slave Trade to America,* Carnegie Institute of Washington, 1931.

Dow, George Francis, *Slave Ships and Slaving,* Dover Publications, New York, 1970.

Drake, Thomas E., *Quakers and Slavery in America,* Yale University Press, New Haven, 1950.

DuBois, W. E. B., *The Suppression of the African Slave-Trade,* Oxford University Press, New York, 2007.

Durden, Robert, F., *The Gray and the Black: The Confederate Debates on Emancipation,* Louisiana State University Press, Baton Rouge, 1972.

Edwards, Bryan, *History of the British Colonies in the West Indies,* John Stockdale, London, 1793.

Elliott, E. N., *Cotton is King, and Pro-Slavery Arguments,* Negro Universities Press, New York, 1969.

Eltis, David, *Atlas of the Transatlantic Slave Trade,* Yale University Press, New Haven, 2010.

Escott, Paul D., *Slavery Remembered,* University of North Carolina Press, Chapel Hill, 1979; also *"What Shall We Do with the Negro?",* University of Virginia Press, Charlottesville, 2009.

Essig, James D. *The Bonds of Wickedness: American Evangelicals Against Slavery,* Temple University Press, Philadelphia, 1982.

Faust, Drew Gilpin, *James Henry Hammond and the Old South,* Louisiana State University Press, Baton Rouge, 1982.

Feldstein, Stanley, *Once A Slave: The Slave's View of Slavery,* William Morrow, New York, 1971.

Fisher, Leslie H. Jr. and Benjamin Quarles, *The Black American: A Documentary History,* William Morrow, New York, 1970.

Fogel, Robert William, *Without Consent or Contract: The Rise and Fall of American Slavery,* W. W. Norton, New York, 1989; also *Time on the Cross: The Economics of American Slavery,* W. W. Norton, New York, 1974.

Franklin, John Hope and Alfred A. Moss, Jnr., *From Slavery to Freedom: A History of African Americans,* Alfred A. Knopf, New York, 2004.

Frey, Sylvia R. *Water from the Rock: Black Resistance in a Revolutionary Age,* Princeton University Press, Princeton, 1991;

Gara, Larry, *The Liberty Line: The Legend of the Underground Railroad,* University of Kentucky Press, Lexington, 1961.

Genovese, Eugene, *Roll, Jordan, Roll,* Vintage Books, New York, 1972.

Hallett, Robin, *The Penetration of Africa,* Frederick A. Praeger, New York, 1965.

Hirschfeld, Fritz, *George Washington and Slavery,* Missouri University Press, Columbia, 1997.

Hoffer, Peter Charles, *Cry Liberty: The Great Stono River Slave Rebellion,* Oxford University Press, New York, 2012.

Howard, Thomas, *Black Voyage: Eyewitness Accounts of the Atlantic Slave Trade,* Little, Brown, Boston, 1971.

Hunt, Alfred, *Haiti's Influence on Antebellum America,* Louisiana State University, Baton Rouge, 1988.

Isaac, Rhys, *Landon Carter's Uneasy Kingdom,* Oxford University Press, New York, 2004.

James, C. L. R., *The Black Jacobins,* Vintage Books, New York, 1968.

Jordan, Winthrop, *White Over Black,* University of North Carolina Press, Chapel Hill, 1968.

Katz, Jonathan, *Resistance at Christiana,* Thomas Y. Crowell, New York, 1974.

Kolchin, Peter, *American Slavery,* Hill & Wang, New York, 1993.

Levtzion, N. and J. F. F. Hopkins, *Corpus of Early Arabic Sources for West African History,* Cambridge University Press, Cambridge, 1981.

Lockley, Timothy James, *Maroon Communities in South Carolina,* University of South Carolina Press, Columbia, 2009.

Mannix, Daniel, *Black Cargoes,* Viking Press, New York, 1962.

Mayer, Henry, *All on Fire: William Lloyd Garrison and the Abolition of Slavery,* W. W. Norton, New York, 1998.

McFeely, William, *Frederick Douglass,* W. W. Norton, New York, 1991.

McManus, Edgar J., *A History of Slavery in New York,* Syracuse University Press, Syracuse, 1965.

McPherson, James, *Battle Cry of Freedom,* Oxford University Press, New York, 1988; also *The Negro's Civil War,* Random House, 1965.

Middlekauf, Robert, *The Glorious Cause: The American Revolution 1763-1789,* Oxford University Press, New York, 1982.

Morgan, Edmund S., *American Slavery, American Freedom,* W. W. Norton, New York, 1975.

Morgan, Philip D., *Slave Counterpoint,* University of North Carolina Press, Charlotte, 1998.

Mullin, Michael, *American Negro Slavery: A Documentary History,* University of South Carolina Press, Columbia, 1976.

Murphy, E. Jefferson, *History of African Civilization,* Thomas Y. Crowell, New York, 1972.

Nichols, Charles H., *Many Thousands Gone,* Indiana University Press, Bloomington, 1963.

Osofsky, Gilbert, *The Burden of Race: A Documentary History,* Harper & Row, New York, 1967.

Patterson, Orlando, *Slavery and Social Death,* Harvard University Press, Cambridge, 1982.

Phillips, Ulrich R., *American Negro Slavery,* Louisiana State University, Baton Rouge, 1966; also *Plantation and Frontier, 1649-1863,* Burt Franklin, New York, 1969.

Pope-Hennessy, James, *Sins of the Fathers,* Alfred A. Knopf, New York, 1968.

Porter, Kenneth W., *The Negro on the American Frontier,* Arno Press, New York, 1971.

Price, Richard, *Maroon Societies*, Johns Hopkins University Press, Baltimore, 1979.

Quarles, Benjamin, *Black Abolitionists*, Oxford University Press, New York, 1969; also *The Negro in the Civil War*, Little, Brown, Boston, 1953.

Raboteau, Albert J., *Slave Religion*, Oxford University Press, New York, 2004.

Rawick, George P., *From Sundown to Sunup*, Greenwood Press, Westport, 1972.

Rediker, Marcus, *The Slave Ship*, Viking Penguin, New York, 2007.

Ripley, C. Peter, *Witness to Freedom*, University of North Carolina Press, Chapel Hill, 1993.

Rose, Willie Lee, *A Documentary History of Slavery in North America*, University of Georgia Press, Athens, 1999.

Russell, Peter, *Prince Henry 'The Navigator'*, Yale University Press, New Haven, 2000.

Schama, Simon, *Rough Crossings*, BBC Books, London, 2005.

Segars, J. H. and Charles Kelley Barrow, *Black Southerners in Confederate Armies*, Pelican Publishing, Gretna, 2007.

Slaughter, Thomas I., *Bloody Dawn: The Christiana Riot*, Oxford University Press, New York, 1991.

Smith, Abbot Emerson, *Colonists in Bondage*, University of North Carolina Press, Chapel Hill, 1947.

Smith, John David, *Black Soldiers in Blue*, University of North Carolina Press, Chapel Hill, 2002.

Stampp, Kenneth, *The Peculiar Institution*, Alfred A. Knopf, New York, 1956; also *America in 1857*, Oxford University Press, New York, 1990.

Starobin, Robert S., *Denmark Vesey*, Prentice Hall, Upper Saddle River, N. J., 1970.

Still, William, *The Underground Railroad*, Dover Publications, Mineola, 2007.

Thomas, Hugh, *The Slave Trade*, Simon and Schuster, New York, 1997.

Tocqueville, Alexis de, *Democracy in America*, Alfred A. Knopf, New York, 1945.

U. S. Government, *The War of the Rebellion: A Compilation of the Official Records*, Government Printing Office, Washington, 1900.

Vaissière, Pierre de, *La Société et la Vie Créole sous l'Ancien Régime*, Perrin et Cie, Paris, 1900.

Walvin, James, *Slavery and the Slave Trade*, University Press of Mississippi, Oxford, 1983.

Wheelan, Joseph, *Mr. Adams's Last Crusade*, Public Affairs, New York, 2008.

Wiencek, Henry, *An Imperfect God*, Farrar, Straus and Giroux, New York, 2003.

Wilson, Edmund, *Patriotic Gore*, Oxford University Press, New York, 1962.

Wilson, Ellen Gibson, *The Loyal Blacks*, G. P. Putnam's Sons, New York, 1976; also *John Clarkson and the African Adventure*, Macmillan Press Ltd., London, 1980.

Wood, Gordon S., *Empire of Liberty*, Oxford University Press, New York, 2009.

Wood, Peter H., *Black Majority*, W. W. Norton, New York, 1974.

ILLUSTRATION CREDITS

p 14. Schomburg Center for Research in Black Culture, Manuscripts, Archives and Rare Books Division, The New York Public Library, Digital Collections.

p 23. From St. Vincent panels, by Nuno Gonçalves, c. 1498, National Museum of Ancient Art, Portugal.

p 39. Schomburg Center for Research in Black Culture, Manuscripts, Archives and Rare Books Division, The New York Public Library, Digital Collections.

p 44. Engraving by Johann Theodor de Bry, Americae pars quinta, 1595. Rosenwald Collection, Library of Congress Prints and Photographs Division.

p 52. "Carte du Golfe de Bénin et partie de la Côte de Guinée" 1700–1799. Schomburg Center for Research in Black Culture, Jean Blackwell Hutson Research and Reference Division, The New York Public Library, Digital Collections.

p 59. Schomburg Center for Research in Black Culture, Jean Blackwell Hutson Research and Reference Division, The New York Public Library, Digital Collections.

p 79. Schomburg Center for Research in Black Culture, Manuscripts, Archives and Rare Books Division, The New York Public, Digital Collections.

p 83. "Branding slaves," 1859. Schomburg Center for Research in Black Culture, Manuscripts, Archives and Rare Books Division, The New York Public, Digital Collections

p 88. Job, son of Solliman Diallo, high priest of Bonda in the country of Foota, Africa, 1750. Schomburg Center for Research in Black Culture, Photographs and Prints Division, The New York Public Library, Digital Collections.

p 103. From *The London Review*, v. 35 (June 1799), frontispiece. Library of Congress Prints and Photographs Division.

p 111. Frontispiece and title page from *The interesting narrative of the life of Olaudah Equiano*, 1794. Library of Congress Prints and Photographs Division.

p 116. "The lower deck of a Guinea-Man, in the last century," 1854. Schomburg Center for Research in Black Culture, Manuscripts, Archives and Rare Books Division, The New York Public Library, Digital Collections.

p 119. "Ombord a ett slafskepp," 1896. Schomburg Center for Research in Black Culture, Jean Blackwell Hutson Research and Reference Division, The New York Public Library, Digital Collections.

p 123. "View of chained African slaves in cargo hold of slave ship." Schomburg Center for Research in Black Culture, Photographs and Prints Division, the New York Public Library, Digital Collections.

p 125. Schomburg Center for Research in Black Culture, Jean Blackwell Hutson Research and Reference Division, The New York Public Library, Digital Collections.

p 133. "Strid ombord pa ett slafskepp," 1896. Schomburg Center for Research in Black Culture, Jean Blackwell Hutson Research and Reference Division, The New York Public Library, Digital Collections.

p 146. Frontispiece engraving by Scipio Moorhead, for A. Bell, bookseller, Aldgate, London, 1773. Library of Congress Rare Book and Special Collections Division.

p 155. E.C. Stedman and E. M. Hutchinson, eds., *A Library of American Literature: From the Earliest Settlement to the Present Time*, vol. 2 (New York: Charles L. Webster, 1889), p. 188.

p 172. Schomburg Center for Research in Black Culture, Manuscripts, Archives and Rare Books Division, The New York Public Library, Digital Collections.

p 197. Courtesy of Hargrett Rare Book and Manuscript Library, University of Georgia Libraries.

p 199. "Plano de la Ciudad y Puerto de San Agustin de la Florida," by Tomas Lopez de Vargas Machura, 1783. Courtesy Florida State Archives.

p 200. Painting, Scottish National Gallery.

p 217. Lithograph by T. Doughty from a drawing by H. Reinagle. Philadelphia: Childs & Inman, 1832. Library of Congress Prints and Photographs Division.

p 229. "A View of the entrance into Sierra-Leone River," by John Matthews, 1791. Schomburg Center for Research in Black Culture, Manuscripts, Archives and Rare Books Division, The New York Public Library, Digital Collections.

p 232. 1830 abolitionist print. Library of Congress Prints and Photographs Division.

p 238. Woodcut illus. in *The Penitential Tyrant* by Thomas Branagan. New York: Samuel Wood, 1807. Library of Congress Rare Book and Special Collections Division.

p 249. "Slave Auction in Virginia," 1861. Schomburg Center for Research in Black Culture, Photographs and Prints Division, The New York Public Library, Digital Collections.

p 262. Engraving by A.H. Ritchie, c. 1870. Liljenquist Family Collection of Civil War Photographs, Library of Congress Prints and Photographs Division.

p 275. Fanny Kemble. Library of Congress Prints and Photographs Division.

p 283. Frederick Law Olmsted. *Century Magazine*, 1903.

p 301. Sarah Grimké, wood engraving. Library of Congress Prints and Photographs Division.

p 306. Illustration from *Twelve Years a Slave, Narrative of Solomon Northup*, 1853. Schomburg Center for Research in Black Culture, Manuscripts, Archives and Rare Books Division, The New York Public Library, Digital Collections.

p 315. 1862 woodcut. Schomburg Center for Research in Black Culture, Manuscripts, Archives and Rare Books Division, The New York Public Library, Digital Collections.

p 347. "Family Worship on a South Carolina Cotton Plantation," engraving by Frank Vizetelly, Illustrated London News, December 5, 1863.

p 352. Photograph between c. 1871 and 1876, by Harvey B. Lindsley. Library of Congress Prints and Photographs Division.

p 361. William Wells Brown, *Narrative of William W. Brown: an American Slave*. London: G. Gilpin, 1849. Schomburg Center for Research in Black Culture, Manuscripts, Archives and Rare Books Division, The New York Public Library, Digital Collections.

p 382. Poster, "$200 Reward," 1847. Library of Congress Prints and Photographs Division.

p 386. "Horrid Massacre in Virginia," woodcut, 1831. Library of Congress Rare Book and Special Collections Division.

p 419. William Still, *Underground Rail Road*. Philadelphia: Porter & Coates, 1872, p. 351.

p 424. Engraving of painting by T. Hicks, from daguerrotype by Brady. New York: A.H. Ritchie & Co., c. 1852. Library of Congress Prints and Photographs Division.

p 438. Frank Leslie's Illustrated Newspaper, December 1857. Library of Congress Prints and Photographs Division.

p 453. Lithograph by Charles L. Magee, 1855.

p 458. National Archives and Records Administration.

p 467. Engraving of painting, 1835. Library of Congress Prints and Photographs Division.

p 495. Reproduction of 1850's photograph. Library of Congress Prints and Photographs Division.

p 504. Wood engraving by John Andrews, c. 1855. Library of Congress Prints and Photographs Division.

p 508. Chicago: Kurz & Allison, c. 1890. Library of Congress Prints and Photographs Division.

p 515. Wood engraving, 1862. Library of Congress Prints and Photographs Division.

p 535. "Cumberland Landing, VA: group of 'contrabands at Follwer's house,'" May 1862. Photograph by James Gibson. Library of Congress Prints and Photographs Division.

p 544. Harper's Weekly, June 1863.

INDEX